Lecture Notes in Computer Science 12912

More information about this subseries at http://www.springer.com/series/7410

Patrick Longa · Carla Ràfols (Eds.)

Progress in Cryptology – LATINCRYPT 2021

7th International Conference on Cryptology
and Information Security in Latin America
Bogotá, Colombia, October 6–8, 2021
Proceedings

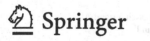 Springer

Editors
Patrick Longa (iD)
Microsoft Research
Redmond, WA, USA

Carla Ràfols (iD)
Universitat Pompeu Fabra
Barcelona, Spain

ISSN 0302-9743   ISSN 1611-3349 (electronic)
Lecture Notes in Computer Science
ISBN 978-3-030-88237-2   ISBN 978-3-030-88238-9 (eBook)
https://doi.org/10.1007/978-3-030-88238-9

LNCS Sublibrary: SL4 – Security and Cryptology

This Springer imprint is published by the registered company Springer Nature Switzerland AG
The registered company address is: Gewerbestrasse 11, 6330 Cham, Switzerland

Preface

This book includes the proceedings of the 7th International Conference on Cryptology and Information Security in Latin America, LATINCRYPT 2021. This event is organized in cooperation with the International Association of Cryptologic Research. The conference was originally planned to take place in 2020 at the Universidad del Rosario in Bogotá, Colombia, but was rescheduled to the next year due to the COVID-19 pandemic and finally changed to be a virtual event.

The 22 accepted papers in this volume were carefully selected, after a double-blind review process, from 47 submissions from authors in 26 countries. All submissions received at least three reviews and committee-member submissions at least four. We wish to thank the Program Committee (PC) for the hard work and the active discussions and, most particularly, those PC members that shepherded a paper.

The program of LATINCRYPT 2021 included three invited talks. Shweta Agrawal (Indian Institute of Technology Madras, India) discussed "Recent Progress and Challenges in Lattice-Based Cryptography", Luca De Feo (IBM Research Zürich, Switzerland) discussed "What's Next for Isogeny-Based Cryptography?", and Dan Boneh (Stanford University, USA) told us about "Recent Developments in Cryptography".

As is usual, the school in cryptography ASCrypto took place on the two days before the conference. It was decided to find speakers who could introduce in more detail some of the topics addressed in the keynote talks. The speakers were Alice Pellet-Mary, Thomas Prest, Riad S. Wahby, Armando Faz-Hernández, and Jesús-Javier Chi-Domínguez. We would like to express our sincere gratitude for their collaboration.

We would also like to thank the general chair Valerie Gauthier Umaña for her tireless effort in organizing the conference and the school, and in particular, for making it as close as it could be to an in-person event in beautiful Bogotá. We are also very grateful to Francisco Rodríguez-Henríquez for sharing his knowledge and experience from previous editions. We thank the steering committee for giving us the chance to edit this volume. The submission and review process was handled with the Websubrev review software, with the kind support of Shai Halevi, who set up the submission server for us.

Finally, the conference would not have been possible without our sponsors, the Technology Innovation Institute, UAE, and the Universidad del Rosario, Colombia, through an "Internal Research Funding" grant.

October 2021

Patrick Longa
Carla Ràfols

Organization

General Chair

Valerie Gauthier Umaña   Universidad del Rosario, Colombia

Program Committee Chairs

Patrick Longa   Microsoft Research, USA
Carla Ràfols   Universitat Pompeu Fabra, Spain

Steering Committee

Michel Abdalla   CNRS and DI/ENS, Université PSL, France
Diego Aranha   Aarhus University, Denmark
Paulo Barreto   University of Washington Tacoma, USA
Ricardo Dahab   Universidade Estadual de Campinas, Brazil
Alejandro Hevia   Universidad de Chile, Chile
Kristin Lauter   Facebook, USA
Julio López   Universidade Estadual de Campinas, Brazil
Daniel Panario   Carleton University, Canada
Francisco Rodríguez-Henríquez   CRC-TII, UAE, and CINVESTAV-IPN, Mexico
Nicolas Thériault   Universidad de Santiago de Chile, Chile
Alfredo Viola   Universidad de la República de Uruguay, Uruguay

Program Committee

Lejla Batina   Radboud University, The Netherlands
Carsten Baum   Aarhus University, Denmark
Nina Bindel   University of Waterloo, Canada
Debrup Chakraborty   Indian Statistical Institute, India
Céline Chevalier   Université Paris II Panthéon-Assas, France
Jesús-Javier Chi-Domínguez   CRC-TII, UAE
Joan Daemen   Radboud University, The Netherlands
Jan-Pieter D'Anvers   imec-COSIC/KU Leuven, Belgium
Bernardo David   IT University of Copenhagen, Denmark
Luca De Feo   IBM Research Zürich, Switzerland
Orr Dunkelman   University of Haifa, Israel
Antonio Faonio   EURECOM, France

Oriol Farràs	Universitat Rovira i Virgili, Spain
Pooya Farshim	University of York, UK
Gina Gallegos García	Instituto Politécnico Nacional, Mexico
Alonso González	Toposware, Japan
Aurore Guillevic	Inria Nancy, France
Tim Güneysu	Ruhr-Universität Bochum and DFKI, Germany
Javier Herranz	Universitat Politècnica de Catalunya, Spain
Julia Hesse	IBM Research Zürich, Switzerland
Alejandro Hevia	Universidad de Chile, Chile
Sorina Ionica	Université de Picardie Jules Verne, France
Patrick Longa (Co-chair)	Microsoft Research, USA
Marine Minier	Université de Lorraine, France
Rafael Misoczki	Google, USA
Anderson Nascimento	University of Washington Tacoma, USA
Khoa Nguyen	Nanyang Technological University, China
Geovandro Pereira	University of Waterloo and evolutionQ, Canada
Peter Pessl	Infineon Technologies, Germany
Christiane Peters	IBM Security, Belgium
Carla Ràfols (Co-chair)	Universitat Pompeu Fabra, Spain
Joost Renes	NXP Semiconductors, The Netherlands
Oscar Repáraz	Square, USA, and COSIC/KU Leuven, Belgium
Matthieu Rivain	CryptoExperts, France
Francisco Rodríguez-Henríquez	CINVESTAV-IPN, Mexico, and CRC-TII, UAE
Sven Schäge	Ruhr-Universität Bochum, Germany
Peter Schwabe	MPI-SP, Germany, and Radboud University, The Netherlands
Douglas Stebila	University of Waterloo, Canada
Nicolas Thériault	Universidad de Santiago de Chile, Chile
Alfredo Viola	Universidad de la República de Uruguay, Uruguay
Greg Zaverucha	Microsoft Research, USA

Additional Reviewers

Gorjan Alagic	Chelsea Komlo	John Schanck
Norica Bacuieti	Benjamin Kuykendall	Jan Schoone
Gustavo Banegas	Loïc Masure	Joachim Schäfer
Sanjit Chatterjee	Conor McMenamin	Florian Speelman
Thomas Debris	Ilana Mergudich	Monika Trimoska
Koustabh Ghosh	Mridul Nandi	Fernando Virdia
Yonglin Hao	Shahram Rasoolzadeh	Hendrik Waldner
Senyang Huang	Jordi Ribes-González	Alexandros Zacharakis
Neal Koblitz	Édouard Rousseau	
Stefan Kolbl	Simona Samardjiska	

Contents

Quantum Cryptography

Tight Bounds for Simon's Algorithm

Xavier Bonnetain[✉]

Institute for Quantum Computing, Department of Combinatorics and Optimization,
University of Waterloo, Waterloo, Canada
xbonnetain@uwaterloo.ca

Abstract. Simon's algorithm is the first example of a quantum algorithm exponentially faster than any classical algorithm, and has many applications in cryptanalysis. While these quantum attacks are often extremely efficient, they are generally missing some precise cost estimate. This article aims at resolving this issue by computing precise query costs for the different use cases of Simon's algorithm in cryptanalysis.

We show that it requires little more than n queries to succeed in most cases. We perform the first concrete cost analysis for the offline Simon's algorithm, and show that it require little more than $n + k$ queries. We also find that for parameter sizes of cryptographic relevance, it is possible to truncate the output of the periodic function to a dozen of bits without any impact on the number of queries, which can save roughly a factor 3 in qubits in reversible implementations of Simon's algorithm.

Keywords: Simon's algorithm · Quantum cryptanalysis · Symmetric cryptanalysis · Query complexity

1 Introduction

Simon's algorithm [30] is the first example of a quantum algorithm exponentially faster than any classical one, and lead the way to Shor's algorithm [29]. This algorithm aims at solving the following problem:

Definition 1 (Simon's problem (informal)). *Let $f : \{0,1\}^n \to X$ be a periodic function. Find its period.*

For a long time, this algorithm had no concrete application. This changed in 2010, with a polynomial-time quantum distinguisher on the 3-round Feistel cipher [20], which is classically proven secure. This opened the way to many other attacks [1,2,6,9,11,13,15,17,18,21,24,27,28], including the Grover-meets-Simon technique, which uses Simon's algorithm as a test in a quantum search [22]. All these attacks have an important restriction: they only fit in the *quantum query model*, that is, they require access to a quantum circuit that can compute the corresponding construction *including its secret material*.

This last restriction was overcomed in 2019, with the offline Simon's algorithm [4] that uses Simon's algorithm in a quantum search in a novel way, and

© Springer Nature Switzerland AG 2021
P. Longa and C. Ràfols (Eds.): LATINCRYPT 2021, LNCS 12912, pp. 3–23, 2021.
https://doi.org/10.1007/978-3-030-88238-9_1

makes some of the previous attacks applicable when we only have access to classical queries to the secret function, but with a polynomial gain only.

The Grover-meets-Simon and its specialization, the offline Simon's algorithm, aim at solving the following problem:

Definition 2 (Grover-Meets-Simon (Informal)). *Let $f_1, \ldots, f_{2^k}$ be a set of functions from $\{0,1\}^n$ to X, such that exactly one of them is periodic. Find the index of the periodic function.*

In the literature, the query cost of these attacks is often left as a $\mathcal{O}(n)$. Very few concrete estimates are proposed, and they tend to be loose estimates. Hence, in the current situation, we have asymptotically efficient attacks, but their effiency in practice is less clear, and we are lacking tools to compare between these attacks and others. Moreover, in many attacks, an ad-hoc analysis was required to ensure that Simon's algorithm was efficient. This work aims at resolving this issue, by providing results allowing to directly compute the query cost of a Simon-based attack in any cryprographical use case. It has already been used in [5] to provide concrete circuits for the offline Simon's algorithm. Our analysis is crucial for many of the optimizations they propose.

We focus here on giving precise bounds on the number of queries required by Simon's algorithm in its different use cases. Note that we do not give here concrete lower bounds for Simon's *problem*. To our knowledge, the sole work in this direction is [19], where a lower bound in $n/8$ queries is proven.

Previous Works. The first concrete estimate comes from [18, Theorem 1 and 2], where it is shown that cn queries, for $c > 3$ that depends on the function, is enough to have a success probability exponentially close to 1. In [22, Theorem 2], a bound of $2(n + \sqrt{n})$ queries for the Grover-meets-Simon algorithm with a perfect external test is shown, for a success probability greater than 0.4, assuming that the periodic function has been sampled uniformly at random, and that the output and input size are equal. In [1], a heuristic cost of $1.2n + 1$ for Simon's algorithm is used. In the recent [23, Theorem 3.2], it is shown that for 2-to-1 functions, Simon's algorithm needs on average less than $n + 1$ queries, and that for functions with 1 bit of output, on average less than $2(n + 1)$ queries are needed, if each query uses a function sampled independently uniformly over the set of functions with the same period.

Contributions. Our contributions can be summarized around three axis:

- We propose an exact query analysis of all the proposed variant of Simon's algorithm in the litterature, and in particular give the first non-asymptotical cost estimate for the offline Simon's algorithm and the exact variant of Simon's algorithm.
- We study comprehensively the algorithm's behaviour with random functions.
- We show the algorithm's behaviour is not impacted by a significant reduction of the function's output size.

This allows us to propose heuristics, meant to be directly used in quantum cryptanalysis. They are heuristics, in the sense that technically, some counter-examples exists. Still, we show the functions that do not satisfy these heuristics are completely degenerate, and are far too rare to appear in practice.

The results we obtain can be summarized by the following heuristic:

Heuristic 1 (Simplified Estimates). *Simon's algorithm needs n queries, except in its offline version, where it needs $n + k$ queries, assuming the output size of the function is at least $\lceil 3.5 + \log_2(q) \rceil$ bits, with q the number of queries.*

We also propose more refined heuristics with an exact query cost in function of the success probability in Subsect. 7.2, as well as theorems to support them.

Cryptographic Applications. In general, our work can be used as-is to propose concrete costs estimates for any Simon-based cryptanalysis. Moreover, this work also has some interesting consequences:

- The original concrete proof for Grover-meets-Simon [22] assumed a large output size, while the original proof of the Offline Simon's algorithm [4] focuses on the asymptotical behaviour. We propose concrete estimates with a very small output size limitation. This allows to give concrete estimates for attacks that were missing them, such as some slide attacks [6] or some cryptanalyses of Chaskey [16].
- Some attacks apply Simon's algorithm in a nested fashion [6,9]. Our improvement in query is multiplied in that case, and the gain of a small constant becomes much larger in that case.
- Fewer queries and a smaller output size means a reduced memory footprint for reversible applications of Simon's algorithm (such as the nested algorithms, Grover-meets-Simon or the Offline Simon's algorithm). While the exact gain depends on the concrete attack, we can estimate these two improvements allow to save around a factor 10 in memory, without any drawback nor preventing any other optimization.

Outline. Sect. 2 recalls the amplitude amplification results useful in the following paper. Sections 3, 4, 5 and 6 respectively presents and analyze precisely Simon's algorithm, its exact variant, the Grover-meets-Simon algorithm and the offline Simon's algorithm. We present a survey of the Simon-based attacks and discuss what the previous analysis means in practice for concrete attacks in Sect. 7.

2   Amplitude Amplification

We assume basic knowledge of quantum computing. For a detailed introduction, we refer to [25]. We will use amplitude amplification [8] with Simon's algorithm as a test function in the following sections. We recall here these standard results.

Lemma 1 (Amplitude Amplification [8]). *Let C be a quantum circuit such that $C\,|0\rangle = \sqrt{p}\,|Good\rangle + \sqrt{1-p}\,|Bad\rangle$,*

Let O_g be an operator that fulfills $O_g\,|Good\rangle = -\,|Good\rangle$ and $O_g\,|Bad\rangle = |Bad\rangle$, and O_0 the operator $I - 2\,|0\rangle\,\langle 0|$, let $\theta = \arcsin(\sqrt{p})$. Then $(CO_0C^\dagger O_g)^t C\,|0\rangle = \sin((2t+1)\theta)\,|Good\rangle + \cos((2t+1)\theta)\,|Bad\rangle$.

Lemma 2 (Exact Amplitude Amplification for $p = 1/2$ [7]). *Let C be a quantum circuit such that $C\,|0\rangle = \frac{1}{\sqrt{2}}\,|Good\rangle + \frac{1}{\sqrt{2}}\,|Bad\rangle$,*

Let S_g be an operator that fulfills $S_g\,|Good\rangle = i\,|Good\rangle$ and $S_g\,|Bad\rangle = |Bad\rangle$, and S_0 the operator $I - (1 - i)\,|0\rangle\,\langle 0|$. Then $CS = S_0 C^\dagger S_g C\,|0\rangle = |Good\rangle$.

Remark 1. The operators O_g and S_g can be easily implemented given a quantum circuit T that computes 1 for the good elements and 0 for the bad ones.

For our numerical analysis, we propose slight variants of the amplitude amplification lemma that will be used for the Grover-meets-Simon and Offline Simon analysis.

Proposition 1 (Unprecise Amplitude Amplification). *Let C be a quantum circuit such that $C\,|0\rangle = \sqrt{p}\,|Good\rangle + \sqrt{1-p}\,|Bad\rangle$, If $p \in [(1-\beta)p_0, p_0]$, then after $\frac{\pi}{4\arcsin\sqrt{p_0}}$ iterations, the probability of measuring an element in $|Good\rangle$ is at least $1 - (2\beta + 2p_0 + \sqrt{p_0})^2$. If $p \in [p_0, p_0(1 + \beta)]$, then after $\frac{\pi}{4\arcsin\sqrt{p_0}}$ iterations, the probability of measuring an element in $|Good\rangle$ is at least $1 - (\beta + \sqrt{(1+\beta)p_0} + 2\sqrt{1+\beta}^3 p_0)^2$.*

Proof. See the full version [3].

Proposition 2 (Amplitude Amplification with Aapproximate Test). *Let C be a quantum circuit such that $C\,|0\rangle = \sqrt{p}\,|Good\rangle + \sqrt{1-p}\,|Bad\rangle$,*

Let O_g be an operator that fulfills $O_g\,|Good\rangle = -\,|Good\rangle$ and $O_g\,|Bad\rangle = |Bad\rangle$, and O_0 the operator $I - 2\,|0\rangle\,\langle 0|$, let $\theta = \arcsin(\sqrt{p})$.

Let $\widehat{O}_g$ be an approximation of O_g, such that for all $|x\rangle$, $\widehat{O}_g\,|x\rangle = O_g\,|x\rangle + |\delta\rangle$, with $|\delta\rangle$ an arbitrary vector such that $\||\delta\rangle\| \le \varepsilon$. Then if $t\varepsilon \le \sin((2t+1)\theta)$, a measurement of $(CO_0C^\dagger\widehat{O}_g)^t C\,|0\rangle$, will give an element in $|Good\rangle$ with probability at least $(\sin((2t+1)\theta) - t\varepsilon)^2$.

Proof. See the full version [3].

3   Simon's Algorithm

3.1   Algorithm Description

Simon's algorithm [30] tackles the Hidden Subgroup problem when the group is $\{0,1\}^n$. We can formulate the problem as follows:

Problem 1 (Simon's Problem). Let $n \in \mathbb{N}$, $\mathcal{H}$ a subgroup of $\{0,1\}^n$ and X a set. Let $f : \{0,1\}^n \to X$ be a function such that for all $(x, y) \in (\{0,1\}^n)^2$, $[f(x) = f(y) \Leftrightarrow x \oplus y \in \mathcal{H}]$. Given oracle access to f, find a basis of $\mathcal{H}$.

The promise in the problem can also be relaxed:

Problem 2 (Relaxed Simon's Problem). Let $n \in \mathbb{N}$, $\mathcal{H}$ a subgroup of $\{0,1\}^n$ and X a set. Let $f : \{0,1\}^n \to X$ be a function such that for all $(x,y) \in (\{0,1\}^n)^2$, $[x \oplus y \in \mathcal{H} \Rightarrow f(x) = f(y)]$ and that for all $h \notin \mathcal{H}$, there exists an x such that $f(x) \neq f(x \oplus h)$. Given oracle access to f, find a basis of $\mathcal{H}$.

We consider two types of functions, depending on the problem we solve:

Definition 3 (Periodic permutations, periodic functions). *We call a periodic permutation a function f that fulfills the promise of Problem 1. If f is constant over the cosets of $\mathcal{H}$, but not necessarily injective over $\{0,1\}^n/(\mathcal{H})$, we say that f is a periodic function.*

Algorithm Description. Circuit 1 is the circuit of Simon's algorithm. It produces a random value orthogonal to $\mathcal{H}$, and can be described as Algorithm 1.

Circuit 1 Simon's circuit

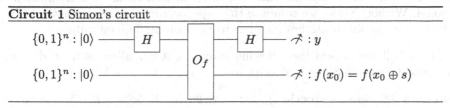

Algorithm 1. Simon's routine

    Input: n, $O_f : |x\rangle |0\rangle \mapsto |x\rangle |f(x)\rangle$ with $f : \{0,1\}^n \to X$ hiding $\mathcal{H}$
    Output: y orthogonal to $\mathcal{H}$
1: Initialize two n-bits registers : $|0\rangle |0\rangle$
2: Apply H gates on the first register, to compute $\sum_{x=0}^{2^n-1} |x\rangle |0\rangle$
3: Apply O_f, to compute $\sum_{x=0}^{2^n-1} |x\rangle |f(x)\rangle$
4: Reapply H gates on the register, to compute

$$\sum_x \sum_{j=0}^{2^n-1} (-1)^{x \cdot j} |j\rangle |f(x)\rangle = \sum_{x_0 \in \{0,1\}^n/(\mathcal{H})} \sum_{x_1 \in \mathcal{H}} \sum_{j=0}^{2^n-1} (-1)^{(x_0 \oplus x_1) \cdot j} |j\rangle |f(x_0)\rangle$$

5: The register is in the state

$$\sum_{x_0 \in \{0,1\}^n/(\mathcal{H})} \sum_{j=0}^{2^n-1} (-1)^{x_0 \cdot j} \sum_{x_1 \in \mathcal{H}} (-1)^{x_1 \cdot j} |j\rangle |f(x_0)\rangle$$

6: Measure $j, f(x_0)$, return them.

Lemma 3 (Adapted from [18, Lemma 1]**).** *Let $\mathcal{H}$ be a subgroup of $\{0,1\}^n$. Let $y \in \{0,1\}^n$. Then*

$$\sum_{h \in \mathcal{H}} (-1)^{y \cdot h} = \begin{cases} |\mathcal{H}| & \text{if } y \in \mathcal{H}^{\perp} \\ 0 & \text{otherwise} \end{cases}$$

Proof. See the full version [3]. $\square$

Hence, at the end of Simon's algorithm, the amplitude of j is nonzero if and only if $j \in \mathcal{H}^{\perp}$. Hence, this routine samples uniformly values orthogonal to $\mathcal{H}$.

The complete algorithm calls the routine until the values span a space of maximal rank or, if the rank is unknown, a fixed T times. Finally, with linear algebra, we can recover a basis of $\mathcal{H}$. In practice, we'll see in the next sections that $T = n + \mathcal{O}(1)$ is sufficient to succeed.

Remark 2 (Reversible Implementations). In Algorithm 1, the measurements are optional. Without them, we compute the superposition of the elements of $\mathcal{H}^{\perp}$. In that case, the linear algebra part has to be computed quantumly.

First of all, we present the following lemma that will allow us to study only the aperiodic case in Simon's algorithm.

Lemma 4 (Simon Reduction). *Let $n \in \mathbb{N}$, let X be a set. There exists a bijection φ_c from $\{f \in \{0,1\}^n \to X | f$ hides a subgroup of dimension $c\}$ to*

$$\{\mathcal{H} \subset \{0,1\}^n | \dim(\mathcal{H}) = c\} \times \left\{ \widehat{f} \in \{0,1\}^{n-c} \to X \Big| \widehat{f} \text{ is aperiodic} \right\}$$

such that, with $\varphi_c(f) = (\mathcal{H}, \widehat{f})$, the behaviour of Simon's algorithm with f and $\widehat{f}$ is identical, up to isomorphism. Moreover, f is a periodic permutation if and only if $\widehat{f}$ is a permutation.

Proof. See the full version [3]. $\square$

3.2 Analysis with Periodic Permutations

Proposition 3 (Simon's Algorithm Success Probability). *Let f be a function on n bits that fullfils the promise of Problem 1, $\mathcal{H}$ its hidden subgroup. With $T \geq n - \dim(\mathcal{H})$ queries, Simon's algorithm succeeds with probability*

$$pr_T = \prod_{i=0}^{n-\dim(\mathcal{H})-1} \left(1 - \frac{1}{2^{T-i}} \right).$$

Moreover, $\left(1 - 2^{n-T-dim(\mathcal{H})-1} \right)^2 \leq pr_T \leq 1 - 2^{n-T-dim(\mathcal{H})-1}$.

Proof. See the full version [3]. $\square$

Theorem 1 (Simon's Algorithm Query Complexity). *Let f be a function on n bits that fullfils the promise of Problem 1, $\mathcal{H}$ its hidden subgroup. To succeed, Simon's algorithm requires, on average:*

- *$n - dim(\mathcal{H}) + 2$ queries if $n - dim(\mathcal{H}) \geq 2$.*
- *2 queries if $n - dim(\mathcal{H}) = 1$.*

Proof. See the full version [3].

3.3 Limitations of Simon's Algorithm

We might want to apply Simon's algorithm on functions that are only periodic functions, and can have more preimages per image. However, we cannot expect to have a functioning algorithm in all cases. Indeed, let's consider

$$f_s : \begin{array}{ccc} \{0,1\}^n & \to & \{0,1\} \\ x & \mapsto & \begin{cases} 1 \text{ if } x \in \{0, s\} \\ 0 \text{ otherwise} \end{cases} \end{array}.$$

The function f_s has the hidden subgroup $\{0, s\}$. This function can be constructed from oracle access to a test function $t_s(x) = \delta_{x,s}$. Hence, as finding the hidden subgroup from f_s is equivalent to recovering s, and as quantum search is optimal to recover s given quantum oracle access to $t_s(x)$ [31], we cannot hope for a polynomial, over even subexponential algorithm in this case.

This inherent limitation of Simon's algorithm forces to estimate wether the periodic function will work well. The general argument to support the efficiency of Simon's algorithm in practice is, as we will prove below, that it works well for random functions, and that the functions that makes Simon's algorithm fail are degenerate enough to be distinguishable classically from random, which makes the cryptosystem likely to be breakable classically. We present here two approaches in this direction, which amounts in either ensuring that the function does not have any unwanted collision, or showing that these unwanted collisions are not a problem in practice.

Long Outputs. The first approach amounts in remarking that if the output of the function is long enough, there is a very low chance to find a collision in the function. This principle of lenght extension is for example used in [27].

Proposition 4 (Functions with Long Output). *The fraction of functions from $\{0,1\}^n$ to $\{0,1\}^{2n+\alpha}$ that are not a permutation is lower than $2^{-\alpha}$.*

Proof. See the full version [3].

If the output is not large enough, we can extend it by considering the function $g(x) = (f(x), f(x \oplus 1), f(x \oplus 2), \dots)$. This function will have a lower probability to have unwanted collisions than f, and with enough queries, will likely be a permutation.

There is however two limitations with this approach: first, the number of queries is multiplied by the number of copies of f we have in g, which is especially significant as the number of queries, from the previous section, is linear. Second, this may not be sufficient to prevent unwanted collisions to occur, and there are functions for which $f(\cdot)$ and $(f(\cdot), f(\cdot \oplus 1))$ have exactly as many collisions. Hence, there is still a need for a more precise analysis.

We will now present the other approach, which aims at showing that even with unwanted collisions, the pathological cases that prevent Simon's algorithm to succeed in a reasonable number of queries are too scarce to be an issue.

3.4   A General Criterion

To quantify how bad a function is, we define $\varepsilon(f)$ similarly to [18]:

$$\varepsilon(f) = \max_{t \in \{0,1\}^n/(\mathcal{H})} \Pr_x[f(x \oplus t) = f(x)].$$

This value estimates the probability that any given t is present as an additional period for some of the output vectors of Algorithm 1. It allows to bound the success probability of Simon's algorithm.

Proposition 5 (Success probability with More Preimages, adapted from [18, Theorem 1]). *Let f be a periodic function, $\mathcal{H}$ its hidden subgroup, and $\varepsilon(f)$ be defined as above. After $c(n - \dim(\mathcal{H}))$ steps, Simon's algorithm on f succeeds with probability greater than $1 - \left(2 \left(\frac{1+\varepsilon(f)}{2}\right)^c\right)^{n-\dim(\mathcal{H})}$.*

Proof. See the full version [3]. ∎

Theorem 2 (Number of Queries in General). *Let f be a periodic function, $\mathcal{H}$ its hidden subgroup, $\varepsilon(f)$ be defined as above. Simon's algorithm on f fails with probability lower than $2^{-\alpha}$ after $\frac{1}{1-\log_2(1+\varepsilon(f))}(n - \dim(\mathcal{H}) + \alpha)$ queries.*

Proof. See the full version [3]. ∎

3.5   With Random Functions

Now, we want to estimate the value of $\varepsilon(f)$. We show below that for all but a negligible fraction of functions, as long as the domain of the function is large enough, it is too small to have any impact on the number of queries.

Lemma 5. *Let $\mathcal{F} = \{0,1\}^n \to \{0,1\}^m$. Then $\left|\{f \in \mathcal{F} | \varepsilon(f) \geq \frac{2\ell}{2^n}\}\right| \leq 2^n \frac{2^{(n-m)\ell}}{\ell!} |\mathcal{F}|$*

Proof. See the full version [3]. ∎

Theorem 3 (ε for large enough m). *Let $\mathcal{F} = \{0,1\}^n \to \{0,1\}^m$. The proportion of functions in $\mathcal{F}$ such that $\varepsilon \geq e2^{1-m} + 2^{1-n}(n + \alpha)$ is upper bounded by $2^{-\alpha}$.*

Proof. See the full version [3].

Theorem 4 (Success Probability of Simon's Algorithm with Random Functions). *Assume* $m \geq \log_2(4e(n-h+\alpha+1))$. *Then the fraction of functions in* $\{0,1\}^n \to \{0,1\}^m$ *with a hidden subgroup of dimension* h *such that, after* $n-h+\alpha+1$ *queries, Simon's algorithm fails with a probability greater than* $2^{-\alpha}$ *is bounded by* $2^{n-h-\frac{2^{n-h}}{4(n-h+\alpha+1)}}$.

Proof. See the full version [3].

Theorem 5 (Average Complexity of Simon's Algorithm with Random Functions). *Assume* $m \geq \log_2(4e((n-h)+1))$. *Then the fraction of functions in* $\{0,1\}^n \to \{0,1\}^m$ *with a hidden subgroup of dimension* h *such that, on average, Simon's algorithm requires more than* $n-h+3$ *queries is bounded by* $2^{n-h-\frac{2^{n-h}}{4(2(n-h)+2)}}$.

Proof. See the full version [3].

4   Exact Variant of Simon's Algorithm

An exact version of Simon's algorithm was proposed by Brassard and Høyer in 1997 [7]. We propose here a more efficient variant of this algorithm, and prove that its query complexity is bounded by $3n - h + 1$ if the function operates on n bits and the hidden subgroup has dimension h. Note that this algorithm is only exact for periodic permutations.

4.1   The Algorithm of Brassard and Høyer

The idea of Algorithm 2 is to ensure that any measurement we perform gives us some information about the period. This is done by doing exact amplitude amplification over a subset of the values outputted by Simon's algorithm. Moreover, the subset we seek can be empty. In the original algorithm, the empty case meant that we should try with another subset until we find a non-empty one, or, if there is none, that the algorithm can end. As there is at most n such subsets, the algorithm is polynomial.

4.2   Our Improved Variant

We improve over the previous algorithm by remarking that the knowledge that a subset is empty actually gives some information on the hidden subgroup: it shows that a given vector is not in he subgroup's dual. Moreover, we show that this case is actually better, that is, we can reuse the quantum state, and save 1 query each time this occurs. This is Algorithm 3.

Theorem 6 (Complexity and Correctness of Algorithm 3). *Let* f *be a periodic permutation from* $\{0,1\}^n$ *with a hidden subgroup of dimension* h. *Algorithm 3 returns a basis of* $\mathcal{H}$ *in less than* $\min(3n - h + 1, 3n)$ *queries.*

Proof. See the full version [3].

Algorithm 2. Exact Simon's algorithm, from [7]

Input: n, $O_f : |x\rangle |0\rangle \mapsto |x\rangle |f(x)\rangle$ with $f : \{0,1\}^n \to X$ hiding $\mathcal{H}$
Output: a basis of $\mathcal{H}$

1: $V = \emptyset$ ▷ Basis of $\mathcal{H}^\perp$
2: **for** i from 1 to n **do**
3:     Choose a set W such that V, W forms a basis of $\{0,1\}^n$.
4:     **for** j from i to n **do**
5:         Apply Algorithm 1, without measuring

The state is $\displaystyle\sum_{x_0 \in \{0,1\}^n/(\mathcal{H})} \sum_{y=0}^{2^n-1} (-1)^{x_0 \cdot y} \sum_{x_1 \in \mathcal{H}} (-1)^{x_1 \cdot y} |y\rangle |f(x_0)\rangle$

6:         **amplify** the marked vectors: ▷ Exact amplitude amplification
7:             Decompose y as $\sum_{v_k \in V} \delta_k v_k + \sum_{w_j \in W} \gamma_\ell w_\ell$
8:             Mark if $\gamma_j = 1$
9:         **end amplify**
10:         Measure $|\gamma_j\rangle$
11:         **if** $\gamma_j = 1$ **then** measure the first register, add the result to V, break
12:         **end if**
13:     **end for**
14:     **if** V has not been updated **then** break
15:     **end if**
16: **end for**
17: **return** a basis of $V^\perp$

---

5   Grover-meets-Simon

5.1   Algorithm Description

The Grover-meets-Simon algorithm [22] aims at solving the following problem[1]:

Problem 3 (Grover-meets-Simon). Let $f : \{0,1\}^k \times \{0,1\}^n \to \{0,1\}^m$ be a function such that there exists a unique k_0 such that $f(k_0, \cdot)$ hides a non-trivial subgroup $\mathcal{H}$. Find k_0 and $\mathcal{H}$.

The idea to solve this problem is to use Simon's algorithm as a distinguisher: for the wrong k, Simon's algorithm should return the trivial subgroup, while for k_0 it will always return a non-trivial subgroup. We can then use it as a test function to find k_0, as in Algorithm 4.

The issue with this test is that it allows many false positives: indeed, even for some incorrect k, Simon's algorithm may return a non-trivial subgroup, and these bad cases will also be amplified.

The idea to overcome this issue is to use a test outside of Simon's algorithm to check if its output is correct.

---

[1] In [22], the algorithm they introduce is in fact a special case of what we call here Grover-meets-Simon with a perfect external test.

Algorithm 3. Improved variant of the exact Simon's algorithm

    Input: n, $O_f : |x\rangle\,|0\rangle \mapsto |x\rangle\,|f(x)\rangle$ with $f : \{0,1\}^n \to X$ hiding $\mathcal{H}$
    Output: a basis of $\mathcal{H}$
1: $V = \emptyset$ ▷ Basis of $\mathcal{H}^\perp$
2: $W = \emptyset$ ▷ Basis of $\{0,1\}^n/(\mathcal{H}^\perp)$
3: **for** i from 1 to n **do**
4:     **if** No quantum state is available **then**
5:         Apply Algorithm 1, without measuring
        The state is $\displaystyle\sum_{x_0 \in \{0,1\}^n/(\mathcal{H})} \sum_{y=0}^{2^n-1} (-1)^{x_0 \cdot y} \sum_{x_1 \in \mathcal{H}} (-1)^{x_1 \cdot y} \, |y\rangle\,|f(x_0)\rangle$
6:     **end if**
7:     **amplify** the marked vectors: ▷ Exact amplification
8:         Choose a set Z such that V, W, Z forms a basis of $\{0,1\}^n$.
9:         Decompose each y as $\sum_{v_k \in V} \delta_k v_k + \sum_{z_j \in Z} \gamma_j z_j$, mark if $\gamma_1 = 1$
10:     **end amplify**
11:     Measure $|\gamma_1\rangle$
12:     **if** $\gamma_1 = 1$ **then** Measure the first register, add the result to V, discard the quantum state
13:     **else** Add z_1 to W, uncompute steps 7–10   ▷ Get the state from step 5
14:     **end if**
15: **end for**
16: **return** a basis of $V^\perp$

Algorithm 4. Grover-meets-Simon

    Input: n, $O_f : |k\rangle\,|x\rangle\,|0\rangle \mapsto |x\rangle\,|f(k,x)\rangle$ with $f(k_0, \cdot)$ of Hidden subgroup $\mathcal{H}$
    Output: k_0, a basis of $\mathcal{H}$.
1: **amplify** over k with the following test:
2:     $H \leftarrow$ Simon's algorithm over $f(k, \cdot)$
3:     **return** $H \neq \{0\}$
4: **end amplify**

Hence, instead of only checking the dimension of the subgroup, we compute the subgroup and check if it is correct. This is something we can always do if $\dim(\mathcal{H}) \geq 1$ and $f(k, \cdot)$ is aperiodic if $k \neq k_0$, as presented in Algorithm 5. This test is only perfect with periodic permutations, otherwise it may happen that these equalities hold for an aperiodic function, but it can in general rule out false positives more efficiently than by adding more queries in Simon's algorithm.

Algorithm 5. Periodicity test

    Input: k, H

    Output: $(k, H) \overset{?}{=} (k_0, \mathcal{H})$

1: **for** some $x, h \in \{0,1\}^n \times H \setminus \{0\}$ **do**

2:      **if** $f(k, x) \neq f(k, x \oplus h)$ **then**

3:          **return** False

4:      **end if**

5: **end for**

6: **return** True

5.2 Cost Analysis

Here, Simon's algorithm is used to identify one function among a family. The main issue is that there can be false positives, that is, functions that are identified as periodic while they are not, which create terms in $k - \alpha$ in Theorem 7.

Theorem 7 (Success Probability for Plain Grover-meets-Simon). *Let $f : \{0,1\}^k \times \{0,1\}^n \rightarrow \{0,1\}^m$ be a function such that there exists a unique i_0 such that $f(i_0, \cdot)$ hides a non-trivial subgroup $\mathcal{H}$. If for all $i \neq i_0$, Simon's algorithm on $f(i, \cdot)$, succeeds with probability at least $1 - 2^{-\alpha}$, then Algorithm 4 succeeds in $\frac{\pi}{4 \arcsin \sqrt{2^{-k}}}$ iterations with probability at least $1 - 2^{k-\alpha} - 2^{2(k-\alpha)+1} - 2^{-k+2} - 2^{-\alpha+2} - 2^{-2k+6} + 2^{k-3\alpha+6}$.*

Proof. See the full version [3]. ∎

Now, we study the situation with external tests, either when we have perfect external tests, or using Algorithm 5, with Theorem 8.

Theorem 8 (Grover-meets-Simon with Perfect External Test). *Let $f : \{0,1\}^k \times \{0,1\}^n \rightarrow \{0,1\}^m$ be a function such that there exists a i_0 such that $f(i_0, \cdot)$ hides a subgroup $\mathcal{H}$, and there exists a test function T such that $T(i, H) = 1$ if and only if $(i, H) = (i_0, \mathcal{H})$. If for $f(i_0, \cdot)$, Simon's algorithm succeeds with probability at least $1 - 2^{-\alpha}$, then Algorithm 4 with a perfect external test succeeds in $\frac{\pi}{4 \arcsin \sqrt{2^{-k}}}$ iterations with probability at least $1 - (2^{-\alpha+1} + 2^{-k/2} + 2^{-k+1})^2$.*

Proof. See the full version [3]. ∎

Remark 3 (Grover-meets-Simon for Periodic permutation). There is a perfect test for periodic permutations which costs only 2 queries. It amounts in testing wether or not the function fullfils $f(0) = f(h_i)$, with (h_i) a basis of the guessed hidden subgroup H. This will only be the case if the function is indeed periodic.

Remark 4. The external test allows to remove the error terms in $k - \alpha$, which means that there is no longer a dependency in k for the nimimal number of queries. We only need n plus a constant number of queries to succeed.

When there is no perfect external test (for example in the case of quantum distinguishers), we can still do better than Theorem 7 using Algorithm 5.

Theorem 9 (Grover-meets-Simon with Periodicity Test). *Let $k \geq 3$, f : $\{0,1\}^k \times \{0,1\}^n \to \{0,1\}^m$ be a function such that there exists a unique i_0 such that $f(i_0, \cdot)$ hides a non-trivial subgroup $\mathcal{H}$. If for all $f(i, \cdot)$, Simon's algorithm succeeds with probability at least $1 - 2^{-\alpha}$ and for all $i \neq i_0$, $\varepsilon(f(i, \cdot)) \leq \varepsilon$, then Algorithm 4 with γ queries in Algorithm 5 succeeds in $\frac{\pi}{4 \arcsin \sqrt{2^{-k}}}$ iterations with probability at least $1 - \varepsilon^\gamma 2^{k-\alpha+1} - (2^{-\alpha+1} + 2^{-k/2} + 2^{-k+1})^2$.*

Proof. See the full version [3].

6 The Offline Simon's Algorithm

6.1 Algorithm Description

The offline Simon's algorithm [4] is the only known application of Simon's algorithm that does not require quantum access to a secret function. It can be seen as a variant of the Grover-meets-Simon algorithm that leverages a special structure of the periodic function. Concretely, the algorithm can solve the following problem:

Problem 4 (Constructing and Finding a Periodic Function). Let E_k : $\{0,1\}^n \to \{0,1\}^\ell$ be a function, $f : \{0,1\}^k \times \{0,1\}^n \to \{0,1\}^\ell$ be a family of functions. Let P be a quantum circuit such that

$$P \ket{i} \sum_{x \in \{0,1\}^n} \ket{x} \ket{E_k(x)} = \ket{i} \sum_{x \in \{0,1\}^n} \ket{x} \ket{f(i,x)}$$

Assume that there exists a unique $i_0 \in \{0,1\}^k$ such that $f(i_0, \cdot)$ hides a non-trivial subgroup. Given oracle access to E_k and P, find i_0 and the period of $f(i_0, \cdot)$.

Here, the compared to Grover-meets-Simon, we add the assumption that the family of functions can be efficiently computed from a fixed function E_k. In most cases, we can restrict ourselves to the following simpler problem, with f the sum of two functions:

Problem 5 (Asymmetric Search of a Periodic Function). Let g : $\{0,1\}^m \times \{0,1\}^n \to \{0,1\}^\ell$ and E_k : $\{0,1\}^n \to \{0,1\}^\ell$ be some functions.
Assume that there exists a unique $i_0 \in \{0,1\}^m$ such that $g(i_0, \cdot) \oplus E_k$ hides a non-trivial subgroup. Given oracle access to g and E_k, find i_0.

The idea to solve Problem 4 is to see Simon's algorithm slightly differently than usual. Instead of querying an oracle to a function, we suppose that the algorithm is given as input a *database* of E_k, a set of superpositions $\sum_x \ket{x} \ket{E_k(x)}$. It then computes the periodic function from this set, and finally extracts the period. We note $\ket{\psi_{E_k}^m} = \bigotimes_{j=1}^m \sum_x \ket{x} \ket{E_k(x)}$, a state which contains m copies of the superpositions of input/outputs of E_k.

Hence, the algorithm is very similar to Algorithm 4, but instead of querying the function E_k, the test function fetches $|\psi_{E_k}^m\rangle$, uses it to check if the function is periodic, and finally uncomputes everything, to get back a state close to $|\psi_{E_k}^m\rangle$, which can then be reused in the next iteration. This is Algorithm 6. Thus, m corresponds to the number of queries required by Simon's algorithm.

Algorithm 6. The offline Simon's algorithm

    Input: n, An oracle O_{E_k} and a quantum circuit P that fullfils the constraints of Problem 4
    Output: i_0.
1: Query m times O_{E_k}, to construct $|\psi_{E_k}^m\rangle$
2: **amplify** over i with the following test:
3:     Compute m copies of $\sum_x |x\rangle |f(i,x)\rangle$ from $|\psi_{E_k}^m\rangle$ and P.
4:     Apply a Hadamard gate on the first register of each copy.
5:     Compute in superposition the rank r of the values in each first register.
6:     $b \leftarrow r \neq n$
7:     Uncompute everything but the value of b, to recover $|\psi_{E_k}^m\rangle$.
8:     Return b
9: **end amplify**

Remark 5. In this algorithm, all the queries have to be done at the beginning of Simon's algorithm. Hence, it is not possible to use the exact variant of Algorithm 3 here.

Now, it remains to estimate the deviation due to the fact that we are not exactly testing if i is equal to i_0.

Lemma 6 (Deviation for the Offline Simon's Algorithm). *If Simon's algorithm fails with probability at most $2^{-\alpha}$, then the test function in Algorithm 6 tests if $i = i_0$ and adds a noise of amplitude smaller than $2^{-\alpha/2+1}$.*

Proof. See the full version [3].   □

Algorithm 6 allows to only make the quantum queries to E_k once, at the beginning. Now, the idea to use only classical queries is to construct manually the quantum superposition over E_k *from the classical queries of all its 2^n possible inputs.* This is presented in Algorithm 7. As this is can only be done in $\mathcal{O}(2^n)$ time, we really need to reuse the queries to still have a time-efficient algorithm.

Algorithm 7. Generation of $|\psi_{E_k}^m\rangle$ from classical queries

    Input: A classical oracle to E_k, m
    Output: $|\psi_{E_k}^m\rangle$
1: $|\phi\rangle \leftarrow \bigotimes_m \sum_x |x\rangle |0\rangle$
2: **for** $0 \leq i < 2^n$ **do**
3:      Query $E_k(i)$
4:      Apply to each register in $|\phi\rangle$ the operator

$$|x\rangle |y\rangle \mapsto \begin{cases} |x\rangle |y \oplus E_k(i)\rangle & \text{if } x = i \\ |x\rangle |y\rangle & \text{otherwise} \end{cases}$$

5: **end for**
6: **return** $|\phi\rangle$

6.2 Cost Analysis

The offline Simon's algorithm reuses the quantum queries between the tests. This allows to make the algorithm work with classical queries, at the expense of having more noise than with the Grover-meets-Simon algorithm.

Theorem 10 (Success Probability for the Offline Simon's Algorithm). *Let $f : \{0,1\}^k \times \{0,1\}^n \to \{0,1\}^m$ be a function such that there exists a unique i_0 such that $f(i_0, \cdot)$ hides a non-trivial subgroup $\mathcal{H}$. If for all $i \neq i_0$, Simon's algorithm on $f(i, \cdot)$ succeeds with probability at least $1 - 2^{-\alpha}$, then Algorithm 6 succeeds in $\frac{\pi}{4 \arcsin \sqrt{2^{-k}}}$ iterations with probability at least $1 - 2^{k-\alpha} - (2^{k/2-\alpha/2+1} + 2^{k-\alpha} + \sqrt{2^{-k} + 2^{-\alpha}} + 2^{-k+1}\sqrt{1 + 2^{k-\alpha}}^3)^2$*

Proof. See the full version [3]. □

Remark 6. Contrary to the Grover-meets-Simon case, we cannot remove the error terms in $2^{k-\alpha}$ with an external test, which means that we cannot remove the direct dependency in k in the number of queries.

Theorem 11 (The Offline Simon's Algorithm with Random Functions). *Assume that $m \geq \log_2(4e(n + k + \alpha + 1))$ and $k \geq 5$. The fraction of functions in $\{0,1\}^k \times \{0,1\}^n \to \{0,1\}^m$ such that the offline Simon's algorithm with $n + k + \alpha + 1$ queries per iterations succeeds in $\frac{\pi}{4 \arcsin \sqrt{2^{-k}}}$ iterations with probability lower than*

$$1 - 2^{-\alpha} - \left(2^{-\alpha/2+1} + 2^{-\alpha} + 2^{-k/2+1}\right)^2$$

is lower than $2^{n+k - \frac{2^n}{4(n+k+\alpha+1)}}$.

Proof. See the full version [3]. □

7   Applications in Cryptanalysis

We separate three use cases of Simon's algorithm in cryptanalysis:

- Quantum distinguishers, that aims at telling wether the input oracle has a given structure or has been chosen uniformly at random,
- Forgeries, in which the knowledge of the hidden subgroup is not sufficient to compute fully the secret oracle (but is enough to forge valid ciphertext),
- Key recoveries, in which all the secret information is recovered.

7.1   Landscape of Known Simon-Based Attacks

We present the distinguishers in the literature in Table 1, the forgeries in Table 2 and the key recoveries in Table 3. There are two models for these attacks: the quantum chosen-plaintext model (qCPA) assumes we can query the encryption oracle quantumly. The more powerful quantum chosen-ciphertext model (qCCA) assumes that we can also query the decryption oracle.

From these tables, we can see that periodic permutations are almost never used, that the hidden subgroup is generally of dimension 1, the only known exception being the quantum cryptanalysis of AEZ [1]. Finally, in these attacks, the domain of the function has generally almost the same size as the codomain, or a larger size with the offline Simon's algorithm, as it fixes part of the input. The dimension of the problem can be estimated between 32 and 256, as the block size of the affected symetric constructions generally ranges between 64 and 256 bits. Hence, if we restrict ourselves to an error probability greater than 2^{-256}, the probability that a function does not satisfy Theorem 4 is *at best* $2^{-2^{20}}$.

7.2   Cost Estimates in Practice

Dimension of the Subgroup. In almost all cases, the dimension is 0 or 1. Hence, we consider that it is 0, which is an increase of at most 1 query.

Simon's Algorithm. For plain Simon's algorithm, we can directly apply Theorem 5 and Theorem 4 to get the following heuristic:

Heuristic 2 (Simon's algorithm). *Simon's algorithm succeeds in $n + 3$ queries on average and with $n + \alpha + 1$ queries, it succeeds with probability $1 - 2^{-\alpha}$.*

Table 1. Known Simon-based distinguishers. n is the input size, d is the number of branches. GFN means generalized Feistel Network. The algorithm is always plain Simon's algorithm, but the distinguishers can be converted to key recoveries and extended to more rounds with a quantum search or a nested Simon, as proposed in [9,12,24]. *Note that if the distinguisher is given a random permutation/function, Simon's algorithm will not operate on a permutation.

Target	Number of rounds	Periodic permutation	Group dim.	Input size	Output size	Source
Feistel	3 (qCPA)	Yes*	0–1	$n/2+1$	$n/2$	[20]
	4 (qCCA)		0–1	$n/2+1$	$n/2$	[17]
Type-1 GFN	$3d-3$ (qCPA)		0–1	$n/d+1$	n/d	[24]
	d^2-d+1 (qCCA)		0–1	$n/d+1$	n/d	[24]
Type-2 GFN	$d+1$ (qCPA)		0–1	$n/d+1$	n/d	[11]
Type-3 GFN	d (qCPA)		0–1	$n/d+1$	n/d	[13]
Contracting GFN	$2d-1$ (qCPA)		0–1	$n/d+1$	n/d	[9]

Table 2. Known Simon-based forgeries. No attack use a periodic permutation. Forgeries for Chaskey and other versions of AEZ are not presented, as a key recovery exists.

Target		Group dim.	Input size	Output size	Algorithm	Source
MAC	CBC-MAC	1	$n+1$	n	Simon	[18,28]
	PMAC	1	$n+1$	n	Simon	[18]
	GMAC	1	$n+1$	n	Simon	[18]
Modes	LRW	1	$n+1$	n	Simon	[18]
	OCB	1	$n+1$	n	Simon	[18]
	GCM	1	$n+1$	n	Simon	[18]
AE schemes	Minalpher	1	257	256	Simon	[18]
	OMD	1	129	128	Simon	[18]
	AEZ10	1–2	128	128	Simon	[1]

Nested Simon's Algorithm. A few attacks require a mested use of Simon's algorithm. This still makes for some polynomial attacks, albeit of larger degree. In that case, precise estimates have a larger impact, as a cost estimate of $cn+o(n)$ lead to a nested cost of $c^k n^k + o(n^k)$. Our work shows that we can use $c=1$.

External Tests in Grover-meets-Simon. In general, a perfect external test amounts to checking if the output of a secret function (say, a block cipher) matches the output of the guessed function, secret function whose size will be, in practice, around the dimension of the Simon instance. Hence, this test will fail with probability 2^{-n}, which means that we need $\lceil \frac{k}{n} \rceil$ tests to filter out all the false positives. This is close to what we have with a periodicity test. However, the external test might use a cheaper function than the periodic function, which would then allow a small gain.

Table 3. Known Simon-based key recoveries. No attack use a periodic permutation. Chaskey's output size is a parameter to be chosen by the user. *The 4 articles present distinct models of quantum related-keys.

	Target	Group dim.	Input size	Output size	Algorithm	Offline variant	Source
	Even-Mansour	1	n	n	Simon	Yes	[21]
	FX construction	0–1	n	n	Grover+Simon	Yes	[22]
	AEZ	1–3	128	128	Simon		[1]
	Feistel-MiMC/GMiMC	1	$n/2$	$n/2$	Simon	Yes	[2]
	8-round SMS4	0–1	33	32	Grover+Simon	Yes	[14]
	Chaskey	1	128	$t \le 128$	Simon	Yes	[16]
	HCTR/HCH	1	n	n	Simon	Yes	[26]
	Round-keys						
Self-similar Feistel	1	1	$n/2$	$n/2$	Simon		[6,10]
	2	1	$n+1$	n	Simon		[6,10]
	4	1	$n/2+1$	$n/2$	Nested Simon		[6]
	4+Whitening	0–1	$n+1$	$n/2$	Grover+Simon		[6]
	any in related-key*	1	$n/2$	$n/2$	Variable		[9]
Self-similar SPN	1	1	$n+1$	n	Simon		[18]
	any	0–1	$n+1$	n	Grover+Simon	Yes	[4]
	any in related-key*	1	$n+1$	n	Simon		[15]
	Block ciphers in related-key*	1	n	n	Simon	Yes	[4,27]

Grover-meets-Simon. We use Theorem 8 or Theorem 9, depending on whether an external test is available. We assume that testing the periodicity $\lceil \frac{k}{n} \rceil$ times is enough to rule out the false positives. Moreover, we assume that the dominant term in the error will be the term in $2^{-2\alpha+2}$, which means that $\alpha \ll k/2 - 1$. Under that assumption, we have the following heuristic:

Heuristic 3 (Grover-meet-Simon). *Grover-meet-Simon succeeds with probability* $1 - 2^{-\alpha}$ *in* $n + \alpha/2 + 2 \lceil \frac{k}{n} \rceil$ *queries per iteration.*

With a perfect external test, it succeeds with probability $1 - 2^{-\alpha}$ *in* $n + \alpha/2$ *queries plus one query to the external test per iteration.*

The Offline Simon's Algorithm. Using external tests does not really improve the offline Simon's algorithm, and we can directly rely on Theorem 11. We assume that the dominant term in the term in the square is $2^{-\alpha/2+1}$, which implies $\alpha \ll k$. Under that assumption, we have the following heuristic:

Heuristic 4 (The offline Simon's algorithm). *The offline Simon's algorithm succeeds with probability* $1 - 2^{-\alpha}$ *in* $n + k + \alpha + 4$ *queries per iteration.*

Truncating the Output. For the functions we consider, we generally have the same input and output size, which is more than enough for Simon's algorithm to be efficient. From Theorem 4, with q queries, we only need $\log_2(4eq)$ bits of output, any longer would have no impact on the query cost. Hence, we can propose the following heuristic:

Heuristic 5 (Truncating functions in reversible implementations). *A reversible implementation of Simon's algorithm with q queries only needs a periodic function with $\lceil 3.5 + \log_2(q) \rceil$ bits of output.*

Memory Gain. The truncation technique allows to gain memory in reversible implementations, as all the oracle calls have to be made in parallel. For the offline Simon's algorithm, we typically have an input size of $n/3$ bits and an output size of n bits. Thus, we can improve from $4n/3$ qubits to $n/3 + log_2(n) + 3.5$ per query. With typical parameters, this corresponds to $n/3 + 15$ which is a free gain of around a factor 3 in memory. Combined with the reduction in query, depending on the concrete attack, we can estimate an overall gain of around a factor 10 in memory.

8 Conclusion

We computed precise concrete query estimates for all use cases of Simon's algorithm, including the first concrete estimates for the exact variant of Simon's algorithm and the offline Simon's algorithm. With a query cost of $3n$ queries, it is not competitive for cryptographic applications, as the success probability of the plain algorithm with $3n$ queries is overwhelming. We showed that relaxing the promise of Simon's algorithm has a negligible impact on its complexity. These estimates pave the way to quantum circuits for concrete Simon-based attacks, which would give precise and optimized *time* cost estimates. For example, the recent [5] crucially relies on our results.

Our analysis showed that there is a gap between the Grover-meets-Simon and offline Simon's algorithm, the latter being less precise, and requiring more queries to succeed. Finally, it showed that it is possible to truncate the periodic function without any impact on the query cost, which allows to save memory in all reversible implementations of Simon's algorithm for free.

Open Problems. There is still one case out of reach with our current techniques: periodic functions with 1 bit of output, which were proposed in [23]. More generally, there is the question of how reduced the output size can be while still having a negligible impact on the query cost.

While we showed a matching lower bound on the query cost of Simon's algorithm, our analysis does not rule out the existence of a different algorithm that needs less than $n - h$ queries. It would be of interest to prove this lower bound, or, in the unlikely event that it exists, propose a more efficient algorithm.

Acknowledgements. The author would like to thank André Schrottenloher and Akinori Hosoyamada for interesting discussions.

References

1. Bonnetain, X.: Quantum key-recovery on full AEZ. In: Adams, C., Camenisch, J. (eds.) SAC 2017. LNCS, vol. 10719, pp. 394–406. Springer, Cham (2018). https://doi.org/10.1007/978-3-319-72565-9_20
2. Bonnetain, X.: Collisions on Feistel-MiMC and univariate GMiMC. Cryptology ePrint Archive, Report 2019/951 (2019). https://eprint.iacr.org/2019/951
3. Bonnetain, X.: Tight bounds for Simon's algorithm. IACR Cryptol. ePrint Arch. 2020, 919 (2020). https://eprint.iacr.org/2020/919
4. Bonnetain, X., Hosoyamada, A., Naya-Plasencia, M., Sasaki, Y., Schrottenloher, A.: Quantum attacks without superposition queries: the offline Simon's algorithm. In: Galbraith, S.D., Moriai, S. (eds.) ASIACRYPT 2019, Part I. LNCS, vol. 11921, pp. 552–583. Springer, December 2019
5. Bonnetain, X., Jaques, S.: Quantum period finding against symmetric primitives in practice. CoRR abs/2011.07022 (2020), https://arxiv.org/abs/2011.07022
6. Bonnetain, X., Naya-Plasencia, M., Schrottenloher, A.: On quantum slide attacks. In: Paterson, K.G., Stebila, D. (eds.) SAC 2019. LNCS, vol. 11959, pp. 492–519. Springer, August 2019
7. Brassard, G., Hoyer, P.: An exact quantum polynomial-time algorithm for Simon's problem. In: Proceedings of the Fifth Israeli Symposium on Theory of Computing and Systems, pp. 12–23 (1997)
8. Brassard, G., Høyer, P., Mosca, M., Tapp, A.: Quantum amplitude amplification and estimation. In: Lomo-naco, S.J., Brandt, H.E. (eds.) Quantum Computation and Information, AMS Contemporary Mathematics, vol. 305 (2002)
9. Cid, C., Hosoyamada, A., Liu, Y., Sim, S.M.: Quantum cryptanalysis on contracting feistel structures and observation on related-key settings. In: Bhargavan, K., Oswald, E., Prabhakaran, M. (eds.) INDOCRYPT 2020. LNCS, vol. 12578, pp. 373–394. Springer, Cham (2020). https://doi.org/10.1007/978-3-030-65277-7_17
10. Dong, X., Dong, B., Wang, X.: Quantum attacks on some Feistel block ciphers. Des. Codes Cryptogr. **88**(6), 1179–1203 (2020)
11. Dong, X., Li, Z., Wang, X.: Quantum cryptanalysis on some generalized Feistel schemes. Sci. China Inf. Sci. **62**(2), 22501:1–22501:12 (2019)
12. Dong, X., Wang, X.: Quantum key-recovery attack on feistel structures. Sci. China Inf. Sci. **61**(10), 102501:1–102501:7 (2018)
13. Hodžić, S., Knudsen Ramkilde, L., Brasen Kidmose, A.: On quantum distinguishers for Type-3 generalized Feistel network based on separability. In: Ding, J., Tillich, J.-P. (eds.) PQCrypto 2020. LNCS, vol. 12100, pp. 461–480. Springer, Cham (2020). https://doi.org/10.1007/978-3-030-44223-1_25
14. Hodžić, S., Knudsen, L.: A quantum distinguisher for 7/8-round sms4 block cipher. Quant. Inf. Process. **19**, 411 (2020)
15. Hosoyamada, A., Aoki, K.: On quantum related-key attacks on iterated even-mansour ciphers. In: Obana, S., Chida, K. (eds.) IWSEC 2017. LNCS, vol. 10418, pp. 3–18. Springer, Cham (2017). https://doi.org/10.1007/978-3-319-64200-0_1
16. Hosoyamada, A., Sasaki, Y.: Cryptanalysis against symmetric-key schemes with online classical queries and offline quantum computations. In: Smart, N.P. (ed.) CT-RSA 2018. LNCS, vol. 10808, pp. 198–218. Springer, Cham, April 2018
17. Ito, G., Hosoyamada, A., Matsumoto, R., Sasaki, Yu., Iwata, T.: Quantum chosen-ciphertext attacks against feistel ciphers. In: Matsui, M. (ed.) CT-RSA 2019. LNCS, vol. 11405, pp. 391–411. Springer, Cham (2019). https://doi.org/10.1007/978-3-030-12612-4_20

18. Kaplan, M., Leurent, G., Leverrier, A., Naya-Plasencia, M.: Breaking symmetric cryptosystems using quantum period finding. In: Robshaw, M., Katz, J. (eds.) CRYPTO 2016, Part II. LNCS, vol. 9815, pp. 207–237. Springer, August 2016

19. Koiran, P., Nesme, V., Portier, N.: The quantum query complexity of the abelian hidden subgroup problem. Theor. Comput. Sci. **380**(1–2), 115–126 (2007)

20. Kuwakado, H., Morii, M.: Quantum distinguisher between the 3-round feistel cipher and the random permutation. In: IEEE Proceedings of the International Symposium on Information Theory (ISIT 2010), June 13–18, 2010, pp. 2682–2685. Austin (2010)

21. Kuwakado, H., Morii, M.: Security on the quantum-type even-mansour cipher. In: Proceedings of ISITA 2012, . October 28–31, pp. 312–316. Honolulu, HI (2012)

22. Leander, G., May, A.: Grover meets Simon - quantumly attacking the FX-construction. In: Takagi, T., Peyrin, T. (eds.) ASIACRYPT 2017, Part II. LNCS, vol. 10625, pp. 161–178. Springer, December 2017

23. May, A., Schlieper, L.: Quantum period finding with a single output qubit - factoring n-bit RSA with n/2 qubits. CoRR abs/1905.10074 (2019)

24. Ni, B., Ito, G., Dong, X., Iwata, T.: Quantum attacks against type-1 generalized Feistel ciphers and applications to CAST-256. In: Hao, F., Ruj, S., Sen Gupta, S. (eds.) INDOCRYPT 2019. LNCS, vol. 11898, pp. 433–455. Springer, December 2019

25. Nielsen, M.A., Chuang, I.L.: Quantum Computation and Quantum Information, 10th Anniversary edn. Cambridge University Press, Cambridge (2016)

26. Rahman, M., Paul, G.: Quantum attacks on HCTR and its variants. IACR Cryptol. ePrint Arch. **2020**, 802 (2020)

27. Roetteler, M., Steinwandt, R.: A note on quantum related-key attacks. Inf. Process. Lett. **115**(1), 40–44 (2015)

28. Santoli, T., Schaffner, C.: Using Simon's algorithm to attack symmetric-key cryptographic primitives. Quant. Inf. Comput. **17**(1 & 2), 65–78 (2017)

29. Shor, P.W.: Algorithms for quantum computation: Discrete logarithms and factoring. In: 35th FOCS, pp. 124–134. IEEE Computer Society Press, November 1994

30. Simon, D.R.: On the power of quantum computation. In: 35th FOCS, pp. 116–123. IEEE Computer Society Press, November 1994

31. Zalka, C.: Grover's quantum searching algorithm is optimal. Phys. Rev. A **60**(4), 2746 (1999)

Constructions for Quantum Indistinguishability Obfuscation

Anne Broadbent[1]([⊠]) and Raza Ali Kazmi[1,2]

[1] Department of Mathematics and Statistics, University of Ottawa, Ottawa, Canada
abroadbe@uottawa.ca
[2] Fintech Research, Bank of Canada, Ottawa, Canada
RKazmi@bank-banque-canada.ca

Abstract. An *indistinguishability obfuscator* is a polynomial-time probabilistic algorithm that takes a circuit as input and outputs a new circuit that has the same functionality as the input circuit, such that for any two circuits of the same size that compute the *same* function, the outputs of the indistinguishability obfuscator are indistinguishable. Here, we study schemes for indistinguishability obfuscation for *quantum* circuits. We present two definitions for indistinguishability obfuscation: in our first definition ($qi\mathcal{O}$) the outputs of the obfuscator are required to be indistinguishable if the input circuits are perfectly equivalent, while in our second definition ($qi\mathcal{O}_\mathbf{D}$), the outputs are required to be indistinguishable as long as the input circuits are approximately equivalent with respect to a pseudo-distance $\mathbf{D}$. Our main results provide (1) a computationally-secure scheme for $qi\mathcal{O}$ where the size of the output of the obfuscator is exponential in the number of non-Clifford (T gates), which means that the construction is efficient as long as the number of T gates is logarithmic in the circuit size and (2) a statistically-secure $qi\mathcal{O}_\mathbf{D}$, for circuits that are close to the kth level of the Gottesman-Chuang hierarchy (with respect to $\mathbf{D}$); this construction is efficient as long as k is small and fixed.

1 Introduction

At the intuitive level, an *obfuscator* is a probabilistic polynomial-time algorithm that transforms a circuit C into another circuit C' that has the same functionality as C but that does not reveal anything about C, except its functionality *i.e.*, anything that can be learned from C' about C can also be learned from black-box access to the input-output functionality of C. This concept is formalized in terms of *virtual black-box obfuscation*, and was shown [11] to be unachievable in general. Motivated by this impossibility result, the same work proposed a weaker notion called *indistinguishability obfuscation* ($i\mathcal{O}$).

In the classical context, an *indistinguishability obfuscator* is a probabilistic polynomial-time algorithm that takes a circuit C as input and outputs a circuit $i\mathcal{O}(C)$ such that $i\mathcal{O}(C)(x) = C(x)$ for all inputs x and the size of $i\mathcal{O}(C)$ is at most polynomial in the size of C. Moreover, it must be that for any two circuits C_1 and C_2 of the same size and that compute the same function, their

P. Longa and C. Ràfols (Eds.): LATINCRYPT 2021, LNCS 12912, pp. 24–43, 2021.
https://doi.org/10.1007/978-3-030-88238-9_2

obfuscations are computationally indistinguishable. It is known that $i\mathcal{O}$ achieves the notion of *best possible obfuscation*, which states that any information that is not hidden by the obfuscated circuit is also not hidden by any circuit of similar size computing the same functionality [28]. Indistinguishability obfuscation is a very powerful cryptographic tool which is known to enable, among others: digital signatures, public key encryption [38], multiparty key agreement, broadcast encryption [13], fully homomorphic encryption [18] and witness-indistinguishable proofs [12]. Notable in the context of these applications is the *punctured programming technique* [38] which manages to render an $i\mathcal{O}(C)$ into an intriguing cryptographic building block, and this, despite that fact that the security guarantees of $i\mathcal{O}(C)$ appear quite weak as they are applicable only if the two original circuits have *exactly* the same functionality.

The first candidate construction of $i\mathcal{O}$ was published in [24], with security relying on the hardness of multilinear maps [20,26,34]. Unfortunately, there have been many quantum attacks on multilinear maps [6,19,21]. Recently, new $i\mathcal{O}$ schemes were proposed under different assumptions [9,25,32]. Whether or not these schemes are resistant against quantum attacks remains to be determined.

Indistinguishability obfuscation has been studied for *quantum* circuits in [4, 5]. In a nutshell (see Sect. 1.2 for more details), [5] shows a type of obfuscation for quantum circuits, but without a security reduction. On the other hand, the focus of [4] is on impossibility of obfuscation for quantum circuits in various scenarios. Thus, despite these works, until now, the achievability of indistinguishability obfuscation for quantum circuits has remained wide open.

1.1 Overview of Results and Techniques

Our contribution establishes indistinguishability obfuscation for certain families of quantum circuits. Below we overview each of our two main definitions, and methods to achieve them. We then compare the two approaches.

Indistinguishability Obfuscation for Quantum Circuits. First, we define indistinguishability obfuscation for quantum circuits ($qi\mathcal{O}$) (Sect. 3) as an extension of the conventional classical definition. This definition specifies that on input a classical description of a quantum circuit C_q, the obfuscator outputs a *pair* $(|\phi\rangle, C_q')$, where $|\phi\rangle$ is an auxiliary quantum state and C_q' is a quantum circuit. For correctness, we require that $||C_q'(|\phi\rangle, \cdot) - C_q(\cdot)||_\diamond = 0$, whereas for security, we require that, on input two functionally equivalent quantum circuits, the outputs of $qi\mathcal{O}$ are indistinguishable. As a straightforward extension of the classical results, we then argue that *inefficient* indistinguishability obfuscation exists.

In terms of constructing $qi\mathcal{O}$, we first focus on the family of *Clifford* circuits and show two methods of obfuscation: one straightforward method based on the canonical representation of Cliffords, and another based on the principle of gate teleportation [30]. Clifford circuits are quantum circuits that are built from the gate-set $\{X, Z, P, CNOT, H\}$. They are known not to be universal for quantum computation and are, in a certain sense, the quantum equivalent of classical *linear circuits*. It is known that Clifford circuits can be efficiently simulated on a classical computer [29]; however, note that this simulation is with respect to a *classical* distribution, hence for a purely quantum computation, quantum circuits are required, which motivates the obfuscation of this circuit class. Furthermore, Clifford circuits are an important building block for fault-tolerant quantum computing, for instance, due to the fact that Cliffords admit transversal computations in many fault-tolerant codes. We provide two methods to achieve $qi\mathcal{O}$ for Clifford circuits.

Obfuscating Cliffords Using a Canonical Form. Our first construction of $qi\mathcal{O}$ for Clifford circuits starts with the well-known fact that a canonical form is an $i\mathcal{O}$. We point out that a canonical form for Clifford circuits was presented in [2]; this completes this construction (we also note that an alternative canonical form was also presented in [39]). This canonical form technique does not require any computational assumptions. Moreover, the obfuscated circuits are classical, and hence can be easily communicated, stored, used and copied.

Obfuscating Cliffords Using Gate Teleportation. Our second construction of $qi\mathcal{O}$ for Clifford circuits takes a very different approach. We start with the gate teleportation scheme [30]: according to this, it is possible to *encode* a quantum computation C_q into a quantum state (specifically, by preparing a collection of entangled qubit pairs, and applying C_q to half of this preparation). Then, in order to perform a quantum computation on a target input $|\psi\rangle$, we *teleport* $|\psi\rangle$ *into* the prepared entangled state. This causes the state $|\psi\rangle$ to undergo the evolution of C_q, *up to some corrections*, based on the teleportation outcome. If C_q is chosen from the Clifford circuits, these corrections are relatively simple[1] and thus we can use a classical $i\mathcal{O}$ to provide the correction function. In contrast to the previous scheme, the gate teleportation scheme requires the assumption of quantum-secure classical $i\mathcal{O}$ for a certain family of functions (see [16]) and the obfuscated circuits include a quantum system. While this presents a technological challenge to communication, storage and also usage, there could be advantages to storing quantum programs into quantum states, for instance to take advantage of their *uncloneability* [1,17].

Obfuscating Beyond Cliffords. Next, in our main result for Sect. 5, we generalize the gate teleportation scheme for Clifford circuits, and show a $qi\mathcal{O}$ obfuscator for all quantum circuits where the number of non-Clifford gates is at most logarithmic in the circuit size. For this, we consider the commonly-used Clifford+T gate-set, and we note that the T relates to the X, Z as: $\mathsf{TX}^b\mathsf{Z}^a = \mathsf{X}^b\mathsf{Z}^{a\oplus b}\mathsf{P}^b\mathsf{T}$. This means that, if we implement a circuit C with T gates as in the gate teleportation scheme above, then the *correction* function is no longer a simple Pauli update (as in the case for Cliffords). However, this is only partially true: since the Paulis form a basis, there is always a way to represent an update as a complex, linear combination of Pauli matrices. In particular, for the case of a T, we note that $\mathsf{P} = (\frac{1+i}{2})\mathsf{I} + (\frac{1-i}{2})\mathsf{Z}$. Hence, it *is* possible to produce an update function for general quantum circuits that are encoded via gate teleportation. To illustrate this, we first analyze the case of a general Clifford+T quantum circuit on a *single* qubit (Sect. 5.1). Here, we are able to provide $qi\mathcal{O}$ for all circuits. Next, for

---

[1] The correction is a tensor products of *Pauli* operators, which is computed as a function of C_q and of the teleportation outcome.

general quantum circuits, (Sect. 5.2), we note that the update function exists for all circuits, but becomes more and more complex as the number of T gates increases. We show that if we limit the number of T gates to be logarithmic in the circuit size, we can reach an efficient construction. Both of these constructions assume a quantum-secure, classical indistinguishability obfuscation.

To the best of our knowledge, our gate teleportation provides the first method for indistinguishability obfuscation that is efficient for a large class of quantum circuits, beyond Clifford circuits. Note, however that canonical forms (also called *normal* forms) are known for *single* qubits universal quantum circuits [27,36]. We note that, for many other quantum cryptographic primitives, it is the case that the T-gate is the bottleneck (somewhat akin to a *multiplication* in the classical case). This has been observed, *e.g.*, in the context of *homomorphic quantum encryption* [15,23], and instantaneous quantum computation [41]. Because of these applications, and since the T is also typically also the bottleneck for fault-tolerant quantum computing, techniques exist to reduce the number of T gates in quantum circuits [7,8,22] (see Sect. 1.2 for more on this topic).

Indistinguishability Obfuscation for Quantum Circuits, with Respect to a Pseudo-distance. Next in Sect. 6, we define indistinguishability obfuscation for quantum circuits with respect to some pseudo-norm $\mathbf{D}$, which we call $qi\mathcal{O}_\mathbf{D}$. This definition specifies that on input a classical description of a quantum circuit C_q, the obfuscator outputs a *pair* $(|\phi\rangle, C'_q)$, where $|\phi\rangle$ is an auxiliary quantum state and C'_q is a quantum circuit. For correctness, we require that $\mathbf{D}(C'_q(|\phi\rangle, \cdot), C_q(\cdot)) \leq \texttt{negl}(n)$, whereas for security, we require that, on input two *approximately* equivalent quantum circuits (Definition 7), the outputs of $qi\mathcal{O}_\mathbf{D}$ are statistically indistinguishable. This definition is more in line with [4].

We show how to construct a statistically-secure quantum indistinguishability obfuscation with respect to the pseudo-distance $\mathbf{D}$ (see Algorithm 4) for quantum circuits that are very close to kth level of the Gottesman-Chuang hierarchy [30], for some fixed k (see [16]). The construction takes a circuit U_q as an input with a promise that the distance $\mathbf{D}(U_q, C) \leq \epsilon < \frac{1}{2^{k+1}/2}$ for some $C \in \mathcal{C}_k$. It computes the conjugate circuit $U_q^\dagger$ and then runs Low's learning algorithm as a subroutine on inputs U_q and $U_q^\dagger$ [35]. The algorithm outputs whatever Low's learning algorithm outputs. Note that Low's learning algorithm runs in time super-polynomial in k, therefore for our construction to remain efficient the parameter k is some small fixed integer (say $k = 5$). Note that for $k > 2$, the set $\mathcal{C}_k$ includes all Clifford unitaries as well as some non-Clifford unitaries [35].

Comparison of the Two Approaches. Our notions of $qi\mathcal{O}$ and $qi\mathcal{O}_\mathbf{D}$ are incomparable. To see this, on one hand, note that the basic instantiation of an indistinguishability obfuscator that outputs a canonical form is no longer secure in the definition of indistinguishability with respect to a pseudo-norm.[2] On the other hand, the construction for $qi\mathcal{O}_\mathbf{D}$ that we give in Algorithm 4 does not satisfy the definition of $qi\mathcal{O}$, because the functionality is not perfectly preserved,

---

[2] If two different circuits are close in functionality but not identical, then we have no guarantee that their canonical forms are close.

which is a requirement for $qi\mathcal{O}$. We recall that in the classical case, it is generally considered an *advantage* that $i\mathcal{O}$ is a relatively weak notion (since it is more easily attained) and that, despite this, a host of uses of $i\mathcal{O}$ are known. We thus take $qi\mathcal{O}$ as the more natural extension of classical indistinguishability obfuscation to the quantum case, but we note that issues related to the continuity of quantum mechanics and the inherent approximation in any universal quantum gateset justify the relevance for our approach to $qi\mathcal{O}_{\mathbf{D}}$.

We now compare the schemes that we achieve. The most general scheme that we give as a construct for $qi\mathcal{O}$ (Algorithm 3) allows to obfuscate any polynomial-size quantum circuit (with at most logarithmic number of non-Clifford gates). While this is a restricted class, it is well-understood and we believe that this technique may be amenable to an extension that would result into a full $qi\mathcal{O}$.

In comparison, the scheme that we give for $qi\mathcal{O}_{\mathbf{D}}$, based on Low's learning algorithm [35] has some advantages over the teleportation-based constructions. Firstly, the circuits to be obfuscated don't need to be of equal size or perfectly equivalent and the outputs of the obfuscator remain statistically indistinguishable as long as the circuits are approximately equivalent (with respect to the pseudo-distance $\mathbf{D}$). Secondly, Algorithm 4 does not require any computational assumptions, whereas the teleportation-based constructions require a quantum-secure classical indistinguishability obfuscator. However, beyond the fact that $\mathcal{C}_k$ contains all Clifford circuits, it is not clear how powerful unitaries are in the kth level of the Gottesman-Chuang hierarchy (especially for a fixed small k). Even when $k \to \infty$, the hierarchy does not include all unitaries. In terms of extending this technique, Low's learning algorithm exploits the structure of the Gottesman-Chuang hierarchy and it not obvious how one can apply this technique to arbitrary quantum circuits.

1.2   More on Related Work

Quantum Obfuscation. Quantum obfuscation was first studied in [5], where a notion called (G, Γ)-*indistinguishability obfuscation* was proposed, where G is a set of gates and Γ is a set of relations satisfied by the elements of G. In this notion, any two circuits over the set of gates G are perfectly indistinguishable if they differ by some sequence of applications of the relations in Γ. Since perfect indistinguishability obfuscation is known to be impossible under the assumption that $\mathsf{P} \neq \mathsf{NP}$ [28], one of the motivations of this work was to provide a weaker definition of perfectly indistinguishable obfuscation, along with possibility results. However, to the best of our knowledge, (G, Γ)-*indistinguishability obfuscation* is incomparable with computational indistinguishability obfuscation [11,24], which is the main focus of our work.

Quantum obfuscation is studied in [4], where the various notions of quantum obfuscation are defined (including quantum black-box obfuscation, quantum indistinguishability obfuscation, and quantum best-possible obfuscation). A contribution of [4] is to extend the classical impossibility results to the quantum setting, including *e.g.* showing that each of the three variants of quantum indistinguishability obfuscation is equivalent to the analogous variant of quantum best-possible obfuscation, so long as the obfuscator is efficient. This work shows that the existence of a computational quantum indistinguishability obfuscation implies a witness encryption scheme for all languages in QMA. Various impossibility results are also shown: that efficient statistical indistinguishability obfuscation is impossible unless PSPACE is contained in QSZK[3] (for the case of circuits that include measurements), or unless coQMA[4] is contained in QSZK (for the case of unitary circuits). Notable here is that [4] defines a notion of indistinguishability obfuscation where security must hold for circuits that are *close* in functionality (this is similar to our definition of $qi\mathcal{O}_D$); it is however unclear if their impossibility results hold for a notion of quantum indistinguishability along the lines of our definition of $qi\mathcal{O}$. See Sect. 3 for further discussion of the links between this definition and ours. We note that [4] does not provide any concrete instantiation of obfuscation.

Recently it has been shown that virtual black-box obfuscation of classical circuits via quantum mechanical means is also impossible [3,10].

Quantum Homomorphic Encryption. In *quantum homomorphic encryption*, a computationally-weak client is able to send a ciphertext to a quantum server, such that the quantum server can perform a quantum computation on the encrypted data, thus producing an encrypted output which the client can decrypt, and obtaining the result of the quantum computation.

This primitive was formally defined in [15] (see also [14,23]), where it was shown how to achieve homomorphic quantum computation for quantum circuits of low T-depth, by assuming quantum-secure classical fully homomorphic encryption. We note that even the simplest scheme in [15] (which allows the homomorphic evaluation of *any* Clifford circuit), requires computational assumptions in order for the server to update homomorphically the classical portion of the ciphertext, based on the choice of Clifford. In contrast, here we are able to give information-theoretic constructions for this class of circuits (essentially, because the choice of Clifford is chosen by the obfuscator, not by the evaluator). We thus emphasize that in $i\mathcal{O}$, we want to hide the *circuit*, whereas in homomorphic encryption, we want to hide the *plaintext* (and allow remote computations on the ciphertext). Since the evaluator in homomorphic encryption has control of the circuit, but not of the data, the evaluator knows which types of gates are applied, and the main obstacle is to perform a correction after a T-gate, controlled on a classical value that is held only in an encrypted form by the evaluator. In contrast to this, in $i\mathcal{O}$, we want to hide the inner workings of the circuit. By using gate teleportation, we end up in a situation where the evaluator *knows* some classical values that have affected the quantum computation in some undesirable way, and then we want to hide the inner workings of *how* the

---

[3] PSPACE is the class of decision problems solvable by a Turing machine in polynomial space and QSZK is the class of decision problems that admit a quantum statistical zero-knowledge proof system.

[4] coQMA is the *complement* of QMA, which is the class of decision problems that can be verified by a one-message quantum interactive proof.

evaluator should compensate for these undesirable effects. Thus, the techniques of quantum homomorphic encryption do not seem directly applicable, although we leave as an open question if they could be used in some indirect way, perhaps towards efficient $qi\mathcal{O}$ for a larger family of circuits.

1.3 Open Questions

The main open question is efficient quantum indistinguishability obfuscation for quantum circuits with super-logarithmic number of T-gates. Another open question is about the applications of quantum indistinguishability obfuscation. While we expect that many of the uses of classical $i\mathcal{O}$ carry over to the quantum case, we leave as future work the formal study of these techniques.

Outline. The remainder of this paper is structured as follows. Section 2 overviews basic notions required in this work. In Sect. 3, we formally define indistinguishability obfuscation for quantum circuits. In Sect. 4, we provide the construction for Clifford circuits. In Sect. 5, we give our main result which shows quantum indistinguishability obfuscation for quantum circuits, which is efficient for circuits having at most a logarithmic number of T gates. Finally in Sect. 6, we consider the notion of quantum indistinguishability obfuscation with respect to a pseudo-distance, and show how to instantiate it for a family of circuits close to the Gottesman-Chuang hierarchy.

2 Preliminaries

2.1 Basic Classical Cryptographic Notions

Let $\mathbb{N}$ be the set of positive integers. For $n \in \mathbb{N}$, we set $[n] = \{1, \cdots, n\}$. We denote the set of all binary strings of length n by $\{0, 1\}^n$. An element $s \in \{0, 1\}^n$ is called a bitstring, and $|s| = n$ denotes its length. Given two bit strings x and y of equal length, we denote their bitwise XOR by $x \oplus y$. For a finite set X, the notation $x \xleftarrow{\$} X$ indicates that x is selected uniformly at random from X. We denote the set of all $d \times d$ unitary matrices by $\mathcal{U}(d) = \{U \in \mathbb{C}^{d \times d} \mid UU^\dagger = \mathbf{I}\}$, where $U^\dagger$ denotes the conjugate transpose of U. A function $\mathtt{negl} : \mathbb{N} \to \mathbb{R}^+ \cup \{0\}$ is *negligible* if for every positive polynomial $p(n)$, there exists a positive integer n_0 such that for all $n > n_0$, $\mathtt{negl}(n) < 1/p(n)$. A typical use of negligible functions is to indicate that the probability of success of some algorithm is too small to be amplified to a constant by a feasible (*i.e.*, polynomial) number of repetitions.

2.2 Classical Circuits and Algorithms

A deterministic polynomial-time (or **PT**) algorithm $\mathcal{C}$ is defined by a polynomial-time uniform[5] family $\mathcal{C} = \{C_n \mid n \in \mathbb{N}\}$ of classical Boolean circuits over some

---

[5] Recall that polynomial-time uniformity means that there exists a polynomial-time Turing machine which, on input n in unary, prints a description of the nth circuit in the family.

gate set, with one circuit for each possible input size $n \in \mathbb{N}$. For a bitstring x, we define $\mathcal{C}(x) := \mathcal{C}_{|x|}(x)$. We say that a function family $f : \{0,1\}^n \to \{0,1\}^m$ is **PT**-computable if there exists a polynomial-time $\mathcal{C}$ such that $\mathcal{C}(x) = f(x)$ for all x; it is implicit that m is a function of n which is bounded by some polynomial, e.g., the same one that bounds the running time of $\mathcal{C}$. Note that in the literature, circuits that compute functions whose range is $\{0,1\}^m$ are often called multi-output Boolean circuits [31], but in this paper we simply called them Boolean circuits [40]. A probabilistic polynomial-time algorithm (or **PPT**) is again a polynomial-time uniform family of classical Boolean circuits, one for each possible input size n. The nth circuit still accepts n bits of input, but now also has an additional "coins" register of $p(n)$ input wires. Note that uniformity enforces that the function p is bounded by some polynomial. For a **PPT** algorithm $\mathcal{C}$, n-bit input x and $p(n)$-bit coin string r, we set $\mathcal{C}(x;r) := \mathcal{C}_n(x;r)$. In contrast with the PT case, the notation algorithm $\mathcal{C}(x)$ will now refer to the random variable algorithm $\mathcal{C}(x;r)$ where $r \xleftarrow{\$} \{0,1\}^{p(n)}$.

2.3   Classical Indistinguishability and Obfuscation

Here, we define indistinguishability for classical random variables, against a quantum distinguisher (Definition 2), as well as classical indistinguishability obfuscation.

Definition 1. *(Statistical Distance) Let X and Y be two random variables over some countable set Ω. The statistical distance between X and Y is*

$$\Delta(X,Y) = \frac{1}{2} \left\{ \sum_{\omega \in \Omega} |Pr[X(\omega)] - Pr[Y(\omega)]| \right\}.$$

Definition 2. *(Indistinguishability) Let $\mathcal{X} = \{X_n\}_{n \in \mathbb{N}}$ and $\mathcal{Y} = \{Y_n\}_{n \in \mathbb{N}}$ be two distribution ensembles indexed by a parameter n. We say*

1. $\mathcal{X}$ *and* $\mathcal{Y}$ *are* perfectly indistinguishable *if for all n, $\Delta(X_n, Y_n) = 0$.*
2. $\mathcal{X}$ *and* $\mathcal{Y}$ *are* statistically indistinguishable *if there exists a negligible function* negl *such that for all sufficiently large n, $\Delta(X_n, Y_n) \leq \mathtt{negl}(n)$.*
3. $\{X_n\}_{n \in \mathbb{N}}$ *and* $\{Y_n\}_{n \in \mathbb{N}}$ *are* computationally indistinguishable *if for quantum distinguisher $\mathcal{D}_q$ that runs in polynomial-time, there exists a negligible function* negl *such that* $\left| \Pr[\mathcal{D}_q(X_n) = 1] - \Pr[\mathcal{D}_q(Y_n) = 1] \right| \leq \mathtt{negl}(n)$.

Let $\mathcal{C}$ be a family of probabilistic polynomial-time circuits. For $n \in \mathbb{N}$, let $\mathcal{C}_n$ be the circuits in $\mathcal{C}$ of input length n. We now provide a definition of classical indistinguishability obfuscation $(i\mathcal{O})$ as defined in [28], but where we make a few minor modifications.[6]

---

[6] We make a few design choices that are more appropriate for our situation, where we show the *possibility* of $i\mathcal{O}$ against quantum adversaries: our adversary is a probabilistic polynomial-time quantum algorithm, we dispense with the mention of the random oracle, and note that our indistinguishability notions are defined to hold for all inputs.

Definition 3. (Indistinguishability Obfuscation, $i\mathcal{O}$) *A polynomial-time probabilistic algorithm is a* quantum-secure indistinguishability obfuscator $(i\mathcal{O})$ *for a class of circuits $\mathcal{C}$, if the following conditions hold:*

1. `Preserving Functionality`: *For any $C \in C_n$:*

$$i\mathcal{O}(x) = C(x), \text{ for all } x \in \{0,1\}^n$$

   The probability is taken over the $i\mathcal{O}$'s coins.
2. `Polynomial Slowdown`: *There exists a polynomial $p(n)$ such that for all input lengths, for any $C \in C_n$, the obfuscator $i\mathcal{O}$ only enlarges C by a factor of $p(|C|)$:*

$$|i\mathcal{O}(C)| \leq p(|C|).$$

3. `Indistinguishability`: *An $i\mathcal{O}$ is said to be a computational/statistical/ perfect indistinguishability obfuscation for the family $\mathcal{C}$, if for all large enough input lengths, for any circuit $C_1 \in C_n$ and for any $C_2 \in C_n$ that computes the same function as C_1 and such that $|C_1| = |C_2|$, the distributions $i\mathcal{O}(C_1))$ and $i\mathcal{O}(C_2)$ are (respectively) computationally/statistically/perfectly indistinguishable.*

2.4   Basic Quantum Notions

Given an n-bit string x, the corresponding n-qubit quantum computational basis state is denoted $|x\rangle$. The 2^n-dimensional Hilbert space spanned by n-qubit basis states is denoted: $\mathcal{H}_n := \mathbf{span}\{|x\rangle : x \in \{0,1\}^n\}$. We denote by $\mathcal{D}(\mathcal{H}_n)$ the set of density operators (*i.e.*, valid quantum states) on $\mathcal{H}_n$. These are linear operators on $\mathcal{D}(\mathcal{H}_n)$ which are positive-semidefinite and have trace equal to 1.

We refer to [16] for background information and notation on quantum circuits and algorithms, quantum teleportation, gate teleportation and the Gottesman-Chuang hierarchy.

2.5   Norms and Pseudo-distance

The trace distance between two quantum states $\rho, \sigma \in \mathcal{D}(\mathcal{H}_n)$ is given by: $||\rho - \sigma||_{tr} := \frac{1}{2}\mathrm{Tr}\left(\left|\sqrt{(\rho - \sigma)^\dagger(\rho - \sigma)}\right|\right)$, where $|\cdot|$ denotes the positive square root of the matrix $\sqrt{(\rho - \sigma)^\dagger(\rho - \sigma)}$.

Let Φ and Ψ be two admissible operators of type (n, m)[7]. The *diamond norm* between two quantum operators is $||\Phi - \Psi||_\diamond := \max_{\rho \in \mathcal{D}(\mathcal{H}_{2n})} ||(\Phi \otimes I_n)\rho - (\Psi \otimes I_n)\rho||_{tr}$.

The Frobenius norm of a matrix $A \in \mathbb{C}^{n \times m}$ is defined as $||A||_F = \sqrt{\mathrm{Tr}(AA^\dagger)}$. Let $U_1, U_2 \in \mathcal{U}(d)$ be two $d \times d$ unitary matrices. The phase invariant

---

[7] An operator is admissible if its action on density matrices is linear, trace-preserving, and completely positive. A operator's type is (n, m) if it maps n-qubit states to m-qubit states.

distance between U_1 and U_2 is $\mathbf{D}(U_1, U_2) = \frac{1}{\sqrt{2d^2}} \|U_1 \otimes U_1^* - U_2 \otimes U_2^*\|_F = \sqrt{1 - \left|\frac{\mathrm{Tr}(U_1 U_2^\dagger)}{d}\right|^2}$, where U_i^* denotes the matrix with only complex conjugated entries and no transposition and $|z|$ denotes the norm of the complex number z. Note that $\mathbf{D}$ is a pseudo-distance since $\mathbf{D}(U_1, U_2) = 0$ does not imply $U_1 = U_2$, but that U_1 and U_2 are equivalent up to a phase so the difference is unobservable. It is easy to see that $\mathbf{D}$ satisfies the axioms of symmetry ($\mathbf{D}(U_1, U_2) = \mathbf{D}(U_2, U_1)$), the triangle inequality ($\mathbf{D}(U_1, U_2) \le \mathbf{D}(U_1, U) + \mathbf{D}(U, U_2)$) and nonnegativity ($\mathbf{D}(U_1, U_2) \ge 0$).

2.6 Quantum Indistinguishability

Here, we define indistinguishability for quantum states and define the case of *perfectly* equivalent quantum circuits.

Definition 4. *(Indistinguishability of Quantum States) Let $\mathcal{R} = \{\rho_n\}_{n \in \mathbb{N}}$ and $\mathcal{S} = \{\sigma_n\}_{n \in \mathbb{N}}$ be two ensembles of quantum states such that ρ_n and σ_n are n-qubit states. We say*

1. *$\mathcal{R}$ and $\mathcal{S}$ are perfectly indistinguishable if for all n, $\rho_n = \sigma_n$.*
2. *$\mathcal{R}$ and $\mathcal{S}$ are statistically indistinguishable if there exists a negligible function $\mathtt{negl}$ such that for all sufficiently large n, $\|\rho_n - \sigma_n\|_{tr} \le \mathtt{negl}(n)$.*
3. *$\mathcal{R}$ and $\mathcal{S}$ are computationally indistinguishable if there exists a negligible function $\mathtt{negl}$ such that for every state $\rho_n \in \mathcal{R}$, $\sigma_n \in \mathcal{S}$ and for all polynomial-time quantum distinguisher $\mathcal{D}_q$, we have*

$$\left|\Pr[\mathcal{D}_q(\rho_n) = 1] - \Pr[\mathcal{D}_q(\sigma_n) = 1]\right| \le \mathtt{negl}(n).$$

Definition 5. *(Perfectly Equivalent Quantum Circuits): Let C_{q_0} and C_{q_1} be two n-qubit quantum circuits. We say C_{q_0} and C_{q_1} are perfectly equivalent if $\|C_{q_0} - C_{q_1}\|_\diamond = 0$.*

3   Indistinguishability Obfuscation for Quantum Circuits

We now define our notion of quantum indistinguishability obfuscation for equivalent circuits (Sect. 3) and make an observation about the existence of inefficient quantum indistinguishability obfuscation.

Definition 6. *(Quantum Indistinguishability Obfuscation for Perfectly Equivalent Quantum Circuits): Let $\mathcal{C}_Q$ be a polynomial-time family of reversible quantum circuits. For $n \in \mathbb{N}$, let C_q^n be the circuits in $\mathcal{C}_Q$ of input length n. A polynomial-time quantum algorithm for $\mathcal{C}_Q$ is a Computational/Statistical/Perfect quantum indistinguishability obfuscator (qiO) if the following conditions hold:*

1. **Functionality:** *There exists a negligible function* `negl(n)` *such that for every* $C_q \in C_q^n$

$$(|\phi\rangle, C_q') \leftarrow qi\mathcal{O}(C_q) \quad and \quad ||C_q'(|\phi\rangle, \cdot) - C_q(\cdot)||_\diamond = 0.$$

Where $|\phi\rangle$ *is an* ℓ-*qubit state, the circuits* C_q *and* C_q' *are of type* (n, n) *and* (m, n) *respectively* $(m = \ell + n)$.[8]

2. **Polynomial Slowdown:** *There exists a polynomial* $p(n)$ *such that for any* $C_q \in C_q^n$, $\ell \leq p(|C_q|)$, $m \leq p(|C_q|)$, *and* $|C_q'| \leq p(|C_q|)$.

3. **Computational/Statistical/Perfect Indistinguishability:** *For any two perfectly equivalent quantum circuits* $C_{q_1}, C_{q_2} \in C_q^n$, *of the same size, the two distributions* $qi\mathcal{O}(C_{q_1})$ *and* $qi\mathcal{O}(C_{q_2})$ *are (respectively) computationally/statistically/perfectly indistinguishable.*

Remark 1. A subtlety that is specific to the quantum case is that Definition 6 only requires that $(|\phi\rangle, C_q')$ enable a *single* evaluation of C_q. We could instead require a k-time functionality, which can be easily achieved by executing the single-evaluation scheme k times in parallel. This justifies our focus here on the single-evaluation scheme.

Note 1. As described in Sect. 1.2, our Definition 6 differs from [4] as it requires security only in the case of equivalent quantum circuits (see Definition 8 for a definition that addresses this). Compared to [4], we note that in this work we focus on unitary circuits only.[9] Another difference is that the notion of indistinguishability (computational or statistical) in [4] is more generous than ours, since it allows a finite number of inputs that violate the indistinguishability inequality. Since our work focuses on *possibility* of obfuscations, our choice leads to the strongest results; equally, since [4] focuses on impossibility, their results are strongest in their model. We also note that that [4] defines the efficiency of the obfuscator in terms of the number of qubits. We believe that our definition, which bounds the size of the output of the obfucation by a polynomial in the *size* of the input circuit, is more appropriate[10] and follows the lines of the classical definitions. As far as we are aware, further differences in our definition are purely a choice of style. For instance, we do not include an *interpreter* as in [4], but instead we let the obfuscator output a quantum circuit together with a quantum state; we chose this presentation since it provides a clear separation between the quantum circuit output by the $qi\mathcal{O}$ and the "quantum advice state".

Inefficient Quantum Indistinguishability Obfuscators Exist Finally, we note a simple extension of a result in [11]: *inefficient indistinguishability obfuscators exist for all quantum circuits*. This is achieved by letting $qi\mathcal{O}(C_q)$ be the lexicographically first circuit of size $|C_q|$ that computes the same map as C_q.

---

[8] A circuit is of type (i, j) if it maps i qubits to j qubits.

[9] This is without loss of generality, since a $qi\mathcal{O}$ for a generalized quantum circuit can be obtained from a $qi\mathcal{O}$ for a reversible version of the circuit, followed by a trace-out operation (see [16]).

[10] It would be unreasonable to allow an obfuscator that outputs a circuit on n qubits, but of depth super-polynomial in n.

4 Quantum Indistinguishability Obfuscation for Clifford Circuits

Here, we show how to construct $qi\mathcal{O}$ for Clifford circuits with respect to definition Definition 6. The first construction (Sect. 4.1) is based on a canonical form, and the second is based on gate teleportation (Sect. 4.2).

4.1 $qi\mathcal{O}$ for Clifford Circuits via a Canonical Form

Aaronson and Gottesman developped a polynomial-time algorithm that takes a Clifford circuit C_q and outputs its canonical form (see [2], section VI), which is invariant for any two equivalent n-qubit circuits[11]. Moreover the size of the canonical form remains polynomial in the size of the input circuit. Based on this canonical form, we define a $qi\mathcal{O}$ in Algorithm 1. The proof is in [16].

Algorithm 1. $qi\mathcal{O}$-Canonical

- Input: An n-qubit Clifford Circuit C_q.
  1. Using the Aaronson and Gottesman algorithm [2], compute the canonical form
     of $C'_q \xleftarrow{\text{canonical form}} C_q$.
  2. Let $|\phi\rangle$ be an empty register.
  3. Output $\left(|\phi\rangle, C'_q\right)$.

Lemma 1. *Algorithm 1 is a Perfect Quantum Indistinguishability Obfuscation for all Clifford Circuits.*

4.2 $qi\mathcal{O}$ for Clifford Circuits via Gate Teleportation

In this section, we show how gate teleportation (see [16,30]) can be used to construct a quantum indistinguishability obfuscation for Clifford circuits. Our construction, given in Algorithm 2, relies on the existence of a quantum-secure $i\mathcal{O}$ for classical circuits; however, upon closer inspection, our construction relies on the assumption that a quantum-secure classical $i\mathcal{O}$ exists for a very specific class of classical circuits[12]. In fact, it is easy to construct a perfectly secure $i\mathcal{O}$ for this class of circuits: like Clifford circuits, the circuits that compute the update functions also have a canonical form. Then the $i\mathcal{O}$ takes as input a Clifford circuit and outputs a canonical form of a classical circuit that computes the update function for C_q. The $i\mathcal{O}$ is described formally in [16].

Theorem 1. (See [16] for the proof). *Algorithm 2 is a perfect quantum indistinguishability obfuscation for all Clifford Circuits.*

---

[11] Their algorithm outputs a canonical form (unique form) provided it runs on the standard initial tableau see pages 8–10 of [2].

[12] Circuits that compute update functions for Clifford circuits, see [16].

Algorithm 2. $qi\mathcal{O}$ via Gate Teleportation for Clifford

- Input: An n-qubit Clifford Circuit C_q.
    1. Prepare a tensor product of n Bell states: $|\beta^{2n}\rangle = |\beta_{00}\rangle \otimes \cdots \otimes |\beta_{00}\rangle$.
    2. Apply the circuit C_q on the right-most n qubits to obtain a system $|\phi\rangle = (I_n \otimes C_q)|\beta^{2n}\rangle$.
    3. Compute a classical circuit C that computes the update function F_{C_q}. The classical circuit C can be computed in polynomial-time [16].
    4. Set $C' \leftarrow i\mathcal{O}(C)$, where $i\mathcal{O}(C)$ is a perfectly secure indistinguishability obfuscation defined in [16].
    5. Description of the circuit C_q' :
        (a) Perform a general Bell measurement on the leftmost $2n$-qubits on the system $|\phi\rangle \otimes |\psi\rangle$, where $|\phi\rangle$ is an auxiliary state and $|\psi\rangle$ is an input state. Obtain classical bits $(a_1, b_1 \ldots, a_n, b_n)$ and the state

$$C_q(\mathsf{X}^{\otimes_{i=1}^n b_i} \cdot \mathsf{Z}^{\otimes_{i=1}^n a_i})|\psi\rangle. \tag{1}$$

        (b) Compute the correction bits

$$(a_1', b_1', \ldots, a_n', b_n') = C'(a_1, b_1 \ldots, a_n, b_n). \tag{2}$$

        (c) Using the above, the correction unitary is $U' = (\mathsf{X}^{\otimes_{i=1}^n b_i'} \cdot \mathsf{Z}^{\otimes_{i=1}^n a_i'})$.
        (d) Apply U' to the system $C_q(\mathsf{X}^{\otimes_{i=1}^n b_i} \cdot \mathsf{Z}^{\otimes_{i=1}^n a_i})|\psi\rangle$ to obtain the state $C_q(|\psi\rangle)$.
    6. Output $(|\phi\rangle, C_q')$.

---

5   Obfuscating Beyond Clifford Circuits

In this section, we extend the gate teleportation technique to show how we can construct $qi\mathcal{O}$ for *any* quantum circuit. Our construction is efficient as long as the circuit has T-count at most logarithmic in the circuit size. For the sake of simplicity, we first construct a $qi\mathcal{O}$ for an arbitrary 1-qubit quantum circuit (Sect. 5.1), then extend the 1-qubit construction to any n-qubit quantum circuit (Sect. 5.2).

We first start with some general observations on quantum circuits which are relevant to this section. Consider the application of the T-gate on an encrypted system using the quantum one-time pad. The following equation relates the T-gate to the X- and Z-gates:

$$\mathsf{T}\mathsf{X}^b\mathsf{Z}^a = \mathsf{X}^b\mathsf{Z}^{a\oplus b}\mathsf{P}^b\mathsf{T}. \tag{3}$$

If $b = 0$, then P^b is the identity; otherwise we have a P-gate correction. This is undesirable as P does not commute with X, making the update of the encryption key (a, b) complicated (since it is no longer a tensor product of Paulis). Note that we can write $\mathsf{P} = \left(\frac{1+i}{2}\right)I + \left(\frac{1-i}{2}\right)\mathsf{Z}$, therefore Eq. (3) can be rewritten as:

$$\mathsf{T}\mathsf{X}^b\mathsf{Z}^a = \mathsf{X}^b\mathsf{Z}^{a\oplus b}\left[\left(\frac{1+i}{2}\right)I + \left(\frac{1-i}{2}\right)\mathsf{Z}\right]^b\mathsf{T} \tag{4}$$

Since $\left[\left(\frac{1+i}{2}\right)I + \left(\frac{1-i}{2}\right)Z\right]^b = \left(\frac{1+i}{2}\right)I + \left(\frac{1-i}{2}\right)Z^b$ for $b \in \{0,1\}$, we can rewrite Eq. (4) as,

$$TX^bZ^a = X^bZ^{a\oplus b}\left[\left(\frac{1+i}{2}\right)I + \left(\frac{1-i}{2}\right)Z^b\right]T = \left[\left(\frac{1+i}{2}\right)X^bZ^{a\oplus b} + \left(\frac{1-i}{2}\right)X^bZ^a\right]T.$$

It follows from the above that for any $a, b \in \{0,1\}$, we can represent TX^bZ^a as a linear combination of X and Z: $TX^bZ^a = (\alpha_1 I + \alpha_2 X + \alpha_3 Z + \alpha_4 XZ)T$, where $\alpha_j \in \{0, 1, \frac{1+i}{2}, \frac{1-i}{2}\}$, for $j \in [4]$.

We further note that for a general n-qubit quantum unitary U and n-qubit Pauli P, there exists a Clifford C such that $UP|\psi\rangle = CU|\psi\rangle$. This is due to the *Clifford hierarchy* [30]. We also mention that if an n-qubit Clifford operation is given in matrix form, an efficient procedure exists in order to produce a circuit that executes this Clifford [37]. This is a special case of the general problem of *synthesis* of quantum circuits, which aims to produce quantum circuits, based on an initial description of a unitary operation.

5.1 Single-Qubit Circuits

Here, we show an indistinguishability obfuscation for single-qubit circuits. As previously mentionned, we note that for the single-qubit case, an efficient indistinguishability obfuscation can also be built using the Matsumoto-Amano normal form [27,36]. Here, we give an alternate construction based on gate teleportation. Let C_q be a 1-qubit circuit we want to obfuscate and $|\psi\rangle$ be the quantum state on which we want to evaluate C_q. Note that we can write any 1-qubit circuit as a sequence of gates from the set $\{H, T\}$[13]

$$C_q = (g_{|C_q|}, \ldots, g_2, g_1), \ g_i \in \{H, T\}.$$

For the indistinguishability obfuscation of a single-qubit circuit, we use the gate teleportation protocol ([16,30]), which leaves us (after the teleportation) with a subsystem of the form $C_q X^b Z^a(|\psi\rangle)$

$$C_q X^b Z^a(|\psi\rangle) = (g_{|C_q|}, \ldots, g_2, g_1)X^b Z^a(|\psi\rangle), \tag{5}$$

and to evaluate the circuit on $|\psi\rangle$, we have to apply a correction unitary. Now suppose we apply the gate g_1. We can write the system in Eq. (5) as

$$C_q X^b Z^a(|\psi\rangle) = (g_{|C_q|}, \ldots, g_2)(\alpha_0 I + \alpha_1 X + \alpha_2 Z + \alpha_3 XZ)g_1(|\psi\rangle) \tag{6}$$

where $\alpha_i \in \{0, 1, \frac{1+i}{2}, \frac{1-i}{2}\}$. Since $\{I, X, Z, XZ\}$, forms a basis, after applying the remaining gates in the sequence $(g_{|C_q|}, \ldots, g_3, g_2)$, we can write Eq. (6) as

$$C_q X^b Z^a(|\psi\rangle) = (\beta_1 I + \beta_2 X + \beta_3 Z + \beta_4 XZ)(g_{|C_q|}, \ldots, g_2, g_1)(|\psi\rangle) \tag{7}$$

---

[13] The set $\{H, T\}$ is universal for 1-qubit unitaries [33].

where each $\beta_i \in \mathbb{C}$ and is computed by multiplying and adding numbers from the set $\{0, 1, \frac{1+i}{2}, \frac{1-i}{2}\}$. We show in [16] that the size of the coefficients β_i grows at most as a polynomial in the number of T-gates. Therefore it follows from Eq. (7) that the update function for any 1-qubit circuit C_q can be defined as a map of the form: $F_{C_q} : \{0,1\}^2 \rightarrow \mathbb{C}^4$, $(a, b) \mapsto (\beta_1, \beta_2, \beta_3, \beta_4)$, and is in one-to-one correspondence with the correction unitary $\beta_1 I + \beta_2 X + \beta_3 Z + \beta_4 XZ$. As indicated, our construction for 1-qubit circuits is nearly the same as the gate teleportation scheme for Clifford circuits (Algorithm 2). The proof that this is a $qi\mathcal{O}$ scheme is also very similar to the proof for the Clifford construction (Sect. 4.2); we thus omit the formal proof here (it can also be seen as a special case of the proof of Theorem 2). Some subtleties, however are addressed below: the equivalence of the update functions (Lemma 2) and the circuit synthesis (Lemma 3).[14]

Lemma 2. (See [16] for the proof). *Let C_{q_1} and C_{q_2} be two equivalent 1-qubit circuits. Then their corresponding update functions in the gate teleportation protocol are also equivalent.*

Lemma 3. *Based on the classical $i\mathcal{O}$ that computes the coefficients in Eq. (7), it is possible to build a quantum circuit that performs the correction efficiently.*

Proof. Given a 2×2 unitary matrix that represents a Clifford operation as in Eq. (7), it is simple to efficiently derive the Clifford circuit that implements the unitary. This is a special case of the general efficient synthesis for Clifford circuits as presented in [37].

5.2 $qi\mathcal{O}$ via Gate Teleportation for all Quantum Circuits

In this section, we construct a $qi\mathcal{O}$ for all quantum circuits. The construction is efficient whenever the number of T-gates is at most logarithmic in the circuit size (see Algorithm 3). The reason for this limitation is that the update function blows up once the number of T-gates is greater than logarithmic in the circuit size. The construction is very similar to the gate teleportation for Clifford circuits (Sect. 4.2) and assumes the existence of a quantum-secure $i\mathcal{O}$ for classical circuits. We are now ready to present our main theorem (Theorem 2); see [16] for the proof.

Theorem 2. *(Main Theorem) If $i\mathcal{O}$ is a perfect/statistical/computational quantum-secure indistinguishability obfuscation for classical circuits, then Algorithm 3 is a perfect/statistical/computational quantum indistinguishability obfuscator for any quantum circuit C_q with T-count $\in O(\log |C_q|)$.*

---

[14] We note that, on top of being equal, the circuits that compute the update functions $F_{C_{q_1}}$, $F_{C_{q_2}}$ can be assumed to be of the same size. This follows by an argument very similar to the one in [16].

Algorithm 3. $qi\mathcal{O}$ via Gate Teleportation for Quantum Circuits

- Input: A n-qubit quantum Circuit C_q with T-count $\in O(\log(|C_q|))$.
  1. Prepare a tensor product of n Bell states: $|\beta^{2n}\rangle = |\beta_{00}\rangle \otimes \cdots \otimes |\beta_{00}\rangle$.
  2. Apply the circuit C_q on the right-most n qubits to obtain a system $|\phi\rangle = (I_n \otimes C_q)|\beta^{2n}\rangle$.
  3. Set $\hat{C} \leftarrow i\mathcal{O}(C)$. Where C is a circuit that computes the update function F_{C_q} as in [16] Note the size of C is at most a polynomial in $|C_q|$ (see [16]).
  4. Description of the circuit C_q' :
     (a) Perform a general Bell measurement on the leftmost $2n$-qubits on the system $|\phi\rangle \otimes |\psi\rangle$, where $|\phi\rangle$ is an auxiliary state and $|\psi\rangle$ is an input state. Obtain classical bits $(a_1, b_1 \ldots, a_n, b_n)$ and the state $C_q(\mathsf{X}^{\otimes_{i=1}^{n} b_i} \cdot \mathsf{Z}^{\otimes_{i=1}^{n} a_i})|\psi\rangle$.
     (b) Compute the correction using the obfuscated circuit $((\beta_1, \mathbf{s}_1), \ldots, (\beta_n, \mathbf{s}_k)) = \hat{C}(a_1, b_1 \ldots, a_n, b_n)$.
     (c) Using the above, the correction unitary is $U_{F_{C_q}} = \sum_{i=1}^{4^k} \beta_i \mathsf{X}^{b_{i1}} \mathsf{Z}^{a_{i1}} \otimes \cdots \otimes \mathsf{X}^{b_{in}} \mathsf{Z}^{a_{in}}$. Compute a quantum circuit that applies $U_{F_{C_q}}$, using the circuit synthesis method of [37].
     (d) Apply the quantum circuit for $U_{F_{C_q}}$ to the system $C_q(\mathsf{X}^{\otimes_{i=1}^{n} b_i} \cdot \mathsf{Z}^{\otimes_{i=1}^{n} a_i})|\psi\rangle$ to obtain the state $C_q(|\psi\rangle)$.

---

6 Quantum Indistinguishability Obfuscation with Respect to a Pseudo-Distance

In this section, we provide a definition for circuits that are approximately equivalent (with respect to a pseudo-distance) (Definition 7). In Sect. 6.2, we present a definition of quantum indistinguishability obfuscation with respect to a pseudo-distance, and in Sect. 6.3, we present a scheme that satisfies this definition, for circuits close to a fixed level of the Gottesman-Chuang hierarchy.

6.1 Approximately Equivalent Quantum Circuits

Definition 7. (Approximately Equivalent Quantum Circuits): *Let C_{q_0} and C_{q_1} be two n-qubit quantum circuits and $\mathbf{D}$ be a pseudo-distance. We say C_{q_0} and C_{q_1} are* approximately equivalent *with respect to $\mathbf{D}$ if there exists a negligible function $\mathtt{negl}(n)$ such that $\mathbf{D}(C_{q_0}, C_{q_1}) \leq \mathtt{negl}(n)$.*

6.2 Indistinguishability Obfuscation for Approximately Equivalent Quantum Circuits

In this section, we provide a definition of quantum indistinguishability obfuscation for approximately equivalent circuits, $qi\mathcal{O}_{\mathbf{D}}$. To be consistent with Definition 6, we require that the obfuscator, on input a quantum circuit C_q, outputs an auxiliary quantum state $|\phi\rangle$ and a quantum circuit C_q', but note in the actual construction (Algorithm 4), the state $|\phi\rangle$ is an empty register. Here, we consider only the case of *statistical* security. Notable here is the indistinguishability property is required to hold not only for equivalent quantum circuits, but also for *approximately* equivalent quantum circuits. Also, contrary to Definition 6, we only require the indistinguishability for large values of n.

Definition 8. *Let C_Q be a polynomial-time family of reversible quantum circuits and let $\mathbf{D}$ be a pseudo-distance. For $n \in \mathbb{N}$, let C_q^n be the circuits in C_Q of input length n. A polynomial-time quantum algorithm for C_Q is a statistically secure quantum indistinguishability obfuscator ($qi\mathcal{O}_\mathbf{D}$) for C_Q with respect to $\mathbf{D}$ if the following conditions hold:*

1. **Functionality:** *There exists a negligible function $\mathtt{negl}(n)$ such that for every $C_q \in C_q^n$*

$$(|\phi\rangle, C_q') \leftarrow qi\mathcal{O}_\mathbf{D}(C_q) \quad and \quad \mathbf{D}(C_q'(|\phi\rangle, \cdot), C_q(\cdot)) \leq \mathtt{negl}(n).$$

   Where $|\phi\rangle$ is an ℓ-qubit state, the circuits C_q and C_q' are of type (n,n) and (m,n) respectively $(m = \ell + n)$.[15]

2. **Polynomial Slowdown:** *There exists a polynomial $p(n)$ such that for any $C_q \in C_q^n$, $\ell \leq p(|C_q|)$, $m \leq p(|C_q|)$ and $|C_q'| \leq p(|C_q|)$.*

3. **Statistically Secure Indistinguishability:** *For any two **approximately equivalent** quantum circuits $C_{q_0}, C_{q_1} \in C_q^n$, of the same size **and for large enough** n, the two distributions $qi\mathcal{O}_\mathbf{D}(C_{q_0})$ and $qi\mathcal{O}_\mathbf{D}(C_{q_1})$ are statistically indistinguishable.*

6.3 $qi\mathcal{O}_\mathbf{D}$ for Circuits Close to the Gottesman-Chuang Hierarchy

Here, we present a quantum indistinguishability obfuscation (Definition 6) for a family of circuits that are approximately equivalent (Definition 7) with respect to the pseudo-distance $\mathbf{D}(U_1, U_2) = \frac{1}{\sqrt{2d^2}} ||U_1 \otimes U_1^* - U_2 \otimes U_2^*||_F$ (see Sect. 2.5). There are two main ingredient in our construction, one is Low's learning algorithm [35] (described below) and the second is Lemma 4.

In [35] Low presents a learning algorithm that, given oracle access to a unitary U and its conjugate $U^\dagger$ with the promise that the distance $\mathbf{D}(U, C) \leq \epsilon < \frac{1}{2^{k-1/2}}$ for some $C \in \mathcal{C}_k$, outputs a circuit C_q for computing C with probability at least $1 - \delta$ with $O\left(\frac{1}{\epsilon'^2}(2n)^{k-1} \log\left(\frac{(2n+1)^{k-1}}{\delta}\right)\right)$ queries. Where $\epsilon' := \sqrt{2(1 - (2^{k-1}\epsilon)^2)} - 1 > 0$ and $\mathbf{D}(U_1, U_2) = \frac{1}{\sqrt{2d^2}} ||U_1 \otimes U_1^* - U_2 \otimes U_2^*||_F$ is the pseudo-distance defined in Sect. 2.5.

Based on Low's work, we construct an quantum indistinguishability obfuscation $qi\mathcal{O}_\mathbf{D}$ with respect to this pseudo-distance $\mathbf{D}$ for circuits that are very close to $\mathcal{C}_k$. Note that the run-time of Low's algorithm is exponential in k. Moreover, the algorithm becomes infeasible if ϵ' is very small. Therefore, to ensure that our construction in Algorithm 4 runs in polynomial-time we set k to be some fixed positive integer and $\epsilon \leq \mathtt{negl}(n) < \frac{1}{2^{k-1/2}}$ for all n. Note if $\epsilon < \frac{1}{2^{k-1/2}}$, then $\epsilon' \geq \frac{\sqrt{7}}{2} - 1$.

---

[15] A circuit is of type (i,j) if it maps i qubits to j qubits.

Lemma 4 (from [35]). *Let U and C be unitaries. If the distance $\mathbf{D}(U, C) < \frac{1}{2^{k-1/2}}$ for some $C \in \mathcal{C}_k$, then C is unique up to phase.*

Theorem 3 (See [16] for the proof). *Consider the polynomial-time family of reversible quantum circuits $\mathcal{C}_Q = \{U_{q^{n,k}} \mid n \in \mathbb{N} \text{ and } k \text{ is fixed positive integer}\}$. Here, $U_{q^{n,k}}$ denotes the n-qubit circuits for which there exists a negligible function $\mathtt{negl}(n)$ such that for any $U_q \in U_{q^{n,k}}$, there exists a $C_q \in \mathcal{C}_k$ that satisfies $\mathbf{D}(U_q, C_q) < \mathtt{negl}(n) < \frac{1}{2^{k+1/2}}$. Then Algorithm 4 is a statistically-secure quantum indistinguishability obfuscation for $\mathcal{C}_Q$ with respect to $\mathbf{D}$.*

Algorithm 4. $qi\mathcal{O}$-Gottesman-Chuang

- Input: An n-qubit circuit $U_q \in U_{q^{n,k}}$, k and $\delta = \mathtt{negl}(n)$).
  1. From U_q compute the circuit $U_q^\dagger$.
  2. Using Low's approximate learning algorithm on inputs U_q and $U_q{}^\dagger$ compute the circuit C_q [35].
  3. Output the circuit C_q.

Acknowledgements. We thank an anonymous reviewer for pointing out the work of [35]; we would also like to thank Yfke Dulek for related discussions. This material is based upon work supported by the Air Force Office of Scientific Research under award number FA9550-20-1-0375, Canada's NRF, Canada's NSERC, an Ontario ERA, and the University of Ottawa's Research Chairs program.

References

1. Aaronson, S.: Quantum copy-protection and quantum money. In: 24th Annual Conference on Computational Complexity–CCC 2009, pp. 229–242 (2009). https://doi.org/10.1109/CCC.2009.42
2. Aaronson, S., Gottesman, D.: Improved simulation of stabilizer circuits. Phys. Rev. A **70**(5), 052328 (2004). https://doi.org/10.1103/PhysRevA.70.052328
3. Alagic, G., Brakerski, Z., Dulek, Y., Schaffner, C.: Impossibility of quantum virtual black-box obfuscation of classical circuits (2020). https://arxiv.org/abs/2005.06432
4. Alagic, G., Fefferman. G.: On quantum obfuscation (2016). https://arxiv.org/abs/1602.01771
5. Alagic, G., Jeffery, S., Jordan. S.: Circuit obfucation using braids. In: 9th Conference on the Theory of Quantum Computation, Communication and Cryptography–TQC 2014, pp. 141–160 (2014). https://doi.org/10.4230/LIPIcs.TQC.2014.141
6. Albrecht, M., Bai, S., Ducas, L.: A subfield lattice attack on overstretched NTRU assumptions. In : Advances in Cryptology–CRYPTO 2016, vol. 1, pp. 153–178 (2016). https://doi.org/10.1007/978-3-662-53018-4_6
7. Amy, M., Maslov, D., Mosca, M.: Polynomial-time T-depth optimization of Clifford$+T$ circuits via matroid partitioning. IEEE Trans. Comput.-Aided Des. Integr. Circ. Syst. **33**(10), 1476–1489 (2014). https://doi.org/10.1109/TCAD.2014.2341953

8. Amy, M., Maslov, D., Mosca, M., Roetteler, M.: A meet-in-the-middle algorithm for fast synthesis of depth-optimal quantum circuits. IEEE Trans. Comput.-Aid. Des. Integr. Circ. Syst. **32**(6), 818–830 (2013). https://doi.org/10.1109/TCAD.2013.2244643

9. Ananth, P., Jain, A., Lin, H., Matt, C., Sahai, A.: Indistinguishability obfuscation without multilinear maps: new paradigms via low degree weak pseudorandomness and security amplification. In: Advances in Cryptology–CRYPTO 2019, vol. 3, pp.284–332 (2019). https://doi.org/10.1007/978-3-030-26954-8_10

10. Ananth, P., La Placa, R.L.: Secure software leasing (2020). https://arxiv.org/abs/2005.05289

11. Barak, B., Goldreich, O., Impagliazzo, R., Rudich, S., Sahai, A., Vadhan, S., Yang, K.: On the (im)possibility of obfuscating programs. J. ACM **59**(2), 6 (2012). https://doi.org/10.1145/2160158.2160159

12. Bitansky, N., Paneth, O.: ZAPs and non-interactive witness indistinguishability from indistinguishability obfuscation. In: 12th Theory of Cryptography Conference–TCC 2015, vol. II, pp. 401–427 (2015). https://doi.org/10.1007/978-3-662-46497-7_16

13. Boneh, D., Zhandry, M.: Multiparty key exchange, efficient traitor tracing, and more from indistinguishability obfuscation. In: Advances in Cryptology–CRYPTO 2014, vol. I, pp. 480–499 (2014). https://doi.org/10.1007/978-3-662-44371-2_27

14. Brakerski, Z.: Quantum FHE: (almost) as secure as classical. In: Advances in Cryptology–CRYPTO 2018, vol. 3, pp. 67–95 (2018). https://doi.org/10.1007/978-3-319-96878-0_3

15. Broadbent, A., Jeffery, S.: Quantum homomorphic encryption for circuits of low T-gate complexity. In: Advances in Cryptology–CRYPTO 2015, vol. 2, pp. 609–629 (2015). https://doi.org/10.1007/978-3-662-48000-7_30

16. Broadbent, A., Kazmi, R.A.: Constructions for quantum indistinguishability obfuscation (2020). https://eprint.iacr.org/2020/639

17. Broadbent, A., Lord, S.: Uncloneable quantum encryption via oracles. In: Theory of Quantum Computation, Communication, and Cryptography–TQC 2020, pp. 4:1–4:22 (2020). https://doi.org/10.4230/LIPIcs.TQC.2020.4

18. Canetti, R., Lin, H., Tessaro, S., Vaikuntanathan, V.: Obfuscation of probabilistic circuits and applications. In: 12th Theory of Cryptography Conference–TCC 2015, vol. II, pp. 468–497 (2015). https://doi.org/10.1007/978-3-662-46497-7_19

19. Chen, Y., Gentry, C., Halevi, S.: Cryptanalyses of candidate branching program obfuscators. In: Advances in Cryptology–EUROCRYPT 2017, vol. 3, pp. 278–307 (2017). https://doi.org/10.1007/978-3-319-56617-7_10

20. Coron, J.-S. Lepoint, T., Tibouchi, M.: Practical multilinear maps over the integers. In: Advances in Cryptology–CRYPTO 2013, vol. 1, pp. 476–493 (2013). https://doi.org/10.1007/978-3-642-40041-4_26

21. Cramer, R., Ducas, L., Peikert, C., Regev, O.: Recovering short generators of principal ideals in cyclotomic rings. In: Advances in Cryptology–EUROCRYPT 2016, vol. 2, pp. 559–585 (2016). https://doi.org/10.1007/978-3-662-49896-5_20

22. Di Matteo, O., Mosca, M.: Parallelizing quantum circuit synthesis. Quant. Sci. Technol. **1**(1), 015003 (2016). https://doi.org/10.1088/2058-9565/1/1/015003

23. Dulek, Y., Schaffner, C., Speelman, F.: Quantum homomorphic encryption for polynomial-sized circuits. In: Advances in Cryptology–CRYPTO 2016, pp. 3–32 (2016). https://doi.org/10.1007/978-3-662-53015-3_1

24. Garg, S., Gentry, C., Halevi, S., Raykova, M., Sahai, A., Waters, B.: Candidate indistinguishability obfuscation and functional encryption for all circuits. In: 54th

Annual Symposium on Foundations of Computer Science–FOCS 2013, pp.40–49 (2013). https://doi.org/10.1109/FOCS.2013.13

25. Gay, R., Jain, A., Lin, H., Sahai, A.: Indistinguishability obfuscation from simple-to-state hardness assumptions (2021). https://eprint.iacr.org/2020/764.pdf

26. Gentry, C., Gorbunov, S., Halevi, S.: Graph-induced multilinear maps from lattices. In: 12th Theory of Cryptography Conference–TCC 2015, vol. 2, pp. 498–527 (2015). https://doi.org/10.1007/978-3-662-46497-7_20

27. Giles, B., Selinger, P.: Remarks on Matsumoto and Amano's normal form for single-qubit Clifford+T operators (2019). https://arxiv.org/abs/1312.6584

28. Goldwasser, S., Rothblum, G.N.: On best-possible obfuscation. J. Cryptol. **27**(3), 480–505 (2014). https://doi.org/10.1007/s00145-013-9151-z

29. Gottesman, D.: The Heisenberg representation of quantum computers. In: 22nd International Colloquium on Group Theoretical Methods in Physics–GROUP 22, pp. 32–43 (1998). http://arxiv.org/abs/quant-ph/9807006

30. Gottesman, D., Chuang, I.L.: Demonstrating the viability of universal quantum computation using teleportation and single-qubit operations. Nature **402**, 390–393 (1999). https://doi.org/10.1038/46503

31. Guo, S., Malkin, T., Oliveira, I.C., Rosen, A.: The power of negations in cryptography. In: 12th Theory of Cryptography Conference–TCC 2015, vol. 1, pp. 36–65 (2015). https://doi.org/10.1007/978-3-662-46494-6_3

32. Jain, A., Lin, H., Sahai, A.: Indistinguishability obfuscation from well-founded assumptions (2020). https://eprint.iacr.org/2020/1003

33. Kaye, P., Laflamme, R., Mosca, R.: An Introduction to Quantum Computing. Oxford University Press, Oxford (2007)

34. Langlois, A., Stehlé, D., Steinfeld, R.: GGHLite: more efficient multilinear maps from ideal lattices. In: Advances in Cryptology–EUROCRYPT 2014, pp. 239–256 (2014). https://doi.org/10.1007/978-3-642-55220-5_14

35. Low, R.A.: Learning and testing algorithms for the Clifford group. Phys. Rev. **80**(5):052314 (2009). http://dx.doi.org/https://doi.org/10.1103/PhysRevA.80.052314

36. Matsumoto, K., Amano, K.: Representation of quantum circuits with Clifford and $\pi/8$ gates (2008). https://arxiv.org/abs/0806.3834

37. Niemann, P., Wille, R., Drechsler, R.: Efficient synthesis of quantum circuits implementing Clifford group operations. In: 19th Asia and South Pacific Design Automation Conference–ASP-DAC 2014, pp. 483–488 (2014). https://doi.org/10.1109/ASPDAC.2014.6742938

38. Sahai, A., Waters, B.: How to use indistinguishability obfuscation: deniable encryption, and more. In: 46th Annual ACM Symposium on Theory of Computing–STOC 2014, pp. 475–484 (2014). https://doi.org/10.1145/2591796.2591825

39. Selinger, R.: Generators and relations for n-qubit Clifford operators (2013). https://arxiv.org/abs/1310.6813

40. Sipser, M.: Introduction to the Theory of Computation. Cengage Learning, 3rd edn. Cengage, Boston (2012)

41. Speelman. F.: Instantaneous non-local computation of low T-depth quantum circuits. In: 11th Conference on the Theory of Quantum Computation, Communication and Cryptography–TQC 2016, pp. 9:1–9:24 (2016). https://doi.org/10.4230/LIPIcs.TQC.2016.9

On Forging SPHINCS+-Haraka Signatures on a Fault-Tolerant Quantum Computer

Robin M. Berger and Marcel Tiepelt[✉]

KASTEL, Karlsruhe Institute of Technology, Karlsruhe, Germany
{robin.berger,marcel.tiepelt}@kit.edu

Abstract. SPHINCS+ is a state-of-the-art hash based signature scheme, the security of which is either based on SHA-256, SHAKE-256 or on the Haraka hash function. In this work, we perform an in-depth analysis of how the hash functions are embedded into SPHINCS+ and how the quantum pre-image resistance impacts the security of the signature scheme. Subsequently, we evaluate the cost of implementing Grover's quantum search algorithm to find a pre-image that admits a universal forgery.

In particular, we provide quantum implementations of the Haraka and SHAKE-256 hash functions in Q# and consider the efficiency of attacks in the context of fault-tolerant quantum computers. We restrict our findings to SPHINCS+-128 due to the limited security margin of Haraka. Nevertheless, we present an attack that performs better, to the best of our knowledge, than previously published attacks.

We can forge a SPHINCS+-128-Haraka signature in about $1.5 \cdot 2^{90}$ surface code cycles and $2.03 \cdot 10^6$ physical qubits, translating to about $1.55 \cdot 2^{101}$ logical-qubit-cycles. For SHAKE-256, the same attack requires $8.65 \cdot 10^6$ qubits and $1.6 \cdot 2^{84}$ cycles resulting in about $2.65 \cdot 2^{99}$ logical-qubit-cycles.

Keywords: Post-quantum cryptography · Quantum implementation · Resource estimation · Cryptanalysis

1 Introduction

Overview and Related Work. Ongoing research in the area of quantum technologies has led to the belief that quantum computers will be able to break current public-key cryptosystems within the coming decades. On the contrary, symmetric-key primitives are believed to be somewhat resistant against quantum attacks, with the most promising generic attack being Grover's search algorithm [15]; Its quadratic improvement over a classical brute force search can easily be countered by doubling the key length of the underlying primitives.

In order to prepare for the (public-key) quantum menace the National Institute for Standards and Technology (NIST) started the post-quantum standardization competition in 2017. From the initial 69 submissions, only 7 were selected

© Springer Nature Switzerland AG 2021
P. Longa and C. Ràfols (Eds.): LATINCRYPT 2021, LNCS 12912, pp. 44–63, 2021.
https://doi.org/10.1007/978-3-030-88238-9_3

as finalists [24]. Additionally, 8 schemes were chosen as alternate candidates based on a high confidence of their security, but with a drawback in performance compared to the 7 finalists. Briefly speaking, they may be considered as *Backup* candidates for standardization. Among the alternate candidates is the stateless hash-based signature scheme SPHINCS$^+$ [16]. SPHINCS$^+$ builds on the hardness of inverting one-way functions, i.e., Haraka [20], SHAKE-256 [22] or SHA-256 [11], the first of which can be derived from block-ciphers and thus is believed to provide similar security guarantees against quantum adversaries.

An estimate of the security of SPHINCS$^+$, based on cryptographic assumptions, was given within the scope of the NIST submission: The authors considered general attacks [16, Sec. 9.3.1] on the distinct-function multi-target second preimage resistance of the underlying hash functions and estimated the success probability of such an attack as $\Theta\left((q_{hash}+1)^2/2^n\right)$, where q_{hash} is the number of hash queries and n a security parameter. Generally, they quantify the security based on the number of required hash function invocations and thus on the probability of an successful adversary.

The NIST competition features 5 security levels [23, 24]: The first level provides security equivalent to performing a key search on AES-128, the second a collision attack on SHA-256 and the fifth a key search on AES-256. Moreover they categorize attacks with quantum computers according to the maximal circuit depth, where each level resembles a number of gates that can be serially computed over a plausible time period. Specifically, NIST estimates that quantum circuits up to a depth of 2^{40} gates can be computed within a single year, up to a depth of 2^{64} in a single decade and up to 2^{96} in a millennium. Respectively, the number of quantum gates to break AES is estimated by NIST to be $2^{170}/\text{MAXDEPTH}$, i.e. 2^{130}, 2^{104} and 2^{74}. [17] gave precise estimates for attacking AES-128 for different values of maxdepth and respective parallelization. Equivalently, NISt estimates 2^{143} classical computational steps. However, we note the most promising attack on AES-128 can be performed in $2^{126.1}$ classical steps as shown by [4]. SPHINCS$^+$ features parameters for each security levels, i.e. SPHINCS$^+$-SHAKE-256 and SPHINCS$^+$-SHA-256 both provide a sufficient amount of security for all 5 NIST security levels. On the other side, SPHINCS$^+$-Haraka achieves security level 1 or 2 at most.

An analysis of the security of SHAKE-256 has been given by [1], whose result is the main motivation for our work. They present a quantum circuit to implement a Grover search and attack the 256-bit pre-image resistance of the SHA3-256 hash function and give concise and fault-tolerant estimates for the resources required to implement such a circuit: They claim that their circuit requires $2^{153.8}$ surface code cycles using $2^{12.6}$ logical qubits, resulting in an overall requirement of about $2^{166.4}$ logical-qubit-cycles using 2^{128} black box queries for a 256-bit preimage search. Their results may be adapted to estimate the work required to break the hash function for the SPHINCS$^+$ signature scheme. However, there is still considerable ambiguity on the specific construction to forge a signature.

The quantum security of Haraka has not been explicitly analyzed yet. However, due to the capacity of the sponge construction in SPHINCS$^+$-Haraka using only 256 bits, attacking the second-preimage-resistance as described in [3] only requires about $2^{129.5}$ classical hash function invocations, producing a collision on the internal state of the hash function in the process. The best known generic quantum collision attacks on hash functions is the BTH algorithm by [7], which finds a collision using $\mathcal{O}(2^{n/3})$ Grover iterations, (where n is a security parameter), however, also requiring $\mathcal{O}(2^{n/3})$ quantum RAM (QRAM). The concept of QRAM is highly controversial, as quantum states that interact with the environment eventually decay. [10, Thm 2] presented a trade-off using only $\tilde{\mathcal{O}}(n)$ QRAM but $\tilde{\mathcal{O}}(2^{2n/5})$ Grover iterations, resulting in a work effort of about 2^{102} iterations for a collision search with $n - 256$ on Haraka.

The (quantum) invocation of the hash function induces a significant overhead and has to be accounted for. Moreover the implementation on a fault-tolerant quantum computer requires additional overhead to compensate for error correction within the circuit. In our analysis we adapt the concept of logical-qubit-cycles as quantum cost metric, such that each cycle is roughly equivalent to a single (classical) hash function invocation [1]. Briefly speaking, a logical-qubit-cycle is the time-space product of the (fault-tolerant) number of quantum gates and the number of qubits (space) that is used during the computation. The cost to implement the generic attack on a fault-tolerant quantum computer has not been analyzed yet. Instead we can consider the time-space product of Grover iterations and memory, which is $\tilde{\mathcal{O}}(2^{3n/5})$, resulting in a cost of about 2^{153}.

Contribution. In this work we consider attacks on SPHINCS$^+$ based on inverting the underlying hash functions at specific points, i.e. attacking the XMSS or FORS structure. We chose particularly Haraka, because of its placement as a potential component within the NIST competition. Moreover, preimage resistance of the Haraka [20] hash function has not, to the best of our knowledge, been explicitly evaluated in the quantum setting in any literature. We evaluate the logical resources required to implement our attacks on the Haraka as well as the SHAKE-256 hash-functions and further estimate the fault-tolerant cost to attack the SPHINCS$^+$-128 scheme. For the sake of completeness and comparability we also present the numbers to attack the SPHINCS$^+$-256 scheme.

In Sect. 2 we recall parts of the SPHINCS$^+$, Haraka and SHAKE-256 scheme, and review the Grover algorithm with respective metrics for fault-tolerant quantum computing. In our work, we use the logical-qubit-cycles metric (introduced in [1]) which compares to classical hash function invocations. Section 3 shows the results for our implementation[1] of the hash functions in Q#. To construct a circuit for Haraka, we partially reused the work of [17] on AES functions, resulting in the first implementation of the Haraka hash function in the quantum setting. The implementation for SHAKE-256 was built from scratch. For both circuits, we consider the number of qubits as well as different metrics based on the gate count and T-Depth. As a result, our implementation of the Haraka512 permutation in the hash function consumes about $2.2 \cdot 10^6$ quantum gates on 1144 logical qubits. Our Keccak permutation in the SHAKE-256 hash function consumes about $3.3 \cdot 10^6$ quantum gates on 3200 logical qubits.

---

[1] https://github.com/RobinBerger/Grover-Sphincs.

In Sect. 4, we analyze the most promising points of attack in the SPHINCS$^+$ signature scheme. We propose that the weakest link is the XMSS authentication path for a given WOTS$^+$ public key, as this allows a universal forgery attack. Our most promising attack on SPHINCS$^+$-128-Haraka requires about $1.6 \cdot 2^{86}$ quantum gates. The same circuit to attack SPHINCS$^+$-128-SHAKE-256 has about $1.2 \cdot 2^{86}$ gates.

In Sect. 5, we partially follow the approach of [1] to estimate the resources for this attack in the context of fault-tolerant quantum computing. We compute the amount of error correction in terms of surface code cycles and the optimal scheme for magic state distillation.

For the Haraka hash function, our attack requires $3.91 \cdot 10^{30} \approx 1.55 \cdot 2^{101}$ logical-qubit-cycles on $2.03 \cdot 10^6$ physical qubits, which is better than the generic quantum collision attack on the hash function, which requires 2^{102} quantum hash function invocations (without considering the cost of implementing the hash function), or a time-space product of 2^{153}, which appears to be the more realistic comparison to the cost of logical-qubit-cycles. Performing our attack with the SHAKE-256 hash function instead requires $7.44 \cdot 10^{29} \approx 2.65 \cdot 2^{99}$ logical-qubit-cycles on $8.65 \cdot 10^6$ physical qubits.

2 Preliminaries

2.1 The SPHINCS$^+$ Signature Scheme

In this section we partially review the SPHINCS$^+$ signature scheme as proposed and submitted by [16] to the second and third round of NIST's post-quantum cryptography competition. The structure of the SPHINCS$^+$-scheme combines a hypertree (HT) of eXtended Merkle Signature Schemes (XMSS) and Winternitz One-Time Signature schemes (WOTS) with a Forest Of Random Subsets (FORS) as represented in the attack Fig. 3.

In the following, we consider a signature σ_y^x using the scheme y to sign the message x and a hash function $\mathcal{H} \in \{\text{SHAKE-256, Haraka-512, Haraka-sponge}\}$ for all the subsequent hashes. Moreover, each scheme is associated with a $KeyGen(\cdot)$, $Sign(\cdot)$ and $Verify(\cdot)$ functionality. Let $\text{pk}_{\text{SPHINCS+}}, \text{sk}_{\text{SPHINCS+}}$ be a SPHINCS$^+$ key pair associated with seeds to deterministically generate the subsequent keys of the scheme. Then a signature of a message m is a tuple of value σ_r and signatures from the hypertree and FORS: $\sigma_{\text{SPHINCS+}}^m :=$ $(\sigma_r \| \sigma_{FORS}^m \| \sigma_{HT}^{\text{pk}_{FORS}})$. The value σ_r will be mostly ignored in the remaining paper.

During signing, one generates a FORS instance, signs a message digest with the FORS key, and signs the FORS pk with the hypertree. The hypertree consists of several layers of XMSS instances. Each XMSS instance is a binary hash tree with WOTS schemes at the leaves, where the value of each node is the output of hashing its child nodes. Each XMSS tree is associated with a root node pk_{XMSS} and a set of WOTS keys $\text{pk}_{WOTS}, \text{sk}_{WOTS}$. An XMSS signature consists of a WOTS signature and an authentication path $\sigma_{XMSS}^x := (\sigma_{WOTS}^x, \text{path}_{XMSS})$,

---

Algorithm 1: SPHINCS$^+$ − KeyGen()

---

1 $sk_{\text{seed}} \xleftarrow{\$} \{0,1\}^n$, $sk_{\text{prf}} \xleftarrow{\$} \{0,1\}^n$, $pk_{\text{seed}} \xleftarrow{\$} \{0,1\}^n$

2 $pk_{\text{root}} \leftarrow KeyGen_{\text{HT}}(sk_{\text{seed}}, pk_{\text{seed}})$

3 **return** ($\text{pk}_{\text{SPHINCS+}} := (pk_{\text{seed}}, pk_{\text{root}}), \text{sk}_{\text{SPHINCS+}} := (sk_{\text{seed}}, sk_{\text{prf}})$)

Algorithm 2: SPHINCS$^+$ − Sign($m := \{0,1\}^*, \text{sk}_{\text{SPHINCS+}}$)

---

1 $r \xleftarrow{\$} \{0,1\}^n$

2 $\sigma_r \leftarrow prf\_msg(sk_{\text{prf}}, r, m)$

3 $md \leftarrow \mathcal{H}(\sigma_r, pk_{\text{seed}}, pk_{\text{root}}, m)$

4 $\sigma_{FORS}^{md} \leftarrow Sign_{\text{FORS}}(md, sk_{\text{seed}}, pk_{\text{seed}})$

5 $\text{pk}_{FORS} \leftarrow pkFromSig_{\text{FORS}}(\sigma_{FORS}, m, pk_{\text{seed}})$

6 $\sigma_{HT}^{\text{pk}_{FORS}} \leftarrow Sign_{\text{HT}}(\text{pk}_{FORS}, sk_{\text{seed}}, pk_{\text{seed}}, md)$

7 **return** ($\sigma := (\sigma_r || \sigma_{FORS}^{md} || \sigma_{HT}^{\text{pk}_{FORS}})$)

---

where path$_{XMSS}$ consists of all sibling nodes on the path from a leaf to the root of the tree. The WOTS instances at the leaf nodes are then used to sign the root node of the next layer, resulting in a hypertree. The root node of the top tree is the public key of the hypertree. The bottom WOTS instances represent the respective secret key of the hypertree that is used to create the signature $\sigma_{HT}^{\text{pk}_{FORS}}$.

To validate a signature $\sigma_{\text{SPHINCS+}}^m$, one first computes a FORS public key from σ_{FORS}^m and then verifies the hypertree signature $\sigma_{HT}^{\text{pk}_{FORS}}$. For the latter, one has to compute the authentication path through the hypertree and finally compare the resulting public key pk_{HT}' to the key associated with the SPHINCS$^+$ signature scheme. The Algorithms 1, 2, 3 review these procedures using the respective signature schemes and a function prf_msg, that generates a pseudo-random value as part of the signature. We note that the description is not complete (as in [16]), i.e. it is restricted to a level appropriate to follow the remaining paper.

2.2 Quantum Computing

We assume the reader to be familiar with the basics of quantum information theory (e.g. see [25]). In the following we first describe the general attack strategy using Grover's algorithm [15]. Then, we recall the setup to estimate quantum resources on a fault-tolerant quantum computing architecture based on the excellent description of [19] using surface codes [13] and magic state distillation [8].

2.3 Grover's Algorithm on Preimage Resistance

For a fixed n, given a predicate $p : \{0,1\}^n \rightarrow \{0,1\}$ marking M elements $x \in \{0,1\}^n$, Grover's algorithm finds an element x, for which $p(x) = 1$. Let the initial

---

Algorithm 3: SPHINCS$^+$ $-$ Verify
$(\sigma := (\sigma_r || \sigma_{FORS}^{md} || \sigma_{HT}^{pk_{FORS}}), m, pk_{SPHINCS^+})$

---

1   $md \leftarrow \mathcal{H}(\sigma_r, pk_{seed}, pk_{root}, m)$
2   $pk_{FORS} \leftarrow pkFromSig_{FORS}(\sigma_{FORS}, m, pk_{seed})$
3   **return** $Verify_{HT}(pk_{FORS}, \sigma_{HT}, pk_{seed}, md, pk_{root})$

---

superposition be $|\phi\rangle = \sqrt{(N-M)/N}\,|\{x|p(x)=0\}\rangle + \sqrt{M/N}\,|\{x|p(x)=1\}\rangle$. Then the algorithm of Grover operates in the space spanned by $|\phi\rangle$ and $|\{x|p(x)=1\}\rangle$, where $\langle\phi||\{x|p(x)=1\}\rangle = \sin(\theta)$. The initial value is $\theta = \arcsin(\sqrt{M/N})$, and is increased in every iteration by roughly $\sqrt{M/N}$, where the advance diminishes during the last few iterations. Thus the probability to measure a marked element is the largest after $R = \lfloor \pi/4\sqrt{N/M} \rfloor$ Grover iterations. Our implementation of the Grover iteration follows the principle construction for oracle invocations.

If the number of matches M is not (exactly) known, and one performs too many iterations, the value of θ decreases. Instead one can run Grover's algorithm multiple times with different values for M. [6, Theorem 3] have shown that the expected number of iterations remains in $\mathcal{O}(\sqrt{N/M})$.

In the context of hash functions and the random oracle model, we assume the number of matches to be $M = 1$, i.e. we are given a value y and we are looking for a single value x, so that $y = \mathcal{H}(x)$. Whereas there is no guarantee that there are no collisions (i.e. $M > 1$), $M = 1$ is to be expected, since the input and output domain of the hash functions are of equal size in our case.

2.4 Fault-Tolerant Resource Estimation

The layered architecture in [19] describes the physical design of a fault-tolerant quantum computer. The first and second layer cover the physical processes and the virtual interfaces of the hardware and are not considered in the analysis. The third layer provides reliable QubitClifford-gates, but not T-gates, by performing a series of measurements and faulty gate applications on physical qubits to correct errors. Each of these intervals is called a surface code cycle. Then, the logical layer provides a universal gate set. The final layer consists of the application of Grover's algorithm.

In the following we describe the layers in more detail, review the cost metrics of [1] in our setting and explicitly mention the assumptions (since quantum benchmarks are not available) required for the analysis. Our description of the different layers, which are pictured in Fig. 1, is tailored to our resource estimate. We combine these with the cost metrics used by [1] for comparability.

Assumption 1. The cost for a computation of a large-scale fault-tolerant quantum computer is well approximated using surface codes [1,18,26].

The following parameters approximate today's state of the art [1,12]. We use these for comparability, but note that other values have also been suggested [19].

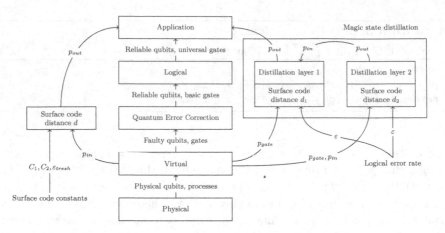

Fig. 1. Layered architecture for quantum computers including parameters for the error correction layer (left) and exemplary magic state distillation (right).

While Assumption 3 does not hold for our oracle implementation per se, it does so for the Grover algorithm over multiple Grover iterations.

Assumption 2. p_{in} is the initial error probability of a quantum state, i.e. before any layer of error correction $p_{in} \approx 10^{-4}$. $p_{gate} \approx p_{in}/10$ is the gate error rate. $T_{sc} = 200$ ns is the approximate time for a single surface code cycle.

Assumption 3. All quantum gates are distributed uniformly across all layers.

Quantum Error Correction. Let $C_1, C_2, \varepsilon_{tresh}$ be parameters determined by the implementation of the surface code with distance d. Given an initial error rate of p_{in} one can calculate the distance d for a targeted error rate p_{out} as per $p_{out} \approx C_1 \left(C_2 p_{in}/\varepsilon_{tresh} \right)^{\lfloor d+1/2 \rfloor}$ [19, Sec. IV.B]. We follow the suggestion in [14, Fig. 8] and estimate that each logical qubit requires $2 \cdot (d+1)^2$ physical qubits to be implemented in a surface code with distance d.

Logical Layer. We deploy the Reed-Muller-15-to-1 distillation introduced by [8], each layer uses 15 magic states with an input error rate of p_{in} and produces one magic state with lower error rate $p_{dist} \approx 35 p_{in}^3$. We follow the work of [1] and assume that the amount of logical errors introduced during distillation is already covered in the process resulting in $p_{out} = (1 + \varepsilon) p_{dist}$, hence $p_{in} \approx \sqrt[3]{p_{out}/35(1+\varepsilon)}$ The distillation is repeated until p_{out} reaches a target value.

Let d_i be a surface code distance for layer i with $i = 1$ being the top layer of distillation, where each distillation requires $10 \cdot d_i$ cycles. For this, [12, Sec. II] gives an example calculation, [1, Alg. 4] gives an explicit algorithm that takes an initial gate error p_{gate} and calculates the number of layers of magic state distillation as well as their respective surface code distance. Each layer i requires $16 \cdot 15^{(i-1)}$ logical qubits. The number of physical qubits in the code is calculated based on the respective surface code.

Algorithm 4: Haraka512Permutation($A[x] : \{0,1\}^{128}, 0 \leq x < 4$)

---

1 for $0 \leq i < 5$ **do**
2   **for** $0 \leq j < 4$ **do**
3 $A[j] := aesEnc(aesEnc(A[j], key_{i,j,1}), key_{i,j,0})$
4 $A := mix(A)$
5 return A

Application Layer. For our implemented circuits we consider the total count for T-, CNOT- and QubitClifford gates, along with the T-depth and T-width, motivated in [1,17]. For a circuit implementing our attacks, i.e. using Grover's algorithm, let G^d be the total depth (i.e. number of layers) of a circuit and let SCC be the number of surface code cycles for each layer. First, we consider the total number of surface code cycles as $\text{COST}_{\text{SCC}} = \text{SCC} \cdot \text{G}^d$. Then, we consider the number of logical qubits Q_G^{log} required to implement the Grover algorithm and the number of logical qubits Q_{MD}^{log} to perform the magic state distillation. Finally, we consider the metric of logical-qubit-cycles from [1, As. 4 and Cost Metric 1], where each cycle is comparable to one (classical) hash function invocation. The number of logical-qubit-cycles is considered to be the total cost of the attack: $\text{COST}_{\text{lqc}} = \text{COST}_{\text{SCC}} \cdot (\text{Q}_G^{log} + \text{Q}_{MD}^{log})$. We consider this metric to be the most fitting in comparison to the time-space product given for the best generic attack in [10].

3 Reversible Implementations

We implemented[2] the Haraka and SHAKE-256 hash functions in Q#. We briefly review the schemes and describe our reversible implementations. To the best of our knowledge, this is the first reversible implementation of Haraka.

3.1 Haraka

Haraka, as specified in [20], consists of AES encryptions (*aesEnc*) and a mixing step (*mix*) for the permutation, which is used in turn to instantiate a sponge construction with a capacity of 256 bits, resulting in the Haraka-Sponge hash function. The Haraka512 hash function is defined as the truncated XOR of the input value and the output of the Haraka512 permutation on said input. Algorithm 4 describes the Haraka512 permutation. We partially reuse the AES implementation from [17] and adjust it to our use case.

For the AES encryption [21], we implement each of its four steps. The *SubBytes* step consists of applying the AES S-Box on each 8-bit block of the input. We use the implementation of [17] for the S-Box and additionally implement its inverse based on the proposed circuit in [5] using 120 ancillary qubits. This allows us to compute the output of the operation into new qubits and then

---

[2] https://github.com/RobinBerger/Grover-Sphincs.

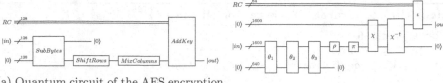

(a) Quantum circuit of the AES encryption step.

(b) Quantum circuit of the Keccak round function.

Fig. 2. Implementation of the round function components of Haraka and SHAKE-256.

using the adjoint inverse S-Box to reset the input qubits. In contrast to the implementation in [17], this allows us to recursively apply AES multiple times without needing additional qubits for every application, at the cost of additional quantum gates required. The *ShiftRows* step swaps qubits. Thus we simply apply all following gates to different qubits (resulting in no additional cost). The *MixColumns* operation is the same implementation as the one by [17]. The *AddKey* operation is implemented using classically controlled NOT gates, as we use classical AES round keys, whereas [17] use quantum round keys. Figure 2a shows the complete circuit for the AES encryption.

Similarly to the *ShiftRows* operation, we implemented the mixing step for the Haraka permutation by redirecting the quantum wires.

The AES encryption operation computes the output into a new set of qubits, freeing up the input qubits. We apply this twice on each input block, alternating the input and output qubits, followed by the mixing step. This completes the round function that is repeated a total of 6 times for the Haraka512 permutation.

We implement the Haraka512 hash function by *copying* the input into ancillary qubits using CNOT gates, then applying the Haraka512 permutation on these qubits. Next, the relevant qubits from the output of the permutation and the input of the hash function are XORed into the output qubits using CNOT gates. Finally, the ancilla qubits are freed up again by applying the adjoint Haraka512 permutation. The Haraka-based sponge construction is implemented by instantiating a sponge construction with the Haraka512 permutation.

The quantum gate count for our implementations of the Haraka permutation and hash function can be seen in Table 1. Note that Q# optimizes the width of the quantum circuit, reusing ancillary qubits whenever possible, even if this results in a significantly higher depth of the quantum circuit. As the exact amount of quantum gates required depends on the SPHINCS+ instance, all round constants for determining the gate count here and in the rest of this work are assumed to be zero. When using the default round constants, 2582 additional NOT gates are required for every application of the Haraka512 permutation, which is negligible compared to the gates required for the rest of the implementation.

Table 1. Resources for our implementation of the Haraka512 permutation and hash function. The width of the circuit includes the input and output qubits.

	T	CNOT	QubitClifford	T-Depth	Width
Permutation	609 289	1 383 040	189 440	69 125	1144
Hash function	1 218 560	2 767 616	378 880	138 250	1912

Algorithm 5: KeccakPermutation($A[x][y][z]$: $\{0,1\}, 0 \leq x,y < 5, 0 \leq z < 64$)

---

1 **for** $0 \leq i < 24$ **do**
2 $\quad \lfloor \; A := \iota((\chi \circ \pi \circ \rho \circ \theta)(A), i)$
3 **return** A

3.2 SHAKE-256

The SHAKE-256 hash function, as specified in [22], consists of the Keccak permutation, which is used to instantiate a sponge construction. The Keccak permutation consists of iterating the steps θ, ρ, π, χ and ι 24 times. The complete permutation is described in Algorithm 5, where the five steps are defined as

$$\theta: \qquad C[x][z] := \bigoplus_{0 \leq j < 5} A[x][j][z]$$

$$D[x][z] := C[x-1][z] \oplus C[x+1][z-1]$$

$$A'[x][y][z] := A[x][y][z] \oplus D[x][z]$$

$$\rho: \qquad A'[x][y][z] := A[x][y][z + c[x][y]]$$

$$\pi: \qquad A'[x][y][z] := A[x + 3y][x][z]$$

$$\chi: \qquad A'[x][y][z] := A[x][y][z] \oplus ((A[x+1][y][z] \oplus 1) \cdot A[x+2][y][z])$$

$$\iota: \qquad A'[x][y][z] := \begin{cases} A[x][y][z] \oplus RC_i[z] & x = 0 \wedge y = 0 \\ A[x][y][z] & \text{otherwise} \end{cases}.$$

We note that our implementation follows closely the definition in [22] and thus has a similar structure to the one used by [1]. The operation θ is split into three parts $\theta_{1,2,3}$. θ_1 and θ_2 are a straight forward implementation of the SHA-3 specification, where we compute intermediate values in step θ_1 which are used in θ_2 to compute the output of the θ step. θ_3 implements θ^{-1} to uncompute intermediate values and is based on the KeccakTools reference implementation [2]. All XOR operations are implemented using CNOT gates. ρ and π are permuting the input and output bits by adjusting the subsequent quantum wires. The χ step of the Keccak permutation is a straight forward implementation of the specification with binary addition and multiplication based on CNOT and Toffoli gates, χ^{-1} is the respective inverse, where the adjoint χ^{-1} uncomputes the input qubits. This is the design also used by [1]. The ι step XORS a round constant on the state, which is implemented using classically controlled NOT gates.

Table 2. Quantum gate count for our implementation of the Keccak permutation and for the work by [1]. Gate counts for θ and χ are given for one round. Gate counts for ι, and the complete Keccak permutation are given for all 24 rounds.

	Step	T	CNOT	QubitClifford	T-Depth	Width
Our implementation	$\theta_{1,2,3}$	0	63 040	0	0	2240
	χ	11 200	19 200	3200	25	3200
	χ^{-1}	13 440	23 360	3840	30	3200
	ι	0	0	86	0	1600
	Keccak	591 360	2 534 400	169 046	1176	3200
Implementation in [1]	Keccak	591 360	33 269 760	169 045	792	3200
	Optimized	499 200	34 260 480	169 045	432	3200

The padding for the sponge construction is implemented using classically controlled NOT gates on the state.

The quantum circuit for the round function is represented in Fig. 2b. The Keccak permutation consists of applying this implementation 24 times while alternating input and output qubits.

The quantum gates for our implementation of the Keccak permutation and a comparison with [1] can be seen in Table 2. The most notable differences are that we use more than an order of magnitude fewer CNOT gates, because we use ancilla qubits for the θ operation and that we use the T-depth 5 Toffoli gate provided by Q# while [1] use a T-depth 3 Toffoli gate.

4   Attacking the SPHINCS$^+$ Signature Scheme

We analyzed the WOTS, FORS and XMSS components of the SPHINCS$^+$ scheme to identify weak points and compared resources to mount an attack. Briefly speaking, we determined that forging an XMSS signature requires the fewest logical resources to forge a complete SPHINCS$^+$ signature. In the following sections we describe two of our attacks in more detail.

4.1   Forging a SPHINCS$^+$ Signature on the XMSS component

To compute a universal forgery for a signature of a message $\tilde{m}$, we create a new SPHINCS$^+$ instance associated with a secret key $\tilde{sk}_{SPHINCS^+}$. The root node of the topmost XMSS instance of our new hypertree evaluates to the original public key $pk_{SPHINCS^+}$ as in Fig. 3.

Let $\tilde{\sigma}^{\tilde{m}}_{SPHINCS^+} := (\tilde{\sigma}^{\tilde{m}}_{FORS}, \tilde{\sigma}^{pk_{FORS}}_{HT})$ be a forged signature. The FORS signature is a freshly generated signature and the validation of which depends only on the new key pair. To forge the signature $\tilde{\sigma}^{pk_{FORS}}_{HT}$ we use the public key of the topmost WOTS instance generated from $\tilde{sk}_{SPHINCS^+}$ and replace the respective XMSS signature with a forged signature $\tilde{\sigma}_{XMSS}$: Therefore, we need to find an authentication path $\tilde{path}_{XMSS}$ in the respective tree, so that computing the root

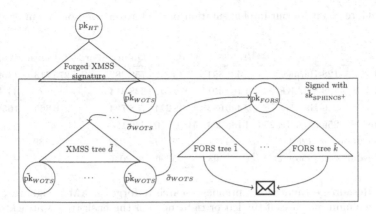

Fig. 3. Forged SPHINCS$^+$ signature using a forged XMSS signature.

node of the tree along the path with the respective WOTS public key results in the given XMSS public key.

Let $p_1 \ldots p_{h'}$ be the nodes on the path from the given WOTS public key node to the root of the XMSS tree with p_1 being the leaf and $p_{h'}$ being the root node. Also, let $v_1 \ldots v_{h'-1}$ be the respective sibling nodes. p_1 is the WOTS public key and p_i is computed from p_{i-1} and v_{i-1} for $i > 0$.

To find values v_i for an authentication path, we select the first $h' - 2$ values $v_1 \ldots v_{h'-2}$ at random from $\{0, 1\}^n$. This results in fixed values $p_1 \ldots p_{h'-1}$. Then we can forge the authentication path $\tilde{\text{path}}_{XMSS}$ if we can find a value $v_{h'-1}$ to complete the path. We can estimate the probability of such a preimage $v_{h'-1}$ existing for a fixed $v_1 \ldots v_{h'-2}$ and a given public key, if we assume that the deployed hash function behaves like a random oracle, i.e. with each value $\mathcal{H}(x)$ being chosen uniformly at random independently from each other:

$$\mathbb{P}\left(\exists x \in \{0,1\}^n : \mathcal{H}(x) = pk\right) = 1 - \mathbb{P}\left(\forall x \in \{0,1\}^n : \mathcal{H}(x) \neq pk\right)$$
$$\geq 1 - \frac{1}{e} \tag{1}$$

This means that a preimage $v_{h'-1}$ exists with probability $\geq 1 - 1/e$. Therefore, forging a valid signature for a message depends only on finding the value $v_{h'-1}$. In the remaining paper we are concerned with estimating the resources to find this value using Grover's algorithm on a fault-tolerant quantum computer.

While this attack can be modified by generating WOTS instances for one half of the attacked XMSS instance, allowing to easily forge signatures for multiple messages if they fall on that side of the XMSS tree, the setup and the cost for the preimage search is the same, so we will not go into more detail with this.

Resource Estimate. To forge the XMSS signature, we need to find a preimage of the Haraka-based sponge or the SHAKE-256 hash function using Grover's algorithm. In the following estimate, let n be the security parameter in bits.

Table 3. Gate count for our implementation of the Grover components in one Grover iteration.

	T	CNOT	QubitClifford	T-Depth	Width
SPHINCS+-128-Haraka	2 438 891	5 535 202	758 282	275 713	1400
SPHINCS+-128-SHAKE-256	1 184 491	5 071 842	338 614	3635	3456
SPHINCS+-256-Haraka	2 440 683	5 538 274	758 794	276 865	1656
SPHINCS+-256-SHAKE-256	1 186 283	5 076 450	339 126	4787	3712
Grover diffusion (128 bit)	1771	2530	1022	1139	–
Grover diffusion (256 bit)	3563	5090	2046	2291	–

Table 4. Resource estimate for a preimage search to forge an XMSS signature, where the target column indicates if the left or right node of the hash tree is attacked.

SPHINCS+ instantiation	Gate count	T-Depth	T-Depth-Times-Width
SPHINCS+-128-Haraka	$1.6 \cdot 2^{86}$	$1.7 \cdot 2^{81}$	$1.1 \cdot 2^{92}$
SPHINCS+-128-SHAKE-256	$1.2 \cdot 2^{86}$	$1.8 \cdot 2^{75}$	$1.5 \cdot 2^{87}$
SPHINCS+-256-Haraka	$1.6 \cdot 2^{150}$	$1.7 \cdot 2^{145}$	$1.4 \cdot 2^{156}$
SPHINCS+-256-SHAKE-256	$1.2 \cdot 2^{150}$	$1.4 \cdot 2^{140}$	$1.2 \cdot 2^{152}$

For the Haraka instantiation, the input to the hash function consists of a 256 bit address and two n-bit values, one of which is the hash value of a node in the XMSS tree, the other one is the value searched for by Grover's algorithm to forge the signature. For the SHAKE-256 instantiation, the input to the hash function consists of a n-bit public key seed and the same inputs as with Haraka.

Using $n = 128$ for the Haraka instantiation, we can save resources by precomputing one iteration of the Haraka512 permutation. As the rate of the sponge instantiation is 256 bits, the first iteration absorbing the address can always be precomputed, so the quantum circuit is implemented using a different initial state, skipping this iteration. Using the same security parameter for the SHAKE-256 instantiation, none of the iterations can be precomputed. The gate count for the implementation of these Grover oracles as well as for the Grover diffusion operator for the SPHINCS+-128 and SPHINCS+-256 parameter sets as determined by Q# are shown in Table 3. While we include the 256-bit parameter sets for comparison, we want to note that for the Haraka hash function, more efficient attacks exist for that parameter set.

For $n = 128$, Grover's algorithm requires roughly $1.6 \cdot 2^{63}$ iterations. Combining these gate counts with the amount of Grover iterations, we can evaluate two cost metrics for this attack. These results are shown in Table 4.

We can see that the attack using the SHAKE-256 hash function performs better on both cost metrics than the attack using Haraka. This results from the additional iterations of the Haraka permutation compared to SHAKE-256.

4.2   Forging a SPHINCS$^+$ Signature on the WOTS Component

An alternate approach to forging SPHINCS$^+$ signatures is to attack the WOTS component. Similarly to the previous attack, this is a universal forgery attack, however we also require a message m, that already has a valid signature σ.

The general attack strategy is similar to [9], i.e. the selection of the WOTS instance and the construction of the SPHINCS$^+$ signature from the other components: We generate a SPHINCS$^+$ signature for a new message using a new secret key, making sure that this signature uses the first-layer WOTS instance at the same position as the one in σ. We then forge a WOTS signature, that authenticates our second-layer XMSS public key for the first-layer WOTS public key in the original structure. In comparison to [9], who use a fault injection attack, we forge the WOTS signature using a quantum preimage attack.

Custom Selection of WOTS Instances. Similarly to [9], when creating a SPHINCS$^+$ signature σ^* for a message m^*, we need to use a FORS instance, that results in σ^* using the first-layer WOTS instance at the same position as σ does. They state that this is possible on a classical computer with feasible effort. In the setting of SPHINCS$^+$-128 [16], this takes an average of $\approx 2^9$ hash function invocations.

Forging WOTS Signatures. As the WOTS signature scheme divides a message into message and checksum blocks and then signs each block individually, forging a WOTS signature requires forging a signature for each block. A signature for a block containing a message m_i consists of the m_i-th element of a hash chain.

Let m_i and m_i^* be the message in the i-th block of m and m^* respectively. For $m_i \leq m_i^*$, a signature for block i can be computed, by advancing in the hash chain $m_i^* - m_i$ times by applying the hash function. For $m_i > m_i^*$, we need to go back $m_i - m_i^*$ times in the hash chain. To do this, we can apply Grover's algorithm.

Such a preimage to a value of the hash chain must exist, as σ was generated using this value. As it might not be unique, but only the value used to generate σ is guaranteed to have a preimage again, this means that instead of applying Grover's algorithm multiple times, to go back in the hash chain once in each step, we need to do a preimage search on a recursive application of the hash function in a single step. If multiple preimages of the recursive application of the hash function exist, any one of them produces a valid signature for that block.

Let the length of each block be $\log_2 w$. As the messages for the WOTS signature scheme are outputs of a hash function and therefore the message blocks m_i and m_i^* are blocks of an output of a hash function, it is reasonable to assume, that they are distributed uniformly at random from the set $\{0, \ldots, w - 1\}$, independently from each other. However we cannot assume this assumption to hold for the checksum blocks. Using this assumption for the message blocks, we can estimate the recursion depth of the hash function required for this attack.

Table 5. Gate count required by our implementation of the Grover oracles for a recursion depth 5 of the hash functions.

	T	CNOT	QubitClifford	T-Depth	Width
SPHINCS$^+$-128-Haraka	12 187 371	27 667 810	3 789 310	1 369 814	1912
SPHINCS$^+$-128-SHAKE-256	11 828 971	50 694 370	3 381 550	26 098	3968
SPHINCS$^+$-256-Haraka	12 189 163	27 674 850	3 789 822	1 357 142	2680
SPHINCS$^+$-256-SHAKE-256	11 830 763	50 700 770	3 382 062	27 250	4736
Grover diffusion (128 bit)	1771	2530	1022	1139	–
Grover diffusion (256 bit)	3563	5090	2046	2291	–

We will follow a simple approach, only considering a single preimage search for a message block, neglecting the amount of preimage searches required for checksum blocks and the possibility of searching for weak instances. A more detailed approach also considering the aforementioned aspects is beyond the scope of this work.

For the recursion depth required for a preimage search we take the value d, so the probability of a recursion depth of $\geq d$ and $\leq d$ being required for the preimage search is $\geq 1/2$. For the SPHINCS$^+$ parameters proposed in [16] with $\log w = 4$, this results in $d = 5$.

Resource Estimate. For forging a WOTS signature and carrying out this attack, we need to do multiple preimage searches of a recursive application of the SHAKE-256 or Haraka512 hash function. Let n be the security parameter in bits in the following resource estimate.

For the Haraka instantiation, the input to the hash function consists of a 256 bit address and the n bit value searched for. The SHAKE-256 instantiation additionally gets an n bit public key seed as input.

Using $n = 128$, we will only go into detail for a hash function recursion depth of 5, as calculated previously. The gate count required for the Grover oracles for this attack for both of the hash functions and for the diffusion operator are shown in Table 5.

As with the previous attack, for $n = 128$, $\approx 1.6 \cdot 2^{63}$ Grover iterations are required for one preimage attack. We can again combine this with the gate counts from Table 5 to evaluate the cost metrics for this attack. This is shown in Table 6. As mentioned previously, the cost metric does not capture that this attack requires multiple preimage attacks of variable recursion depths.

As the Haraka512 hash function is used here and not the Haraka-Sponge hash function used in the previous attack, the amount of applications of the underlying permutation is the same for the Haraka and SHAKE-256 instantiation, with Haraka permutation requiring fewer quantum gates explaining the results of the gate count metric. As in the previous attack, Haraka performs worse in the T-Depth-Times-Width metric, as the Haraka permutation has a significantly higher T-Depth.

Table 6. Resource estimate for a preimage search to forge a WOTS signature.

SPHINCS$^+$ instantiation	Gate count	T-Depth	T-Depth-Times-Width
SPHINCS$^+$-128-Haraka	$1.0 \cdot 2^{89}$	$1.0 \cdot 2^{84}$	$1.9 \cdot 2^{94}$
SPHINCS$^+$-128-SHAKE-256	$1.5 \cdot 2^{89}$	$1.3 \cdot 2^{78}$	$1.3 \cdot 2^{90}$
SPHINCS$^+$-256-Haraka	$1.0 \cdot 2^{153}$	$1.0 \cdot 2^{116}$	$1.3 \cdot 2^{159}$
SPHINCS$^+$-256-SHAKE-256	$1.5 \cdot 2^{153}$	$1.4 \cdot 10^{142}$	$1.6 \cdot 2^{154}$

5 Fault-Tolerant Cost

In this section, we give tight cost estimates of carrying out the *most promising* attack on XMSS signatures in Sect. 4.1. In particular, we analyze the resource requirements for the SPHINCS$^+$-128 parameter sets, i.e. Haraka and SHAKE-256 hash function. A comparison of all results can be found in Table 7. The analysis follows the approach by [1], but optimizes the parallelization of the magic state distillation.

5.1 Haraka

Setup. The entire Grover circuit for the attack using the Haraka hash function consists of $T_{\text{Haraka}} = 3.54 \cdot 10^{25}$ T-gates, $G_{\text{Haraka}}^{cnot} = 8.02 \cdot 10^{25}$ CNOT-gates and $G_{\text{Haraka}}^{c} = 1.1 \cdot 10^{25}$ QubitClifford-gates with the Hadamard-gates dominating, thus other types of gates are ignored. The circuit has a width of $Q_{\text{Haraka}}^{w} = 1400$ and a T-depth of $T_{\text{Haraka}}^{d} = 4.01 \cdot 10^{24}$.

Magic State Distillation. Given the desired output error rate relative to the size of the circuit $p_{\text{out}} = 1/T_{\text{Haraka}}^{d}$ and the assumptions given in Sect. 2.4 one can determine the number of layers of magic distillation required. We require two layers as in Fig. 4a, each with a surface code distance d_i, number of logical Q_i^{log} and respectively physical qubits Q_i^{phy}. In total, the number of logical qubits for a single distillery is $Q_{\text{MD, Haraka}}^{\text{log}} = 240$.

The layers can be optimized based on the cost metrics from Sect. 2.4, i.e. $\text{COST}_{\text{lqc}} = \text{COST}_{\text{SCC}} \cdot (Q_G + Q_{MD})$ and $\text{COST}_{\text{SCC}} = \text{SCC} \cdot G^d$, thus increasing the number of cycles scales the cost by both, cycles and qubits. Consider an increase of cycles by a factor X and an increase of qubits by a factor Y. Then the optimal distillery can be found by computing $\min_{X,Y} X Q_G + XY Q_{MD}$.

Surface Code. The gates in the circuit are embedded into a surface code of distance $D_{G,\text{Haraka}} = 25$, with $p_{\text{out}} = 1/(G_{\text{Haraka}}^{cnot} + G_{\text{Haraka}}^{c})$ as targeted error rate. This results in each of the $Q_{G,\text{Haraka}}^{\text{log}} = 1400$ logical qubits to require 1352 physical qubits. In total, the algorithm requires $Q_{G,\text{Haraka}}^{phy} \approx 1.89 \cdot 10^{6}$ physical qubits.

Results. On average, about 9 T-gates are applied in each layer of T-depth. The number of physical qubits is dominated by the surface code, therefore we suggest

(a) Distance of the error correcting code d_i and number of logical and physical qubits for each layer i.

Layer	i	d_i	$Q_i^{\log}$	Q_i^{phy}
Top	1	19	16	12800
Bottom	2	9	240	48000

(b) Pipelining the production of 3 magic states allows to reuse the qubits from the bottom layer in the top layer.

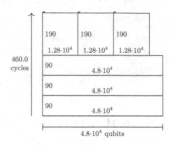

Fig. 4. Magic state distillation scheme for attacking SPHINCS$^+$-128.

to compute all magic states in parallel using 3 magic state distilleries and $Q_{MD}^{\text{phy}} = 3 \cdot 48000 = 1.6 \cdot 10^4$ physical qubits in $\text{SCC}_{\text{Haraka}}^m = 460$ cycles. The average number of gates per layer of T-depth for each CNOT and QubitClifford gates, $G_{\text{Haraka}}^{cnot}/Q_{\text{Haraka}}^w \cdot T_{\text{Haraka}}^d \approx 0.0143$ and $G_{\text{Haraka}}^c/Q_{\text{Haraka}}^w \cdot T_{\text{Haraka}}^d \approx 0.002$, is significantly smaller than the number of surface code cycles required to implement a single layer required for magic state distillation.

Therefore, the total number of surface code cycles for the entire algorithm is dominated by the magic state distilleries, which is $\text{COST}_{\text{SCC}} = \text{SCC}_{\text{Haraka}}^m \cdot T_{\text{Haraka}}^d = 460 \cdot 4.01 \cdot 10^{24} \approx 1.5 \cdot 2^{90}$. The total number of logical qubits required is 2120. With 200 ns per surface code cycle, this would take $1.17 \cdot 10^{13}$ years. The total cost of running the attack is then $\text{COST}_{\text{lqcHaraka}} = \text{COST}_{\text{SCC}} \cdot (1400 + 3 \cdot 240) = 1.5 \cdot 2^{90} \cdot (2120) \approx 3.91 \cdot 10^{30} \approx 1.55 \cdot 2^{101}$.

5.2   SHAKE-256

Setup. When using the SHAKE-256 hash function, our quantum circuit for the entire Grover algorithm for the attack contains $G_{\text{SHAKE-256}}^T = 1.72 \cdot 10^{25}$ T-gates and $G_{\text{SHAKE-256}}^{cnot} = 7.35 \cdot 10^{25}$ CNOT-gates. It also contains $G_{\text{SHAKE-256}}^c = 4.92 \cdot 10^{24}$ QubitClifford gates, most of which are Hadamard-gates. We will ignore any QubitClifford gates, that are not Hadamard-gates. The quantum circuit has a logical width of $Q_{\text{SHAKE-256}}^w = 3456$ qubits and a T-Depth of $T_{\text{SHAKE-256}}^d = 6.92 \cdot 10^{22}$.

Magic State Distillation. The number of layers and thus the values for magic state distillation are reminiscent to those of Sect. 5.1, in particular, of Fig. 4a.

Surface Code. The distance of the surface code remains as $D_{G,\text{SHAKE-256}} = 25$, with the same targeted error rate. This results in each of the $Q_{G,\text{SHAKE-256}}^{\log}$ 3456 logical qubits to require 1953 physical qubits. In total the algorithm requires $Q_{G,\text{SHAKE-256}}^{\text{phy}} \approx 6.75 \cdot 10^6$ physical qubits.

Table 7. Fault-tolerant cost for our attack from Sect. 4.1 using the SHAKE-256 and Haraka hash functions. The collision attack of [10] refers to attacking the internal state of Haraka.

SPHINCS$^+$-			SHAKE-256	Haraka
Collision attack [10]	#Grover Iterations		–	$1.32 \cdot 2^{102}$
	Time-Space Product		–	$1.51 \cdot 2^{153}$
	#Classical hash function invocations		–	$2^{129.5}$
Our attack on 128	#Distilleries	ϕ	83×3	3×3
	#Log. Qubits	Q^{log}	23876	2120
	#Total Phys. Qubits	Q^{phy}	$8.65 \cdot 10^6$	$2.03 \cdot 10^6$
	#Total ECC cycles	COST$_{SCC}$	$1.6 \cdot 2^{84}$	$1.5 \cdot 2^{90}$
	logical-qubit-cycles	COST$_{lqc}$	$2.65 \cdot 2^{99}$	$1.55 \cdot 2^{101}$
Our attack on 256	#Distilleries	ϕ	42×4	9×1
	#Log. Qubits	Q^{log}	$1.7 \cdot 10^5$	$0.38 \cdot 10^5$
	#Total Phys. Qubits	Q^{phy}	$5.8 \cdot 10^7$	$1.5 \cdot 10^7$
	#Total ECC cycles	COST$_{SCC}$	$1.02 \cdot 2^{152}$	$3.95 \cdot 2^{154}$
	logical-qubit-cycles	COST$_{lqc}$	$1.31 \cdot 2^{169}$	$1.44 \cdot 2^{171}$

Results. On average, about 249 T-gates are applied in each layer of T-depth. Therefore, we suggest to use 83 distilleries each generating 3 states in parallel, using a total of $Q^{phy}_{MD} = 83 \cdot 48000 = 3.98 \cdot 10^6$ physical qubits in SCC$^m_{SHAKE-256} = 460$ cycles. The average number of CNOT gates per layer of T-depth is 0.31, and 0.021 Hadamard gates.

Again, magic state distillation dominates resulting in a total number of COST$_{SCC}$ = SCC$^m_{SHAKE-256} \cdot$ T$^d_{SHAKE-256} = 460 \cdot 6.92 \cdot 10^{22} \approx 1.6 \cdot 2^{84}$ surface code cycles.

The total number of logical qubits required is 23876. With 200 ns per surface code cycle, this would take $2.02 \cdot 10^{11}$ years. The total cost of running the attack is then COST$_{lqcSHAKE-256}$ = COST$_{SCC} \cdot (3456 + 83 \cdot 240) = 1.6 \cdot 2^{84} \cdot (23876) \approx 7.44 \cdot 10^{29} \approx 2.65 \cdot 2^{99}$.

6   Conclusion

We presented quantum implementations for the Haraka (and respectively SHAKE-256) hash function in the context of the SPHINCS$^+$ signature scheme. Subsequently, we proposed and reviewed multiple points of attack in the SPHINCS$^+$-128-Haraka signature scheme based on applying Grover's algorithm to find pre-images. A tight estimate of the resources required to carry out the most promising attack on a fault tolerant quantum computer is given. Our attack, that forges a signature in $1.55 \cdot 2^{101}$ steps, improves over the previously best known attack on SPHINCS$^+$-128-Haraka.

Following the suggestion by NIST to review the security in terms of a maximal depth for quantum circuits, it is clear that for a depth of 2^{96} the attack can be implemented without any further constraints and would be more efficient than the classical counter part. For a depth of 2^{40} and 2^{64} the overhead induced by error correction needs to be reevaluated and optimized to the respective depth. A detailed analysis is out of scope for this paper and left as future work.

Acknowledgements. This work was supported by funding of the Helmholtz Association (HGF) through the Competence Center for Applied Security Technology (KASTEL) under project number 46.23.01 and 46.23.02. We thank the reviewers for the useful comments and remarks.

References

1. Amy, M., Di Matteo, O., Gheorghiu, V., Mosca, M., Parent, A., Schanck, J.: Estimating the cost of generic quantum pre-image attacks on SHA-2 and SHA-3. In: Avanzi, R., Heys, H. (eds.) SAC 2016. LNCS, vol. 10532, pp. 317–337. Springer, Cham (2017). https://doi.org/10.1007/978-3-319-69453-5_18
2. Bertoni, G., Daemen, J., Peeters, M., Van Assche, G.: Keccaktools. https://github.com/KeccakTeam/KeccakTools
3. Bertoni, G., Daemen, J., Peeters, M., Van Assche, G.: Cryptographic sponge functions (2011). https://keccak.team/sponge_duplex.html
4. Bogdanov, A., Khovratovich, D., Rechberger, C.: Biclique cryptanalysis of the full AES. In: Lee, D.H., Wang, X. (eds.) ASIACRYPT 2011. LNCS, vol. 7073, pp. 344–371. Springer, Heidelberg (2011). https://doi.org/10.1007/978-3-642-25385-0_19
5. Boyar, J., Peralta, R.: A small depth-16 circuit for the AES S-Box. In: Gritzalis, D., Furnell, S., Theoharidou, M. (eds.) SEC 2012. IAICT, vol. 376, pp. 287–298. Springer, Heidelberg (2012). https://doi.org/10.1007/978-3-642-30436-1_24
6. Boyer, M., Brassard, G., Høyer, P., Tapp, A.: Tight bounds on quantum searching. Fortschr. Phys. **46**(4–5), 493–505 (1998). https://doi.org/10.1002/(SICI)1521-3978(199806)46:4/5h493::AID-PROP493i3.0.CO;2-P
7. Brassard, G., HØyer, P., Tapp, A.: Quantum cryptanalysis of hash and claw-free functions. In: Lucchesi, C.L., Moura, A.V. (eds.) LATIN 1998. LNCS, vol. 1380, pp. 163–169. Springer, Heidelberg (1998). https://doi.org/10.1007/BFb0054319
8. Bravyi, S., Kitaev, A.: Universal quantum computation with ideal Clifford gates and noisy ancillas. Phys. Rev. A **71**, 022316 (2005). https://doi.org/10.1103/PhysRevA.71.022316
9. Castelnovi, L., Martinelli, A., Prest, T.: Grafting trees: a fault attack against the SPHINCS framework. In: Lange, T., Steinwandt, R. (eds.) PQCrypto 2018. LNCS, vol. 10786, pp. 165–184. Springer, Cham (2018). https://doi.org/10.1007/978-3-319-79063-3_8
10. Chailloux, A., Naya-Plasencia, M., Schrottenloher, A.: An efficient quantum collision search algorithm and implications on symmetric cryptography. In: Takagi, T., Peyrin, T. (eds.) ASIACRYPT 2017. LNCS, vol. 10625, pp. 211–240. Springer, Cham (2017). https://doi.org/10.1007/978-3-319-70697-9_8

11. Dang, Q.H.: Secure hash standard (SHS). National Institute for Standards and Technology (2008). https://doi.org/10.6028/NIST.FIPS.180-4
12. Fowler, A.G., Devitt, S.J., Jones, C.: Surface code implementation of block code state distillation. Sci. Rep. **3**(1) (2013). Article number: 1939. https://doi.org/10.1038/srep01939
13. Fowler, A.G., Mariantoni, M., Martinis, J.M., Cleland, A.N.: Surface codes: towards practical large-scale quantum computation. Phys. Rev. A **86**, 032324 (2012). https://doi.org/10.1103/PhysRevA.86.032324
14. Gidney, C., Ekerå, M.: How to factor 2048 bit RSA integers in 8 hours using 20 million noisy qubits. Quantum **5**, 433 (2021). https://doi.org/10.22331/q-2021-04-15-433
15. Grover, L.K.: A fast quantum mechanical algorithm for database search. In: Proceedings of the Twenty-Eighth Annual ACM Symposium on Theory of Computing, STOC 1996, pp. 212–219. Association for Computing Machinery, New York (1996). https://doi.org/10.1145/237814.237866
16. Hulsing, A., et al.: SPHINCS+-Submission to the 3rd round of the NIST post-quantum project (2020)
17. Jaques, S., Naehrig, M., Roetteler, M., Virdia, F.: Implementing Grover oracles for quantum key search on AES and LowMC. In: Canteaut, A., Ishai, Y. (eds.) EUROCRYPT 2020. LNCS, vol. 12106, pp. 280–310. Springer, Cham (2020). https://doi.org/10.1007/978-3-030-45724-2_10
18. Jaques, S.: Quantum cost models for cryptanalysis of isogenies. Master's thesis, University of Waterloo (2019). http://hdl.handle.net/10012/14612
19. Jones, N.C., et al.: Layered architecture for quantum computing. Phys. Rev. X **2**, 031007 (2012). https://doi.org/10.1103/PhysRevX.2.031007
20. Külbl, S., Lauridsen, M.M., Mendel, F., Rechberger, C.: Haraka v2 - efficient short-input hashing for post-quantum applications. IACR Trans. Symmetric Cryptol. **2016**(2), 1–29 (2017). https://doi.org/10.13154/tosc.v2016.i2.1-29
21. National Institute for Standards and Technology: Advanced Encryption Standard (AES) (2001). https://doi.org/10.6028/NIST.FIPS.197
22. National Institute for Standards and Technology: SHA-3 standard: permutation-based hash and extendable-output functions (2015). https://doi.org/10.6028/NIST.FIPS.202
23. National Institute for Standards and Technology: Post-quantum cryptography call for proposals (2017). https://csrc.nist.gov/CSRC/media/Projects/Post-Quantum-Cryptography/documents/call-for-proposals-final-dec-2016.pdf
24. National Institute for Standards and Technology: Post-quantum cryptography round 3 (2020). https://csrc.nist.gov/projects/post-quantum-cryptography/round-3-submissions
25. Nielsen, M.A., Chuang, I.L.: Quantum Computation and Quantum Information. Cambridge University Press, Cambridge (2010)
26. Roetteler, M., Naehrig, M., Svore, K.M., Lauter, K.: Quantum resource estimates for computing elliptic curve discrete logarithms. In: Takagi, T., Peyrin, T. (eds.) ASIACRYPT 2017. LNCS, vol. 10625, pp. 241–270. Springer, Cham (2017). https://doi.org/10.1007/978-3-319-70697-9_9

Post-quantum Cryptography

Post-quantum Key-Blinding for Authentication in Anonymity Networks

Edward Eaton[✉], Douglas Stebila, and Roy Stracovsky

University of Waterloo, Waterloo, Canada
{eeaton,dstebila,rstracovsky}@uwaterloo.ca

Abstract. Anonymity networks, such as the Tor network, are highly decentralized and make heavy use of ephemeral identities. Both of these characteristics run in direct opposition to a traditional public key infrastructure, so entity authentication in an anonymity network can be a challenge. One system that Tor relies on is key-blinded signatures, which allow public keys to be transformed so that authentication is still possible, but the identity public key is masked. This is used in Tor during onion service descriptor lookup, in which a .onion address is resolved to a rendezvous point through which a client and an onion service can communicate. The mechanism currently used is based on elliptic curve signatures, so a post-quantum replacement will be needed.

We consider three fully post-quantum key-blinding schemes, and prove the unlinkability and unforgeability of all schemes in the random-oracle model. We provide a generic framework for proving unlinkability of key-blinded schemes by reducing to two properties, signing with oracle reprogramming and independent blinding. Of the three schemes, one is based on a Round 3 candidate in NIST's post-quantum signature standardization process, Dilithium. The other two are based on much newer schemes, CSI-FiSh and LegRoast, which have more favourable characteristics for blinding. CSI-FiSh is based on isogenies and boasts a very small public key plus signature sizes, and its group action structure allows for key-blinding in a straightforward way. LegRoast uses the Picnic framework, but with the Legendre symbol PRF as a symmetric primitive, the homomorphic properties of which can be exploited to blind public keys in a novel way. Our schemes require at most small changes to parameters, and are generally almost as fast as their unblinded counterparts.

1 Introduction

Among the many difficulties in building a robust anonymity network, how entities are authenticated can be a unique challenge that cannot be solved with direct cryptographic techniques. Most networks will accomplish authenticity goals through the use of a signature scheme, but in a network with anonymity goals, the public keys used for signing can run contrary to those goals. One technique to overcome this contradiction is used in the Tor network: *key-blinding*.

A signature scheme with key-blinding works similarly to a regular signature scheme, but with the added property that given a public key pk and a nonce

© Springer Nature Switzerland AG 2021
P. Longa and C. Ràfols (Eds.): LATINCRYPT 2021, LNCS 12912, pp. 67–87, 2021.
https://doi.org/10.1007/978-3-030-88238-9_4

τ, a new public key pk_τ can be derived, which in turn can be used for signing and verification. This is useful in contexts where two parties wish to exchange signed material, but must do so in the presence of a potential eavesdropper who may attempt to de-anonymize them. Tor describes such a scheme, and its use, in version 3 of the rendezvous specification, describing how clients connect to onion services in the network [28]. In Subsect. 2.1 we will describe precisely how key-blinding is used in Tor, and the security it is meant to provide.

It is useful to describe the key-blinding scheme as it exists in Tor, to gain some intuition for how such a scheme works and what security it provides. Key-blinding in Tor today uses the Ed25519 signature scheme [7]. Keys in this signature scheme are made with respect to a generator B of a cyclic group of size ℓ (written with additive notation). Secret keys are an integer $a \in \{1, \ldots, \ell - 1\}$ and the corresponding public key is $A = aB$. We refer to [7] for a complete description of the signing and verification processes, but for our description, it suffices to know that any such (a, A) pair are a valid key pair for Ed25519.

To blind a public key with a nonce τ, one computes a value $t \leftarrow H(\tau \| A)$, with $t \in \{1, \ldots, \ell - 1\}$. Then the blinded public key is tA, with corresponding secret key $t \cdot a \pmod{\ell}$. This forms a new key pair that is entirely compatible with Ed25519, so that it can be used for signing and verification.

It is fairly easy to see why this scheme has the desired security properties. Given two blinded keys and the associated nonces, there is no way to tell if they come from the same identity public key or not. Without knowledge of the identity public key, the distribution of the blinded public key is entirely uniform over the public key space, so that these keys are entirely unlinkable to each other. Furthermore, the keys retain their unforgeability, as the blinded secret key ta requires both t and a to be known. Formal proofs of the security properties can be found in a tech report posted to the Tor developer mailing list [20].

This system works quite well for Tor today, but with the development of quantum computers, cryptography based on the discrete logarithm problem will eventually be rendered insecure. To ensure the long-term security of Tor, a replacement post-quantum signature scheme with key-blinding will be needed.

1.1 Our Contributions and Paper Structure

In our work we address the challenge of extending post-quantum signature schemes to have a key-blinding functionality. We focus on three promising post-quantum signature schemes. *Dilithium* is a lattice-based signature scheme that is currently under consideration in NIST's Post-Quantum Cryptography standardization effort [17]. Instead of directly working with Dilithium, we will work with the Dilithium-QROM variant [22]. Dilithium-QROM has simpler provable guarantees by neatly fitting into the 'Lossy ID scheme' framework [1], so to ensure that our scheme has similar guarantees we work within the same framework. *CSI-FiSh* is a relatively new post-quantum signature scheme based on the CSIDH group action [12]. *LegRoast* is based on the Picnic framework, but replaces the more traditional symmetric function used with the Legendre PRF, the homomorphic properties of which allow for small signatures [10,15]. In the

Scheme	$|pk|$	$|\sigma|$	KeyGen	Blind	Sign	Verify
Dilithium-QROM	7.7 kB	5.7 kB	3810 ms	-	9360 ms	2890 ms
blDlithium-QROM	10 kB	5.7 kB	2180 ms	1650 ms	28300 ms	717 ms
Increase from blinding	1.3×	1×	0.6×	-	3×	0.25×
LegRoast	0.50 kB	7.94 kB	0.9 ms	-	12.4 ms	11.7 ms
blLegRoast	0.50 kB	11.22 kB	0.9 ms	0.9 ms	18.6 ms	17.8 ms
Increase from blinding	1.0×	1.4×	1.0×	-	1.5×	1.5×
CSI-FiSh-Merkleized	32 B	1.8–2.1 kB	10900 ms	-	559 ms	559 ms
CSI-FiSh-unMerkleized	16 kB	0.45 kB	10800 ms	-	554 ms	553 ms
blCSI-FiSh	16 kB	0.45 kB	10600 ms	10600 ms	546 ms	540 ms
Increase from blinding	1.0×	1.0×	1.0×	-	1.0×	1.0×

Fig. 1. Performance results from the implemented key-blinding schemes. Note that we emphasize the increase over the raw numbers for the timing information. Implementations are not optimized and may not reflect how long a 'proper' implementation will take. Nonetheless, the increase reflects how much additional work is required to use the scheme for key-blinding. For all schemes, blinded public keys have the same size as their unblinded version and so we do not distinguish between the two.

full version of this paper, available on the IACR Cryptology ePrint archive, we also consider Picnic itself. *Picnic* is another submission to NIST's efforts, which constructs a signature scheme out of the 'MPC-in-the-head' paradigm [14,21]. We show how all of these signature schemes can be extended to support key-blinding. For CSI-FiSh, Dilithium, and LegRoast this process is done similarly to the existing Ed25519 scheme, by homomorphically incorporating a blinding factor into the public key. In all the schemes, blinding is generally around as efficient as key generation, while signing is either as efficient, or at worst half as fast. We provide a generic framework for proving the unlinkability property, showing that it reduces to two easily proven properties. We prove all these schemes both unlinkable and unforgeable in the random oracle model. Note that each of the signature schemes we have discussed are built out of the Fiat-Shamir paradigm. We discuss why this is the case, and what some of the challenges are for building a key-blinded scheme out of a trapdoor signature scheme. Finally, we provide prototype implementations out of the CSI-FiSh, LegRoast, and Dilithium-QROM schemes and discuss aspects of their performance as it applies to Tor. Our results from the three implemented schemes are shown in Fig. 1.

Section 2 provides background information on Tor and definitions for key-blinding, which is needed to follow discussion in the remainder of the paper. We discuss the property of unlinkability, and how it can be achieved in all of our schemes in Sect. 3. In Sect. 4 we extend Dilithium-QROM with key-blinding and discuss the proof of security, then repeat this process with CSI-FiSh in Sect. 5, and LegRoast in Sect. 6. Finally we provide details of our implementations and their performance in Sect. 7 before concluding in Sect. 8.

In the full version, we include an outline of a key-blinded Picnic scheme, as well as the detailed descriptions of the other schemes and the associated proofs of unlinkability and unforgeability.

1.2 Related Work

As mentioned, the schemes that we choose to base blinded signature schemes off of are Dilithium [17,22], CSI-FiSh [12], LegRoast/PorcRoast [10], and, in the full version, Picnic [14]. While to our knowledge, this is the first attempt to construct post-quantum key-blinded signatures, there are a few other papers who have attempted to build similar primitives, for different reasons. In a 2018 preprint [3], the authors considered post-quantum PKIs in vehicle-to-anything (V2X) communications. One of the techniques they developed to provide anonymity to vehicles in such a context involved transformations on public key materials similar to that of key-blinding. Their construction was based on the lattice scheme qTESLA, which was a candidate for standardisation in the first two rounds of NIST's process. The process of key-blinding also bears a similarity to hierarchical deterministic wallets used for Bitcoin [18,23]. These wallets allow a user to create child public and secret keys for the delegation of abilities for spending. Such a protocol has much stronger requirements than simple key-blinding, which does not need to be hierarchical and does not need for the child secret keys to contain no information about parent secret keys. Some work on post-quantum deterministic wallets has been published [2], with their scheme also based on qTESLA.

It is important to distinguish between the key-blinding schemes we discuss here and the notion of 'blind signatures', for which post-quantum schemes already exist [19,25]. Blind signatures are an interactive protocol that allow a user to obtain a signature on a message without the signer knowing the message. This is very different from key-blinded schemes, which have the same functionality as a traditional signature scheme, but with the extra ability to randomize public keys.

2   Background

2.1   Onion Services

The Tor network serves millions of clients a day, providing anonymity to users from the websites they connect to, and concealing what they are connecting to from their Internet service provider and any other intermediary in their path [27]. An important part of the Tor networks is *onion services* (previously known as hidden services). Onion services allow users to not only *access* content with Tor's strong privacy guarantees, but also *serve* content.

At a high level, onion services work by uploading a three hop path (called a *circuit* in Tor terminology) to a Tor node called a *introduction point*. This path begins at the introduction point and ends at the onion service. Because of

Tor's layered encryption, the introduction point does not know where the onion service lives, only where the next node in the path lives. For a client to connect to the onion service, they use the .onion address to find the introduction point, who will then direct their communication towards the onion service.

In the most recent version of the rendezvous specification (the specification that describes the process of connecting to an onion service), the .onion address is the long-lived EdDSA public key of the onion service. Time in the Tor network is divided into periods, with the period length a consensus parameter and the period number the number of periods that have occurred since the Unix epoch. So given a public key, a nonce, and consensus parameters of the Tor network, the *blinding factor t* is computed by hashing together the public key, the nonce, and the current period number, as well as some parameters of both the Tor network and the signature scheme. As mentioned in the introduction, this value t is treated as an integer in the range 1 to $\ell - 1$, with ℓ the order of the cyclic group, so that public keys are transformed by simply multiplying by t.

The blinded key can then be used to index the descriptors while they are held by the HSDir. Clients can derive the blinded key from the .onion address and query for a descriptor by providing the blinded key. So, the blinded key serves as a private *index* from which the descriptor may be queried. This also implicitly means that the client is implicitly checking the connection between the identity public key from the .onion address and the blinded public key. For security it is important that only the actual owner of the .onion address can upload a descriptor to a given index. This is where the signing functionality of key-blinding is used. Onion services also upload a signature on the descriptor, which can be verified with the blinded key. When HSDirs verify this signature, they ensure that the descriptor is being uploaded by the actual owner of the identity public key—all without knowing what the .onion address is.

A malicious actor with a quantum computer could forge a signature with respect to a chosen blinded public key, and use this to upload false information about an introduction point. This would mean that queries to the onion service could be redirected to the adversary.

2.2 Key-Blinding Signature Scheme Definitions

Definition 1. *A key-blinding signature scheme* Δ *consists of four algorithms* (KeyGen, BlindPk, Sign, Verify) *where*

- KeyGen() *generates an identity key pair* (pk, sk).
- BlindPk(pk, τ) *deterministically generates a blinded public key* pk_τ.
- Sign(m, sk, τ) *may deterministically or probabilistically generate a signature* σ *for the message* m *using the identity secret key* sk *and epoch* τ.
- Verify(m, σ, pk_τ) *accepts if the signature is valid under the message* m *and epoch* τ *used to generate* pk_τ, *otherwise it rejects*.

We require the usual correctness properties for signature schemes, but extended for key-blinding. That is, if (pk, sk) is a keypair generated from KeyGen,

pk_τ is then derived from BlindPk with a given nonce τ, and $\sigma \leftarrow \text{Sign}(m, sk, \tau)$, then with overwhelming probability $\text{Verify}(m, \sigma, pk_\tau)$ will accept. Anyone without knowledge of the identity public key can verify using the pk_τ given in the descriptor, while someone with knowledge of the identity key can take the additional step of checking $pk_\tau = \text{BlindPk}(pk, \tau)$. Note that we do not require that blinded keys can be blinded again.

Signatures with key-blinding must satisfy two security requirements. First, they must be *unlinkable*, which means that an adversary without knowledge of the identity public key who observes many public key blindings as well as signatures under those blindings cannot distinguish a fresh blinding of the public key from an entirely unrelated key. Second, the scheme must satisfy *unforgeability*. This property is largely the same for signature schemes with key-blinding as it is for typical signature schemes. However, rather than just devising an (m, σ) such that $\text{Verify}(m, \sigma, pk)$ accepts, the adversary must be able to provide an (m, σ, τ) such that $\text{Verify}(m, \sigma, pk_\tau)$ accepts where $pk_\tau \leftarrow \text{BlindPk}(pk, \tau)$.

Earlier versions of both of these formulations appear in [20]. The security definitions that we present here are more general. The definitions in [20] were tied to the exact usage of key-blinding in Tor, and do not consider security in situations where the blinding process is decoupled from the signing process, so that multiple signatures can be issued under the same blinded public key.

Definition 2 (Unlinkability). *Let* $\Delta = (\text{KeyGen}, \text{BlindPk}, \text{Sign}, \text{Verify})$ *be a key-blinding signature scheme. Define* $\text{Exp}_\Delta^{\text{UL}-\text{CMEA}}(\mathcal{A})$ *as follows:*

- *Let* $(pk, sk) \leftarrow \text{KeyGen}()$ *be freshly generated identity keys.*
- *$\mathcal{A}$ may query τ to a public key-blinding oracle to get $pk_\tau \leftarrow \text{BlindPk}(pk, \tau)$.*
- *$\mathcal{A}$ may query (m, τ) to a signing oracle to receive $\sigma_{m,\tau} \leftarrow \text{Sign}(m, sk, \tau)$ for any τ previously queried to the public key-blinding oracle.*
- *$\mathcal{A}$ makes a challenge query τ^* not previously queried to the public key-blinding oracle. A bit b is uniformly sampled, $pk_0 \leftarrow pk$, and a fresh pair of identity public keys $(pk_1, sk_1) \leftarrow \text{KeyGen}()$ is generated. $\mathcal{A}$ receives $pk_b^* \leftarrow \text{BlindPk}(pk_b, \tau^*)$.*
- *$\mathcal{A}$ may additionally query the public key-blinding oracle or the signing oracle, except that if the queried $\tau = \tau^*$, the oracles use pk_b^*.*
- *$\mathcal{A}$ provides a bit b^* after expending t-bounded computational resources, q_B-bounded public key-blinding oracle queries, and q_S-bounded signing queries; and the game outputs 1 if $b^* = b$, otherwise it outputs 0.*

The UL $-$ CMEA *(unlinkability under chosen message and epoch attack) advantage is defined as* $\text{Adv}_\Delta^{\text{UL}-\text{CMEA}}(\mathcal{A}) = \left| \Pr[\text{Exp}_\Delta^{\text{UL}-\text{CMEA}}(\mathcal{A}) = 1] - \frac{1}{2} \right|$.

Definition 3 (Unforgeability). *Let* $\Delta = (\text{KeyGen}, \text{BlindPk}, \text{Sign}, \text{Verify})$ *be a key-blinding signature scheme. Define* $\text{Exp}_\Delta^{\text{EUF}-\text{CMEA}}(\mathcal{A})$ *as follows:*

- *Let* $(pk, sk) \leftarrow \text{KeyGen}()$ *be freshly generated identity keys.*
- *$\mathcal{A}$ may query (m, τ) to a signing oracle which generates $pk_\tau \leftarrow \text{BlindPk}(pk, \tau)$ and $\sigma_{m,\tau} \leftarrow \text{Sign}(m, sk, \tau)$, and sends $(pk_\tau, \sigma_{m,\tau})$ to $\mathcal{A}$.*

- $\mathcal{A}$ submits (m^*, σ^*, τ^*) after expending t-bounded computational resources and q_S-bounded signing queries, and the game outputs 1 if (m^*, τ^*) was not previously queried and $\mathsf{Verify}(m^*, \sigma^*, \mathsf{BlindPk}(pk, \tau^*)) = 1$, otherwise it outputs 0.

The $\mathsf{EUF} - \mathsf{CMEA}$ (existential unforgeability under chosen message and epoch attack) advantage is defined as $\mathbf{Adv}_{\mathcal{A}}^{\mathsf{EUF-CMEA}}(\mathcal{A}) = \Pr[\mathbf{Exp}_{\mathcal{A}}^{\mathsf{EUF-CMEA}}(\mathcal{A}) = 1]$.

3   Unlinkability of Signature Schemes with Key-Blinding

We want to establish that an adversary who has access to a blinding oracle and a signing oracle still cannot distinguish a new blinding of the identity public key from the blinding of a fresh public key. We observed a common technique that could be used for showing unlinkability among the signature schemes we consider. To establish unlinkability, we devise a property we call *independent blinding*, which asks that the distribution of the output of the blinding function is independent from its input. This means that seeing any number of blindings of a public key leaks no information on the identity public key.

While our techniques provide a generic framework to establish unlinkability, they do not extend to showing unforgeability or provide a way to generically *construct* schemes with key-blinding out of Fiat–Shamir style signature schemes. This is because the mechanism by which blinding is accomplished changes depending on the scheme. As a result, there is no common framework for constructing a key-blinding scheme, and the proof of unforgeability similarly must take the blinding mechanism into account.

To guarantee that the signing oracle leaks no information about the identity public key, we require that the distribution of signatures is dependent only on the public key. This is best characterized by a property we call *signing with oracle reprogramming*, which states that if we have the ability to reprogram the random oracle used in the signature scheme, then we can create signatures indistinguishable from real ones for any message.

Many signature schemes show their security by first establishing just such a property. As an example, for signature schemes built from an identification protocol and the Fiat–Shamir heuristic, the zero-knowledge property is typically proven by establishing the ability to simulate transcripts given only the public key. When given control of the random oracle, we can sample transcripts and reprogram the random oracle to generate a signature.

To formalize this notion, we require a concept we call a *reprogrammed point extractor*. This is a simple function, efficiently computable and publicly known to all, which, given a signature σ, public key, and message, can extract the point on which the random oracle is reprogrammed to make the signature verify.

It is best to illustrate this with an example. Consider a generic form of the Probabilistic Signature Scheme [6] defined with respect to a trapdoor permutation T. To sign a message, sample a random salt r and compute $x = T^{-1}(H(pk\|m\|r))$. The signature is $\sigma = (x, r)$. To verify a signature, simply check that $T(x) = H(pk\|m\|r)$. It is straightforward to show that signatures can be generated if the random oracle can be reprogrammed. On input of a message m, sample a random (x, r) and reprogram H so that $H(pk\|m\|r) = T(x)$. If T is a permutation, it is easy to see that (x, r) will have the same distribution as in a real signature, and the reprogramming cannot be detected as long as r is sufficiently long (so that the adversary is unlikely to have queried $pk\|m\|r$ beforehand). Let Ext denote our reprogrammed point extractor. For the example above, we have $\mathsf{Ext}((x, r), pk, m) = pk\|m\|r$.

Definition 4 (Signing with oracle reprogramming). *Let Σ be a signature scheme that relies on a random oracle H. We say that the signature scheme admits signing with oracle reprogramming if there exists a reprogrammed point extractor* Ext *and a forgery function* Forge *that takes in pk, m and returns (y, σ) such that $\Sigma.\mathsf{Verify}^{H:\mathsf{Ext}(\sigma, pk, m) \mapsto y}(pk, m, \sigma) \to$ 'accept', where $H : x \mapsto y$ denotes the random oracle reprogrammed such that $H(x) = y$.*

In order to use oracle reprogramming to sign a message, we need to consider the probability that an adversary is capable of noticing that the real signing algorithm wasn't used. This amounts to considering the joint distribution of the signature as well as the input and output of the hash function on the reprogrammed point.

Definition 5. *Let $\Sigma = (\mathsf{Sign}, \mathsf{Verify})$ be a signature scheme defined with respect to a random oracle H and a public key space $\mathcal{PK}$ that admits signing with oracle reprogramming via a point extractor* Ext *and a forgery function* Forge.

For a public key and message pk, m, we consider the adversary's ability to distinguish the distribution of $(y_{forged}, \sigma_{forged}) \leftarrow \mathsf{Forge}(pk, m)$ from the distribution of $(y_{real}, \sigma_{real})$ where $\sigma_{real} \leftarrow \mathsf{Sign}(pk, m)$ and $y_{real} = H(\mathsf{Ext}(\sigma_{real}, pk, m))$ (i.e., the output of the hash on the input that would be reprogrammed).

We denote $L1$ distance between these distributions as δ, that is

$$\delta = \sum_{\sigma, y} \left| \Pr[\sigma_{real} = \sigma, y_{real} = y] - \Pr[\sigma_{forged} = \sigma, y_{forged} = y] \right|.$$

As well, we need to consider the ability of an adversary to detect that reprogramming has occurred. This can be evaluated by considering the min-entropy of the point that is reprogrammed, to ensure that the probability that an adversary queries this point prior to reprogramming is low. Let h_{min} denote the min-entropy of $\mathsf{Ext}(\sigma, pk, m)$, where $(y, \sigma) \leftarrow \mathsf{Forge}(pk, m)$.

Note that in the above definition we are implicitly assuming that the statistical distance and the entropy are not dependent on m, pk, or H. For all of the schemes that we construct this is the case. Even if these values were dependent on pk, m, or H, the scheme could still be secure as long as they were sufficiently small on average. However to simplify the proof and notation, our definition only considers schemes where they do not depend on pk, m, or H.

We now consider the unlinkability experiment $\mathbf{Exp}_{\Delta}^{\mathsf{UL-CMEA}}$. We will show a reduction from an adversary who makes queries to the signing oracle to an adversary who makes none.

Lemma 1. *Let Δ be a key-blinding signature scheme which admits signing with oracle reprogramming with L1 distance δ and min-entropy of reprogrammed points h_{min}. Let $\mathcal{A}$ be an adversary making q_B queries to the blinding oracle, q_S queries to the signing oracle, and q_H queries to the random oracle. Using $\mathcal{A}$, we construct an adversary $\mathcal{A}^{q_S=0}$ that makes no signing queries (i.e., a key-only adversary) for which* $\mathbf{Adv}_\Delta^{\mathsf{UL-CMEA}}(\mathcal{A}) \leq \mathbf{Adv}_\Delta^{\mathsf{UL-CMEA}}(\mathcal{A}^{q_S=0}) + q_H q_S 2^{-h_{min}} + q_S \delta.$

Proof. To construct the adversary $\mathcal{A}^{q_S=0}$ while relying on the adversary $\mathcal{A}$ as a subroutine, we must show how to handle queries to the blinding oracle and the signing oracle. For queries to the blinding oracle, $\mathcal{A}^{q_S=0}$ can simply pass along these queries to the blinding oracle provided to them.

To handle the signing queries, we rely on signing with oracle reprogramming. Whenever a signing query is made with respect to a blinded public key pk_{τ_i}, we reprogram the random oracle in order to provide a signature. Thus we need to consider the adversary's ability to distinguish that the secret key is not being used to sign messages. To realize this, the adversary either needs to observe that the oracle has been reprogrammed, or notice a difference in the observed distribution of some part of the signature.

To distinguish that reprogramming has occurred during signing, the adversary must have queried the random oracle on the reprogrammed point previously. In total, q_S points will be reprogrammed. So the adversary makes q_H guesses, and then q_S points are chosen to be reprogrammed from a distribution with min entropy h_{min}, and we want to consider the probability of a match between the q_H and q_S points. We can upper-bound this by $q_H q_S 2^{-h_{min}}$.

Next we consider the output distribution of the programmed points. There are q_S reprogrammed points, and the statistical ($L1$) distance between the forged values and the real values is δ, so the adversary's advantage in distinguishing based on the distribution of reprogrammed values is at most $q_S \delta$. $\qquad\square$

We now only need to consider the advantage of $\mathcal{A}^{q_S=0}$, an adversary who makes no queries to the signing oracle. So, we need only consider how the blinding oracle and random oracle provide information to the adversary.

To characterize the security of blinding, we want to insist that the distribution of the public key returned by BlindPk is independent of the identity public key input, so that no knowledge is gained. However care must be taken here, because the BlindPk algorithm is actually deterministic on the inputs pk and τ. So when we refer to the 'distribution' of BlindPk we need to be clear over what randomness.

In practice, the BlindPk function hashes the public key and the nonce τ to generate some randomness, and then uses that randomness to blind the public key. To separate out the process of hashing to generate randomness and using the randomness, we will define a new function randBlind($pk; r$), which takes in a public key and some randomness, and blinds the public key. Then BlindPk is defined by making randBlind deterministic through the random oracle H. Specifically, BlindPk$(pk, \tau) = $ randBlind$(pk; H(pk \| \tau))$.

Definition 6 (Independent Blinding). *Let Δ be a key-blinding signature scheme and let n be a positive integer. Let $pk_0, pk_1, \ldots, pk_n$ be public keys generated from* KeyGen. *Sample uniform randomness $r_1, r_2, \ldots, r_n$. The independent blinding advantage, denoted $\mathbf{Adv}_{\Delta,n}^{\mathsf{Ind-Blind}}(\mathcal{A})$, is the advantage that an adversary has in distinguishing the following two distributions:*

1) $\mathsf{randBlind}(pk_0; r_1), \mathsf{randBlind}(pk_0; r_2), \ldots, \mathsf{randBlind}(pk_0; r_n)$

2) $\mathsf{randBlind}(pk_1; r_1), \mathsf{randBlind}(pk_2; r_2), \ldots, \mathsf{randBlind}(pk_n; r_n)$

This ensures that the adversary $\mathcal{A}^{qs=0}$ may observe many blindings of the public key with respect to arbitrary nonces but what they see is close to a distribution independent of the identity public key.

Lemma 2. *Let Δ be a key-blinding signature scheme and let h_{pk} be the min-entropy of the public key returned from $\Delta.$KeyGen. Let $\mathcal{A}^{qs=0}$ be an* UL − CMEA *adversary that makes no queries to its signing oracle. Then there exists an algorithm $\mathcal{B}$ such that $\mathbf{Adv}_{\Delta}^{\mathsf{UL-CMEA}}(\mathcal{A}^{qs=0}) \leq \mathbf{Adv}_{\Delta,n}^{\mathsf{Ind-Blind}}(\mathcal{B}) + q_H 2^{-h_{pk}}$, where n is the number of blinding queries $\mathcal{A}^{qs=0}$ makes to its public key-blinding oracle and the runtime of $\mathcal{B}$ is approximately the same as the runtime of $\mathcal{A}$.*

Proof. We use a simple game-hopping proof to bound the adversary's success probability. Game G_0 proceeds according to $\mathbf{Exp}^{\mathsf{UL-CMEA}}$ with the adversary making no signing queries by assumption. In game G_1, when the adversary queries the blinding oracle with input τ, rather than responding with $\mathsf{BlindPk}(pk, \tau) = \mathsf{randBlind}(pk, H(pk\|\tau))$, we sample a uniformly random r and return $\mathsf{randBlind}(pk, r)$. Note that there is no difference between these games until an adversary queries $H(pk\|\tau)$ for some τ; we let bad be the event that the adversary makes such a query. Games G_0 and G_1 are identical-until-bad [5].

In game G_2 we modify the response to each blinding query from $\mathsf{randBlind}(pk, r)$ by sampling a fresh pk' each time from KeyGen and returning $\mathsf{randBlind}(pk', r)$. We can construct, from an adversary that distinguishes G_1 from G_2, a reduction $\mathcal{B}$ that distinguishes the two distributions in the independent blinding property: G_1 uses the first distribution in Definition 6, whereas G_2 uses the second. Thus G_2 can be distinguished from G_1 with advantage at most $\mathbf{Adv}_{\Delta,n}^{\mathsf{Ind-Blind}}(\mathcal{B})$.

We now consider the probability of event bad—i.e., the adversary querying $H(pk\|\tau)$—in G_2. Since none of the blindings actually use pk, the success probability is bounded by the adversary's ability to guess the public key. For this we use the min-entropy of the public key returned from key-generation. Over q_H queries, the probability that an adversary is able to guess the public key is bounded by $q_H 2^{-h_{pk}}$. By the fundamental lemma of game playing [5], this is the probability that an adversary is able to distinguish between game G_0 and G_1.

Finally, in game G_2 all blinded public keys are independent of the original key, so everything the adversary sees is independent of the challenge bit b, and thus the adversary's advantage in G_2 is 0, yielding the desired result (Fig. 2). □

blDilithium-QROM.KeyGen()	blDilithium-QROM.BlindPk($pk = \mathbf{t}_1, \tau$)
1: $K \leftarrow \{0, 1\}^{256}$	1: $(\mathbf{s}_1', \mathbf{s}_2') \leftarrow G(pk \| \tau)$
2: $(\mathbf{s}_1, \mathbf{s}_2) \xleftarrow{\$} S_\eta^\ell \times S_\eta^k$	2: $\mathbf{t}' \leftarrow \mathbf{A}\mathbf{s}_1' + \mathbf{s}_2'$
3: $\mathbf{t} \leftarrow \mathbf{A}\mathbf{s}_1 + \mathbf{s}_2$	3: $\mathbf{t}_1' \leftarrow \text{Power2Round}_q(\mathbf{t}', d - 1)$
4: $\mathbf{t}_1 \leftarrow \text{Power2Round}_q(\mathbf{t}, d - 1)$	4: $\mathbf{t}_{1,\tau} \leftarrow \mathbf{t}_1 + \mathbf{t}_1'$
5: $\mathbf{t}_0 \leftarrow \mathbf{t} - \lfloor \mathbf{t}_1/2 \rfloor \cdot 2^d$	5: $pk_\tau \leftarrow \mathbf{t}_{1,\tau}$
6: $pk \leftarrow \mathbf{t}_1$	6: return pk_τ
7: $sk \leftarrow (\mathbf{s}_1, \mathbf{s}_2, \mathbf{t}_0, K)$	
8: return (pk, sk)	

Fig. 2. Key generation and blinding algorithms for blDilithium-QROM.

One could go to the effort of computing or bounding the min-entropy h_{pk} of the public key returned from KeyGen for each scheme. It is convenient to observe that $2^{-h_{pk}} \leq \mathbf{Adv}_\Delta^{\text{EUF-CMEA}}(\mathcal{A})$ for any adversary $\mathcal{A}$: otherwise, for a scheme where certain public keys have abnormally high change of being generated, an adversary could break unforgeability by repeatedly running KeyGen until the desired public key (and a corresponding secret key) is generated. Thus,

Corollary 1. *Let Δ and $\mathcal{A}^{qs=0}$ be as in Lemma 2. Then there exist algorithms $\mathcal{B}_1, \mathcal{B}_2$ such that $\mathbf{Adv}_\Delta^{\text{UL-CMEA}}(\mathcal{A}^{qs=0}) \leq \mathbf{Adv}_{\Delta,n}^{\text{Ind-Blind}}(\mathcal{B}_1) + q_H \mathbf{Adv}_\Delta^{\text{EUF-CMEA}}(\mathcal{B}_2)$, where n is the number of blinding queries $\mathcal{A}^{qs=0}$ makes to its public key-blinding oracle and the runtimes of $\mathcal{B}_1$ and $\mathcal{B}_2$ are approximately the same as that of $\mathcal{A}$.*

4 A Lattice-Based Key-Blinding Scheme

Dilithium [17] is a finalist in the NIST post-quantum signature standardization process and comes from a long line of lattice-based signature schemes. We present a key-blinded version of Dilithium-QROM [22] which modifies Dilithium to permit lossy key generation, hence allowing a reduction from the scheme to Module Learning with Errors (MLWE) assumption. Later, in Sect. 4.3, we discuss the challenges in blinding Dilithium itself.

Our construction, blDilithium-QROM utilizes the fact addition is homomorphic. As a result, the $\mathbf{A}$ matrix is a public matrix used by all parties in the network. In addition, both signing and verification use the public key when sampling the challenge c. Finally, the identity public key consists of an extra bit as this permits key-blinding.

4.1 blDilithium-QROM Description

We make use of functions defined in [22]. In addition, our notation mirrors that in [22]. A complete description is in the full version.

Signing is performed by using G to sample blinding secrets adding these to the identity public key secrets, and performing the operations in KeyGen. Then, the procedure in [22] is followed except that the public key is added to the hash to produce the challenge c. Verification is also similar to that in [22] except that $ct_{1,\tau}$ is multiplied by 2^{d-1}. The full scheme is supplied in the full version.

The parameters are identical to the parameters in [22], except that $d = 7$ and $\beta = 644$.

4.2   blDilithium-QROM Security

We now consider the security of blDilithium-QROM by addressing unforgeability and unlinkability as defined in Sect. 2. Since the proof of unforgeability closely follows the proof of unforgeability for Dilithium-QROM in [22], we give a summary here and provide the detailed proof in the full version. In addition, the proof of unlinkability can be found in the full version due to space constraints.

We first address unforgeability, in which we follow the framework set out in [22]. To begin, we create a version of blDilithium-QROM where the identity public key $pk = \mathbf{t}$, which we then use to construct an identification protocol ID whose Fiat-Shamir transform is equivalent to the scheme with the larger public key. We then follow the techniques in [22] to show that ID is non-abort honest verifier zero knowledge (naHVZK) and lossy, and establish bounds on its correctness and min-entropy. This allows us to use Theorem 3.1 of [22] to establish the following bound:

Theorem 1. *Let $\mathcal{A}$ be any adversary that makes at most q_H hash queries and q_S signing queries against the unforgeability of* blDilithium-QROM *with parameters as specified in Subsect. 4.1. Then there exists an algorithm $\mathcal{B}$ such that*

$$\mathbf{Adv}_{\text{blDilithium-QROM}}^{\text{EUF-CMEA}}(\mathcal{A}) \leq \mathbf{Adv}_{k,\ell,\mathcal{U}}^{\text{SA-MLWE}}(\mathcal{B}) + 8(q_H + 1) \cdot 2^{-137} + 2^{-2899}$$

In general, the proof of naHVZK and bounds on correctness and min-entropy are identical to those in [22], except that the blinding factor is introduced and $\|2cs\|_\infty$ must be bounded by β. Lossiness differs in that the added blinding factor contributes to the bound on size of the solutions of a specific equation, hence raising the bound ε_{ls}.

We now turn our attention to unlinkability and discuss independent blinding and signing with oracle reprogramming discussed in Sect. 3.

Theorem 2. *For any adversary $\mathcal{A}$ that makes q_S signing queries and q_H random oracle queries, there exists an algorithm $\mathcal{B}$ such that*

$$\mathbf{Adv}_{\text{blDilithium-QROM},t}^{\text{UL-CMEA}}(\mathcal{A}) \leq 2t\mathbf{Adv}_{m,k,\mathcal{U},\mathbf{A}}^{\text{SA-MLWE}}(\mathcal{B}_1) + q_H\mathbf{Adv}_{\text{blDilithium-QROM}}^{\text{EUF-CMEA}}(\mathcal{B}_2) + q_Hq_S2^{-2899}$$

At a high level, the theorem follows from the fact a blinded public key $\mathbf{t} + \mathbf{t}'$ can be replaced by $\mathbf{t} + \tilde{\mathbf{t}}'$ where $\tilde{\mathbf{t}}'$ is uniformly sampled. Since we are working in R_q^k, then $\mathbf{t} + \tilde{\mathbf{t}}'$ is itself uniformly random. We make t hops away from independent blindings of a single public key using the replacement as above, then use another t hops to return to independent blindings of independent public keys.

We also know that blDilithium-QROM permits signing with oracle reprogramming as we can use the simulator from unforgeability to create a forgery function with $\delta = 0$ and the min-entropy bound comes directly from the min-entropy bound in unforgeability.

As we make no changes to the set of parameters that contributes to MLWE hardness, the classical and quantum bit-security from [22] apply here. In particular, they argue that as there is no known attack that leverages the module structure of the assumption, it is common to directly apply LWE bit security directly to MLWE security. We make the further assumption that the SA-MLWE assumption is also as secure as the MLWE assumption.

4.3 Key-Blinding Dilithium

We briefly describe a key-blinded version of Dilithium [17] but we provide no security analysis or guarantees.

As is with blDilithium-QROM, **A** is a public parameter of the network and thus ρ can be omitted from the scheme. In addition, Power2Round is modified to release one extra bit for $\mathbf{t}_1$ while keeping $\mathbf{t}_0$ the same. The appropriate changes to Sign and Verify are made in a similar fashion to the changes made from Dilithium-QROM to blDilithium-QROM.

Note that during signing, tr may be recomputed as it is dependent solely on the identity public key and not the blinded public key. One possibility could be to set $tr = \mathsf{CRH}(\mathbf{s}_{1,\tau}, \|\mathbf{s}_{2,\tau})$.

No parameters need to be changed to modify the correctness of the blinded scheme.

5 An Isogeny-Based Key-Blinding Scheme

In this section we briefly describe how to realize a key-blinding signature scheme from CSI-FiSh [12], which is an isogeny-based signature scheme that uses the structure of the CSIDH [13] group action. The 'group' here refers to class group $\mathrm{Cl}(\mathcal{O})$, with $\mathcal{O}$ being the endomorphism ring $\mathrm{End}_{\mathbb{F}_p}(E)$, the ring of endomorphisms from a curve E to itself defined over $\mathbb{F}_p$, which is an order in the imaginary quadratic field $\mathbb{Q}(\sqrt{-p})$. A main contribution of the CSI-FiSh paper was to calculate the precise structure of this group, so that it can be described as a cyclic group of order N. This allows for two crucial operations with respect to the group action: group elements can now be sampled *uniformly* from the group, and group elements can now be given a *canonical representation* as a member of $\mathbb{Z}_N$, so that for example, when revealing to an adversary a group element $g = g_1 \cdot g_2$, we can be assured that no information about g_1 or g_2 is leaked by how g is represented.

For our purpose, we will describe the scheme as an abstract group action, and avoid notation that refers to how the group is actually constructed. For complete details about the group action we refer to the CSI-FiSh paper [12].

We briefly recall the details of a group action. We have a group G and a set $\mathcal{E}$ along with an operation $\star : G \times \mathcal{E} \rightarrow E$. The operation $\star$ satisfies the property that if $id \in G$ is the identity group element, then $id \star E = E$ for all $E \in \mathcal{E}$. Furthermore, for $g_1, g_2 \in G$, it must be the case that $g_1 \star (g_2 \star E) = (g_1 \cdot g_2) \star E$. In fact, the group action described in [12] is both *free* and *transitive*, meaning that for $E_1, E_2 \in \mathcal{E}$ there is one and only one $g \in G$ such that $g \star E_1 = E_2$. Furthermore, the group G in our case is cyclic, and we will denote the order N.

In CSI-Fish, signatures correspond to a zero-knowledge proof of knowledge of a secret group element g_{sk} such that $g_{sk} \star E_0 = E_{pk}$, with E_{pk} being the public key and E_0 being a system parameter. Proving knowledge of such a g_{sk} is done via a simple sigma protocol. The commitment is created by uniformly sampling $g \overset{\$}{\leftarrow} G$ and computing $E_{com} = g \star E_{pk}$ as the commitment. The verifier then selects a bit $b \overset{\$}{\leftarrow} \{0,1\}$ as the challenge, and the prover responds by sending g if $b = 0$, and $g \cdot g_{sk}$ if $b = 1$.

The verifier then checks: if $b = 0$ that $g \star E_{pk} = E_{com}$; and if $b = 1$ that $(g \cdot g_{sk}) \star E_0 = E_{com}$. Soundness follows from the fact that, from two responses g and $g \cdot g_{sk}$, the secret key g_{sk} can quickly be recovered. Honest-verifier zero-knowledge can be shown by simulating transcripts in a straightforward way (here we rely on the fact that group elements have a canonical representation).

The basic idea of how key-blinding functionality can be added to the scheme is already apparent. From a value τ, a group element g_τ can be generated, and the public key E_{pk} is blinded to $E_\tau = g_\tau \star E_{pk}$. Anyone who knows the public key and τ can perform this operation, but to sign a message, one must know g_τ and g_{sk} so the scheme is still unforgeable. Furthermore, because the group action is transitive, the action of g_τ entirely hides E_{pk}. Observing many blindings still leaks no information about E_{pk}, ensuring that the scheme is unlinkable.

Of course, the soundness of this zero-knowledge scheme is only $1/2$, and would have to be repeated many times in order for the signature scheme to be existentially unforgeable. The authors of CSI-FiSh employed many clever techniques in order to improve on the efficiency of the scheme over just repeating the signature scheme 128 times. Most notably, the public keys of CSI-FiSh consist of many curves $E_{pk,1}, E_{pk,2}, \ldots, E_{pk,L}$, generated by computing $g_{sk,1} \star E_0$, $g_{sk,2} \star E_0$, etc. Then rather than choosing a single bit for the challenge, an index from 0 to L can be chosen. This increases the soundness significantly, and so the protocol can be repeated fewer times to achieve the same level of security, allowing for a trade-off between the signature size and the public key size. To blind, we can similarly sample independent blinding factors $g_{\tau,1}, g_{\tau,2}, \ldots$ and apply each of them to each part of the public key.

A further advantage that CSI-FiSh optionally takes is to then 'Merkleize' the public key. Rather than including each of $E_{pk,1}, \ldots, E_{pk,L}$, key generation commits to these public keys by constructing a Merkle tree with each curve as a leaf node. When signing a message, each $E_{pk,i}$ that gets used, as well as the Merkle path that proves the commitment, is provided. This causes the public key to be only 32 Bytes, at the expense of increasing the size of signatures and making signing and verification slightly slower. Unfortunately, it is not possible to use this technique for a blinded version. The raw $E_{pk,i}$ values must be available in order to construct the blinded version of the public key, and so 'Merkleization' is impossible.

In the full version we describe signing and verification, which are essentially unchanged from in CSI-FiSh. There we also prove the unlinkability of the scheme, and discuss the proof of unforgeability of the scheme.

bICSI-FiSh.KeyGen()	bICSI-FiSh.BlindPk($(E_{pk,i})_{i \in [L]}, \tau$)
1 : **for** $i \in [L]$ **do**	1 : $(g_{\tau,i})_{i \in [L]} \leftarrow KDF((E_{pk,i})_{i \in [L]} \| \tau)$
2 : $\quad g_{sk,i} \xleftarrow{\$} \mathbb{Z}_N$	2 : **for** $i \in [L]$ **do**
3 : $\quad E_{pk,i} \leftarrow g_{sk,i} \star E_0$	3 : $\quad E_{\tau,i} \leftarrow g_{\tau,i} \star E_{pk,i}$
4 : **endfor**	4 : **endfor**
5 : **return** $(pk, sk) = ((E_{pk,i})_{i \in [L]}, (g_{sk,i})_{i \in [L]})$	5 : **return** $pk_\tau = (E_{\tau,i})_{i \in [L]}$

6 A Number-Theoretic Key-Blinding Scheme

LegRoast and PorcRoast are new adaptations of Picnic that use the Legendre Symbol as a symmetric PRF [10,15]. In this section we show how the mathematical structure of LegRoast enables a more efficient key-blinding signature scheme.

Recall that the Legendre symbol modulo a prime p, denoted $(\frac{a}{p})$, is defined as 0 if $a \equiv 0 \pmod{p}$, 1 if a is a quadratic residue modulo p, and -1 if it is not. To use the Legendre symbol as a 1-bit keyed PRF with input X and key K, we can define a function that returns values in $\{0,1\}$. For an odd prime p, define $\mathcal{L}_K(X)$ to return 0 if $K + X$ is a quadratic residue or 0 $\pmod{p}$, and 1 otherwise. This concept can be generalized to consider the ℓ-th power residue, instead of just quadratic residues. This allows for a keyed PRF with $\log \ell$ bits of output to be defined as

$$\mathcal{L}_K^\ell(X) = \begin{cases} i, & \text{if } (X + K)/g^i \equiv h^\ell \pmod{p} \text{ for some } h \in \mathbb{F}_p^\times \\ 0, & \text{if } K + X \equiv 0 \pmod{p}. \end{cases}$$

A key property of this PRF is that it is a group homomorphism from $\mathbb{F}_p^\times$ to $\mathbb{Z}_\ell$. This is helpful for proving statements in zero-knowledge about preimages of the PRF. To prove knowledge of a K such that $\mathcal{L}_K^\ell(X) = s$, one can sample a random value $r \in \mathbb{F}_p^\times$ and send $(K+X) \cdot r$ and $\mathcal{L}_0^\ell(r)$. The prover then only needs to prove that the multiplication of $(K + X) \cdot r$ was computed correctly for the verifier to calculate s and be convinced of knowledge of K.[1] Since the equation being proven consists of a single multiplication gate, the resulting proof can be comparatively short.

---

[1] The verifier must also be convinced that the prover did not lie about the value of $\mathcal{L}_0^\ell(r)$. This is accomplished by having the prover commit to this value before the challenge X is issued, so that the prover cannot choose the output of the PRF in a way to help them.

Algorithm 1. blLegRoast.BlindPk

Input: identity public key $pk = (w_1, w_2, \ldots, w_L)$, epoch τ
Output: blinded public key $pk_\tau = (w_{1,\tau}, w_{2,\tau}, \ldots, w_{L,\tau})$
1: $T \leftarrow KDF(pk\|\tau)$
2: $v_1 \leftarrow \mathcal{L}_T^\ell(j_1), \ldots, v_L \leftarrow \mathcal{L}_T^\ell(j_L)$
3: $w_{1,\tau} \leftarrow w_1 + v_1 \pmod{\ell}, \ldots, w_{L,\tau} \leftarrow w_L + v_L \pmod{\ell}$
4: **return** pk_τ

LegRoast and PorcRoast [10] expand this idea into a signature scheme that uses the Fiat–Shamir heuristic. Public keys consist of the output of L computations of the Legendre PRF, with inputs $\mathcal{I} = i_1, \ldots, i_L$, which can be public parameters. We define the function F, which is parameterized by ℓ and $\mathcal{I}$, as taking in the secret key K and returning $\mathcal{L}_K^\ell(i_m)$ for $m \in [L]$. Hence, key generation consists of sampling a random secret key $K \in \mathbb{F}_p^\times$ and computing the public key $F_\mathcal{I}^\ell(K) = \left(\mathcal{L}_K^\ell(i_1), \ldots, \mathcal{L}_K^\ell(i_L)\right)$.

The same homomorphic property that makes the Legendre symbol an attractive option for zero knowledge proofs is also what allows for a blinding mechanism. Hashing the nonce and public key to a value $T \in \mathbb{F}_p^\times$, we can calculate L computations of the Legendre PRF with separate inputs $j_1, \ldots, j_L$. The public key blinded under the value T becomes $\left(\mathcal{L}_K^\ell(i_1) + \mathcal{L}_T^\ell(j_1), \ldots, \mathcal{L}_K^\ell(i_L) + \mathcal{L}_T^\ell(j_L)\right)$, where addition is performed modulo ℓ. Due to the homomorphic property of $\mathcal{L}$, this can also be written as $\left(\mathcal{L}_0^\ell((K + i_m) \cdot (T + j_m))\right)_{m \in [L]}$.

As mentioned, LegRoast works by presenting parts of the public key multiplied by random values $r^{(j)} \in \mathbb{F}_p^\times$, the results of which are denoted by $o^{(j)}$. Then the signer proves knowledge of K by presenting a zero knowledge proof that a random linear combination of B $(K + I^{(j)}) \cdot r^{(j)} - o^{(j)}$ terms is equal to 0; here the $I^{(j)}$ values are a random re-indexing of the $i^{(j)}$ values in the public key. We call such a linear combination the error term, which should be equal to zero. Once the coefficients $\{\lambda^{(j)}\}$ of the linear combination are defined, the error term is $E = \sum_{j=1}^B \lambda^{(j)}\left((K + I^{(j)}) \cdot r^{(j)} - o^j\right) = K \cdot \left(\sum_{j=1}^B \lambda^{(j)} r^{(j)}\right) + \sum_{j=1}^B \lambda^{(j)}(I^{(j)} r^{(j)} - o^{(j)})$. Since only the K and $r^{(j)}$ values are secret, the only time we have a secret value multiplied by a secret value is in the $K \cdot \sum \lambda^{(j)} r^{(j)}$ term, so this can be verified to be 0 with only one multiplication gate.

If we are using a blinded public key, then the corresponding error term is the summation of $\lambda^{(j)}((K + I^{(j)})(T + J^{(j)})r^{(j)} - o^{(j)})$ terms. Through rearranging in a similar way to that of LegRoast, we get an error term that has three multiplication gates as opposed to one. Due to the nature of the zero-knowledge proof system used, the complete description of signing and verifying is quite large, and so we move it to the full version. We focus on a description of the blinding process.

To complete the security assessment for blLegRoast, we still need to establish (i) the independent blinding property, (ii) the signing with oracle reprogramming property, and (iii) the existential unforgeability of the scheme. As the scheme uses the Fiat–Shamir heuristic, signing with reprogramming is possible by choosing the output of the hash function in advance and constructing the signature accordingly. The existential unforgeability of the scheme follows from how finding a K and T that satisfy the relations informed by the public key is still hard. As these proofs require careful details of the scheme itself, we present them in the full version, where the complete description of the scheme can be found.

7   Implementation Details

We implemented the blDilithium-QROM, the blCSI-FiSh, and blLegRoast schemes; code for each is available at http://github.com/tedeaton/pq-key-blinding. The code for blCSI-FiSh and blLegRoast is forked from the CSI-FiSh and LegRoast code respectively [9,11] and is written primarily in C. The code for blDilithium-QROM is written in Sage. Results can be seen in Fig. 1 in Sect. 1. Our performance metrics indicate that the increase over the unblinded version of schemes is quite reasonable.

blDilithium-QROM. For blDilithium-QROM, key generation and verification are in fact *faster* since a fixed parameter $\mathbf{A}$ is used for all users and can be pre-generated, rather than being pseudorandomly generated each time. The signing procedure of blDilithium-QROM is three times slower than that of Dilithium-QROM. We caution that, since our blDilithium-QROM implementation is written in Sage, the implementation is non-optimized and results not be used an absolute measure of performance, but can still give insight when *compared* to a similar Sage implementation of non-blinded Dilithium-QROM.

blLegRoast. Blinded LegRoast's performance is compelling both in absolute terms (under 1 ms for key generation and blinding, under 20 ms for signing and verifying) and comparative terms (no worse than 1.5× slower than unblinded LegRoast).

blPicnic. We leave an implementation of blPicnic as future work. New advancements to the zero knowledge protocol that Picnic uses are still being made [4], so the performance of the scheme, and any blinded version, will change. We can summarize what we expect to see in a blPicnic implementation however. Public keys should be maintained at a straightforward 32 bytes, which is very attractive. We do not have exact calculations for the signature size, but the circuit being used is twice as large (for two encryptions), so we would expect the size to be roughly twice as large. In practice it may not be quite twice as large, however, as some of the values sent are independent of the length of the circuit.

blCSI-FiSh. Our blCSI-FiSh implementation achieves sizes and performance effectively matching that of CSI-FiSh-unMerkleized. The CSI-FiSh and blCSI-FiSh implementations use the CSIDH-512 parameter set. This parameter set aims to achieve NIST level 1 security (comparable to the security of AES-128 against a quantum adversary), though whether it achieves this level of security has been a matter of contention [24]. Unfortunately, increasing the parameters in CSI-FiSh is a matter of great difficulty. It is essential to CSI-FiSh that the structure of the class group be known. Calculating the order N of the group was a subexponential computation that took the CSIDH authors 52 core years. If the parameters are increased, then a new computation must happen, which will almost certainly be infeasible. Quantum computers could calculate the structure of the class group much more easily, so by the time CSI-FiSh is needed, there may also be the ability to use it by computing the class group number.

Tor Integration. Recall that Tor uses identity public keys as the URL for `.onion` addresses. This means that, unless the onion service lookup process changes, users directly interact with an onion service's public key, whether by clicking on it as a link or copying and pasting it into a browser window. This motivates keeping public keys as small as possible. For this purpose, blPicnic and blLegRoast are the most attractive of the schemes considered. In the context of Tor, the process for connecting to an onion service is quite lengthy (several seconds, usually), so there may be less sensitivity to increased computation time.

8 Conclusion

We have considered the problem of building post-quantum key blinding schemes. We have shown that the unlinkability property can be reduced to two properties that are often relatively easy to establish: that blinding properly re-randomizes the public key (independent blinding) and that the distribution of signatures is only dependent on the public key (signing with oracle reprogramming). We have shown four different ways that post-quantum key blinding can be achieved: with supersingular isogenies via CSI-FiSh, lattices via Dilithium-QROM, with only symmetric primitives via Picnic, and by a number theoretic construction via LegRoast. We implemented blDilithium-QROM, blCSI-FiSh, and blLegRoast, and saw small performance impact compared to the unblinded versions.

Each of these four schemes is built out of the Fiat–Shamir paradigm. We did not consider any schemes built out of other ways to build signature schemes, such as hash-based signatures like SPHINCS+ [8], or the hash-and-sign paradigm like Rainbow [16] or Falcon [26].

It is difficult to envision a hash-based key blinding scheme. As public keys are the root of a Merkle tree, the only simple operation to blind a public key would be to hash it again. This could satisfy independent blinding, but not signing with oracle reprogramming: hash-based signatures work by providing paths up to the root, so the identity public key would be revealed on that path.

Hash-and-sign algorithms appear to have the opposite problem. A blinded version would almost certainly satisfy the signing with oracle programming property. If the trapdoored function is F, then by choosing a point x in the domain of F and programming the hash function so that $H(msg) = F(x)$, we obtain a signature; this is how hash-and-sign signature schemes often prove security.

But it is not clear how to justify the independent blinding property. The most simple blinding mechanism would be to compose the trapdoor function F with another mapping G based on the blinding factor. This requires the range of F to match the domain of G, which makes it an interesting problem to be used with a hash-and-sign scheme. As well, to ensure the independent blinding property, we need that $F \circ G$ cannot be decomposed into the two mappings, which is a more novel security assumption. Because RSA is a trapdoor *permutation*, the structure of its mapping may allow for key-blinding, but it is not clear if any post-quantum primitive immediately does.

For these reasons, signature schemes that follow the Fiat–Shamir paradigm appear to admit key blinding much more readily. While homomorphic properties over the key space are certainly useful for key blinding (as in Dilithium and CSI-FiSh), they are not actually necessary, as the Picnic construction shows.

Acknowledgements. E.E. was supported by a Natural Sciences and Engineering Research Council of Canada (NSERC) Alexander Graham Bell Canada Graduate Scholarship. D.S. was supported by NSERC Discovery grant RGPIN-2016-05146 and a Discovery Accelerator Supplement.

References

1. Abdalla, M., Fouque, P.-A., Lyubashevsky, V., Tibouchi, M.: Tightly secure signatures from lossy identification schemes. J. Cryptol. **29**(3), 597–631 (2016)
2. Alkadri, N.A., et al.: Deterministic wallets in a quantum world. In: ACM Conference on Computer and Communications Security (CCS) 2020, pp. 1017–1031 (2020)
3. Barreto, P.S.L.M., Ricardini, J.E., Simplício, M.A., Jr., Patil, H.K.: qSCMS: post-quantum certificate provisioning process for V2X. Cryptology ePrint Archive, Report 2018/1247 (2018)
4. Baum, C., et al.: Banquet: short and fast signatures from AES. In: Garay, J.A. (ed.) PKC 2021. LNCS, vol. 12710, pp. 266–297. Springer, Cham (2021). https://doi.org/10.1007/978-3-030-75245-3_11
5. Bellare, M., Rogaway, P.: Code-based game-playing proofs and the security of triple encryption. In: Vaudenay, S. (ed.) Eurocrypt 2006. LNCS, vol. 4004, pp. 40–426. Springer, Heidelberg (2006). https://doi.org/10.1007/11761679
6. Bellare, M., Rogaway, P.: The exact security of digital signatures-how to sign with RSA and Rabin. In: Maurer, U. (ed.) EUROCRYPT 1996. LNCS, vol. 1070, pp. 399–416. Springer, Heidelberg (1996). https://doi.org/10.1007/3-540-68339-9_34
7. Bernstein, D.J., Duif, N., Lange, T., Schwabe, P., Yang, B.-Y.: High-speed high-security signatures. In: Preneel, B., Takagi, T. (eds.) CHES 2011. LNCS, vol. 6917, pp. 124–142. Springer, Heidelberg (2011). https://doi.org/10.1007/978-3-642-23951-9_9
8. Bernstein, D.J., Hülsing, A., Kölbl, S., Niederhagen, R., Rijneveld, J., Schwabe, P.: The SPHINCS$^+$ signature framework. In: ACM Conference on Computer and Communications Security (CCS) 2019, pp. 2129–2146 (2019)
9. Beullens, W., de Saint Guilhem, C.D.: LegRoast. GitHub Repository (2020). https://github.com/WardBeullens/LegRoast. Accessed May 2021

10. Beullens, W., Delpech de Saint Guilhem, C.: LegRoast: efficient post-quantum signatures from the legendre PRF. In: Ding, J., Tillich, J.-P. (eds.) PQCrypto 2020. LNCS, vol. 12100, pp. 130–150. Springer, Cham (2020). https://doi.org/10.1007/978-3-030-44223-1_8

11. Beullens, W., Kleinjung, T., Vercauteren, F.: CSI-FiSh. GitHub Repository (2019). https://github.com/KULeuven-COSIC/CSI-FiSh. Accessed May 2021

12. Beullens, W., Kleinjung, T., Vercauteren, F.: CSI-FiSh: efficient isogeny based signatures through class group computations. In: Galbraith, S.D., Moriai, S. (eds.) ASIACRYPT 2019. LNCS, vol. 11921, pp. 227–247. Springer, Cham (2019). https://doi.org/10.1007/978-3-030-34578-5_9

13. Castryck, W., Lange, T., Martindale, C., Panny, L., Renes, J.: CSIDH: an efficient post-quantum commutative group action. In: Peyrin, T., Galbraith, S. (eds.) ASIACRYPT 2018. LNCS, vol. 11274, pp. 395–427. Springer, Cham (2018). https://doi.org/10.1007/978-3-030-03332-3_15

14. Chase, M., et al.: Post-quantum zero-knowledge and signatures from symmetric-key primitives. In: ACM Conference on Computer and Communications Security (CCS) 2017, pp. 1825–1842 (2017)

15. Damgård, I.B.: On the randomness of Legendre and Jacobi sequences. In: Goldwasser, S. (ed.) CRYPTO 1988. LNCS, vol. 403, pp. 163–172. Springer, New York (1990). https://doi.org/10.1007/0-387-34799-2_13

16. Ding, J., Chen, M.-S., Petzoldt, A., Schmidt, D., Yang, B.-Y.: Rainbow (2019). https://csrc.nist.gov/projects/post-quantum-cryptography/round-2-submissions

17. Ducas, L., Kiltz, E., Lepoint, T., Lyubashevsky, V., Schwabe, P., Seiler, G., Stehlé, D.: CRYSTALS-Dilithium: a lattice-based digital signature scheme. IACR Trans. Cryptogr. Hardw. Embed. Syst. **2018**(1), 238–268 (2018)

18. Gutoski, G., Stebila, D.: Hierarchical deterministic bitcoin wallets that tolerate key leakage. In: Böhme, R., Okamoto, T. (eds.) FC 2015. LNCS, vol. 8975, pp. 497–504. Springer, Heidelberg (2015). https://doi.org/10.1007/978-3-662-47854-7_31

19. Hauck, E., Kiltz, E., Loss, J., Nguyen, N.K.: Lattice-based blind signatures, revisited. In: Micciancio, D., Ristenpart, T. (eds.) CRYPTO 2020. LNCS, vol. 12171, pp. 500–529. Springer, Cham (2020). https://doi.org/10.1007/978-3-030-56880-1_18

20. Hopper, N.: Proving security of Tor's hidden service identity blinding protocol (2013). https://www-users.cs.umn.edu/~hoppernj/basic-proof.pdf

21. Ishai, Y., Kushilevitz, E., Ostrovsky, R., Sahai, A.: Zero-knowledge from secure multiparty computation. In: ACM Symposium on Theory of Computing (STOC) 2007, pp. 21–30 (2007)

22. Kiltz, E., Lyubashevsky, V., Schaffner, C.: a concrete treatment of Fiat-Shamir signatures in the quantum random-oracle model. In: Nielsen, J.B., Rijmen, V. (eds.) EUROCRYPT 2018. LNCS, vol. 10822, pp. 552–586. Springer, Cham (2018). https://doi.org/10.1007/978-3-319-78372-7_18

23. Liu, Z., Nguyen, K., Yang, G., Wang, H., Wong, D.S.: a lattice-based linkable ring signature supporting stealth addresses. In: Sako, K., Schneider, S., Ryan, P.Y.A. (eds.) ESORICS 2019. LNCS, vol. 11735, pp. 726–746. Springer, Cham (2019). https://doi.org/10.1007/978-3-030-29959-0_35

24. Peikert, C.: He gives C-sieves on the CSIDH. In: Canteaut, A., Ishai, Y. (eds.) EUROCRYPT 2020. LNCS, vol. 12106, pp. 463–492. Springer, Cham (2020). https://doi.org/10.1007/978-3-030-45724-2_16

25. Petzoldt, A., Szepieniec, A., Mohamed, M.S.E.: A practical multivariate blind signature scheme. In: Kiayias, A. (ed.) FC 2017. LNCS, vol. 10322, pp. 437–454. Springer, Cham (2017). https://doi.org/10.1007/978-3-319-70972-7_25

26. Prest, T., et al.: Falcon (2019). https://csrc.nist.gov/projects/post-quantum-cryptography/round-2-submissions
27. The Tor Project, Inc., Tor Metrics (2020). https://metrics.torproject.org/. Accessed May 2020
28. The Tor Project, Inc., Tor Rendezvous Specification - Version 3 (2020). https://gitweb.torproject.org/torspec.git/tree/rend-spec-v3.txt

Implementing and Measuring KEMTLS

Sofía Celi[1]([✉])[iD], Armando Faz-Hernández[1,2][iD], Nick Sullivan[1,2],
Goutam Tamvada[3][iD], Luke Valenta[1,2][iD], Thom Wiggers[4][iD], Bas
Westerbaan[5][iD], and Christopher A. Wood[1,2][iD]

[1] Cloudflare, Inc., Lisbon, Portugal
{sceli,armfazh,nick,lvalenta,chriswood}@cloudflare.com
[2] Cloudflare, Inc., San Francisco, United States
[3] University of Waterloo, Waterloo, Canada
goutam.tamvada@uwaterloo.ca
[4] Radboud University, Nijmegen, Netherlands
thom@thomwiggers.nl
[5] PQShield, Ltd, Oxford, UK
bas@westerbaan.name

Abstract. KEMTLS is a novel alternative to the Transport Layer Security (TLS) handshake that integrates post-quantum algorithms. It uses key encapsulation mechanisms (KEMs) for both confidentiality and authentication, achieving post-quantum security while obviating the need for expensive post-quantum signatures. The original KEMTLS paper presents a security analysis, Rust implementation, and benchmarks over emulated networks. In this work, we provide full Go implementations of KEMTLS and other post-quantum handshake alternatives, describe their integration into a distributed system, and provide performance evaluations over real network conditions. We compare the standard (non-quantum-resistant) TLS 1.3 handshake with three alternatives: one that uses post-quantum signatures in combination with post-quantum KEMs (PQTLS), one that uses KEMTLS, and one that is a reduced round trip version of KEMTLS (KEMTLS-PDK). In addition to the performance evaluations, we discuss how the design of these protocols impacts TLS from an implementation and configuration perspective.

Keywords: Post-quantum cryptography · KEMTLS · Transport Layer Security · Cryptographic engineering

1 Introduction

Transport Layer Security (TLS) is one of the most widely used protocols on the Internet today [11,22], and provides confidentiality, integrity, and authenticity to communications between two parties. The most recent version, TLS 1.3 [29], uses ephemeral (elliptic curve) Diffie-Hellman (-EC-DH) to establish keys, which are used to encrypt parts of the handshake and the traffic that will be sent in

Bas Westerbaan—Cloudflare, Inc, Amsterdam, Netherlands

ⓒ Springer Nature Switzerland AG 2021
P. Longa and C. Ràfols (Eds.): LATINCRYPT 2021, LNCS 12912, pp. 88–107, 2021.
https://doi.org/10.1007/978-3-030-88238-9_5

the connection. Authentication of the server and (optionally) of the client can be achieved by using digital signatures. The corresponding public keys for those signatures are transmitted during the handshake in digital certificates, which are signed by a certificate authority (CA).

Given that TLS 1.3 is the most widely used protocol today to secure connections [22], it is vital to start thinking about how to integrate post-quantum cryptography into it to protect from the imminent threat of quantum computing. Advances in quantum computing are promising and motivate a swift move to quantum-resistant algorithms. However, widespread adoption and protocol standardization are slow processes that can take several years to reach consensus among the parties[1]. In fact, the National Institute of Standards and Technologies (NIST) is organizing a multi-year competition to select post-quantum algorithms for standardization [27]. Several proposals on how to integrate post-quantum cryptography into TLS have already been suggested in the form of specifications, implementations, and experiments.

Related Work. Many early experiments focused on *transitional security* to protect against adversaries capable of recording today's communications with the hope of decrypting them in the future with a quantum computer. They focus on the key exchange phase of the handshake and add quantum-resistant confidentiality. This latter property is achieved by replacing the (EC-)DH key exchange by one based on a post-quantum Key Encapsulation Mechanism (KEM). However, this strategy does not address quantum-resistant authentication.

In 2016, a post-quantum experimentation project was initiated by Google [7], and was later expanded to a large-network scale in collaboration with Cloudflare in 2019 [21, 24]. In the latter experiment, connections made from experimental versions of the Chrome browser to Cloudflare's edge servers used post-quantum key exchange algorithms in the TLS 1.3 handshake to secure connections and provide quantum-resistant confidentiality. The handshake used a "hybrid" key exchange protocol that combined post-quantum key exchange algorithms with traditional algorithms in order to safely use experimental cryptography without sacrificing any security guarantees. The experiment included two hybrid post-quantum key exchange protocols: X25519 [5] with the lattice-based KEM NTRU-HRSS [14] and X25519 with the supersingular-isogeny-based KEM SIKE [16]. These experiments focused on post-quantum *confidentiality*, but still relied on traditional authentication using non-quantum-resistant digital signature algorithms.

From a specification level, these works on quantum-resistant *confidentiality* mechanisms have taken priority [8,13,19,31,32,37,42], without much actual integration into real-world systems.

While these previous experiments provided valuable insights about the performance impact of post-quantum cryptography in real networks, post-quantum confidentiality is only one part of the picture: full post-quantum security also requires post-quantum authentication. In this sense, there are some research efforts towards this goal by using post-quantum signatures. But, most post-quantum signature schemes participating in the NIST competition have large

---

[1] It took, for example, 5 years to standardize TLS 1.3 [39].

public keys or signatures, and/or have significant performance considerations in their cryptographic operations. Sikeridis et al. [35] suggest that only the lattice-based candidates Dilithium [25] and Falcon [28] are viable contenders to be used in the TLS handshake, taking into account the trade-off between lengthy signatures and computationally heavy cryptographic operations.

Post-quantum KEM operations are, in practice, more efficient than post-quantum signature operations. A new approach, called KEMTLS [33], achieves authentication using KEMs instead of relying on digital signatures. This technique consists of encapsulating under the long-term KEM public key advertised in the peer's certificate, obtaining a shared secret in the process. Only the peer that has the private key corresponding to the public key in the advertised certificate can decapsulate the shared secret and decrypt any encrypted data sent under that key. Thus, KEMTLS uses post-quantum KEMs for both *confidentiality* and *authentication* to achieve full post-quantum security. A tweaked version of KEMTLS, called KEMTLS-PDK [34], achieves the same properties while reducing the number of round-trips needed.

Contributions. The focus of this paper is analyzing how the integration of post-quantum cryptography impacts the TLS 1.3 handshake from a performance, implementation, and configuration perspective. We developed a framework for establishing TLS 1.3 handshakes using post-quantum algorithms on a real-world system: a distributed network that is subject to actual Internet traffic conditions and that spans two continents. We examined several handshake configurations: one that uses KEMs for confidentiality and post-quantum signature schemes for authentication, which we called PQTLS; and we evaluate the KEMTLS protocol and its reduced round trip version called KEMTLS-PDK. We measured the latency of these handshakes and compare them against the baseline TLS 1.3 handshake by considering both server-only and mutual authentication. Additionally, we touch upon the engineering process of implementing all these protocols in the Go language, and report some constraints found in the design of KEMTLS. Our implementations are publicly available for further experimentation.

Organization. In Sect. 2, we describe the integration of post-quantum algorithms into the TLS 1.3 handshake. Section 3 covers details of our implementation and our integration into the testbed network used for experimentation. In Sect. 4, we discuss our experimental methodology and measurement results, and finally in Sect. 5, we state our conclusions.

2   Post-quantum Cryptography in TLS 1.3

We first give an overview of the TLS 1.3 handshake, and then discuss proposed specifications, implementations, and experiments for integrating the PQTLS, KEMTLS and KEMTLS-PDK post-quantum handshakes.

2.1   Reviewing the TLS 1.3 Protocol

Standardized in 2018, the TLS 1.3 protocol emerged in response to dissatisfaction with the outdated design of the TLS 1.2 handshake, its two-round-trip overhead, and the increasing number of practical attacks on older versions of TLS [1–3,6]. The pressure to increase efficiency also motivated the creation of alternative protocols such as the QUIC protocol [15]. In light of this, the main improvements of TLS 1.3 are: reducing the handshake's latency, encrypting as many messages as possible of the handshake itself, improving resilience to cross-protocol attacks, and removing legacy features [39]. It achieves a one-round-trip time (1-RTT) handshake and even a 0-RTT handshake through a resumption mode.

The default[2] mode of the protocol uses certificates for authentication and (EC-)DH for shared secret generation. In this mode, the handshake starts with the client sending a ClientHello (CH) message to the server. This message advertises the supported (EC-)DH groups and the ephemeral (EC-)DH keyshares offered by the client and specified in the supported_groups and key_shares extensions, respectively. The CH message also advertises the signature algorithms supported in the signature_algorithms extension. It also contains a nonce and a list of supported symmetric-key algorithms (ciphersuites).

The server processes the ClientHello message and chooses the appropriate cryptographic parameters to be used in the connection. If (EC-)DH key exchange is in use (meaning the client sent the key_shares extension), the server sends a ServerHello (SH) message containing a key_share extension with the server's (EC-)DH key corresponding to one of the key_shares advertised by the client. The SH message also contains a server-generated nonce and the ciphersuite chosen.

An ephemeral shared secret is then computed at both ends (the client computes it when it receives SH). After this point, all subsequent handshake messages are encrypted using keys derived from this secret.

The server then sends a certificate chain (ServerCertificate message) and a message that contains a proof that the server possesses the private key corresponding to the public key advertised in its leaf certificate. This proof is a signature over the handshake transcript and it is sent in the ServerCertificateVerify message. The advertised signature_algorithms in CH are used to decide which algorithms can be used to generate this signature. The goal of this message is to provide proof of possession of the server's private key, which is essential for achieving authentication. The server also sends the ServerFinished message that provides integrity of the handshake up to this point. It contains a message authentication code (MAC) over the entire transcript providing key confirmation and binding the server's identity to any computed keys.

Optionally, the server can send a CertificateRequest message, prior to sending its ServerCertificate message, requesting a certificate from the client for authentication. At this point, the server can immediately send application data to the unauthenticated client. Upon receiving the server's messages, the client verifies the signature of the ServerCertificateVerify message and the MAC of the ServerFinished message. If requested, the client must respond with their own authentication messages, ClientCertificate and ClientCertificateVerify, to achieve mutual authentication. Finally, the client

---

[2] Advanced modes of the TLS 1.3 handshake can also use a pre-shared key (PSK) exchange, PSK with ephemeral key exchange, and password-based authentication.

must confirm their view of the handshake by sending a MAC over the handshake transcript in the `ClientFinished` message.

It is only after this process that the handshake is completed, and the client and server can derive the keying material required by the record layer to exchange application data protected with authenticated encryption.

2.2 PQTLS: Signed Post-quantum TLS 1.3

A variety of specifications, implementations and experiments explain how to integrate post-quantum cryptography into the TLS 1.3 handshake. Regarding the post-quantum key exchange phase of TLS 1.3 (without addressing post-quantum authentication), several Internet-Drafts are proposed [13,19,31,37,42], as well as some experimental demonstrations [9,21,23,24]. On the other hand, fewer works have focused on post-quantum authentication. In [18,35], the authors recommended that the adoption of at least two post-quantum signature algorithms is viable for the TLS 1.3 handshake.

There are no theoretical obstacles for transitioning TLS 1.3 to a post-quantum world. One can use post-quantum signature algorithms for authentication and the (EC-)DH key exchange can be replaced by a post-quantum KEM; we call this approach PQTLS.

In practice, however, this replacement is not so simple. CAs must adapt their software to include post-quantum signatures, and, historically, the Web Public Key Infrastructure (PKI) and other X.509 PKIs have limited which algorithms can be used. It could take a long time until new algorithms are widely deployed. These changes may occur in the future but, for the purpose of experimentation and rapid deployment, these issues become limitations.

We propose a practical approach for overcoming this problem. Specifically, we rely on a delegation mechanism for credentials. A Delegated credential (DC) is an authenticated credential valid for a short period (at most 7 days) that can be used to decouple the handshake authentication algorithm from the authentication algorithms used in the certificate chain: a delegated credential can contain an algorithm to be used in the handshake and, in turn, it is cryptographically bound to the end-entity certificate as it is authenticated by it. The process of authenticating the DC is executed at the TLS stack level.

Using DCs in itself does not give us full post-quantum security, but it allows us to support post-quantum authentication algorithms that are not supported by existing CAs. An existing certificate is used to authenticate this delegated credential (by signing in a classical way in our experiments), and the advertised algorithm in the DC is used to authenticate the handshake.[3] The Internet

---

[3] Authentication is as strong as its weakest link, so until the entire certificate chain has post-quantum security we do not have a fully post-quantum authenticated protocol. However, the approach suffices for the purpose of our experiments.

Engineering Task Force (IETF) draft describing this technique, "Delegated Credentials for TLS" [4], is on track for standardization.[4]

Using delegated credentials comes with other advantages for our cases. Unlike a regular certificate, a delegated credential is smaller and has no other extensions, such as revocation lists and certificate statuses, which makes it a perfect fit for experiments where the size of parameters is important. Also, DCs are validated only at the TLS stack level, which reduces the number of codebases or systems where we needed to roll out new algorithms.

If full post-quantum security is wanted, the whole certificate chain will need to contain post-quantum algorithms. A peer wanting to authenticate another peer with its certificate (and the public key in it) in the TLS 1.3 handshake requires confidence that the associated private key is owned by the certificate owner's peer. This confidence is obtained through the use of public key certificates that bind these values to an identity. A CA signs certificates after asserting proof of possession of the private key. If the peer does not hold the public key of the CA that signed the other peer's certificate, then it might need an additional certificate to obtain that public key. These certificates are called 'intermediates'.

For a client to authenticate a server it uses this chain of certificates: a root CA's one, followed by at least one intermediate CA certificate, and then the leaf certificate of the server. Certificates can be cached, pre-installed or suppressed, which means that less data needs to be transmitted during the handshake; but these mechanisms are not widely deployed. In turn what this means is that for a full post-quantum TLS 1.3 handshake, peers will need to transmit the whole certificate chain and verify all their authentication proofs (at least three signatures or other proofs of authentication). If a DC is used in this scenario, data transmitted is increased, as well of the number of authentication operations.

2.3 KEMTLS: KEMs Everywhere

Using post-quantum signatures for authentication comes with another challenge. The proposed signature schemes participating in the NIST post-quantum competition have public keys or signatures much larger than their classical counterparts. For most algorithms, this size increase for post-quantum signatures is bigger than for post-quantum KEMs. The large size of cryptographic material can become an issue in the PQTLS scenario.

KEMTLS suggests the use of KEMs as the primary asymmetric building block for both the key exchange and authentication phases of the TLS 1.3 handshake. Its goal is to achieve a TLS 1.3 handshake that provides full post-quantum security (confidentiality and authentication) in an efficient way. KEMs instead of signatures are used for authentication because the KEM's public keys and ciphertexts are smaller.

---

[4] While it is stated in the draft that the DC signature algorithm *"is expected to be the same as the sender's Certificate Verify.algorithm"*, this is not a hard requirement, and in KEMTLS the Certificate Verify messages are not sent.

Like in PQTLS, the client advertises their support of post-quantum KEMs as part of the `supported_groups` extension, and their supported ephemeral KEM public keys as part of their `key_shares` extension. Support for KEMTLS authentication, via KEM leaf certificates or DCs with KEMs, is indicated by including KEMs in the `signature_algorithms` extension.

The server, in turn, determines the appropriate cryptographic parameters to be used in the connection, and replies with a ciphertext: an encapsulation against one of the advertised ephemeral KEM public keys of the `ClientHello` message. The encapsulation generates a second output: an unauthenticated ephemeral shared secret. From this point onward, all subsequent messages will be encrypted under the secret, after applying the appropriate key schedule operations. The server also sends its certificate chain (`ServerCertificate` message): the leaf certificate (or DC) should advertise a post-quantum KEM public key. Optionally, the server can send a `CertificateRequest` message, which is sent prior to the `ServerCertificate` message, asking the client to authenticate.

Contrary to TLS 1.3, the server cannot provide explicit proof of possession (using digital signatures) of the private key corresponding to the public key advertised as part of the leaf certificate (or DC). Instead, in KEMTLS, the client must receive the `ServerCertificate` message first, and reply with the encapsulation of the public key advertised in it. This encapsulation (a ciphertext) is sent as part of a new TLS message called `ClientKEMCiphertext`. The KEMTLS handshake diverges from the TLS 1.3 standard, as the server must wait for this message adding another flight or half round-trip to the protocol.

The second output of the client key encapsulation is an implicitly authenticated shared secret. This secret is mixed into the key schedule operations and will afterwards be used to encrypt all subsequent messages. Only the intended server can decrypt any messages encrypted under this key. By being able to do so, the server proves possession of the private key corresponding to the public key in it's certificate. If the server did not request client authentication (server-only authentication), the client can immediately send their `ClientFinished` message in this flight, which contains a MAC over the entire transcript. The client can also send at this point application data, which is implicitly authenticated, and has slightly weaker downgrade resilience and forward secrecy compared to when digital signatures are used.

When receiving the `ClientKEMCiphertext` message and decapsulating their parameters, the server can send their confirmation message `ServerFinished`, authenticating the handshake transcript. In the same flight, the server can now send application data encrypted by the shared secret of the decapsulation mechanism. Once the client receives and verifies the `ServerFinished` message, the server is explicitly authenticated, and the handshake has full downgrade resilience and strong forward secrecy.

Ciphersuite Negotiation and Middlebox Compatibility. TLS 1.3 allows clients and servers to negotiate the used algorithms. For key exchange, the supported algorithms are advertised in the `supported_groups` extension. For authentication, the mandatory `signature_algorithms` extension contains a list of algorithms that can be used by the peer to pick the appropriate certificate advertised by the corresponding peer. Post-quantum KEMs can simply be added to these lists and negotiated accordingly.

Any compliant TLS 1.3 implementation that does not understand or wish to negotiate KEMTLS will simply ignore any advertised post-quantum KEMs for the key exchange, and will not send a leaf certificate (or DC) with a KEM public key. As all messages following ServerHello are encrypted, changes in the protocol should be opaque to any non-decryption traffic interception; otherwise, a barrier on its adoption will be observed, similar to the "Middlebox" issues that arose when moving from TLS 1.2 to TLS 1.3 [20,38]. Issues may still arise if traffic interception servers enforce stricter constraints on key sizes than those required by the TLS 1.3 standard; these kinds of issues are harder to control.

Mutual Authentication. TLS 1.3 requires that *"the client's identity should be protected against both passive and active attackers"* [29, Sec. E.1]. Thus, both TLS 1.3 and KEMTLS cannot send the client's certificate (its identity) before the server has been authenticated. In TLS 1.3, the client can authenticate to the server, after receiving a request to do so from it, by providing its certificate and a signature over the handshake transcript.

In the sketch of client authentication in KEMTLS [33, App. C], upon request from the server, the client responds with the ClientCertificate message, where the leaf certificate (or DC) must contain a post-quantum KEM public key. This message must be sent in the same flight as when the ClientKEMCiphertext message is sent (but after it). In turn, the server sends the ServerKEMCiphertext message containing an encapsulation against the client certificate's KEM public key after processing the ClientKEMCiphertext and ClientCertificate messages. The client must wait for a ServerKEMCiphertext message from the server prior to sending their ClientFinished or any other message. Therefore, the client proves their identity by showing that both sides can arrive to the same shared key: the output of the encapsulation of the client's public key sent in the leaf certificate (or DC). Finally, once the server receives the ClientFinished, it can send ServerFinished, which achieves full downgrade resilience and forward secrecy.

The straightforward addition of these messages adds a round-trip to the handshake, as they can not be sent until the server has been authenticated. This extra round does not occur in the TLS 1.3 handshake because an explicit proof of authentication (the signature) is sent in the same flight as the certificate.

For a practical instantiation for our experiments, we use classically signed DCs that wrap KEM public keys to provide certified KEM keys.

2.4 KEMTLS-PDK: Reducing Round Trips

KEMTLS-PDK is a technique that relies on pre-distributed keys and has the goal of improving KEMTLS round-trips. It assumes the client knows the server's public key beforehand. This is not an uncommon situation as, for example, web browsers cache certificates of frequently accessed servers, mobile apps pin certificates, or server certificates are pre-distributed through DNS [17].

During the handshake, servers can authenticate earlier to the client, when KEM authentication keys are pre-distributed. We implement this mechanism using the TLS cached information extension[5] [30], so the client sends an encapsulation against the server's public KEM key in the first flight (alongside the `ClientHello` message: either as a separate message or as an extension for it). This allows the server to be explicitly authenticated by sending `ServerFinished` in the first message to the client and to immediately send application data.

On the other hand, the situation is more complex for achieving earlier client authentication since the client has to *proactively know* that the server will ask for its authentication. Nonetheless, this assumption does occur in certain applications such as in virtual private networks (VPN), where the client could send the certificate as early as possible.

Recall that for privacy reasons, TLS 1.3 requires that the server must be authenticated prior to transmitting the client certificate, and that this certificate must be sent encrypted. For the former requirement, KEMTLS-PDK assumes the client knows the server's certificate so it is sent after the `ClientKEMCiphertext` message in the first flight (as a separate message from the `ClientHello` one). For the latter requirement, the client certificate is encrypted under the shared secret resulting from the encapsulation mechanism used for `ClientKEMCiphertext`. Thus, it is possible to remove a full round-trip from KEMTLS with mutual authentication.

Early client authentication can be secured by caching a `CertificateRequest` message using the TLS cached information extension. The client certificate will then contain a key with an authentication algorithm that is likely known to be supported by the server. However, further investigation is needed for coming with a mechanism to encrypt the client's certificate.

3   Implementation Details

3.1   Implementation in Go

Go is a high-level programming language with support for the TLS protocol (including version 1.3). Its standard library is open, which allowed us to made modifications to its internals without requiring third-party libraries. While Go is well-known for developing web server applications, it also has mechanisms to interact with low-level features of the computer architecture. This is particularly useful for accessing architecture-specific capabilities, which are only available through assembler code.

Some implementations of post-quantum algorithms are available. The teams currently contending at the ongoing NIST's post-quantum competition provide implementations in C/C++. The Open-Quantum Safe [36] project wraps C implementations to run in Go through the cgo programming interface. However, performance degradation in it can be observed due to this wrapping procedure. The CIRCL [10] library implements a number of post-quantum algorithms natively in

---

[5] This extension is only available for TLS 1.2, so we adapted it to be used in TLS 1.3.

Go, including SIDH and SIKE [16]. As part of our contributions, we integrate to the CIRCL library AVX2-optimized implementations of the Dilithium signature scheme (round 2) and the Kyber key encapsulation mechanism.

Go provides a clean implementation of TLS 1.3. However, the implementation is conservative in regards to the type of extensions and algorithms that it supports. Changing the TLS 1.3 implementation to include delegated credentials and PQTLS required including some extensions and adding certain algorithm identifiers. It also meant adding a way for generating and validating delegated credentials, as well as adding the ability to include the delegated credentials X.509 extension to generated certificates. We also added the cached information extension [30] and modified it to work with TLS 1.3 for KEMTLS-PDK.

Integrating KEMTLS and KEMTLS-PDK was more challenging. Doing so required the interruption of the handshake's flow depending on whether there is cached information, whether it is server-only authentication, or whether it is mutual authentication. As noted, the flow of messages in KEMTLS and KEMTLS-PDK is different depending on the authentication modes: server-only, mutual or with cached information. This differs from the standard TLS 1.3 handshake that follows the same flow of messages regardless if server-only or mutual authentication is performed. These differences were an important lesson learned during our implementation as it was often a source of errors.

We made available all of these modifications in a fork of Go at https://github. com/cloudflare/go/tree/cf-pq-kemtls. This code integrates CIRCL and can be used as a replacement of the standard Go to compile other Go programs. Hence, anyone wanting to use post-quantum algorithms or the new handshake protocols can benefit from our code by compiling programs with our modified Go.

3.2 A Testbed Network

To test and measure TLS connections, we looked for a service that operates under common Internet conditions and spans across different geographical locations. We chose Drand [40], a distributed randomness beacon written in Go, as the target of our experimentation. In this network, Drand servers are linked so they can collectively produce publicly-verifiable random numbers at fixed intervals of time. A threshold signature scheme prevents collusion or biasing the generation of numbers. Nodes in the network communicate with one another using a gRPC protocol [26] with TLS authentication. Additionally, the Drand service exposes public randomness through an HTTPS endpoint.

Changes in the Drand code base are minimal. We needed to provide and configure a certificate with the DCs extension enabled for servers and clients. We also needed to state which protocol will be initiated (KEMTLS or PQTLS) by stating so at the TLS configuration level. If KEMTLS-PDK wanted to be used, a "regular" KEMTLS handshake is first run, information is cached (the ServerCertificate message), and then cached information is used in a fresh KEMTLS-PDK handshake by configuring it at the TLS configuration level. We added those configuration options for ease of experimentation: in a more realistic scenario stating which key exchange and signature algorithms are supported should be enough to trigger the appropriate protocol execution.

At run time, fresh delegated credentials are generated each time that a request arrives. However, these credentials can be further cached and stored so they can be reused between connections. A mechanism that routinely checks the validity of these credentials can also be implemented. This shows that delegated credentials can be easily implemented and used without needing to constantly modify certificate storage or retrieval. It is worth noting that adding delegated credentials increases the number of validations that need to be executed: the certificate has to be validated, the delegated credential has to be validated and the handshake has to be validated.

4   Measurement Experiment and Discussion

The goal of our experiment is to analyze the effects on the TLS handshake when using post-quantum algorithms. To do that, we measure the time it takes for a TLS 1.3 handshake using certificate-based authentication to complete, and compare all experiments to this standard measure.

4.1   Experiment Setup

We build a Drand cluster with one leader node and three worker peers. Each node independently ran in a data center located in Portland, USA. The connection of each internal node and the external HTTPS interface are configured to support post-quantum handshake protocols.

A Drand client retrieves randomness from the Drand network. We opted for locating the client far from the Drand network itself, so it is located in Lisbon, Portugal. With this setup our experiment faces the same traffic conditions found in transatlantic connections. Source codes of the client program are available at https://github.com/claucece/KEMTLS-local-measurements.

We choose a combination of cryptographic algorithms for setting up the following handshake configurations:

TLS 1.3 handshake using Ed25519 certificates for authentication (baseline).

TLS 1.3+DC handshake with Ed25519 certificate and delegated credentials either using Ed25519 or Ed448 algorithms for authentication.

PQTLS handshake with SIKEp434 and Kyber512 for key exchange, and hybrid signatures using round-two Dilithium mode 3 and mode 4, respectively, paired with Ed25519 and Ed448 for authentication (the authentication algorithms are advertised in DCs).

KEMTLS handshake with SIKEp434 and Kyber512 for both key exchange and authentication (the authentication algorithms are advertised in DCs).

KEMTLS-PDK handshake using the same configuration as KEMTLS (server authentication only).

4.2   Measurements

For each client to server connection, we measured the time elapsed until completion of the TLS handshake, that is until the client can send encrypted application data, for each different handshake configuration. We also measured the elapsed time for each flight of the handshake, i.e., the time elapsed that a peer (server or client) waits for receiving messages from their counterpart. We initiated two timers: one for the client (which started when the CH message was constructed and sent) and one for the server (which started when the CH message is received). Therefore, the first and second flight, as seen in the tables, do not include network latency, as the timer is started prior to the message being sent or just when it is received, respectively. Note that the round trip times (RTT) from the third flight onward are affected by the conditions of the state of the network. We tested the scenarios over an average-latency network.

To reduce the effects caused by the state of the network, the Drand client was instructed to fetch randomness from the Drand server consecutively during one hour. The total number of connections during this period amounts to approximately 5×10^3 connections. From them, we calculated the average time of the connections and report the timings in Table 1 and Table 2. We also measured the total average time until the handshake is completed (note that these times include the sending and receiving of encrypted application data). These measures are listed in Table 3 and Table 4.

In server-only authentication, the handshake performs the following flights:

1st ($C \Rightarrow S$) Sending ClientHello for all cases.
KEMTLS-PDK: this message includes the ClientKEMCiphertext message, and a hash of the cached server's ServerCertificate message.
2nd ($C \Leftarrow S$) Processing of ClientHello.
Standard and PQTLS: reply with the ServerHello, ServerCertificate, ServerCertificateVerify and ServerFinished messages.
KEMTLS: reply with the ServerHello and ServerCertificate.
KEMTLS-PDK: reply with the ServerHello and ServerFinished messages.
3rd ($C \Rightarrow S$) Processing of received messages based on the protocol.
Standard and PQTLS: processing of ServerHello, ServerCertificate, ServerCertificateVerify and ServerFinished messages.
Reply with ClientFinished and immediate sending of encrypted application data.
KEMTLS: processing of ServerHello and ServerCertificate. Reply with ClientKEMCiphertext and ClientFinished messages and immediate sending of encrypted application data.
KEMTLS-PDK: processing of ServerHello and ServerFinished messages. Reply with ClientFinished and immediate sending of encrypted application data.
4th ($C \Leftarrow S$) Processing of received messages based on the protocol.
Standard and PQTLS: processing of ClientFinished message and of encrypted application data.

KEMTLS: processing of `ClientKEMCiphertext` and `ClientFinished` messages. Reply with `ServerFinished` message.
KEMTLS-PDK: processing of `ClientFinished` message and of encrypted application data.

In mutual authentication, the handshake performs the following flights:

1st $(C \Rightarrow S)$ Sending `ClientHello` for all cases.
2nd $(C \Leftarrow S)$ Processing of `ClientHello`.
Standard and PQTLS: reply with the `ServerHello`, `ServerCertificate`, `ServerCertificateVerify`, `CertificateRequest` messages followed by the `ServerFinished` message.
KEMTLS: reply with the `ServerHello`, the `ServerCertificate` and the `CertificateRequest` messages.
3rd $(C \Rightarrow S)$ Processing of received messages based on the protocol.
Standard and PQTLS: processing of `ServerHello`, `ServerCertificate`, `ServerCertificateVerify`, `CertificateRequest` messages followed by the `ServerFinished` message.
Reply with the `ClientCertificate`, the `ClientCertificateVerify` and the `ClientFinished` messages, and immediate sending of encrypted application data.
KEMTLS: processing of the `ServerHello`, the `ServerCertificate` and the `CertificateRequest` messages.
Reply with `ClientKEMCiphertext` and `ClientCertificate` messages.
4th $(C \Leftarrow S)$ Processing of received messages based on the protocol.
Standard and PQTLS: processing of the received `ClientCertificate`, `ClientCertificateVerify` and `ClientFinished` messages, and received encrypted application data.
KEMTLS: processing of `ClientKEMCiphertext` and `ClientCertificate` messages. Reply with `ServerKEMCiphertext` message.
5th $(C \Rightarrow S)$ This case only happens in KEMTLS. It includes the processing of `ServerKEMCiphertext` message and sending of the `ClientFinished` message. Immediate sending of encrypted application data.
$(C \Leftarrow S)$ This case only happens in KEMTLS. It includes the processing of `ClientFinished` message and any application data. Sending of the `ServerFinished` message.

4.3   Discussion

As noted, we initiated two timers for our measurements: one for the client (which started when the CH message was constructed and sent) and one for the server (which started when the CH message is received). This is the reason why the first and second flights see small timings as they do not take into account network latency. Starting from the third flight, the impact of network latency can be seen. An important point to note as well is that encrypted application data is sent already on the 3rd flight of all experiments except for KEMTLS for mutual

Table 1. Average time in 10^{-3} s of messages for server-only authentication. Note that timings are measured per-client and per-server: each one has its own timer. The 'KEX' label refers to the Key Exchange and the 'Auth' label refers to authentication.

Handshake	KEX	Auth	Handshake flight			
			1st	2nd	3rd	4th
TLS 1.3	X25519	Ed25519	0.227	0.436	123.838	180.202
TLS 1.3+DC	X25519	Ed25519	0.243	0.489	156.954	186.868
TLS 1.3+DC	X25519	Ed448	0.242	0.907	165.395	183.124
PQTLS	Kyber512	Dilithium3	0.350	0.701	173.814	198.256
PQTLS	SIKEp434	Dilithium4	2.533	4.856	441.732	212.924
KEMTLS	Kyber512	Kyber512	0.412	0.217	157.123	187.147
KEMTLS	SIKEp434	SIKEp434	3.058	7.215	352.840	291.592
KEMTLS-PDK	Kyber512	Kyber512	0.623	0.327	181.132	189.442
KEMTLS-PDK	SIKEp434	SIKEp434	9.573	12.507	396.818	287.550

authentication (as the client has to wait two flights in order to be able to send application data), which can increase the timing numbers.

When adding delegated credentials to the TLS 1.3 handshake, a peer receiving a delegated credential must validate that it was signed by the appropriate end-entity certificate (which is sent as part of the handshake) and must validate the certificate chain, as well. In our measurements, we observed a short increase in the latency of the flights when DCs are added; but the impact is almost negligible (specially, in the second flight when the DCs are received).

This is not the case when adding either post-quantum signatures or post-quantum KEMs for certain algorithms. The first observable difference appears in the ClientHello in both server-only authentication and mutual authentication: this message advertises both classic and post-quantum key exchange algorithms because this could be the realistic scenario for systems when transitioning to post-quantum cryptography. The timings increase specially when using SIKEp434 as a KEM in both KEMTLS and PQTLS, because its KEM decapsulation time takes in average 8.92 ms (when using the implementation of the CIRCL library). The predominant factor that slows down PQTLS is the number of signature validations; but this is similar (when using Kyber512) to using Ed448.

In regards to KEMTLS, its biggest drawback is the number of round-trips that it has to perform, specially when performing mutual authentication. The KEM cryptographic operations do not seem to heavily impact the connection if the underlying algorithm operations are fast. An ideal scenario for post-quantum cryptography is the use of KEMs for both confidentiality and authentication provided that the number of round trips do not increase, which is the case of KEMTLS-PDK for server authentication. This prediction matches with the

Table 2. Average time in 10^{-3} s of messages for mutual authentication. Note that timings are measured per-client and per-server: each one has its own timer. The 'KEX' label refers to the Key Exchange and the 'Auth' label refers to authentication.

Handshake	KEX	Auth	Handshake flight					
			1st	2nd	3rd	4th	5th	6th
TLS 1.3	X25519	Ed25519	0.113	0.420	111.358	121.349		
TLS 1.3+DC	X25519	Ed25519	0.148	0.546	129.638	178.90		
TLS 1.3+DC	X25519	Ed448	0.154	0.221	137.131	192.283		
PQTLS	Kyber512	Dilithium3	0.125	1.326	231.232	191.187		
PQTLS	SIKEp434	Dilithium4	3.324	7.294	459.888	216.077		
KEMTLS	Kyber512	Kyber512	0.244	0.303	231.752	175.490	375.202	346.308
KEMTLS	SIKEp434	SIKEp434	2.450	6.206	431.445	228.414	510.591	436.301

timings in tables: note that the best scenario is KEMTLS-PDK for server-only authentication, specifically, when it is used with Kyber512.

Let's look now at the measurements in regards to the kind of peer authentication they perform:

In the case of server-only authentication, KEMTLS performs faster than PQTLS and, in both cases, a client can immediately send application data on the third flight (when the client sends its ClientFinished). Nevertheless, for KEMTLS the server still has to wait for the ClientFinished to arrive and to send their ServerFinished in turn, in order to be able to send application data. Sending of the ServerFinished completes the handshake for the server, and provides full downgrade-resilience and forward-secrecy for the whole connection. However, this extra half-round trip forces the server to wait for a time before sending application data, which could not be an ideal scenario for real-world systems. In contrast, the client can send application data after sending their ClientFinished (as noted in the measurements) but it has weaker security protections (weak downgrade-resilience and forward-secrecy), and, therefore, a client might also wait until receiving the ServerFinished message to send its data in turn. This adds an extra round-trip which is not noted in the measurements. If we look at Fig. 1, we see that the best protocol to use is KEMTLS, if we don't take into consideration that application data sent at that point has weaker security properties. The ideal case is using KEMTLS-PDK which allows the sending of application data much earlier and with the stronger notions of the security properties.

For mutual authentication, KEMTLS has the biggest impact on the handshake completion timings, as an extra flight is needed prior to be able to send encrypted application data, as seen in Fig. 1. SIKEp434, on average, increases the handshake timings by approximate 10ms compared with Kyber512 for the verification of the peer's Certificate in both cases. For this reason, the PQTLS completion time is also slowed down when using SIKEp434 even without the extra round-trip addition. Although, we do not provide timings for the KEMTLS-

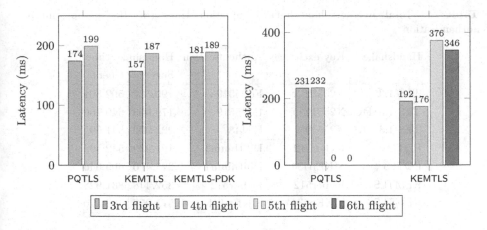

Fig. 1. Comparison of: on the left, server authentication flows for the 3rd, and 4th flights; on the right, mutual authentication flows for the 5th and 6th flights. Both using Kyber512.

Table 3. Total average handshake completion time (in 10^{-3} s) for server-only authentication.

Handshake	Key Exchange	Authentication	Handshake time	
			Server	Client
TLS 1.3	X25519	Ed25519	187.296	552.518
TLS 1.3+DC	X25519	Ed25519	197.568	578.097
TLS 1.3+DC	X25519	Ed448	220.576	614.366
PQTLS	Kyber512	Dilithium3	199.025	556.203
PQTLS	SIKEp434	Dilithium4	219.401	634.546
KEMTLS	Kyber512	Kyber512	200.237	792.168
KEMTLS	SIKEp434	SIKEp434	277.304	901.292
KEMTLS-PDK	Kyber512	Kyber512	209.872	583.582
KEMTLS-PDK	SIKEp434	SIKEp434	200.126	561.068

PDK handshake with mutual authentication, our timings can provide an insight about the cost of the operations and the relevance of the algorithm selection.

4.4 Optimizations

The cost of transmitting post-quantum parameters is tangible in our measurements. These costs can be further optimized by using a form of certificate compression [12] or of suppression of the intermediate certificates [41]. Still, the costs of post-quantum operations needed remains.

Table 4. Total average handshake completion time (in 10^{-3} s) for mutual authentication.

Handshake	Key exchange	Authentication	Handshake time	
			Server	Client
TLS 1.3	X25519	Ed25519	190.587	592.801
TLS 1.3+DC	X25519	Ed25519	179.653	549.760
TLS 1.3+DC	X25519	Ed448	222.902	541.695
PQTLS	Kyber512	Dilithium3	191.939	542.599
PQTLS	SIKEp434	Dilithium4	223.470	609.646
KEMTLS	Kyber512	Kyber512	352.448	881.928
KEMTLS	SIKEp434	SIKEp434	571.057	1096.708

5   Conclusions

Our experimental results are the first ones that integrate different post-quantum handshake alternatives to the TLS 1.3 handshake into a real-world system. These results have shown us how post-quantum algorithms can impact the handshake completion time, and, therefore, impact the establishment of real-world connections. In general, on the reliable network that we used, the different post-quantum TLS 1.3 handshake alternatives do not have a handshake completion time that is ostensibly different to a regular TLS 1.3 handshake. The only somewhat exception to this is KEMTLS, as the extra half or full round trip that is added does increase the completion time. For this reason, it is vital to think more in depth around KEMTLS-PDK, as it could reduce the completion time.

In this paper, we dive into the implementation of post-quantum algorithms in native Go language, adapt different handshake configurations and modify TLS extensions, and we explore the deployment of a test bed distributed network for enabling measurements. As a result, we developed a measurement framework that allows to perform transatlantic post-quantum TLS 1.3 connections for retrieving random numbers from a Drand network.

We remark that an important piece to achieve crypto-agility on the transition to post-quantum algorithms is the use of delegated credentials. They allowed us to advertise post-quantum KEMs or post-quantum signatures without generating new certificates or asking certificate authorities to support new algorithms.

Future work can involve increasing the number of connections tested, modifying the latency of the network, and testing with more post-quantum algorithms; we intend to continue our experiments. We further can extend our experiments to implement KEMTLS-PDK with mutual authentication, but more investigation is needed to determine the security requirements for encrypting the `ClientCertificate` message. Another interesting topic for further investigation lies around on how to properly integrate post-quantum algorithms into certificate chains and experiment with certificate authorities.

Acknowledgements. Authors wish to thank Latincrypt's reviewers for their useful suggestions. A special mention to Jonathan Hoyland for reviewing an early version of this document. Thom Wiggers was supported during this work by the European Commission through the ERC Starting Grant 805031 (EPOQUE). Goutam Tamvada was supported by the Natural Sciences and Engineering Research Council of Canada (NSERC) Discovery grant RGPIN-2016-05146.

References

1. Adrian, D., et al.: Imperfect forward secrecy: how Diffie-Hellman fails in practice. In: Proceedings of the 22nd ACM SIGSAC Conference on Computer and Communications Security, CCS 2015, pp. 5–17. Association for Computing Machinery, New York (2015). https://doi.org/10.1145/2810103.2813707
2. Arai, K., Matsuo, S.: Formal verification of TLS 1.3 full handshake protocol using proverif (Draft-11). IETF TLS mailing list (2016). https://mailarchive.ietf.org/arch/msg/tls/NXGYUUXCD2b9WwBRWbvrccjjdyI
3. Aviram, N., et al.: DROWN: breaking TLS using SSLv2. In: 25th USENIX Security Symposium (USENIX Security 2016), pp. 689–706. USENIX Association, Austin, August 2016. https://www.usenix.org/conference/usenixsecurity16/technical-sessions/presentation/aviram
4. Barnes, R., Iyengar, S., Sullivan, N., Rescorla, E.: Delegated credentials for TLS. Internet-Draft draft-ietf-tls-subcerts-10, Internet Engineering Task Force, January 2021. https://datatracker.ietf.org/doc/html/draft-ietf-tls-subcerts-10. Work in Progress
5. Bernstein, D.J.: Curve25519: new Diffie-Hellman speed records. In: Yung, M., Dodis, Y., Kiayias, A., Malkin, T. (eds.) PKC 2006. LNCS, vol. 3958, pp. 207–228. Springer, Heidelberg (2006). https://doi.org/10.1007/11745853_14
6. Beurdouche, B., et al.: A messy state of the union: taming the composite state machines of TLS. In: 2015 IEEE Symposium on Security and Privacy, pp. 535–552 (2015). https://doi.org/10.1109/SP.2015.39
7. Braithwaite, M.: Experimenting with post-quantum cryptography. Google Security Blog, Google Online Security, July 2016. https://security.googleblog.com/2016/07/experimenting-with-post-quantum.html. Accessed 16 Feb 2021
8. Campagna, M., Crockett, E.: Hybrid post-quantum key encapsulation methods (PQ KEM) for transport layer security 1.2 (TLS). Internet-Draft draft-campagna-tls-bike-sike-hybrid-06, Internet Engineering Task Force, March 2021. https://datatracker.ietf.org/doc/html/draft-campagna-tls-bike-sike-hybrid-06. Work in Progress
9. Crockett, E., Paquin, C., Stebila, D.: Prototyping post-quantum and hybrid key exchange and authentication in TLS and SSH. In: Second PQC Standardization Conference, University of California, Santa Barbara, August 2019. https://csrc.nist.gov/Presentations/2019/prototyping-post-quantum-and-hybrid-key-exchange
10. Faz-Hernández, A., Kwiatkowski, K.: Introducing CIRCL: An Advanced Cryptographic Library. Cloudflare, Inc, June 2019. https://blog.cloudflare.com/introducing-circl/. Accessed Feb 2021
11. Feman, R.C., Willis, T.: Securing the web, together. Google Security Blog, March 2016. https://security.googleblog.com/2016/03/securing-web-together_15.html. Accessed 16 May 2021

12. Ghedini, A., Vasiliev, V.: TLS Certificate Compression. RFC 7924, RFC Editor, December 2020. https://doi.org/10.17487/RFC8879
13. Hoyland, J., Wood, C.: TLS 1.3 extended key schedule. Internet-Draft draft-jhoyla-tls-extended-key-schedule-03, Internet Engineering Task Force, December 2020. https://datatracker.ietf.org/doc/html/draft-jhoyla-tls-extended-key-schedule-03. Work in Progress
14. Hülsing, A., Rijneveld, J., Schanck, J., Schwabe, P.: High-speed key encapsulation from NTRU. In: Fischer, W., Homma, N. (eds.) CHES 2017. LNCS, vol. 10529, pp. 232–252. Springer, Cham (2017). https://doi.org/10.1007/978-3-319-66787-4_12
15. Iyengar, J., Thomson, M.: QUIC: A UDP-Based Multiplexed and Secure Transport. RFC 9000, May 2021. https://doi.org/10.17487/RFC9000
16. Jao, D., et al.: SIKE. Technical report, National Institute of Standards and Technology (2020). https://csrc.nist.gov/projects/post-quantum-cryptography/round-3-submissions
17. Josefsson, S.: Storing Certificates in the Domain Name System (DNS). RFC 4398, RFC Editor, March 2006. https://doi.org/10.17487/RFC4398
18. Kampanakis, P., Sikeridis, D.: Two post-quantum signature use-cases: non-issues, challenges and potential solutions. In: 7th ETSI/IQC Quantum Safe Cryptography Workshop 2019, November 2019. https://eprint.iacr.org/2019/1276
19. Kiefer, F., Kwiatkowski, K.: Hybrid ECDHE-SIDH Key Exchange for TLS. Internet-Draft draft-kiefer-tls-ecdhe-sidh-00, Internet Engineering Task Force, May 2019. https://datatracker.ietf.org/doc/html/draft-kiefer-tls-ecdhe-sidh-00. Work in Progress
20. Kumar, D., et al.: Security challenges in an increasingly tangled web. In: Barrett, R., Cummings, R., Agichtein, E., Gabrilovich, E. (eds.) Proceedings of the 26th International Conference on World Wide Web, WWW 2017, Perth, Australia, 3–7 April 2017, pp. 677–684. ACM (2017). https://doi.org/10.1145/3038912.3052686
21. Kwiatkowski, K., Langley, A., Sullivan, N., Levin, D., Mislove, A., Valenta, L.: Measuring TLS key exchange with post-quantum KEM. University of California, Santa Barbara, August 2019. https://csrc.nist.gov/Presentations/2019/measuring-tls-key-exchange-with-post-quantum-kem
22. Lamik, M.: Introducing Cloudflare Radar. The Cloudflare Blog, September 2020. https://blog.cloudflare.com/introducing-cloudflare-radar. Accessed 16 May 2021
23. Langley, A.: CECPQ2. ImperialViolet, December 2018. https://www.imperialviolet.org/2018/12/12/cecpq2.html. Accessed 16 Feb 2021
24. Langley, A.: Real-world measurements of structured-lattices and supersingular isogenies in TLS. ImperialViolet, October 2019. https://www.imperialviolet.org/2019/10/30/pqsivssl.html. Accessed 16 Feb 2021
25. Lyubashevsky, V., et al.: CRYSTALS-DILITHIUM. Technical report, National Institute of Standards and Technology (2020). https://csrc.nist.gov/projects/post-quantum-cryptography/round-3-submissions
26. Marculescu, M.: Introducing gRPC, a new open source HTTP/2 RPC framework. Google Developers, February 2015. https://developers.googleblog.com/2015/02/introducing-grpc-new-open-source-http2.html
27. National Institute of Standards and Technology: Post-Quantum Cryptography Standardization, January 2017. https://csrc.nist.gov/projects/post-quantum-cryptography/post-quantum-cryptography-standardization. Accessed 16 May 2021
28. Prest, T., et al.: FALCON. Technical report, National Institute of Standards and Technology (2020). https://csrc.nist.gov/projects/post-quantum-cryptography/round-3-submissions

29. Rescorla, E.: The Transport Layer Security TLS Protocol Version 1.3. RFC 8446, RFC Editor, August 2018. https://doi.org/10.17487/RFC8446
30. Santesso, S., Tschofenig, H.: Transport Layer Security (TLS) Cached Information Extension. RFC 7924, RFC Editor, July 2016. https://doi.org/10.17487/RFC7924
31. Schanck, J.M., Stebila, D.: A Transport Layer Security (TLS) Extension For Establishing An Additional Shared Secret. Internet-Draft draft-schanck-tls-additional-keyshare-00, Internet Engineering Task Force, April 2017. https://datatracker.ietf.org/doc/html/draft-schanck-tls-additional-keyshare-00. Work in Progress
32. Schanck, J.M., Whyte, W., Zhang, Z.: Quantum-Safe Hybrid (QSH) Ciphersuite for Transport Layer Security (TLS) version 1.2. Internet-Draft draft-whyte-qsh-tls12-02, Internet Engineering Task Force, January 2017. https://datatracker.ietf.org/doc/html/draft-whyte-qsh-tls12-02. Work in Progress
33. Schwabe, P., Stebila, D., Wiggers, T.: Post-quantum TLS without handshake signatures. In: Ligatti, J., Ou, X., Katz, J., Vigna, G. (eds.) ACM CCS 2020: 27th Conference on Computer and Communications Security, pp. 1461–1480. ACM Press, Virtual Event, 9–13 November 2020. https://doi.org/10.1145/3372297.3423350
34. Schwabe, P., Stebila, D., Wiggers, T.: More efficient post-quantum KEMTLS with pre-distributed public keys (2021). https://eprint.iacr.org/2021/779
35. Sikeridis, D., Kampanakis, P., Devetsikiotis, M.: Post-quantum authentication in TLS 1.3: a performance study. In: ISOC Network and Distributed System Security Symposium - NDSS 2020. The Internet Society, San Diego, 23–26 February 2020
36. Stebila, D., Mosca, M.: Post-quantum Key exchange for the internet and the open quantum safe project. In: Avanzi, R., Heys, H. (eds.) SAC 2016. LNCS, vol. 10532, pp. 14–37. Springer, Cham (2017). https://doi.org/10.1007/978-3-319-69453-5_2
37. Steblia, D., Fluhrer, S., Gueron, S.: Hybrid key exchange in TLS 1.3. Internet-Draft draft-ietf-tls-hybrid-design-03, Internet Engineering Task Force, April 2021. https://datatracker.ietf.org/doc/html/draft-ietf-tls-hybrid-design-03. Work in Progress
38. Sullivan, N.: Why TLS 1.3 isn't in browsers yet. The Cloudflare Blog, December 2017. https://blog.cloudflare.com/why-tls-1-3-isnt-in-browsers-yet/. Accessed 15 April 2021
39. Sullivan, N.: A detailed look at RFC 8446 (a.k.a. TLS 1.3). The Cloudflare Blog, August 2018. https://blog.cloudflare.com/rfc-8446-aka-tls-1-3/. Accessed 16 February 2021
40. Syta, E., et al.: Scalable bias-resistant distributed randomness. In: 2017 IEEE Symposium on Security and Privacy (SP), pp. 444–460 (2017). https://doi.org/10.1109/SP.2017.45. https://drand.love
41. Thomson, M.: Suppressing intermediate certificates in TLS. Internet-Draft draft-thomson-tls-sic-00, Internet Engineering Task Force, March 2019. https://datatracker.ietf.org/doc/html/draft-thomson-tls-sic-00. Work in Progress
42. Whyte, W., Zhang, Z., Fluhrer, S., Garcia-Morchon, O.: Quantum-Safe Hybrid (QSH) Key Exchange for Transport Layer Security (TLS) version 1.3. Internet-Draft draft-whyte-qsh-tls13-06, Internet Engineering Task Force, October 2017. https://datatracker.ietf.org/doc/html/draft-whyte-qsh-tls13-06. Work in Progress

A Monolithic Hardware Implementation of Kyber: Comparing Apples to Apples in PQC Candidates

Mojtaba Bisheh-Niasar[1]([✉]), Reza Azarderakhsh[1,2],
and Mehran Mozaffari-Kermani[3]

[1] Department of Computer and Electrical Engineering and Computer Science,
Florida Atlantic University, Boca Raton, FL, USA
{mbishehniasa2019,razarderakhsh}@fau.edu
[2] PQSecure Technologies, LLC, Boca Raton, FL, USA
[3] Department of Computer Science and Engineering, University of South Florida,
Tampa, FL, USA
mehran2@usf.edu

Abstract. With the advent of large-scale quantum computers, factoring
and discrete logarithm problems could be solved using the polynomial-
time quantum algorithms. To ensure public-key security, a transition to
quantum-resistant cryptographic protocols is required. Performance of
hardware accelerators targeting different platforms and diverse application goals plays an important role in PQC candidates' differentiation.
Hardware accelerators based on FPGAs and ASICs also provide higher
flexibility to create a very low area or ultra-high performance implementations at the high cost of the other. While the hardware/software co-
design development of PQC schemes has already received an increasing
research effort, a cost analysis of efficient pure hardware implementation
is still lacking. On the other hand, since FPGA has various types of hardware resources, evaluating and making the accurate and fair comparison
of hardware-based implementations against each other is very challenging. Without a common foundation, apples are compared to oranges.
This paper demonstrates a pure hardware architecture for Kyber as one
of the finalists in the third round of the NIST post-quantum cryptography standardization process. To enable real, realistic, and comparable
evaluations in PQC schemes over hardware platforms, we compare our
architecture over the ASIC platform as a common foundation showing
that it outperforms the previous works in the literature.

Keywords: ASIC · Hardware architecture · Kyber · Lattice-based
cryptography · NTT · Post-quantum cryptography

1 Introduction

The hard problems of traditional public-key cryptosystems, e.g., RSA and ECC,
can be easily solved using Shor's algorithm [1], so current cryptographic algorithms cannot be secure anymore against quantum attacks. To prepare for

© Springer Nature Switzerland AG 2021
P. Longa and C. Ràfols (Eds.): LATINCRYPT 2021, LNCS 12912, pp. 108–126, 2021.
https://doi.org/10.1007/978-3-030-88238-9_6

security concerns caused by building large-scale quantum computers, in 2016, the National Institute of Standards and Technology (NIST) started the post-quantum cryptography (PQC) standardization process for the quantum-safe cryptographic algorithm. After several rounds, NIST announced finalist candidates in July 2020, including four key encapsulation mechanisms (KEM), i.e., Classic-McEliece, Kyber, NTRU, and Saber. The majority of the finalists are based on lattice-based cryptography offering a high-performance scheme and relatively small ciphertext and key sizes. Kyber KEM [2] is one of the PQC finalists, which is constructed on the hardness of the module learning-with-errors problem (M-LWE) in module lattices [3].

Performance of hardware accelerators plays an important role in the NIST standardization process because the overall complexity of the winner schemes will have to be minimal to be implemented in widely-deployed cryptosystems [4]. As a consequence, hardware benchmarking of PQC candidates is crucial considering the advantages of hardware-based designs to exploit parallelism, which leads to improvements in the efficiency of the overall system. While software (SW) implementations for embedded systems have more flexibility than hardware-based approaches, they have a lower performance. Hardware/Software (HW/SW) co-design approaches increase the performance but keeping the flexibility of a SW solution to cope with embedded constraints. Although the HW/SW approach offers flexibility and a shorter design cycle than pure HW schemes, they may not lead to the best performance. Simultaneously, pure hardware implementation of PQC schemes is extremely challenging due to their high algorithmic complexity, considering both algorithmic and architectural alternatives, and also the lack of hardware description language libraries for the basic building blocks.

An accurate and fair comparison between hardware accelerators is very challenging. One of the main challenges is they target different optimization perspectives, including performance, required resources, power consumption, and energy usage. To address this challenge, one can consider efficiency as an area-time product for a comprehensive comparison. Additionally, another challenge for a fair comparison is that most HW/SW designs proposed a unified core for several schemes [5–7]. Therefore, there appear to be very few hardware implementations that focus only on a specific scheme and make the best of all its features. Moreover, the comparisons are too complicated and cannot indicate the advantage of one architecture over another, especially when they do not belong to the same platform. NIST's recommendation to use the Xilinx Artix-7 FPGA family for hardware prototyping is in an effort to improve the accuracy of comparison in the same chip architecture family. Nevertheless, the effect of different resources, e.g., DSPs and BRAMs, has not been taken into consideration in the calculation of the total area. Consequently, ASIC results can be chosen as a benchmark to have a fair comparison with existing implementations with respect to efficiency.

In this paper, we propose a monolithic hardware implementation, including polynomial sampling, NTT, and point-wise multiplication, that is parallelized by virtue of the Kyber algorithm that is naturally parallelizable to accelerate

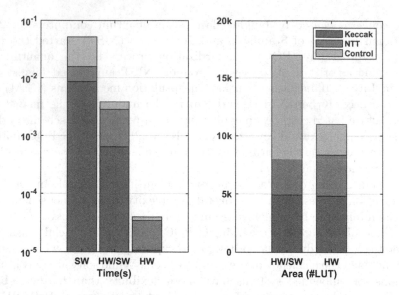

Fig. 1. Performance (in $\log_{10}$) and resource utilization comparison in three different Kyber-512 implementation approaches: software (SW), hardware/software (HW/SW), and hardware (HW). Kyber architecture is breakdown into three main cores, including Keccak (hashing and sampling), NTT (polynomial multiplication), and Control (controller and all other required functions).

lattice-based PQC exploiting fewer resources. The efficiency of our proposed PQC implementation has performance levels comparable to or even significantly better than ECC-based schemes [8–10].

The first hardware implementation of Kyber was proposed in [11] employing the high-level synthesis (HLS) approach. In this work, the authors designed a map of high-level C specifications of round 2 candidates into FPGA and ASIC implementations. Although some dedicated optimizations, particularly for Kyber, are applied, the results are significantly less efficient from other hardware-based implementations. The authors in [5] presented a configurable core based on RISC-V architecture over ASIC targeting power consumption optimization. To provide FPGA results, the authors extended their work in [12]. In [6], another RISC-V accelerator called RISQ-V was introduced synthesized for an FPGA prototype and an ASIC. The authors in [7] proposed a lightweight design for NewHope and Kyber based on the RISC-V processor integrated with a finite field multiplier for FPGA. A vector processor was proposed in [13] for ASIC implementations targeting a high-performance architecture. The first pure hardware implementation of Kyber is reported in [14] based on RTL methodology in FPGA. The work of [15] also presented a pure hardware approach for Kyber. However, this design heavily relies on memory units between components. Moreover, a compact architecture was proposed in [16] to reduce the required block RAMs. In [17], the authors proposed a highly optimized NTT core to achieve significant speedup for Kyber KEM. The hardware architecture for polynomial multiplication targeting Kyber parameters has been studied by several implementations [18–21]; however, these architectures cannot perform the complete Kyber protocols.

Figure 1 illustrates the comparison between different development approaches, i.e., SW, HW/SW, and HW implementations of Kyber KEM based on the required time and resources. The reported cycle counts for SW implementation in [22–24] show 60–80% of the overall computation time is spent on hashing and sampling. Thus, Keccak is the most performance-critical part of SW implementation. However, this core can be accelerated in a hardware architecture since Keccak is a hardware-friendly design of SHA. For HW/SW co-design approach, a wide range of results was reported for polynomial multiplication. While the work of [13] occupied 55% of the total area for vectorized NTT core, in [6], only 12% of resources were utilized for NTT. Additionally, implementing a software-based processor, e.g., RISC-V architecture, increases the occupied resources for the controller in HW/SW compared to the HW approach. For example, the controller requires 31% and 71% of total resources in [5] and [6], respectively. However, in pure HW implementation of lattice-based PQC, the controller cost was reduced to 5% [25]. Accordingly, the pure HW can significantly accelerate the Kyber KEM by parallelizing NTT and hiding the Keccak latency on the one hand, and reduces the required resources compared to HW/SW approach on the other hand.

1.1 Contributions

Polynomial multiplication computations take a significant portion of Kyber KEM latency on hardware implementation. To improve the efficiency of Kyber, one should increase efficiency on the NTT core, providing higher throughput using fewer hardware resources. This paper proposes an efficient hardware implementation of the module lattice-based post-quantum KEM CRYSTALS-Kyber on the application-specific integrated circuit (ASIC) platform. Our proposed architecture provides a monolithic hardware implementation to accelerate lattice-based PQC exploiting compact resources. The contributions of this paper are itemized in the following:

1. We propose a compact hardware architecture for NTT and INTT, supporting both decimation-in-frequency (DIF) and decimation-in-time (DIT) NTT algorithms. Our proposed reconfigurable architecture avoids utilizing additional resources for the same computations while reduces the pre-processing cost of NTT and post-processing cost of INTT. The proposed architecture significantly reduces the overall area and memory consumption with no impact on performance.
2. We highly parallelize the operations in polynomial sampling cores through tightly coupling with Keccak core to decrease the required cycles. The performance of proposed parallel scheduling for binomial sampler indicates a significant improvement, while our rejection sampler latency can be completely absorbed by the Keccak core.

3. We propose a high-performance coprocessor architecture for lattice-based public-key cryptography with Kyber KEM as a case study. Our result utilizes the proposed high-speed NTT core and outperforms all reported implementations by reducing the total time.

The rest of the paper is organized as follows. In Sect. 2, we discuss the preliminaries of lattice-based cryptography and the relevant mathematical background based on the Kyber algorithm. In Sect. 3, our proposed algorithms and architectures for implementing a high-performance Kyber KEM are discussed. We discuss our results and compare them to the counterparts in Sect. 4. Finally, we conclude the paper in Sect. 5.

2   Preliminaries

In this section, employed notation, Kyber protocols and relevant mathematical background are briefly described.

2.1   Symbol Definition

In this paper, to make the paper more readable, regular font lower-case letters (a) shows polynomials, bold lower-case letters $(\mathbf{a})$ determines vectors of polynomials, bold upper-case letters $(\mathbf{A})$ indicates matrices of polynomials, and their NTT-domain representation are referred by $(\hat{a})$, $(\hat{\mathbf{a}})$ and $(\hat{\mathbf{A}})$, respectively. For a vector $\mathbf{a}$ (or matrix $\mathbf{A}$), its transpose is $\mathbf{a}^T$ (or $\mathbf{A}^T$). Also, the lower-case Greek letters ρ, σ, and μ stand for random bit-strings. The polynomial ring $\mathcal{R}_q = \mathbb{Z}_q[X]/(X^n+1)$ is defined over the field of $\mathbb{Z}_q = \mathbb{Z}/q\mathbb{Z}$ in which n is the dimension and q is the prime modulo. Let $\mathbf{a}$ and $\mathbf{b}$ be polynomial vectors in $\mathcal{R}_q$, we denote point-wise multiplication by $\mathbf{a} \circ \mathbf{b} \in \mathcal{R}_q$. The $\circ$ product between a matrix and a vector is the natural generalization of point-wise multiplication between their polynomial vectors.

2.2   The Kyber Protocol

Kyber is an IND-CCA secure KEM [26], including three algorithms, i.e., key generation, encryption, and decryption. In key generation, a matrix $\mathbf{A}$ and a secret key $\mathbf{s}$ are sampled from a uniform and binomial distribution, respectively. Then a public key is computed by multiplication between $\mathbf{A}$ and $\mathbf{s}$ in the NTT domain and adding noise to the product. In encryption, a message m should be added to the product of the public key and a sampled random $\mathbf{r}$ in the normal domain to generate a vector v. Additionally, another polynomial multiplication is performed between $\mathbf{r}$ and uniform distribution matrix $\hat{\mathbf{A}}$ to compute matrix $\mathbf{u}$. The encryption output, called ciphertext ct, is composed of compression of $\mathbf{u}$ and v, while the message can then be decrypted by recovering an approximation of v by computing the product of secret key and $\mathbf{u}$.

Table 1. Parameter sets for Kyber Implementation [2]

Algorithm	NIST-Level	Parameters					Size (in Bytes)		
		n	k	q	(η_1, η_2)	(d_u, d_v)	Secret key (sk)	Public key (pk)	Ciphertext (ct)
Kyber-512	1 (AES-128)	256	2	3,329	(3, 2)	(10, 3)	1,632	800	768
Kyber-768	3 (AES-192)	256	3	3,329	(2, 2)	(10, 4)	2,400	1,184	1,088
Kyber-1024	5 (AES-256)	256	4	3,329	(2, 2)	(11, 5)	3,168	1,568	1,568

All polynomials in the Kyber scheme have 256 coefficients over k-dimensional vectors, where $k = 2, 3, 4$ indicates the three different post-quantum security levels. Kyber parameter sets corresponding to these levels are reported in Table 1 to construct a Chosen Plaintext Attack (CPA) secure public-key encryption scheme. Moreover, a CCA-secure Kyber KEM can be constructed using an adapted Fujisaki-Okamoto transformation [27]. For details, we refer interested readers to [2].

2.3 Polynomial Multiplication

The most important operation in lattice-based cryptography is polynomial multiplication, which can be performed using different methods, e.g., NTT or schoolbook polynomial multiplication algorithm. Polynomial multiplication in NTT domain can be computed efficiently over a polynomial ring $\mathbb{Z}_q[X]/\langle X^n + 1 \rangle$ when the modulus provides m-th primitive roots of unity for a sufficiently high power of two m (ideally, $m = 2n$ or $m = n$). The NTT is defined as a fast Fourier transform (FFT) in a finite field. Let f be a polynomial of degree n, where $f = \sum_{i=0}^{n-1} f_i X^i$ and $f_i \in \mathbb{Z}_q$, and ω_n be n-th primitive root of unity such that $\omega_n^n = 1 \bmod q$. The forward NTT is defined by $\hat{f} = NTT(f)$, such that:

$$\hat{f}_i = \sum_{j=0}^{n-1} f_j \omega_n^{ij} \bmod q \tag{1}$$

The inverse NTT, shown by INTT, as a back transformation form NTT domain to normal domain is shown by $f = INTT(\hat{f})$, such that:

$$f_i = n^{-1} \sum_{j=0}^{n-1} \hat{f}_j \omega_n^{-ij} \bmod q \tag{2}$$

Accordingly, a polynomial multiplication between polynomial vectors f and g employing NTT and INTT results in a polynomial vector which can be performed such that:

$$f \cdot g = \text{INTT}(\text{NTT}(f) \circ \text{NTT}(g)) \tag{3}$$

To avoid the overhead of zero padding in the polynomial multiplication over $\mathbb{Z}_q[X]/\langle X^n + 1 \rangle$, the negative wrapped convolution (NWC) was proposed in

[28] at the cost of pre-processing of NTT and post-processing of INTT. Let $\psi = \sqrt{\omega_n}$ be a primitive $2n$-th root of unity. Pre-processing of NTT includes multiplication between the coefficients of the input polynomials and ψ^i, while the post-processing of INTT is multiplication between the coefficients of the output polynomial and ψ^{-i}.

However, the work of [29] merged the pre-processing of NTT into butterfly operations. The work of [30] presented an algorithm to avoid the post-processing overhead of INTT. The KRED reduction algorithm was proposed in [31] to accelerate the NTT and reduce the post-processing overhead of INTT. NTT computation can be implemented by Cooley-Turkey (CT) [32] or Gentleman-Sande (GS) [33] butterfly configuration. Employing the CT as NTT and the GS as INTT [31,34] is a well-known trick in the literature to avoid the bit-reverse permutation.

Algorithm 1 presents the NTT computation. Figure 2 illustrates an 8-point NTT-based multiplication employing both CT and GS butterfly operations. The matrix-vector multiplication $\hat{\mathbf{A}} \circ \hat{\mathbf{s}}$ in NTT domain for Kyber-512 is shown in (4).

$$\hat{\mathbf{A}} \circ \hat{\mathbf{s}} = \begin{bmatrix} \hat{\mathbf{A}}_{00} & \hat{\mathbf{A}}_{01} \\ \hat{\mathbf{A}}_{10} & \hat{\mathbf{A}}_{11} \end{bmatrix} \circ \begin{bmatrix} \hat{\mathbf{s}}_0 \\ \hat{\mathbf{s}}_1 \end{bmatrix} = \begin{bmatrix} \hat{\mathbf{A}}_{00} \circ \hat{\mathbf{s}}_0 + \hat{\mathbf{A}}_{01} \circ \hat{\mathbf{s}}_1 \\ \hat{\mathbf{A}}_{10} \circ \hat{\mathbf{s}}_0 + \hat{\mathbf{A}}_{11} \circ \hat{\mathbf{s}}_1 \end{bmatrix} \tag{4}$$

A point-wise multiplication includes 128 multiplications of polynomial of degree 2 modulo $X^2 - \zeta^{2\text{br}_7(i)+1}$. For example, multiplication between two coefficients $\hat{\mathbf{A}}_{j,i} \circ \hat{\mathbf{s}}_i$ can be performed as shown in (5) where $\zeta = 17$ is the first primitive 256-th root of unity modulo q, and br_7 is the bit reversal function.

$$\begin{aligned} &(\hat{a}_{j,2i} + \hat{a}_{j,2i+1}X) \cdot (\hat{s}_{2i} + \hat{s}_{2i+1}X) \\ &= (\hat{a}_{j,2i}\hat{s}_{2i} + \hat{a}_{j,2i+1}\hat{s}_{2i+1}\zeta^{2\text{br}_7(i)+1}) \\ &+ (\hat{a}_{j,2i}\hat{s}_{2i+1} + \hat{a}_{j,2i+1}\hat{s}_{2i})X \quad (\text{mod } X^2 - \zeta^{2\text{br}_7(i)+1}) \end{aligned} \tag{5}$$

3 Proposed Architecture

In this section, the proposed components to design a high-performance and efficient Kyber KEM are described.

3.1 Keccak Core

Keccak core is required in KEM to compute four different functions, including two hash functions SHA3-256 and SHA3-512, SHAKE-128 as an extendable output function (XOF), and SHAKE-256 as a pseudo random function (PRF) and key-derivation function (KDF). Keccak is a hardware-oriented design based on bit-oriented operations. Since we compute 24 rounds for Keccak-f[1600], various architectures can be employed considering different optimization perspectives, i.e., high-performance, lightweight, or anything in between. In our proposed high-performance core, we slightly modify the implementation of the high-speed core by the Keccak team [36] by designing a serial-in parallel-out (SIPO) buffer in

Algorithm 1. Iterative In-Place NTT Algorithm Based on Cooley-Tukey Butterfly [35]

Input: a polynomial $a(x) \in \mathbb{Z}_q[X]/(X_n + 1)$, n-th primitive root of unity $\omega_n \in \mathbb{Z}_q$, $n = 2^l$
Output: $\hat{a}(x) = \mathrm{NTT}_{\omega_n}(a) \in \mathbb{Z}_q[X]/(X_n + 1)$
1: $\hat{a} \leftarrow$ bit-reverse(a)
2: **for** ($i = 1$; $i < l$; $i++$) **do**
3:    $m = 2^{l-i}$
4:    $\omega_m \leftarrow \omega_n^{n/m}$
5:    **for** ($j = 0$; $j < n$; $j = j + m$) **do**
6:       $\omega \leftarrow 1$
7:       **for** ($k = 0$; $k < m/2$; $k++$) **do**
8:          $T \leftarrow \omega \cdot \hat{a}[k + j + m/2] \bmod q$
9:          $U \leftarrow \hat{a}[k + j]$
10:        $\hat{a}[k + j] = U + T \bmod q$
11:        $\hat{a}[k + j + m/2] = U - T \bmod q$
12:        $\omega \leftarrow \omega \cdot \omega_m \bmod q$
13:      **end for**
14:    **end for**
15: **end for**
16: **return** $\hat{a}(x)$

Table 2. Failure probabilities in Kyber rejection sampling for performing different Keccak rounds

Total round	Keccak outputs (bit)	Total samples	Required valid sample	Failure probability
3	4,032	336	256	0.0083
4	5,376	448	256	2.2E−32
5	6,720	560	256	2.3E−79

input and parallel-in serial-out (PISO) buffer for accelerating the data transition with this core. The serial data width for these buffers is set to 64-bit, and the parallel line is 1344-bit. A maximum of 21 cycles is needed to read/write to/from these buffers in serial mode, while the Keccak sponge function takes 24 cycles. Therefore, data transforming can be hidden by simultaneously performing Keccak computation without resource conflict and data dependency to reduce clock cycles.

3.2 Rejection Sampling

This unit takes 64-bit data from the output of SHAKE-128 stored in a PISO buffer. The required cycles for this unit are variable due to the non-deterministic pattern of rejection sampling. Since the public key computed by rejection sampling is not secret, the SCA countermeasure against timing attack is not required. Nevertheless, since most SCA evaluation methods, e.g., t-test, can be performed

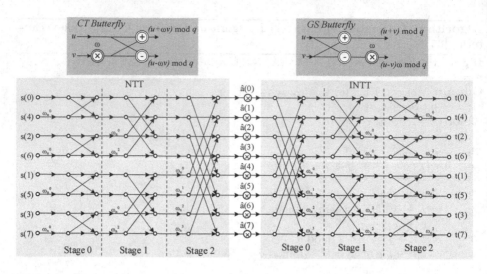

Fig. 2. An 8-point NTT-based polynomial multiplication. Dataflow graph includes CT butterfly-based NTT, point-wise multiplication, and GS butterfly-based INTT. Polynomial $\hat{a}$ is in NTT domain and s and t are in normal domain.

on a constant-time design, we perform constant rounds of SHAKE-128 to form a constant-time implementation. While 112 samples can be evaluated by rejection unit for each round of Keccak core, the failure probability that 256 valid coefficients can be sampled by performing different rounds of SHAKE-128 is listed in Table 2. As a result, four rounds are performed for each required vector of **A** while the failure probability is negligible. In our optimized architecture, this unit works in parallel with the Keccak core. Therefore, the latency for rejection sampling is completely absorbed within the latency for a concurrently running Keccak core. An alternative approach is to sample directly on the Keccak state; however, this approach increases the complexity of hardware-based architecture.

3.3   Binomial Sampling

There are two different configurations for binomial sampling unit corresponding to $\eta = 2$ and $\eta = 3$. We propose an optimized configurable architecture that can compute the Hamming weight for both values of η. To support both architectures, the data from PISO is buffered in a 96-bit register, of which only 64-bit is utilized in $\eta = 2$. The results are in $[-\eta, \eta]$ are presented in 13-bit signed representation to simplify the addressing. Our proposed binomial sampling architecture for two first sampled data is depicted in Fig. 3.

3.4   Configurable Butterfly Core

To avoid the bit-reverse cost in polynomial multiplication, two different butterfly configurations, i.e., CT and GS, are required for NTT and INTT, respectively.

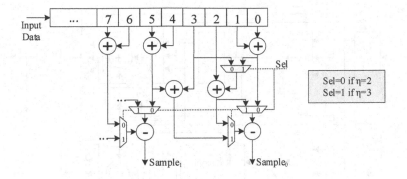

Fig. 3. Proposed configurable binomial sampling unit.

In our proposed architecture, a configurable butterfly core is proposed to support both CT and GS operations and reduce required hardware resources. In order to design a high-performance architecture, the resource sharing technique from [5,37] is extended by using compact storage for pre-computed twiddle factors from [35] and doubled bandwidth scheme from [18,30].

Since CT configuration is used in NTT, we assume that the input polynomials are in normal order, while the public and secret keys are in bit-reverse order. Hence, the point-wise multiplication works in bit-reverse order in the NTT domain, and the results are transformed back to the normal domain with normal order employing GS configuration. We take advantage of the NTT definition in the Kyber scheme to perform two independent NTT computations for odd and even coefficients based on (6) and (7).

$$\hat{a}_{2i} = \sum_{j=0}^{127} a_{2j} \zeta^{(2i+1)j} \tag{6}$$

$$\hat{a}_{2i+1} = \sum_{j=0}^{127} a_{2j+1} \zeta^{(2i+1)j} \tag{7}$$

Two butterfly cores are employed in parallel for NTT computation to reduce execution time to $\frac{N}{2} \log_2 \frac{N}{4}$. Each line of RAM block stores two consecutive coefficients, i.e., $s_{i,2j}$ and $s_{i,2j+1}$, in two columns to feed both butterfly cores. Reading from two addresses of memory provides four coefficients, i.e., $s_{i,2j}$ and $s_{i,2j+1}$ from address j, and $s_{i,2k}$ and $s_{i,2k+1}$ from address k of memory. The lower columns storing the even coefficients, i.e., $s_{i,2j}$ and $s_{i,2k}$, are used for the first butterfly, while the higher columns including the odd coefficients, i.e., $s_{i,2j+1}$ and $s_{i,2k+1}$, are fed into the second core. The results should be stored similarly in the second RAM.

Our proposed NTT architecture includes five different main modules: two RAM blocks, an address generator (working in three modes for NTT, INTT, and point-wise multiplication), a pre-computed twiddle factor ROM, and an

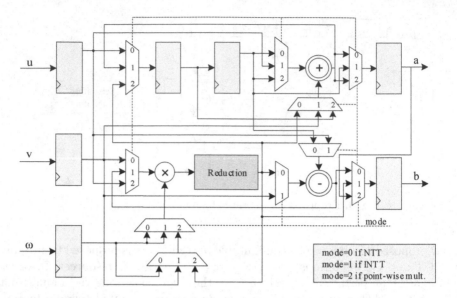

Fig. 4. Proposed configurable butterfly architecture.

arithmetic unit. The dual-port capabilities of the RAM blocks are exploited in our proposed design to increase efficiency. Moreover, the address generator computes the two read and write addresses to load and store the required coefficients as well as the corresponding address for the twiddle factor in each operation.

The arithmetic unit consists of a multiplier, a modular reduction, an addition, and a subtraction, while there are also some registers to balance the pipeline latency in different configurations. The proposed architecture is depicted in Fig. 4. Different reduction units have been studied in the literature. While Barrett reduction works in the normal domain, Montgomery reduction needs more resources and latency to perform the transformation into and out of the Montgomery domain. The proposed architecture employing Barrett reduction is implemented in a pipelined fashion to increase the throughput to 1 output per cycle.

3.5 Area/Performance Trade-Offs

The main goal of the proposed architecture is to achieve high-speed computation employing small area requirements. However, we can target different area/performance trade-offs by increasing the number of butterfly cores, taking advantage of polynomial vector structure in the Kyber algorithm. For example, in Kyber-512 having 2 polynomial vectors, increasing the number of implemented butterfly core from 2 to 4 can drastically reduce to a half of NTT/INTT latency. Nevertheless, implementing more arithmetic units needs higher bandwidth. In this case, the number of occupied RAM blocks will be doubled while they are implemented in parallel to provide the required bandwidth.

Table 3. Implementation results for Kyber KEM on 65-nm ASIC

Protocol	Area		Freq [MHz]	Cycles			Total time† [μs]
	Logic gates [kGE]	SRAM [kB]		KeyGen [CCs]	Encaps [CCs]	Decaps [CCs]	
Kyber-512	95	10	200	4,267	6,769	10,015	83.9
Kyber-768	93	22	200	6,641	9,683	13,569	116.3
Kyber-1024	104	24	200	9,971	13,278	17,676	154.8

† Total time includes Encaps + Decaps, as the key generation can be done offline.

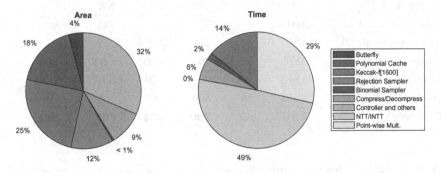

Fig. 5. Area breakdown (left) and time breakdown (right) during encapsulation of Kyber-512.

4   Implementation Results And Comparisons

Our proposed architecture is synthesized using a 65-nm TSMC cell library [38] to show the required area. VHDL has been used as the design entry to the Synopsys Design Compiler [38]. In addition, using the area of a NAND gate in the utilized 65-nm library, which is 1.35 μm², we have provided the gate equivalent (GE) so that area comparisons among different technologies are meaningful. Although similar to the previous work presented in [13], we have not fabricated a chip on silicon, our detailed results are intended for benchmarking the metrics for the previous and proposed research works. All the designs are synthesized with a 5 ns clock period.

Table 3 reports the required hardware resources and latency specifications for our proposed architecture in three different security levels. The total time is the summation of key encapsulation and key decapsulation (Encaps + Decaps), as the key generation can be done offline. We implement 2, 3, and 4 of our proposed NTT architecture for security levels 1, 3, and 5, respectively. As one can see, for NIST level 1 security, our proposed architecture occupies 95 kGE, and 10 kB SRAM. It also runs at 200 MHz and performs the whole Kyber protocol in 83.9 μs.

The area breakdown of our design and the latency breakdown in encapsulation of Kyber-512 is illustrated in Fig. 5. Our proposed Keccak, butterfly, and sampling units utilize 4%, 25%, and 13% of the total area. For reporting latency breakdown, when the butterfly is parallel with other units, the latency is consid-

Table 4. Comparisons with existing hardware-based implementations of NTT for Kyber KEM.

Work	Platform	Tech [nm]	Freq [MHz]	NTT [CCs]	INTT [CCs]	Point-wise Mult. [CCs]
Karabulut et al. [19]	Virtex-7	–	NA	43,756	NA	NA
Alkim et al. [7]	Artix-7	–	59	6,868	6,367	2,395
Chen et al. [18]	Artix-7	–	130	2,055	NA	7,197
Huang et al. [15]	Artix-7	–	155	1,834	NA	NA
Bisheh-Niasar et al. [17]	Artix-7	–	222	324	324	NA
Fritzmann et al. [21]	ASIC	65	25	2,056	NA	NA
Fritzmann et al. [6]	ASIC	65	45	1,935	1,930	NA
Banerjee et al. [5]	ASIC	40	72	1,289	NA	NA
Xin et al. [13]	ASIC	28	300	41	NA	NA
This work	**ASIC**	**65**	**200**	**474**	**602**	**1,289**

ered for NTT or point-wise multiplication. As one can see, the more expensive operation from a resource utilization point of view in Kyber KEM is Keccak core. However, using the compact version of Keccak core results in more delay in sampling units which reduces the total efficiency. In the timing breakdown, the point-wise multiplication and NTT are the first two time-consuming operations. It should be noted that although Kyber reduces the number of required stages for NTT computation from 8 stages to 7, the special form of multiplication in this scheme increases the computation overhead in point-wise multiplication.

Table 4 reports area and latency specifications for our NTT architecture which works in three different modes, i.e., NTT and INTT, and point-wise multiplication. Other state-of-the-art NTT designs for the Kyber scheme over hardware platforms are also listed. We report the results for both Kyber parameters in the previous rounds and round-3, i.e., $q = 3329$ and $q = 7681$, respectively.

Our results show a significant improvement requiring only 474, 602, and 1,289 clock cycles for NTT, INTT, and point-wise multiplication, respectively. We presented a highly optimized FPGA-based NTT core in our previous work [17] which shows 31% NTT performance improvement at the cost of occupying a 2×2 butterfly units. The work in [6] optimized an NTT core based on hardware/software approach over RISC-V architecture, while it works at 45 MHz on the ASIC platform. Our architecture results in 4× and 18× speedup in terms of required cycles and time for NTT computation, respectively. The works in [19] and [7] also presented an NTT architecture over RISC-V, which requires considerably greater cycle count, while our optimized design achieves 92× and 49× speedup, respectively. The FPGA-based design was proposed in [15] employing Montgomery reduction; however, our design reduces the required cycles achieving a speedup factor of 3.9. Our design also improves almost 6.7× and 8.6× the required latency for NTT and point-wise multiplication, respectively. In [5],

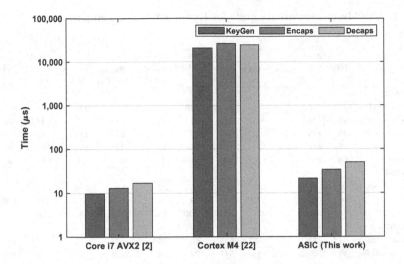

Fig. 6. Comparisons with other software implementations of Kyber-512.

a RISC-V-based architecture proposed working at 72 MHz over a 40-nm ASIC platform. Our proposed architecture achieves 7.5× better timing results compared to this work. The work of [13] employed the vectorized architecture at the cost of utilizing 521 kGE. Although the proposed architecture in [13] shows 17.3× speedup, it consumes 137× more resources compared to our design.

Figure 6 depicts the comparison of timing results for our proposed architecture and software implementations of Kyber on a mainstream desktop Intel Core i7 CPU with the optimization of AVX2 and an embedding Cortex-M4 CPU. The Core i7 CPU works at 3,492 MHz, while the results for the Discovery board are reported in 24 MHz. As one can see, our proposed ASIC architecture is 2.8× slower than Intel core [2]. However, ours achieves more than 600× speedup compared to [22]. Nevertheless, this speedup is not surprising since HW significantly reduces total time compared to SW employing parallel computation.

Table 5 lists the detailed resource consumption and performance results (frequency, required cycles, and execution time) of Kyber coprocessor designs for all NIST security levels. There are several hardware/software implementations targeting Kyber KEM in the literature. However, a direct comparison is not possible between the listed hardware implementations due to the varying techniques of different platforms, targeting different optimization goals, and using different design methodologies. The work in [5] implemented a configurable coprocessor based on a RISC-V architecture that can be used for multiple lattice-based schemes, including Kyber. Its architecture performs almost 263 KEM per second for Kyber-512, which is 45× slower than our design. In [6], another RISC-V-based architecture was proposed to accelerate NTT-based schemes. This design requires 23× more cycles for encapsulation and decapsulation while consuming 2.8× more resources. Additionally, in [13], a high-performance hardware architecture was proposed based on RISC-V. Nevertheless, our design achieves 5×

Table 5. ASIC Implementation results for Kyber KEM and comparison with state-of-the-art.

Work	Tech [nm]	Area		Total Area[†] [kGE]	Freq [MHz]	Latency			Total Time[‡] [µs]	$A \times T$ [GE×s]
		Logic gates [kGE]	SRAM [kB]			KeyGen [kCCs]	Encaps [kCCs]	Decaps [kCCs]		
Kyber-512										
Basu et al. [11]	65	1,341	–	3,531	200	–	–	43	–	–
Fritzmann et al. [6]	65	170	465[§]	635	45	150	193	205	8,844	5,615
Banerjee et al. [5]	40	106	40.25	547	72	75	132	142	3,806	2,081
Xin et al. [13]	28	979	12	1,131	300	19	46	80	420	475
This work	**65**	**95**	**10**	**222**	**200**	**4**	**7**	**10**	**84**	**18**
Kyber-768										
Fritzmann et al. [6]	65	170	465[§]	635	45	273	326	340	14,800	9,398
Banerjee et al. [5]	40	106	40.25	547	72	112	178	191	5,125	2,803
This work	**65**	**93**	**22**	**372**	**200**	**7**	**10**	**14**	**116**	**43**
Kyber-1024										
Fritzmann et al. [6]	65	170	465[§]	635	45	350	405	425	18,444	11,711
Banerjee et al. [5]	40	106	40.25	547	72	149	223	241	6,444	3,524
Xin et al. [13]	28	979	12	1,131	300	40	82	136	727	822
This work	**65**	**104**	**24**	**409**	**200**	**10**	**14**	**18**	**155**	**63**

[†] The total area is calculated based on the reported fabric dimension corresponding to their technology. For non-fabricated results, a rough estimation of 55% area overhead is considered for implementing SRAM similar to [39].
[‡] Total time includes Encaps + Decaps, as the key generation can be done offline.
[§] The reported numbers are in kGE.

faster KEM and improves 80% resource utilization while occupying 5× fewer area compared to [13]. An HLS evaluation was proposed in [11] for Kyber-512 employing different implementations for encapsulation and decapsulation. However, this approach comes at a considerably far larger area consumption. Hence, our design achieves almost 16 and 4.3 times better are and timing results compared to HLS-based implementation. For the other security level, the same trend can be seen.

We also illustrated a summary of comparison with other ASIC implementation of Kyber-512 in Fig. 7. For different implementations, the total time (T) and the equivalent area (A), including the required logic gates and SRAM are shown. The efficiency in terms of $A \times T$ is also computed. As one can see, our proposed design achieves better latency using significantly fewer resources. Furthermore, the proposed Kyber-512 implementation improves 312×, 116×, and 26× efficiency compared to [5,6] and [13], respectively.

The experimental result shows that taking advantage of the proposed NTT architecture to implement lattice-based KEM schemes as full-hardware architecture results in high-speed and efficient design. For Kyber KEM, our coprocessor architecture outperforms the reported implementations in the literature in terms of efficiency. Furthermore, although one of the drawbacks of various post-quantum cryptosystems is requiring larger key sizes and more computational power than the current pre-quantum algorithms, the efficiency of our proposed implementation already has performance levels comparable to or even significantly better than pre-quantum algorithms [8,9,40].

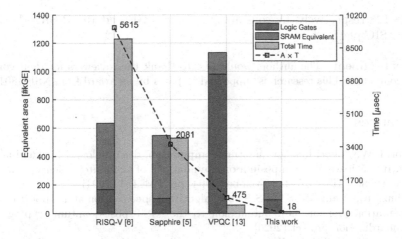

Fig. 7. Comparisons with other ASIC implementations of Kyber-512.

Table 6. Comparisons with existing FPGA-based PQC implementations of CCA-secure KEM schemes in NIST security level 1.

Protocol	Platform	Area (Gates Equivalent) or (LUTs/FFs/Slices/DSPs/BRAMs)	Freq [MHz]	Time [us]
SIKEp434 [43]	Virtex-7	12,818/18,271/5,527/195/32	249.6	8,800
Frodo-640 [44][†]	Artix-7	6,881/5,081/1,947/16/12.5	149	2,621
LightSaber [45]	ASIC	742 kGE[‡]	400	5
Kyber-512 [This work]	**ASIC**	**222 kGE**	**200**	**84**

[†] Different architectures for Encaps and Decaps are used.
[‡] The reported area is 0.38 mm² in 40 nm process.

Several performance optimizations of other PQC schemes were proposed recently [41–45]. Table 6 lists other PQC scheme results implemented on the hardware platform for NIST security level 1. Elkhatib *et al.* in [43] implemented a supersingular isogeny-based KEM performed in 8.8 ms. Howe *et al.* [44] presented a flexible FrodoKEM architecture that performs 825 and 710 encapsulations and decapsulation. The work of [45] proposed an energy-efficient architecture for Saber employing 8-level hierarchical Karatsuba, which consumes 859 and 1,075 clock cycles for encapsulation and decapsulation, respectively.

5 Conclusion

This paper proposed a high-performance and efficient architecture for NTT-based polynomial multiplication and lattice-based public-key cryptography coprocessor with Kyber KEM as a case study. We optimize the implementation of the NTT core by creating a configurable butterfly core. Besides, we propose a coprocessor architecture that can perform all KEM operations for Kyber. The proposed Kyber coprocessor architecture performs key generation, encapsulation, and decapsulation in 21.3, 33.8, and 50 μs for a security level comparable to AES-128 respectively, by consuming only 95 kGE and 10 kB SRAM, on an 65-nm ASIC platform.

Acknowledgment. The authors would like to thank the reviewers for their conservative comments. This research is supported in parts by an award from NSF 1801341.

References

1. Shor, P.W.: Algorithms for quantum computation: discrete logarithms and factoring. In: 35th Annual Symposium on Foundations of Computer Science, Santa Fe, New Mexico, USA, 20–22 November 1994, pp. 124–134 (1994)
2. Avanzi, R., et al.: CRYSTALS-Kyber: algorithm specification and supporting documentation (version 3.0). Submission to the NIST post-quantum cryptography standardization project (2020)
3. Langlois, A., Stehlé, D.: Worst-case to average-case reductions for module lattices. Des. Codes Cryptogr. **75**(3), 565–599 (2015)
4. NIST: Submission requirements and evaluation criteria for the post-quantum cryptography standardization process. National Institute of Standards and Technology (2016)
5. Banerjee, U., Ukyab, T.S., Chandrakasan, A.P.: Sapphire: a configurable cryptoprocessor for post-quantum lattice-based protocols. IACR Trans. Cryptogr. Hardw. Embed. Syst. **2019**(4), 17–61 (2019)
6. Fritzmann, T., Sigl, G., Sepúlveda, J.: RISQ-V: tightly coupled RISC-V accelerators for post-quantum cryptography. IACR Trans. Cryptogr. Hardw. Embed. Syst. **2020**(4), 239–280 (2020)
7. Alkim, E., Evkan, H., Lahr, N., Niederhagen, R., Petri, R.: ISA extensions for finite field arithmetic accelerating Kyber and NewHope on RISC-V. IACR Trans. Cryptogr. Hardw. Embed. Syst. **2020**(3), 219–242 (2020)
8. Bisheh Niasar, M., Elkhatib, R., Azarderakhsh, R., Mozaffari Kermani, M.: Fast, small, and area-time efficient architectures for key-exchange on Curve25519. In: 27th IEEE Symposium on Computer Arithmetic, ARITH 2020, Portland, OR, USA, 7–10 June 2020, pp. 72–79 (2020)
9. Bisheh Niasar, M., Azarderakhsh, R., Kermani, M.M.: Efficient hardware implementations for elliptic curve cryptography over curve448. In: Bhargavan, K., Oswald, E., Prabhakaran, M. (eds.) INDOCRYPT 2020. LNCS, vol. 12578, pp. 228–247. Springer, Cham (2020). https://doi.org/10.1007/978-3-030-65277-7_10
10. Bisheh-Niasar, M., Azarderakhsh, R., Mozaffari-Kermani, M.: Cryptographic accelerators for digital signature based on Ed25519. IEEE Trans. Very Large Scale Integr. Syst. **29**(7), 1297–1305 (2021)
11. Basu, K., Soni, D., Nabeel, M., Karri, R.: NIST post-quantum cryptography-a hardware evaluation study. IACR Cryptol. ePrint Arch. 2019, 47 (2019)
12. Banerjee, U., Ukyab, T.S., Chandrakasan, A.P.: Sapphire: a configurable cryptoprocessor for post-quantum lattice-based protocols (extended version). IACR Cryptol. ePrint Arch. 2019, 1140 (2019)
13. Xin, G., et al.: VPQC: a domain-specific vector processor for post-quantum cryptography based on RISC-V architecture. IEEE Trans. Circuits Syst. I Regul. Pap. **67-I**(8), 2672–2684 (2020)

14. Dang, V.B., Farahmand, F., Andrzejczak, M., Mohajerani, K., Nguyen, D.T., Gaj, K.: Implementation and benchmarking of round 2 candidates in the NIST post-quantum cryptography standardization process using hardware and software/hardware co-design approaches. IACR Cryptol. ePrint Arch. 2020, 795 (2020)
15. Huang, Y., Huang, M., Lei, Z., Wu, J.: A pure hardware implementation of CRYSTALS-Kyber PQC algorithm through resource reuse. IEICE Electronics Express advpub (2020)
16. Xing, Y., Li, S.: A compact hardware implementation of CCA-secure key exchange mechanism CRYSTALS-KYBER on FPGA. IACR Trans. Cryptogr. Hardw. Embed. Syst. 2021(2), 328–356 (2021)
17. Bisheh-Niasar, M., Azarderakhsh, R., Mozaffari-Kermani, M.: High-speed NTT-based polynomial multiplication accelerator for CRYSTALS-Kyber post-quantum cryptography. IACR Cryptol. ePrint Arch. 2021, 563 (2021)
18. Chen, Z., Ma, Y., Chen, T., Lin, J., Jing, J.: Towards efficient Kyber on FPGAs: a processor for vector of polynomials. In: 25th Asia and South Pacific Design Automation Conference, ASP-DAC 2020, Beijing, China, 13–16 January 2020, pp. 247–252 (2020)
19. Karabulut, E., Aysu, A.: RANTT: A RISC-V architecture extension for the number theoretic transform. In: 2020 30th International Conference on Field-Programmable Logic and Applications (FPL), pp. 26–32 (2020)
20. Mert, A.C., Karabulut, E., Öztürk, E., Savas, E., Aysu, A.: An extensive study of flexible design methods for the number theoretic transform. IEEE Trans. Comput., 1–1 (2020)
21. Fritzmann, T., Sepúlveda, J.: Efficient and flexible low-power NTT for lattice-based cryptography. In: IEEE International Symposium on Hardware Oriented Security and Trust, HOST 2019, McLean, VA, USA, 5–10 May 2019, pp. 141–150 (2019)
22. Botros, L., Kannwischer, M.J., Schwabe, P.: Memory-efficient high-speed implementation of kyber on cortex-M4. In: Buchmann, J., Nitaj, A., Rachidi, T. (eds.) AFRICACRYPT 2019. LNCS, vol. 11627, pp. 209–228. Springer, Cham (2019). https://doi.org/10.1007/978-3-030-23696-0_11
23. Alkim, E., Bilgin, Y.A., Cenk, M., Gérard, F.: Cortex-m4 optimizations for R, M LWE schemes. IACR Trans. Cryptogr. Hardw. Embed. Syst. 2020(3), 336–357 (2020)
24. Kannwischer, M.J., Rijneveld, J., Schwabe, P., Stoffelen, K.: PQM4: post-quantum crypto library for the ARM Cortex-M4 (2018)
25. Xing, Y., Li, S.: An efficient implementation of the NewHope key exchange on FPGAs. IEEE Trans. Circuits Syst. I Regul. Pap. 67-I(3), 866–878 (2020)
26. Bos, J.W., et al.: CRYSTALS-Kyber: a CCA-secure module-lattice-based KEM. In: 2018 IEEE European Symposium on Security and Privacy, EuroS&P 2018, London, United Kingdom, 24–26 April 2018, pp. 353–367 (2018)
27. Fujisaki, E., Okamoto, T.: Secure integration of asymmetric and symmetric encryption schemes. In: Wiener, M. (ed.) CRYPTO 1999. LNCS, vol. 1666, pp. 537–554. Springer, Heidelberg (1999). https://doi.org/10.1007/3-540-48405-1_34
28. Pöppelmann, T., Güneysu, T.: Towards efficient arithmetic for lattice-based cryptography on reconfigurable hardware. In: Hevia, A., Neven, G. (eds.) LATIN-CRYPT 2012. LNCS, vol. 7533, pp. 139–158. Springer, Heidelberg (2012). https://doi.org/10.1007/978-3-642-33481-8_8
29. Roy, S.S., Vercauteren, F., Mentens, N., Chen, D.D., Verbauwhede, I.: Compact ring-LWE cryptoprocessor. In: Batina, L., Robshaw, M. (eds.) CHES 2014. LNCS, vol. 8731, pp. 371–391. Springer, Heidelberg (2014). https://doi.org/10.1007/978-3-662-44709-3_21

30. Zhang, N., Yang, B., Chen, C., Yin, S., Wei, S., Liu, L.: Highly efficient architecture of NewHope-NIST on FPGA using low-complexity NTT/INTT. IACR Trans. Cryptogr. Hardw. Embed. Syst. 2020(2), 49–72 (2020)
31. Longa, P., Naehrig, M.: Speeding up the number theoretic transform for faster ideal lattice-based cryptography. In: Foresti, S., Persiano, G. (eds.) CANS 2016. LNCS, vol. 10052, pp. 124–139. Springer, Cham (2016). https://doi.org/10.1007/978-3-319-48965-0_8
32. Cooley, J., Tukey, J.W.: An algorithm for the machine calculation of complex Fourier series. Math. Comput. **19**, 297–301 (1965)
33. Gentleman, W.M., Sande, G.: Fast Fourier transforms: for fun and profit. In: American Federation of Information Processing Societies: Proceedings of the AFIPS 1966 Fall Joint Computer Conference, San Francisco, California, USA, 7–10 November 1966, pp. 563–578 (1966)
34. Pöppelmann, T., Oder, T., Güneysu, T.: High-performance ideal lattice-based cryptography on 8-bit ATxmega microcontrollers. In: Lauter, K., Rodríguez-Henríquez, F. (eds.) LATINCRYPT 2015. LNCS, vol. 9230, pp. 346–365. Springer, Cham (2015). https://doi.org/10.1007/978-3-319-22174-8_19
35. Du, C., Bai, G.: Towards efficient polynomial multiplication for lattice-based cryptography. In: IEEE International Symposium on Circuits and Systems, ISCAS 2016, Montréal, QC, Canada, 22–25 May 2016, pp. 1178–1181 (2016)
36. Bertoni, G., Daemen, J., Hoffert, S., Peeters, M., Assche, G.V.: Keccak in VHDL (2020)
37. Kuo, P.C., et al.: High performance post-quantum key exchange on FPGAs. IACR Cryptology ePrint Archive, 690 (2017)
38. Synopsys. http://Synopsys.com
39. van der Leest, V., van der Sluis, E., Schrijen, G.-J., Tuyls, P., Handschuh, H.: Efficient implementation of true random number generator based on SRAM PUFs. In: Naccache, D. (ed.) Cryptography and Security: From Theory to Applications. LNCS, vol. 6805, pp. 300–318. Springer, Heidelberg (2012). https://doi.org/10.1007/978-3-642-28368-0_20
40. Bisheh-Niasar, M., Azarderakhsh, R., Mozaffari-Kermani, M.: Area-time efficient hardware architecture for signature based on Ed448. IEEE Trans. Circ. Syst. II Express Briefs, **68**(8), 2942–2946 (2021). https://doi.org/10.1109/TCSII.2021.3068136
41. Anastasova, M., Azarderakhsh, R., Mozaffari Kermani, M.: Fast strategies for the implementation of SIKE round 3 on ARM Cortex-M4. IACR Cryptol. ePrint Arch. 2021, 115 (2021)
42. Seo, H., Anastasova, M., Jalali, A., Azarderakhsh, R.: Supersingular isogeny key encapsulation (SIKE) round 2 on ARM Cortex-M4. IACR Cryptol. ePrint Arch. 2020, 410 (2020)
43. Elkhatib, R., Azarderakhsh, R., Mozaffari Kermani, M.: Highly optimized montgomery multiplier for SIKE primes on FPGA. In: 27th IEEE Symposium on Computer Arithmetic, ARITH 2020, Portland, OR, USA, 7–10 June 2020, pp. 64–71 (2020)
44. Howe, J., Martinoli, M., Oswald, E., Regazzoni, F.: Exploring parallelism to improve the performance of frodokem in hardware. Cryptology ePrint Archive, Report 2021/155 (2021)
45. Zhu, Y., et al.: A high-performance hardware implementation of saber based on Karatsuba algorithm. IACR Cryptol. ePrint Arch. 2020, 1037 (2020)

Attribute-Based Access Control for Inner Product Functional Encryption from LWE

Tapas Pal[✉] and Ratna Dutta

Department of Mathematics, Indian Institute of Technology Kharagpur,
Kharagpur, India
tapas.pal@iitkgp.ac.in, ratna@maths.iitkgp.ernet.in

Abstract. The notion of functional encryption (FE) was proposed as a generalization of plain public-key encryption to enable a much more fine-grained handling of encrypted data, with advanced applications such as cloud computing, multi-party computations, obfuscating circuits or Turing machines. While FE for general circuits or Turing machines gives a natural instantiation of the many cryptographic primitives, existing FE schemes are based on indistinguishability obfuscation or multilinear maps which either rely on new computational hardness assumptions or heuristically claimed to be secure. In this work, we present new techniques directly yielding FE for inner product functionality where secret-keys provide access control via polynomial-size bounded-depth circuits. More specifically, we encrypt messages with respect to attributes and embed policy circuits into secret-keys so that a restricted class of receivers would be able to learn certain property about the messages. Recently, many inner product FE schemes were proposed. However, none of them uses a general circuit as an access structure. Our main contribution is designing the *first* construction for an attribute-based FE scheme in *key-policy setting* for inner products from well-studied Learning With Errors (LWE) assumption. Our construction takes inspiration from the attribute-based encryption of Boneh et al. from Eurocrypt 2014 and the inner product functional encryption of Agrawal et al. from Crypto 2016. The scheme is proved in a *stronger setting* where the adversary is allowed to ask secret-keys that can decrypt the challenge ciphertext. Doing so requires a careful setting of parameters for handling the noise in ciphertexts to enable correct decryption. Another main advantage of our scheme is that the size of ciphertexts and secret-keys *depends on the depth of the circuits* rather than its size. Additionally, we extend our construction in a much desirable *multi-input* variant where secret-keys are associated with multiple policies subject to different encryption slots. This enhances the applicability of the scheme with finer access control.

Keywords: Functional encryption · Attribute-based encryption · Inner product functional encryptions

P. Longa and C. Ràfols (Eds.): LATINCRYPT 2021, LNCS 12912, pp. 127–148, 2021.
https://doi.org/10.1007/978-3-030-88238-9_7

1   Introduction

Controlling access to encrypted data is an essential requirement in today's world of cloud computing and data privacy. Plain public-key encryption either hides the entire data or reveals nothing depending on the availability of the secret-key. In many applications of cloud computing, such all-or-nothing type encryption is insufficient. For example, we often need to embed a decryption policy into the secret-key so that only users who satisfy the policy can decrypt the cipher-text. In another scenario, we may want to issue a secret-key that can only let a user learn a specific statistical property of the encrypted data such as average or weighted sum. The notion of (key-policy) *attribute-based encryption* (ABE), introduced by [25,33], is a solution to the former example and the latter can be resolved using *inner product functional encryption* (IPFE) [1] which is a particular class of functional encryption [14]. We consider more general situation where a decryption key requires to serve the functionality of both ABE and IPFE.

To illustrate the potential of the proposed scheme we consider the following example. Suppose in a pandemic, a vaccine developing company stores some characteristics in an encrypted form of the patients who are undergoing trials of a newly created vaccine. The authority wants to issue a decryption key that can be used by selected members of the company (e.g. a specific group of scientists and the members in the board of directors). The key only decrypts a specific statistical computation on the characteristics of patients that may help to determine the usability of the vaccine in a larger scale. However, such statistics should not be revealed to all the members and the secret-key should not be able to decrypt the whole data-set due to the welfare of the company. Therefore, we need to embed a policy (indicating the members who are eligible to learn) and a specific vector (which will be operated on the data-set to compute a specific statistic) into a single key that can be given to the selected members. In other words, we need to have attribute-based access control in IPFE scheme.

A natural solution to the above problem is given by the notion of functional encryption (FE) [14,30] which allows us to compute a secret-key sk_F corresponding to a function F that consists of a policy f^1 and a vector $\boldsymbol{y}$. Given an encryption of message $m = (att, \boldsymbol{x})$, one learns $F(m) = \langle \boldsymbol{x}, \boldsymbol{y} \rangle$ if $f(att) = 0$, using the secret-key sk_F. The indistinguishability security requires that an adversary should be unable to distinguish between encryptions of $m_0 = (att, \boldsymbol{x}_0)$ and $m_1 = (att, \boldsymbol{x}_1)$ even if it possesses many secret-keys for the functions $F_1, \ldots, F_n$ satisfying $F_i(m_0) = F_i(m_1)$, for all i. However, candidate FEs supporting the required function class exist from indistinguishable obfuscation (IO) or multilinear maps (Mmaps) [10,21] the security of which is not well-understood. While some candidate Mmaps (with degree ≥ 2) based constructions [9,22] are still conjectured to be secure, the other FE constructions relying on IO are currently going through a break-and-repair cycle [11]. Therefore, the security of existing FEs for general functions cannot be guaranteed from well-known standard assumptions. Looking into the current state of the art, it is more preferable to

---

[1] A policy is a boolean function and we say an input a satisfies the policy f if $f(a) = 0$.

construct FE for the needed functionality instead of focusing on FE for general function class. Our goal is to build an efficient FE scheme from standard assumption for a class containing only functions like F as described above. This motivation leads us to the following question.

Is it possible to construct a public-key FE scheme where we can embed any boolean function along with a predicate vector into the secret-keys and encrypt a message vector with respect to an attribute so that decryption outputs the inner product between the predicate and message vectors only when the attribute satisfies the boolean function?

Our Contribution. To address the above concern, we present a primitive called *attribute-based IPFE* (ABIPFE) where policies are associated with the secret-keys and attributes are taken while encrypting messages. Our main contribution is a construction of such ABIPFE from Learning With Errors (LWE) assumption in the standard model. The policies can be represented by any polynomial-size bounded-depth boolean circuits and the size of secret-keys or ciphertext relies on the depth of the circuits. Our work takes inspiration from the framework of Abdalla et al. [3]. To obtain an ABIPFE supporting general class of policies, we devise a technique to combine the LWE-based ABE scheme of Boneh et al. [13] (which we call BGG$^+$-ABE) and the LWE-based IPFE scheme of Agrawal et al. [5] (which is abbreviated as ALS-IPFE).

In an ABIPFE scheme, using a master secret-key msk, a central authority generates secret-keys of the form $\mathsf{sk}_{f,y}$ for a tuple (f, y) where f is a depth-d circuit and y is a predicate vector that belongs to $\mathbb{Z}_q^\ell$ for an integer (possibly prime) q. The sender uses the master public-key mpk to encrypt a message vector $x \in \mathbb{Z}_q^\ell$ with respect to an attribute a which is a binary string of length k and produces a ciphertext ct. A receiver having $\mathsf{sk}_{f,y}$, can recover $\langle x, y \rangle$ from ct if $f(a) = 0$. We prove the co-selective indistinguishability (coSel-IND) of the ABIPFE where the adversary $\mathcal{A}$ submits a challenge attribute a^* and a function f^* such that $f^*(a^*) = 0$ before seeing mpk. However, $\mathcal{A}$ can adaptively choose a polynomial number of predicate vectors y and gets secret-keys of the form $\mathsf{sk}_{f^*,y}$. So, $\mathcal{A}$ is given access to many secret-keys that can decrypt the challenge ciphertext. The adversary can also query a secret-key for (f, y) such that $f(a^*) = 1$. If x_0, x_1 are the challenge messages (which can be picked adaptively), we require that $\langle x_0, y \rangle = \langle x_1, y \rangle$ for all y for which a secret-key $\mathsf{sk}_{f^*,y}$ is released during key query phase. Note that using a standard complexity leveraging argument as in [12], we can also allow $\mathcal{A}$ to choose the challenge attribute adaptively.

Theorem 1 (Informal). *Assuming subexponential LWE, there exists a coSel-IND secure ABIPFE scheme with short secret-keys, the size of which depends on the maximum depth of the functions supported by the scheme.*

We show that our single input ABIPFE can be extended to a multi-input variant of ABIPFE which we call *attribute-based multi-input IPFE* (ABMIPFE) scheme. Suppose there are n encryption slots and each slot is associated with a single attribute a_i which is linked to a party that belongs to the system. The i-th party can encrypt a vector $\boldsymbol{x}_i$ with respect to $\mathbf{a}_i$ to produce a ciphertext ct_i. The secret-keys are associated to tuples of form $(\{f_i, \boldsymbol{y}_i\}_{i=1}^n)$ which can be used to learn $\sum_{i=1}^n \langle \boldsymbol{x}_i, \boldsymbol{y}_i \rangle$ if $f_i(\mathbf{a}_i) = 0$ for all $i = 1, \ldots, n$. For security, we define a co-adaptive indistinguishability (coAdp-IND) notion where the adversary is forced to submit n functions $f_1, \ldots, f_n$ before setup whereas it can choose the predicate vectors $(\{\boldsymbol{y}_i\}_{i=1}^n)$ adaptively for key queries. If $\{\boldsymbol{x}_i^0, \boldsymbol{x}_i^1\}_{i=1}^n$ are the challenge messages then all the secret-key queries should satisfy $\sum_{i=1}^n \langle \boldsymbol{x}_i^0, \boldsymbol{y}_i \rangle = \sum_{i=1}^n \langle \boldsymbol{x}_i^1, \boldsymbol{y}_i \rangle$.

Theorem 2 (Informal). *Assuming subexponential* LWE, *there exists a* coAdp-IND *secure ABMIPFE scheme with short secret-keys, the size of which depends on the maximum depth of the functions supported by the scheme and linear to the number of parties in the scheme.*

Comparison to Existing Approaches. We briefly compare our resulting IPFE schemes in reference to existing approaches. The notion of attribute-based functional encryption (ABFE) was formalized by Chen, Zang and Yiu [17] where they proposed a ciphertext-policy ABIPFE (CP-ABIPFE) scheme for limited functionality based on three decisional assumptions in bilinear groups of composite order. They prove the adaptive security in a comparatively weaker setting where the adversary is not allowed to query any secret-key that can decrypt the challenge ciphertext. Improving the security and efficiency, Abdalla et al. [3] gave constructions of CP-ABIPFE based on Decisional Diffie-Hellman (DDH) assumption in bilinear groups of prime order. They utilized the DDH-based IPFE of [5] and any ABE schemes that support dual-system encryption methodology [35] to achieve access control in IPFE setting that can mainly handle policies of equality testing, orthogonality testing, read-once monotone span programs whereas one of the appealing feature of our construction compared to these schemes is that we can embed any general policy represented by a boolean function into the secret-keys of our ABIPFE. The first construction of [3] is selectively secure in simulation setting and the other is adaptively secure in indistinguishability setting. Both of these schemes allow the adversary to have many secret-keys for different attributes that can decrypt the challenge ciphertext, but the advantage of the adversary grows linearly with the number of secret-key queries. In the same work, they also present a natural extension of their pairing-based CP-ABIPFEs to MIPFEs using a generic transformation originally presented in the work of [2]. In this context, it is worth mentioning that our ABIPFE and ABMIPFE are based on standard LWE assumption and hence they are post-quantum secure.

The second main contribution of [3] is the constructions of two adaptively secure identity-based IPFE (IBIPFE) schemes based on the hardness of LWE problem. They combined the ALS-IPFE with two existing LWE-based IBEs. The first one uses the IBE from [24] to get a scheme secure in the random oracle model and the second one relies on the IBE from [4] to obtain a scheme secure in the standard model. In another work [20], Dufour-Sans and Pointcheval built a selectively secure identity-based FE scheme for unbounded inner product functionality in the random-oracle model under Bilinear Decisional Diffie-Hellman assumption. The main advantage of their scheme is the constant size master public-key and secret-keys, in particular, each of them consists of only one group element. Compared to all these IPFE schemes, our IPFE undoubtedly provides a much more finer access control that covers almost all practical applications.

In the context of constructing indistinguishability obfuscation, the authors of [8,26,27] built a primitive called *restricted* FE (latterly renamed as *partially-hiding* FE or PHFE) where the supported function class can execute degree-2 computation on its private input and offers a variety of computations on the public input such as degree-2 functions, NC_0 or NC_1 circuits. While all these PHFEs are described in secret-key setting, recently in [23], the authors proposed a public-key PHFE scheme supporting degree-2 functions in the private input and arithmetic NC_1 functions over the public attribute. The PHFEs are proven secure relying on pairing-based assumptions. On the other hand, our ABIPFE is the first to support any polynomial-size boolean functions over the attributes in public-key setting with security based on standard LWE assumption.

Technical Overview. The starting point is the IBIPFE construction of Abdalla et al. [3] where secret-keys and ciphertexts need to be associated with the same identity for a successful decryption. We use BGG$^+$-ABE and ALS-IPFE to build our ABIPFE and its multi-input variant. The challenge comes in controlling the noise in the ciphertexts for correct decryption and handling secret-key queries that decrypts the challenge ciphertext. We briefly describe the technical road towards achieving this goal. Our core approach utilizes the homomorphic evaluation procedure of [13] which can handle any polynomial-size bounded-depth (unbounded fan-in) boolean circuits of the form $f : \{0,1\}^k \to \{0,1\}$. Given matrices $\overrightarrow{\mathbf{B}} = (\mathbf{B}_1, \ldots, \mathbf{B}_k)$, there are encoding mechanisms such that for any $\mathbf{a} \in \{0,1\}^k$ and function f we have $\mathbf{B_a} \leftarrow \mathsf{Encode}_\mathbf{a}(\overrightarrow{\mathbf{B}}, \mathbf{a})$ and $\mathbf{B}_f \leftarrow \mathsf{Encode}_f(\overrightarrow{\mathbf{B}}, f)$. When a Regev encryption (as described in [24,32]) $c_\mathbf{a} = \mathbf{B_a}^\top s + \text{noise}$ with respect to the public matrix $\mathbf{B_a}$ is available, one can apply a conversion algorithm $\mathsf{Convert}_\mathsf{ct}$ to compute $\mathsf{Convert}_\mathsf{ct}(c_\mathbf{a}, \mathbf{a}, f) = \mathbf{B}_f^\top s + \text{noise}'$ whenever $f(\mathbf{a}) = 0$. The master public-key mpk of our ABIPFE consists of matrices $\mathbf{A} \in \mathbb{Z}_q^{n \times m}, \overrightarrow{\mathbf{B}} \in (\mathbb{Z}_q^{n \times m})^k, \mathbf{D} \in \mathbb{Z}_q^{n \times \ell}$ and the master secret-key is a short basis $\mathbf{T_A}$ of the lattice $\Lambda_q^\perp(\mathbf{A})$. To generate a secret-key $\mathsf{sk}_{f,y}$ for a tuple $(f, \boldsymbol{y})$, the authority first computes $\mathbf{B}_f \leftarrow \mathsf{Encode}_f(\overrightarrow{\mathbf{B}}, f)$ and generates a low-norm matrix $\mathbf{R}_f$ using $\mathbf{T_A}$ such that $(\mathbf{A}|\mathbf{B}_f) \cdot \mathbf{R}_f = \mathbf{D}$. Finally, it sets $\mathsf{sk}_{f,y} = \mathbf{R}_f \cdot \boldsymbol{y}$.

An encryption of a message vector $\boldsymbol{x} \in \mathbb{Z}_q^\ell$ with respect to an attribute $\mathbf{a} \in \{0,1\}^k$ proceeds to compute $\mathbf{B_a} \leftarrow \mathsf{Encode}_\mathbf{a}(\overrightarrow{\mathbf{B}}, \mathbf{a})$ and a Dual-Regev encryption $(c_0 = \mathbf{A}^\top s + e_0, c_\mathbf{a} = \mathbf{B_a}^\top s + e_1)$. It encrypts the message as $c = \mathbf{D}^\top s + e_2 + \boldsymbol{x}$. Here, e_0, e_1, e_2 denote the noise vectors. The ciphertext ct consists of $(c_0, c_\mathbf{a}, c)$.

A receiver holding a secret-key $\mathsf{sk}_{f,y}$ such that $f(\mathbf{a}) = 0$ first obtains $c_f = \mathsf{Convert}_\mathsf{ct}(c_\mathbf{a}, \mathbf{a}, f)$ and then computes the inner product as

$$\boldsymbol{y}^\top c - \mathsf{sk}_{f,y}^\top(c_0|c_f) \approx (\mathbf{D}\boldsymbol{y})^\top s + \boldsymbol{y}^\top \boldsymbol{x} - (\mathbf{R}_f \cdot \boldsymbol{y})^\top (\mathbf{A}|\mathbf{B}_f)^\top s$$
$$= (\mathbf{D}\boldsymbol{y})^\top s + \langle \boldsymbol{x}, \boldsymbol{y} \rangle - \boldsymbol{y}^\top ((\mathbf{A}|\mathbf{B}_f) \cdot \mathbf{R}_f)^\top s = \langle \boldsymbol{x}, \boldsymbol{y} \rangle$$

We prove coSel-IND security for our ABIPFE scheme using the proof techniques of BGG^+-ABE and IBIPFE scheme of [3]. The main technical difference is to program the public matrix $\mathbf{D}$ in such a way that we can generate secret-keys for a fixed function f while varying the associated predicate vectors without using msk. In other words, we need to generate a matrix $\mathbf{Z}$ satisfying $(\mathbf{A}|\mathbf{B}_f)\mathbf{Z} = \mathbf{D}$ such that each row of $\mathbf{Z}$ follows the same distribution $\mathcal{D}$ as that of $\mathbf{R}_f$. For that, we first pick a matrix $\mathbf{Z}_1$ whose rows are coming from $\mathcal{D}$ and define a matrix $\mathbf{D}_1 = \mathbf{A}\mathbf{Z}_1$. Then, we choose another matrix $\mathbf{Z}_2$ following the same distribution as of $\mathbf{Z}_1$ and set $\mathbf{D} = \mathbf{D}_1 + \mathbf{B}_f\mathbf{Z}_2$. Since $\mathbf{Z}_1$ is a low-norm matrix, $\mathbf{D}_1 = \mathbf{A}\mathbf{Z}_1$ is uniformly distributed over $\mathbb{Z}_q^{n \times \ell}$ by a left-over hash lemma [4]. This ensures that $\mathbf{D}$ is also uniform over $\mathbb{Z}_q^{n \times \ell}$ and we can set $\mathbf{Z} = \begin{pmatrix} \mathbf{Z}_1 \\ \mathbf{Z}_2 \end{pmatrix}$ which is distributed according to $\mathbf{R}_f$. We can now generate a secret-key $\text{sk}_{f,\boldsymbol{y}}$ for any vector $\boldsymbol{y}$ as $\mathbf{Z} \cdot \boldsymbol{y}$. The secret matrix $\mathbf{Z}_1$ plays the role of master secret-key in the ALS-IPFE scheme when we finally depend on the hardness of LWE problem to conclude the security of our scheme.

We convert any single-input ABIPFE into an ABMIPFE via a generic transformation inspired from the works of Abdalla et al. [2,3] where they generically convert an IPFE into a multi-input IPFE (MIPFE) without using any additional primitive. The fact that our ABIPFE satisfies certain additional structural properties, namely *two-step decryption* and *linear encryption* [2], helps us to build the *first* ABMIPFE based on LWE assumption.

2   Preliminaries

Notations. For $n \in \mathbb{N}$, we denote by $[n]$ the set $\{1, \ldots, n\}$. We denote by $x \leftarrow \mathcal{D}$ the process of sampling a value x according to the distribution of $\mathcal{D}$. We consider $x \leftarrow S$ as the process of random sampling of a value x according to the uniform distribution over a finite set S. We denote by $\mathbf{A} \otimes \mathbf{B}$ the tensor product between the matrices $\mathbf{A}$ and $\mathbf{B}$. The inner product between two vectors $\boldsymbol{x}, \boldsymbol{y} \in \mathbb{Z}^\ell$ is written as $\langle \boldsymbol{x}, \boldsymbol{y} \rangle = \sum_{i=1}^{\ell} x_i y_i = \boldsymbol{y}^T \boldsymbol{x}$. For any $\lambda > \lambda_0$, if a non-negative function negl satisfies $\text{negl}(\lambda) < 1/\lambda^c$, c is a constant, then negl is called a *negligible* function over the positive integers.

2.1   Attribute-Based Inner Product Functional Encryption

An attribute-based inner product functional encryption (ABIPFE) scheme for a class of functions $\mathcal{F}_\lambda = \{f : \mathcal{S}_\lambda \to \{0, 1\}\}$, a predicate space $\mathcal{Y}_\lambda$ and a message space $\mathcal{X}_\lambda$ consists of four probabilistic polynomial time (PPT) algorithms ABIPFE = (Setup, KeyGen, Enc, Dec) satisfying the following requirement:

- (mpk, msk) $\leftarrow$ Setup$(1^\lambda, 1^\ell, \mathcal{F}_\lambda)$: The setup algorithm on input a security parameter λ, a vector length parameter ℓ and a function class $\mathcal{F}_\lambda$, outputs a master public-key mpk and a master secret-key msk.

- $\mathsf{sk}_{f,y} \leftarrow \mathsf{KeyGen}(\mathsf{mpk}, \mathsf{msk}, f, \boldsymbol{y})$: The key generation algorithm takes as input the key pairs $(\mathsf{mpk}, \mathsf{msk})$, a function $f \in \mathcal{F}_\lambda$ and a vector $\boldsymbol{y} \in \mathcal{Y}_\lambda$ of length ℓ. It outputs a secret-key $\mathsf{sk}_{f,y}$ which also includes the description of f and the vector $\boldsymbol{y}$.
- $\mathsf{ct} \leftarrow \mathsf{Enc}(\mathsf{mpk}, a, \boldsymbol{x})$: The encryption algorithm takes input the master public-key mpk, an attribute $a \in \mathcal{S}_\lambda$ and a message vector $\boldsymbol{x} \in \mathcal{X}_\lambda$. It outputs a ciphertext ct which contains the attribute a.
- $\bot$ or $\zeta \leftarrow \mathsf{Dec}(\mathsf{mpk}, \mathsf{sk}_{f,y}, \mathsf{ct})$: The decryption algorithm is deterministic. It takes as input the master public-key mpk, a secret-key $\mathsf{sk}_{f,y}$ and a ciphertext ct. It outputs either a message $\zeta \in \mathbb{Z}$ or a symbol $\bot$ indicating failure.

Definition 1 (Correctness). An ABIPFE is said to be correct if for all $\lambda \in \mathbb{N}, f \in \mathcal{F}_\lambda, \boldsymbol{y} \in \mathcal{Y}_\lambda, a \in \mathcal{S}_\lambda, \boldsymbol{x} \in \mathcal{X}_\lambda$ we have

$$\Pr\left[\begin{array}{c} \langle \boldsymbol{x}, \boldsymbol{y} \rangle = \mathsf{Dec}(\mathsf{mpk}, \mathsf{sk}_{f,y}, \mathsf{ct}) \\ \wedge \quad f(a) = 0 \end{array} : \begin{array}{c} (\mathsf{mpk}, \mathsf{msk}) \leftarrow \mathsf{Setup}(1^\lambda, 1^\ell, \mathcal{F}_\lambda), \\ \mathsf{sk}_{f,y} \leftarrow \mathsf{KeyGen}(\mathsf{mpk}, \mathsf{msk}, f, \boldsymbol{y}), \\ \mathsf{ct} \leftarrow \mathsf{Enc}(\mathsf{mpk}, a, \boldsymbol{x}) \end{array} \right] = 1 - \mathsf{negl}(\lambda)$$

where the probability is taken over the random coins of Setup, KeyGen and Enc.

We define Q-bounded coSel-IND security for ABIPFE. Let $a^* \in \mathcal{S}_\lambda$ be the target attribute. We call f a *target accepting* function if $f(a^*) = 0$. In Q-bounded coSel-IND game, the adversary $\mathcal{A}$ submits the target attribute a^* and Q target accepting functions before seeing mpk. Note that, $\mathcal{A}$ is allowed to adaptively choose associated predicate vectors and functions which output 1 on input a^*.

Definition 2 (Q-bounded coSel-IND security for ABIPFE). For an ABIPFE scheme $\mathsf{ABIPFE} = (\mathsf{Setup}, \mathsf{Keygen}, \mathsf{Enc}, \mathsf{Dec})$ for a function family $\mathcal{F}_\lambda$, a predicate space $\mathcal{Y}_\lambda$, an attribute space $\mathcal{S}_\lambda$, a message space $\mathcal{X}_\lambda$ and for any PPT adversary $\mathcal{A}$, we define Q-bounded coSel-IND security experiment $\mathsf{Expt}^{\mathsf{coSel\text{-}IND}}_{\mathcal{A}, \mathsf{ABIPFE}}(1^\lambda)$ as follows.

1. **Pre-Setup Phase.** The adversary $\mathcal{A}$ on input 1^λ, outputs a target attribute $a^* \in \mathcal{S}_\lambda$ and a set $\{f_1, \ldots, f_Q\}$ of Q target accepting functions.
2. **Setup Phase.** On input $1^\lambda, 1^\ell$ and $\mathcal{F}_\lambda$, the challenger samples $(\mathsf{mpk}, \mathsf{msk}) \leftarrow \mathsf{Setup}(1^\lambda, 1^\ell, \mathcal{F}_\lambda)$. It gives mpk to $\mathcal{A}$.
3. **Query Phase.** During the experiment $\mathcal{A}$ can make the following queries in any arbitrary order. $\mathcal{A}$ can make unbounded many key queries, however, it is allowed to make only one challenge query.
   (a) **Key Queries.** $\mathcal{A}$ sends $(f, \boldsymbol{y}) \in \mathcal{F}_\lambda \times \mathcal{Y}_\lambda$ and the challenger returns $\mathsf{sk}_{f,y} \leftarrow \mathsf{KeyGen}(\mathsf{mpk}, \mathsf{msk}, f, \boldsymbol{y})$.
   (b) **Challenge Query.** $\mathcal{A}$ submits a pair of messages $(\boldsymbol{x}_0, \boldsymbol{x}_1) \in \mathcal{X}_\lambda^2$. The challenger samples a bit $b \leftarrow \{0, 1\}$ and returns $\mathsf{ct} \leftarrow \mathsf{Enc}(\mathsf{mpk}, a^*, \boldsymbol{x}_b)$.
   We require that any secret-key query $(f_j, \boldsymbol{y}_j)$ should satisfy $(j \in [Q] \wedge \langle \boldsymbol{x}_0, \boldsymbol{y}_j \rangle = \langle \boldsymbol{x}_1, \boldsymbol{y}_j \rangle)$ or $f_j(a^*) = 1$.
4. **Guess Phase.** $\mathcal{A}$ outputs a guess bit b'. The experiment outputs 1 if $b = b'$.

The ABIPFE is said to satisfy Q-bounded coSel-IND security (or simply co-selective security when Q is clear from the context) if the advantage

$$\mathsf{Adv}^{\mathsf{coSel\text{-}IND}}_{\mathcal{A},\mathsf{ABIPFE}}(\lambda) = \left| \Pr[\mathsf{Expt}^{\mathsf{coSel\text{-}IND}}_{\mathcal{A},\mathsf{ABIPFE}}(1^\lambda) = 1] - \frac{1}{2} \right|$$

of $\mathcal{A}$ in the above game is negligible in λ.

We can also define stronger versions of the security such as selective and adaptive experiments. In Sel-IND security game the adversary $\mathcal{A}$ submits the target attribute a^* in the pre-setup phase and it is allowed to choose the target accepting functions adaptively. We give more power to $\mathcal{A}$ in the Adp-IND security experiment. In particular, $\mathcal{A}$ has the freedom to choose the target attribute a^* in the challenge phase and target accepting functions in the key query phase. Accordingly, we can define the advantages by the functions $\mathsf{Adv}^{\mathsf{Sel\text{-}IND}}_{\mathcal{A},\mathsf{ABIPFE}}(\lambda)$ and $\mathsf{Adv}^{\mathsf{Adp\text{-}IND}}_{\mathcal{A},\mathsf{ABIPFE}}(\lambda)$ in the selective and adaptive security experiments respectively.

2.2 Lattice Preliminaries [3, 13]

We recall basics of lattices and some important results related to our construction of ABIPFE. Let n, m, q be positive integers such that $n = \mathsf{poly}(\lambda)$ and $m \geq n\lceil \log q \rceil$. For a matrix $\mathbf{A} \in \mathbb{Z}_q^{n \times m}$, we let $\Lambda_q^\perp(\mathbf{A})$ denotes the lattice $\{\boldsymbol{x} \in \mathbb{Z}^m : \mathbf{A}\boldsymbol{x} = \mathbf{0} \text{ in } \mathbb{Z}_q\}$. More generally for $\boldsymbol{u} \in \mathbb{Z}_q^n$, we let $\Lambda_q^u(\mathbf{A})$ denote the lattice $\{\boldsymbol{x} \in \mathbb{Z}^m : \mathbf{A}\boldsymbol{x} = \boldsymbol{u} \text{ in } \mathbb{Z}_q\}$.

Matrix Norms. For a vector $\boldsymbol{u}$, we let $||\boldsymbol{u}||$ denote its ℓ_2 norm. For a matrix $\mathbf{R} \in \mathbb{Z}^{k \times m}$, let $\widetilde{\mathbf{R}}$ be the result of applying Gram-Schmidt (GS) orthogonalization to the columns of $\mathbf{R}$. We define the following norms.

– $||\mathbf{R}||$ denotes the ℓ_2 norm of the longest column of $\mathbf{R}$.
– $||\mathbf{R}||_2$ denotes the operator norm of $\mathbf{R}$ defined as $||\mathbf{R}||_2 = \sup_{||\boldsymbol{x}||=1}||\mathbf{R}\boldsymbol{x}||$.
– $s_1(\mathbf{R})$ denotes the spectral norm of $\mathbf{R}$ (largest singular value of $\mathbf{R}$).

In addition, we know that $||\widetilde{\mathbf{R}}|| \leq ||\mathbf{R}|| \leq ||\mathbf{R}||_2 \leq \sqrt{k}\mathbf{R}$. The spectral norm of concatenating matrices are bounded as $s_1(\mathbf{R}|\mathbf{S}) \leq \sqrt{s_1(\mathbf{R})^2 + s_1(\mathbf{S})^2}$. The following lemma provides a bound on spectral norm.

Lemma 1 [19]. *Let $\mathbf{X} \in \mathbb{R}^{n \times m}$ be a sub-Gaussian random matrix with parameter s. There exists a universal constant $C \approx \frac{1}{\sqrt{2\pi}}$ such that for any $t \geq 0$, we have $s_1(\mathbf{X}) \leq C \cdot s \cdot (\sqrt{m} + \sqrt{n} + t)$ except with probability at most $2 \cdot exp(-\pi t^2)$.*

Lemma 2 (Gram-Schmidt minimum [15]). *For any arbitrary n-dimensional integer lattice Λ, it holds that:*

$$1 \leq \lambda_1(\Lambda^*) \cdot \min_{\mathbf{B}}||\widetilde{\mathbf{B}}|| \leq \gamma^2 n,$$

where the minimum is over all (ordered) bases $\mathbf{B}$ of lattice Λ and γ is a constant.

Gaussian Distribution. For any n-dimensional lattice Λ, the discrete Gaussian distribution over Λ with center $c \in \mathbb{R}^n$ and parameter $\sigma > 0$ is defined as $\mathcal{D}_{\Lambda,\sigma,c}(x) = \rho_{\sigma,c}(x)/\rho_{\sigma,c}(\Lambda)$, $\forall x \in \mathbb{R}^n$ where $\rho_{\sigma,c}(x) = \exp(-\pi\|x - c\|_2^2/\sigma^2)$ and $\rho_{\sigma,c}(\Lambda) = \sum_{x \in \Lambda} \rho_{\sigma,c}(x)$. When $c = 0$, we use $\mathcal{D}_\sigma(\Lambda_q^u(\mathbf{A}))$ for a parameter $\sigma > 0$ to denote a discrete Gaussian distribution over the lattice $\Lambda_q^u(\mathbf{A})$. For a random matrix $\mathbf{A} \in \mathbb{Z}_q^{n \times m}$ and $\sigma = \tilde{\Omega}(\sqrt{n})$, a vector x sampled from $\mathcal{D}_\sigma(\Lambda_q^u(\mathbf{A}))$ has ℓ_2 norm less than $\sigma\sqrt{m}$ with probability at least $1 - \mathsf{negl}(m)$. For a matrix $\mathbf{U} = (u_1|\cdots|u_k) \in \mathbb{Z}_q^{n \times k}$, we let $\mathcal{D}_\sigma(\Lambda_q^{\mathbf{U}}(\mathbf{A}))$ be a distribution on matrices in $\mathbb{Z}^{m \times k}$ where the i-th column is sampled from $\mathcal{D}_\sigma(\Lambda_q^{u_i}(\mathbf{A}))$ independently for $i = 1, \ldots, k$. Clearly if $\mathbf{R}$ is sampled from $\mathcal{D}_\sigma(\Lambda_q^{\mathbf{U}}(\mathbf{A}))$ then $\mathbf{A}\mathbf{R} = \mathbf{U}$ in $\mathbb{Z}_q$.

Learning with Errors (LWE) [32]. Fix integers n, m, a prime integer q and a noise distribution χ over $\mathbb{Z}$. The $\mathsf{LWE}_{q,\chi,n}$ problem is to distinguish between the distributions $(\mathbf{A}, \mathbf{A}^\top s + e)$ and $(\mathbf{A}, u)$ where $\mathbf{A} \in \mathbb{Z}_q^{n \times m}, s \in \mathbb{Z}_q^n, u \in \mathbb{Z}_q^m$ are independently sampled.

Proposition 1 [32]. *Let $\alpha = \alpha(n) \in (0,1)$ and let $q = q(n)$ be a prime such that $\alpha \cdot q > 2\sqrt{n}$. If there exists an efficient (possibly quantum) algorithm that solves $\mathsf{LWE}_{q,\Psi_\alpha}$, then there exists an efficient quantum algorithm for approximating SIVP and GapSVP in the ℓ_2 norm, in the worst case, to within $\tilde{O}(n/\alpha)$ factors.*

Here Ψ_α is distributed as $\lceil qX \rfloor \bmod q$ where X is a normal random variable with mean 0 and standard deviation $\alpha/\sqrt{2\pi}$.

Solving $\mathbf{A}\mathbf{Z} = \mathbf{U}$. We review algorithms for finding a low-norm matrix $\mathbf{Z} \in \mathbb{Z}_q^{m \times k}$ such that $\mathbf{A}\mathbf{Z} = \mathbf{U}$.

Theorem 3 [24]. *There is a PPT SampleD that, given a basis $\mathbf{B}$ of an n-dimensional lattice $\Lambda = \mathcal{L}(\mathbf{B})$, a parameter $\sigma \geq \|\widetilde{\mathbf{B}}\| \cdot \omega(\sqrt{\log n})$ and a center $c \in \mathbb{R}^n$, outputs a sample from a distribution that is statistically close to $\mathcal{D}_{\sigma,c}(\Lambda)$.*

Proposition 2 [6]. *For any prime $q = poly(n)$ and any $m \geq 5n \lg q$, there is a probabilistic polynomial-time algorithm SampleMat that, on input 1^n, outputs a matrix $\mathbf{A} \in \mathbb{Z}_q^{n \times m}$ and a full-rank set $\mathbf{S} \subset \Lambda_q^\perp(\mathbf{A})$, where the distribution of $\mathbf{A}$ is statistically close to uniform over $\mathbb{Z}_q^{n \times m}$ and the length $\|\mathbf{S}\| \leq L = m^{2.5}$.*

Also, $\mathbf{S}$ can be converted efficiently to a "good" basis $\mathbf{T}$ of $\Lambda_q^\perp(\mathbf{A})$ such that $\|\widetilde{\mathbf{T}}\| \leq \|\widetilde{\mathbf{S}}\| \leq L$.

Lemma 3 (Preimage samplable functions [24]). *For any prime $q = poly(n)$, any $m \geq 6n \log q$, and any $\sigma \geq L \cdot \omega(\sqrt{\log m})$, it holds that there exists PPT algorithms TrapGen, SampleD, SamplePre such that:*

1. *TrapGen computes $(\mathbf{A}, \mathbf{T_A}) \leftarrow \mathsf{TrapGen}(1^n, 1^m, q)$, where $\mathbf{A}$ is statistically close to uniform over $\mathbb{Z}_q^{n \times m}$ and $\mathbf{T_A} \subset \Lambda_q^\perp(\mathbf{A})$ is a good basis with $\|\widetilde{\mathbf{T_A}}\| \leq L$. The matrix $\mathbf{A}$ is public and $\mathbf{T_A}$ is the trapdoor.*
2. *SampleD is used to sample vectors from $\mathcal{D}_\sigma(\mathbb{Z}^{m \times k})$.*

3. *The trapdoor inversion algorithm* SamplePre$(\mathbf{A}, \mathbf{T_A}, \mathbf{U}, \sigma)$ *outputs a matrix* $\mathbf{Z} \in \mathbb{Z}^{m \times k}$ *such that* $\mathbf{A}\mathbf{Z} = \mathbf{U}$.

In addition, it holds that the following distributions are statistically close:

$$\text{Dist}_1 := (\mathbf{A}, \mathbf{Z}, \mathbf{U}) \; s.t. \; (\mathbf{A}, \mathbf{T_A}) \leftarrow \text{TrapGen}(1^n, 1^m, q), \; \mathbf{U} \leftarrow \mathbb{Z}^{n \times k},$$
$$\mathbf{Z} \leftarrow \text{SamplePre}(\mathbf{A}, \mathbf{T_A}, \mathbf{U}, \sigma)$$

$$\text{Dist}_2 := (\mathbf{A}, \mathbf{Z}, \mathbf{A}\mathbf{Z}) \; s.t. \; \mathbf{A} \leftarrow \mathbb{Z}_q^{n \times m}, \; \mathbf{Z} \leftarrow \mathcal{D}_\sigma(\mathbb{Z}^{m \times k}) : ||z_i|| \leq \sigma\sqrt{m}, i \in [k],$$
$$\text{where } z_i \text{ is the } i\text{-th column of } \mathbf{Z}$$

Trapdoor Generators. The following Lemma states properties of algorithms for generating short basis of lattices.

Lemma 4 [13]. *Let* $n, m, q > 0$ *be integers with* q *prime. There are polynomial-time algorithms with the properties below:*

1. $(\mathbf{A}, \mathbf{T_A}) \leftarrow \text{TrapGen}(1^n, 1^m, q)$ ([6,7,29]): *a randomized algorithm that, when* $m = \Theta(n \log q)$, *outputs a full-rank matrix* $\mathbf{A} \in \mathbb{Z}_q^{n \times m}$ *and basis* $\mathbf{T_A} \in \mathbb{Z}^{m \times m}$ *for* $\Lambda_q^\perp(\mathbf{A})$ *such that* $\mathbf{A}$ *is negl(n)-close to uniform and* $||\tilde{\mathbf{T}}_\mathbf{A}|| = O(\sqrt{n \log q})$, *with all but negligible probability in* n.
2. $\mathbf{T_{A|B}} \leftarrow \text{ExtendRight}(\mathbf{A}, \mathbf{T_A}, \mathbf{B})$ ([16]): *a deterministic algorithm that given full-rank matrices* $\mathbf{A}, \mathbf{B} \in \mathbb{Z}_q^{n \times m}$ *and a basis* $\mathbf{T_A}$ *of* $\Lambda_q^\perp(\mathbf{A})$ *outputs a basis* $\mathbf{T_{A|B}}$ *of* $\Lambda_q^\perp(\mathbf{A}|\mathbf{B})$ *such that* $||\tilde{\mathbf{T}}_\mathbf{A}|| = ||\tilde{\mathbf{T}}_{\mathbf{A|B}}||$.
3. $\mathbf{T_H} \leftarrow \text{ExtendLeft}(\mathbf{A}, \mathbf{G}, \mathbf{T_G}, \mathbf{S})$ *where* $\mathbf{H} = (\mathbf{A}|\mathbf{G}+\mathbf{A}\mathbf{S})$ ([4]): *a deterministic algorithm that given full-rank matrices* $\mathbf{A}, \mathbf{G} \in \mathbb{Z}_q^{n \times m}$ *and a basis* $\mathbf{T_G}$ *of* $\Lambda_q^\perp(\mathbf{G})$ *outputs a basis* $\mathbf{T_H}$ *of* $\Lambda_q^\perp(\mathbf{H})$ *such that* $||\tilde{\mathbf{T}}_\mathbf{H}|| = ||\tilde{\mathbf{T}}_\mathbf{G}|| \cdot (1 + ||\mathbf{S}||_2)$
4. *For* $m = n\lceil \log q \rceil$ *there is a fixed full-rank matrix* $\mathbf{G} \in \mathbb{Z}_q^{n \times m}$ *such that the lattice* $\Lambda_q^\perp(\mathbf{G})$ *has a publicly known basis* $\mathbf{T_G} \in \mathbb{Z}^{m \times m}$ *with* $||\tilde{\mathbf{T}}_\mathbf{G}|| \leq \sqrt{5}$.

Lemma 5 [4,16]. *Let* $n, m, \ell, q > 0$ *be integers with* q *prime. There exist the following polynomial-time algorithms.*

1. $\mathbf{Z} \leftarrow \text{SampleRight}(\mathbf{A}, \mathbf{T_A}, \mathbf{B}, \mathbf{U}, \sigma)$: *a randomized algorithm that given full-rank matrices* $\mathbf{A}, \mathbf{B} \in \mathbb{Z}_q^{n \times m}$, *matrix* $\mathbf{U} \in \mathbb{Z}_q^{n \times \ell}$, *a basis* $\mathbf{T_A}$ *of* $\Lambda_q^\perp(\mathbf{A})$ *and* $\sigma \geq ||\tilde{\mathbf{T}}_\mathbf{A}|| \cdot \omega(\sqrt{\log m})$, *outputs a random sample* $\mathbf{Z} \in \mathbb{Z}_q^{2m \times \ell}$ *from a distribution that is statistically close to* $\mathcal{D}_\sigma(\Lambda_q^\mathbf{U}(\mathbf{A}|\mathbf{B}))$. *This algorithm is the composition of two algorithms:* $\mathbf{T_{A|B}} \leftarrow \text{ExtendRight}(\mathbf{A}, \mathbf{T_A}, \mathbf{B})$ *and* $\mathbf{Z} \leftarrow \text{SamplePre}((\mathbf{A}|\mathbf{B}), \mathbf{T_{A|B}}, \mathbf{U}, \sigma)$.
2. $\mathbf{Z} \leftarrow \text{SampleLeft}(\mathbf{A}, \mathbf{S}, y, \mathbf{U}, \sigma)$: *a randomized algorithm that given full-rank matrix* $\mathbf{A} \in \mathbb{Z}_q^{n \times m}$, *matrices* $\mathbf{S} \in \mathbb{Z}_q^{m \times m}, \mathbf{U} \in \mathbb{Z}_q^{n \times \ell}$, $y \neq 0 \in \mathbb{Z}_q$ *and* $\sigma \geq \sqrt{5} \cdot (1 + ||\mathbf{S}||_2) \cdot \omega(\sqrt{\log m})$, *outputs a random sample* $\mathbf{Z} \in \mathbb{Z}_q^{2m \times \ell}$ *from a distribution that is statistically close to* $\mathcal{D}_\sigma(\Lambda_q^\mathbf{U}(\mathbf{A}|y\mathbf{G}+\mathbf{A}\mathbf{S}))$. *This algorithm is the composition of two algorithms:* $\mathbf{T_{(A|yG+AS)}} \leftarrow \text{ExtendLeft}(\mathbf{A}, y\mathbf{G}, \mathbf{T_G}, \mathbf{S})$ *and* $\mathbf{Z} \leftarrow \text{SamplePre}((\mathbf{A}|y\mathbf{G}+\mathbf{A}\mathbf{S}), \mathbf{T_{(A|yG+AS)}}, \mathbf{U}, \sigma)$.

Randomness Extraction. We consider a version of left-over hash lemma.

Lemma 6 [4]. *Suppose that $m > (n+1)\log_2 q + \omega(\log n)$ and that $q > 2$ is a prime. Let $\mathbf{S}$ be an $m \times k$ matrix chosen uniformly in $\{\pm 1\}^{m \times k}$ mod q where $k = k(n)$ is a polynomial in n. Let $\mathbf{A}$ and $\mathbf{B}$ be matrices chosen uniformly in $\mathbb{Z}_q^{n \times m}$ and $\mathbb{Z}_q^{n \times k}$ respectively. Then, for all vectors $e \in \mathbb{Z}_q^m$, the distribution $(\mathbf{A}, \mathbf{AS}, \mathbf{S}^\top e)$ is statistically close to the distribution $(\mathbf{A}, \mathbf{B}, \mathbf{S}^\top e)$.*

Note that the Lemma holds for every vector e in $\mathbb{Z}_q^m$ including low norm vectors.

Noise Rerandomization. We describe the algorithm $\mathsf{NoiseGen}(\mathbf{R}, s)$ from [28]. On input a matrix $\mathbf{R} \in \mathbb{Z}^{m \times t}$ and $s \in \mathbb{R}^+$ such that $s > s_1(\mathbf{RR}^\top)$, it first samples $\mathbf{e}_1 := \mathrm{Re} + (s^2\mathbf{I}_m - \mathbf{RR}^\top)^{\frac{1}{2}}\mathbf{e}'$, where $\mathbf{I}_m$ denotes the identity matrix of order m, and $\mathbf{e} \leftarrow \mathcal{D}_\sigma^t, \mathbf{e}' \leftarrow \mathcal{D}_{\sqrt{2}\sigma}^m$ are independent spherical continuous Gaussian noises. Then, it samples $\mathbf{e}_2 \leftarrow \mathcal{D}_{s\sqrt{2}\sigma}(\mathbb{Z}^m - \mathbf{e}_1)$, and returns $\mathbf{e}_1 + \mathbf{e}_2$. We have the following Lemma:

Lemma 7 (Noise distribution [28]**).** *Let $\mathbf{R} \leftarrow \mathbb{Z}^{m \times t}$ and $s > s_1(\mathbf{R})$. Then, for all vectors $e \leftarrow \mathcal{D}_\sigma(\mathbb{Z}^t)$, the distribution of $\mathrm{Re} + \mathsf{NoiseGen}(\mathbf{R}, s)$ is statistically close to $\mathcal{D}_{2s\sigma}(\mathbb{Z}^m)$.*

2.3   Homomorphic Evaluation Procedures

We follow the abstraction of evaluation procedure in the LWE-based ABE scheme of [13]. Let $n, m, k, q = q(n)$ be positive integers such that $m = \Theta(n\log q)$ and $\mathbf{G} \in \mathbb{Z}_q^{n \times m}$ be a fixed matrix obtained by padding $\mathbf{I}_n \otimes (1, 2, 4, 8, \ldots, 2^{\lceil \log q \rceil})$ with zero columns.

Theorem 4. *There exist efficient deterministic algorithms $\mathsf{Eval}_{pk}, \mathsf{Eval}_{ct}, \mathsf{Eval}_{sim}$ such that for any sequence of matrices $(\mathbf{B}_1, \ldots, \mathbf{B}_k) \in (\mathbb{Z}_q^{n \times m})^k$, for any family of boolean functions $\mathcal{F} = \{f : \{0,1\}^k \to \{0,1\}\}$ with maximum depth d and for every $\mathbf{a} = (a_1, \ldots, a_k) \in \{0,1\}^k$, the following properties hold:*

1. $\mathbf{B}_f \leftarrow \mathsf{Eval}_{pk}(f, (\mathbf{B}_1, \ldots, \mathbf{B}_k))$: *On input a function $f \in \mathcal{F}$ and matrices $\{\mathbf{B}_i\}_{i \in [k]}$, it outputs a matrix $\mathbf{B}_f \in \mathbb{Z}_q^{n \times m}$.*
2. $\mathbf{c}_f \leftarrow \mathsf{Eval}_{ct}(f, ((a_i, \mathbf{B}_i, \mathbf{c}_i))_{i=1}^k)$: *On input a function $f \in \mathcal{F}$, $a_i \in \{0,1\}$, $\mathbf{B}_i \in \mathbb{Z}_q^{n \times m}$ and $\mathbf{c}_i \in \mathbb{Z}_q^m$ for $i \in [k]$, it outputs a vector $\mathbf{c}_f \in \mathbb{Z}_q^m$ such that*

   $$\text{if } \{\mathbf{c}_i = (a_i\mathbf{G} + \mathbf{B}_i)^\top s + \mathbf{e}_i\}_{i \in [k]} \text{ then } \mathbf{c}_f = (f(\mathbf{a})\mathbf{G} + \mathbf{B}_f)^\top s + \mathbf{e}_f$$

   where $\mathbf{a} = (\mathbf{a}_1, \ldots, \mathbf{a}_k) \in \{0,1\}^k$ and $\mathbf{B}_f = \mathsf{Eval}_{pk}(f, (\mathbf{B}_1, \ldots, \mathbf{B}_k))$. Furthermore, we require that $\|\mathbf{e}_f\| < \gamma_\mathcal{F} \cdot \max_{i \in [k]} \|\mathbf{e}_i\|$.
3. $\mathbf{S}_f \leftarrow \mathsf{Eval}_{sim}(f, ((a_i, \mathbf{S}_i))_{i=1}^k, \mathbf{A})$: *On input a function $f \in \mathcal{F}$, $a_i \in \{0,1\}, \mathbf{S}_i \in \{\pm 1\}^{m \times m}$ for $i \in [k]$ and $\mathbf{A} \in \mathbb{Z}_q^{n \times m}$, it outputs a matrix $\mathbf{S}_f \in \mathbb{Z}_q^{m \times m}$ that satisfies*

   $$\mathbf{AS}_f + f(\mathbf{a})\mathbf{G} = \mathbf{B}_f \text{ where } \mathbf{B}_f = \mathsf{Eval}_{pk}(f, (\mathbf{AS}_1 + a_1\mathbf{G}, \ldots, \mathbf{AS}_k + a_k\mathbf{G})).$$

   Furthermore, we require that $\|\mathbf{S}_f\|_2 \leq \gamma_\mathcal{F}$.

For any family $\mathcal{F}$ of depth-d boolean functions the noise $\gamma_\mathcal{F}$ (in worst case) is upper bounded by $O(\sqrt{m}m^d)$.

3   Our Construction of ABIPFE from LWE

In this section, we describe our construction of an ABIPFE scheme based on the hardness of LWE problem in standard model. In particular, we use the ABE scheme of [13] and the ALS-IPFE scheme [5] with a slight modification [3,34] in the distribution of the master secret-key matrix. We describe the modified ALS-IPFE in Sect. 3 of the full version of this paper [31]. We present our ABIPFE for a class of functions $\mathcal{F}_\lambda = \{f : \{0,1\}^k \to \{0,1\}\}$, a predicate space $\mathcal{Y}_\lambda = \{0, \ldots, V(\lambda) - 1\}^\ell$ and a message space $\mathcal{X}_\lambda = \{0, \ldots, X(\lambda) - 1\}^\ell$. In addition, we assume that $|\langle \boldsymbol{x}, \boldsymbol{y} \rangle| < K$ where $K = \ell V X$ and $\mathcal{F}_\lambda$ is the class of all circuits having input length $k = k(\lambda)$ and depth at most $d(\lambda) = O(\log \lambda)$. We use the matrix $\mathbf{G}$, defined in Sect. 2.3, in our construction and security proof.

Setup($1^\lambda, 1^\ell, \mathcal{F}_\lambda$): On input 1^λ, 1^ℓ and $\mathcal{F}_\lambda$, the setup algorithm defines the parameters $n = n(\lambda), m = m(\lambda), q = q(\lambda)$. It then proceeds as follows.
   1. Sample $(\mathbf{A}, \mathbf{T_A}) \leftarrow \mathsf{TrapGen}(1^n, 1^m, q)$ such that $\mathbf{A} \in \mathbb{Z}_q^{n \times m}$.
   2. Sample random matrices $(\mathbf{B}_1, \ldots, \mathbf{B}_k) \leftarrow (\mathbb{Z}_q^{n \times m})^k, \mathbf{D} \leftarrow \mathbb{Z}_q^{n \times \ell}$.
   3. Output the master public-key $\mathsf{mpk} = (\mathbf{A}, \mathbf{B}_1, \ldots, \mathbf{B}_k, \mathbf{D})$ and the master secret-key $\mathsf{msk} = \mathbf{T_A}$. We assume that mpk also contains a set of public parameters $\mathsf{param} = \{n, m, q, \ell, X, V, K, \rho, \sigma, \tau\}$.
KeyGen($\mathsf{mpk}, \mathsf{msk}, f, \boldsymbol{y}$) : The key generation algorithm takes as input $\mathsf{mpk}, \mathsf{msk}$, a function $f \in \mathcal{F}_\lambda$ and a vector $\boldsymbol{y} \in \mathcal{Y}_\lambda$, and works as follows.
   1. Compute $\mathbf{B}_f = \mathsf{Eval}_{\mathrm{pk}}(f, (\mathbf{B}_1, \ldots, \mathbf{B}_k))$ where $\mathbf{B}_f \in \mathbb{Z}_q^{n \times m}$.
   2. Compute $\mathbf{R}_f \leftarrow \mathsf{SampleRight}(\mathbf{A}, \mathbf{T_A}, \mathbf{B}_f, \mathbf{D}, \rho)$ so that $(\mathbf{A}|\mathbf{B}_f) \cdot \mathbf{R}_f = \mathbf{D}$.
   3. Output the secret-key as $\mathsf{sk}_{f,\boldsymbol{y}} = \mathbf{R}_f \cdot \boldsymbol{y}$. We assume that the secret-key trivially includes f and $\boldsymbol{y}$.
Enc($\mathsf{mpk}, \mathbf{a}, \boldsymbol{x}$) : The encryption algorithm takes as input mpk, an attribute $\mathbf{a} = (a_1, \ldots, a_k) \in \{0,1\}^k$ and a message $\boldsymbol{x} \in \mathcal{X}$. It proceeds as follows.
   1. Compute $\mathbf{H_a} = (\mathbf{A}|a_1\mathbf{G} + \mathbf{B}_1| \cdots |a_k\mathbf{G} + \mathbf{B}_k) \in \mathbb{Z}_q^{n \times m(k+1)}$.
   2. Sample $\boldsymbol{s} \leftarrow \mathbb{Z}_q^n$ and $\boldsymbol{e}_1 \leftarrow \mathcal{D}_\sigma(\mathbb{Z}^m), \boldsymbol{e}_2 \leftarrow \mathcal{D}_\sigma(\mathbb{Z}^\ell), \boldsymbol{e}_3 \leftarrow \mathcal{D}_\tau(\mathbb{Z}^\ell)$, and matrices $\mathbf{S}_i \leftarrow \{\pm 1\}^{m \times m}$ for $i \in [k]$.
   3. Set $\boldsymbol{v} = (\mathbf{I}_m|\mathbf{S}_1| \cdots |\mathbf{S}_k)^\top \cdot \boldsymbol{e}_1 \in \mathbb{Z}_q^{m(k+1)}$.
   4. Compute $\mathsf{ct}_1 = \mathbf{H_a}^\top \boldsymbol{s} + \boldsymbol{v} \in \mathbb{Z}_q^{m(k+1)}$, $\mathsf{ct}_2 = \mathbf{D}^\top \boldsymbol{s} + \boldsymbol{e}_2 + \boldsymbol{e}_3 + \lfloor \frac{q}{K} \rfloor \cdot \boldsymbol{x} \in \mathbb{Z}_q^\ell$.
   5. Output the ciphertext $\mathsf{ct} = (\mathsf{ct}_1, \mathsf{ct}_2)$. We assume that the ciphertext includes the attribute $\mathbf{a}$.
Dec($\mathsf{mpk}, \mathsf{sk}_{f,\boldsymbol{y}}, \mathsf{ct}$) : The decryption algorithm takes as input mpk, a secret-key $\mathsf{sk}_{f,\boldsymbol{y}}$ corresponding to a function f and a predicate vector $\boldsymbol{y}$ and a ciphertext ct associated with an attribute $\mathbf{a}$. It proceeds as follows.
   1. Parse $\mathsf{ct} = (\mathsf{ct}_1, \mathsf{ct}_2)$ where $\mathsf{ct}_1 = (\boldsymbol{c}_0, \boldsymbol{c}_1, \ldots, \boldsymbol{c}_k) \in (\mathbb{Z}_q^m)^{k+1}, \mathsf{ct}_2 \in \mathbb{Z}_q^\ell$ and $\mathsf{sk}_{f,\boldsymbol{y}} \in \mathbb{Z}^{2m}$.
   2. Compute $\boldsymbol{c}_f = \mathsf{Eval}_{\mathrm{ct}}(f, ((a_i, \mathbf{B}_i, \boldsymbol{c}_i))_{i=1}^k)$ where $\mathbf{a} = (a_1, \ldots, a_k)$.
   3. Compute $\zeta' = \boldsymbol{y}^\top \mathsf{ct}_2 - \mathsf{sk}_{f,\boldsymbol{y}}^\top \cdot (\boldsymbol{c}_0|\boldsymbol{c}_f)$.
   4. Output $\zeta \in \{0, \ldots, K\}$ which minimizes $||\lfloor \frac{q}{K} \rfloor \cdot \zeta - \zeta'|$.

Correctness. For correctness we first observe that $c_i = (a_i\mathbf{G} + \mathbf{B}_i)^\top \mathbf{s} + \mathbf{S}_i^\top \mathbf{e}_1$ with $||\mathbf{S}_i^\top \mathbf{e}_1|| < \sigma\sqrt{m}$ for all $i \in [k]$. Therefore, using Theorem 4, we have $c_f = (f(\mathbf{a})\mathbf{G} + \mathbf{B}_f)^\top \mathbf{s} + \mathbf{e}_f \in \mathbb{Z}_q^m$ where $||\mathbf{e}_f|| < \sigma\sqrt{m} \cdot \gamma_{\mathcal{F}}$. Consequently,

$$(c_0|c_f) = (\mathbf{A}|f(\mathbf{a})\mathbf{G} + \mathbf{B}_f)^\top \mathbf{s} + (\mathbf{e}_1|\mathbf{e}_f) \in \mathbb{Z}_q^{2m}.$$

Now, the secret-key $\mathsf{sk}_{f,y} = \mathbf{R}_f \cdot \mathbf{y}$ where $\mathbf{R}_f$ is sampled from $\mathcal{D}_\sigma(\Lambda_q^{\mathbf{D}}(\mathbf{A}|\mathbf{B}_f))$. Thus, $(\mathbf{A}|\mathbf{B}_f) \cdot \mathbf{R}_f = \mathbf{D}$ and $||\mathbf{R}_f|| < \rho\sqrt{2m\ell}$. Since $\mathbf{e}_2 \leftarrow \mathcal{D}_\sigma(\mathbb{Z}^\ell), \mathbf{e}_3 \leftarrow \mathcal{D}_\tau(\mathbb{Z}^\ell)$, with overwhelming probability we have $||\mathbf{e}_2|| < \sigma\sqrt{\ell}$ and $||\mathbf{e}_3|| < \tau\sqrt{\ell}$. Finally, if $f(\mathbf{a}) = 0$ then the element ζ' can be viewed as

$$\zeta' = \mathbf{y}^\top \mathsf{ct}_2 - \mathsf{sk}_{f,y}^\top \cdot (c_0|c_f)$$
$$= \mathbf{y}^\top (\mathbf{D}^\top \mathbf{s} + \mathbf{e}_2 + \mathbf{e}_3 + \left\lfloor \frac{q}{K} \right\rfloor \cdot \mathbf{x}) - (\mathbf{R}_f \cdot \mathbf{y})^\top \cdot ((\mathbf{A}|\mathbf{B}_f)^\top \mathbf{s} + (\mathbf{e}_1|\mathbf{e}_f))$$
$$= \left\lfloor \frac{q}{K} \right\rfloor \cdot \langle \mathbf{x}, \mathbf{y} \rangle + \mathbf{y}^\top (\mathbf{e}_2 + \mathbf{e}_3) - (\mathbf{R}_f\mathbf{y})^\top (\mathbf{e}_1|\mathbf{e}_f) = \left\lfloor \frac{q}{K} \right\rfloor \cdot \langle \mathbf{x}, \mathbf{y} \rangle + error$$

and $|error| < V\ell(\sigma + \tau) + 2\rho\sigma V\ell m(1 + \gamma_{\mathcal{F}})$ with overwhelming probability. To ensure the correct decryption we need to set $q > 4KV\ell(\sigma+\tau) + 8\rho\sigma KV\ell m(1 + \gamma_{\mathcal{F}})$ so that $\zeta = \langle \mathbf{x}, \mathbf{y} \rangle$ minimizes $||\lfloor \frac{q}{K} \rfloor \cdot \zeta - \zeta'|$.

Theorem 5 (1-bounded coSel-IND Security). *Assuming the modified variant of ALS-IPFE scheme (see [31]) with parameters $n, q, m, \sigma, \rho, \alpha$ is secure under $\mathsf{LWE}_{q,\alpha,n}$ and the parameters additionally satisfy $m \geq 6n\log q, q > 4KV\ell(\sigma + \tau) + 8\rho\sigma KV\ell m(1 + \gamma_{\mathcal{F}})$, the above ABIPFE scheme with $\tau > 2C\rho\sigma(2\sqrt{m} + \sqrt{\ell})\gamma_{\mathcal{F}}$ for a constant C is 1-bounded coSel-IND secure under the $\mathsf{LWE}_{q,\alpha,n}$ assumption.*

Proof. The proof is done by considering the sequence of games used in the selectively secure ABE of [13]. We also incorporate the idea of [3] to simulate the secret-key queries correspond to the target accepting function. However, we make crucial changes along the way to let proof go through. As in Definition 2 with $Q = 1$, we assume that the adversary $\mathcal{A}$ submits a target attribute $\mathbf{a}^*$ and a target accepting function f^* (i.e. $f^*(\mathbf{a}^*) = 0$) before seeing the master public-key. A secret-key query $(f, \mathbf{y})$ should satisfy either $f(\mathbf{a}^*) = 1$ or $(f = f^* \wedge \langle \mathbf{x}_0, \mathbf{y} \rangle = \langle \mathbf{x}_1, \mathbf{y} \rangle)$ where $\mathbf{x}_0, \mathbf{x}_1$ are the challenge messages chosen adaptively from $\mathcal{X}_\lambda$.

Game 0: The is the standard ABIPFE experiment as defined in Definition 2.

Game 1: We modify the setup algorithm. The challenger selects a random matrix $\mathbf{A}$ distributed uniformly over $\mathbb{Z}_q^{n\times m}$, instead of sampling $(\mathbf{A}, \mathbf{T_A}) \leftarrow \mathsf{TrapGen}(1^n, 1^m, q)$. However, a short basis of $\Lambda_q^\perp(\mathbf{A})$ is required to answer $\mathcal{A}$'s secret-key queries. For that, we enumerate all short bases of $\Lambda_q^\perp(\mathbf{A})$ and select one of these bases as $\mathbf{T_A}$. Note that, from Lemma 2, we have $\min||\widetilde{\mathbf{B}}|| < O(m)$

where minimum is taken over all ordered bases of $\Lambda_q^{\perp}(\mathbf{A})$. To apply SampleD with the input basis $\mathbf{B}$ (Theorem 3), we need to set $\rho > ||\widetilde{\mathbf{B}}|| \cdot \omega(\sqrt{\log m})$. Since $m = \Theta(n \log q)$, this suggests to set $\rho > n \cdot \omega(\sqrt{n})$.

The challenger is inefficient in this game, but this should not be a problem as long as we establish statistical indistinguishability between the games [3]. The matrix $\mathbf{A}$ used in game 0 is generated by $\mathsf{TrapGen}(1^n, 1^m, q)$ and Lemma 3 states that the distribution of $\mathbf{A}$ is statistically close to uniform over $\mathbb{Z}_q^{n \times m}$. Therefore, game 0 and game 1 are statistically indistinguishable as required.

Game 2: In this game the public matrix $\mathbf{D} \in \mathbb{Z}_q^{n \times \ell}$ is programmed by the challenger as follows. First, it samples $\mathbf{Z}_1, \mathbf{Z}_2 \leftarrow \mathcal{D}_\rho(\mathbb{Z}^{m \times \ell})$ and set $\mathbf{D}_1 = \mathbf{A}\mathbf{Z}_1$. Since $\mathcal{A}$ submits the target accepting function f^* before setup, the challenger computes $\mathbf{B}_{f^*} \leftarrow \mathsf{Eval}_{pk}(f^*, (\mathbf{B}_1, \ldots, \mathbf{B}_k))$ and set $\mathbf{D} = \mathbf{D}_1 + \mathbf{B}_{f^*}\mathbf{Z}_2$. In particular, if we take $\mathbf{Z} = \begin{pmatrix} \mathbf{Z}_1 \\ \mathbf{Z}_2 \end{pmatrix} \in \mathbb{Z}^{2m \times \ell}$, then $\mathbf{D} = (\mathbf{A}|\mathbf{B}_{f^*})\mathbf{Z}$. Instead of computing $\mathbf{R}_{f^*} \leftarrow \mathsf{SampleRight}(\mathbf{A}, \mathbf{T_A}, \mathbf{B}_{f^*}, \mathbf{D}, \rho)$, the challenger uses $\mathbf{Z}$ and answers secret-key queries for $(f^*, \boldsymbol{y})$ as $\mathsf{sk}_{f^*, \boldsymbol{y}} = \mathbf{Z} \cdot \boldsymbol{y}$. Note that, both $\mathbf{R}_{f^*}$ and $\mathbf{Z}$ follow the same distribution $\mathcal{D}_\rho(\mathbb{Z}^{2m \times \ell})$, as given in Lemma 5. However, the challenger still computes $\mathbf{R}_f \leftarrow \mathsf{SampleRight}(\mathbf{A}, \mathbf{T_A}, \mathbf{B}_f, \mathbf{D}, \rho)$ and outputs $\mathbf{R}_f \cdot \boldsymbol{y}$ as a reply to a secret-key query corresponding to $(f, \boldsymbol{y})$ if $f(\mathbf{a}^*) = 1$.

We show that $\mathbf{D}$ is uniformly distributed over $\mathbb{Z}_q^{n \times \ell}$. Specifically, we observe that for a matrix $\mathbf{A}$ uniform over $\mathbb{Z}_q^{n \times m}$ and a short basis $\mathbf{T_A}$ the distributions

$$\mathrm{Dist}_1 := (\mathbf{A}, \mathbf{Z}_1, \mathbf{D}_1) \text{ s.t. } \mathbf{D}_1 \leftarrow \mathbb{Z}^{n \times \ell}, \; \mathbf{Z}_1 \leftarrow \mathsf{SamplePre}(\mathbf{A}, \mathbf{T_A}, \mathbf{D}_1, \rho),$$
$$\mathrm{Dist}_2 := (\mathbf{A}, \mathbf{Z}_1, \mathbf{A}\mathbf{Z}_1) \text{ s.t. } \mathbf{Z}_1 \leftarrow \mathcal{D}_\rho(\mathbb{Z}^{m \times \ell})$$

are statistically close by Lemma 3. Therefore, $\mathbf{D}_1 = \mathbf{A}\mathbf{Z}_1$ is statistically close to uniform over $\mathbb{Z}_q^{n \times \ell}$ and hence the matrix $\mathbf{D} = \mathbf{D}_1 + \mathbf{B}_{f^*}\mathbf{Z}_2$ of game 2 is also statistically close to uniform over $\mathbb{Z}_q^{n \times \ell}$. Thus, game 1 and game 2 are statistically indistinguishable.

Game 3: Instead of selecting $(\mathbf{B}_1, \ldots, \mathbf{B}_k)$ uniformly from $(\mathbb{Z}_q^{n \times m})^k$, the challenger first chooses random matrices $\mathbf{S}_i^* \leftarrow \{\pm 1\}^{m \times m}$ in advance and uses the challenge attribute $\mathbf{a}^* = (a_1^*, \ldots, a_k^*)$ to set $\mathbf{B}_i = \mathbf{A}\mathbf{S}_i^* + a_i^* \mathbf{G}$ for all $i \in [k]$. Note that, the matrices $\mathbf{S}_1^*, \ldots, \mathbf{S}_k^*$ will be utilized to create the challenge ciphertext $\mathsf{ct}^* = (\mathsf{ct}_1^*, \mathsf{ct}_2^*)$. In particular, a fixed $\boldsymbol{e}_1 \leftarrow \mathcal{D}_\sigma(\mathbb{Z}^m)$ and low-norm vectors $\mathbf{S}_i^* \cdot \boldsymbol{e}_1 \in \mathbb{Z}^m$ for all $i \in [k]$ are used to create ct_1^*.

Observe that the distribution $(\mathbf{A}, \mathbf{A}\mathbf{S}_i^*, \mathbf{S}_i^* \boldsymbol{e}_1)$ is statistically close to the distribution $(\mathbf{A}, \mathbf{B}', \mathbf{S}_i^* \boldsymbol{e}_1)$ by lest-over hash lemma (Lemma 6) where $\mathbf{B}'$ is uniform over $\mathbb{Z}_q^{n \times m}$. This holds for all $i \in [k]$ and hence all matrices $\mathbf{A}\mathbf{S}_i^*$ are statistically close to uniform over $\mathbb{Z}_q^{n \times m}$. In other words, given $(\mathbf{S}_1^*| \cdots |\mathbf{S}_k^*) \cdot \boldsymbol{e}_1$, all matrices $\mathbf{B}_i = \mathbf{A}\mathbf{S}_i^* + a_i^* \mathbf{G}$ of game 3 are statistically close to uniform as in game 2. Thus, game 2 and game 3 are statistically indistinguishable.

Game 4: In this game, we make the challenger efficient, that is the short basis $\mathbf{T_A}$ is not required in the key query phase. Recall that a secret-key query $(f, \boldsymbol{y})$ of $\mathcal{A}$ should satisfy either $f(\mathbf{a}^*) = 1$ or $(f = f^* \wedge \langle \boldsymbol{x}_0, \boldsymbol{y} \rangle = \langle \boldsymbol{x}_1, \boldsymbol{y} \rangle)$. If $f = f^*$, the challenger uses the secret matrix $\mathbf{Z}$ to send the secret-key as $\mathsf{sk}_{f^*, \boldsymbol{y}} = \mathbf{Z} \cdot \boldsymbol{y}$ as in the previous game. When $f(\mathbf{a}^*) = 1$, instead of sampling $\mathbf{R}_f \leftarrow$ $\mathsf{SampleRight}(\mathbf{A}, \mathbf{T_A}, \mathbf{B}_f, \mathbf{D}, \rho)$ satisfying, $(\mathbf{A}|\mathbf{B}_f)\mathbf{R}_f = \mathbf{D}$ the challenger does the following.

1. Compute $\mathbf{S}_f = \mathsf{Eval}_{\mathsf{sim}}(f, ((a_i^*, \mathbf{S}_i))_{i=1}^k, \mathbf{A})$ which satisfies $\mathbf{AS}_f + \mathbf{G} = \mathbf{B}_f$ and $\|\mathbf{S}_f\|_2 < \gamma_{\mathcal{F}}$ by Theorem 4.
2. Sample $\mathbf{R}_f \leftarrow \mathsf{SampleLeft}(\mathbf{A}, \mathbf{S}_f, 1, \mathbf{D}, \rho)$ which is distributed according to $\mathcal{D}_\rho(\Lambda_q^{\mathbf{D}}(\mathbf{A}|\mathbf{AS}_f + \mathbf{G}))$ by Lemma 5.
3. Finally, the challenger outputs $\mathsf{sk}_{f, \boldsymbol{y}} = \mathbf{R}_f \cdot \boldsymbol{y}$.

Observe that $\mathbf{R}_f$ satisfies $(\mathbf{A}|\mathbf{AS}_f + \mathbf{G})\mathbf{R}_f = (\mathbf{A}|\mathbf{B}_f)\mathbf{R}_f = \mathbf{D}$ as required. To apply $\mathsf{SampleLeft}$, we need to set $\rho \geq \sqrt{5} \cdot (1 + \|\mathbf{S}_f\|_2) \cdot \omega(\sqrt{\log m})$. We also require $\rho > n \cdot \omega(\sqrt{n})$ as suggested in game 2. Combining, we set $\rho > n\gamma_{\mathcal{F}} \cdot \omega(\sqrt{n})$. The public parameters and secret-key queries in this game are statistically close to that of game 3. Hence, $\mathcal{A}$'s advantage in distinguishing between game 3 and game 4 is at most negligible in λ.

Game 5: In this game, we rely on the security of ALS-IPFE (Sect. 3 of the full version [31]) to establish the indistinguishability of the challenge ciphertext encrypting $\boldsymbol{x}_b$ for $b \leftarrow \{0, 1\}$. We consider an intermediate adversary $\mathcal{B}$ that interacts with the ALS-IPFE challenger. Let $\mathcal{B}$ receives the master public-key $\mathsf{mpk}_{\mathsf{ALS}} = (\mathbf{A}_{\mathsf{ALS}}, \mathbf{D}_{\mathsf{ALS}})$ from the ALS-IPFE challenger and a pair of attribute and target accepting function $(\mathbf{a}^*, f^*)$ from $\mathcal{A}$. Now, $\mathcal{B}$ simulates $\mathcal{A}$ as follows. $\mathcal{B}(1^\lambda, \mathsf{mpk}_{\mathsf{ALS}}, \mathbf{a}^*, f^*)$:

Setup. Pick $\mathbf{Z}_2 \leftarrow \mathcal{D}_\rho(\mathbb{Z}^{m \times \ell})$ and $\mathbf{S}_i^* \leftarrow \{\pm 1\}^{m \times m}$ for $i \in [k]$, and set

$$\mathbf{A} = \mathbf{A}_{\mathsf{ALS}}^\top, \quad \mathbf{B}_i = \mathbf{AS}_i^* - a_i^*\mathbf{G} \; \forall \, i \in [k], \quad \mathbf{D} = \mathbf{D}_{\mathsf{ALS}}^\top + \mathbf{B}_{f^*}\mathbf{Z}_2,$$

where $\mathbf{a}^* = (a_1^*, \ldots, a_k^*)$ and $\mathbf{B}_{f^*} = \mathsf{Eval}_{\mathsf{pk}}(f^*, (\mathbf{B}_1, \ldots, \mathbf{B}_k))$. It sends the master public-key as $\mathsf{mpk} = (\mathbf{A}, \mathbf{B}_1, \ldots, \mathbf{B}_k, \mathbf{D})$.

Secret-Key Queries. Suppose $\mathcal{A}$ asks a secret-key for a tuple $(f, \boldsymbol{y})$.

(a) If $f = f^*$ then $\mathcal{B}$ requests a secret-key for $\boldsymbol{y}$ from the ALS-IPFE challenger. Let $\mathsf{sk}_{\boldsymbol{y}}^{\mathsf{ALS}}$ be the secret-key. Then $\mathcal{B}$ sends $\mathsf{sk}_{f^*, \boldsymbol{y}} = \begin{pmatrix} (\mathsf{sk}_{\boldsymbol{y}}^{\mathsf{ALS}})^\top \\ \mathbf{Z}_2 \boldsymbol{y} \end{pmatrix}$ as the secret-key for $(f^*, \boldsymbol{y})$.

(b) If $f(\mathbf{a}^*) = 1$ then $\mathcal{B}$ uses $\mathsf{Eval}_{\mathsf{sim}}$ and $\mathsf{SampleLeft}$ to obtain a matrix $\mathbf{R}_f \in \mathbb{Z}^{2m \times \ell}$ and outputs $\mathbf{R}_f \cdot \boldsymbol{y}$ as in the previous game.

Challenge Ciphertext. Let $(\boldsymbol{x}_0, \boldsymbol{x}_1)$ be the challenge messages submitted by $\mathcal{A}$. Then, $\mathcal{B}$ submits the same to the ALS-IPFE challenger and receives $\mathsf{ct}_b^{\mathsf{ALS}} = (\mathsf{ct}_1^{\mathsf{ALS}}, \mathsf{ct}_2^{\mathsf{ALS}})$. Now, $\mathcal{B}$ computes and sends the challenge ciphertext $\mathsf{ct}^* = (\mathsf{ct}_1^*, \mathsf{ct}_2^*)$ for $\mathcal{A}$ as

$$\mathsf{ct}_1^* = \mathsf{ct}_1^{\mathsf{ALS}} + (\mathbf{S}^*)^\top \cdot \mathsf{ct}_1^{\mathsf{ALS}} \text{ and } \mathsf{ct}_2^* = \mathsf{ct}_2^{\mathsf{ALS}} + \mathbf{Z}_2^\top \cdot c_{f^*} + \mathsf{NoiseGen}(\mathbf{Z}_2^\top, s)$$

where we take $\mathbf{S}^* = (\mathbf{S}_1^* | \cdots | \mathbf{S}_k^*) \in \{\pm 1\}^{m \times km}$, $\mathsf{ct}_1^* = (c_0, c_1, \ldots, c_k) \in (\mathbb{Z}_q^m)^{k+1}$, $c_{f^*} = \mathsf{Eval}_{\mathsf{ct}}(f^*, ((a_i^*, \mathbf{B}_i, c_i))_{i=1}^k)$ and $\mathsf{NoiseGen}$ is the randomized algorithm with $s > s_1(\mathbf{Z}_2^\top)$ from Lemma 7.

We show that the distribution of the master public-key, secret-key queries and the challenge ciphertext are statistically close to that of in game 4. Let $\mathbf{D}_{\mathrm{ALS}} = \mathbf{Z}_{\mathrm{ALS}}\mathbf{A}_{\mathrm{ALS}}$ for some matrix $\mathbf{Z}_{\mathrm{ALS}} \leftarrow \mathcal{D}_\rho(\mathbb{Z}^{\ell \times m})$. Therefore, we have

$$\mathbf{D} = (\mathbf{Z}_{\mathrm{ALS}}\mathbf{A}_{\mathrm{ALS}})^\top + \mathbf{B}_{f^*}\mathbf{Z}_2 = \mathbf{A}\mathbf{Z}_{\mathrm{ALS}}^\top + \mathbf{B}_{f^*}\mathbf{Z}_2 = (\mathbf{A}|\mathbf{B}_{f^*})\mathbf{Z}$$

where $\mathbf{Z} = \begin{pmatrix} \mathbf{Z}_{\mathrm{ALS}}^\top \\ \mathbf{Z}_2 \end{pmatrix}$ is distributed according to $\mathcal{D}_\rho(\mathbb{Z}^{2m \times \ell})$. Note that, $\mathbf{Z}_{\mathrm{ALS}}$ plays the role of master secret-key of ALS-IPFE and the secret-keys of the form $\mathsf{sk}_{f^*,\boldsymbol{y}} = \begin{pmatrix} \mathbf{Z}_{\mathrm{ALS}}^\top \boldsymbol{y} \\ \mathbf{Z}_2 \boldsymbol{y} \end{pmatrix} = \mathbf{Z} \cdot \boldsymbol{y}$ are distributed similar to the previous game. Thus, the master public-key mpk and the secret-keys $\mathsf{sk}_{f^*,\boldsymbol{y}}$ for $(f^*, \boldsymbol{y})$ are distributed according to game 4. Moreover, secret-keys for $(f, \boldsymbol{y})$ satisfying $f(\mathbf{a}^*) = 1$ are identically distributed as in game 4.

Now, let $\mathsf{ct}_1^{\mathrm{ALS}} = \mathbf{A}_{\mathrm{ALS}}s + e_1$ and $\mathsf{ct}_2^{\mathrm{ALS}} = \mathbf{D}_{\mathrm{ALS}}s + e_2 + \lfloor \frac{q}{K} \rfloor \cdot \boldsymbol{x}_b$ for some $e_1 \leftarrow \mathcal{D}_\sigma(\mathbb{Z}^m)$ and $e_2 \leftarrow \mathcal{D}_\sigma(\mathbb{Z}^\ell)$. Hence, we can write the challenge ciphertext

$$\mathsf{ct}_1^* = \mathsf{ct}_1^{\mathrm{ALS}} + (\mathbf{S}^*)^\top \cdot \mathsf{ct}_1^{\mathrm{ALS}} = \mathbf{A}^\top s + e_1 + (\mathbf{S}^*)^\top \cdot (\mathbf{A}^\top s + e_1)$$
$$= (\mathbf{A}|\mathbf{A}\mathbf{S}^*)^\top s + (\mathbf{I}_m|\mathbf{S}^*)^\top \cdot e_1 = \mathbf{H}_{\mathbf{a}^*}^\top s + \boldsymbol{v}$$

where $\mathbf{H}_{\mathbf{a}^*} = (\mathbf{A}|a_1^*\mathbf{G} + \mathbf{B}_1| \cdots |a_k^*\mathbf{G} + \mathbf{B}_k) = (\mathbf{A}|\mathbf{A}\mathbf{S}^*)$ and $\boldsymbol{v} = (\mathbf{I}_m|\mathbf{S}^*)^\top \cdot e_1$. Observe that, by Theorem 4, $\mathsf{Eval}_{\mathsf{ct}}(f^*, ((a_i^*, \mathbf{B}_i, c_i))_{i=1}^k) = (f^*(\mathbf{a}^*)\mathbf{G} + \mathbf{B}_{f^*})^\top s + e_{f^*} = \mathbf{B}_{f^*}^\top s + e_{f^*} = c_{f^*}$ with $\|e_{f^*}\| < \sigma\sqrt{m} \cdot \gamma_{\mathcal{F}}$ which implies

$$\mathsf{ct}_2^* = \mathsf{ct}_2^{\mathrm{ALS}} + \mathbf{Z}_2^\top \cdot c_{f^*} + \mathsf{NoiseGen}(\mathbf{Z}_2^\top, s)$$
$$= (\mathbf{D} - \mathbf{B}_{f^*}\mathbf{Z}_2)^\top s + e_2 + \lfloor \frac{q}{K} \rfloor \cdot \boldsymbol{x}_b + \mathbf{Z}_2^\top \cdot (\mathbf{B}_{f^*}^\top s + e_{f^*}) + \mathsf{NoiseGen}(\mathbf{Z}_2^\top, s)$$
$$= \mathbf{D}^\top s + e_2 + \mathbf{Z}_2^\top e_{f^*} + \mathsf{NoiseGen}(\mathbf{Z}_2^\top, s) + \lfloor \frac{q}{K} \rfloor \cdot \boldsymbol{x}_b$$

From Lemma 1, we have $s_1(\mathbf{Z}_2^\top) \leq C\rho(2\sqrt{m} + \sqrt{\ell})$ and Lemma 7 implies that $\mathbf{Z}_2^\top e_{f^*} + \mathsf{NoiseGen}(\mathbf{Z}_2^\top, s)$ is distributed statistically close to $\mathcal{D}_\tau(\mathbb{Z}^\ell)$ where $\tau > 2C\rho\sigma(2\sqrt{m} + \sqrt{\ell})\gamma_{\mathcal{F}}$. Therefore, we can write $\mathsf{ct}_2^* = \mathbf{D}^\top s + e_2 + e_3 + \lfloor \frac{q}{K} \rfloor \cdot \boldsymbol{x}_b$ where e_2, e_3 are distributed as $\mathcal{D}_\sigma(\mathbb{Z}^\ell)$ and $\mathcal{D}_\tau(\mathbb{Z}^\ell)$ respectively. This proves that the challenge ciphertext is distributed statistically close to that of in the previous game. Also, the advantage of $\mathcal{A}$ in guessing the challenge bit is upper bounded by the advantage of $\mathcal{B}$ in breaking the security of ALS-IPFE scheme.

Parameter Setting. First we choose n, m, q, σ, ρ as in ALS-IPFE described in the full version [31]. We modify them step by step according to our requirement for correctness and security of our ABIPFE scheme. The modifications are made without violating the security of ALS-IPFE.

1. For TrapGen algorithm we set $m \geq 6n \log q$.
2. To obtain a short basis $\mathbf{T_A}$ for a uniformly chosen matrix $\mathbf{A}$ as required in game 1, we set $\rho > n \cdot \omega(\sqrt{n})$.
3. The parameters already satisfy the constrain in the left-over hash lemma (game 3 of the security proof).
4. For SampleRight and SampleLeft we need to set $\rho > \max\{\|\widetilde{\mathbf{T_A}}\| \cdot \omega(\sqrt{\log m}), \sqrt{5}(1 + \|\mathbf{S}_f\|_2)\omega(\sqrt{\log m})\}$ where $\|\mathbf{S}_f\|_2 < \gamma_{\mathcal{F}}$. This is due to correctness and game 4 of the security proof. Thus, combining with step 2, we can set $\rho > n\gamma_{\mathcal{F}} \cdot \omega(\sqrt{n})$.
5. To apply NoiseGen in game 5, we need to keep $\tau > 2C\rho\sigma(2\sqrt{m} + \sqrt{\ell})\gamma_{\mathcal{F}}$.
6. For the hardness of $\mathsf{LWE}_{q,\alpha,n}$ we want the standard deviation to satisfy $\alpha q > 2\sqrt{n}$.

Finally, the parameters of our ABIPFE can be set as

$$q > 4KV\ell(\sigma + \tau) + 8\rho\sigma KV\ell m(1 + \gamma_{\mathcal{F}}), \quad \sigma = 2C'\alpha q(\sqrt{m} + \sqrt{n} + \sqrt{\ell})$$

$$m \geq 6n \log q, \quad \rho > n\gamma_{\mathcal{F}} \cdot \omega(\sqrt{n}), \quad \tau > 2C\rho\sigma(2\sqrt{m} + \sqrt{\ell})\gamma_{\mathcal{F}}$$

where C (as in game 5), C' (as in ALS-IPFE) are constants.

4 Generic Construction of ABMIPFE from ABIPFE

We define an $\mathsf{ABMIPFE}_{n,m}$ scheme with access control given by a class of polynomial size circuits where n denotes the number of encryption slots and m denotes the number of attributes supported by each slot. Consider a class of attributes $\mathsf{Att} = \{((\mathbf{a}_1^{(j)}, \ldots, \mathbf{a}_n^{(j)}))_{j=1}^m\}$ where i-th encryption slot is associated to the attribute set $\mathsf{Att}_i = \{\mathbf{a}_i^{(1)}, \ldots, \mathbf{a}_i^{(m)}\}$ and $\mathbf{a}_i^{(j)} \in \{0,1\}^k$ for all $i \in [n], j \in [m]$. We represent the attribute class as $\mathsf{Att} = [\mathsf{Att}_1| \cdots |\mathsf{Att}_n]$. The i-th encryption slot encrypts a vector $\boldsymbol{x} \in \mathbb{Z}_q^\ell$ with respect to an attribute $\mathbf{a}_i^{(j)}$ for $j \in [m]$. We denote $\mathcal{F}_\lambda^{d,k}$ by the set of all polynomial size circuits with input space $\{0,1\}^k$ and depth bounded by d. A secret-key is generated for a tuple $(\mathsf{S} \subseteq [n], (f_i, \boldsymbol{y}_i)_{i \in \mathsf{S}})$ where $f_i \in \mathcal{F}_\lambda^{d,k}$, $\boldsymbol{y}_i \in \mathbb{Z}_q^\ell$ for all $i \in \mathsf{S}$. The secret-key allows a receiver to learn $\sum_{i \in \mathsf{S}} \langle \boldsymbol{x}_i, \boldsymbol{y}_i \rangle$ if $f_i(\mathbf{a}_i^{(j)}) = 0$ for all $i \in \mathsf{S}$ where $\boldsymbol{x}_i$ is encrypted for the i-th slot with an attribute $\mathbf{a}_i^{(j)} \in \mathsf{Att}_i$. For security, we first consider adaptive indistinguishability (Adp-IND) where the adversary $\mathcal{A}$ has the freedom to choose secret-key queries and encryption queries depending on the mpk. We also define a weaker security notion called Q-bounded co-adaptive indistinguishability (coAdp-IND) where $\mathcal{A}$ is restricted to submit all functions $f_1, \ldots, f_Q$ to be queried along with the predicate vectors in the key query phase before seeing the mpk. This is similar to the coSel-IND notion of ABIPFE. We formally define $\mathsf{ABMIPFE}_{n,m}$ and its security notions in the full version [31].

We utilize the transformation of [2,3] to convert a single input ABIPFE into an $\mathsf{ABMIPFE}_{n,1}$. Let us consider an ABIPFE for the function class

$\mathcal{F}_\lambda^{k,d}$ along with the predicates space $\{0,\ldots,V(\lambda)-1\}^\ell$ and message space $\{0,\ldots,X(\lambda)-1\}^\ell$. Combining we say that the ABIPFE is associated with a class $(\mathcal{F}_\lambda^{k,d},\mathcal{F}_\lambda^{\ell,V,X})$. We construct an $\text{ABMIPFE}_{n,1}$ for a class $(\mathcal{F}_\lambda^{k,d},\mathcal{F}_\lambda^{\ell,V,X})$ using an ABIPFE associated with a class $(\mathcal{F}_\lambda^{k,d},\mathcal{F}_\lambda^{\ell,V,3X})$. The ABIPFE should satisfy the structural properties namely *two step decryption* and *linear encryption* as required for the transformation of [2,3]. We describe the properties as follows:

1. *Two step decryption.* An ABIPFE scheme (Setup, KeyGen, Enc, Dec) admits additional PPT algorithms $\text{Setup}^*, \text{Dec}_1, \text{Dec}_2$ and an encoding function $\mathcal{E}$ such that
   (a) For all λ, ℓ, n, V, X, $\text{Setup}^*(1^\lambda, \mathcal{F}_\lambda^{\ell,V,X}, \mathcal{F}_\lambda^{k,d}, 1^n)$ uses $\text{Setup}(1^\lambda, 1^\ell, \mathcal{F}_\lambda^{k,d})$ to outputs (mpk, msk) where mpk includes a bound $B \in \mathbb{N}$, a group description $(\mathbb{G}, \circ)$ of order $L > n\ell V X$, which defines an encoding function $\mathcal{E} : \mathbb{Z}_L \times \mathbb{Z} \to \mathbb{G}$.
   (b) For all $\boldsymbol{x} \in \mathbb{Z}^\ell, \boldsymbol{a} \in \{0,1\}^k, \text{ct} \leftarrow \text{Enc}(\text{mpk}, \boldsymbol{a}, \boldsymbol{x})$ and $\boldsymbol{y} \in \mathbb{Z}^\ell, f \in \mathcal{F}_\lambda^{k,d}, \text{sk}_{f,\boldsymbol{y}} \leftarrow \text{KeyGen}(\text{sk}, f, \boldsymbol{y})$, we have

   $$\text{Dec}_1(\text{mpk}, \text{sk}_{f,\boldsymbol{y}}, \text{ct}) = \mathcal{E}(\langle \boldsymbol{x}, \boldsymbol{y} \rangle \bmod L, \text{noise})$$

   for some $\text{noise} \in \mathbb{N}$. Furthermore, for all $\boldsymbol{x}, \boldsymbol{y} \in \mathbb{Z}^\ell$ we have $\Pr[\text{noise} < B] = 1 - \text{negl}(\lambda)$. We also require that $\mathcal{E}(\gamma, 0)$ is efficiently computable for any $\gamma \in \mathbb{Z}_L$. Moreover, the encoding is linear, that is for $\gamma, \gamma' \in \mathbb{Z}_L, \text{noise}, \text{noise}' \in \mathbb{Z}$, we have

   $$\mathcal{E}(\gamma, \text{noise}) \circ \mathcal{E}(\gamma', \text{noise}') = \mathcal{E}(\gamma + \gamma' \bmod L, \text{noise} + \text{noise}')$$

   (c) For all $\gamma < n\ell V X$ and $\text{noise} < nB$, $\text{Dec}_2(\mathcal{E}(\gamma, \text{noise})) = \gamma$.
2. *Linear encryption.* There exists a deterministic algorithm Add such that for all $\boldsymbol{a} \in \{0,1\}^k, \boldsymbol{x}, \boldsymbol{x}' \in \mathbb{Z}^\ell$, the distributions $\text{Add}(\text{Enc}(\text{mpk}, \boldsymbol{a}, \boldsymbol{x}), \boldsymbol{x}')$ and $\text{Enc}(\text{mpk}, \boldsymbol{a}, \boldsymbol{x} + \boldsymbol{x}' \bmod L)$ are identically distributed. This property will be used in the security proof.

We present the transformation of $\text{ABMIPFE}_{n,1}$ from $\text{ABIPFE} = (\text{Setup}', \text{KeyGen}', \text{Enc}', \text{Dec}')$ which satisfies the above properties.

$\text{Setup}(1^\lambda, 1^\ell, \mathcal{F}_\lambda^{d,k}, \text{Att})$: It computes $(\text{mpk}_i, \text{msk}_i) \leftarrow \text{Setup}^*(1^\lambda, \mathcal{F}_\lambda^{\ell,V,3X}, \mathcal{F}_\lambda^{k,d}, 1^n)$ and samples $\boldsymbol{u}_i \leftarrow \mathbb{Z}_L^\ell$ for $i \in [n]$. Then it outputs $(\text{mpk} = \{\text{mpk}_i\}_{i\in[n]}, \text{msk} = (\{\text{msk}_i, \boldsymbol{u}_i\}_{i\in[n]}), \{\text{ek}_i = \boldsymbol{u}_i\}_{i\in[n]})$. We take $\text{Att} = (\mathbf{a}_1, \ldots, \mathbf{a}_n) \in \{0,1\}^{kn}$ as each party has a single attribute.
$\text{KeyGen}(\text{msk}, S, (f_i, \boldsymbol{y}_i)_{i\in S})$: If $f_i(\mathbf{a}_i) = 1$ for some $i \in S$ then returns $\bot$. Otherwise, it computes $\text{sk}_{f_i,\boldsymbol{y}_i} \leftarrow \text{KeyGen}'(\text{msk}_i, f_i, \boldsymbol{y}_i)$ for $i \in S$ and outputs $(S, \text{sk}_{f,\boldsymbol{y}} = (\{\text{sk}_{f_i,\boldsymbol{y}_i}\}_{i\in S}, z = \sum_{i\in S}\langle \boldsymbol{u}_i, \boldsymbol{y}_i\rangle))$. We assume that the secret-key includes a description of $(f_i, \boldsymbol{y}_i)_{i\in S}$.
$\text{Enc}(\text{mpk}, \text{ek}_i, \mathbf{a}_i, \boldsymbol{x}_i)$: It returns $\text{ct}_i \leftarrow \text{Enc}'(\text{mpk}_i, \mathbf{a}_i, \boldsymbol{x}_i + \text{ek}_i \bmod L)$.
$\text{Dec}(\text{mpk}, S, \text{sk}_{f,\boldsymbol{y}}, \{\text{ct}_i\}_{i=1}^n)$: It parses $\text{sk}_{f,\boldsymbol{y}} = (\{\text{sk}_{f_i,\boldsymbol{y}_i}\}_{i\in S}, z)$ and computes $\zeta_i \leftarrow \text{Dec}_1(\text{mpk}_i, \text{sk}_{f_i,\boldsymbol{y}_i}, \text{ct}_i)$ for $i \in S$. Then it returns $\text{Dec}_2(\circ_{i\in S} \zeta_i \circ \mathcal{E}(-z, 0))$.

Correctness. Let us assume that $f_i(\mathbf{a}_i) = 0$ for all $i \in S$. By the correctness of Dec_1 and Dec_2 of ABIPFE, we see $\zeta_i = \mathcal{E}(\langle \boldsymbol{x}_i + \boldsymbol{u}_i, \boldsymbol{y}_i \rangle \bmod L, \mathsf{noise}_i)$ for all $i \in S$ where $|\mathsf{noise}_i| < B$ with high probability. Since $z = \sum_{i \in S} \langle \boldsymbol{u}_i, \boldsymbol{y}_i \rangle$, by the linearity of $\mathcal{E}$, we have $\circ_{i \in S} \zeta_i \circ \mathcal{E}(-z, 0) = \mathcal{E}(\sum_{i \in S} \langle \boldsymbol{x}_i + \boldsymbol{u}_i, \boldsymbol{y}_i \rangle - z \bmod L, \mathsf{noise}) = \mathcal{E}(\sum_{i \in S} \langle \boldsymbol{x}_i, \boldsymbol{y}_i \rangle \bmod L, \mathsf{noise})$ where $|\mathsf{noise}| < nB$. Finally, $|\sum_{i \in S} \langle \boldsymbol{x}_i, \boldsymbol{y}_i \rangle| < L$ implies $\mathsf{Dec}_2(\circ_{i \in S} \zeta_i \circ \mathcal{E}(-z, 0))$ returns $\sum_{i \in S} \langle \boldsymbol{x}_i, \boldsymbol{y}_i \rangle$.

Theorem 6. *Assuming the single input ABIPFE is* Sel-IND *secure (respectively, Q-bounded* coSel-IND *secure) for a class $(\mathcal{F}_\lambda^{k,d}, \mathcal{F}_\lambda^{\ell,V,3X})$, then the above construction of* $\mathsf{ABMIPFE}_{n,1}$ *for the class $(\mathcal{F}_\lambda^{k,d}, \mathcal{F}_\lambda^{\ell,V,X})$ is* Adp-IND *secure (respectively, Q-bounded* coAdp-IND *secure). More specifically, for any PPT adversary $\mathcal{A}$, there exists a PPT adversary $\mathcal{B}$ such that*

$$\mathsf{Adv}^{\mathsf{xx\text{-}IND}}_{\mathsf{ABMIPFE}_{n,1},\mathcal{A}}(\lambda) \leq n \cdot \mathsf{Adv}^{\mathsf{yy\text{-}IND}}_{\mathsf{ABIPFE},\mathcal{B}}(\lambda) + \mathsf{negl}(\lambda)$$

where $(\mathsf{xx}, \mathsf{yy}) \in \{(\mathsf{Adp}, \mathsf{Sel}), (\mathsf{coAdp}, \mathsf{coSel})\}$.

We prove this Theorem in the full version [31]. Our 1-bounded coSel-IND secure ABIPFE of Sect. 3 can be fit into the above transformation. Formally, we state the result in the following corollary which is proved in the full version [31].

Corollary 1. *Assuming* $\mathsf{LWE}_{q,\alpha,n}$ *is hard with q, α, n are as defined at the end of Sect. 3, there exists a κ-bounded* coAdp-IND *secure* $\mathsf{ABMIPFE}_{\kappa,1}$ *scheme.*

5 Conclusion

We have shown the way of embedding any polynomial-size boolean circuit into the secret-keys of the existing IPFE scheme [5] and its multi-input variants [2]. The secret-keys are short and both the secrete-keys and ciphertexts of our ABIPFEs depend on the depth of the circuits. Moreover, the security is based on LWE assumption which makes our ABIPFEs post-quantum secure. The notion of 1-bounded coSel-IND security permits the adversary to query many secret-keys that can decrypt the challenge ciphertexts. This delivers a partial solution to the open problem in the key-policy setting given by Abdalla et al. [3].

However, the secret-keys that decrypt challenge messages are all corresponding to a single function. Achieving Q-bounded coSel-IND security with $Q > 1$ or (stronger) Sel-IND security for ABIPFE is a challenging open problem. Other than strengthening the security of ABIPFE, we can also investigate decentralized ABIPFE [34], attribute-based access control in case of unbounded IPFE [20] or traceable ABIPFE [18] for a specific class of policies.

References

1. Abdalla, M., Bourse, F., De Caro, A., Pointcheval, D.: Simple functional encryption schemes for inner products. In: Katz, J. (ed.) PKC 2015. LNCS, vol. 9020, pp. 733–751. Springer, Heidelberg (2015). https://doi.org/10.1007/978-3-662-46447-2_33

2. Abdalla, M., Catalano, D., Fiore, D., Gay, R., Ursu, B.: Multi-input functional encryption for inner products: function-hiding realizations and constructions without pairings. In: Shacham, H., Boldyreva, A. (eds.) CRYPTO 2018. LNCS, vol. 10991, pp. 597–627. Springer, Cham (2018). https://doi.org/10.1007/978-3-319-96884-1_20

3. Abdalla, M., Catalano, D., Gay, R., Ursu, B.: Inner-product functional encryption with fine-grained access control. IACR Cryptol. ePrint Arch. **2020**, 577 (2020)

4. Agrawal, S., Boneh, D., Boyen, X.: Efficient lattice (H)IBE in the standard model. In: Gilbert, H. (ed.) EUROCRYPT 2010. LNCS, vol. 6110, pp. 553–572. Springer, Heidelberg (2010). https://doi.org/10.1007/978-3-642-13190-5_28

5. Agrawal, S., Libert, B., Stehlé, D.: Fully secure functional encryption for inner products, from standard assumptions. In: Robshaw, M., Katz, J. (eds.) CRYPTO 2016. LNCS, vol. 9816, pp. 333–362. Springer, Heidelberg (2016). https://doi.org/10.1007/978-3-662-53015-3_12

6. Ajtai, M.: Generating hard instances of the short basis problem. In: Wiedermann, J., van Emde Boas, P., Nielsen, M. (eds.) ICALP 1999. LNCS, vol. 1644, pp. 1–9. Springer, Heidelberg (1999). https://doi.org/10.1007/3-540-48523-6_1

7. Alwen, J., Peikert, C.: Generating shorter bases for hard random lattices (2009)

8. Ananth, P., Jain, A., Khurana, D., Sahai, A.: Indistinguishability obfuscation without multilinear maps: IO from LWE, bilinear maps, and weak pseudorandomness. IACR Cryptol. ePrint Arch. **2018**, 615 (2018)

9. Ananth, P., Jain, A., Lin, H., Matt, C., Sahai, A.: Indistinguishability obfuscation without multilinear maps: new paradigms via low degree weak pseudorandomness and security amplification. In: Boldyreva, A., Micciancio, D. (eds.) CRYPTO 2019. LNCS, vol. 11694, pp. 284–332. Springer, Cham (2019). https://doi.org/10.1007/978-3-030-26954-8_10

10. Ananth, P., Sahai, A.: Functional encryption for turing machines. In: Kushilevitz, E., Malkin, T. (eds.) TCC 2016. LNCS, vol. 9562, pp. 125–153. Springer, Heidelberg (2016). https://doi.org/10.1007/978-3-662-49096-9_6

11. Barak, B., Hopkins, S.B., Jain, A., Kothari, P., Sahai, A.: Sum-of-Squares meets program obfuscation, revisited. In: Ishai, Y., Rijmen, V. (eds.) EUROCRYPT 2019. LNCS, vol. 11476, pp. 226–250. Springer, Cham (2019). https://doi.org/10.1007/978-3-030-17653-2_8

12. Boneh, D., Franklin, M.: Identity-Based encryption from the Weil pairing. In: Kilian, J. (ed.) CRYPTO 2001. LNCS, vol. 2139, pp. 213–229. Springer, Heidelberg (2001). https://doi.org/10.1007/3-540-44647-8_13

13. Boneh, D., et al.: Fully key-homomorphic encryption, arithmetic circuit ABE and compact garbled circuits. In: Nguyen, P.Q., Oswald, E. (eds.) EUROCRYPT 2014. LNCS, vol. 8441, pp. 533–556. Springer, Heidelberg (2014). https://doi.org/10.1007/978-3-642-55220-5_30

14. Boneh, D., Sahai, A., Waters, B.: Functional encryption: definitions and challenges. In: Ishai, Y. (ed.) TCC 2011. LNCS, vol. 6597, pp. 253–273. Springer, Heidelberg (2011). https://doi.org/10.1007/978-3-642-19571-6_16

15. Cai, J.Y.: A relation of primal-dual lattices and the complexity of shortest lattice vector problem. Theoret. Comput. Sci. **207**(1), 105–116 (1998)

16. Cash, D., Hofheinz, D., Kiltz, E., Peikert, C.: Bonsai trees, or how to delegate a lattice basis. In: Gilbert, H. (ed.) EUROCRYPT 2010. LNCS, vol. 6110, pp. 523–552. Springer, Heidelberg (2010). https://doi.org/10.1007/978-3-642-13190-5_27

17. Chen, Y., Zhang, L., Yiu, S.M.: Practical attribute based inner product functional encryption from simple assumptions. IACR Cryptol. ePrint Arch. **2019**, 846 (2019)

18. Do, X.T., Phan, D.H., Pointcheval, D.: Traceable inner product functional encryption. In: Jarecki, S. (ed.) CT-RSA 2020. LNCS, vol. 12006, pp. 564–585. Springer, Cham (2020). https://doi.org/10.1007/978-3-030-40186-3_24

19. Ducas, L., Micciancio, D.: Improved short lattice signatures in the standard model. In: Garay, J.A., Gennaro, R. (eds.) CRYPTO 2014. LNCS, vol. 8616, pp. 335–352. Springer, Heidelberg (2014). https://doi.org/10.1007/978-3-662-44371-2_19

20. Dufour-Sans, E., Pointcheval, D.: Unbounded inner-product functional encryption with succinct keys. In: Deng, R.H., Gauthier-Umaña, V., Ochoa, M., Yung, M. (eds.) ACNS 2019. LNCS, vol. 11464, pp. 426–441. Springer, Cham (2019). https://doi.org/10.1007/978-3-030-21568-2_21

21. Garg, S., Gentry, C., Halevi, S., Raykova, M., Sahai, A., Waters, B.: Candidate indistinguishability obfuscation and functional encryption for all circuits. SIAM J. Comput. 45(3), 882–929 (2016)

22. Garg, S., Miles, E., Mukherjee, P., Sahai, A., Srinivasan, A., Zhandry, M.: Secure obfuscation in a weak multilinear map model. In: Hirt, M., Smith, A. (eds.) TCC 2016. LNCS, vol. 9986, pp. 241–268. Springer, Heidelberg (2016). https://doi.org/10.1007/978-3-662-53644-5_10

23. Gay, R., Jain, A., Lin, H., Sahai, A.: Indistinguishability obfuscation from simple-to-state hard problems: new assumptions, new techniques, and simplification. IACR Cryptol. ePrint Arch 2020, 764 (2020)

24. Gentry, C., Peikert, C., Vaikuntanathan, V.: Trapdoors for hard lattices and new cryptographic constructions. In: Proceedings of the Fortieth Annual ACM symposium on Theory of Computing, pp. 197–206 (2008)

25. Goyal, V., Pandey, O., Sahai, A., Waters, B.: Attribute-based encryption for fine-grained access control of encrypted data. In: Proceedings of the 13th ACM Conference on Computer and Communications Security, pp. 89–98 (2006)

26. Jain, A., Lin, H., Matt, C., Sahai, A.: How to leverage hardness of constant-degree expanding polynomials over $\mathbb{R}$ to build $i\mathcal{O}$. In: Ishai, Y., Rijmen, V. (eds.) EUROCRYPT 2019. LNCS, vol. 11476, pp. 251–281. Springer, Cham (2019). https://doi.org/10.1007/978-3-030-17653-2_9

27. Jain, A., Lin, H., Sahai, A.: Simplifying constructions and assumptions for IO. Technical Report, Cryptology ePrint Archive, Report 2019/1252. https ... (2019)

28. Katsumata, S., Yamada, S.: Partitioning via non-linear polynomial functions: more compact IBEs from ideal lattices and bilinear maps. In: Cheon, J.H., Takagi, T. (eds.) ASIACRYPT 2016. LNCS, vol. 10032, pp. 682–712. Springer, Heidelberg (2016). https://doi.org/10.1007/978-3-662-53890-6_23

29. Micciancio, D., Peikert, C.: Trapdoors for lattices: simpler, tighter, faster, smaller. In: Pointcheval, D., Johansson, T. (eds.) EUROCRYPT 2012. LNCS, vol. 7237, pp. 700–718. Springer, Heidelberg (2012). https://doi.org/10.1007/978-3-642-29011-4_41

30. O'Neill, A.: Definitional issues in functional encryption. IACR Cryptol. ePrint Arch. 2010, 556 (2010)

31. Pal, T., Dutta, R.: Attribute-based access control for inner product functional encryption from LWE. Cryptology ePrint Archive, Report 2021/178 (2021)

32. Regev, O.: On lattices, learning with errors, random linear codes, and cryptography. In: Proceedings of the Thirty-Seventh Annual ACM Symposium on Theory of Computing, pp. 84–93 (2005)

33. Sahai, A., Waters, B.: Fuzzy identity-based encryption. In: Cramer, R. (ed.) EUROCRYPT 2005. LNCS, vol. 3494, pp. 457–473. Springer, Heidelberg (2005). https://doi.org/10.1007/11426639_27

34. Wang, Z., Fan, X., Liu, F.-H.: FE for inner products and its application to decentralized ABE. In: Lin, D., Sako, K. (eds.) PKC 2019. LNCS, vol. 11443, pp. 97–127. Springer, Cham (2019). https://doi.org/10.1007/978-3-030-17259-6_4
35. Waters, B.: Dual system encryption: realizing fully secure IBE and HIBE under simple assumptions. In: Halevi, S. (ed.) CRYPTO 2009. LNCS, vol. 5677, pp. 619–636. Springer, Heidelberg (2009). https://doi.org/10.1007/978-3-642-03356-8_36

Asymmetric Cryptanalysis

Classical Attacks on a Variant of the RSA Cryptosystem

Abderrahmane Nitaj[1(✉)], Muhammad Rezal Bin Kamel Ariffin[2],
Nurul Nur Hanisah Adenan[2], and Nur Azman Abu[3]

[1] Normandie Univ, UNICAEN, CNRS, LMNO, 14000 Caen, France
abderrahmane.nitaj@unicaen.fr
[2] Institute for Mathematical Research, Universiti Putra Malaysia,
43400 Serdang, Selangor, Malaysia
[3] Faculty of Information Technology and Communication Technology,
Universiti Teknikal Malaysia, Melaka, Malaysia

Abstract. Let $N = pq$ be an RSA modulus with balanced prime factors. In 2018, Murru and Saettone presented a variant of the RSA cryptosystem based on a cubic Pell equation in which the public key (N, e) and the private key (N, d) satisfy $ed \equiv 1 \pmod{(p^2 + p + 1)(q^2 + q + 1)}$. They claimed that the classical small private attacks on RSA such as Wiener's continued fraction attack do not apply to their scheme. In this paper, we show that, on the contrary, Wiener's method as well as the small inverse problem technique of Boneh and Durfee can be applied to attack their scheme. More precisely, we show that the proposed variant of RSA can be broken if $d < N^{0.5694}$. This shows that their scheme is in reality more vulnerable than RSA, where the bound of vulnerability is $d < N^{0.292}$.

Keywords: RSA · Factorization · Continued fractions · Small inverse problem · Coppersmith's method

1 Introduction

Data transaction during early 70's was conducted using symmetric cryptosystems which means the same key were used for encryption and decryption processes. However, problems on distributing keys arose as the number of users increased. In 1976, this problem was solved mathematically by Diffie and Hellman [10], and improved in 1978 by Rivest, Shamir and Adleman [23]. Rivest, Shamir and Adleman invented an elegant cryptosytem named RSA which utilized different keys for encryption and decryption algorithms. The construction of RSA begins with key generation process. Let $N = pq$ be the modulus of RSA where p and q are large primes. To resist the factorization attacks, it is recommended that p and q should be of the same bitsize, that is $q < p < 2q$. Let e be an integer such that $\gcd(e, \phi(N)) = 1$ where $\phi(N) = (p-1)(q-1)$ is Euler-totient function. Let $d \equiv e^{-1} \pmod{\phi(N)}$. The key (N, e) is public while $p, q, d, \phi(N)$ are kept secret. For encryption and decryption processes, both involve modulo

© Springer Nature Switzerland AG 2021
P. Longa and C. Ràfols (Eds.): LATINCRYPT 2021, LNCS 12912, pp. 151–167, 2021.
https://doi.org/10.1007/978-3-030-88238-9_8

operations. To encrypt a message m, one needs to compute $c \equiv m^e \pmod{N}$ while to decrypt and retrieve back the message, one needs to compute $m \equiv c^d \pmod{N}$.

It can be seen that the private exponent d is needed to decrypt the ciphertext c. Note that the cost incurred to decrypt increases directly proportional with the size of d. Thus, one would prefer to use small value of d. Unfortunately, Wiener [27] showed that the cryptosystem that employ a small value of d is vulnerable. Wiener showed that for $d < \frac{1}{3} N^{\frac{1}{4}}$, one could retrieve d via the continued fraction expansion of $\frac{e}{N}$ and thus factor the modulus N. This bound was then improved by Boneh and Durfee [6] up to $d < N^{0.292}$. Later in 2004, Blömer and May [2] described a generalized Wiener's attack. Utilizing the combination of lattice reduction and continued fraction, Blömer and May showed that if there exists three integers x, y, z such that $ex - y\phi(N) = z$ with $x < \frac{1}{3} N^{\frac{1}{4}}$ and $|z| < exN^{-3/4}$, then N can be factored.

Since then, researchers studied thoroughly on this cryptosystem in order to find any other weakness that could lead to the vulnerabilities of RSA. They found that, any leakage on either of the primes could lead to the factorization of N. In 1996, Coppersmith [8] showed that RSA is susceptible given only half of the most significant bits of one of the primes. Later, Boneh et al. [4] showed that if one knew half of the least significant bit of either prime p or q, then RSA can be factored. Ernest et al. [11] and Boneh et al. [4] also worked upon this matter and they showed that indeed RSA is susceptible if one knows some information on bits of either most significant bits (MSBs) or least significant bits (LSBs) of private exponents.

Meanwhile, some researchers began to design variants of the RSA cryptosystem purposely to enhance its security. Takagi [25] was the first that designed a variant of RSA using the modulus $N = p^{r-1}q$ for $r \geq 3$ and showed that this scheme is more efficient in both its key generation and decryption algorithms. However, the studies from [1,5,24] showed that this variant of RSA is also insecure from attacks if certain conditions are satisfied.

In 2018, another scheme was invented by Murru and Saettone [21]. They introduced a new variant of the RSA cryptosystem based on the cubic Pell equation $x^3 + ry^3 + r^2 z^3 - 3rxyz = 1$. In their cryptosystem, they utilized the standard modulus $N = pq$, a public exponent e, a private exponent d, and the key equation $ed - k\psi(N) = 1$ with $\psi(N) = (p^2 + p + 1)(q^2 + q + 1)$. The authors investigated the proposed cryptosystem for efficiency and security, and claimed that the attack of Wiener is not usable against their scheme.

In this paper, we show that the attack of Wiener, as well as the method of Boneh and Durfee, can be applied to factor $N = pq$ with $q < p < 2q$ when the decryption exponent d is sufficiently small. More precisely, we set $e = N^\alpha$, and $d = N^\delta$, and we show that Wiener's attack can solve the equation $ed - k\psi(N) = 1$ and factor N if $\delta < \frac{5}{4} - \frac{1}{2}\alpha$. In the normal case where $e \approx N^2$, the bound becomes $d < N^{\frac{1}{4}}$. Astonishingly, this is roughly the same bound than the classical bound obtained by Wiener's method for standard RSA. Similarly, we show that the method of Boneh and Durfee can be applied if $\delta < \frac{7}{3} - \frac{2}{3}\sqrt{3\alpha + 1}$. When $e \approx N^2$, the bound reduces to $d < N^{0.5694}$. Here, we observe that 0.5694 is twice the weaker bound 0.2847 obtained by Boneh and Durfee [6] with the small inverse problem attack on RSA.

The framework of this paper is as follows. In Sect. 2 and Sect. 3, we describe some important tools and useful lemmas respectively. In Sect. 4, we present our first results while Sect. 5 presents our second results. We conclude the paper in Sect. 6.

2   Preliminaries

In this section, we summarize the scheme of Murru and Saettone [21], and describe briefly on some important tools that are needed in our attacks.

2.1   The Scheme of Murru and Saettone

Let $(\mathbb{F}, +, \cdot)$ be a field, and $r \in \mathbb{F}$ be a non-cubic integer. Then the polynomial $t^3 - r$ is irreducible in $\mathbb{F}[t]$, and the quotient field $\mathbb{A} = \mathbb{F}[t]/\left(t^3 - r\right)$ is the set of elements of the form $x + ty + t^2 z$ with $(x, y, z) \in \mathbb{F}^3$. A product $\bullet$ between the elements of $\mathbb{A}$ can be conducted by the rule

$$(x_1, y_1, z_1) \bullet (x_2, y_2, z_2)$$
$$= ((x_1 x_2 + (y_2 z_1 + y_1 z_2)r, x_2 y_1 + x_1 y_2 + r z_1 z_2, y_1 y_2 + x_2 z_1 + x_1 z_2).$$

The norm of an element $x + ty + t^2 z \in \mathbb{A}$ is defined by

$$N(x, y, z) = x^3 + ry^3 + r^2 z^3 - 3rxyz.$$

The cubic Pell equation is defined by the solutions $(x, y, z) \in \mathbb{F}^3$ of the equation $N(x, y, z) = 1$. The solutions form the commutative group $(\mathcal{C}, \bullet)$ where

$$\mathcal{C} = \left\{ (x, y, z) \in \mathbb{F}^3, \ x^3 + ry^3 + r^2 z^3 - 3rxyz = 1 \right\}.$$

In $(\mathcal{C}, \bullet)$, the identity is $(1, 0, 0)$ and the inverse of $(x, y, z) \in \mathcal{C}$ is $(x, y, z)^{-1} = \left(x^2 - ryz, rz^2 - xy, y^2 - xz\right)$. Next, let $B = \mathbb{A}^*/\mathbb{F}^*$ be the quotient group. Let $\alpha \notin \mathbb{F}$ be fixed. The elements of B are of one of the forms $m + nt + t^2$, or $m + t$, or 1. As a consequence, B reduces to

$$B = (\mathbb{F} \times \mathbb{F}) \cup (\mathbb{F} \times \{\alpha\}) \cup \{(\alpha, \alpha)\},$$

where (α, α) will play the point at infinity for the addition operation $\odot$ defined by the following cases

- $(m, \alpha) \odot (p, \alpha) = (mp, m + p)$,
- if $n + p \neq 0$, then $(m, n) \odot (p, \alpha) = \left(\frac{mp+r}{n+p}, \frac{m+np}{n+p} \right)$,
- if $n + p = 0$ and $m - n^2 \neq 0$, then $(m, n) \odot (p, \alpha) = \left(\frac{mp+r}{m-n^2}, \alpha \right)$,
- if $n + p = 0$ and $m - n^2 = 0$, then $(m, n) \odot (p, \alpha) = (\alpha, \alpha)$,

- if $m + p + nq \neq 0$, then $(m, n) \odot (p, q) = \left(\frac{mp+(n+q)r}{m+p+nq}, \frac{np+mq+r}{m+p+nq} \right)$,
- if $m+p+nq = 0$ and $np+mq+r \neq 0$, then $(m, n) \odot (p,q) = \left(\frac{mp+(n+q)r}{np+mq+r}, \alpha \right)$,
- if $m + p + nq = 0$ and $np + mq + r = 0$, then $(m, n) \odot (p, q) = (\alpha, \alpha)$,

Then $(B, \odot)$ is a commutative group, and the scheme of Murru and Saettone [21] is based on the cubic Pell equation $x^3 + ry^3 + r^2z^3 - 3rxyz = 1$ where r is a non-cubic integer. When $\mathbb{F} = \mathbb{Z}/p\mathbb{Z}$ where p is a prime number, one can take $\alpha = \infty$, and $\mathbb{A} = \mathbb{F}_{p^3}$ is the Galois field with p^3 elements. Hence, $B = B_p$ is a cyclic group of order $p^2 + p + 1$, and for every $(m, n) \in B_p$, one has $(m, n)^{\odot(p^2+p+1)} = (\alpha, \alpha) \pmod{p}$ where $x^{\odot k} = x \odot x \odot \cdots x$ (k times). Using these facts, a variant of the RSA cryptosystem can be built by choosing an RSA modulus $N = pq$, an integer r which is non-cubic modulo p, q, and N, and by combing the cyclic groups B_p and B_q. In this scheme, the public exponent is an integer e satisfying $\gcd\left(e, (p^2 + p + 1)(q^2 + q + 1)\right) = 1$. To encrypt a message $M \in B$, the operation is $C = M^{\odot e} \pmod{N}$, and to decrypt C, the operation is $M = C^{\odot d} \pmod{N}$ where $d \equiv e^{-1} \pmod{(p^2 + p + 1)(q^2 + q + 1)}$. We notice that the idea of constructing a variant of RSA based on a cubic curve has already been used in [7,16–18]. We also notice that the XTR cryptosystem [20] uses the arithmetic that consists of representing the elements of $\mathbb{F}_{p^6}^*$ with order dividing $p^2 - p + 1$ by their trace over $\mathbb{F}_{p^2}$.

In [21], the efficiency and the security of the RSA variant are studied. The authors claim that classical small exponent attacks such as Wiener's continued fraction attack can not be applied since the trapdoor function is not a simple monomial power as in RSA. In this paper, we show that Wiener's attack as well as Boneh and Durfee lattice reduction based attack can be applied to this variant of RSA. Moreover, we show that it is more vulnerable in general than RSA.

2.2   Continued Fraction

The continued fraction expansion of a real number ξ can be written in the form

$$\xi = a_0 + \cfrac{1}{a_1 + \cfrac{1}{a_2 + \cfrac{1}{a_3 + \cfrac{1}{a_4 + \cdots}}}} \tag{1}$$

where $a_0 \in \mathbb{Z}$ and $a_i \in \mathbb{Z}^+$ are the partial quotients. The form in (1) is often expressed as $\xi = [a_0, a_1, \ldots, a_n]$. Thus, for $i \geq 0$, every rational number $\frac{r}{s}$, such that

$$\frac{r}{s} = [a_0, a_1, \ldots, a_n]$$

is a convergent of the continued fraction expansion of ξ. The continued fraction expansion is finite if ξ is a rational number. Moreover, r and s are coprime. The following theorem is a tool to test if a rational number $\frac{r}{s}$ is a convergent of ξ (see [12], Theorem 184).

Theorem 1. *Let ξ be a positive number. Suppose that $\gcd(r, s) = 1$ and*

$$\left| \xi - \frac{r}{s} \right| < \frac{1}{2s^2}.$$

Then $\frac{r}{s}$ is a convergent of the continued fraction expansion of ξ.

2.3 Lattices and Coppersmith's Method

Let ω and n be two positive integers. Let $u_1, \cdots, u_\omega \in \mathbb{R}^n$ be a set of ω linearly independent vectors. A lattice $\mathcal{L}$ is constructed based on the linear combinations of $u_1, \ldots, u_\omega$ such that $\mathcal{L} = \{\sum_{i=1}^{\omega} \lambda_i u_i | \lambda_i \in \mathbb{Z}\}$. For full ranked lattice which means $\omega = n$, the determinant is defined as $\det(\mathcal{L}) = (\det(UU^T))^{\frac{1}{2}} = |\det(U)|$. In 1982, Lenstra, Lenstra, and Lovász [19] introduced an important algorithm called LLL that is used to produce a reduced basis with optimal properties. Their result is described as follows.

Theorem 2 (LLL). *Let $\mathcal{L}$ be a lattice that is constructed by a basis $(u_1, \ldots, u_\omega)$. The LLL algorithm yields a new basis $(b_1, \ldots, b_\omega)$ of L satisfying*

$$\|b_1\| \leq \cdots \leq \|b_i\| \leq 2^{\frac{\omega(\omega-1)}{4(\omega+1-i)}} \det(\mathcal{L})^{\frac{1}{\omega+1-i}},$$

for $i = 1, 2, \ldots, \omega$.

One of the numerous applications of the LLL algorithm is Coppersmith's method [8]. The method is suited to find the small solutions of an univariate polynomial modular equation $f(x) = 0 \pmod{N}$, or a bivariate polynomial equation $f(x, y) = 0$. Coppersmith's method has various applications, especially in cryptanalysis, and has been extended to more variables. Two of the key ingredients in Coppersmith's method are lattice reduction and the following result, as reformulated by Howgrave-Graham [14].

Theorem 3 (Howgrave-Graham). *Let $h(x, y) = \sum a_{ij} x^i y^j \in \mathbb{Z}[x, y] \in \mathbb{Z}[x, y]$ be a polynomial with at most ω monomials and norm $\|h(x, y)\| = \sqrt{\sum a_{ij}^2}$. If $|x_0| < X$, $|y_0| < Y$, and*

$$h(x_0, y_0) \equiv 0 \pmod{e^m}, \quad \|h(xX, yY)\| < \frac{e^m}{\sqrt{\omega}},$$

then $h(x_0, y_0) = 0$ holds over the integers.

In this paper, we will consider the bivariate modular polynomial equation $f(x, y) = x(y^2 + ay + b) + 1 \equiv 0 \pmod{e}$, where a, b, and e are fixed integers. To find the small solutions of this equation, we build a lattice $\mathcal{L}$ of dimension ω with a basis formed by the coefficients of a class of polynomials $G(x, y)$ derived from $f(x, y)$. Each polynomial $G(x, y)$ is such that $G(x, y) \equiv 0 \pmod{e^m}$ for a fixed integer m. Then, applying the LLL algorithm, we reduce the basis and construct new polynomials $h(x, y)$ such that $h(x, y) \equiv 0 \pmod{e^m}$. Under certain conditions, we have also $h(x, y) = 0$ over the integers for some polynomials. Then, assuming that such polynomials are algebraically independent, we use Gröbner basis technique to find the common roots. The assumption can be formulated as follows.

Assumption 1. *The lattice reduced basis yields algebraically independent polynomials, and the common roots of these polynomials can be efficiently computed using the Gröbner basis technique.*

3 Useful Lemmas

Let $N = pq$ be an RSA modulus with $q < p < 2q$. The following result gives the bounds for p, and q in terms of N (see [22]).

Lemma 1. *Let $N = pq$ be the product of two unknown integers with $q < p < 2q$. Then*

$$\frac{\sqrt{2}}{2}\sqrt{N} < q < \sqrt{N} < p < \sqrt{2}\sqrt{N}.$$

The former lemma can be used to find an upper and a lower bound for $\psi(N)$.

Proposition 1. *Let $N = pq$ be the product of two unknown prime integers with $q < p < 2q$, and $\psi(N) = (p^2 + p + 1)(q^2 + q + 1)$. Then*

$$\left(N + \sqrt{N} + 1\right)^2 < \psi(N) < \left(N + \frac{3}{4}\sqrt{2}\sqrt{N} + 1\right)^2 - \frac{3}{8}N.$$

Proof. Plugging $q = \frac{N}{p}$ in $\psi(N) = (p^2 + p + 1)(q^2 + q + 1)$, we get a function f with p as a variable, namely

$$f(p) = (p^2 + p + 1)\left(\frac{N^2}{p^2} + \frac{N}{p} + 1\right).$$

The derivative of f at p is

$$f'(p) = \frac{(p^2 - N)(2p^2 + (N+1)p + 2N)}{p^3}.$$

By Lemma 1, we have $p^2 > N$, which implies $f'(p) > 0$. It follows that f is increasing with p. Also, by Lemma 1, we have $\sqrt{N} < p < \sqrt{2}\sqrt{N}$. Hence $f\left(\sqrt{N}\right) < f(p) < f\left(\sqrt{2}\sqrt{N}\right)$, which leads to

$$\left(N + \sqrt{N} + 1\right)^2 < \psi(N) < \left(N + \frac{3}{4}\sqrt{2}\sqrt{N} + 1\right)^2 + \frac{3}{8}N.$$

This terminates the proof.   □

The former proposition can be used to find a good approximation for $\psi(N)$.

Proposition 2. *Let $N = pq$ be the product of two unknown prime integers with $q < p < 2q$, and*

$$\psi_0(N) = \frac{1}{2}\left(N + \sqrt{N} + 1\right)^2 + \frac{1}{2}\left(N + \frac{3}{4}\sqrt{2}\sqrt{N} + 1\right)^2 + \frac{3}{16}N.$$

Then

$$|\psi(N) - \psi_0(N)| < \frac{1}{2}N^{\frac{3}{2}}.$$

Proof. By Proposition 1, $\psi_0(N)$ is the mean value of the two bounds $\left(N + \sqrt{N} + 1\right)^2$ and $\left(N + \frac{3}{4}\sqrt{2}\sqrt{N} + 1\right)^2 + \frac{3}{8}N$. Then

$$
\begin{aligned}
|\psi(N) - \psi_0(N)| &\leq \frac{1}{2}\left(\left(N + \frac{3}{4}\sqrt{2}\sqrt{N} + 1\right)^2 - \left(N + \sqrt{N} + 1\right)^2 + \frac{3}{8}N\right) \\
&= \frac{1}{2}\left(\frac{3}{4}\sqrt{2} - 1\right)\sqrt{N}\left(2N + \left(\frac{3}{4}\sqrt{2} + 1\right)\sqrt{N} + 2\right) + \frac{3}{16}N \\
&= \left(\frac{3}{4}\sqrt{2} - 1\right)N^{\frac{3}{2}}\left(1 + \left(\frac{3}{8}\sqrt{2} + \frac{1}{2}\right)N^{-\frac{1}{2}} + N^{-2}\right) + \frac{3}{16}N \\
&< \frac{1}{2}N^{\frac{3}{2}},
\end{aligned}
$$

which is valid for all $N > 2$. This terminates the proof. $\square$

The following result shows that one can factor the modulus $N = pq$ if $\psi(N)$ is known.

Proposition 3. *Let $N = pq$ be the product of two unknown integers with $q < p$. Suppose that $\psi(N) = \left(p^2 + p + 1\right)\left(q^2 + q + 1\right)$ is known. Then*

$$p = \frac{1}{2}\left(S + \sqrt{S^2 - 4N}\right), \quad q = \frac{1}{2}\left(S - \sqrt{S^2 - 4N}\right),$$

where

$$S = \frac{1}{2}\left(\sqrt{(N+1)^2 + 4\left(\psi(N) - (N^2 - N + 1)\right)} - (N + 1)\right).$$

Proof. Expanding $\psi(N) = \left(p^2 + p + 1\right)\left(q^2 + q + 1\right)$ and rearranging, we get

$$(p + q)^2 + (N + 1)(p + q) + N^2 - N + 1 - \psi(N) = 0.$$

Solving for $p + q$, we get

$$p + q = \frac{1}{2}\left(\sqrt{(N+1)^2 + 4\left(\psi(N) - (N^2 - N + 1)\right)} - (N + 1)\right).$$

Let $S = \frac{1}{2}\left(\sqrt{(N+1)^2 + 4\left(\psi(N) - (N^2 - N + 1)\right)} - (N + 1)\right)$. Using $q = \frac{N}{p}$, we get $p^2 - Sp + N = 0$. Then solving this equation for p, we get

$$p = \frac{1}{2}\left(S + \sqrt{S^2 - 4N}\right), \text{ and } q = \frac{1}{2}\left(S - \sqrt{S^2 - 4N}\right).$$

This gives the result. $\square$

4   Application of Continued Fractions

In this section, we give an upper bound for d for which the continued fractions algorithm will succeed to find d and factor the modulus $N = pq$.

4.1   The Attack

Theorem 4. *Let $N = pq$ be the product of two unknown prime numbers with $q < p < 2q$. Suppose that $ed - k\psi(N) = 1$ with $\psi(N) = (p^2 + p + 1)(q^2 + q + 1)$, $e = N^\alpha$, and $d = N^\delta$. Then, for $\frac{3}{2} < \alpha < \frac{5}{2}$, one can find d and factor N in polynomial time if*

$$\delta < \frac{5}{4} - \frac{1}{2}\alpha.$$

Proof. Suppose that $ed - k\psi(N) = 1$ with $\psi(N) = (p^2 + p + 1)(q^2 + q + 1)$. Let

$$\psi_0(N) = \frac{1}{2}\left(N + \sqrt{N} + 1\right)^2 + \frac{1}{2}\left(N + \frac{3}{4}\sqrt{2}\sqrt{N} + 1\right)^2 + \frac{3}{16}N.$$

Then

$$\left|\frac{k}{d} - \frac{e}{\psi_0(N)}\right| = \frac{|ed - k\psi_0(N)|}{d\psi_0(N)} \le \frac{|ed - k\psi(N)| + k|\psi(N) - \psi_0(N)|}{d\psi_0(N)}.$$

We have $|ed - k\psi(N)| = 1$, and, by Proposition 2, we have $|\psi(N) - \psi_0(N)| < \frac{1}{2}N^{\frac{3}{2}}$. Also, by Proposition 1, we have

$$\psi(N) > \left(N + \sqrt{N} + 1\right)^2 > N^2.$$

Using this, we get

$$\left|\frac{k}{d} - \frac{e}{\psi_0(N)}\right| < \frac{1 + \frac{1}{2}kN^{\frac{3}{2}}}{d\psi_0(N)} < \frac{k}{2d} \cdot \frac{2 + N^{\frac{3}{2}}}{\psi_0(N)}$$

By Proposition 1, we have

$$\psi_0(N) > \left(N + \sqrt{N} + 1\right)^2 > N^2 + 2\sqrt{N}.$$

Then

$$\left|\frac{k}{d} - \frac{e}{\psi_0(N)}\right| < \frac{k}{2d} \cdot \frac{2 + N^{\frac{3}{2}}}{N^2 + 2\sqrt{N}} = \frac{k}{2d\sqrt{N}}.$$

Now, we have $k\psi(N) = ed - 1 < ed$, which leads to

$$\frac{k}{d} < \frac{e}{\psi(N)} < \frac{N^\alpha}{N^2} = N^{\alpha - 2}.$$

We then obtain

$$\left|\frac{k}{d} - \frac{e}{\psi_0(N)}\right| < \frac{1}{2}\frac{N^{\alpha-2}}{\sqrt{N}} = \frac{1}{2}N^{\alpha-\frac{5}{2}}.$$

Now, if $\alpha - \frac{5}{2} < -2\delta$, that is $\delta < \frac{5}{4} - \frac{1}{2}\alpha$, then

$$\left| \frac{k}{d} - \frac{e}{\psi_0(N)} \right| < \frac{1}{2d^2}.$$

Consequently, by Theorem 1, $\frac{k}{d}$ is a convergent of $\frac{e}{\psi_0(N)}$ that can be computed by the continued fraction algorithm. Using $\frac{k}{d}$ in $ed - k\psi(N) = 1$, we get $\psi(N) = \frac{ed-1}{k}$. By Proposition 3, this leads to the values of the prime factors p and q. Observe that we must have $\delta > 0$, which implies that $\frac{5}{4} - \frac{1}{2}\alpha > 0$, and consequently $\alpha < \frac{5}{2}$. Also, we must have $\delta + \alpha > 2$. This implies that $\alpha > \frac{3}{2}$. □

If e is a full size exponent, that is $e \approx N^2$, then the bound on δ becomes $\delta < \frac{1}{4}$, which is the bound that can be attained by applying Wiener's method to the standard RSA.

4.2   A Numerical Example

As an example for the continued fraction attack, let us consider the small public key

$$N = 23213379103433965595553921193777061637232329967339982 07,$$

$$e = 38045049044229768209422371670354854749091332518178618 2\backslash$$
$$1424765273464173530009100734162450325021258033591800 3.$$

We have $e \approx N^\alpha$ with $\alpha \approx 1.997$. We apply the continued fraction algorithm to $\frac{e}{\psi_0(N)}$ and get the first 30 partial quotients

$$[0, 1, 2, 2, 2, 23, 2, 12, 5, 2, 2, 8, 8, 1, 10, 1, 1, 1, 17, 6, 1, 1, 29, 1, 2, 1, 34, 22, 2, 1, 10, \ldots].$$

All the corresponding convergents are candidates for $\frac{k}{d}$. We consider only the convergents such that $\psi = \frac{ed-1}{k}$ is an integer. This happens for the 2th, 3th, 4th and 26th convergents. Among them, we consider only the convergents such that the system of equations

$$\begin{cases} \left(p^2 + p + 1\right)\left(q^2 + q + 1\right) & = \psi, \\ pq & = N, \end{cases}$$

has a solution as given in Proposition 3. This happens only for the 26th convergent, that is for $\frac{k}{d} = \frac{14646831653369}{20745421813476}$. It leads to

$$\psi(N) = 53886096939974470038369301629051749283201431422018206\backslash$$
$$725952642886800244273357202657271138657794039600145283,$$

and, by Proposition 3, we get

$$p = 54472665980815171246 0129079,$$
$$q = 42614729214115439878 1533433.$$

We observe that $d \approx N^\delta$ with $\delta \approx 0.249$, which satisfies the condition of Theorem 4, that is $\delta < \frac{5}{4} - \frac{1}{2}\alpha \approx 0.251$.

5   Application of Coppersmith's Method

Let e and d be the public and the private exponent such that $ed - k\psi(N) = 1$ with $\psi(N) = (p^2 + p + 1)(q^2 + q + 1)$. In this section, we focus on solving the small inverse problem $x(y^2 + ay + b) + 1 \pmod{e}$, where $a = N+1$ and $b = N^2 - N + 1$. We then apply the method to show that one can factor N if k or d is sufficiently small.

5.1   The Small Inverse Problem

Theorem 5. *Let $N = pq$ be the product of two unknown prime factors with $q < p < 2q$. Let $a = N + 1$ and $b = N^2 - N + 1$. Suppose that $x(y^2 + ay + b) + 1 \equiv 0 \pmod{e}$ with $e = N^\alpha$, $y < 2\sqrt{2}N^{\frac{1}{2}}$, and $x = N^\gamma$. Then, for $1 < \alpha < \frac{15}{4}$, one can find x and y in polynomial time if*

$$\gamma < \alpha + \frac{1}{3} - \frac{2}{3}\sqrt{3\alpha + 1}.$$

Proof. Let $N = pq$ be an RSA modulus. Let e be a public exponent satisfying $x(y^2 + ay + b) + 1 \equiv 0 \pmod{e}$ where $a = N + 1$ and $b = N^2 - N + 1$. Consider the polynomial $f(x,y) = x(y^2 + ay + b) + 1$. The small solutions of the former equation could be found by Coppersmith's method [8] combined with the extended strategy of Jochemsz and May [15]. Let m and t be positive integers. For $0 \leq k \leq m$, define the set

$$M_k = \bigcup_{0 \leq h \leq t} \{ x^i y^{j+h} \mid x^i y^j \text{ is a monomial of } f^m(x,y)$$

$$\text{and} \quad \frac{x^i y^j}{(xy^2)^k} \text{ is a monomial of } f^{m-k}(x,y) \}.$$

We have

$$f^m(x,y) = \sum_{i_1=0}^{m} \sum_{j_1=0}^{i_1} \sum_{j_2=0}^{i_1-j_1} \binom{m}{i_1}\binom{i_1}{j_1}\binom{i_1-j_1}{j_2} a^{j_2} b^{i_1-j_1-j_2} x^{i_1} y^{2j_1+j_2}.$$

It follows that $x^i y^j$ is a monomial of $f^m(x,y,z)$ if

$$i = 0, \ldots, m, \quad j = 0, \ldots, 2i.$$

Then, we deduce that $x^i y^j$ is a monomial of $f^{m-k}(x,y)$ if

$$i = 0, \ldots, m - k, \quad j = 0, \ldots, 2i.$$

It follows that, if $x^i y^j$ is a monomial of $f^m(x,y)$, then $\frac{x^i y^j}{(xy^2)^k}$ is a monomial of $f^{m-k}(x,y)$ if $i = k, \ldots, m, j = 2k, \ldots, 2i$. Hence, the set M_k is as follows

$$x^i y^j \in M_k \text{ if } i = k, \ldots, m, \quad j = 2k, \ldots, 2i + t.$$

Classical Attacks on a Variant of the RSA Cryptosystem 161

Similarly, we have

$$x^i y^j \in M_{k+1} \text{ if } i = k+1, \ldots, m, \; j = 2k+2, \ldots, 2i+t.$$

Then $x^i y^j \in M_k \backslash M_{k+1}$ if

$$i = k, \ldots, m, \; j = 2k, 2k+1 \text{ or } i = k, \; j = 2k+2, \ldots, 2i+t.$$

For $0 \le k \le m$, we define the polynomials

$$g_{k,i,j}(x,y) = \frac{x^i y^j}{(xy^2)^k} f(x,y)^k e^{m-k} \quad \text{with} \quad x^i y^j \in M_k \backslash M_{k+1}.$$

They reduce to one of the following polynomials

$$g_{k,i,j}(x,y) = x^{i-k} y^{j-2k} f(x,y)^k e^{m-k},$$
$$\text{for} \quad k = 0, \ldots m, \; i = k, \ldots, m, \; j = 2k, 2k+1,$$
$$\text{or} \quad k = 0, \ldots m, \; i = k, \; j = 2k+2, \ldots, 2i+t.$$

Next, define the lattice $\mathcal{L}$ spanned by the coefficient vectors of the polynomials $g_{k,i,j}(xX, yY)$ where X and Y are positive integers satisfying

$$X = N^\gamma, Y = 2\sqrt{2}N^{\frac{1}{2}}.$$

The rows of the matrix of the lattice are denoted $g_{k,i,j}$ and ordered following the natural order of (i,j), completed by k. Similarly, the monomials $x^i y^j$ are ordered as in the natural order of (i,j). In Table 1, we present an example of the matrix of the lattice for $m = 2$, $t = 2$, where every symbol ⊛ is a non zero entry.

We obtain a left triangular matrix and its determinant is the product of the diagonal terms, where only X, Y, and e are used. Hence, the determinant is of the form

$$\det(\mathcal{L}) = X^{n_X} Y^{n_Y} e^{n_e}. \tag{2}$$

Table 1. The matrix of the lattice for $m = 2$, $t = 2$.

	1	y	y^2	x	xy	xy^2	xy^3	xy^4	x^2	x^2y	x^2y^2	x^2y^3	x^2y^4	x^2y^5	x^2y^6
$g_{0,0,0}$	e^2	0	0	0	0	0	0	0	0	0	0	0	0	0	0
$g_{0,0,1}$	0	Ye^2	0	0	0	0	0	0	0	0	0	0	0	0	0
$g_{0,0,2}$	0	0	Y^2e^2	0	0	0	0	0	0	0	0	0	0	0	0
$g_{0,1,0}$	0	0	0	Xe^2	0	0	0	0	0	0	0	0	0	0	0
$g_{0,1,1}$	0	0	0	0	XYe^2	0	0	0	0	0	0	0	0	0	0
$g_{1,1,2}$	⊛	0	0	⊛	⊛	XY^2e	0	0	0	0	0	0	0	0	0
$g_{1,1,3}$	0	⊛	0	0	⊛	⊛	XY^3e	0	0	0	0	0	0	0	0
$g_{1,1,4}$	0	0	⊛	0	0	⊛	⊛	XY^4e	0	0	0	0	0	0	0
$g_{0,2,0}$	0	0	0	0	0	0	0	0	X^2e^2	0	0	0	0	0	0
$g_{0,2,1}$	0	0	0	0	0	0	0	0	0	X^2Ye^2	0	0	0	0	0
$g_{1,2,2}$	0	0	0	⊛	0	0	0	0	⊛	⊛	X^2Y^2e	0	0	0	0
$g_{1,2,3}$	0	0	0	0	⊛	0	0	0	0	⊛	⊛	X^2Y^3e	0	0	0
$g_{2,2,4}$	⊛	0	0	⊛	⊛	⊛	0	0	⊛	⊛	⊛	⊛	X^2Y^4	0	0
$g_{2,2,5}$	0	⊛	0	0	⊛	⊛	⊛	0	0	⊛	⊛	⊛	⊛	X^2Y^5	0
$g_{2,2,6}$	0	0	⊛	0	0	⊛	⊛	⊛	0	0	⊛	⊛	⊛	⊛	X^2Y^6

Define

$$S(z) = \sum_{k=0}^{m}\sum_{i=k}^{m}\sum_{j=2k}^{2k+1} z + \sum_{k=0}^{m}\sum_{i=k}^{k}\sum_{j=2k+2}^{t} z$$

We set $t = m\tau$, where $\tau \geq 0$ will be optimised later. The exact values of n_X, n_Y, and n_e, as well as the dimension ω of the lattice, and their approximations are

$$n_X = S(i) = \frac{1}{6}m(m+1)(4m+3\tau+5)$$

$$= \frac{1}{6}(3\tau+4)m^3 + o(m^3)$$

$$n_Y = S(j) = \frac{1}{6}(m+1)\left(4m^2 + 6m\tau + 3\tau^2 + 5m + 3\tau\right)$$

$$= \frac{1}{6}\left(3\tau^2 + 6\tau + 4\right)m^3 + o(m^3) \qquad (3)$$

$$n_e = S(m-k) = \frac{1}{6}m(m+1)(4m+3\tau+5)$$

$$= \frac{1}{6}(3\tau+4)m^3 + o(m^3)$$

$$\omega = S(1) = (m+1)(m+1+\tau)$$

$$= (\tau+1)m^2 + o(m^2).$$

In order to combine Theorem 3 and Theorem 2 for $i = 2$, we need

$$2^{\frac{\omega}{4}}\det(\mathcal{L})^{\frac{1}{\omega-1}} < \frac{e^m}{\sqrt{\omega}},$$

which gives

$$\det(\mathcal{L}) < \frac{2^{-\frac{\omega(\omega-1)}{4}}}{(\sqrt{\omega})^{\omega-1}}e^{m(\omega-1)}.$$

Combining with (2), we get

$$e^{n_e - m\omega}X^{n_X}Y^{n_Y} < \frac{2^{-\frac{\omega(\omega-1)}{4}}}{(\sqrt{\omega})^{\omega-1}}e^{-m}. \qquad (4)$$

Substituting the values of n_X, n_Y, n_e, and ω from (3) as well as $X = N^\gamma$ and $Y = 2\sqrt{2}N^{\frac{1}{2}}$ in (4), taking logarithms, and dividing by $\log(N)$, we get

$$3\tau^2 + 6(\gamma - \alpha + 1)\tau + 4(2\gamma - \alpha + 1) < -\varepsilon_1,$$

where ε_1 is a small positive constant, that depends on m and N. The optimal value for τ in the left side is $\tau_0 = \alpha - \gamma - 1$. It gives

$$-3\gamma^2 + 2(1 + 3\alpha)\gamma - 3\alpha^2 + 2\alpha + 1 < -\varepsilon_1,$$

which is true if

$$\gamma < \alpha + \frac{1}{3} - \frac{2}{3}\sqrt{3\alpha + 1}.$$

We need $\gamma \geq 0$. This is satisfied if

$$\alpha + \frac{1}{3} - \frac{2}{3}\sqrt{3\alpha + 1} \geq 0,$$

that is $\alpha \geq 1$. On the other hand, we need $\tau_0 = \alpha - \gamma - 1 \geq 0$, that is $\gamma \leq \alpha - 1$. Hence, for $\alpha \geq 1$, we have

$$\gamma < \min\left(\alpha - 1, \alpha + \frac{1}{3} - \frac{2}{3}\sqrt{3\alpha + 1}\right) = \alpha + \frac{1}{3} - \frac{2}{3}\sqrt{3\alpha + 1}.$$

Using two vectors in the LLL reduced basis, we form two polynomials $G_1(x, y)$, $G_2(x, y)$ satisfying

$$G_1(x, y) = G_2(x, y) = 0.$$

Assuming that the polynomials are algebraically independent, we apply resultant techniques or Gröbner basis method to find the solution (x, y). This terminates the proof. □

5.2   The Attack with Small k

As an application of the method of Theorem 1, we have the following result.

Corollary 1. *Let $N = pq$ be the product of two unknown prime factors with $q < p < 2q$. Suppose that $ed - k\psi(N) = 1$ with $\psi(N) = \left(p^2 + p + 1\right)\left(q^2 + q + 1\right)$, $e = N^\alpha$, and $k = N^\gamma$. Then, for $1 < \alpha$, one can factor N in polynomial time if*

$$\gamma < \alpha + \frac{1}{3} - \frac{2}{3}\sqrt{3\alpha + 1}.$$

Proof. Let $N = pq$ be an RSA modulus. Let e be a public exponent satisfying $ed - k\psi(N) = 1$, with $\psi(N) = \left(p^2 + p + 1\right)\left(q^2 + q + 1\right)$, $e = N^\alpha$, and $k = N^\gamma$. Since

$$\left(p^2 + p + 1\right)\left(q^2 + q + 1\right) = (p + q)^2 + a(p + q) + b$$

where $a = N + 1$ and $b = N^2 - N + 1$, then the equation $ed - k\psi(N) = 1$ can be rewritten as

$$k\left((p + q)^2 + a(p + q) + b\right) + 1 \equiv 0 \pmod{e}.$$

Consider the polynomial $f(x, y) = x\left(y^2 + ay + b\right) + 1$. Then $(x_0, y_0) = (k, p + q)$ is a solution of the polynomial modular equation $f(x, y) \equiv 0 \pmod{e}$. The equation can be solved by the method of Theorem 5 if $\gamma < \alpha + \frac{1}{3} - \frac{2}{3}\sqrt{3\alpha + 1}$. Using $p + q = y_0$, and $pq = N$, this leads to the factorization of N. □

Let us present a small numerical example for Corollary 1. Consider

$$N = 437444022784453, e = 370036391765209395740044739800.$$

Since $e \approx N^{1.951}$, then the bound is $\gamma < \alpha + \frac{1}{3} - \frac{2}{3}\sqrt{3\alpha + 1} \approx 0.539$. So we take $X = \lfloor N^{0.6} \rfloor$, $Y = 3 \lfloor \sqrt{N} \rfloor$, $m = 4$, and $t = 3$. We build a lattice with a dimension $\omega = 40$. Then applying our method, we get the solution

$$x = k = 164427, y = p + q = 42593626.$$

Combining with $pq = N$, we finally get $p = 25310567$, and $q = 17283059$, which factors the modulus.

5.3   The Attack with Small d

Now, we focus on the attack on the scheme when d is small.

Theorem 6. *Let $N = pq$ be the product of two unknown prime factors with $q < p < 2q$. Suppose that $ed - k\psi(N) = 1$ with $\psi(N) = (p^2 + p + 1)(q^2 + q + 1)$, $e = N^\alpha$, and $d = N^\delta$. Then, for $1 < \alpha < \frac{15}{4}$, one can find d, and factor N in polynomial time if*

$$\delta < \frac{7}{3} - \frac{2}{3}\sqrt{3\alpha + 1}.$$

Proof. Let $N = pq$ be an RSA modulus. Let e be a public exponent satisfying $ed - k\psi(N) = 1$, where $\psi(N) = (p^2 + p + 1)(q^2 + q + 1)$. We use the bounds $e = N^\alpha$, $d = N^\delta$. By Proposition 1, we have $(p+q)^2 + a(p+q) + b = \psi(N) > N^2$. Then

$$k = \frac{ed - 1}{(p+q)^2 + a(p+q) + b} < N^{\alpha + \delta - 2}.$$

We apply Corollary 1 with $\gamma = \alpha + \delta - 2$. The condition is

$$\gamma = \alpha + \delta - 2 < \alpha + \frac{1}{3} - \frac{2}{3}\sqrt{3\alpha + 1},$$

which is true if

$$\delta < \frac{7}{3} - \frac{2}{3}\sqrt{3\alpha + 1}.$$

Since $ed = k\psi(N) + 1 > \psi(N) > N^2$, then we need $\alpha + \delta > 2$. The condition is satisfied if

$$\alpha + \frac{7}{3} - \frac{2}{3}\sqrt{3\alpha + 1} > 2,$$

and is valid if $\alpha > 1$. On the other hand, we need $\delta > 0$. This is satisfied if

$$\alpha + \frac{7}{3} - \frac{2}{3}\sqrt{3\alpha + 1} > 0,$$

leading to $\alpha < \frac{15}{4}$. This terminates the proof.   □

If e is a full size exponent, that is $e \approx N^2$, then the bound on δ becomes $\delta < \frac{7}{3} - \frac{2}{3}\sqrt{7} \approx 0.569$. This is twice the bound obtained by Boneh and Durfee [6] with the small inverse problem attack on RSA.

5.4   Experimental Results

We implemented the method described in Theorem 6, and conducted intensive experiments in Windows 10 environment on a computer with Intel(R) Core(TM) i5-8250U CPU 1.60 GHz, 8.0 GO. We experimented the method with the following process

- We generate two random prime numbers p, q of various sizes up to 1024 bits.
- We compute $N = pq$, and $\psi(N) = (p^2 + p + 1)(q^2 + q + 1)$.
- We generate a random integer $d = N^\delta$ with $\delta < 0.56$ and $\gcd(d, \psi(N)) = 1$.
- We compute $e \equiv d^{-1} \pmod{\psi(N)}$.
- We apply the method described in Theorem 6 to find the small solutions of the equation $x(y^2 + ay + b) + 1 \equiv 0 \pmod{e}$.
- Using $p + q = y$ and $pq = N$, we retrieve p and q.

The longest phase in the method is the computation of the reduced basis when applying the LLL algorithm. It depends mainly on the dimension ω and the size of N.

So far, we succeeded to factor the very small RSA modulus $N = 601396198489$ for $e = 1569479955769308430$. Since $e \approx N^{1.544}$, then the bound on δ is $\delta < \frac{7}{3} - \frac{2}{3}\sqrt{3\alpha + 1} \approx 0.750$. So we applied our method with $X = \lfloor N^{0.75} \rfloor$, $Y = 3\lfloor \sqrt{N} \rfloor$, $m = 6$, and $t = 3$. We get a lattice with a dimension $\omega = 70$. We solved the equation $x(y^2 + ay + b) + 1 \equiv 0 \pmod{e}$, and get the solution $x = 13$, $y = 1559590$. Then, using $p + q = y$ and $pq = N$, we get $p = 861551$, and $q = 698039$. We notice here that $d = N^\delta$ with $\delta \approx 0.55$. The whole process took less than 240 s.

When N is a 1024 bit modulus, we were able to factor N with $d = N^\delta$ for $\delta < 0.43$, with $m = 4$, $t = 2$, $\omega = 35$, $X = \lfloor N^{0.5} \rfloor$, and $Y = 3\lfloor \sqrt{N} \rfloor$. The computation took approximately 8372 s.

6   Conclusion

In this paper, we presented two distinct attacks on a cubic Pell equation variant of the RSA cryptosystem presented by Murru and Saettone in 2018. The variant is based on an RSA modulus $N = pq$, with a public exponent $e = N^\alpha$, a private exponent d and a key equation of the form $ed - k\psi(N) = 1$ where $\psi(N) = (p^2 + p + 1)(q^2 + q + 1)$. For the first attack, we extended Wiener's attack and showed that one can factor the modulus N via the continued fraction expansion provided $d = N^\delta$ for $\delta < \frac{5}{4} - \frac{1}{2}\alpha$. Moreover, we showed that this variant of RSA is more vulnerable by our second attack which is based on Coppersmith's method. We extended the method of Boneh and Durfee and showed that the RSA variant is insecure whenever $\delta < \frac{7}{3} - \frac{2}{3}\sqrt{3\alpha + 1}$. When $\alpha \approx 2$, the bound resumes to $d < N^{0.5694}$, which is much larger than the classical bound $d < N^{0.292}$ for RSA. As a conclusion, the variant RSA scheme is more vulnerable than the RSA cryptosystem.

References

1. Adenan, N.N.H., Ariffin, M.R.K., Sapar, S.H., Ghafar, A.H.A., Asbullah, M.A.: New Jochemsz-May cryptanalytic bound for RSA system utilizing common modulus $N = p^2q$. Mathematics **9**(4), 340 (2021). https://www.mdpi.com/2227-7390/9/4/340

2. Blömer, J., May, A.: A generalized Wiener attack on RSA. In: Bao, F., Deng, R., Zhou, J. (eds.) PKC 2004. LNCS, vol. 2947, pp. 1–13. Springer, Heidelberg (2004). https://doi.org/10.1007/978-3-540-24632-9_1

3. Boneh, D.: Twenty years of attacks on the RSA cryptosystem. Notices Amer. Math. Soc. **46**(2), 203–213 (1999)

4. Boneh, D., Durfee, G., Frankel, Y.: An attack on RSA given a small fraction of the private key bits. In: Ohta, K., Pei, D. (eds.) ASIACRYPT 1998. LNCS, vol. 1514, pp. 25–34. Springer, Heidelberg (1998). https://doi.org/10.1007/3-540-49649-1_3

5. Boneh, D., Durfee, G., Howgrave-Graham, N.: Factoring $N = p^r q$ for large r. In: Wiener, M. (ed.) CRYPTO 1999. LNCS, vol. 1666, pp. 326–337. Springer, Heidelberg (1999). https://doi.org/10.1007/3-540-48405-1_21

6. Boneh, D., Durfee, G.: Cryptanalysis of RSA with private key d less than $N^{0.292}$. In: Stern, J. (ed.) EUROCRYPT 1999. LNCS, vol. 1592, pp. 1–11. Springer, Heidelberg (1999). https://doi.org/10.1007/3-540-48910-X_1

7. Boudabra, M., Nitaj, A.: A new generalization of the KMOV cryptosystem. J. Appl. Math. Comput. **57**(1-2), 229–245 (2018)

8. Coppersmith, D.: Small solutions to polynomial equations, and low exponent RSA vulnerabilities. J. Cryptol. **10**(4), 233–260 (1997)

9. Demytko, N.: A new elliptic curve based analogue of RSA. In: Helleseth, T. (ed.) EUROCRYPT 1993. LNCS, vol. 765, pp. 40–49. Springer, Heidelberg (1994). https://doi.org/10.1007/3-540-48285-7_4

10. Diffie, W., Hellman, M.: New directions in cryptography. IEEE Trans. Inf. Theory **22**(6), 644–654 (1976)

11. Ernst, M., Jochemsz, E., May, A., de Weger, B.: Partial key exposure attacks on RSA up to full size exponents. In: Cramer, R. (ed.) EUROCRYPT 2005. LNCS, vol. 3494, pp. 371–386. Springer, Heidelberg (2005). https://doi.org/10.1007/11426639_22

12. Hardy, G.H., Wright, E.M.: An Introduction to the Theory of Numbers, 5th edition. The Clarendon Press, Oxford University Press, New York (1979)

13. Hinek, M.: Cryptanalysis of RSA and its Variants. Cryptography and Network Security Series, Chapman & Hall/CRC, Boca Raton (2009)

14. Howgrave-Graham, N.: Finding small roots of univariate modular equations revisited. In: Darnell, M. (ed.) Cryptography and Coding 1997. LNCS, vol. 1355, pp. 131–142. Springer, Heidelberg (1997). https://doi.org/10.1007/BFb0024458

15. Jochemsz, E., May, A.: A strategy for finding roots of multivariate polynomials with new applications in attacking RSA variants. In: Lai, X., Chen, K. (eds.) ASIACRYPT 2006. LNCS, vol. 4284, pp. 267–282. Springer, Heidelberg (2006). https://doi.org/10.1007/11935230_18

16. Koyama, K.: Fast RSA-type schemes based on singular cubic curves $y^2 + axy \equiv x^3 \pmod{n}$. In: Guillou, L.C., Quisquater, J.-J. (eds.) EUROCRYPT 1995. LNCS, vol. 921, pp. 329–340. Springer, Heidelberg (1995). https://doi.org/10.1007/3-540-49264-X_27

17. Koyama, K., Maurer, U.M., Okamoto, T., Vanstone, S.A.: New public-key schemes based on elliptic curves over the ring $\mathbb{Z}_n$. In: Feigenbaum, J. (ed.) CRYPTO 1991. LNCS, vol. 576, pp. 252–266. Springer, Heidelberg (1992). https://doi.org/10.1007/3-540-46766-1_20

18. Kuwakado H., Koyama K., Tsuruoka, Y.: A new RSA-type scheme based on singular cubic curves $y^2 \equiv x^3 + bx^2 \pmod{n}$. IEICE Trans. Fundamentals **E78-A**, 27–33 (1995)

19. Lenstra, A.K., Lenstra, H.W., Lovász, L.: Factoring polynomials with rational coefficients. Mathematische Annalen **261**, 513–534 (1982)

20. Lenstra, A.K., Verheul, E.R.: The XTR public key system. In: Bellare, M. (ed.) CRYPTO 2000. LNCS, vol. 1880, pp. 1–19. Springer, Heidelberg (2000). https://doi.org/10.1007/3-540-44598-6_1

21. Murru, N., Saettone, F.M.: A novel RSA-like cryptosystem based on a generalization of the Rédei rational functions. In: Kaczorowski, J., Pieprzyk, J., Pomykała, J. (eds.) NuTMiC 2017. LNCS, vol. 10737, pp. 91–103. Springer, Cham (2018). https://doi.org/10.1007/978-3-319-76620-1_6

22. Nitaj, A.: Another generalization of Wiener's attack on RSA. In: Vaudenay, S. (ed.) AFRICACRYPT 2008. LNCS, vol. 5023, pp. 174–190. Springer, Heidelberg (2008). https://doi.org/10.1007/978-3-540-68164-9_12

23. Rivest, R., Shamir, A., Adleman, L.: A method for obtaining digital signatures and public-key cryptosystems. Commun. ACM **21**(2), 120–126 (1978)

24. Sarkar, S.: Small secret exponent attack on RSA variant with modulus $N = p^r q$. Des. Codes Cryptogr. **73**(2), 383–392 (2014)

25. Takagi, T.: A fast RSA-type public-key primitive modulo $p^k q$ using Hensel lifting. IEICE Trans. **87-A**, 94–101 (2004)

26. de Weger, B.: Cryptanalysis of RSA with small prime difference. Appl. Algebra Eng. Commun. Comput. **13**(1), 17–28 (2002)

27. Wiener, M.: Cryptanalysis of short RSA secret exponents. IEEE Trans. Inf. Theory **36**, 553–558 (1990)

Improved Attacks Against Key Reuse in Learning with Errors Key Exchange

Nina Bindel[(⊠)], Douglas Stebila[Ⓘ], and Shannon Veitch

University of Waterloo, Waterloo, ON, Canada
{nlbindel,dstebila,ssveitch}@uwaterloo.ca

Abstract. Basic key exchange protocols built from the learning with errors (LWE) assumption are insecure if secret keys are reused in the face of active attackers. One example of this is Fluhrer's attack on the Ding, Xie, and Lin (DXL) LWE key exchange protocol, which exploits leakage from the signal function for error correction.

In this work, we demonstrate improved and new attacks exploiting key reuse in several LWE-based key exchange protocols. First, we show how to greatly reduce the number of samples required to carry out Fluhrer's attack and reconstruct the secret period of a noisy square waveform, speeding up the attack on DXL key exchange by a factor of over 200. We show how to adapt this to attack a protocol of Ding, Branco, and Schmitt (DBS) designed to be secure with key reuse, breaking the claimed 128-bit security level in 12 min. Our results show that building secure key exchange protocols directly from LWE that resist key reuse attacks remains a challenging and mostly open problem.

Keywords: Learning with errors · Key exchange · Key reuse

1 Introduction

The learning with errors (LWE) problem [22] can be used to construct a variety of post-quantum cryptographic algorithms, such as digital signatures, public-key encryption, key encapsulation mechanisms (KEMs), and key exchange, the latter being the focus of this paper. LWE-based key exchange protocols are appealingly similar to the Diffie–Hellman (DH) protocol [7] which is the prototypical unauthenticated key exchange protocol. Authenticated key exchange (AKE) can be built from unauthenticated DH through two main techniques, either explicit authentication using digital signatures, or implicit authentication where public-key encryption or DH keys are used as long-term credentials for authentication.

Passively Secure LWE-Based Key Exchange. LWE-based key exchange can be constructed from LWE-based public-key encryption [19,22]: the core idea is that two (plain or ring) LWE samples $as_A + e_A$ and $as_B + e_B$ are combined to form approximately equal shared secrets close to $as_A s_B$ (where a is a public parameter, s_A and s_B are the initiator and responder's secret keys, and e_A and

© Springer Nature Switzerland AG 2021
P. Longa and C. Ràfols (Eds.): LATINCRYPT 2021, LNCS 12912, pp. 168–188, 2021.
https://doi.org/10.1007/978-3-030-88238-9_9

e_B are secret noise). Reliable passively secure key exchange can be achieved by transmitting error correcting hints about the shared secret, such as the signal function of Ding, Xie, and Lin (DXL) [13] or Peikert's reconciliation function [21]. The basic idea of DXL's signal function is as follows. In the ring-LWE variant of DXL key exchange, both Alice and Bob derive a polynomial that is their copy of the approximately equal shared secret. The signal function is applied to each coefficient of the polynomial, and returns a bit indicating whether the coefficient is within a certain range, namely, within $\{-\lfloor q/4 \rfloor, \ldots, \lfloor q/4 \rfloor\}$, where q is the modulus defining the ring. These signal bits are computed by Bob and transmitted to Alice. This extra information allows both parties to derive from each coefficient one or more exactly equal secret bits with high probability.

Attacks Against Passively Secure LWE-Based Key Exchange. Bare LWE public key encryption [19,22] and key exchange [13,21] are not designed to be secure against active adversaries, and in fact are insecure against active adversaries. For example, Regev's search-to-decision equivalence for LWE [22] is a chosen ciphertext attack that recovers the LWE secret given an oracle for decision LWE. Fluhrer [14] constructed an active attack against a simplified form of DXL key exchange [13], in which an attacker Eve sends malicious public keys and uses information leaked via the signal function to recover a party's secret key. [9] refines this to work on the full DXL protocol using signal leakage.

Prevention of Key Reuse Attacks in LWE-Based Protocols. Authenticated key exchange should be secure against active attacks. There is a small selection of literature building AKE from generic building blocks such as public key encryption [2] or KEMs [5,6,15,23]. There have also been attempts to build AKE protocols directly from LWE such as [26], in many cases using techniques paralleling some DH-based AKE protocols such as MQV [18,20] and HMQV [16].

Ding, Branco, and Schmitt (DBS) [10] propose two key exchange protocols from LWE that are designed to be secure against key reuse and inspired by the HMQV design of combining the ephemeral and static keys alongside pseudorandom masking values. Their first protocol, which we call the DBS reusable-keys protocol, aims to achieve what they call "key reuse robustness" with an approximately equal shared secret of the form $a(s_A + c)(s_B + d)$ for public values c and d. Their second protocol, which we call the DBS AKE protocol, achieves AKE security in the Bellare–Rogaway (BR) model [3] with weak forward secrecy, using an approximate shared secret of the form $a(r_A + s_A + c)(r_B + s_B + d)$.

Our Contributions. In this paper, we improve the query complexity of the key reuse attack using signal leakage and apply the improved attack in several settings. Table 1 compares our improvements and new attacks to the literature.

Improved Attack Using Signal Leakage. The key reuse attack exploiting signal leakage [9,14] sends malformed public keys $p_A = k$ for all $k \in \{0, \ldots, q-1\}$. This obtains a full picture of the noisy "waveform" $\approx k s_B[i]$ induced for each coefficient $s_B[i]$ of the secret key, then recovers the period from that binary waveform. To assemble the full waveform formerly q samples were used, with a rather large value of q, e.g. ≈ 26 million in [10].

Table 1. Summary of attacks on LWE key exchange protocols with key reuse

Attack	Protocol	Security model		Query complexity
		Claimed	Of attack	
[9]	DXL [13]	Passive	Key reuse rob.	$(1+z)q$
[11, §5]	DXL [13]	Passive	Key reuse rob.	$\approx 32000n^2\alpha$
[11, §7]	DXL [13]	Passive	Key reuse rob.	$(1+z)\frac{q}{2}+O(1)$
Ours, Sect. 4	DXL [13]	Passive	Key reuse rob.	$\approx 36(1+2z)\alpha$
Ours, Sect. 5	DBS reusable [10]	Key reuse rob.	Key reuse rob.	$\approx 3600(1+4z)\alpha^2$
Ours (full v.)	DBS AKE [10]	BR	eCK	$\approx 1467(1+4z)\alpha^2$

Legend: n: LWE dimension; q: modulus; α: standard deviation of the secret/noise distribution; z: number of consecutive zeros in the secret key, typically $z \approx 4$.

We show that far fewer samples suffice for determining the period of the noisy waveform, given that the period—which depends on the secret key—is bounded by some known value h (for example, for reasonable parameters, the secret key coefficients have magnitude less than 15 with high probability). If there was no noise, then the waveform would be square and have exactly $2s_B[i]$ switches, equally distributed. With noise, there will be many switches bunched around the period. However, based on the standard deviation of the noise distribution, we can bound the region in which these noisy switches occur with high probability. If we could sample from the stable regions, where noisy switches do not occur, we would be able to reconstruct the period and thus the secret key coefficient. Our technique is to sample every tth value, where t is chosen so that we will collect at least one value from each stable region and at most one value from each noisy region around period switches, allowing efficient computation of the period.

Our optimizations yield an active key recovery attack against the DXL protocol that uses $(1+2z)8C\alpha$ queries, where α is the standard deviation of the noise distribution, z is the maximum number of consecutive zeros in a secret key plus one, and C is a small constant; for the parameters we consider, $C \approx 5$ and $z = 4$ suffice for the attack to work with high probability. We implemented our attack against the same parameters used in the previous best attack [9]: $n = 1024$, $\alpha = 3.197$, $q = 2^{14} + 1$. Our attack succeeds with probability 0.97 in on average 62 s, compared to 3.8 h of [9].

Attack on DBS Reusable-Keys Protocol. In Sect. 5, we examine the DBS reusable-keys protocol and observe that its countermeasure for achieving security against key reuse is unfortunately not sufficient. Using our improved attack, we experimentally recover the key of the proposed 128-bit security parameters successfully.

The main idea of our attack is as follows. Recall that the approximate shared secret is $a(s_A + c)(s_B + d)$, for pseudorandom values c and d distributed according to the error distribution. From Bob's perspective, this is computed (ignoring small error terms) as $\approx (p_A + ac)(s_B + d) = p_A s_B + (p_A d + acs_B + acd)$, where p_A is the attacker's public key. DBS calls the process of adding ac to p_A before multiplying by the secret key s_B "pasteurization" and claims it "force[s] the

parties involved in the KE scheme to behave honestly". In fact, this pasteurization does not force honest behaviour. Consider an attacker who uses the basic
signal leakage attack described above, and sends malformed public keys $p_A = k$
for $k \in \{0, \dots, q-1\}$. Noting that as_B is approximately equal to Bob's public
key p_B, from the attacker's perspective, the shared secret is $p_A s_B$ (which the
attacker does not know) plus $p_A d + p_B c + acd$ (which is known to the adversary).
This known sum is approximately uniformly distributed, so each coefficient will
be 0 with probability around $1/q$, and most importantly the adversary *knows
when it is 0*. Thus, when the ith coefficient of this known sum is 0, the signal
function is being applied to the ith coefficient of $(p_A s_B)[i]$ directly—with no
"pasteurization"—and we are able to apply the original attack! We discuss the
potential gap in the proof of "key reuse robustness" in Sect. 5.8.

Our optimizations to the attack against DXL key exchange also apply in this
scenario, yielding an attack that runs in $(1 + 4z) \cdot 144 C^2 \alpha^2$, where α, z, and C
are as above. We implemented our attack against the parameters proposed by
DBS for 128-bit security, with $n = 512$, $\alpha = 4.19$, and $q \approx 26$ million, and on
average successfully recovered the key in less than 12 min; see Sect. 5.7.

The pasteurization technique has also been adopted by Seyhan et al. [24] in a
module-LWE-based analogue of the DBS reusable keys protocol. We are similarly
able to deconstruct the shared secret as the sum of a single unknown term plus
several known terms, effectively eliminating pasteurization. A full attack on the
Seyhan et al. protocol would need to use the "key mismatch oracle" technique
[11] since the protocol does not transmit a signal value.

Attack on LWE-Based AKE Protocols in the eCK Model. Briefly in Sect. 6 and
with more detail in the full version of this paper [4], we consider whether our
attack applies to two more LWE-based AKE protocols, the ZZDSD AKE protocol [26] and the DBS AKE protocol [10], which are shown secure in the Bellare–
Rogaway (BR) security model [3]. Our attack does not immediately apply in the
BR security model. We *could* attack the DBS AKE protocol using the ephemeral
key reveal capabilities in the stronger eCK security model [17], but were unable
to apply our attack to the ZZDSD AKE protocol even in the eCK model.

2   Background

Notation. An instance of the ring learning with errors (RLWE) problem will
be specified by a prime modulus q, a dimension n, and distribution χ_α with
standard deviation α which is used for both the secrets and errors. The ring is
$R_q[x] = \mathbb{Z}_q[x]/\langle f(x) \rangle$ for an irreducible polynomial $f(x)$. Elements of $\mathbb{Z}_q$ may
be represented as either $\{0, \dots, q-1\}$ or $\{-(q-1)/2, \dots, (q-1)/2\}$ as required. The
coefficient of x^i of $y \in R_q[x]$ is denoted by $y[i]$. We write $\#S$ to denote the
number of elements in set S. $x \leftarrow_\$ S$ denotes sampling x uniformly from set S.
If χ is a distribution on S, $x \leftarrow_\$ \chi$ denotes sampling from S according to χ.

Initiator (Alice)	Responder (Bob)
$s_A, e_A \leftarrow^\$ \chi_\alpha$ $p_A \leftarrow as_A + 2e_A \in R_q$	$s_B, e_B \leftarrow^\$ \chi_\alpha$ $p_B \leftarrow as_B + 2e_B \in R_q$ $g_B \leftarrow^\$ \chi_\alpha$
$\xrightarrow{\quad p_A \quad}$	
$g_A \leftarrow^\$ \chi_\alpha$ $k_A \leftarrow p_B s_A + 2g_A$ $sk_A \leftarrow \mathrm{Mod}_2(k_A, w_B)$	$k_B \leftarrow p_A s_B + 2g_B$ $w_B \leftarrow \mathrm{Sig}(k_B) \in \{0,1\}^n$ $sk_B \leftarrow \mathrm{Mod}_2(k_B, w_B)$
$\xleftarrow{\quad p_B, w_B \quad}$	

$\mathrm{Sig}(v) = 0$ if $v \in E$ else 1 (extended component-wise)

$E = \{-\lfloor q/4 \rfloor + r, \cdots, \lfloor q/4 \rfloor + r\}$ for $r \leftarrow^\$ \{0,1\}$

$\mathrm{Mod}_2(v, w) = \left(\left(v + w\frac{q-1}{2}\right) \bmod q\right) \bmod 2$ for $(v, w) \in \mathbb{Z}_q \times \{0,1\}$

Fig. 1. Ring-LWE-based key exchange protocol of Ding, Xie, and Lin (DXL) [13].

Basic Ring-LWE Key Exchange. The basic ring-LWE-based key exchange protocol of Ding, Xie, and Lin (DXL) [13] is shown in Fig. 1, and was the basis of the NIST PQC Round 1 submission "Ding Key Exchange". It makes use of a component-wise "signal" function $\mathrm{Sig}(v)$ shown on the right-side of Fig. 1.

Key Reuse. Let Π be a 2-pass key exchange protocol between two parties A and B. *Key reuse* means that each party is willing to run multiple sessions using the same long-term secret. To model this, [9] defines a key reuse oracle $\mathcal{S}$ which executes party B's responses. The oracle $\mathcal{S}$ has access to the (fixed) secret key of party B (e.g., s_B, e_B in Fig. 1). On receiving p_A from party A, $\mathcal{S}$ computes and returns p_B according to the protocol using the same secret key for every response. *Key reuse robustness* [10] means that it is safe for a party to reuse a key, even in the face of maliciously generated messages from the other party.

2.1 Fluhrer's Key Reuse Attack on DXL RLWE-Based Key Exchange

The original key reuse attack by Fluhrer [14] and refined by [9] against RLWE-based key exchange protocols, such as the DXL protocol depicted in Fig. 1, takes advantage of the signal function to determine the coefficients of the reused secret s_B. The attack can be described by the following two steps.

Absolute Value Recovery. Adversary $\mathcal{A}$ invokes oracle $\mathcal{S}$ with input $p_A = k$ for $k = 0, \ldots, q - 1$. As k changes from 0 to $q - 1$, the corresponding signal $w_B[i]$ of the ith coefficient will essentially be a noisy version of a periodic function with $|2s_B[i]|$ signal changes between zero and one. By recovering the period from this noisy signal, $\mathcal{A}$ can determine $|s_B[i]|$. Applied component-wise to all coefficients of w_B, the adversary can reveal the absolute values of all coefficients of s_B.

Relative Sign Recovery. To determine the sign of each secret coefficient, the adversary $\mathcal{A}$ invokes the oracle $\mathcal{S}$ with input $(1 + x)p_A$ where $p_A = k$ for $k = 0, \ldots, q - 1$. Again, by recovering the period from this noisy signal, $\mathcal{A}$ can determine the value of the coefficients of $(1 + x)s_B$, up to sign. The coefficients of $(1 + x)s_B$ are $s_B[0] - s_B[n-1], s_B[1] + s_B[2], \ldots, s_B[n-2] + s_B[n-1]$. With this information, $\mathcal{A}$ can determine the relative signs of adjacent pairs of coefficients in s_B. If there are $z - 1$ consecutive zeros in the s_B (which can be seen from the absolute value recovery stage), this technique must be repeated

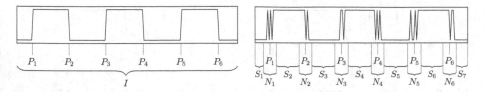

Fig. 2. Periodic function f (left) and noisy version g (right) over interval I with $m = 6$ signal changes at points P_i, split into stable (S_i) and noisy (N_i) regions.

with $(1 + x^z)k$ to determine relative signs between coefficients z positions apart. Once all relative signs are recovered, this narrows the possibilities down to two options: $\pm s_B$.

Although the values $p_A = k$ sent by the adversary look atypical and one could try to protect against this attack by filtering such values out, it is possible to adapt the attack to work with values that look random [8, §4.4].

3   Sparse Signal Collection

As described in the previous section, the main tool in Fluhrer's attack is recovering the secret period from the noisy binary signal induced by $\mathrm{Sig}(k_B)$. In this section, we present our improvements which use a much smaller number of samples from the signal, hence we call this *sparse signal collection*.

We aim to keep our presentation in this section generic, but it helps to keep in mind the application to RLWE-based key exchange protocols like DXL (Fig. 1). In DXL, as a result of the error term g_B, there are frequent changes in the value of the signal function when $k_B[i]$ is near the boundary of E. As $k_B[i]$ moves away from the boundary, the impact of the error term g_B decreases and the signal stabilizes. Filtering out the fluctuations near the boundaries of E, the noiseless signal changes would determine $s_B[i]$. The attack as described in [9] collects all signals but does not specify a general algorithm to determine the secret coefficients. In this section, we describe a new method of signal collection that determines the period with high probability while substantially reducing the number of samples needed to carry out the attack.

Requirements. Let I be a finite integer interval and b some bound specified below. Let $f : I \to \{0, 1\}$ be a periodic signal function, changing signals at points $P_1, ..., P_m$, equally spaced out over the interval I, i.e., $P_{i+1} - P_i = \#I/m$ for $1 \le i \le m - 1$. Without loss of generality, assume $f(x) = 0$ for $x < P_1$ and $x \ge P_m$. Let $g : I \to \{0, 1\}$ be a function that *approximates* f. By this we mean the following: there exist $m + 1$ non-empty ("stable") intervals $S_i \subset I$, with $S_i \cap S_j = \emptyset$ for $i \ne j$ such that $f(S_i) = g(S_i)$ for $i = 1, ..., m + 1$. Let the intervals be ordered in the sense that all elements of S_i are strictly smaller than all elements in S_j for $i < j$. Furthermore, let $\#S_1 = \#S_{m+1} = \#S_i/2$ for $1 < i < m + 1$. (Strictly speaking, this requirement is not needed in general but simplifies our explanation and is closer to the case of RLWE-based key exchange.)

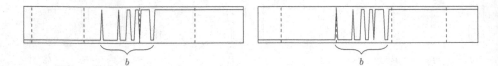

Fig. 3. Two different sets of collected signals (marked with dashed vertical lines).

In addition, we define the (ordered) set of remaining ("noisy") intervals (in between the S_i) to be $N_1, ..., N_m$, with $P_i \in N_i$. We assume that for all i it holds that $\#N_i \leq b$ for some integer bound $b \leq \#S_k$ for $1 < k < m + 1$ and $N_i \cap N_j = \emptyset$ for $i \neq j$. We visualize the above definitions in Fig. 2.

The problem of interest is recovering the unknown period m using samples from g. The problem may be constrained in the sense that m is upper bounded.

Description. Rather than collecting signals for every k in the interval I, we only collect a few signals in the intervals S_i skipping the areas N_j; or at least limiting the number of samples coming from noisy periods. In particular, if we could guarantee that we collect (i) *at least* one sample from every *stable* region and (ii) *at most* one signal from every *noisy* region, we could still determine the period. The main task becomes bounding the width b of the noisy region and determining how far apart samples should be taken to ensure that both (i) and (ii) are satisfied while trying to minimize the number of samples collected.

Figure 3 shows two examples that involve collecting every $(b + 1)$th signal. Since the width of the noisy region is bounded by b, no matter where the signal collection begins, at most one sample will be collected from each noisy region.

In order for the count of signal changes to be correct, we must ensure that at least one value from every stable interval S_i is collected. There are $m + 1$ stable periods, where the intervals $S_2, ..., S_m$ and $\#(S_1 \cup S_{m+1})$ have width $\#I/m - b$. Thus, at least every $(\#I/2m - b/2)$th value of $g(x)$ must be collected. Since we assumed that the values of g during the first and last stable interval are equal to zero, actually only at least every $(\#I/m - b)$th value of $g(x)$ needs to be collected.

4   Improvements to Existing Key Reuse Attacks

We now apply the sparse signal collection strategy of Sect. 3 to Fluhrer's attack [9,14] against the DXL RLWE-based key exchange protocol [13] in Fig. 1.

4.1   Determining Sparse Signal Collection Parameters

For the remainder of this section, we focus on recovering the ith coefficient of k_B, i.e., $k_B[i] = (p_A s_B + 2g_B)[i]$. In the notation of Sect. 3, the interval I corresponds to $[0, ..., q - 1]$; the approximation function f corresponds to the response of the oracle $\mathcal{S}$ except that $g_B = 0$, i.e., $f(p_A) = \text{Sig}(p_A s_B)[i]$, while g is defined as $g(p_A) = \text{Sig}(p_A s_B + 2g_B)[i]$. We say that a signal at some index i is noisy if the addition of $2g_B[i]$ causes the signal to be flipped.

Determining b. In the case of a signal change from 0 to 1, a noisy signal occurs if $2g_B[i]$ and $\lfloor q/4 \rfloor + r - (p_A s_B)[i]$ have the same sign and $|2g_B[i]| \geq |\lfloor q/4 \rfloor + r - (p_A s_B)[i]|$. Similarly, in the case of a signal change from 1 to 0, a noisy signal occurs if $2g_B[i]$ and $\lfloor 3q/4 \rfloor + r - (p_A s_B)[i]$ have the same sign and $|2g_B[i]| \geq |\lfloor 3q/4 \rfloor + r - (p_A s_B)[i]|$.

As p_A changes, the difference between $(p_A s_B)[i]$ and the closest point of signal change P_j changes as well. This means that the farther away the absolute value of $(p_A s_B)[i]$ is from $\lfloor q/4 \rfloor + r$, the larger must be $|2g_B[i]|$ in order to cause a noisy signal. Since g_B is sampled from a discrete Gaussian distribution, there is some value, say h, where it is highly unlikely that $|2g_B[i]| > h$. So suppose $h \geq |2g_B[i]|$. (Many practical LWE and ring-LWE protocols have bounded s_B since they use approximate Gaussian distributions, e.g., FrodoKEM has errors between ± 12.) Our choice of h will determine the success probability of the attack. As $s_B[i]$ increases, the distance between $(p_A s_B)[i]$ and the boundaries of E changes at a faster rate as p_A increases. Hence, the noisy intervals are largest when $s_B[i] = 1$ (when $s_B[i] = 0$, the noise changes the signal when $|2g_B[i]| \geq \lfloor q/4 \rfloor + r$ which we assume does not occur). Thus, we choose b such that it upper bounds the size of N_i corresponding to $s_B[i] = 1$; namely, $b = 2h$.

Determining the Maximum Number of Signal Changes m. In Fluhrer's attack, signals are collected for two different purposes: to find the absolute value of a coefficient, and to determine the relative sign of two coefficients. In the first case, the number m of signal changes observed in our sparse signal collection corresponds to the maximum absolute value of $s_B[i]$ times two. If s_B is chosen with discrete Gaussian distribution, the maximum number of signal changes is $m = 2h$, following the same reasoning as for b. In case of finding the relative sign of two coefficients, the number m of signal changes corresponds to the maximum value of $s_B[i] + s_B[j]$, i.e., $m = 4h$.

Number of Signals Needed to be Collected. Following Sect. 3, in order to ensure we collect *at least* one value from every stable period, we must collect at least every $(q/2m - b/2)$th signal. Moreover, in order to ensure we collect *at most* one value from every noisy period, we must collect at most every bth signal, with $b = 2h$. Say we collect every t_1th signal when recovering absolute value and every t_2th signal when recovering the sign of a coefficient; this means that we must choose t_1 such that $2h < t_1 < q/4h - h$ and t_2 such that $2h < t_2 < q/8h - h$.

4.2 Description of the Improved Attack

Absolute Value Recovery. The adversary $\mathcal{A}$ invokes the oracle $\mathcal{S}$ with input $p_A = k$ where k takes on every t_1th value from 0 to $q - 1$. The signal returned, $w_B[i]$, will change exactly $|2s_B[i]|$ times. So, $\mathcal{A}$ can determine the value of $s_B[i]$ up to the $\pm$ sign for each coefficient of s_B.

Relative Sign Recovery. The adversary $\mathcal{A}$ invokes the oracle $\mathcal{S}$ with input $p_A = (1+x)k$ where k takes on every t_2th value from 0 to $q - 1$. Again, by checking the number of signal changes, $\mathcal{A}$ can determine the absolute value of the coefficients of $(1+x)s_B$. As in Sect. 2.1, $\mathcal{A}$ can determine the relative signs of adjacent pairs of coefficients in s_B. Repeat this step as necessary with $(1+x^z)p_A$ to determine relative signs of coefficients between which there are $z-1$ zeros. This narrows the possibilities down to two options, namely s_B or $-s_B$.

4.3 Success Probability

Next, we determine the success probability of our attack. In particular, we analyze the probability that coefficients of s_B, g_B exceed the bound h.

Suppose $|s_B[i]| > h$ for some coefficient i, which might hinder collecting at least one signal from every stable interval. The probability that this occurs is $\rho_1 \approx 2\sum_{x=h+1}^{\infty} \frac{1}{\sqrt{2\pi}\cdot\alpha^2} \exp(-x^2/2\alpha^2)$; otherwise, $|s_B[i]| \le h$. When $|s_B[i]| \le h$, the attack may fail if there is some error that causes enough noise which results in the collection of an incorrect signal. This occurs if $g_B[i]$ is greater than or equal to $t_1/2 + r$. This probability is given by $\rho_2 = 2\sum_{x=t_1/2+1}^{\infty} \frac{1}{\sqrt{2\pi}\cdot\alpha^2} \exp(-x^2/2\alpha^2)$.

There are $2|s_B[i]| + 1$ noisy intervals, $|s_B[i]| \le h$, n coefficients of s_B, and $1/t_1$ chance that we collect this incorrect signal. Given that each $s_B[i], g_B[i]$ is chosen independently, it is reasonable to assume that the probability of collecting an incorrect signal at each noisy interval is independent. Then, the probability of failure of absolute value recovery is at most $n(\rho_1 + (1-\rho_1)(2h+1)\frac{1}{t_1}\rho_2)$. Similarly, the probability of failure in one iteration of relative sign recovery is $n(\rho_1 + (1-\rho_1)(4h+1)\frac{1}{t_2}\rho_3)$, where $\rho_3 = 2\sum_{x=t_2/2+1}^{\infty} \frac{1}{\sqrt{2\pi}\cdot\alpha^2} \exp(-x^2/2\alpha^2)$. Putting this all together, the probability of failure of the entire attack is $n\left(\rho_1 + (1-\rho_1)(2h+1)\frac{1}{t_1}\rho_2\right) + zn\left(\rho_1 + (1-\rho_1)(4h+1)\frac{1}{t_2}\rho_3\right)$, where z is the maximum number of consecutive zeros in the key plus one. We compute the number of needed queries next.

4.4 Query Complexity

The key reuse attack requires $q_S = (z+1)q$ queries where z denotes the number of times the relative sign recovery step must be taken, i.e., the maximum number of consecutive zeros between two nonzero coefficients plus one. The probability of sampling $z-1$ consecutive zeros is $1 - (1-1/(\sqrt{2\pi\alpha^2})^{z-1})^{n-z}$.

To improve the query complexity, [11] suggested collecting signals for values of k until the signal changes and stabilizes. That method requires $q/2+c$ queries to recover $|s_B[i]|$, where c is a small constant, leading to a total of $(1+z)(q/2+c)$ queries. Suppose we choose $h = C\alpha$, where C is a constant such that it is highly unlikely that $|s_B[i]| \ge C\alpha$, and $t_1 = q/8h$, which satisfies $2h < t_1 < q/4h - h$ for parameters we consider. Our method requires only $8C\alpha$ queries to recover $|s_B[i]|$. Since $t_2 \approx 2t_1$, the total number of queries we require is $q_S = 8C\alpha + z(16C\alpha) = (1+2z)8C\alpha$. This is a significant improvement since $\alpha \ll q$. We compare the number of queries from [9,11] with sparse signal collection in Table 1.

The choice of the constant C will affect the efficiency and the success probability. For practical LWE parameters, $C \approx 4.5$, accompanied with a reasonable choice of t_1 and t_2, provides high success probability of approximately 97%.

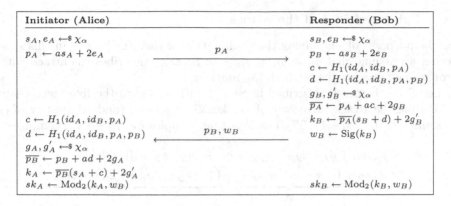

Initiator (Alice)		Responder (Bob)
$s_A, e_A \xleftarrow{\$} \chi_\alpha$		$s_B, e_B \xleftarrow{\$} \chi_\alpha$
$p_A \leftarrow a s_A + 2 e_A$	$\xrightarrow{\quad p_A \quad}$	$p_B \leftarrow a s_B + 2 e_B$
		$c \leftarrow H_1(id_A, id_B, p_A)$
		$d \leftarrow H_1(id_A, id_B, p_A, p_B)$
		$g_B, g'_B \xleftarrow{\$} \chi_\alpha$
		$\overline{p_A} \leftarrow p_A + ac + 2 g_B$
$c \leftarrow H_1(id_A, id_B, p_A)$		$k_B \leftarrow \overline{p_A}(s_B + d) + 2 g'_B$
$d \leftarrow H_1(id_A, id_B, p_A, p_B)$	$\xleftarrow{\quad p_B, w_B \quad}$	$w_B \leftarrow \mathrm{Sig}(k_B)$
$g_A, g'_A \xleftarrow{\$} \chi_\alpha$		
$\overline{p_B} \leftarrow p_B + ad + 2 g_A$		
$k_A \leftarrow \overline{p_B}(s_A + c) + 2 g'_A$		
$sk_A \leftarrow \mathrm{Mod}_2(k_A, w_B)$		$sk_B \leftarrow \mathrm{Mod}_2(k_B, w_B)$

Fig. 4. DBS reusable-keys protocol [10]

4.5   Experimental Results

For the parameters proposed in [9] $n = 1024, q = 2^{14} + 1, \alpha = 3.197$, we choose $h = 14$, hence the noisy intervals have at most $b = 2 \cdot 28 = 56$ elements. Moreover, the stable interval has at least 264 elements during absolute value recovery and 118 elements when recovering relative signs. Thus, collecting every tth value with $t_1 = t_2 = t$, for any $56 < t < 118$ is sufficient.

Suppose we collect every $t = 100$th signal value. Following Sect. 4.3, the probability that some coefficient of s_B exceeds h is approximately $2^{-17.53}$. The probability that some coefficient of the error term exceeds $t/2 = 50$ is approximately $2^{-50.25}$. Therefore, the probability of failure is at most 0.027, i.e., the success probability is at least 97.3%.

Our experimental implementation obtains correct results up to sign in an average of 62.82 s over ten runs (with an average of 766 queries), compared to 3.8 h of the original attack [9]. The execution of our attack was performed using a MacBook Air equipped with a 1.6 GHz dual-core Intel Core i5 CPU.

5   Attack on DBS Reusable-Keys Protocol

In this section, we show a new variant of Fluhrer's attack [9,14] that, combined with our sparse signal collection technique, yields a successful and efficient key recovery attack against a protocol by Ding, Branco, and Schmitt [10] that was designed to be secure against key reuse attacks.

The protocol in question is the DBS reusable-keys protocol as shown in Fig. 4. It relies on a public parameter $a \xleftarrow{\$} R_q$ and a hash function $H_1 : \{0,1\}^* \rightarrow \chi_\alpha$ whose outputs follow the discrete Gaussian distribution χ_α with standard deviation α. In [10], the protocol is claimed to provide key reuse robustness for the initiator and responder, under the assumption that the Hermite-normal-form ring-LWE assumption is hard and H_1 is a random oracle. For the purpose of key reuse, the values that the responder reuses are s_B, e_B, and p_B. We discuss the potential gap in the proof of the security in Sect. 5.8.

5.1   High-Level Idea of the Attack

For the purposes of simplifying the explanation of the attack idea, in this sub-section we assume that $e_B = g_B = g'_B = 0$; Sect. 5.2 describes the attack with error terms following the original distribution.

Let $\mathcal{S}$ be the oracle described in Sect. 2 with access to the fixed secret key s_B. During the attack, adversary $\mathcal{A}$ invokes $\mathcal{S}$ on $p_A = k$ (and an identity id_A) for some $k \in \{0, ..., q-1\}$. The oracle $\mathcal{S}$ then samples $g_B, g'_B \leftarrow^{\$} \chi_\alpha$, computes

$$k_B - \overline{p_A}(s_B + d) + 2g'_B = (p_A + ac + 2g_B)(s_B + d) + 2g'_B$$
$$= p_A s_B + \underbrace{(cp_B + acd + dp_A)}_{\Delta} + \underbrace{(2g_B s_B + 2g_B d + 2g'_B - 2ce_B)}_{\varepsilon},$$

and returns $(p_B, w_B) = (p_B, \text{Sig}(k_B))$. Notice that $g_B, e_B, c, d, g'_B, s_B$ are all distributed according to χ_α, and hence, $\varepsilon = 2g_B s_B + 2g_B d + 2g'_B - 2ce_B$ is the sum of small values. Furthermore, $\mathcal{A}$ knows a, controls p_A, receives p_B, is able to compute d and c, and hence, is able to compute the value of $\Delta = cp_B + acd + dp_A$.

The core idea of our attack is as follows: an adversary is able to find p_A and an identity id_A such that the ith coefficient of Δ is equal to zero. Invoking the oracle $\mathcal{S}$ with such p_A, id_A, returns $\text{Sig}(p_A s_B + \Delta)$ (assuming $\varepsilon = 0$ for simplicity), with $\text{Sig}(p_A s_B[i] + \Delta[i]) = \text{Sig}(p_A s_B[i]) = \text{Sig}(p_A s_B)[i]$.

The key observation is that the probability that $\Delta[i] = 0$ is close to $1/q$, as analyzed in Sect. 5.4. Moreover, the adversary can tell when $\Delta[i] = 0$ occurs. When it does occur, the adversary can determine the coefficient of $s_B[i]$ up to its sign by counting the number of signal changes as in the original key reuse attack. Now, this only succeeds $1/q$th of the time, specifically when $\Delta[i] = 0$, but since q is not cryptographically large, it is feasible to repeat this $\approx q$ times. (We show how to do this with fewer than q repetitions below.) Thus, for each p_A ranging from $k = 0, \ldots, q-1$, we repeat this with different id_A (different p_A and id_A will induce random c and d, thereby randomizing Δ) until observing a sample with $\Delta[i] = 0$, which we then use as for k in the original key reuse attack. Having done this for all $k \in \{0, \ldots, q-1\}$ for every coefficient, we have the information needed to recover the entire secret s_B up to sign.

5.2   The Complete Attack

We now assume $e_B, g_B, g'_B \leftarrow^{\$} \chi_\alpha$ and, hence, upon input p_A, id_A the oracle $\mathcal{S}$ returns $\text{Sig}(p_A s_B + \Delta + \varepsilon)$. In our description below, we will follow the notation from Sect. 3 and 4. Table 2 summarizes the tuneable parameters of the attack.

Table 2. Attack parameters

Symbol	Description
h_1	Upper bound on error terms added to key
h_2	Upper bound on known terms used during absolute value collection
h_3	Upper bound on secret coefficients
t_1	Collect every t_1-th signal in absolute value recovery
h_2'	Upper bound on known terms used during relative sign collection
h_3'	Upper bound on difference of secret coefficients
t_2	Collect every t_2-th signal in relative sign recovery
z	Maximum number of consecutive zeros in the secret plus one

Adversary Construction of p_A and Deconstructing Corresponding k_B. In the simple form of the attack, the adversary uses values of the form $p_A = k$ for $k = 0, ..., q - 1$. Party B could in principle thwart this attack by checking whether p_A is a constant polynomial. To undermine such countermeasures, we pick p_A to take the form of a RLWE sample, namely $p_A = as_A + ke_A$ with $s_A \leftarrow^s \chi_\alpha$ and $e_A = 1$. The key determined by the oracle S is then $k_B = (p_A + ac + 2g_B)(s_B + d) + 2g_B' = as_As_B + ks_B + \Delta + \varepsilon$. The value as_As_B is constant as we loop over values of k. Hence, the number of signal changes will still be $|2s_B|$ for each coefficient. The first ith signal will correspond to the value of $as_As_B[i]$ (plus some error term), so it is not guaranteed to start at 0. In fact, all signals of the ith coefficient will be shifted by the value of $as_As_B[i]$. Hence, we cannot assume the first and last signal to be 0. However, a simple modification of the signal processing, which checks if there is a signal change between the last and first signal received, is sufficient to correctly account for this shift. Also, the known value will be different due to the factor of dp_A but is still expected to be approximately uniform.

Determine the Number of Signals Needed. To determine the number of signals needed during absolute value and relative sign recovery, t_1 and t_2 respectively, we first need to bound the width b of the noisy intervals and the number of signal changes m (see Sect. 4.1). To this end, we make the following observations.

The terms $\Delta = cp_B + acd + dp_A$ and $\varepsilon = 2g_Bs_B + 2g_Bd + 2g_B' - 2ce_B$ add noise which may change the value of the signal. In the simplified form of the attack, we demanded $\Delta[i] = 0$ in order to make use of a sample. However in the complete attack we can relax this and just demand that this is sufficiently small. At some boundary, $\beta \in \{\lfloor q/4 \rfloor, \lfloor 3q/4 \rfloor\}$, the signal may change if $|\Delta + \varepsilon| > |\beta - p_As_B|$. Thus, in order to bound b and m, we need find bounds h_1, h_2 and h_3 (compare with h in Sect. 4.1) such that (1) $h_1 \geq |\varepsilon|$ with high probability, (2) $h_2 \geq |\Delta|$ with probability $2h_2/q$, since the known values are indistinguishable from uniform (see Sect. 5.4), and (3) $h_3 \geq |s_B|$ with high probability.

In Sect. 5.3, we show that the sum ε of error terms is normally distributed with some standard deviation α_e. Choosing $h_1 \approx 4.5\alpha_e$ means the probability

n	128		256		512		1024	
q	2 255 041		9 205 761		26 038 273		28 434 433	
α	4.19	2.6	4.19	2.6	4.19	2.6	4.19	2.6
h_2	17 000	30 000	75 000	125 000	220 000	350 000	240 000	380 000
t_1	40 000	63 000	164 000	255 000	465 000	720 000	500 000	790 000
h_2'	6 500	14 000	35 000	62 000	110 000	175 000	115 000	190 000
t_2	20 000	31 000	82 000	128 000	230 000	360 000	253 000	395 000

Fig. 5. Parameters of attack on DBS reusable-keys protocol

that ε is greater than h_1 is at most 2^{-17}. Similarly, we choose $h_3 \approx 4.5\alpha$ and, hence, the probability that $|s_B| \geq h_3$ is at most 2^{-17}. Additionally, we choose h_2 such that $2(h_1 + h_2) < q/2h_3 - 2(h_1 + h_2)$. That is, $h_2 < 1/4(q/2h_3 - 4h_1) = q/8h_3 - h_1$. A larger value of h_2 will increase the efficiency but decrease the success probability.

Following Sect. 4.4, we can now determine the number of signals needed for absolute and sign recovery, t_1 and t_2 respectively. Namely, collecting every t_1th signal for any t_1 satisfying $2(h_1 + h_2) < t_1 < \frac{q}{2h_3} - 2(h_1 + h_2)$ ensures that at most one signal in every noisy interval N_i and at least one signal for every stable interval S_j is collected. The value of h_2 will determine how large this range is. A t_1 value closer to either bound will decrease the success probability, so, to optimize the success probability, choose some t_1 value in the middle of either bound. However, a larger value of t_1 will improve the efficiency of the attack.

During relative sign recovery, we are collecting values corresponding to the difference between two coefficients. These coefficients are bounded by $2h_3$ with high probability. Similarly, we can compute a collection interval t_2 for relative sign recovery using $h_3' = 2h_3$ and $h_2' < q/8h_3' - h_1$. The parameter choices used for experimental results in Sect. 5.7 are given in Fig. 5.

To summarize, the two stages of the attack are as follows.

Absolute Value Recovery. Invoke the oracle $\mathcal{S}$ with input $p_A = as_A + k$ (taking $e_A = 1$) where k takes on every t_1th value from 0 to $q - 1$. For each of these k, collect signals $w_B[i]$ where the value of the known term Δ at coefficient i is less than or equal to h_2 (a single sample w_B may provide satisfying samples for several indices). Stop when a signal has been collected for every $i \in [0, n]$ for each k. For each coefficient i, as k changes, the signal returned, $w_B[i]$, will change exactly $|2s_B[i]|$ times. Thus, the value of $s_B[i]$ can be determined up to $\pm$ sign by dividing the number of signal changes by 2.

Relative Sign Recovery. Invoke the oracle $\mathcal{S}$ with input $(1 + x)p_A$ where $p_A = as_A + k$ (taking $e_A = 1$) where k takes on every t_2th value from 0 to $q - 1$. For each of these k, collect signals when the value of the known term Δ is less than or equal to h_2'. Checking the number of signal changes, the value of the coefficients of $(1 + x)s_B$ can be determined up to sign. The coefficients of $(1 + x)s_B$ are $s_B[0] - s_B[n - 1], s_B[1] + s_B[2], \ldots, s_B[n - 2] + s_B[n - 1]$, which determine the relative signs of adjacent pairs of coefficients in s_B. Repeat this step as necessary with $(1 + x^z)p_A$ based on the number of consecutive zeroes.

The following subsections provide our theoretical analysis and experimental results. More concretely, they can be summarized as follows:

Section 5.3 Determining the distribution of the error terms ε. We find that each coefficient of the error term ε is distributed according to a Gaussian distribution with standard deviation $\sqrt{12n\alpha^4 + 4\alpha^2}$.

Section 5.4 Determining the distribution of the known term Δ. Under the decision RLWE assumption for appropriate parameters, the known term Δ is indistinguishable from uniform. We check experimentally that for our parameters of interest the distribution appears sufficiently uniform.

Section 5.5 Calculating the number of queries required to collect sufficiently many samples. By extending the query complexity analysis of sparse signal recovery on DXL key exchange as in show that the number of queries Sect. 4.4, we show that the number of queries required to collect samples to carry out our attack against the DBS reusable-keys protocol is $(1 + 4z) \cdot 144C^2\alpha^2$, for a small constant C. For our parameters of interest, $C \approx 5$ and $z \approx 4$ suffice.

Section 5.6 Calculating the success probability of the attack. By extending the success probability analysis of sparse signal recovery on DXL key exchange as in Sect. 4.3, we compute a lower bound on the success probability of our attack against the DBS reusable-keys protocol.

Section 5.7 Providing our experimental results.

Section 5.8 Discussing a mistake in [10] that might have lead to the wrong conclusion that the DBS reusable-keys protocol is robust against key reuse attacks.

5.3   Distribution of the Error Terms

Recall that the key computed by the oracle $\mathcal{S}$ is given by $k_B = p_A s_B + \Delta + \varepsilon$, where $\varepsilon = 2g_B s_B + 2g_B d + 2g'_B - 2ce_B$. During the attack, values such that $\Delta[i] = 0$ (or is small) and thus $k_B[i] = (p_A s_B + \varepsilon)[i]$ are found, where the polynomials g_B, d, g'_B, c, e_B are sampled with discrete Gaussian distribution with standard deviation α. In what follows, we argue that we can assume that the error ε also follows a discrete Gaussian distribution with standard deviation γ to be determined.

The Central Limit Theorem (CLT) says that, for a set of N independent random variables $X_1, ..., X_N$ with a common distribution with mean μ and variance α^2, the distribution of $X_1 + ... + X_N$ follows the normal distribution with variance $N\alpha^2$ (for sufficiently large N). Moreover, the sum $X_1 + X_2$ of two independent random variables X_1 and X_2 with normally distribution $\mathcal{N}(\mu_1 = 0, \alpha_1)$ and $\mathcal{N}(\mu_2 = 0, \alpha_2)$, respectively, is of normal distribution $\mathcal{N}(\mu = 0, \sqrt{\alpha_1^2 + \alpha_2^2})$. Thus, one coefficient of $2g_B s_B$, $2g_B d$, or $2ce_B$ is normally distributed standard deviation $2\sqrt{n}\alpha^2$. Hence, each coefficient of ε is normally distributed with standard deviation $\sqrt{12n\alpha^4 + 4\alpha^2}$.

Although the Central Limit Theorem only holds asymptotically, its results are good enough for our concrete parameters. For example, we experimentally measured the variance of ε observed over 10000 samples for $\alpha = 4.19$, $n = 512$ and $q = 26\,038\,273$, which was 1.862 million, compared to the variance of 10000 samples from $\mathcal{N}(0, \sqrt{12n\alpha^4 + 4\alpha^2})$ which was 1.894 million.

5.4 Distribution of the Known Term Δ

We now take a look at the distribution of the so-called *known* terms $\Delta = cp_B + acd + dp_A = a(cs_B + cd + ds_A) + (ce_B + de_A)$ in the computation of k_B. We define $s = cs_B + cd + ds_A$ and $e = ce_B + de_A$. Applying the CLT, we can assume that $s \sim \chi_\psi$ and $e \sim \chi_\phi$ with standard deviations ψ and ϕ, respectively. Let $A_{q,\psi,\phi}$ be the distribution of the pair $(a, as + e) \in R_q \times R_q$ where $a \leftarrow_\$ R_q$, $s \leftarrow_\$ \chi_\psi$ and $e \leftarrow_\$ \chi_\phi$. Under the decision RLWE assumption on $A_{q,\psi,\phi}$, (a, Δ) is indistinguishable from uniform. Rather than trying to calculate the specific ψ and ϕ in question and arguing these are reasonable ϕ and ψ for which the RLWE assumption might hold, it suffices for our purposes to observe experimentally that $\Delta[i] \leq h_2$ with reasonable probability. As a check, we collected samples of approximately 133 million coefficients of randomly-constructed Δ for RLWE parameters suggested in [10], i.e., $\alpha = 4.19$, $n = 512$ and $q = 26\,038\,273$. We found that the distribution at this granularity of bucketing is close to uniform, and that the proportion of $\Delta[i]$ values satisfying $\Delta[i] \leq h_2$ was approximately h_2/q. Thus, we proceed assuming that the coefficients of Δ follow a distribution close to uniform over R_q, and consequently that the probability of observing values such that $(cp_B + acd + dp_A)[i] = 0$, is close to $1/q$.

5.5 Query Complexity

In this section, we calculate the number of queries required to collect samples to carry out our attack against the DBS reusable-keys protocol as $(1 + 4z) \cdot 144C^2\alpha^2$, for a small constant C. For the range of parameters we consider in our experiments (see Sect. 5.7), $C \approx 5$ and $z \approx 4$ suffice.

The query complexity depends on choices of h_1, h_2, h_3, t_1, and t_2. For the following argument, we assume that $n \geq 2C^2\alpha$ and $\alpha > 1$. Suppose we choose some constant C such that $h_3 = C\alpha$ and $h_1 = C\sqrt{12n\alpha^4 + 4\alpha^2}$. Also, suppose we choose $t_1 = q/4h_3$, i.e., the midpoint between $2(h_1 + h_2)$ and $q/2h_3 - 2(h_1 + h_2)$. Then the number of signals collected for each coefficient is $q/t_1 = 4C\alpha$.

For each of these signals, we require the corresponding coefficient of δ to have absolute value less than or equal to h_2, where $h_2 < q/4h_3 - h_1 = q/8C\alpha - C\sqrt{12n\alpha^4 + 4\alpha^2}$. We want to choose some h_2 that is close to but does not exceed this bound. One way of doing so is to find some value γ that is close to, but slightly greater than $C\sqrt{12n\alpha^4 + 4\alpha^2}$. Then we can let $h_2 = q/8C\alpha - \gamma$.

Lemma 1. *For $C > 0$, $n, \alpha > 1$, $Cq/4.5n > C\sqrt{12\alpha^4 + 4\alpha^2}$.*

Proof. By the correctness lemma [10], we must have $q > 16\alpha^2 n^{\frac{3}{2}} + 2\alpha\sqrt{n}$, so it is enough to show that $\frac{C}{4.5n}\left(16\alpha^2 n^{\frac{3}{2}} + 2\alpha\sqrt{n}\right) > C\sqrt{12\alpha^4 + 4\alpha^2}$. If $C, n > 0$, this statement simplifies to $13n^2\alpha^2 + 64n\alpha - 81n + 4 > 0$. Since $n, \alpha > 0$, this is true

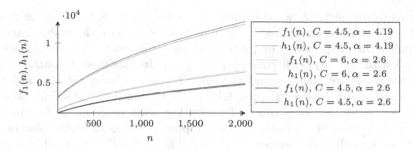

Fig. 6. Closeness of $f_1(n) = \frac{C}{4.5}\frac{16\alpha^2 n^{3/2}+2\alpha\sqrt{n}}{n}$ to $h_1(n) = C\sqrt{12n\alpha^4 + 4\alpha^2}$

if and only if $\alpha > \frac{9\sqrt{13n+12}-32}{13n}$. As a function of n, $\frac{9\sqrt{13n+12}-32}{13n}$ is decreasing for $n \geq 1$ and $\frac{9\sqrt{13n+12}-32}{13n} = 1$ when $n = 1$. So, since $n, \alpha > 1$ by assumption, it follows that $\alpha > \frac{9\sqrt{13n+12}-32}{13n}$ as required. $\qquad\square$

Applying this fact, let $\gamma = \frac{Cq}{4.5n}$ and $h_2 = \frac{q}{8C\alpha} - \frac{Cq}{4.5n} < \frac{q}{8C\alpha} - C\sqrt{12n\alpha^4 + 4\alpha^2}$.

In addition, Fig. 6 exemplifies that for parameters of interest, $h_1(n) = C\sqrt{12n\alpha^4 + 4\alpha^2}$ is indeed slightly less than $f_1(n) = \frac{C}{4.5n}\left(16\alpha^2 n^{3/2} + 2\alpha\sqrt{n}\right)$, and hence, it seems $\gamma = \frac{Cq}{4.5n}$ is a reasonable choice.

This choice of h_2 is positive when $n > (16/9)C^2\alpha$, which is true by assumption. Since the known values are approximately uniform (see Sect. 5.4), we expect to find some known value with absolute value less than h_2 in approximately $q/2h_2 = \frac{36Cn\alpha}{9n-16C^2\alpha}$ queries. Moreover, by assumption, it holds that $n \geq 2C^2\alpha$ so $\frac{q}{2h_2} = \frac{36Cn\alpha}{9n-16C^2\alpha} \leq \frac{36Cn\alpha}{n} = 36C\alpha$. Thus, we expect that $4C\alpha \cdot 36C\alpha = 144C^2\alpha^2$ queries will be sufficient to collect enough signals to complete absolute value recovery and obtain $|s_B[i]|$.

For relative sign collection, we can choose h_2' to be $h_2/2$ and t_2 to be $t_1/2$. Then we expect the number of queries for each iteration of relative sign collection to be $4 \cdot 144C^2\alpha^2$. Therefore, $(1 + 4z)144C^2\alpha^2$ queries suffice to complete relative sign recovery and retrieve s_B or $-s_B$.

As n increases and α decreases, z becomes larger; however, we still expect z to be small in practice. Average values of z from experimental results are given in Fig. 7. Although z does depend on n, larger values of n only increase z by a small amount. Different choices for h_1, h_2, h_3, and t_1 will affect the query complexity, but we note that our analysis shows that it is possible to make choices such that the complexity does not depend on q and depends very little on n. Thus, as q becomes large, the query complexity remains the same and as n becomes large, the query complexity increases at a slow rate.

5.6 Success Probability

We now compute the success probability of our attack. In particular, the attack may fail if any of the bounds h_1, h_2 or h_3 are exceeded.

184 Ni. Bindel et al.

Similarly to Sect. 4.3, we start with the case $|s_B[i]| > h_3$ for some i; this would lead to not counting enough signal changes because the stable intervals are smaller than expected. The probability that this occurs is ρ_1 as defined in Sect. 4.3 with $h = h_3$. Otherwise, $|s_B[i]| \leq h_3$. In this case, the attack may fail if we count too many signal changes. That is, a noisy interval is larger than expected, i.e., when $2\left(|\varepsilon[i]| + |\Delta[i]|\right) > t_1$. Since the absolute value of the known value $\Delta[i]$ is guaranteed to be less than or equal to h_2, and we chose t_1 such that $2(h_1 + h_2) < t_1$, this implies that the absolute value of the error term at coefficient i exceeds $t_1/2 - h_2$. The probability that this occurs is

$\rho_2 = 2\sum_{x=\frac{t_1}{2}-h_2+1}^{\infty} \frac{\exp\left(\frac{-x^2}{2(12n\alpha^4+4\alpha^2)}\right)}{\sqrt{2\pi \cdot (12n\alpha^4+4\alpha^2)}}$. There are $2|s_B[i]| + 1$ boundary periods where this error could occur (note $|s_B[i]| \leq h_3$) and a $1/t_1$ chance we actually collect the incorrect signal so the probability that this occurs (for any coefficient) is at most $n\left(\rho_1 + (1 - \rho_1)(2h_3 + 1)\rho_2/t_1\right)$. Similarly, the probability of failure of relative sign recovery is at most $zn\left(\rho_1 + (1 - \rho_1)(4h_3 + 1)\rho_3/t_2\right)$, where $\rho_3 = 2\sum_{x=\frac{t_2}{2}-h_2'+1}^{\infty} \frac{\exp\left(\frac{-x^2}{2(12n\alpha^4+4\alpha^2)}\right)}{\sqrt{2\pi \cdot (12n\alpha^4+4\alpha^2)}}$. Then, the overall failure probability is at most $n\left(\rho_1 + (1 - \rho_1)(2h_3 + 1)\frac{\rho_2}{t_1}\right) + zn\left(\rho_1 + (1 - \rho_1)(4h_3 + 1)\frac{\rho_3}{t_2}\right)$.

To demonstrate the high success probability while needing only a small number of queries, we instantiate the above parameters using parameters proposed in [10], i.e., $n = 512$, $\alpha = 4.19$, $q = 26\,038\,273$. Moreover, recall our choice of parameters in Sect. 5.5: $h_1 = C\sqrt{12n\alpha^4 + 4\alpha^2}$, $h_2 = q/(8C\alpha) - Cq/(4.5n)$, $h_2' = h_2/2$, $h_3 = C\alpha$, $t_1 = q/(4h_3) = 2$ and $t_2 = t_1/2$. Then $\frac{t_1}{2} - h_2 = \frac{Cq}{4.5n}$ and $\frac{t_2}{2} - h_2' = \frac{Cq}{9n}$. Hence, the probability of failure is at most $n\left(\rho_1 + (1 - \rho_1)(2C\alpha + 1)\frac{4C\alpha}{q}\rho_2\right) + zn\left(\rho_1 + (1 - \rho_1)(4C\alpha + 1)\frac{8C\alpha}{q}\rho_3\right)$.

Continuing our example, suppose $z = 3$ and $C = 4.5$, leading to some secret coefficient being greater than $h_3 = 19$ with probability $\approx 2^{-18.3}$. Moreover, since $Cq/9n > h_1 = 6193$, the probability that some coefficient of an error term is greater than h_1 is $\approx 2^{-19.1}$. Thus, the overall failure probability is at most ≈ 0.00634, i.e., the success probability is at least 99.36%. Using the query complexity derived in the previous section, this success probability is achieved with only $\frac{q}{t_1} \cdot \frac{q}{h_2} + z \cdot \frac{q}{t_2} \cdot \frac{q}{h_2'} \leq 2^{17.7} \approx 212\,900$ queries to the oracle S in total.

5.7   Experimental Results

We ran our attack against the DBS reusable-keys protocol for the two parameter sets proposed in [10] and additional sets for $n = 128$, 256, 512, and 1024, with two different choices of $\alpha = 4.19$ and 2.6. The corresponding q were chosen based on the correctness requirement [10, Lemma 16].

Figure 7 shows the experimental results which are the average over 15 tests, on a 2.4 GHz Intel Xeon CPU E7-8870 with 80 cores and 1 TB RAM. Our code is publicly available at https://git.uwaterloo.ca/ssveitch/improved-key-reuse.

As n increases, the runtime increases largely due to more time spent on polynomial multiplication, since polynomial multiplication increases quadratically in

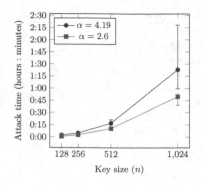

n	128	256	512	1024
q	2 255 041	9 205 761	26 038 273	28 434 433
$\alpha = 4.19$				
z (avg.)	2.73	3.00	3.20	3.73
max. (h:m:s)	3:37	5:06	21:13	2:18:12
avg. (h:m:s)	2:12	4:46	16:56	1:22:54
min. (h:m:s)	1:20	4:35	15:09	59:16
$\alpha = 2.6$				
z (avg.)	3	3.47	3.93	4.8
max. (h:m:s)	0:59	3:07	11:59	53:47
avg. (h:m:s)	0:43	2:54	10:23	49:39
min. (h:m:s)	0:31	2:00	8:02	39:06
# queries (avg.)	202 999.6	239 637.5	305 094.4	401 806.3

Fig. 7. Experimental runtime of attack on DBS reusable-keys protocol

n and key recovery increases linearly in n. The runtime for a set of parameters varies depending on the value of z and the amount of queries it takes to find known values that are sufficiently small.

5.8 Analysis of the Claimed Proof Showing Robustness

As our experiments and theoretical analysis show, the DBS reusable-keys protocol is not robust against key reuse as claimed in [10, Theorem 14]. We point out a mistake in the proof that might have lead to this wrong conclusion.

The idea of the proof of [10, Theorem 14] is essentially that, because of the use of the random oracle H_1 to compute $c = H_1(id_A, id_B, p_A)$ and $d = H_1(id_A, id_B, p_A, p_B)$, the shared secret key k_j is "indistinguishable from a uniformly chosen value of R_q from the point-of-view of [the adversary] $\mathcal{A}$" [10]. In particular, it is said that if $\mathcal{A}$ (impersonating the initiator) samples p_A from an arbitrary distribution, the distribution of $\overline{p_A} = p_A + aH_1(id_A, id_B, p_A) + 2g_B$ (with $g_B \leftarrow_\$ \chi_\alpha$) is "statistically close to the uniform distribution [over R_q]" [10].

At the core of this argument is [10, Lemma 10] (originally stated in [12]): "Let ϕ be an arbitrary distribution over R_q and ψ be a distribution over R_q statistically close to the uniform distribution over R_q. Let $x \leftarrow_\$ \phi$ and $y \leftarrow_\$ \psi$. Then, the distribution of $\bar{x} = x+y$ is statistically close to uniform [over R_q]." The statement assumes implicitly that x and y are *independent* random variables.

In the proof of [10, Theorem 14], the variable x corresponds to p_A (the value controlled by the adversary $\mathcal{A}$) and y corresponds to $aH_1(id_A, id_B, p_A) + 2g_B$. While the output of the random oracle by assumption, it is fixed by the output. Since p_A is given as input to H_1 (the adversary can even choose it themselves), the random variables x and y are *not* independent from each other from the perspective of an adversary who can query the random oracle. Indeed, the dependency of $H_1(id_A, id_B, p_A)$ on p_A is exploited in our attack by finding p_A and id_A such that the ith coefficient of the known values $\Delta = cp_B + acd + dp_A$ is equal to 0 (or small).

Initiator (Alice)	Responder (Bob)
$s_A, e_A \leftarrow^\$ \chi_\alpha$	$s_B, e_B \leftarrow^\$ \chi_\alpha$
$p_A \leftarrow a s_A + 2 e_A$	$p_B \leftarrow a s_B + 2 e_B$
$r_A, f_A \leftarrow^\$ \chi_\alpha$	$r_B, f_B \leftarrow^\$ \chi_\alpha$
$y_A \leftarrow a r_A + 2 f_A$	$y_B \leftarrow a r_B + 2 f_B$
	$c \leftarrow H_1(id_A, id_B, y_A)$
	$d \leftarrow H_1(id_A, id_B, y_A, y_B)$
	$g_B, g'_B \leftarrow^\$ \chi_\alpha$
$c \leftarrow H_1(id_A, id_B, y_A)$	$\overline{y_A} \leftarrow y_A + ac + 2 g_B$
$d \leftarrow H_1(id_A, id_B, y_A, y_B)$	$k_B \leftarrow (p_A + \overline{y_A})(s_B + r_B + d) - p_A s_B + 2 g'_B$
$g_A, g'_A \leftarrow^\$ \chi_\alpha$	$w_B \leftarrow \mathrm{Sig}(k_B)$
$\overline{y_B} \leftarrow y_B + ad + 2 g_A$	$\sigma_B \leftarrow \mathrm{Mod}_2(k_B, w_B)$
$k_A \leftarrow (p_B + \overline{y_B})(s_A + y_A + c) - p_B s_A + 2 g'_A$	
$\sigma_A \leftarrow \mathrm{Mod}_2(k_A, w_B)$	
$sk_A \leftarrow H_2(id_A, id_B, y_A, y_B, w_B, \sigma_A)$	$sk_B \leftarrow H_2(id_A, id_B, y_A, y_B, w_B, \sigma_B)$

with arrows: y_A (Alice → Bob), y_B, w_B (Bob → Alice)

Fig. 8. DBS AKE protocol [10]

5.9 Application to Seyhan et al. Reusable Keys Protocol

Seyhan et al. [24] present a module-LWE-based analogue of the DBS reusable keys protocol that also uses the pasteurization technique. Our core observation also applies here: we can deconstruct the shared secret as the sum of a single unknown term plus several known terms, effectively eliminating pasteurization. In particular, the shared secret is

$$k_B = (s_B^T + d^T)(p_A + Ac + g_B) + g'_B$$
$$= s_B^T p_A + \underbrace{p_B c + d^T p_A + d^T Ac}_{\Delta} \underbrace{- e_B c + s_B^T g_B + c g_B + g'_B}_{\varepsilon}.$$

One difference between the Seyhan et al. reusable keys protocol and the DBS reusable-keys protocol is that the Seyhan et al. protocol does not transmit a signal value, and instead relies on most-significant bit rounding for error correction. (In fact this casts in to doubt the correctness of their protocol.) The lack of signal value is not a fundamental problem, and can be solved by shifting the overall attack to use the "key mismatch oracle" technique of Ding et al. [11].

6 Extension to Authenticated Key Exchange Protocols

We briefly consider the application of our techniques to two different authenticated key exchange protocols with a similar structure; details appear in the full version. Figure 8 shows the DBS AKE protocol [10] which was shown secure in the Bellare–Rogaway (BR) model [3] with weak forward secrecy. The BR model permits the adversary to compromise session keys of any session except the target session, and long-term secret keys of any parties except the two parties involved in the session before the session has completed (weak forward secrecy).

The value k_B can be written as $k_B = y_A s_B + \Delta + \varepsilon$, where $\Delta = p_A r_B + p_A d + c p_B + \overline{y_A} r_B + \overline{y_A} d + 2g'_B$ and $\varepsilon = 2g_B s_B - 2e_B c$. We cannot immediately apply our attack from Sect. 5 in the BR model, since a BR adversary will not be able to determine terms involving r_B. But in the extended Canetti–Krawczyk (eCK) model [17], the adversary *is* permitted to reveal ephemeral keys of certain sessions, giving enough information to allow the adversary to compute all of Δ, and thereby apply our attack. As the authenticated key exchange proposed by Akleylek and Seyhan [1] makes use of the same pasteurization technique, our attack can be applied to their protocol as well.

This in no way invalidates the security claims of [1,10], since our attack is in a stronger model. But we still think it worth observing since the DBS AKE protocol uses a design inspired by the MQV protocol [18,20], some variants of which *are* eCK-secure [25]. The ZZDSD AKE protocol [26] is also inspired by an MQV design, but we were not able to apply our attack in the eCK model to the ZZDSD AKE protocol, in part because the ZZDSD AKE protocol uses the c and d values multiplicatively, rather than additively as in the DBS AKE protocol.

References

1. Akleylek, S., Seyhan, K.: A probably secure BI-GISIS based modified AKE scheme with reusable keys. IEEE Access **8**, 26210–26222 (2020). https://doi.org/10.1109/ACCESS.2020.2970537
2. Bellare, M., Canetti, R., Krawczyk, H.: A modular approach to the design and analysis of authentication and key exchange protocols (extended abstract). In: 30th ACM STOC, pp. 419–428. ACM Press, May 1998
3. Bellare, M., Rogaway, P.: Entity authentication and key distribution. In: Stinson, D.R. (ed.) CRYPTO 1993. LNCS, vol. 773, pp. 232–249. Springer, Heidelberg (1994). https://doi.org/10.1007/3-540-48329-2_21
4. Bindel, N., Stebila, D., Veitch, S.: Improved attacks against key reuse in learning with errors key exchange. Cryptology ePrint Archive, Report 2020/1288 (2021). https://eprint.iacr.org/2020/1288
5. Bos, J., et al.: CRYSTALS - Kyber: a CCA-secure module-lattice-based KEM. In: IEEE European Symposium on Security and Privacy (EuroS&P) 2018, pp. 353–367. IEEE (2018)
6. Boyd, C., Cliff, Y., González Nieto, J.M., Paterson, K.G.: One-round key exchange in the standard model. Int. J. Appl. Cryptogr. **1**(3), 181–199 (2009)
7. Diffie, W., Hellman, M.E.: New directions in cryptography. IEEE Trans. Inf. Theory **22**(6), 644–654 (1976)
8. Ding, J., Alsayigh, S., RV, S., Fluhrer, S., Lin, X.: Leakage of signal function with reused keys in RLWE key exchange. Cryptology ePrint Archive, Report 2016/1176 (2016). http://eprint.iacr.org/2016/1176
9. Ding, J., Alsayigh, S., Saraswathy, R.V., Fluhrer, S., Lin, X.: Leakage of signal function with reused keys in RLWE key exchange. In: 2017 IEEE International Conference on Communications (ICC), pp. 1–6 (2017)
10. Ding, J., Branco, P., Schmitt, K.: Key exchange and authenticated key exchange with reusable keys based on RLWE assumption. Cryptology ePrint Archive, Report 2019/665 (2019). https://eprint.iacr.org/2019/665

11. Ding, J., Fluhrer, S., Rv, S.: Complete attack on RLWE key exchange with reused keys, without signal leakage. In: Susilo, W., Yang, G. (eds.) ACISP 2018. LNCS, vol. 10946, pp. 467–486. Springer, Cham (2018). https://doi.org/10.1007/978-3-319-93638-3_27

12. Ding, J., RV, S., Alsayigh, S., Clough, C.: How to validate the secret of a ring learning with errors (RLWE) key. Cryptology ePrint Archive, Report 2018/081 (2018). https://eprint.iacr.org/2018/081

13. Ding, J., Xie, X., Lin, X.: A simple provably secure key exchange scheme based on the learning with errors problem. Cryptology ePrint Archive, Report 2012/688 (2012). http://eprint.iacr.org/2012/688

14. Fluhrer, S.: Cryptanalysis of ring-LWE based key exchange with key share reuse. Cryptology ePrint Archive, Report 2016/085 (2016). http://eprint.iacr.org/2016/085

15. Fujioka, A., Suzuki, K., Xagawa, K., Yoneyama, K.: Strongly secure authenticated key exchange from factoring, codes, and lattices. In: Fischlin, M., Buchmann, J., Manulis, M. (eds.) PKC 2012. LNCS, vol. 7293, pp. 467–484. Springer, Heidelberg (2012). https://doi.org/10.1007/978-3-642-30057-8_28

16. Krawczyk, H.: HMQV: a high-performance secure Diffie-Hellman protocol. In: Shoup, V. (ed.) CRYPTO 2005. LNCS, vol. 3621, pp. 546–566. Springer, Heidelberg (2005). https://doi.org/10.1007/11535218_33

17. LaMacchia, B., Lauter, K., Mityagin, A.: Stronger security of authenticated key exchange. In: Susilo, W., Liu, J.K., Mu, Y. (eds.) ProvSec 2007. LNCS, vol. 4784, pp. 1–16. Springer, Heidelberg (2007). https://doi.org/10.1007/978-3-540-75670-5_1

18. Law, L., Menezes, A., Qu, M., Solinas, J.A., Vanstone, S.A.: An efficient protocol for authenticated key agreement. Des. Codes Cryptogr. 28(2), 119–134 (2003)

19. Lyubashevsky, V., Peikert, C., Regev, O.: On ideal lattices and learning with errors over rings. In: Gilbert, H. (ed.) EUROCRYPT 2010. LNCS, vol. 6110, pp. 1–23. Springer, Heidelberg (2010). https://doi.org/10.1007/978-3-642-13190-5_1

20. Menezes, A., Qu, M., Vanstone, S.A.: Some new key agreement protocols providing implicit authentication. In: Workshop on Selected Areas in Cryptography (SAC 1995), pp. 22–32 (1995)

21. Peikert, C.: Lattice cryptography for the internet. In: Mosca, M. (ed.) PQCrypto 2014. LNCS, vol. 8772, pp. 197–219. Springer, Cham (2014). https://doi.org/10.1007/978-3-319-11659-4_12

22. Regev, O.: On lattices, learning with errors, random linear codes, and cryptography. In: Gabow, H.N., Fagin, R. (eds.) 37th ACM STOC, pp. 84–93. ACM Press, May 2005

23. Schwabe, P., Stebila, D., Wiggers, T.: Post-quantum TLS without handshake signatures. In: ACM Conference on Computer and Communications Security (CCS) 2020. ACM, November 2020

24. Seyhan, K., Nguyen, T.N., Akleylek, S., Cengiz, K., Islam, S.H.: Bi-GISIS KE: modified key exchange protocol with reusable keys for IoT security. J. Inf. Secur. Appl. 58, 102788 (2021). https://doi.org/10.1016/j.jisa.2021.102788

25. Ustaoglu, B.: Obtaining a secure and efficient key agreement protocol from (H)MQV and NAXOS. Des. Codes Cryptogr. 46(3), 329–342 (2008)

26. Zhang, J., Zhang, Z., Ding, J., Snook, M., Dagdelen, Ö.: Authenticated key exchange from ideal lattices. In: Oswald, E., Fischlin, M. (eds.) EUROCRYPT 2015. LNCS, vol. 9057, pp. 719–751. Springer, Heidelberg (2015). https://doi.org/10.1007/978-3-662-46803-6_24

Cryptanalysis and Side-Channel Analysis

Differential-ML Distinguisher: Machine Learning Based Generic Extension for Differential Cryptanalysis

Tarun Yadav$^{(\boxtimes)}$ and Manoj Kumar

Scientific Analysis Group, DRDO, Metcalfe House Complex, Delhi 110 054, India
{tarunyadav,manojkumar}@sag.drdo.in

Abstract. The differential attack is a basic cryptanalytic technique for block ciphers. Application of machine learning shows promising results for the differential cryptanalysis. In this paper, we present a new technique to extend the classical differential distinguisher using machine learning (ML). We use r-round classical differential distinguisher to build an s-round ML based differential distinguisher. This s-round ML distinguisher is used to construct an $(r+s)$-round differential-ML distinguisher with the reduced data complexity. We demonstrate this technique on the lightweight block ciphers SPECK32, SIMON32, and GIFT64 by constructing the differential-ML distinguishers. The data complexities of distinguishers for 9-round SPECK32, 12-round SIMON32, and 8-round GIFT64 are reduced from 2^{30} to 2^{20}, 2^{34} to 2^{22}, and 2^{38} to 2^{20} respectively. Moreover, the differential-ML distinguisher for SIMON32 is the first 12-round distinguisher with the data complexity less than 2^{32}.

Keywords: Block cipher · Differential cryptanalysis · Machine learning

1 Introduction

Cryptanalysis of block ciphers witnessed the remarkable progress after the proposal of differential attack on DES by Biham and Shamir [8] in 1990. The differential attack is a basic and widely used cryptanalytic approach against the block ciphers. This attack is generalised and combined with other cryptanalytic techniques to reduce the attack complexity. High probability differential characteristics are the first and foremost requirement for the attack to succeed. In 1994, M. Matsui proposed a method based on the branch-and-bound technique [17] to search the high probability differential characteristics. In 2011, Mouha et al. proposed a new technique using mixed integer linear programming (MILP) to search the differential characteristics [18]. The method based on MILP uses optimization problem solvers to construct high probability differential characteristics. Most of the block ciphers follow the Shannon's principles [14] and wide trail design strategy [11] to thwart the differential attack. In practice, we need

© Springer Nature Switzerland AG 2021
P. Longa and C. Ràfols (Eds.): LATINCRYPT 2021, LNCS 12912, pp. 191–212, 2021.
https://doi.org/10.1007/978-3-030-88238-9_10

a differential with the probability greater than 2^{-n} to distinguish r rounds of an n-bit block cipher from the random data. Any r-round characteristic with a probability less than 2^{-n} cannot be used to mount the differential attack on r or more rounds of a block cipher. A differential characteristic is useful till it requires less data than the available limit i.e. 2^n pairs. The motivation of this paper is to find a technique which can be used to extend the classical differential characteristics without (much) increasing the data complexity. Machine learning based differential cryptanalysis approach works well to solve this problem.

Machine learning techniques are used to determine the meticulous relations in the data. Since such relations define the security strength of the cipher, identification of these relations plays an important role. In cryptanalysis domain, the machine learning techniques are explored very recently to mount the key recovery attack using differential cryptanalysis [12].

In this paper, we combine the classical and machine learning techniques to design an ML based generic extension for any classical differential distinguisher. This approach provides the better results with (much) lower data complexity. We extend an r-round high probability classical differential distinguisher with an s-round ML based differential distinguisher. The extended distinguisher is used to distinguish the $(r + s)$ rounds of a block cipher using less data. With this extension, the hybrid distinguisher outperforms both the classical and ML based distinguisher. We call this hybrid distinguisher a *differential-ML distinguisher*. This technique is experimented on three different types of lightweight block ciphers SPECK32 [4], SIMON32 [4], and GIFT64 [3] and better results are obtained with very high accuracy.

The remaining part of the paper is organised as follows. In Sect. 2, we compare our technique with the previous work. In Sect. 3, we provide a brief description of the lightweight block ciphers SIMON32, SPECK32 and GIFT64. We discuss the classical differential distinguisher and machine learning based differential distinguisher in Sect. 4 and describe the existing work on differential distinguishers using machine learning. In Sect. 5, we propose a novel technique to construct the differential-ML distinguisher. We demonstrate our technique on SPECK32, SIMON32, and GIFT64 block ciphers and present the results in Sect. 6. The paper is concluded in Sect. 7.

Notations: We have used the following notations in this paper:

- Δ_r :Output difference after r rounds
- 2^{-p_r} :Probability of r-round differential characteristic
- $D_{x \cdots y}$:Distinguisher for $(y - x + 1)$ rounds; x and y are round indices
- $D_{x \cdots y}^{CD}$:Classical differential distinguisher
- $D_{x \cdots y}^{ML}$:Machine learning based differential distinguisher
- $D_{x \cdots y}^{CD \rightarrow ML}$:Differential-ML distinguisher

Conventions: Throughout the paper, we refer an r-round differential distinguisher with the single input and single output difference as a classical differential distinguisher $D_{1 \cdots r}^{CD}$.

2   Comparison with the Previous Work

A. Gohr [12] used machine learning techniques and proposed the idea of learning the differences to mount a key recovery attack. He presented a technique to construct the ML based differential distinguisher and used it for the key recovery attack on SPECK32. Gohr compared this technique with the classical differential attack and showed that complexity of the key recovery attack is reduced by using the ML distinguisher. Baksi et al. [2] also used the same approach to design the ML distinguisher for GIMLI cipher and GIMLI hash [5]. Various ML architectures are compared in [2] and it is claimed that ML distinguisher for GIMLI outperforms the classical differential distinguisher.

A. Gohr presented the 11-round key recovery attack on SPECK32. In this attack, 7-round ML based distinguisher is used and it is extended to 9 rounds by pre-pending a 2-round high probability differential distinguisher. In Gohr's approach, the accuracy and the data complexity of the 9-round extended distinguisher is not discussed explicitly. Although, the accuracy of extended distinguisher is quite low, yet it is used in the key recovery with various cipher specific optimizations. In this paper, we present a new technique to extend r-round classical differential distinguisher using an s-round ML distinguisher. Now, the extended distinguisher works as the $(r + s)$ rounds differential-ML distinguisher. The proposed technique ensures that the accuracy of differential-ML distinguisher is high and comparable to the classical differential distinguisher. We experimentally show that there is an exponential reduction in the data complexity of the $(r + s)$-round distinguisher by using the proposed differential-ML distinguisher.

3   Block Ciphers: SPECK32, SIMON32, and GIFT64

SPECK and SIMON are two families of the block ciphers proposed by Beaulieu et al. [4] in 2013. These block ciphers are designed to provide the high performance across a range of devices. There are 10 versions of each cipher based on the block and key size combinations which makes them suitable for a wide range of applications. We discuss the encryption algorithm for 32-bit block size and 64-bit key variants of each block cipher. We omit the key expansion algorithm and original paper [4] can be referred for more details.

GIFT is designed by improving the bit permutation of the lightweight block cipher PRESENT. Based on the input plaintext block size, there are two versions of GIFT namely GIFT64 and GIFT128. In each version, the 128-bit key is used to encrypt the input plaintext. A brief description of SPECK32, SIMON32, and GIFT64 block ciphers is provided in the following subsections.

3.1   Description of SPECK32

SPECK32 is a block cipher with 32-bit block size and 64-bit key size. There are total 22 rounds in SPECK32. It is based on the Feistel network and can be represented by the composition of two Feistel maps. Its encryption algorithm divides the 32-bit input into the two 16-bit words (L_r, R_r) and the key expansion algorithm extracts the 16-bit round subkeys (RK_r) for each round. The round function comprises of addition modulo 2^{16}, bitwise XOR, left and right circular shift operations as described in Algorithm 1.

Algorithm 1: Encryption Algorithm of SPECK32

1 **Input:** $P = (L_0 \| R_0)$ and $RK_r (0 \le r \le 21)$
2 **Output:** $C = (L_{22} \| R_{22})$
3 **for** *r=0 to 21* **do**
4 $\quad L_{r+1} = ((L_r \ggg 7) + R_r) \oplus RK_r$
5 $\quad R_{r+1} = L_{r+1} \oplus (R_r \lll 2)$
6 **end**

3.2   Description of SIMON32

SIMON32 is a block cipher with 32-bit block size and 64-bit key size. There are total 32 rounds in SIMON32 and it is also based on the Feistel network. Its encryption algorithm divides the 32-bit input into two 16-bit words (L_r, R_r). The key expansion algorithm expands the 64-bit master key to provide the 16-bit round subkeys (RK_r) for each round. It applies a round function consisting the bitwise XOR, bitwise AND, and left circular shift operations on the left 16-bit words in each round. The encryption algorithm of SIMON32 is described in Algorithm 2.

Algorithm 2: Encryption Algorithm of SIMON32

1 **Input:** $P = (L_0 \| R_0)$ and $RK_r (0 \le r \le 31)$
2 **Output:** $C = (L_{32} \| R_{32})$
3 **for** *r=0 to 31* **do**
4 $\quad L_{r+1} = (L_r \lll 1 \,\&\, L_r \lll 8) \oplus (L_r \lll 2) \oplus R_r \oplus RK_r$
5 $\quad R_{r+1} = L_r$
6 **end**

3.3   Description of GIFT64

GIFT64 encrypts a 64-bit plaintext block using the 128-bit key and generates a 64-bit ciphertext block [3]. There are total 28 rounds in GIFT64. In each round, S-box, bit permutation, round subkeys and constant additions are applied through the round function. The key expansion algorithm extracts the 32-bit subkeys (RK_r) from the 128-bit key. Its encryption algorithm uses a 4-bit S-box S (Table 1), bit permutation P_{64} (Table 2), 6-bit round constants C_r (Table 3) and 32-bit round subkeys RK_r as described in Algorithm 3.

Algorithm 3: Encryption Algorithm of GIFT64

---

1 **Input:** $P(=X_0) = (x_{63}, x_{62}, \cdots, x_0)$ and $RK_r = (U, V)(0 \leq r \leq 27)$
2 **Output:** $C = X_{28}$
3 **for** $r=0$ to 27 **do**
4   **for** $j=0$ to 15 **do**
5         $(y'_{3+4*j}, y'_{2+4*j}, y'_{1+4*j}, y'_{0+4*j}) = S(x_{3+4*j}, x_{2+4*j}, x_{1+4*j}, x_{0+4*j})$
6   **end**
7     $(y_{63}, y_{62}, \cdots, y_0) = P_{64}(y'_{63}, y'_{62}, \cdots, y'_0)$
8   **for** $k=0$ to 5 **do**
9         $y_{3*(k+1)+k} = c_r \oplus y_{3*(k+1)+k}$
10   **end**
11   **for** $l=0$ to 15 **do**
12         $y_{4l+1} = y_{4l+1} \oplus u_l$
13         $y_{4l} = y_{4l} \oplus v_l$
14   **end**
15     $X_{r+1} = (y_{63}, y_{62}, \cdots, y_0) \oplus (1 \ll 63)$
16 **end**

S-box: The 4-bit S-box (Table 1) is applied 16 times in parallel in each round.

Table 1. S-Box

x	0	1	2	3	4	5	6	7	8	9	A	B	C	D	E	F
S(x)	1	a	4	c	6	f	3	9	2	d	b	7	5	0	8	e

Bit Permutation: The diffusion layer uses a permutation P_{64} (Table 2) on 64 bits in each round.

Table 2. Bit permutation

i	0	1	2	3	4	5	6	7	8	9	10	11	12	13	14	15
$P_{64}(i)$	0	17	34	51	48	1	18	35	32	49	2	19	16	33	50	3
i	16	17	18	19	20	21	22	23	24	25	26	27	28	29	30	31
$P_{64}(i)$	4	21	38	55	52	5	22	39	36	53	6	23	20	37	54	7
i	32	33	34	35	36	37	38	39	40	41	42	43	44	45	46	47
$P_{64}(i)$	8	25	42	59	56	9	26	43	40	57	10	27	24	41	58	11
i	48	49	50	51	52	53	54	55	56	57	58	59	60	61	62	63
$P_{64}(i)$	12	29	46	63	60	13	30	47	44	61	14	31	28	45	62	15

Round Constants: In each round, the 6-bit round constant C_r given in the Table 3 is used, where c_0 refers to the least significant bit. For subsequent rounds, it is updated as follows:

$$(c_5, c_4, c_3, c_2, c_1, c_0) \leftarrow (c_4, c_3, c_2, c_1, c_0, c_5 \oplus c_4 \oplus 1)$$

Table 3. Round constants

Rounds (r)	Constants (C_r)
1–14	01 03 07 0F 1F 3E 3D 3B 37 2F 1E 3C 39 33
15–28	27 0E 1D 3A 35 2B 16 2C 18 30 21 02 05 0B

4 Differential Cryptanalysis

Differential cryptanalysis was applied on DES [19] and its exhaustive attack complexity was reduced. This created a path for other cryptanalytic techniques e.g. linear [16], impossible differential [6], algebraic [10], etc. [9]. While designing a block cipher, its output is tested for indistinguishability from the random permutations. However, there may not exist any relationship between the single input and output occurrences but there may exist the non-random relations between the input and output differences. The basic approach of differential attack is to study the propagation of input differences and exploitation of non-random relations between the input and output differences. This attack works with differential characteristics providing the high probability relation between the input and output differences. The high probability differential characteristics are used in the key recovery attack by adding some rounds on the top and bottom of the differential characteristic.

4.1 Classical Differential Distinguisher

There exists several automated techniques to search the optimal differential distinguishers for block ciphers [13]. In this paper, we use the available differential distinguishers for SPECK32 [1] and SIMON32 [7]. We extend the 6-round distinguisher for SPECK32 and 7-round distinguisher for SIMON32 using the ML distinguisher. For GIFT64, we construct the high probability differential characteristics for 4 rounds using the branch-and-bound based search technique [15] and extend this distinguisher with the ML distinguisher.

4.1.1 Differential Characteristic for SPECK32

Abed et al. [1] presented the 9-round differential characteristics for SPECK32 with the probability of 2^{-31}. We choose 8-round differential characteristic presented in Table 4 [1] and use the 6-round differential characteristic ($\Delta_0 \rightarrow \Delta_6$) with the probability of 2^{-13} in our experiments.

Table 4. Differential characteristic of SPECK32 [1]

Round (r)	Input difference (Δ_r)	Probability (2^{-p_r})
0	0211 0A04	1
1	2800 0010	2^{-4}
2	0040 0000	2^{-6}
3	8000 8000	2^{-6}
4	8100 8102	2^{-7}
5	8000 840A	2^{-9}
6	850A 9520	2^{-13}
7	802A D4A8	2^{-19}
8	81A8 D30B	2^{-26}

4.1.2 Differential Characteristic for SIMON32

Biryukov et al. [7] presented the 12-round differential characteristics for SIMON32 with the probability of 2^{-34}. From the 12-round characteristic presented in Table 5 [7], we use the 7-round differential characteristic ($\Delta_0 \rightarrow \Delta_7$) with the probability of 2^{-16} in our experiments.

Table 5. Differential characteristic of SIMON32 [7]

Round (r)	Input difference (Δ_r)	Probability (2^{-p_r})
0	0400 1900	1
1	0100 0400	2^{-2}
2	0000 0100	2^{-4}
3	0100 0000	2^{-4}
4	0400 0100	2^{-6}
5	1100 0400	2^{-8}
6	4200 1100	2^{-12}
7	1D01 4200	2^{-16}
8	0500 1D01	2^{-24}
9	0100 0500	2^{-27}
10	0100 0100	2^{-29}
11	0500 0100	2^{-31}
12	1500 0500	2^{-34}

4.1.3 Differential Characteristic for GIFT64

We construct the 4-round optimal differential characteristic with high probability using branch-and-bound based search algorithm [15]. We use this 4-round differential characteristic with the probability of 2^{-12} to construct the differential-ML distinguisher for GIFT64 (Table 6).

Table 6. Differential characteristic of GIFT64

Round (r)	Input difference (Δ_r)	Probability (2^{-p_r})
0	0000 0000 0000 000A	1
1	0000 0000 0000 0001	2^{-2}
2	0008 0000 0000 0000	2^{-5}
3	0000 0000 2000 1000	2^{-7}
4	0044 0000 0011 0000	2^{-12}

4.2   Differential Distinguisher Using Machine Learning

For a chosen input difference, we use the neural distinguisher design proposed by A. Gohr [12]. We also consider the improvements in this design suggested by Baksi et al. [2] and use dense layers of MLPs (Multi Layers Perceptrons) instead of the convolution networks. We use two hidden layers with 1024 neurons in each layer and train the model on ciphertext differences rather than ciphertext pairs. These improvements increase the learning efficiency of the model.

The model is trained on the data with chosen and random differences. This approach works well because the model learns sensitivity as well as specificity in the data. The sensitivity corresponds to the true positive predictions while the specificity corresponds to the true negative predictions. Initially, we generate a set of random plaintexts $(P_1, P_2, \cdots, P_N)$ and assign a label 0 or 1 to each plaintext randomly. If label of the plaintext P_i is 1, then we generate another plaintext P_i' having a difference Δ_r with P_i otherwise P_i' is generated randomly. The difference Δ_r corresponds to the output difference of the classical differential distinguisher. We encrypt the plaintexts P_i and P_i' using the s-round CIPHER$_s$ to get the ciphertexts C_i and C_i'. The set of ciphertext differences $(C_i \oplus C_i')$ along with the labels is used as training data (TD) for the training phase. Other than the training data, we also generate the validation data (VD) which is used by the trained model M to determine the validation accuracy. Size of TD and VD is subjected to the available computing resources. We train the model M on training data till the validation accuracy is saturated. The saturation implies that there is a negligible improvement in the validation accuracy of ith training epoch (α_{s_i}) in comparison to the validation accuracies $(\alpha_{s_{i-1}}$ and $\alpha_{s_{i-2}})$ of the last two training epoches. We consider the model M as a valid distinguisher $(D_{r+1\cdots r+s}^{ML})$ if the validation accuracy (α_s) is at least 0.51 (Algorithm 4).

Once a valid ML based distinguisher$(D_{r+1\cdots r+s}^{ML})$ is obtained, we generate a pair of plaintexts with chosen difference (Δ_r). ORACLE is queried for the corresponding ciphertexts and $D_{r+1\cdots r+s}^{ML}$ is used to make the prediction on ciphertexts difference. If the prediction probability is at least 0.51 then we consider that the ciphertext pair belongs to the CIPHER$_s$ otherwise not. The accuracy of such prediction is expected to be α_s.

Algorithm 4: ML based differential distinguisher $D_{r+1\cdots r+s}^{ML}$

---

1 **Function** DataGeneration($N,\Delta_r,s=no.\ of\ rounds$):
2   Data Set (D) $\leftarrow$ (.)
3     $K \leftarrow$ Choose a random key
4     $(P_1, P_2, \cdots, P_N) \leftarrow$ Generate a set of random plaintexts
5     $(b_1, b_2, \cdots, b_N) \leftarrow$ Initialize a set of labels
6   **for** $i \leftarrow 1\ to\ N$ **do**
7         $b_i \leftarrow random(0,1)$ $\triangleright$ $random(0,1)$ return either 0 or 1 randomly
8   **if** $b_i = 0$ **then**
9             $P_i' \leftarrow$ Choose a random plaintext
10   **end**
11   **else**
12             $P_i' = P_i \oplus \Delta_r$
13   **end**
14         $C_i \leftarrow$ CIPHER$_s$(P_i, K) $\triangleright$ s-round encryption
15         $C_i' \leftarrow$ CIPHER$_s$(P_i', K) $\triangleright$ s-round encryption
16   Append D by ($C_i \oplus C_i'$, b_i)
17   **end**
18   **return** D
19 **End Function**
20 **Procedure** Trainig Phase($D_{1\cdots r}^{CD}(\Delta_0 \rightarrow \Delta_r)$,$s=no\ of\ rounds$):
21   Training Data (TD) $\leftarrow$ DataGeneration(2^{25}, Δ_r,s)
22   Validation Data (VD) $\leftarrow$ DataGeneration(2^{22}, Δ_r,s)
23   **for** $i \leftarrow 1\ to\ 10$ **do**
24   Train ML Model (M) on TD
25   Validate M on VD
26         $\alpha_{s_i} \leftarrow$ Validation Accuracy of M
27   **if** ($i \geq 3$ and $\alpha_{s_i} \approx \alpha_{s_{i-1}}$ and $\alpha_{s_{i-1}} \approx \alpha_{s_{i-2}}$) **then**
28             $\alpha_s = \alpha_{s_i}$
29   goto Line 32
30   **end**
31   **end**
32   **if** $\alpha_s \geq 0.51$ **then**
33         $D_{r+1\cdots r+s}^{ML} \leftarrow M$
34   **end**
35   **else**
36   M is not a valid distinguisher
37   **end**
38 **End Procedure**
39 **Procedure** Prediction Phase($D_{1\cdots r}^{CD}(\Delta_0 \rightarrow \Delta_r)$, $D_{r+1\cdots r+s}^{ML}$):
40     $P \leftarrow$ Choose a random plaintext
41     $P' = P \oplus \Delta_r$
42     $C \leftarrow$ ORACLE(P)
43     $C' \leftarrow$ ORACLE(P')
44     $p \leftarrow$ prediction probability for ($C \oplus C'$) using $D_{r+1\cdots r+s}^{ML}$
45   **if** ($p \geq 0.51$) **then**
46   ORACLE = CIPHER$_s$
47   **end**
48   **else**
49   ORACLE $\neq$ CIPHER$_s$
50   **end**
51 **End Procedure**

5   Differential-ML Distinguisher: Extending Classical Differential Distinguisher Using Machine Learning

The accuracy plays an important role to design the machine learning based differential distinguisher. There is a trade-off between the accuracy and the number of rounds covered. If we increase the number of rounds then accuracy of the ML distinguisher may decrease. The data complexity of a low accuracy distinguisher cannot be compared with the classical distinguisher due to high amount of false positive and false negative in the ML distinguisher. Therefore, we propose a new technique which uses the ML distinguisher to extend the existing classical distinguisher. Since, the accuracy of the proposed extended distinguisher is high, we can compare its data complexity with the classical distinguisher.

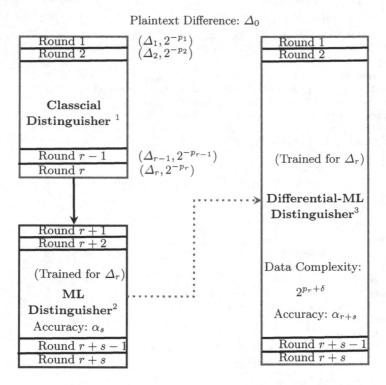

Fig. 1. Extending the classical distinguisher using ML distinguisher (1. Classical distinguisher: $D_{1\cdots r}^{CD}$ 2. ML distinguisher: $D_{r+1\cdots r+s}^{ML}$ 3. Differential-ML distinguisher: $D_{1\cdots r+s}^{CD\to ML}$)

Algorithm 5: Differential-ML distinguisher $D_{1\cdots r+s}^{CD \to ML}$: $(D_{1\cdots r}^{CD}, D_{r+1\cdots r+s}^{ML},$ $T = \alpha_s,\, C_T,\, \beta)$

---

1 **Function** Construction Phase($D_{1\cdots r}^{CD}$ *(Data:* 2^{p_r} *),* $D_{r+1\cdots r+s}^{ML}$, $T = \alpha_s$):
2     $\delta \leftarrow 0$
3   **repeat**
4   **for** $k \leftarrow 1$ *to* 10 **do**
5           $K \leftarrow$ Choose a random key
6           $(P_{\Delta_0}, P'_{\Delta_0}) \leftarrow 2^\delta * 2^{p_r}$ plaintext pairs with difference Δ_0
7           $(P_R, P'_R) \leftarrow 2^\delta * 2^{p_r}$ plaintext pairs with random difference
8           $(C_{\Delta_0}, C'_{\Delta_0}) \leftarrow$ (CIPHER$_{r+s}(P_{\Delta_0}, K)$,CIPHER$_{r+s}(P'_{\Delta_0}, K)$)
9           $(C_R, C'_R) \leftarrow$ (CIPHER$_{r+s}(P_R, K)$,CIPHER$_{r+s}(P'_R, K)$)
10           $p_{\Delta_0} \leftarrow$ prediction probabilities for $(C_{\Delta_0} \oplus C'_{\Delta_0})$ using $D_{r+1\cdots r+s}^{ML}$
11           $p_R \leftarrow$ prediction probabilities for $(C_R \oplus C'_R)$ using $D_{r+1\cdots r+s}^{ML}$
12   TP $\leftarrow$ number of elements with $p_{\Delta_0} \geq T$
13   TN $\leftarrow$ number of elements with $p_R \geq T$
14   Plot the curve for TP and TN values
15   **end**
16        $\delta \leftarrow \delta + 1$
17   **until** *(TP and TN curves do not intersect)*;
18     $C_T \approx$ average of ordinates of closest points on TP and TN curves
19   Data Complexity(β) $\leftarrow 2^\delta * 2^{p_r}$
20   **return** C_T, β
21 **End Function**
22 **Procedure** Prediction Phase($D_{1\cdots r+s}^{CD \to ML}$):
23   Test Data (TD) $\leftarrow$ (.)
24   **for** $i \leftarrow 1$ *to* β **do**
25        $P_i \leftarrow$ Choose a random plaintext
26        $P'_i = P_i \oplus \Delta_0$
27        $C_i \leftarrow$ ORACLE(P_i)
28        $C'_i \leftarrow$ ORACLE(P'_i)
29   Append TD by $C_i \oplus C'_i$
30   **end**
31     $p \leftarrow$ prediction probabilities for elements in TD using $D_{r+1\cdots r+s}^{ML}$
32   **if** *((number of pairs with* $p \geq T$*)* $\geq C_T$*)* **then**
33   ORACLE = CIPHER$_{r+s}$
34   **end**
35   **else**
36   ORACLE $\neq$ CIPHER$_{r+s}$
37   **end**
38 **end Procedure**

To extend the r-round classical differential distinguisher $D_{1\cdots r}^{CD}$ $(\Delta_0 \rightarrow \Delta_r)$, we use the difference Δ_r to model s-round distinguisher $(D_{r+1\cdots r+s}^{ML})$ with an accuracy α_s. The accuracy α_s defines the distinguishing ability of the distinguisher and better accuracy gives better predictions. Now, the distinguisher $D_{r+1\cdots r+s}^{ML}$ can be used to distinguish the output of CIPHER$_s$ with an accuracy α_s.

The data complexity of the r-round classical differential distinguisher $(\Delta_0 \rightarrow \Delta_r$, probability: $2^{-p_r})$ is 2^{p_r} chosen plaintext pairs. It is expected to get at least one occurrence of Δ_r in the output difference. If we provide 2^{p_r} ciphertext pairs after the $(r + s)$ rounds of encryption to the distinguisher $D_{r+1\cdots r+s}^{ML}$ then we expect that the ML distinguisher $D_{r+1\cdots r+s}^{ML}$ will correctly predict one occurrence corresponding to the difference Δ_r. Since ML distinguisher learns the multiple output differences, we expect that it will learn the pattern of differences which are suggested by the classical differential distinguisher. Therefore, we require at least 2^{p_r} data to model the $(r + s)$-round differential-ML distinguisher $(D_{1\cdots r+s}^{CD\rightarrow ML})$. Now, the accuracy α_s of the s-round ML distinguisher plays a significant role. If accuracy α_s is low then the accuracy α_{r+s} of the distinguisher $D_{1\cdots r+s}^{CD\rightarrow ML}$ for 2^{p_r} data will also be low. The accuracy of the differential-ML distinguisher must be high to compare it with the $(r + s)$-round classical differential distinguisher. To increase the accuracy α_{r+s}, we propose a novel technique which requires additional data (2^{δ}). Therefore, data complexity of the differential-ML distinguisher $D_{1\cdots r+s}^{CD\rightarrow ML}$ becomes $2^{p_r+\delta}$, where δ defines the additional data required to increase the accuracy of predictions (Fig. 1).

In our technique, we define the differential-ML distinguisher $D_{1\cdots r+s}^{CD\rightarrow ML}$ with five parameters $(D_{1\cdots r}^{CD}, D_{r+1\cdots r+s}^{ML}, T = \alpha_s, C_T, \beta)$. Where, T is the threshold probability, C_T is the cutoff on the number of pairs with the prediction probability $\geq$ T and β is data complexity of the differential-ML distinguisher. These parameters are required to construct the differential-ML distinguisher. We set α_s as the threshold probability (T) and propose an experimental approach to calculate C_T and β (Algorithm 5). We start with the minimum data (2^{p_r}) and set δ as 0. We generate a set of 2^{p_r} plaintext pairs with the difference Δ_0 and another set of 2^{p_r} plaintext pairs with the random differences. These pairs are encrypted using the CIPHER$_{r+s}$. The distinguisher $D_{r+1\cdots r+s}^{ML}$ is used to get the prediction probabilities p_{Δ_0} and p_R as explained in Algorithm 5.

Using these probabilities, we get the True Positive (TP) and the True Negative (TP) values. We repeat this process 10 times and plot the curve for TP and TN values. If the TP and TN curves intersect, then we increase the data requirement and repeat the process with the increased data. We repeat the process until we get the non intersecting curves. Once such curves are obtained, data complexity (β) of the differential-ML distinguisher $D_{1\cdots r+s}^{CD\rightarrow ML}$ becomes $2^{p_r+\delta}$. To calculate C_T, we take average of the closest points on the TP and TN curves. Closest points correspond to the minimum number of predictions on TP curve and maximum number of predictions on TN curve. The value of C_T is taken as the separation cutoff for TP and TN curves and it is used by the distinguisher $(D_{1\cdots r+s}^{CD\rightarrow ML})$ to distinguish the data sample correctly. The complete procedure to construct the differential-ML distinguisher is described in Algorithm 5.

The differential-ML distinguisher $D_{1 \cdots r+s}^{CD \to ML}$ act as the $(r+s)$-round distinguisher. We choose a set of β plaintext pairs with the difference Δ_0 and get the ciphertext pairs after $(r+s)$ rounds. The distinguisher $D_{1 \cdots r+s}^{CD \to ML}$ makes the prediction for each ciphertext pair. If the number of pairs with the prediction probability greater than T is above the cutoff threshold C_T then the distinguisher $D_{1 \cdots r+s}^{CD \to ML}$ classifies whether the given data is an output from the target CIPHER$_{r+s}$ or not. The prediction procedure is described in the prediction phase of the Algorithm 5.

With the proposed distinguisher $D_{1 \cdots r+s}^{CD \to ML}$, we can achieve very high accuracy to distinguish the output of the CIPHER$_{r+s}$ and it can be used to mount a key recovery attack. The experiments to construct the differential-ML distinguishers are presented in the next section.

6   Experimental Results

We construct the differential-ML distinguisher for the 32-bit variants of the lightweight block ciphers SPECK and SIMON and 64-bit variant of GIFT. We experimented on 32-bit and 64-bit block ciphers due to constraints on available resources. With more computing power, ciphers with larger block size can be explored to construct differential-ML distinguisher. We extend the classical differential distinguisher discussed in Sect. 4 with the ML distinguisher. Using this novel technique, we construct the differential-ML distinguishers for 9-round SPECK32, 12-round SIMON32, and 8-round GIFT64 with (much) less data complexity than the classical distinguishers.

We used Keras-GPU[1] library in Google colab[2] for the model training and predictions. In each experiment, ADAM optimizer is used for the adaptive learning rates and the Mean-Square-Error is used as the loss function. The validation batch accuracy is considered as the accuracy (α_s) of the trained model.

6.1   Differential-ML Distinguisher: SPECK32

For SPECK32, we use the classical differential characteristic for 6 rounds $(\Delta_0 \to \Delta_6)$ as described in the Table 4. We have an output difference 0x850A9520 after 6 rounds with the probability of 2^{-13}. We train the 3-round ML distinguisher using Δ_6 as the input difference and the model is trained with the accuracy of 0.79 using Algorithm 4. The batch accuracy and loss are described in the Appendix A.

6.1.1   Construction
The probability of the 6-round classical differential distinguisher is 2^{-13}. Therefore, we will require at least 2^{13} data to make the predictions with the 9-round differential-ML distinguisher. We calculate T, C_T, and β as discussed in

---

[1] https://keras.io.
[2] https://colab.research.google.com.

Algorithm 5 and construct the 9-round differential-ML distinguisher $D_{1 \cdots r+s}^{CD \rightarrow ML}$
by extending the 6-round classical distinguisher. We draw the graphs for TP and
TN values (Fig. 2) and calculate data complexity (β) and cutoff (C_T). We experimented with the various samples of different sizes and obtained a clear separation
between true positive and true negative curves for a sample size of 2^{20}. We calculate the value of C_T as 73100 and β as 2^{20} with the help of graph (d) in Fig. 2.

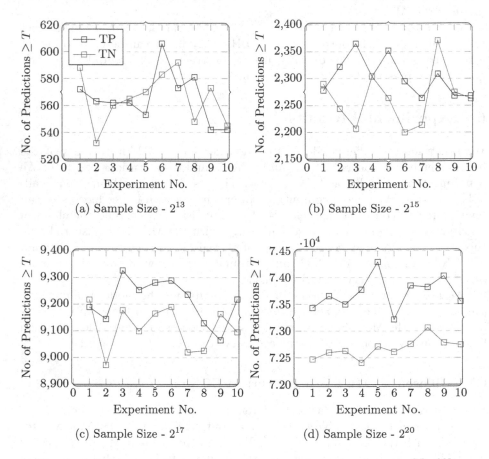

(a) Sample Size - 2^{13}

(b) Sample Size - 2^{15}

(c) Sample Size - 2^{17}

(d) Sample Size - 2^{20}

Fig. 2. Calculation of C_T and data complexity (β) for SPECK32 ($D_{1 \cdots r+s}^{CD \rightarrow ML}$)

6.1.2 Prediction

We constructed the 9-round differential-ML distinguisher $D_{1 \cdots r+s}^{CD \rightarrow ML}$ in the previous subsection. The accuracy (α_{r+s}) of this differential-ML distinguisher for
different experiments is mentioned in the Table 7.

In the experiments, we take 50 samples belonging to the plaintext difference
Δ_0 (=0x0211 0A04) of the classical distinguisher and other 50 samples belonging
to the random input differences. The differential-ML distinguisher $D_{1 \cdots r+s}^{CD \rightarrow ML}$

Table 7. Accuracy for SPECK32 with $T = 0.79$, $C_T = 73100$ and $\beta = 2^{20}$

Experiment no.	Sample size	Correctly distinguished (true positive, true negative)
1	100	98(50,48)
2	100	98(50,48)
3	100	99(49,50)
4	100	97(48,49)
5	100	96(49,47)

predicts whether the given sample belongs to the difference Δ_0 or not by using the Algorithm 5. We used 2^{20} data in each sample and achieved the accuracy (α_{r+s}) more than 96% in each experiment.

Therefore, the data complexity of the 9-round differential-ML distinguisher for SPECK32 is 2^{20}. However, the data complexity of the 9-round classical differential distinguisher is 2^{31} as presented in [1]. The best known differential characteristics for SPECK32 exists for 9-rounds with the data complexity of 2^{30} [7]. Using the differential-ML technique, we have constructed the 9-round distinguisher with the data complexity far less than the existing classical differential distinguisher.

6.2 Differential-ML Distinguisher: SIMON32

For SIMON32, we use the classical differential characteristic for 7 rounds as described in the Table 5. We have an output difference 0x1D014200 (Δ_7) after 7 rounds with the probability of 2^{-16}. We use Δ_7 as the input difference for the training phase of the 5-round ML distinguisher. We train the model with the accuracy of 0.57 using the Algorithm 4. The batch accuracy and loss are described in the Appendix A.

6.2.1 Construction

The probability of the 7-round classical differential distinguisher is 2^{-16}. So, we will require at least 2^{16} data for the 12-round differential-ML distinguisher of SIMON32 and additional data (2^{δ}) will be required to increase the accuracy of the differential-ML distinguisher. Similar to the SPECK32 case, we require T, C_T, and β to construct the 12-round differential-ML distinguisher $D_{1\cdots r+s}^{CD \rightarrow ML}$ which extends the existing 7-round classical distinguisher. We calculate the data complexity (β) and cutoff (C_T) by using the Algorithm 5 and the graphs for TP and TN values (Fig. 3). It is observed from the graphs that a clear separation between true positive and true negative values exists for the sample size of 2^{22}. We calculated the value of C_T as 656300 and data complexity(β) as 2^{22} on the basis of this separation.

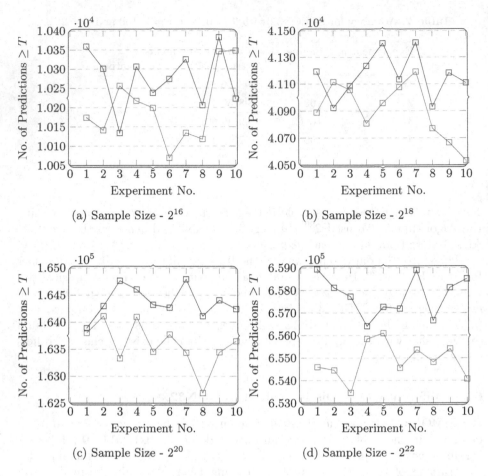

Fig. 3. Calculation of C_T and data complexity (β) for SIMON32 ($D_{1\cdots r+s}^{CD \to ML}$)

6.2.2 Prediction

The 5-round ML distinguisher ($D_{r+1\cdots r+s}^{ML}$) is trained with the validation accuracy of 0.57. It is used to extend the 7-round classical differential distinguisher. The accuracy of the 12-round differential-ML distinguisher $D_{1\cdots r+s}^{CD \to ML}$ for different experiments is mentioned in the Table 8.

Similar to the previous case, we take 50 samples belonging to the initial input difference Δ_0 (=0x04001900) of the classical distinguisher and other 50 samples belonging to the random input differences. We make predictions with 2^{22} data using the value of C_T calculated in the previous step and the accuracy (α_{r+s}) greater than 97% is achieved in each experiment. From these experiments, 12-round differential-ML distinguisher $D_{1\cdots r+s}^{CD \to ML}$ with data complexity of 2^{22} is constructed, while data complexity for the 12-round classical differential distinguisher is 2^{34} (Table 5). In this case, we present the first 12-round distinguisher with the data complexity less than 2^{32}. This shows that the differential-ML

Table 8. Accuracy for SIMON32 with $T = 0.57$, $C_T = 656300$ and $\beta = 2^{22}$

Experiment no.	Sample size	Correctly distinguished (true positive, true negative)
1	100	98(48,50)
2	100	98(48,50)
3	100	98(49,49)
4	100	97(48,49)
5	100	98(48,50)

distinguisher provides the better results than the classical differential distinguisher in case of SIMON32 also.

6.3   Differential-ML Distinguisher: GIFT64

For GIFT64, we searched an optimal differential characteristic for 4 rounds which is described in the Table 6. We obtain the output difference after 4 rounds as Δ_4 = 0x0044000000110000 with the probability of 2^{-12}. The difference Δ_4 is used to train the 4-round ML based distinguisher. We train a model with the accuracy of 0.65 using the Algorithm 4. The batch accuracy and loss are described in Appendix A.

6.3.1 Construction
The probability of the 4-round classical differential characteristic is 2^{-12}. Therefore, data complexity of the 4-round differential distinguisher will be 2^{12}. So, the 8-round differential-ML distinguisher for GIFT64 will require at least 2^{12} data. We calculate T, C_T, and data complexity (β) by using Algorithm 5. These are required to construct the 8-round differential-ML distinguisher by extending the 4-round classical differential distinguisher. It can be easily inferred from the graphs depicted in Fig. 4 that a clear separation between true positive and true negative values exists for the sample size of 2^{20}. We use this separation to get the cutoff threshold ($C_T = 103750$) and data complexity ($\beta = 2^{20}$) for $D_{1\cdots r+s}^{CD \rightarrow ML}$.

6.3.2 Prediction
The 4-round ML distinguisher $D_{r+1\cdots r+s}^{ML}$ is trained with the validation accuracy of 0.65 and it is used to extend the 4-round classical differential distinguisher. Accuracy of the 8-round differential-ML distinguisher $D_{1\cdots r+s}^{CD \rightarrow ML}$ for different experiments is mentioned in the Table 9.

Similar to SPECK32 and SIMON32 cases, we take 50 samples belonging to the input difference Δ_0 (=0x000000000000000A) of the classical distinguisher and other 50 samples belonging to the random input differences. For each sample, we use 2^{20} data to achieve the accuracy (α_{r+s}) greater than 98% in each experiment. Therefore, data complexity of the 8-round differential-ML distinguisher

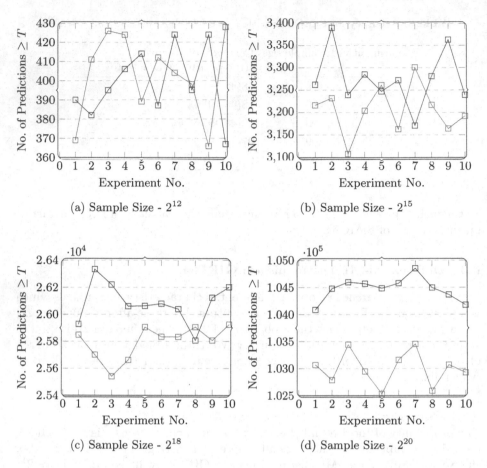

(a) Sample Size - 2^{12}

(b) Sample Size - 2^{15}

(c) Sample Size - 2^{18}

(d) Sample Size - 2^{20}

Fig. 4. Calculation of C_T and data complexity (β) for GIFT64 ($D_{1\cdots r+s}^{CD\rightarrow ML}$)

Table 9. Accuracy for GIFT64 with $T = 0.65$, $C_T = 103650$ and $\beta = 2^{20}$

Experiment no.	Sample size	Correctly distinguished (true positive, true negative)
1	100	99(50,49)
2	100	100(50,50)
3	100	98(50,48)
4	100	100(50,50)
5	100	100(50,50)

is 2^{20}, while data complexity of the 8-round classical differential distinguisher was 2^{38} [20].

6.4   Comparison with the Classical Differential Distinguishers

We have constructed the differential-ML distinguishers for the block ciphers based on three different types of structures (Feistel, SPN, and ARX). We are able to distinguish the same number of rounds using less amount of data in comparison to the classical distinguisher. These results indicate that our technique provides better results for the block ciphers based on all types of structures. The source code for the above mentioned experiments is available on GitHub[3]. We provide a comparison of the data complexities between the differential-ML distinguisher and the classical differential distinguisher in Table 10.

Table 10. Summary of results

Cipher	Distinguisher	Round	Data complexity	Source
SPECK32	Differential	9	2^{30}	[7]
SPECK32	**Differential-ML**	**9**	2^{20}	**Sec. 6.1**
SIMON32	Differential	12	2^{34}	[7]
SIMON32	**Differential-ML**	**12**	2^{22}	**Sec. 6.2**
GIFT64	Differential[7]	8	2^{38}	[20]
GIFT64	**Differential-ML**	**8**	2^{20}	**Sec. 6.3**

There exists differential distinguisher for 12 rounds with the data complexity of 2^{60}.

7   Conclusion

In this paper, we have proposed a novel technique to extend the classical differential distinguisher using machine learning. We have constructed the high accuracy (more than 96%) differential-ML distinguishers for 9-round SPECK32, 12-round SIMON32, and 8-round GIFT64. For SPECK32, we have extended the 6-round classical differential distinguisher with the 3-round ML distinguisher and the data complexity of 9-round differential-ML distinguisher is 2^{20}. For SIMON32, the classical differential distinguisher for 7-rounds is extended with the 5-round ML distinguisher and data complexity of the 12-round differential-ML distinguisher is 2^{22}. For GIFT64, the 8-round differential-ML distinguisher is constructed with the data complexity of 2^{20} whereas data complexity of the 8-round classical differential distinguisher was 2^{38}. The data complexity of the distinguishers for SPECK32, SIMON32, and GIFT64 is significantly reduced using differential-ML distinguishers in comparison to the classical distinguishers.

---

[3] https://github.com/tarunyadav/Differential-ML-Distinguisher.

Appendix A - Accuracy and Loss Graphs

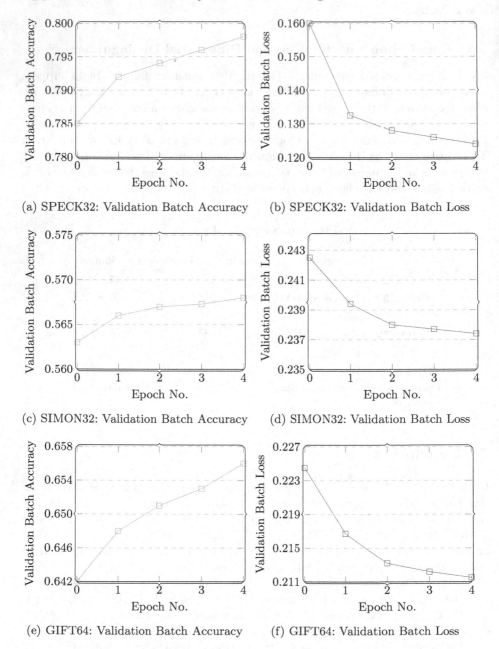

(a) SPECK32: Validation Batch Accuracy

(b) SPECK32: Validation Batch Loss

(c) SIMON32: Validation Batch Accuracy

(d) SIMON32: Validation Batch Loss

(e) GIFT64: Validation Batch Accuracy

(f) GIFT64: Validation Batch Loss

References

1. Abed, F., List, E., Lucks, S., Wenzel, J.: Differential cryptanalysis of round-reduced SIMON and SPECK. In: Cid, C., Rechberger, C. (eds.) FSE 2014. LNCS, vol. 8540, pp. 525–545. Springer, Heidelberg (2015). https://doi.org/10.1007/978-3-662-46706-0_27
2. Baksi, A., Breier, J., Dong, X., Yi, C.: Machine Learning Assisted Differential Distinguishers For Lightweight Ciphers (2020). https://eprint.iacr.org/2020/571
3. Banik, S., Pandey, S.K., Peyrin, T., Sasaki, Y., Sim, S.M., Todo, Y.: GIFT: a small present - towards reaching the limit of lightweight encryption. In: Cryptographic Hardware and Embedded Systems - CHES 2017–19th International Conference, Taipei, Taiwan, 25–28 September 2017, Proceedings, vol. 10529, pp. 321–345 (2017)
4. Beaulieu, R., Shors, D., Smith, J., Treatman-Clark, S., Weeks, B., Wingers, L.: The SIMON and SPECK families of lightweight block ciphers. Cryptology ePrint Archive, Report 2013/404 (2013). https://eprint.iacr.org/2013/404
5. Bernstein, D.J., et al.: Gimli (2019)
6. Biham, E., Biryukov, A., Shamir, A.: Cryptanalysis of skipjack reduced to 31 rounds using impossible differentials. In: Stern, J. (ed.) EUROCRYPT 1999. LNCS, vol. 1592, pp. 12–23. Springer, Heidelberg (1999). https://doi.org/10.1007/3-540-48910-X_2
7. Biryukov, A., Roy, A., Velichkov, V.: Differential analysis of block ciphers SIMON and SPECK. In: Cid, C., Rechberger, C. (eds.) FSE 2014. LNCS, vol. 8540, pp. 546–570. Springer, Heidelberg (2015). https://doi.org/10.1007/978-3-662-46706-0_28
8. Biham, E., Shamir, A.: Differential cryptanalysis of the full 16-round DES. In: Brickell, E.F. (ed.) CRYPTO 1992. LNCS, vol. 740, pp. 487–496. Springer, Heidelberg (1993). https://doi.org/10.1007/3-540-48071-4_34
9. Bogdanov, A.: Analysis and design of block cipher constructions, Ph.D. thesis (2009)
10. Courtois, N.T., Meier, W.: Algebraic attacks on stream ciphers with linear feedback. In: Biham, E. (ed.) EUROCRYPT 2003. LNCS, vol. 2656, pp. 345–359. Springer, Heidelberg (2003). https://doi.org/10.1007/3-540-39200-9_21
11. Daemen, J., Rijmen, V.: The Design of Rijndael. Springer, Heidelberg (2002). https://doi.org/10.1007/978-3-662-04722-4
12. Gohr, A.: Improving attacks on round-reduced Speck32/64 using deep learning. In: Boldyreva, A., Micciancio, D. (eds.) CRYPTO 2019. LNCS, vol. 11693, pp. 150–179. Springer, Cham (2019). https://doi.org/10.1007/978-3-030-26951-7_6
13. Hays, H.M.: A tutorial on linear and differential cryptanalysis. Cryptologia **26**(3), 188–221 (2002)
14. Knudsen, L., Robshaw, M.J.B.: Block Cipher Companion. Springer, Heidelberg (2011). https://doi.org/10.1007/978-3-642-17342-4. ISBN 978-3-642-17341-7
15. Kumar, M., Suresh, T.S., Pal, S.K., Panigrahi, A.: Optimal differential trails in lightweight block ciphers ANU and PICO. Cryptologia **44**(1), 68–78 (2020)
16. Matsui, M.: Linear cryptanalysis method for DES cipher. In: Helleseth, T. (ed.) EUROCRYPT 1993. LNCS, vol. 765, pp. 386–397. Springer, Heidelberg (1994). https://doi.org/10.1007/3-540-48285-7_33
17. Matsui, M.: On correlation between the order of S-boxes and the strength of DES. In: De Santis, A. (ed.) EUROCRYPT 1994. LNCS, vol. 950, pp. 366–375. Springer, Heidelberg (1995). https://doi.org/10.1007/BFb0053451

18. Mouha, N., Wang, Q., Gu, D., Preneel, B.: Differential and linear cryptanalysis using mixed-integer linear programming. In: Wu, C.-K., Yung, M., Lin, D. (eds.) Inscrypt 2011. LNCS, vol. 7537, pp. 57–76. Springer, Heidelberg (2012). https:// doi.org/10.1007/978-3-642-34704-7_5
19. US National Bureau of Standards, Data Encryption Standard. Federal Information Processing Standards Publications, vol. 46 (1977)
20. Zhu, B., Dong, X., Yu, H.: MILP-based differential attack on round-reduced GIFT. In: Matsui, M. (ed.) CT-RSA 2019. LNCS, vol. 11405, pp. 372–390. Springer, Cham (2019). https://doi.org/10.1007/978-3-030-12612-4_19

Train or Adapt a Deeply Learned Profile?

Christophe Genevey-Metat[1], Annelie Heuser[1], and Benoît Gérard[1,2](✉)

[1] Univ Rennes, Inria, CNRS, IRISA, Rennes, France
benoit.gerard@irisa.fr
[2] Direction Générale de l'Armement - Maîtrise de l'Information, Bruz, France

Abstract. In recent years, many papers have shown that deep learning can be beneficial for profiled side-channel analysis. However, to obtain good performance with deep learning, an evaluator or an attacker face the issue of data. Due to the context, he might be limited in the amount of data for training. This can be mitigated with classical Machine Learning (ML) techniques such as data augmentation. However, these mitigation techniques lead to a significant increase in the training time; first, by augmenting the data and second, by increasing the time to perform the learning of the neural network.

Recently, weight initialization techniques using specific probability distributions have shown some impact on the training performances in side-channel analysis. In this work, we investigate the advantage of using weights initialized from a previous training of a network in some different contexts. The idea behind this is that different side-channel attacks share common points in the sense that part of the network has to understand the link between power/electromagnetic signals and the corresponding intermediate variable. This approach is known as Transfer Learning (TL) in the Deep Learning (DL) literature and has shown its usefulness in various domains. We present various experiments showing the relevance and advantage of starting with a pretrained model. In our scenarios, pretrained models are trained on different probe positions/channels/chips. Using TL, we obtain better accuracy and/or training speed for a fixed amount of training data from the target device.

Keywords: Side-channel analysis · Profiling attacks · Neural networks · Electromagnetic emanations · Transfer learning

1 Introduction

Since its introduction at the end of the 90's [14], the exploitation of side-channel information observed from a cryptographic device has grown significantly. Using physical quantities such as time, heat, power, electromagnetic field, photon emission, sound, it is possible to recover secret data. Defenses against side-channel attacks can be found in smart-cards, set-top boxes, video game consoles, or smartphones for instance.

Profiled attacks are considered as the strongest type of side-channel attacks. They are based on the principle that the attacker is able to derive a relevant

© Springer Nature Switzerland AG 2021
P. Longa and C. Ràfols (Eds.): LATINCRYPT 2021, LNCS 12912, pp. 213–232, 2021.
https://doi.org/10.1007/978-3-030-88238-9_11

leakage model for the targeted device. Template attacks [5] are considered as optimal [10] and often the noise distribution is modeled as multivariate Gaussian. However, this approach may not be the most effective in practice due to some limitations. Among them, the Gaussian model that may not be perfectly suited or the spreading of the leakage points (e.g. due to some jitter) that may lead to intractable computations for model estimation. A new trend in side-channel analysis (SCA) is to explore the use of deep learning (DL) tools for profiled attacks [2,20]. These tools may help in solving problems such as trace misalignment, or high dimensional data in combination with masking counter-measures. However, deep learning tools still require a sufficient amount of data to construct relevant models, which may not be possible in particular scenarios.

Data augmentation [4] has been shown as a solution to cope with insufficient amount of data in some contexts. On the downside, adding data increases the amount of resources needed for both generating and processing this additional data. In this paper, we investigate the opportunity of exploiting information previously learnt from a different context to mount a new attack.

Traditionally, the dataset for profiling is assumed to come from a distribution identical to the one of the target device. In the research community, often only one dataset is measured, which is then divided into profiling and attacking datasets. Lately, the problematic of portability has been brought up and investigated [3,6,8]. In these works, portability refers to the differences between training and attacking dataset distributions and the consequences on the learnt model. The differences investigated in these works mostly arise due to fixed key alterations or variations in the manufacturing process of the device. The authors show that indeed the impact of the differences in distribution are notably in the effectiveness of the side-channel attack.

So far, the changes investigated could be mostly considered as minor compared to scenarios tackled, for example, in the field of image classification or computer vision. In the same context, transfer learning has recently[1] gained attention in the deep learning community [9], which allows to refine models that have been built solving different – but still related – problems. These pretrained models may allow to build accurate models for different tasks in a time-saving way as less data and training may be required.

Following this path, we investigate if data coming from sources that are not identical to the target dataset can actually benefit the side-channel attacker or evaluator. In particular, we adapt the concept of pretrained models to the side-channel community and extend the currently used attacker models. One could argue that pretrained models could be open-sourced and available in the community easily as it is done, for example, in the image classification domain.

In this paper, we investigate if using pretrained weights from different contexts, such as

- different EM probe positions,
- different side-channel sources (power instead of EM), and
- different devices,

---

[1] The concept itself has been already discussed in 1995 at NIPS [21].

could benefit an attacker/evaluator. We experiment both the naive approach of directly using the pretrained model itself and the transfer learning approach where the pretrained models are first fine-tuned for the new task with some available labelled data. The latter one can be seen as initializing the network weights with some application-dependent values.

2   State-of-the-Art on Deep Learning Techniques for SCA

First works using machine learning techniques in side-channel analysis showed that Support Vector Machine (SVM) and Random Forest (RF) are effective profiled side-channel attacks [12,17]. Particularly, when the size of the training dataset is limited, SVM can be more efficient than Gaussian templates due to the underlying estimation problem [11]. More recently, deep learning techniques have shown to be even more advantageous in several settings. Using the advantages of deep learning in side-channel analysis is becoming a very "fruitful" topic, with newly published works very frequently. Nevertheless, how to use the full potential of deep learning for side channel analysis has not been developed yet. One of the first works [20] showed that when an implementation is protected with a masking countermeasure, neural networks can reveal sensitive key information even without the need of a higher order combination function [22] or an additional step of point of interest selection. Shortly after the introduction of deep learning techniques for side-channel analysis, a database of side-channel measurements (called ASCAD) has been published [2] to facilitate comparable research works in this direction. The database consists of EM measurements of an AES-128 implementation protected with a masking countermeasure. Furthermore, the authors provide a software tool to artificially add a random delay countermeasure. Together with the database, the authors provide a study of neural network architectures, parameter selection, and pretrained neural network models. On the same lines as against masking countermeasures, neural networks are extremely effective against random delay countermeasures [4].

To strengthen profiled side-channel attacks based on neural networks, recent works showed techniques to further improve their attacking strength. The authors [4] highlighted that data augmentation techniques, i.e., the addition of artificial data, are significantly improving the success of an attack when shuffling (jitter-based) protections are present. A practical parameter selection guide is given by Maghrebi [19], i.e. the author provides some recommendations and practical hints to either enhance the efficiency from an adversary's perspective or to strengthen the resistance of the cryptographic implementations against these attacks from a security developer's perspective. A follow-up on parameter selection has also been published by Zaid et al. [27] where authors try to find minimal networks to greatly improve the training time at a negligible cost in terms of final accuracy, which was further improved by Wouters et al. [26]. The influence of weight initalizations on CNN has been compared in terms of guessing entropy by Li et al. [18]. A realistic real-world study has been performed by Bhasin et al. [3], and similarly by Das et al. [8], and by Wang et al. [25]. These works investigated the scenario when the profiling and attacking devices are different (to some extent), which is relevant in practice, but not always studied in research. In addition the work [25] also investigate how cryptographic algorithm implementation diversity affects classification accuracy. In these works, researchers trained MLP or CNN in order to study their performance on several chips of the same device, and/or different keys, or different modes of operation. To overcome the problem of overfitting to one specific device chip, the authors [3] trained on one device, validated on a second device, and attacked on the third device. A different approach was discussed by Das *et al.* [8], where the authors trained on multiple chips of the same device to avoid influences from cross-devices dissimilarities. Note that all these papers investigated simple devices running an 8-bit microcontroller. In this paper, we consider another variability source also on more complex devices. We investigate several devices, probe positions and types, and we derive a workaround to diversity by fine-tuning a pretrained model (which is known as "transfer learning" in the machine learning community). Transfer learning has been shown to be successful in a simulated environment by Thapar *et al.* [24], where results show that transfer learning may help to lower the requirement on the number of traces in the learning phase.

3   On Transferring Side-Channel Model Knowledge

3.1   Approach

Profiled side-channel analysis requires a sufficient amount of representative data in the learning phase, in particular, when using deep learning techniques. Fortunately, the community has put forward open-source datasets and models trained on these datasets recently. Naturally, the available data and pretrained models may not correspond exactly to the conditions an attacker faces on the target device. This problem of data discrepancy between training and testing datasets or data limitation of the training dataset is already known in other research fields and is tackled, for example, with the concept of transfer learning using neural networks. In particular, the idea of transfer learning is to transfer "knowledge" from a previous task or on related data to reduce the complexity of the learning on the actual suitable training dataset. Using this knowledge is simply achieved by using the weights of an already trained network as initialization instead of random weights according to some distributions. Seeing it from an implementation point of view, an attacker simply needs to download the pretrained model and load it into his framework before starting the training. Then, when reusing previously learnt models, the amount of data needed from the target device and the training time can be reduced. Or to put it the other way around, with less data it is possible to achieve higher effectiveness.

Transfer learning has shown to be efficient in several domains such as food classification [13], illustration classification [16] and for saliency [15].

In SCA, the first publicly known pretrained model is the ASCAD model [2], since then some other pretrained models have been published independently [26,27].

Remark 1 (Clone Dataset). Conditions that are not identical between training and attacking may not only come from device variations, but also from the measurement setup (as in our experiments later on). We therefore use the term "clone dataset" instead of the state-of-the-art term "clone device" if we want to refer to a dataset which is identical to the one in the attacking phase.

Depending on the available amount of data and the attack/evaluation context, multiple choices are available for training. We define three different training strategies that use throughout the paper:

Definition 1 (Training the Model on a Clone Dataset). *A (small) clone profiling dataset is available. This clone dataset is obtained from a setup that is identical to the attack dataset one (illustrated in Fig. 1a and labeled as S0).*

Definition 2 (Training the Model on a Different Dataset). *In this scenario, possessing a clone dataset is not possible at all. One can only take advantage of a pretrained neural network that has been trained on a related (but not identical) setup (illustrated in Fig. 1b and labeled as S1).*

Definition 3 (Fine-tuning the Pretrained Model with a (Small) Clone Dataset). *A (small) clone profiling dataset is available. This dataset is used to fine-tune a model previously trained on some related setup (illustrated in Fig. 1c and labeled as S2).*

Remark 2. Training strategy in Definition 1 corresponds to the traditional profiled attacker that has been originally introduced in the context of template attacks. Definition 3 also corresponds to the traditional profiled view, however, in here we additionally consider pretrained models from the outside. Assuming only a limited clone dataset (without the knowledge of pretrained models) has been investigated in recent works on side-channel attacks using machine or deep learning. For instance, authors [4] suggest to use Data Augmentation by generating new traces by the addition of noise (here temporal noise). Data Augmentation is known as a relevant technique to deal with too small datasets, however adding data increases the resource complexity.

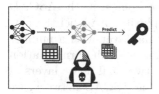  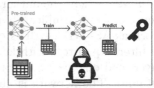

(a) Strategy S0 using a clone dataset; traditional profiled attacker   (b) Strategy S1 using only a pretrained model   (c) Strategy S2 using a pretrained model and a clone dataset to finetune

Fig. 1. Training strategies.

In this paper, we do not consider variations due to the manufacturing process of the chip, but differences arising from the measuring setup, side-channel information source, or from different devices (while still being close enough). We investigate three main scenarios in our experiments.

1. The position and type of the EM probe differ between pretrained model and target dataset.
2. The source of side-channel information differs between pretrained model and target dataset. Here, we investigate the use of power consumption and EM.
3. The device differs between pretrained model and target dataset. In this work, we consider the STM32Fx family as explained in more details later on.

3.2   CNN Architecture

Thorough study of CNN was introduced by Benadjila *et al.* [2] and is commonly called ASCAD network. Its architecture was chosen through exhaustive evaluation of many design principles and parameters. The best performing network (in their selection) is relying on the architecture of VGG-16 [23] with five blocks and 1 convolutional layer per block, a number of filters equal to (64, 128, 256, 512, 512) with kernel size 11 ("same" padding), ReLU activation functions and an average pooling layer for each block. The CNN has two final dense layers of 4 096 units. The network is illustrated in Fig. 2. The weights of the network are initialized with the "Glorot uniform" initializer. To conform to Benadjila et al.'s use-case [2], we have selected time frames for each experiment to reduce the input trace to 700 points based on the highest value of SNR.

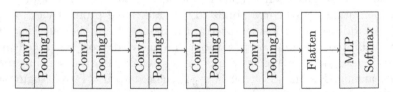

Fig. 2. ASCAD network

A fine-tuned and more efficient version of ASCAD was introduced by Zaid *et al.* [27] where the authors show that their network outperforms the ASCAD network while significantly reducing the network complexity. We label the network as ASCAD++. It is composed of one convolutional layer with a number of filters equal to 4 with kernel size 1 (same padding), one batch normalization layer, and one average pooling layer. The network has two final dense layers of 10 units. The network is illustrated in Fig. 3a. As for the ASCAD network, we used the Glorot uniform initializer for weight initialisation and the size of the time frame for each of our experiments is equal to 700 points.

An enhancement of the ASCAD++ was given by Wouters *et al.* [26]. Authors point out that the convolutional layer of ASCAD++ network acts as a normalization and that it is useless on normalized inputs. Hence, this network does

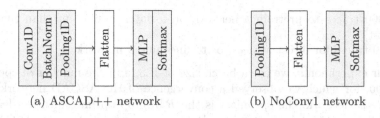

(a) ASCAD++ network   (b) NoConv1 network

Fig. 3. Enhancements of the ASCAD network

not contain any convolutional layers. It is only composed of one average pooling layer, and has two final dense layers of 10 units. The network is illustrated in Fig. 3b. As ASCAD++ and ASCAD network, we use the network with the Glorot uniform initializer and the size of the time frames for our experiments is equal to 700 points. In the following section, this network is called NoConv1.

3.3 CNN Training

Naturally, for S0 and S1, a large enough amount of data is needed to train the neural network, because none of the parameters of both convolutional and dense layers are fitted to the classification problem faced in side-channel analysis when starting from a random initial state.

However, for S2, different strategies using transfer learning are available. For example, an attacker could have only trained dense layers (thus freezing convolutional layers) or could have reset some specific layers while keeping previous parameters for other layers. Those strategies may permit to decrease the amount of data needed to train the neural network. The parameters kept from the first training may be better suited than a random initialization, thus getting the starting point closer to a minimum in the search space. In addition, some strategies where layers are frozen reduce the number of parameters to update in the neural network, which may increase the training speed. We apply two strategies on initial experiments: re-training the complete network during the second step and freezing the convolutional layers[2] (assuming that feature extraction is similar from one context to another but only decision changes). Since both gave similar results on our first runs, we decided to focus on retraining the full network, since then we do not make any hypothesis (that could end up to be false in some cases). Investigating deeply different techniques is clearly an interesting extension of this work.

We used a similar amount of data across experiments. The choices have been made i) to have most of the direct approaches leading to working attacks ii) to show the data requirement drops when performing transfer learning, and iii) to take into account that pretrained models are open-sourced from another party that may have higher available resources than the attacker itself. The number of traces used are hence:

---

[2] If existent.

- 100 000 traces to pretrain a network on a dataset different than the clone dataset,
- 12 500 traces for direct attacks, or to fine-tune a network.

In our experiments, we use a batch size of 128, and the number of epochs is set to 100, for which we observed a convergence of the ASCAD network[3]. For the ASCAD network, the optimizer is the *RMSprop* optimizer with a learning rate equal to 1e–5 as introduced by Benadjila *et al.* [2]. For the ASCAD++ and NoConv1 networks, we used *Adam* optimizer with a learning rate equal to 1e–5. We do not apply an early stopping criterion to stop the training of the neural networks if it reaches a minimal loss error. We simply save the best model according to the lowest (validation) loss error during the training.

3.4   Evaluation Metrics and Targeted Value

Experiments have been performed on first-order leakage from the output of the AES substitution box (SBox) [7]. In Sect. 5 and Sect. 6 we use a simple implementation of AES and target the Sbox output that is $y = \text{SBox}(t \oplus k)$ with t being a plaintext byte and k a key byte. In Sect. 4, we collect datasets with multiple probes for which the setup is similar to the one introduced by Benadjila *et al.* [2]. We then chose the highest first-order leakage source that is the masked output of the Sbox.2

To evaluate the amount of leakage, we use the signal-to-noise ratio (SNR). Let X denote the captured side-channel measurement, let Y be the label that is determined by the plaintext and the secret fixed key, then SNR gives the ratio between the deterministic data-dependent leakage and the remaining noise, i.e. $SNR = \frac{\text{Var}(\text{E}(X|Y))}{\text{E}(\text{Var}(X|Y))}$, where $\text{E}(\cdot)$ is the expectation and $\text{Var}(\cdot)$ the variance of a random variable.

To evaluate the ability to retrieve the key, we use the guessing entropy (GE), by computing the average rank of the secret key k^* within a vector of key guesses. In particular, the vector of key guesses $g_{i,1}, \ldots, g_{i,|K|}$ for the ith measurement is calculated by mapping each key guess k to a label j with probability $\hat{p}_{i,j}$ and applying the maximum-likelihood principle over 1 to m measurements. The rank is then the position of the secret key k^* in the sorted vector of key guesses, where the sorting is applied to the probabilities in descending order. In other words, the guessing entropy gives the expected number of key guesses an attacker needs to perform before he reveals the secret key.

Remark 3. In our experiments, we observed that in some cases, GE inversely converges, i.e., instead of going down towards zero, it increases towards 255. We (and others) have observed this effect already on other datasets and models, yet this observation has not been published or explained. In our experiments, GE is "inverted" as a straightforward solution when seeing this effect.

---

[3] NoConv1 and ASCAD++ may require a larger number of epochs before convergence and thus the guessing entropy might be still improvable using more epochs. An extended evaluation on the convergence and the corresponding guessing entropies will be provided on eprint.

4   Transferring Between EM Probe Position and Type

In this section, we investigate transferring knowledge from a network trained on a dataset obtained using a different probe type or position. The motivation for this scenario is twofold.

First, when using EM as a side-channel source, the type of probe as well as its exact position, i.e., location and angle, play a crucial role (see for example [1]). In some situations, an attacker may not be able to precisely replicate the measurement setup from training on the attacked device.

Second, from an evaluation lab point of view, this scenario is related to the problematical duration of a fine-grained cartography. Leveraging transfer learning between probe positions, it is then possible to decrease the acquisition time since fewer traces are needed to train the network at each new position. The methodology would be to acquire a lot of traces on a seemingly relevant position to train a network, then to measure a few traces on each other position and adapt the network using transfer learning.

Fig. 4. Multi-probe experiment setup

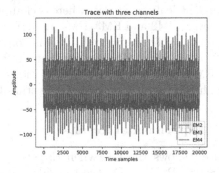

Fig. 5. Measurement trace from each of the three channels

For our experiments, we use a similar measurement setup and device as introduced by Benadjila et al. [2], namely a raw AtMega8515 microcontroller on the AVR STK500 platform[4]. We used the same AES-128 encryption than the one from ASCAD, which is protected using a masking countermeasure. The compiler optimization flag was set to --O0 but we did not embed the SOSSE operating system. The chip frequency was set to 3.686 MHz. Recall that for consistency between experiments, we targeted the masked output of the Sbox while knowing the output mask to target a significant first-order leakage. The measurements are obtained using different Langer near-field EM probes (two RF-B 0,3-3 and one RF-K 7-4) connected to 30 dB amplifiers while the overall is having a bandwidth maximum frequency of 3 GHz. The signal was then digitized by an RTO2014 oscilloscope from Rohde and Schwarz having a bandwidth of 1 GHz (thus being the limiting link).

---

[4] For ASCAD a smart-card embedding this micro-controller has been used.

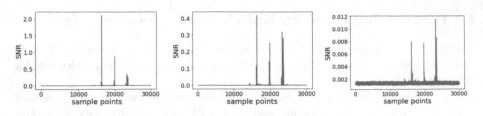

Fig. 6. SNR evaluation for each channel (from left to right: EM2, EM3, EM4)

We focused on the first AES round with a sampling frequency of 1Gs per second and obtained traces containing 20K samples. We observed that the leakages we obtained have a different location than the one reported by Benadjila *et al.* [2], however, we obtained similar leakages for the most informative part of the signal.

We show for example a measurement trace for each of the three channels in Fig. 5. The probes on channels 2 and 3 (EM2, EM3) are placed to capture data-dependent leakage signals, whereas channel 4 (EM4) is capturing mostly noise[5]. Moreover, EM2 and EM3/EM4 are different types of probes, which explains the different amplitude as well. This is confirmed in Fig. 6 showing the SNRs for EM2, EM3, EM4. One can see that EM2 provides higher SNR levels then EM3 and EM4, however, the leakage positions in time are consistent. Note that, even though EM4 is very noisy, one can still observe minor leakages.

4.1   Experimental Results

Figure 7 shows the GE when targeting EM2, which is the channel with the highest SNR value. On the left side, we see that the pretrained model of EM2 (even if limited in traces) is converging quickly towards zero, with ASCAD++ and NoConv1 being slightly more effective. Pretrained models on other EM channels also succeed (even for EM4 which contains a high amount of noise), again on these ASCAD++ is the most effective, closely followed by NoConv1. On the other hand, using transfer learning is not improving the GE in most cases.

Next, Fig. 8 shows the GE when targeting EM3, which has a medium SNR and is using the same probe type as EM4. Interestingly, a pretrained model on EM4 is slightly more effective than using a model trained on EM3 when directly used for attacking EM3. Again, ASCAD++ and NoCOnv1 are performing better than ASCAD. When using transfer learning, the results are slightly improved for the pretrained model of EM4, and improved for ASCAD using EM2.

---

[5] Channel 1 was used for triggering.

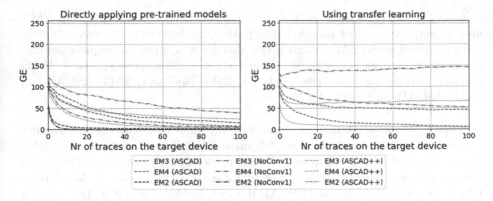

Fig. 7. Guessing entropy when targeting EM2

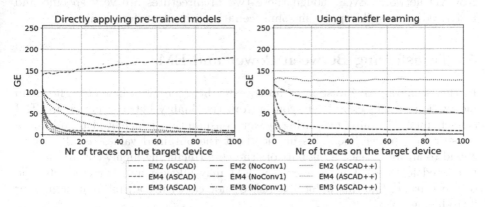

Fig. 8. Guessing entropy when targeting EM3

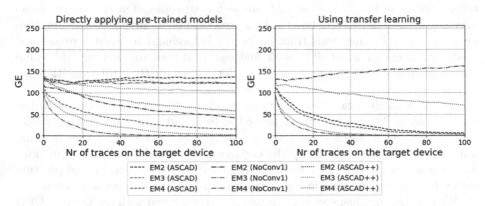

Fig. 9. Guessing entropy when targeting EM4

In Fig. 9 we show the GE targeting EM4 that has the lowest SNR from all three EM positions. Directly applying a pretrained model from EM3 using

NoConv1 works sufficiently well, followed by ASCAD++ network from EM3, and a pretrained model on EM4 using ASCAD. Interestingly, using directly the pretrained model EM2, which is the channel containing the highest amount of information, does not perform better than less informative channels. Using transfer learning improves the result for EM3+NoConv1, EM3+ASCAD++, EM3+ASCAD, and EM2+ASCAD.

Summary. When targeting noisy channels, our results show that the performance increases when using pretrained models on another channel with more available data, compared to training a model that is identical to the one of the target dataset (clone dataset) with less amount of data. In addition, on this dataset which is related to the original ASCAD dataset, NoConv1 and ASCAD++ (that have been fine-tuned on the ASCAD dataset) perform (slightly) better than the ASCAD network. Even though these two architectures are very specific and restricted, they still improve in some scenarios using transfer learning.

5   Transferring Between Power and EM

In this scenario, we investigate the transfer between side-channels. The main motivation for this experiment comes from the duality between power and EM side-channels. Usually, measuring power consumption is achieved by adding a resistor to a power line. This implies that the obtained values usually correspond to all (or at least a big part of) the chip (including highly consuming but unrelated features). On the contrary, EM may allow a more precise selection of the leakage, but this induces a risk of not capturing all relevant signals or introducing noise.

In some contexts, the attacker cannot add a resistor to the PCB of the target and thus has to use an EM probe for attacking. On the contrary, he may buy a clone device and build a dedicated card enabling power consumption measurements. He may thus train on power beforehand to build a pretrained model which makes use of all possible leakages, and then attack using EM where only a part of the signal are available (depending on the probe position for instance).

Again, from the evaluation lab point of view, this scenario is linked to the cartography problem. EM source is more localized and may lead to better results than power, but it needs a fine-grained cartography of the chip. First, training a network with power speeds up the cartography as mentioned in the previous experiment. Using power for a first training prevents from making a bad position choice for the first acquisition run (with no signal or a too specialized one).

We use the chipwhisperer lite capture board combined with the CW308 UFO board on STM32Fx target devices. Like in the previous setup, we measure the beginning of an AES-128 encryption, where we used the TINYAES implementation integrated in the chipwhisperer software. The chip frequency was set to 7.37 MHz and the measurements are sampled at 4×7.37 Ms/s. Power consumption is collected through the measurement shunt on the CW308 UFO board. To capture

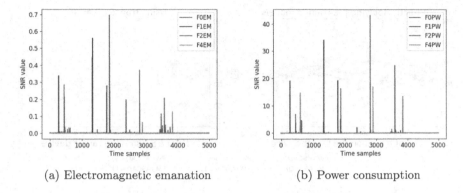

(a) Electromagnetic emanation   (b) Power consumption

Fig. 10. SNR evaluation for each targeted device

EM signals, we used a Langer near-field EM probe (RF-U 5-2) connected to a 20 dB amplifier.

Figure 10a and Fig. 10b show the SNRs obtained with EM emissions and power consumption for each device. Depending on the device, we have different SNR levels for power and EM emissions. However, the shapes corresponding to power and EM are close to each other. The SNR values for power are higher than for EM. Seemingly, the EM emission measurements contain more noise than the ones from power. We expect that transfer learning can use the knowledge given by power to improve the models to target EM.

5.1   Experimental Results

We now compare the effectiveness of applying pretrained models against using transfer learning when targeting EM measurements and having available pretrained models on power consumption. We consider the four previously introduced devices (namely, F0, F1, F2, and F4).

In Fig. 11 we plot the guessing entropy obtained when targeting device F0 with EM (F0em). On the left, one can observe that for all three neural networks the attack does not converge within 1000 traces. When using transfer learning (right side), i.e., using the weights obtained when training on power consumption as initialization, all networks show a decreasing GE, whereas ASCAD is the most effective network nearly reaching a GE of 0.

Figure 12 presents the results when attacking F1 with electromagnetic emission. Similarly as before, when applying pretrained networks directly (even when using EM measurements), none of the networks seem to have a decreasing GE. However, when updating the pretrained model with transfer learning, one can observe that ASCAD is reaching a GE close to 0.

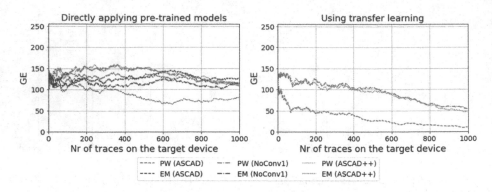

Fig. 11. Guessing entropy when targeting F0em

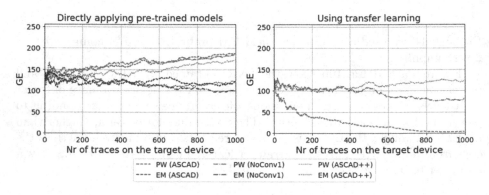

Fig. 12. Guessing entropy when targeting F1em

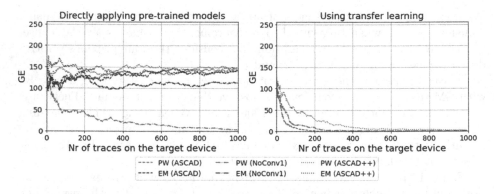

Fig. 13. Guessing entropy when targeting F2em

Targeting F2em, Fig. 13 shows that using a pretrained model on power and the NoConv1 network results in converging GE towards 0, whereas the other two networks trained on power as well as all networks on EM fail to decrease within

1000 traces. Interestingly, we see that in this scenario transfer learning is very effective on all three networks, while ASCAD is the most effective one, reaching a GE of 0 with less than 100 traces.

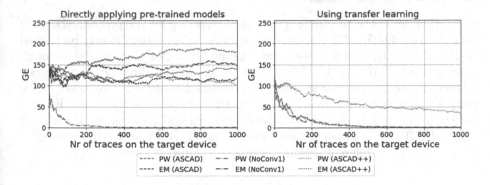

Fig. 14. Guessing entropy when targeting F4em

On device F4, directly applying a pretrained model with the NoConv1 network results in an effective attack converging towards GE 0 rather quickly, where all other pretrained models and networks do not converge. When using transfer learning, one can see that all 3 neural networks pretrained on power consumption are decreasing in GE with NoConv1, while ASCAD is the most effective one.

Summary. In all of the four scenarios, the effectiveness of using pretrained models with transfer learning instead of training on the dataset corresponding to the target dataset can be seen. Moreover, in most of the cases, using transfer learning instead of applying directly the pretrained network is showing superior results. When using transfer learning, the ASCAD network is the most effective one, whereas when directly applying pretrained networks, only NoConv1 converges in the scenario of F2em.

6   Transferring Between Different Devices

In this scenario, we investigate the possible use of pretrained models stemming from different devices. The motivation here is that an attacker may have access to public datasets and/or publicly trained networks corresponding to some other chip. Then, based on this, he may try to attack another device that is different but still close (same architecture for instance). From an evaluation lab perspective, it boils down to leveraging previous analyses with similar enough chips to speed up the current one.

We use the same measurement setup as in the previous section. In Fig. 10b, we show the SNR values obtained from measuring the power consumption of the

devices F0, F1, F2, and F4. We see that the highest SNR levels are obtained by
F2, followed by F1, F4, and finally F0.

6.1 Experimental Results

In Fig. 15 we show the guessing entropy when targeting F0 and pretrained models
are built from F0, F1, F2, F4. One can see that when using directly pretrained
models, the model on F0 is the most effective, that not all pretrained models
converge towards 0, and ASCAD is the best among the three neural networks.
When compared to transfer learning, all pretrained models are improved, where
using ASCAD with a pretrained model on F2 and F4 is the most effective one.
Note that F0 and F2/F4 have different ARM Cortex M versions and the highest
values of SNR are at different time locations (see Fig. 10), still using knowledge
from devices with different architectures brings improvements.

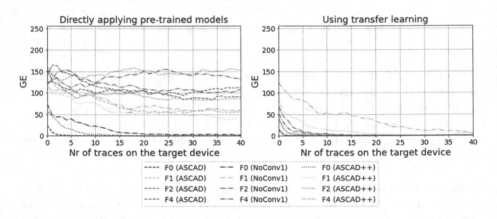

Fig. 15. Guessing entropy when targeting F0

Figure 16 shows a similar trend. When directly applying pretrained models, the most effective pretrained model is the one trained on the target device,
where the ones on F2 may also converge given a higher number of attacking
traces. Using the pretrained models as weight initialisation improves all networks. Again, the ASCAD network is the most effective one, but the difference
between networks is rather marginal.

Figure 17 shows the results when targeting F2, again using a pretrained network on the target device is the best performing one, while transfer learning
improves the results for all pretrained models and architectures. Interestingly, in
this scenario we see a clear advantage of using transfer learning against the network directly trained on the target device. This shows that initializing weights
using a network trained on a similar problem is more suited than using the
classical initialization (here default Glorot uniform initialization).

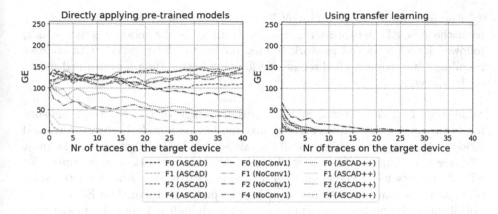

Fig. 16. Guessing entropy when targeting F1

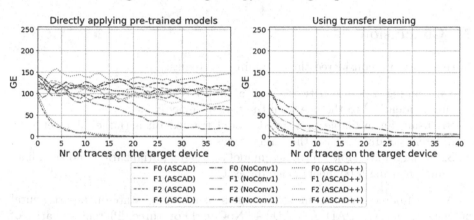

Fig. 17. Guessing entropy when targeting F2

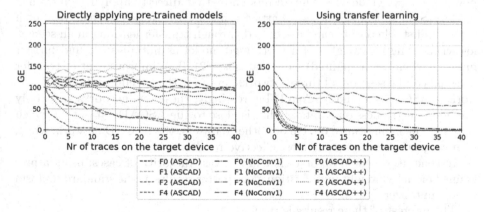

Fig. 18. Guessing entropy when targeting F4

Figure 18 shows the GE of target F4. Using a pretrained model on F2 together with the ASCAD network with transfer learning is the most effective attack, followed by a pretrained network trained on F0 and F1 together with transfer learning. Interestingly, all three are performing better than a pretrained model on F4 directly.

Summary. In this scenario, we see a disadvantage of the NoConv1 network for both cases, using directly pretrained models and updating the pretrained model with transfer learning. In all scenarios, the ASCAD network is the most effective one. This would suggest that the ASCAD network is more suited for STM32 targets when the amount of available data is low. Another interesting observation is that, in all scenarios, using the pretrained model on F4 as weight initialization is the best performing one, even though it is not the model with the highest SNR values.

7   Conclusion

In this work, we considered three training strategies:

- S0: training a neural network with a (limited) clone dataset (i.e. a dataset that is identical to the one from the target device);
- S1: using an available pretrained model trained on a (large) dataset with different conditions than the target dataset;
- S2: using an available pretrained model as weight initialization and then fine-tuning it using a (smaller) clone dataset.

We compared these training strategies using three state-of-the-art neural network models (ASCAD, ASCAD++, NoConv1) on three different scenarios of data discrepancy: EM probe type and/or positions, side-channel sources (EM vs power) and target devices. Our results show that directly applying pretrained models (S1) can lead to successful attacks in a few investigated scenarios. Much better and stable results can be achieved through transfer learning in all scenarios when using the weights of a pretrained model as initialization and further fine-tune them on a (limited) clone dataset (S2). The improvement of transfer learning can be seen on all three networks, even for the specific and limited network of ASCAD++ and NoConv1. Interestingly, these two networks show only the best effectiveness on a dataset that is close to the ASCAD dataset for which they have been fine-tuned on. On our other datasets, the ASCAD network, which is more general, achieves the most effective results.

In general, we could observe that in the vast majority of cases, using a pretrained model as weight initialization gives better results as the standard uniform Glorot initalizer.

The interest of these results is twofold.

1. First, a profiled attacker scenario should not be rejected due to a too small number of available labeled traces.

2. Second, evaluation process (and particularly trace acquisition) can be significantly speed up and improved by using transfer learning with an already trained network (from a previous evaluation or another position in the case of a cartography).

We chose to train the whole network again to avoid misinterpretations due to wrong choices of the frozen layers. However, to improve even more the efficiency of the training, investigating different fine-tuning strategies may be of interest. This is part of the natural extension of the presented work. Another extension which is less straightforward (but may be linked to layer freezing) would be to leverage transfer learning to help a network to converge on a protected (masked) implementation. A network has to understand the signal structure, then extract the information, and then process it. The hope is that the signal structure knowledge could be obtained from an easier setup (unprotected) to focus the second learning on the extraction of relevant information and its smart combination.

References

1. Andrikos, C., et al.: Location, location, location: Revisiting modeling and exploitation for location-based side channel leakages. In: Galbraith, S.D., Moriai, S. (eds.) Advances in Cryptology - ASIACRYPT 2019, pp. 285–314. Springer International Publishing, Cham (2019)
2. Benadjila, R., Prouff, E., Strullu, R., Cagli, E., Dumas, C.: Deep learning for side-channel analysis and introduction to ASCAD database. J. Cryptogr. Eng. **10**(2), 163–188 (2020)
3. Bhasin, S., Chattopadhyay, A., Heuser, A., Jap, D., Picek, S., Shrivastwa, R.R.: Mind the portability: a warriors guide through realistic profiled side-channel analysis. In: 27th Annual Network and Distributed System Security Symposium (NDSS 2020). The Internet Society (2020)
4. Cagli, E., Dumas, C., Prouff, E.: Convolutional neural networks with data augmentation against jitter-based countermeasures - profiling attacks without preprocessing. In: CHES 2017, pp. 45–68 (2017)
5. Chari, S., Rao, J.R., Rohatgi, P.: Template attacks. In: Kaliski, B.S., Koç, K., Paar, C. (eds.) CHES 2002. LNCS, vol. 2523, pp. 13–28. Springer, Heidelberg (2003). https://doi.org/10.1007/3-540-36400-5_3
6. Choudary, O., Kuhn, M.G.: Template attacks on different devices. In: COSADE 2014, pp. 179–198 (2014)
7. Daemen, J., Rijmen, V.: The Design of Rijndael: AES - The Advanced Encryption Standard (Information Security and Cryptography). 1st edn. Springer (2002)
8. Das, D., Golder, A., Danial, J., Ghosh, S., Raychowdhury, A., Sen, S.: X-deepsca: cross-device deep learning side channel attack. In: DAC 2019, pp. 134:1–134:6 (2019)
9. Goodfellow, I., Bengio, Y., Courville, A.: Deep Learning. The MIT Press, Cambridge (2016)
10. Heuser, A., Rioul, O., Guilley, S.: Good Is not good enough - deriving optimal distinguishers from communication theory. In: CHES 2014, pp. 55–74 (2014)
11. Heuser, A., Zohner, M.: Intelligent machine homicide. In: Schindler, W., Huss, S.A. (eds.) COSADE 2012. LNCS, vol. 7275, pp. 249–264. Springer, Heidelberg (2012). https://doi.org/10.1007/978-3-642-29912-4_18

12. Hospodar, G., Gierlichs, B., Mulder, E.D., Verbauwhede, I., Vandewalle, J.: Machine learning in side-channel analysis: a first study. J. Cryptograph. Eng. **1**(4), 293–302 (2011)
13. Islam, K.T., Wijewickrema, S., Pervez, M., O'Leary, S.: An exploration of deep transfer learning for food image classification. In: 2018 Digital Image Computing: Techniques and Applications (DICTA), pp. 1–5, December 2018
14. Kocher, P.C., Jaffe, J., Jun, B.: Differential power analysis. In: CRYPTO 1999, pp. 388–397 (1999)
15. Kümmerer, M., Wallis, T.S.A., Bethge, M.: Deepgaze II: reading fixations from deep features trained on object recognition. CoRR abs/1610.01563 (2016)
16. Lagunas, M., Garces, E.: Transfer learning for illustration classification. CoRR abs/1806.02682 (2018)
17. Lerman, L., Bontempi, G., Markowitch, O.: Side channel attack: an approach based on machine learning. In: COSADE 2011, pp. 29–41 (2011)
18. Li, H., Krček, M., Perin, G.: A comparison of weight initializers in deep learning-based side-channel analysis. In: Zhou, J., et al. (eds.) ACNS 2020. LNCS, vol. 12418, pp. 126–143. Springer, Cham (2020). https://doi.org/10.1007/978-3-030-61638-0_8
19. Maghrebi, H.: Deep learning based side channel attacks in practice. IACR Cryptol. ePrint Arch. **2019**, 578 (2019)
20. Maghrebi, H., Portigliatti, T., Prouff, E.: Breaking cryptographic implementations using deep learning techniques. In: SPACE 2016s, pp. 3–26 (2016)
21. NIPS*95 Post-Conference Workshop: Learning to learn: Knowledge consolidation and transfer in inductive systems. http://plato.acadiau.ca/courses/comp/dsilver/NIPS95_LTL/transfer.workshop.1995.html (1995)
22. Prouff, E., Rivain, M., Bevan, R.: Statistical analysis of second order differential power analysis. IEEE Trans. Comput. **58**(6), 799–811 (2009)
23. Simonyan, K., Zisserman, A.: Very deep convolutional networks for large-scale image recognition. CoRR abs/1409.1556 (2014)
24. Thapar, D., Alam, M., Mukhopadhyay, D.: Deep learning assisted cross-family profiled side-channel attacks using transfer learning. In: 2021 22nd International Symposium on Quality Electronic Design (ISQED), pp. 178–185 (2021)
25. Wang, H., Brisfors, M., Forsmark, S., Dubrova, E.: How diversity affects deep-learning side-channel attacks. Cryptology ePrint Archive, Report 2019/664 (2019)
26. Wouters, L., Arribas, V., Gierlichs, B., Preneel, B.: Revisiting a methodology for efficient CNN architectures in profiling attacks. IACR Trans. Cryptograph. Hardw. Embed. Syst. **2020**(3), 147–168 (2020)
27. Zaid, G., Bossuet, L., Habrard, A., Venelli, A.: Methodology for efficient CNN architectures in profiling attacks. IACR Trans. Cryptogr. Hardw. Embed. Syst. **2020**(1), 1–36 (2020)

Autocorrelations of Vectorial Boolean Functions

Anne Canteaut[1], Lukas Kölsch[2], Chao Li[3,4], Chunlei Li[5], Kangquan Li[3,4], Longjiang Qu[3,4], and Friedrich Wiemer[6,7(✉)]

[1] Inria, Paris, France
anne.canteaut@inria.fr
[2] University of Rostock, Rostock, Germany
lukas.koelsch@uni-rostock.de
[3] College of Liberal Arts and Sciences, National University of Defense Technology, Changsha, China
lichao_nudt@sina.com, likangquan11@nudt.edu.cn
[4] Hunan Engineering Research Center of Commercial Cryptography Theory and Technology Innovation, Changsha, China
[5] Department of Informatics, University of Bergen, Bergen 5020, Norway
chunlei.li@uib.no
[6] Horst Görtz Institute for IT Security, Ruhr University Bochum, Bochum, Germany
[7] Cryptosolutions, Essen, Germany
friedrich@cryptosolutions.de

Abstract. Recently, Bar-On et al. introduced at Eurocrypt'19 a new tool, called the differential-linear connectivity table (DLCT), which allows for taking into account the dependency between the two subciphers E_0 and E_1 involved in differential-linear attacks.

This paper presents a theoretical characterization of the DLCT, which corresponds to an autocorrelation table (ACT) of a vectorial Boolean function. We further provide some new theoretical results on ACTs of vectorial Boolean functions.

Keywords: Vectorial Boolean functions · Differential-linear connectivity table · Autocorrelation table · Absolute indicator

1 Introduction

Let n, m be two arbitrary positive integers. We denote by $\mathbb{F}_{2^n}$ the finite field with 2^n elements and by $\mathbb{F}_2^n$ the n-dimensional vector space over $\mathbb{F}_2$. Vectorial Boolean functions from $\mathbb{F}_2^n$ to $\mathbb{F}_2^m$, also called (n, m)-functions, play a crucial role in block ciphers. Many attacks have been proposed against block ciphers,

The research of Chunlei Li was supported by the Research Council of Norway (No. 311646/O70) and in part by the National Natural Science Foundation of China under Grant (No. 61771021).

The research of Longjiang Qu is supported by National Key R&D Program of China (No.2017YFB0802000), and the National Natural Science Foundation of China (NSFC) under Grant 61722213, 11531002, 61572026.

© Springer Nature Switzerland AG 2021
P. Longa and C. Ràfols (Eds.): LATINCRYPT 2021, LNCS 12912, pp. 233–253, 2021.
https://doi.org/10.1007/978-3-030-88238-9_12

and have led to diverse criteria, such as low differential uniformity, high non-linearity, high algebraic degree, etc., that the implemented cryptographic functions must satisfy. At Eurocrypt'18, Cid et al. [18] introduced a new concept on S-boxes: the boomerang connectivity table (BCT) that analyzes the dependency between the upper part and lower part of a block cipher in a boomerang attack. The work of [18] quickly attracted attention in the study of BCT property of cryptographic functions [6,28,33,40] and stimulated research progress in other crypt-analysis methods. Very recently, in Eurocrypt'19, Bar-On et al. [1] introduced a new tool called the differential-linear connectivity table (DLCT) that similarly analyzes the dependency between the two subciphers in differential-linear attacks, thereby improving the efficiency of the attacks introduced in [26]. The authors of [1] also presented the relation between the DLCT and the differential distribution table (DDT) of S-boxes.

This paper aims to provide a theoretical characterization of the main properties of the DLCT, explicitly of the set formed by all its entries and of the highest magnitude in this set, for generic vectorial Boolean functions. To this end, we first observe that the DLCT coincides (up to a factor 2) with the autocorrelation table (ACT) of vectorial Boolean functions, which is extended from Boolean functions. Based on the study of the autocorrelation of vectorial Boolean functions, we give some characterizations of the DLCT by means of the Walsh transform and the DDT, and provide a lower bound on the absolute indicator (i.e., equivalently, on the highest absolute value in the DLCT excluding the first row and first column) of any (n, m)-function; then we exhibit an interesting divisibility property of the autocorrelation of (n, m)-functions F, which implies that the entries of DLCT of any (n, n)-permutations are divisible by 4. Next, we investigate the invariance property of the autocorrelation (and the DLCT) of vectorial Boolean functions under affine, extended-affine (EA) and Carlet-Charpin-Zinoviev (CCZ) equivalence, and show that the autocorrelation spectrum is affine-invariant and its maximum in magnitude is EA-invariant but not CCZ-invariant. Based on the classification of optimal 4-bit S-boxes by Leander and Poschmann [27], we explicitly calculate their autocorrelation spectra (see [12, Appendix A, Table 2]). Moreover, for certain functions like APN, plateaued and AB functions, we present the relation of their autocorrelation (and DLCT) with other cryptographic criteria. We show that the autocorrelation of APN and AB/plateaued functions can be converted to the Walsh transform of two classes of balanced Boolean functions. Finally, we investigate the autocorrelation spectra of some special polynomials with optimal or low differential uniformity, including monomials, cubic functions, quadratic functions and inverses of quadratic permutations.

The rest of this paper is organized as follows. Section 2 recalls basic definitions, particularly the generalized notion of autocorrelation, the new notion of DLCT, and the connection between them. Most notably, we show that the highest magnitude in the DLCT coincides (up to a factor 2) with the absolute indicator of the function. Section 3 is devoted to the characterization of the autocorrelation: we first characterize the autocorrelation by means of the Walsh transform and of the DDT of the function. We then exhibit generic lower bounds on the absolute indicator of any vectorial Boolean function and study the divisibility of the autocorrelation coefficients. Besides, we study the invariance of the absolute indicator and of the autocorrelation spectrum under the affine, EA and CCZ equivalences. We also present all possible autocorrelation spectra of optimal 4-bit S-boxes. At the end of this section, we study some properties of the autocorrelation of APN, plateaued and AB functions. In Sect. 4, we consider the autocorrelation of some special polynomials. Finally, Sect. 5 draws some conclusions of our work.

2   Preliminaries

In this section, we first recall some basics on (vectorial) Boolean functions and known results that will be useful for our subsequent discussions. Since the vector space $\mathbb{F}_2^n$ can be deemed as the finite field $\mathbb{F}_{2^n}$ for a fixed choice of basis, we will use the notation $\mathbb{F}_2^n$ and $\mathbb{F}_{2^n}$ interchangeably when there is no ambiguity. We will also use the inner product $a \cdot b$ and $\mathrm{Tr}_{2^n}(ab)$ in the context of vector spaces and finite fields interchangeably. For any set E, we denote the nonzero elements of E by E^* (or $E \setminus \{0\}$) and the cardinality of E by $\#E$.

2.1   Walsh Transform, Bent Functions, AB Functions and Plateaued Functions

An n-variable Boolean function is a mapping from $\mathbb{F}_2^n$ to $\mathbb{F}_2$. For any n-variable Boolean function f, $W_f(\omega) := \sum_{x \in \mathbb{F}_2^n} (-1)^{f(x) + \omega \cdot x}$ is its *Walsh transform*, where "$\cdot$" is an inner product on $\mathbb{F}_2^n$. The Walsh transform of f can be seen as the *discrete Fourier transform* of the function $(-1)^{f(x)}$ and yields the well known Parseval's relation [14]: $\sum_{\omega \in \mathbb{F}_2^n} W_f^2(\omega) = 2^{2n}$. The *linearity* of f is defined by $\mathrm{L}(f) := \max_{\omega \in \mathbb{F}_2^n} |W_f(\omega)|$, where $|r|$ denotes the absolute value of any real value r, and the *nonlinearity* of f is defined by $\mathrm{NL}(f) := 2^{n-1} - \frac{1}{2}\mathrm{L}(f)$. According to the Parseval's relation, it is easily seen that the nonlinearity of an n-variable Boolean function is upper bounded by $2^{n-1} - 2^{n/2-1}$. Boolean functions achieving the maximum nonlinearity are called *bent* functions and exist only for even n; their Walsh transforms take only two values $\pm 2^{n/2}$ [38].

For an (n, m)-function F from $\mathbb{F}_2^n$ to $\mathbb{F}_2^m$, its *component* corresponding to a nonzero $v \in \mathbb{F}_2^m$ is the Boolean function given by $F_v(x) := v \cdot F(x)$. For any $u \in \mathbb{F}_2^n$ and nonzero $v \in \mathbb{F}_2^m$, the Walsh transform of F is defined by those of its components F_v, i.e., $W_F(u, v) := \sum_{x \in \mathbb{F}_2^n} (-1)^{u \cdot x + v \cdot F(x)}$. The linear approximation table (LAT) of an (n, m)-function F is the $2^n \times 2^m$ table, in which the entry at position (u, v) is: $\mathrm{LAT}_F(u, v) = W_F(u, v)$, where $u \in \mathbb{F}_2^n$ and $v \in \mathbb{F}_2^m$. The maximum absolute entry of the LAT, ignoring the 0-th column, is the linearity of F denoted as $\mathrm{L}(F)$, i.e., $\mathrm{L}(F) := \max_{u \in \mathbb{F}_2^n, v \in \mathbb{F}_2^m \setminus \{0\}} |W_F(u, v)|$. Similarly, the nonlinearity of F is defined by the nonlinearities of the components, namely, $\mathrm{NL}(F) := 2^{n-1} - \frac{1}{2}\mathrm{L}(F)$.

An (n, m)-function F is called *vectorial bent*, or shortly *bent* if all its components $F_v(x) = v \cdot F(x)$ for each nonzero $v \in \mathbb{F}_2^m$ are bent. It is well known (n, m)-bent functions exist only if n is even and $m \le \frac{n}{2}$. Interested readers can refer to [32,43] for more results on bent functions. For (n, m)-functions F with $m \geq n - 1$, the Sidelnikov-Chabaud-Vaudenay bound

$$\mathrm{NL}(F) \leq 2^{n-1} - \frac{1}{2} \left(\frac{3 \cdot 2^n - 2(2^n - 1)(2^{n-1} - 1)}{2^m - 1} - 2 \right)^{1/2}$$

gives a better upper bound for nonlinearity than the universal bound [16]. When $n = m$ and n is odd, the inequality becomes $\mathrm{NL}(F) \leq 2^{n-1} - 2^{\frac{n-1}{2}}$, and it is achieved by the *almost bent* (AB) functions. It is well known that an (n, n)-function F is AB if and only if its Walsh transform takes only three values $0, \pm 2^{\frac{n+1}{2}}$ [16].

A Boolean function is called *plateaued* if its Walsh transform takes at most three values: 0 and $\pm \mu$, where μ, a positive integer, is called the *amplitude* of the plateaued function. It is clear that bent functions are plateaued. Because of Parseval's relation, the amplitude μ of any plateaued function must be of the form 2^r for certain integer $r \geq n/2$. An (n, m)-function is called *plateaued* if all its components are plateaued, with possibly different amplitudes. In particular, an (n, m)-function F is called *plateaued with single amplitude* if all its components are plateaued with the same amplitude. It is clear that AB functions form a subclass of plateaued functions with the single amplitude $2^{\frac{n+1}{2}}$.

2.2 Differential Uniformity and APN Functions

For an (n, m)-function F and any $u \in \mathbb{F}_2^n \backslash \{0\}$, the function $D_u F(x) := F(x) + F(x + u)$ is called the *derivative of F in direction u*. The *differential distribution table* (DDT) of F is the $2^n \times 2^m$ table, in which the entry at position (u, v) is $\mathrm{DDT}_F(u, v) = \#\{x \in \mathbb{F}_2^n \mid D_u F(x) = v\}$, where $u \in \mathbb{F}_2^n$ and $v \in \mathbb{F}_2^m$. The *differential uniformity* [34] of F is defined as $\max_{u \in \mathbb{F}_2^n \backslash \{0\}, v \in \mathbb{F}_2^m} \mathrm{DDT}_F(u, v)$. Since $D_u F(x) = D_u F(x + u)$ for any x, u in $\mathbb{F}_2^n$, the entries of DDT are always even and the minimum of differential uniformity of F is 2. The functions with differential uniformity 2 are called *almost perfect nonlinear* (APN) functions.

2.3 The DLCT and the Autocorrelation Table

Differential-linear cryptanalysis tries to exploit a strong differential over one part of an iterated block cipher in combination with a strong linear hull over the other part. They are then combined into a relation of the form $v \cdot (F(x) + F(x + u))$ and the differential-linear bias is defined as

$$\varepsilon(u, v) = 2^{-n} \#\{x \in \mathbb{F}_2^n \mid v \cdot (F(x) + F(x + u)) = 0\} - \frac{1}{2},$$

where F is an (n, m)-function. Until recently we had to assume the differential and linear parts of the relation to be independent, while several real world examples observed inaccuracies for the resulting bias. The recent work by Bar-On et al. [1] introduced the concept of the differential-linear connectivity table (DLCT) of (n, m)-functions F, to better handle this combination, when dependencies between the two parts of the differential-linear relation occur.

Definition 1 ([1]). *Let F be an (n, m)-function. The DLCT of F is the $2^n \times 2^m$ table whose rows correspond to input differences to F and whose columns correspond to output masks of F, defined as follows: for $u \in \mathbb{F}_2^n$ and $v \in \mathbb{F}_2^m$, the DLCT entry at (u, v) is defined by*

$$\mathrm{DLCT}_F(u, v) = \#\{x \in \mathbb{F}_2^n \mid v \cdot F(x) = v \cdot F(x + u)\} - 2^{n-1}.$$

The DLCT is then used to analyse the transition between the differential and linear parts, similar to the sandwich extension for boomerang attacks and the recently introduced boomerang connectivity table (BCT).

Since for any $u \in \mathbb{F}_2^n \setminus \{0\}$, $D_u F(x) = D_u F(x + u)$, $\mathrm{DLCT}_F(u, v)$ must be even. Furthermore, for a given $u \in \mathbb{F}_2^n \setminus \{0\}$, if $D_u F(x)$ is a 2ℓ-to-1 mapping for a positive integer ℓ, then $\mathrm{DLCT}_F(u, v)$ is a multiple of 2ℓ. Moreover, it is trivial that for any $(u, v) \in \mathbb{F}_2^n \times \mathbb{F}_2^m$, $|\mathrm{DLCT}_F(u, v)| \leq 2^{n-1}$, and $\mathrm{DLCT}_F(u, v) = 2^{n-1}$ when either $u = 0$ or $v = 0$. Therefore, we only need to focus on the cases for $u \in \mathbb{F}_2^n \setminus \{0\}$ and $v \in \mathbb{F}_2^m \setminus \{0\}$.

Our first observation on the DLCT is that it coincides with the *autocorrelation table* (ACT) of F [45, Sect. 3]. Below we recall the definition of the autocorrelation of Boolean functions, see e.g. [14, P. 277], and extend it to vectorial Boolean functions.

Definition 2 ([44]). *Given a Boolean function f on $\mathbb{F}_2^n$, the autocorrelation of the function f at u is defined as $\mathsf{AC}_f(u) = \sum_{x \in \mathbb{F}_2^n} (-1)^{f(x) + f(x+u)}$. Furthermore, the absolute indicator of f is defined as $\Delta_f = \max_{u \in \mathbb{F}_2^n \setminus \{0\}} |\mathsf{AC}_f(u)|$.*

Similarly to Walsh coefficients, this notion can naturally be generalized to vectorial Boolean functions as follows.

Definition 3. *Let F be an (n, m)-function. For any $u \in \mathbb{F}_2^n$ and $v \in \mathbb{F}_2^m$, the autocorrelation of F at (u, v) is defined as $\mathsf{AC}_F(u, v) = \sum_{x \in \mathbb{F}_2^n} (-1)^{v \cdot (F(x) + F(x+u))}$, the autocorrelation spectrum is $\Lambda_F = \{\mathsf{AC}_F(u, v) \mid u \in \mathbb{F}_2^n \setminus \{0\}, v \in \mathbb{F}_2^m \setminus \{0\}\}$. Moreover, $\Delta_F := \max_{u \in \mathbb{F}_2^n \setminus \{0\}, v \in \mathbb{F}_2^m \setminus \{0\}} |\mathsf{AC}_F(u, v)|$ is the F's absolute indicator.*

In [45], the term Autocorrelation Table (ACT) for a vectorial Boolean function was introduced. Similarly to the LAT, it contains the autocorrelation spectra of the components of F: $\mathsf{ACT}_F(u, v) = \mathsf{AC}_F(u, v)$. It is also worth noticing that $\mathsf{AC}_F(u, v) = W_{D_u F}(0, v)$.

From Definitions 1 and 3, we immediately have the following connection between the DLCT and the autocorrelation of vectorial Boolean functions.

Proposition 1. *Let F be an (n, m)-function. Then for any $u \in \mathbb{F}_2^n$ and $v \in \mathbb{F}_2^m$, the autocorrelation of F at (u, v) is twice the value of the DLCT of F at the same position (u, v), i.e., $\mathrm{DLCT}_F(u, v) = \frac{1}{2} \mathsf{AC}_F(u, v)$. Moreover*

$$\max_{u \in \mathbb{F}_2^n \setminus \{0\}, v \in \mathbb{F}_2^m \setminus \{0\}} |\mathrm{DLCT}_F(u, v)| = \frac{1}{2} \Delta_F.$$

For the remainder of this paper we thus stick to the established notion of the autocorrelation table instead of DLCT, and we will study the absolute indicator of the function since it determines the highest magnitude in the DLCT.

Remark 1. Let us recall some relevant results on the autocorrelation table. The entries $\mathsf{AC}_F(u,v), v \neq 0$ in each nonzero row in the ACT of an (n,n)-function F sum to zero if and only if F is a permutation (see e.g. [3, Proposition 2]). The same property holds when the entries $\mathsf{AC}_F(u,v)$, $u \neq 0$ in each nonzero column in the ACT are considered (see e.g. [3, Eq. (9)]).

3   Properties of the Autocorrelation Table

In this section, we give some characterizations and properties of the ACT of vectorial Boolean functions introduced in Subsect. 2.3.

3.1   Links Between the Autocorrelation and the Walsh Transform

In this subsection, we express the autocorrelation by the Walsh transform of the function. The following proposition shows that the restriction of the autocorrelation function $u \mapsto \mathsf{AC}_F(u,v)$ can be seen as the discrete Fourier transform of the squared Walsh transform of $F_v \colon \omega \mapsto W_F(\omega, v)^2$.

Proposition 2. *Let F be an (n,m)-function. Then for any $u \in \mathbb{F}_2^n$ and $v \in \mathbb{F}_2^m$,*

$$W_F(u,v)^2 = \sum_{\omega \in \mathbb{F}_2^n} (-1)^{\omega \cdot u} \mathsf{AC}_F(\omega, v).$$

Conversely, the inverse Fourier transform leads to

$$\mathsf{AC}_F(\omega, v) = \frac{1}{2^n} \sum_{u \in \mathbb{F}_2^n} (-1)^{u \cdot \omega} W_F(u,v)^2 \tag{1}$$

Moreover, we have

$$\sum_{u \in \mathbb{F}_2^n} \mathsf{AC}_F(u,v) = W_F(0,v)^2 \tag{2}$$

and

$$\sum_{u \in \mathbb{F}_2^n} \mathsf{AC}_F(u,v)^2 = \frac{1}{2^n} \sum_{\omega \in \mathbb{F}_2^n} W_F(\omega, v)^4. \tag{3}$$

Proof. According to the definition, for any $u \in \mathbb{F}_2^n$,

$$W_F(u,v)^2 = \sum_{x \in \mathbb{F}_2^n} (-1)^{u \cdot x + v \cdot F(x)} \sum_{y \in \mathbb{F}_2^n} (-1)^{u \cdot y + v \cdot F(y)}$$

$$= \sum_{x,y \in \mathbb{F}_2^n} (-1)^{u \cdot (x+y) + v \cdot (F(x)+F(y))}$$

$$= \sum_{x,\omega \in \mathbb{F}_2^n} (-1)^{u \cdot \omega + v \cdot (F(x)+F(x+\omega))}$$

$$= \sum_{\omega \in \mathbb{F}_2^n} (-1)^{u \cdot \omega} \sum_{x \in \mathbb{F}_2^n} (-1)^{v \cdot (F(x)+F(x+\omega))}$$

$$= \sum_{\omega \in \mathbb{F}_2^n} (-1)^{u \cdot \omega} \mathsf{AC}_F(\omega, v).$$

The inverse Fourier Transform then leads to Eq. (1). Then Eq. (2) is obtained from Eq. (1) by summing over u. Furthermore, Parseval's equality leads to Eq. (3).

Remark 2. It should be noted that the relations Eq. (1) and Eq. (3) were already obtained in [22] and [44] for Boolean functions. Here we generalize the results to vectorial Boolean functions.

3.2 Links Between the Autocorrelation and the DDT

[45, Section 3] showed that, for an (n, n)-function, the row of index a in the autocorrelation table $b \mapsto \mathsf{AC}_F(a, b)$ corresponds to the Fourier transform of the row of index a in the DDT: $v \mapsto \mathsf{DDT}_F(a, v)$. This relation coincides with the one provided in [1, Proposition 1]. We here express it in the case of (n, m)-functions. It is worth noticing that this correspondence points out the well known relation between the Walsh transform of F and its DDT exhibited by [5, 16].

Proposition 3. *Let F be an (n, m)-function. Then, for any $u \in \mathbb{F}_2^n$ and $v \in \mathbb{F}_2^m$, we have*

$$\mathsf{AC}_F(u, v) = \sum_{\omega \in \mathbb{F}_2^m} (-1)^{v \cdot \omega} \mathsf{DDT}_F(u, \omega) \tag{4}$$

$$\mathsf{DDT}_F(u, v) = 2^{-m} \sum_{\omega \in \mathbb{F}_2^m} (-1)^{v \cdot \omega} \mathsf{AC}_F(u, \omega). \tag{5}$$

Most notably,

$$\sum_{v \in \mathbb{F}_2^m} \mathsf{AC}_F(u, v) = 2^m \mathsf{DDT}_F(u, 0) \tag{6}$$

implying

$$\sum_{u \in \mathbb{F}_2^n, v \in \mathbb{F}_2^m} \mathsf{AC}_F(u, v) = 2^{m+n}, \tag{7}$$

and

$$\sum_{v \in \mathbb{F}_2^m} \mathsf{AC}_F(u, v)^2 = 2^m \sum_{\omega \in \mathbb{F}_2^m} \mathsf{DDT}_F(u, \omega)^2. \tag{8}$$

Proof. The first equation holds since $\mathsf{AC}_F(u, v) = \sum_{x \in \mathbb{F}_2^n} (-1)^{v \cdot (F(x) + F(x+u))} = \sum_{\omega \in \mathbb{F}_2^m} (-1)^{v \cdot \omega} \mathsf{DDT}_F(u, \omega)$. The inverse Fourier transform then leads to Eq. (5). For $v = 0$, we then get Eqs. (6) and (7). Finally, Parseval's relation implies Eq. (8).

Note that Nyberg [36, 37] and Mesnanger et al. [33] linked the boomerang connectivity table (BCT) to the DDT, which results in the following link to the ACT (see e.g., [37, Proposition 1]): $\sum_{v \in \mathbb{F}_2^m} \mathsf{AC}_F(u, v)^2 = 2^m \sum_{\omega \in \mathbb{F}_2^m} \mathsf{BCT}_F(u, \omega)$.

3.3   Bounds on the Absolute Indicator

Similar to other cryptographic criteria, it is interesting and important to know how "good" the absolute indicator of a vectorial Boolean function could be. It is clear that the absolute indicator of any (n, m)-function is upper bounded by 2^n. But finding its smallest possible value is an open question investigated by many authors. From the definition, the autocorrelation spectrum of F equals $\{0\}$ if and only if F is a bent function, which implies that n is even and $m \leq \frac{n}{2}$. However, finding lower bounds in other cases is much more difficult. For instance, Zhang and Zheng conjectured [44, Conjecture 1] that the absolute indicator of a balanced Boolean function of n variables is at least $2^{\frac{n+1}{2}}$. But this was later disproved first for odd values of $n \geq 9$ by modifying the Patterson-Wiedemann construction, namely for $n \in \{9, 11\}$ in [25], for $n = 15$ in [23,29] and for $n = 21$ in [21]. For the case n even, [42] gave a construction for balanced Boolean functions with absolute indicator strictly less than $2^{n/2}$ when $n \equiv 2 \bmod 4$. Very recently, similar examples for $n \equiv 0 \bmod 4$ were exhibited by [24]. However, we now show that such small values for the absolute indicator cannot be achieved for (n, n)-*vectorial functions*.

Proposition 3 leads to the following lower bound on the sum of all squared autocorrelation coefficients in each row. This result can be found in [35] (see also [3, Theorem 2]) in the case of (n, n)-functions. We here detail the proof in the case of (n, m)-functions for the sake of completeness.

Proposition 4. *Let F be an (n, m)-function. Then, for all $u \in \mathbb{F}_2^n$, we have $\sum_{v \in \mathbb{F}_2^m} \mathsf{AC}_F(u, v)^2 \geq 2^{n+m+1}$. Moreover, equality holds for all nonzero $u \in \mathbb{F}_2^n$ if and only if F is APN.*

Proof. From Eq. (8), we have that, for all $u \in \mathbb{F}_2^n$,

$$\sum_{v \in \mathbb{F}_2^m} \mathsf{AC}_F(u, v)^2 = 2^m \sum_{\omega \in \mathbb{F}_2^m} \mathsf{DDT}_F(u, \omega)^2$$

Cauchy-Schwarz inequality implies that

$$\left(\sum_{\omega \in \mathbb{F}_2^m} \mathsf{DDT}_F(u, \omega) \right)^2 \leq \left(\sum_{\omega \in \mathbb{F}_2^m} \mathsf{DDT}_F(u, \omega)^2 \right) \times \#\{\omega \in \mathbb{F}_2^m | \mathsf{DDT}_F(u, \omega) \neq 0\},$$

with equality if and only if all nonzero elements in $\{\mathsf{DDT}_F(u, \omega) | \omega \in \mathbb{F}_2^m\}$ are equal. Using that

$$\#\{\omega \in \mathbb{F}_2^m | \mathsf{DDT}_F(u, \omega) \neq 0\} \leq 2^{n-1}$$

with equality for all nonzero u if and only if F is APN, we deduce that

$$\sum_{\omega \in \mathbb{F}_2^m} \mathsf{DDT}_F(u, \omega)^2 \geq 2^{n+1}$$

with equality for all nonzero u if and only if F is APN. Equivalently, we deduce that

$$\sum_{v \in \mathbb{F}_2^m} \mathsf{AC}_F(u,v)^2 \geq 2^{n+m+1}$$

with equality for all nonzero u if and only if F is APN.

From the previous proposition, we deduce that $\sum_{v \in \mathbb{F}_2^m \setminus \{0\}} \mathsf{AC}_F(u,v)^2 \geq 2^{n+m+1} - 2^{2n}$. Since $\sum_{v \in \mathbb{F}_2^m \setminus \{0\}} \mathsf{AC}_F(u,v)^2 \leq \Delta_F^2 (2^m - 1)$, we get for the absolute indicator $\Delta_F \geq \sqrt{\frac{2^{m+n+1} - 2^{2n}}{2^m - 1}}$. Thus we have the following result.

Theorem 1. *Let F be an (n,m)-function, where $m \geq n$. Then*

$$\Delta_F \geq \sqrt{\frac{2^{m+n+1} - 2^{2n}}{2^m - 1}}. \tag{9}$$

Most notably, if $m = n$, $\Delta_F > 2^{n/2}$.

Note that the condition $m \geq n$ in Theorem 1 is to ensure the term under the square root is strictly greater than 0.

3.4 Divisibility of the Autocorrelation

In this subsection, we investigate the divisibility property of the autocorrelation coefficients of vectorial Boolean functions.

Proposition 5. *Let $n > 2$ and $F : \mathbb{F}_2^n \to \mathbb{F}_2^m$ be a vectorial Boolean function with algebraic degree at most d. Then, for any $u \in \mathbb{F}_2^n$ and $v \in \mathbb{F}_2^m$, $\mathsf{AC}_F(u,v)$ is divisible by $2^{\lceil \frac{n-1}{d-1} \rceil + 1}$. In particular, when $m = n$ and F is a permutation, $\mathsf{AC}_F(u,v)$ is divisible by 8.*

Proof. By definition, for any $u \in \mathbb{F}_2^n$ and $v \in \mathbb{F}_2^m$,

$$\mathsf{AC}_F(u,v) = W_{D_u F_v}(0).$$

Note that for given $u \in \mathbb{F}_2^n$ and $v \in \mathbb{F}_2^m$, the Boolean function

$$h_{u,v}(x) = D_u F_v(x) = v \cdot (F(x) + F(x+u)),$$

satisfies two properties: $\deg(h_{u,v}) \leq d - 1$ since F has degree at most d and $h_{u,v}(x) = h_{u,v}(x+u)$.

We now focus on the divisibility of $W_{h_{u,v}}(0)$. First, assume for simplicity that $u = e_n = (0, \cdots, 0, 1)$, we discuss the general case afterwards. Since $h_{e_n,v}(x + e_n) = h_{e_n,v}(x)$, the value of $h_{e_n,v}(x)$ is actually determined by the first $(n-1)$ coordinates of x. Hence $h_{e_n,v}(x)$ can be expressed as $h_{e_n,v}(x) = h(x') : \mathbb{F}_2^{n-1} \to \mathbb{F}_2$ and the Walsh transform of $h_{e_n,v}$ at point 0 satisfies

$$W_{h_{e_n,v}}(0) = \sum_{x' \in \mathbb{F}_2^{n-1}, x_n \in \mathbb{F}_2} (-1)^{h_{e_n,v}(x', x_n)} = 2 \cdot \sum_{x' \in \mathbb{F}_2^{n-1}} (-1)^{h(x')} = 2 \cdot W_h(0).$$

It is well known that the values taken by the Walsh transform of a Boolean function f from $\mathbb{F}_2^n$ to $\mathbb{F}_2$ with degree d are divisible by $2^{\lceil \frac{n}{d-1} \rceil}$ (see [31] or [14, Section 3.1]). We then deduce that $W_h(0)$ is divisible by $2^{\lceil \frac{n-1}{d-1} \rceil}$, implying that $W_{h_{e_n,v}}(0)$ is divisible by $2^{\lceil \frac{n-1}{d-1} \rceil + 1}$. Most notably, if $m = n$ and F is bijective, then $d < n$. We then have that

$$\left\lceil \frac{n-1}{d-1} \right\rceil \geq 2,$$

implying that $\mathsf{AC}_F(u, v)$ is divisible by 8.

In the case that $u \neq e_n$, we can find a linear transformation L such that $L(e_n) = u$, with which we have the affine equivalent function $G = F \circ L$. We will show in a moment, see the next section, that for affine equivalent functions, their autocorrelation spectra are invariant (Theorem 2). Thus, the same holds for $\mathsf{AC}_G(u, v)$ in this case.

In particular, for (n, m)-functions of algebraic degree 3, we have the following result.

Proposition 6. *Suppose an (n, m)-function F has algebraic degree 3. Then for nonzero u and v, we have*

$$|\mathsf{AC}_F(u, v)| \in \left\{ 0, 2^{\frac{n + \delta(u, v)}{2}} \right\},$$

where $\delta(u, v) = \dim \{ w \in \mathbb{F}_2^n \mid D_u D_w f_v = c \}$ and $c \in \mathbb{F}_2$ is constant.

The proof can be found in [12, Appendix B]. Proposition 6 implies that any entry in the autocorrelation table of a cubic function is divisible by $2^{\frac{n + \psi}{2}}$, where ψ is the smallest integer among $\delta(u, v)$ when u, v run through $\mathbb{F}_2^n \setminus \{0\}$ and $\mathbb{F}_2^m \setminus \{0\}$, respectively. It is clear that $\psi \geq 1$. Furthermore, when $\psi \geq 2$, Proposition 6 improves the result in Proposition 5.

3.5   Invariance Under Equivalence Relations

Let n, m be two positive integers. There are several equivalence relations of functions from $\mathbb{F}_2^n$ to $\mathbb{F}_2^m$ and they play vital roles in classifying functions with good properties, like AB and APN functions [9]. In this subsection, we first recall three equivalence relations, i.e., affine, EA and CCZ [15]. Then we study the autocorrelation and related concepts with respect to these equivalence relations.

Definition 4. *[8] Let n, m be two positive integers. Two functions F and F' from $\mathbb{F}_2^n$ to $\mathbb{F}_2^m$ are called*

1. *affine equivalent (resp. linear equivalent) if $F' = A_1 \circ F \circ A_2$, where the mappings A_1 and A_2 are affine (resp. linear) permutations of $\mathbb{F}_2^m$ and $\mathbb{F}_2^n$, respectively;*
2. *extended affine equivalent (EA equivalent) if $F' = A_1 \circ F \circ A_2 + A$, where the mappings $A : \mathbb{F}_2^n \to \mathbb{F}_2^m, A_1 : \mathbb{F}_2^m \to \mathbb{F}_2^m, A_2 : \mathbb{F}_2^n \to \mathbb{F}_2^n$ are affine and where A_1 and A_2 are permutations;*

3. *Carlet-Charpin-Zinoviev equivalent (CCZ equivalent)* if for some affine permutation $\mathcal{L}$ over $\mathbb{F}_2^n \times \mathbb{F}_2^m$, the image by $\mathcal{L}$ of the graph of F is the graph of F', that is $\mathcal{L}(G_F) = G_{F'}$, where $G_F = \{(x, F(x)) | x \in \mathbb{F}_2^n\}$ and $G_{F'} = \{(x, F'(x)) | x \in \mathbb{F}_2^n\}$.

It is known that affine equivalence is a particular case of EA-equivalence, which is again a particular case of CCZ-equivalence. In addition, every permutation is CCZ-equivalent to its compositional inverse. Two important properties of cryptographic functions, the differential uniformity and the nonlinearity, are invariant under CCZ-equivalence. However, as we will show in this subsection, the autocorrelation spectrum is invariant under affine equivalence, and further its extended autocorrelation spectrum, i.e., the multiset $\{|\mathsf{AC}_F(u, v)| \; : \; u \in \mathbb{F}_2^n, v \in \mathbb{F}_2^m\}$, is invariant under extended affine equivalence. However, they are generally not invariant under compositional inverse, thereby are not invariant under CCZ-equivalence.

Theorem 2. *Assume two (n, m)-functions F and F' are EA-equivalent. Then the extended autocorrelation spectrum of F equals that of F'. In particular, if they are affine equivalent, then the autocorrelation spectrum of F equals that of F'.*

The proof is detailed in [12, Appendix C].

To examine the behavior under CCZ equivalence, we focus on the autocorrelation of a permutation and the autocorrelation of its compositional inverse. When $n = m$ and F permutes $\mathbb{F}_2^n$, Zhang et al. showed in [45, Corollary 1] that

$$\mathsf{ACT}_{F^{-1}} = H^{-1} \cdot \mathsf{ACT}_F \cdot H,$$

where H is the Walsh-Hadamard matrix of order 2^n. In our notation this is

$$\mathsf{AC}_{F^{-1}}(u, v) = \frac{1}{2^n} \sum_{a,b \in \mathbb{F}_2^n} (-1)^{u \cdot b + v \cdot a} \mathsf{AC}_F(a, b). \tag{10}$$

The relation in Eq. (10) indicates that the autocorrelation spectrum of an (n, n)-permutation F is in general not equal to that of F^{-1}.

This observation is indeed confirmed by many examples, in which an (n, n)-permutation F has linear structures but its inverse has not. Recall from [45] that a linear structure for an (n, m)-function F is a tuple $(u, v) \in \mathbb{F}_{2^n} \times \mathbb{F}_{2^m}$ such that $x \mapsto v \cdot (F(x) + F(x + u))$ is constant, zero or one, and $\mathsf{AC}_F(u, v) = \pm 2^n$ if and only (u, v) forms a linear structure. For instance, the S-boxes from SAFER [30], SC2000 [39], and FIDES [4] have linear structures in one direction but not in the other direction. This is also the case of the infinite family formed by the Gold permutations as analyzed in Sect. 4.2.

Below, we also provide an example that demonstrates that the autocorrelation spectrum is not invariant under EA-equivalence.

Example 1. Let $F(x) = \frac{1}{x} \in \mathbb{F}_{2^7}[x]$ and $F'(x) = \frac{1}{x} + x$. Then F and F' are EA-equivalent. However, F's autocorrelation spectrum is $\Lambda_F = \{-24, -16, -8, 0, 8, 16\}$ where as $\Lambda_{F'} = \{-24, -16, -8, 0, 8, 16, 24\}$.

In [27], the authors classified all optimal permutations over $\mathbb{F}_2^4$ having the best differential uniformity and nonlinearity (both 4) up to affine equivalence and found that there are only 16 different optimal S-boxes, see [12, Appendix A, Table 1]. Based on the classification of optimal S-boxes, we exhaust all possibilities of the autocorrelation spectra of optimal S-boxes in [12, Appendix A, Table 2], where the superscript of each autocorrelation value indicates the number of its occurrences in the spectrum.

3.6   Autocorrelation of Plateaued, AB and APN Functions

APN and AB functions provide optimal resistance against differential attacks and linear attacks, respectively. Many researchers have studied some other properties of APN and AB functions (see for example [8]). This subsection will investigate the autocorrelation of these optimal functions. We start with a general result for plateaued functions, which generalizes a result from [22], where the authors studied the autocorrelation of a plateaued Boolean function f in terms of its dual function.

Proposition 7. *Let F be an (n, m)-plateaued function. For $v \in \mathbb{F}_2^m \setminus \{0\}$, we denote the amplitude of the component F_v by 2^{r_v} and define a dual Boolean function of f_v as*

$$\widetilde{f}_v(b) = \begin{cases} 1, & \text{if } W_{f_v}(b) \neq 0, \\ 0, & \text{if } W_{f_v}(b) = 0. \end{cases} \tag{11}$$

Then

$$\mathsf{AC}_F(u, v) = -2^{2r_v - n - 1} W_{\widetilde{f}_v}(u).$$

Furthermore, when F is an AB function from $\mathbb{F}_2^n$ to itself, namely, $r_v = \frac{n+1}{2}$ for any $v \in \mathbb{F}_2^n \setminus \{0\}$,

$$\mathsf{AC}_F(u, v) = -W_{\widetilde{f}_v}(u).$$

Proof. According to Eq. (1), we have

$$\mathsf{AC}_F(u, v) = \frac{1}{2^n} \sum_{\omega \in \mathbb{F}_2^n} (-1)^{u \cdot \omega} W_F(\omega, v)^2 = 2^{2r_v - n} \sum_{\omega \in \mathbb{F}_2^n} (-1)^{u \cdot \omega} \widetilde{f}_v(\omega)$$

$$= 2^{2r_v - n} \sum_{\omega \in \mathbb{F}_2^n} \left(\frac{1}{2} \left(1 - (-1)^{\widetilde{f}_v(\omega)} \right) \right) (-1)^{u \cdot \omega} = -2^{2r_v - n - 1} \sum_{\omega \in \mathbb{F}_2^n} (-1)^{\widetilde{f}_v(\omega) + u \cdot \omega}$$

$$= -2^{2r_v - n - 1} W_{\widetilde{f}_v}(u).$$

Particularly, when F is an AB function, i.e., $r_v = \frac{n+1}{2}$ for any $v \in \mathbb{F}_2^m \setminus \{0\}$, it is clear that $\mathsf{AC}_F(u, v) = -W_{\widetilde{f}_v}(u)$.

Similar to the AB functions, the autocorrelation of APN functions can also be expressed in terms of the Walsh transforms of some balanced Boolean functions.

Proposition 8. *Let F be an APN function from $\mathbb{F}_2^n$ to itself. For any nonzero $u \in \mathbb{F}_2^n$, we define the Boolean function*

$$\gamma_u(x) = \begin{cases} 1, & \text{if } x \in \mathsf{Im}(D_u F), \\ 0, & \text{if } x \in \mathbb{F}_2^n \setminus \mathsf{Im}(D_u F). \end{cases} \tag{12}$$

Then the autocorrelation of F can be expressed by the Walsh transform of γ_u as

$$\mathsf{AC}_F(u, v) = -W_{\gamma_u}(v).$$

Proof. Since the APN function F has a 2-to-1 derivative function $D_u F(x)$ at any nonzero u, we know that $\mathsf{Im}(D_u F)$ has cardinality 2^{n-1}. Then,

$$\mathsf{AC}_F(u, v) = \sum_{x \in \mathbb{F}_2^n} (-1)^{v \cdot (F(x+u)+F(x))} = 2 \sum_{y \in \mathsf{Im}(D_u F)} (-1)^{v \cdot y}$$

$$= \sum_{y \in \mathsf{Im}(D_u F)} (-1)^{v \cdot y} - \sum_{y \in \mathbb{F}_2^n \setminus \mathsf{Im}(D_u F)} (-1)^{v \cdot y} = -\sum_{y \in \mathbb{F}_2^n} (-1)^{\gamma_u(y)+v \cdot y} = -W_{\gamma_u}(v).$$

From Proposition 8, we see that the autocorrelation of any APN function corresponds to the Walsh transform of the Boolean function γ_u in Eq. (12), which is balanced. We then immediately deduce the following corollary.

Corollary 1. *Let n be a positive integer. If there exists an APN function from $\mathbb{F}_2^n$ to $\mathbb{F}_2^n$ with absolute indicator Δ, then there exists a balanced Boolean function of n variables with linearity Δ.*

To our best knowledge, the smallest known linearity for a balanced function is obtained by Dobbertin's recursive construction [20]. For instance, for $n = 9$, the smallest possible linearity for a balanced Boolean function is known to belong to the set $\{24, 28, 32\}$, which implies that exhibiting an APN function over $\mathbb{F}_2^9$ with absolute indicator 24 would determine the smallest linearity for such a function.

One of the functions whose absolute indicator is known is the inverse mapping $F(x) = x^{2^n - 2}$ over $\mathbb{F}_{2^n}$.

Proposition 9 (Charpin et al. [17]). *The autocorrelation spectrum of the inverse function $F(x) = x^{2^n - 2}$ over $\mathbb{F}_{2^n}$ is given by*

$$\Lambda_F = \left\{ K(v) - 1 + 2 \times (-1)^{\mathrm{Tr}_{2^n}(v)} \big| v \in \mathbb{F}_{2^n}^* \right\},$$

where $K(a) = \sum_{x \in \mathbb{F}_{2^n}^*} (-1)^{\mathrm{Tr}_{2^n}(\frac{1}{x}+ax)}$ is the Kloosterman sum over $\mathbb{F}_{2^n}$. Furthermore, the absolute indicator of the inverse function is given by:

i) *when n is even, $\Delta_F = 2^{\frac{n}{2}+1}$;*
ii) *when n is odd, $\Delta_F = \mathsf{L}(F)$ if $\mathsf{L}(F) \equiv 0 \pmod 8$, and $\Delta_F = \mathsf{L}(F) \pm 4$ otherwise.*

When n is odd, the inverse mapping is APN. Then, from Proposition 8, its autocorrelation table is directly determined by the corresponding Boolean function γ. This explains why the absolute indicator of the inverse mapping when n is odd, is derived from its linearity as detailed in the following example.

Example 2 (ACT of the inverse mapping, n odd). For any $u \in \mathbb{F}_{2^n}^*$, the Boolean function γ_u, which characterizes the support of Row u in the DDT of the inverse mapping $F : x \mapsto x^{-1}$, coincides with $(1 + F_{u^{-1}})$ except on two points:

$$\gamma_u(x) = \begin{cases} 1 + \text{Tr}_{2^n}(u^{-1}x^{-1}) & \text{if } x \notin \{0, u^{-1}\} \\ 0 & \text{if } x = 0 \\ 1 & \text{if } x = u^{-1} \end{cases}.$$

This comes from the fact that the equation $(x+u)^{-1} + x^{-1} = v$ for $v \neq u^{-1}$ can be rewritten as $x + (x + u) = v(x + u)x$ or equivalently when $v \neq 0$, by setting $y = u^{-1}x$, $y^2 + y = u^{-1}v^{-1}$. It follows that this equation has two solutions if and only if $\text{Tr}_{2^n}(u^{-1}v^{-1}) = 0$. From the proof of the previous proposition, we deduce

$$\text{AC}_F(u, v) = -W_{\gamma_u}(v) = W_{F_{u^{-1}}}(v) + 2\left(1 - (-1)^{\text{Tr}_{2^n}(u^{-1}v)}\right),$$

where the additional term corresponds to the value of the sum defining the Walsh transform $W_{F_{u^{-1}}}(v)$ at points 0 and u^{-1}.

4   Autocorrelation Spectra and Absolute Indicator of Special Polynomials

This section mainly considers some polynomials of special forms. Explicitly, we investigate the autocorrelation spectra and the absolute indicator of the Gold permutations and their inverses, and of the Bracken-Leander functions. Our study is divided into two subsections.

4.1   Monomials

In the subsection, we consider the autocorrelation of some special monomials of cryptographic interest, mainly APN permutations and one class of permutations with differential uniformity 4, over the finite field $\mathbb{F}_{2^n}$. Firstly, we present a general observation on the autocorrelation of monomials, which is similar with other cryptographic criteria.

Proposition 10. *Let $F(x) = x^d \in \mathbb{F}_{2^n}[x]$. Then $\Lambda_F = \{\text{AC}_F(1, v) \mid v \in \mathbb{F}_{2^n}^*\}$. Moreover, if $\gcd(d, 2^n - 1) = 1$, then $\Lambda_F = \{\text{AC}_F(u, 1) \mid u \in \mathbb{F}_{2^n}^*\}$.*

Proposition 10 implies that it suffices to focus on the autocorrelation of the single component function $\text{Tr}_{2^n}(x^d)$ in the study of the autocorrelation table of the monomial x^d with $\gcd(d, 2^n - 1) = 1$.

We next discuss the autocorrelation of some cubic monomials. From Proposition 6, if $n = m$ is odd, we obviously have that $\Delta_F \geq 2^{\frac{n+1}{2}}$. Furthermore, the equality is achieved when $\dim(\{w \in \mathbb{F}_2^n \mid D_u D_w F_v = c\}) = 1$ for all nonzero u and v. Additionally, an upper bound on the absolute indicator can be established for two cubic APN permutations, namely the Kasami power function and the

Welch function. We denote the Kasami power functions K_i and the Welch power function W by

$$K_i : \mathbb{F}_{2^n} \to \mathbb{F}_{2^n} \qquad \text{and} \qquad W : \mathbb{F}_{2^n} \to \mathbb{F}_{2^n}$$
$$x \mapsto x^{2^{2i}-2^i+1} \qquad\qquad\qquad x \mapsto x^{2^{(n-1)/2}+3} .$$

Proposition 11 (Carlet [13], Lemma 1). *The absolute indicator for W on $\mathbb{F}_{2^n}$ is upper bounded by $\Delta_W \le 2^{\frac{n+5}{2}}$.*

As long as the (regular) degree of the derivatives is small compared to the field size, the Weil bound gives a nontrivial upper bound for the absolute indicator of a vectorial Boolean function. This is particularly interesting for the Kasami functions as the Kasami exponents do not depend on the field size (contrary to for example the Welch exponent).

Proposition 12. *The absolute indicator of K_i on $\mathbb{F}_{2^n}$ is upper bounded by $\Delta_{K_i} \le (4^i - 2^{i+1}) \times 2^{\frac{n}{2}}$. In particular, $\Delta_{K_2} \le 2^{\frac{n+5}{2}}$.*

Proof. Note that the two exponents with the highest degree of any derivative of K_i are $4^i - 2^i$ and $4^i - 2^{i+1} + 1$. The first exponent is even, so it can be reduced using the relation $\mathrm{Tr}_{2^n}(y^2) = \mathrm{Tr}_{2^n}(y)$. The result then follows from the Weil bound. Combining the bound with Proposition 6 yields the bound on K_2.

Some other results on the autocorrelations of cubic Boolean functions $\mathrm{Tr}_{2^n}(x^d)$ are known in the literature, which can be trivially extended to the vectorial functions x^d if $\gcd(d, n) = 1$, see [22, Theorem 5], [13] and [41, Lemmas 2 and 3]. In the case $n = 6r$ and $d = 2^{2r} + 2^r + 1$, the power monomial x^d is not a permutation, but results for all component functions of x^d were derived in [11]. We summarize these results about the absolute indicator in the following proposition.

Proposition 13. *Let $F(x) = x^d$ be a function on $\mathbb{F}_{2^n}$.*

1. *If n is odd and $d = 2^r + 3$ with $r = \frac{n+1}{2}$, then $\Delta_F \in \{2^{\frac{n+1}{2}}, 2^{\frac{n+3}{2}}\}$.*
2. *If n is odd and d is the i-th Kasami exponent, where $3i \equiv \pm 1 \pmod{n}$, then $\Delta_F = 2^{\frac{n+1}{2}}$.*
3. *If $n = 2m$ and $d = 2^{m+1} + 3$, then $\Delta_F \le 2^{\frac{3m}{2}+1}$.*
4. *If $n = 2m$, m odd and $d = 2^m + 2^{\frac{m+1}{2}} + 1$, then $\Delta_F \le 2^{\frac{3m}{2}+1}$.*
5. *If $n = 6r$ and $d = 2^{2r} + 2^r + 1$, then $\Delta_F = 2^{5r}$.*

We now provide a different proof of the second case in the previous proposition that additionally relates the autocorrelation table of K_i with the Walsh spectrum of a Gold function.

Proposition 14 (Dillon [19]). *Let n be odd, not divisible by 3 and $3i \equiv \pm 1 \pmod{n}$. Set $f = \mathrm{Tr}_{2^n}(x^d)$ where $d = 4^i - 2^i + 1$ is the i-th Kasami exponent. Then $\mathrm{Supp}(W_f) = \left\{ x \mid \mathrm{Tr}_{2^n}\left(x^{2^i+1}\right) = 1 \right\}$.*

Proposition 15. *Let n be odd, not divisible by 3 and $3i \equiv \pm 1 \pmod{n}$. Then*

$$\mathsf{AC}_{K_i}(u,v) = - \sum_{x \in \mathbb{F}_{2^n}} (-1)^{\mathrm{Tr}_{2^n}(uv^{1/d}x + x^{2^i+1})},$$

where $d = 4^i - 2^i + 1$ is the i-th Kasami exponent and $1/d$ denotes the inverse of d in $\mathbb{Z}_{2^n-1}$. In particular, $\Delta_{K_i} = 2^{\frac{n+1}{2}}$.

Refer to [12, Appendix D] for the proof. Note that the cases $3i \equiv 1 \pmod{n}$ and $3i \equiv -1 \pmod{n}$ are essentially only one case because the i-th and $(n-i)$-th Kasami exponents belong to the same cyclotomic coset. Indeed, $(4^{n-i} - 2^{n-i} + 1)2^{2i} \equiv 4^i - 2^i + 1 \pmod{2^n - 1}$.

From the known result in the literature, it appears that (n,n)-functions with a low absolute indicator are rare objects, which is also confirmed by experimental results for small integer n.

The Bracken-Leander function [7] is a cubic permutation with differential uniformity 4. In the following, we determine the autocorrelation spectrum and the absolute indicator of the Bracken-Leander function.

Theorem 3. *Let $F(x) = x^{q^2+q+1} \in \mathbb{F}_{q^4}[x]$, where $q = 2^k$. Then for any nonzero u,v, $\mathsf{AC}_F(u,v) \in \{-q^3, 0, q^3\}$ and $\Delta_F = q^3$.*

The proof is listed in [12, Appendix E].

4.2 Quadratic Functions and Their Inverses

In this subsection, we first consider the general quadratic functions and determine the autocorrelation spectra of the Gold functions and of their inverses. The possible values in the autocorrelation table of a quadratic function are easy to be computed since the differential function of a quadratic function is linearized.

Proposition 16. *Let $F(x) = \sum_{0 \le i < j \le n-1} a_{ij} x^{2^i+2^j} \in \mathbb{F}_{2^n}[x]$. Then the autocorrelation table of F takes values from $\{0, \pm 2^n\}$ and $\Delta_F = 2^n$.*

More precisely, we can determine the autocorrelation spectrum of the Gold functions completely.

Corollary 2. *Let $F(x) = x^{2^i+1} \in \mathbb{F}_{2^n}[x]$. Assume $k = \gcd(i,n)$ and $n' = n/k$. Then*

$$\Lambda_F = \begin{cases} \{0, 2^n\} & \text{if } n' \text{ is even,} \\ \{-2^n, 0\} & \text{if } n' \text{ is odd and } k = 1, \\ \{-2^n, 0, 2^n\} & \text{otherwise.} \end{cases}$$

See [12, Appendix F] for the proof.

As previously observed, the autocorrelation spectrum and the absolute indicator are not invariant under compositional inversion. Then, in the following, we consider the absolute indicator of the inverse of a quadratic permutation, which is not obvious at all. Indeed, the absolute indicator depends on the considered function, as we will see later.

Example 3. For $n = 9$, the inverses of the two APN Gold permutations x^3 and x^5, namely x^{341} and x^{409}, do not have the same absolute indicator: the absolute indicator of x^{341} is 56 while the absolute indicator of x^{409} is 72.

Nevertheless, the specificity of quadratic APN permutations for n odd is that they are *crooked* [2], which means that the image set of every derivative $D_u F, u \neq 0$, is the complement of a hyperplane $\langle \pi(u) \rangle^{\perp}$. Moreover, it is known (see e.g. [10, Proof of Lemma 5]) that all these hyperplanes are distinct, which implies that π is a permutation of $\mathbb{F}_2^n$ when we add to the definition that $\pi(0) = 0$. Then, the following proposition shows that, for any quadratic APN permutation F, the autocorrelation of F^{-1} corresponds to the Walsh transform of π.

Proposition 17. *Let n be an odd integer and F be a quadratic APN permutation over $\mathbb{F}_2^n$. Let further π be the permutation of $\mathbb{F}_2^n$ defined by*

$$\mathsf{Im}(D_u F) = \mathbb{F}_2^n \backslash \langle \pi(u) \rangle^{\perp}, \quad when \ u \neq 0,$$

and $\pi(0) = 0$. Then for any nonzero u, v in $\mathbb{F}_2^n$, we have $\mathsf{AC}_{F^{-1}}(u, v) = -W_\pi(v, u)$. It follows that $\Delta_{F^{-1}} \geq 2^{\frac{n+1}{2}}$ with equality if and only if π is an AB permutation.

The proof is given in [12, Appendix G].

It is worth noticing that the previous proposition is valid, not only for quadratic APN permutations, but for all crooked permutations, which are a particular case of AB functions. However, the existence of crooked permutations of degree strictly higher than 2 is an open question.

As a corollary of the previous proposition, we get some more precise information on the autocorrelation spectrum of the quadratic power permutations corresponding to the inverses of the Gold functions. Recall that x^{2^i+1} and $x^{2^{n-i}+1}$ are affine equivalent since the two exponents belong to the same cyclotomic coset modulo $(2^n - 1)$. This implies that their inverses share the same autocorrelation spectrum.

Corollary 3. *Let $n > 5$ be an odd integer and $0 < i < n$ with $\gcd(i, n) = 1$. Let F be the APN power permutation over $\mathbb{F}_{2^n}$ defined by $F(x) = x^{2^i+1}$. Then, for any nonzero u and v in $\mathbb{F}_{2^n}$, we have*

$$\mathsf{AC}_{F^{-1}}(u, v) = -W_\pi(v, u), \quad where \ \pi(x) = x^{2^n - 2^i - 2}.$$

Most notably, the absolute indicator of F^{-1} is strictly higher than $2^{\frac{n+1}{2}}$.

Again, see [12, Appendix H] for the proof.

In the specific case $n = 5$, it can easily be checked that the inverses of all Gold APN permutations $F(x) = x^{2^i+1}$ have absolute indicator 8.

5   Conclusion

This paper intensively investigates the differential-linear connectivity table (DLCT) of vectorial Boolean functions by clarifing its connection to the autocorrelation table of vectorial Boolean functions. The main contributions of this paper are the following. Firstly, we provide bounds on the absolute indicator of (n, m)-functions when $m \geq n$ and we exhibit the divisibility property of the autocorrelation of any vectorial Boolean function. Moreover, we investigate the invariance of the autocorrelation table under affine, EA and CCZ equivalence and exhaustively compute the autocorrelation spectra of optimal 4-bit S-boxes. Secondly, we analyze some properties of the autocorrelation of cryptographically desirable functions, including APN, plateaued and AB functions and express the autocorrelation of APN and AB functions with the Walsh transform of certain Boolean functions. Finally, we investigate the autocorrelation spectra of some special polynomials, including monomials with low differential uniformity, cubic monomials, quadratic functions and inverses of quadratic permutations.

Open Problems

1. Determine a (tight) lower bound on the absolute indicator of vectorial Boolean functions. Are there constructions exhibiting (near) optimal vectorial Boolean functions with respect to that bound?
2. For an odd integer n, are there (n, n)-power functions F with $\Delta_F = 2^{(n+1)/2}$ other than the Kasami APN functions?
3. From Corollary 1 it follows that an APN function with very low absolute indicator is of interest. Is there an APN function in 9 variables with absolute indicator $\Delta = 24$?
4. In addition, the absolute indicators of the Kasami and Welch functions have not been determined completely. Determine the absolute indicators of the Kasami and Welch functions completely.

References

1. Bar-On, A., Dunkelman, O., Keller, N., Weizman, A.: DLCT: A New Tool for Differential-linear Cryptanalysis, pp. 313–342, Springer, Cham (2019)
2. Bending, T.D., Fon-Der-Flaass, D.: Crooked functions, bent functions, and distance regular graphs. Electr. J. Combinat. **5** (1998)
3. Berger, T.P., Canteaut, A., Charpin, P., Laigle-Chapuy, Y.: On almost perfect nonlinear functions over $\mathbb{F}_2^n$. IEEE Trans. Inf. Theory **52**(9), 4160–4170 (2006)
4. Bilgin, B., Bogdanov, A., Knežević, M., Mendel, F., Wang, Q.: FIDES: lightweight authenticated cipher with side-channel resistance for constrained hardware. In: Bertoni, G., Coron, J.-S. (eds.) CHES 2013. LNCS, vol. 8086, pp. 142–158. Springer, Heidelberg (2013). https://doi.org/10.1007/978-3-642-40349-1_9
5. Chabaud, F., Vaudenay, S.: Links between differential and linear cryptanalysis. In: De Santis, A. (ed.) EUROCRYPT 1994. LNCS, vol. 950, pp. 356–365. Springer, Heidelberg (1995). https://doi.org/10.1007/BFb0053450

6. Boura, C., Canteaut, A.: On the boomerang uniformity of cryptographic sboxes. **2018**(3), 290–310 (2018)
7. Bracken, C., Leander, G.: A highly nonlinear differentially 4 uniform power mapping that permutes fields of even degree. Finite Fields Their Appl. **16**(4), 231–242 (2010)
8. Budaghyan, L.: Construction and Analysis of Cryptographic Functions. Springer-Verlag, New York (2014)
9. Budaghyan, L., Carlet, C., Pott, A.: New classes of almost bent and almost perfect nonlinear polynomials. IEEE Trans. Inf. Theory **52**(3), 1141–1152 (2006)
10. Canteaut, A., Charpin, P.: Decomposing bent functions. IEEE Trans. Inf. Theory **49**(8), 2004–2019 (2003)
11. Canteaut, A., Charpin, P., Kyureghyan, G.M.: A new class of monomial bent functions. Finite Fields Their Appl. **14**(1), 221–241 (2008)
12. Canteaut, A., et al.: Autocorrelations of vectorial boolean functions. Cryptol. ePrint Arch. Rep. 2021/947 (2021). https://ia.cr/2021/947
13. Carlet, C.: Recursive lower bounds on the nonlinearity profile of Boolean functions and their applications. IEEE Trans. Inf. Theory **54**(3), 1262–1272 (2008)
14. Carlet, C.: Boolean functions for cryptography and error-correcting codes. In: Crama, Y., Hammer, P.L. (eds) Boolean Models and Methods in Mathematics, Computer Science, and Engineering, pp. 257–397. Cambridge University Press, Cambridge (2010)
15. Carlet, C., Charpin, P., Zinoviev, V.: Codes, bent functions and permutations suitable for DES-like cryptosystems. Des. Codes Cryptograph. **15**(2), 125–156 (1998)
16. Chabaud, F., Vaudenay, S.: Links between differential and linear cryptanalysis. In: De Santis, A. (ed.) EUROCRYPT 1994. LNCS, vol. 950, pp. 356–365. Springer, Heidelberg (1995). https://doi.org/10.1007/BFb0053450
17. Charpin, P., Helleseth, T., Zinoviev, V.: Propagation characteristics of $x^{-1} \mapsto x$ and Kloosterman sums. Finite Fields Their Appl. **13**(2), 366–381 (2007)
18. Cid, C., Huang, T., Peyrin, T., Sasaki, Yu., Song, L.: Boomerang connectivity table: a new cryptanalysis tool. In: Nielsen, J.B., Rijmen, V. (eds.) EUROCRYPT 2018. LNCS, vol. 10821, pp. 683–714. Springer, Cham (2018). https://doi.org/10.1007/978-3-319-78375-8_22
19. Dillon, J.F.: Multiplicative difference sets via additive characters. Des. Codes Cryptogr. **17**(1–3), 225–235 (1999)
20. Dobbertin, H.: Construction of bent functions and balanced Boolean functions with high nonlinearity. In: Preneel, B. (ed.) FSE 1994. LNCS, vol. 1008, pp. 61–74. Springer, Heidelberg (1995). https://doi.org/10.1007/3-540-60590-8_5
21. Gangopadhyay, S., Keskar, P.H., Maitra, S.: Patterson-Wiedemann construction revisited. Discrete Math. **306**(14), 1540–1556 (2006)
22. Gong, G., Khoo, K.: Additive autocorrelation of resilient Boolean functions, pp. 275–290 (2004)
23. Kavut, S.: Correction to the paper: Patterson-Wiedemann construction revisited. Discrete Appl. Math. **202**, 185–187 (2016)
24. Kavut, S., Maitra, S., Tang, D.: Construction and search of balanced Boolean functions on even number of variables towards excellent autocorrelation profile. Des. Codes Cryptogr. **87**(2–3), 261–276 (2019)
25. Kavut, S., Maitra, S., Yücel, M.D.: Search for Boolean functions with excellent profiles in the rotation symmetric class. IEEE Trans. Inf. Theory **53**(5), 1743–1751 (2007)

26. Langford, S.K., Hellman, M.E.: Differential-linear cryptanalysis. In: Desmedt, Y.G. (ed.) CRYPTO 1994. LNCS, vol. 839, pp. 17–25. Springer, Heidelberg (1994). https://doi.org/10.1007/3-540-48658-5_3

27. Leander, G., Poschmann, A.: On the classification of 4 Bit S-Boxes. In: Carlet, C., Sunar, B. (eds.) WAIFI 2007. LNCS, vol. 4547, pp. 159–176. Springer, Heidelberg (2007). https://doi.org/10.1007/978-3-540-73074-3_13

28. Li, K., Longjiang, Q., Sun, B., Li, C.: New results about the boomerang uniformity of permutation polynomials. IEEE Trans. Inf. Theory $65(11)$, 7542–7553 (2019)

29. Maitra, S., Sarkar, P.: Modifications of Patterson-Wiedemann functions for cryptographic applications. IEEE Trans. Inf. Theor $48(1)$, 278–284 (2002)

30. Massey, J.L.: SAFER K-64: A Byte-oriented Block-ciphering Algorithm, pp. 1–17. Springer (1994)

31. McEliece, R.J.: Weight congruences for p-ary cyclic codes. Discrete Math. $3(1–3)$, 177–192 (1972)

32. Mesnager, S.: Bent Functions: Fundamentals and Results. Springer International Publishing (2016). https://doi.org/10.1007/978-3-319-32595-8

33. Mesnager, S., Tang, C., Xiong, M.: On the boomerang uniformity of quadratic permutations. Cryptology ePrint Achieves Report 2019/277 (2019). https://eprint.iacr.org/2019/277

34. Nyberg, K.: Differentially uniform mappings for cryptography. In: Helleseth, T. (ed.) EUROCRYPT 1993. LNCS, vol. 765, pp. 55–64. Springer, Heidelberg (1994). https://doi.org/10.1007/3-540-48285-7_6

35. Nyberg, K.: S-boxes and round functions with controllable linearity and differential uniformity. In: Preneel, B. (ed.) FSE 1994. LNCS, vol. 1008, pp. 111–130. Springer, Heidelberg (1995). https://doi.org/10.1007/3-540-60590-8_9

36. Nyberg, K.: Reverse-engineering hidden assumptions in differential-linear attacks (2015). https://www.cryptolux.org/mediawiki-esc2015/images/8/82/Nyberg_rev.pdf

37. Nyberg, K.: The extended autocorrelation and boomerang tables and links between nonlinearity properties of vectorial boolean functions. Cryptology ePrint Archieves Report 2019/1381 (2019) https://eprint.iacr.org/2019/1381

38. Rothaus, O.S.: On "bent" functions. J. Combinat. Theory Ser. A $20(3)$, 300–305 (1976)

39. Shimoyama, T., et al.: The block cipher SC2000. In: Matsui, M. (ed.) FSE 2001. LNCS, vol. 2355, pp. 312–327. Springer, Heidelberg (2002). https://doi.org/10.1007/3-540-45473-X_26

40. Song, L., Qin, X., Lei, H.: Boomerang connectivity table revisited. IACR Trans. Symmet. Cryptol. $2019(1)$, 118–141 (2019)

41. Sun, G., Chuankun, W.: The lower bound on the second-order nonlinearity of a class of Boolean functions with high nonlinearity. Appl. Algebra Eng. Commun. Comput. $22(1)$, 37–45 (2009)

42. Tang, D., Maitra, S.: Construction of n-variable ($n \equiv 2$ mod 4) balanced boolean functions with maximum absolute value in autocorrelation spectra $<2^{n/2}$. IEEE Trans. Inf. Theory $64(1)$:393–402 (2018)

43. Tokareva, N.: Bent Functions: Results and Applications to Cryptography. Academic Press, London (2015)

44. Zhang, X.M., Zheng, Y.: GAC the criterion for global avalanche characteristics of cryptographic functions. In: Maurer, H., Calude, C., Salomaa, A. (eds.) J.UCS The Journal of Universal Computer Science, pp. 320–337. Springer, Berlin (1996). https://doi.org/10.1007/978-3-642-80350-5_30
45. Zhang, X.-M., Zheng, Y., Imai, H.: Relating differential distribution tables to other properties of of substitution boxes. Des. Codes Cryptogr. **19**(1), 45–63 (2000)

Automatic Search for Bit-Based Division Property

Shibam Ghosh[✉] and Orr Dunkelman

Department of Computer Science, University of Haifa, Haifa, Israel
sghosh03@campus.haifa.ac.il, orrd@cs.haifa.ac.il

Abstract. Division properties, introduced by Todo at Eurocrypt 2015, are an extension of square attack (also called saturation attack or integral cryptanalysis). Given their importance, a large number of works tried to offer automatic tools to find division properties, primarily based on MILP or SAT/SMT. This paper studies better modeling techniques for finding division properties using the Constraint Programming and SAT/SMT-based automatic tools. We use the fact that the Quine-McCluskey algorithm produces a concise CNF representation corresponding to the division trail table of an Sbox. As a result, we can offer significantly more compact models, which allow SAT and Constraint Programming tools to outperform previous results.

To show the strength of our new approach, we look at the NIST lightweight candidate KNOT and Ascon. We show several new distinguishers with a lower data complexity for 17-round KNOT-256, KNOT-384 and 19-round KNOT-512. In addition, for the 5-round Ascon, we get a lower data distinguisher than the previous division-based results.

Finally, we revisit the method to extend the integral distinguisher by composing linear layers at the input and output. We provide a formulation to find the optimal number of linear combinations that need to be considered. As a result of this new formulation, we prove that 18-round KNOT-256 and KNOT-384 have no integral distinguisher using conventional division property and we show this more efficiently than the previous methods.

Keywords: Constraint programming · Division property · Integral cryptanalysis · KNOT · Ascon

1 Introduction

The *Square attack* was introduced by Daemen et al. in [7] to attack the SQUARE block cipher. A variant of this attack was applied to the Twofish cipher by Lucks in [18] and named the *Saturation attack*. These were formalized by Knudsen and

Electronic supplementary material The online version of this chapter (https://doi.org/10.1007/978-3-030-88238-9_13) contains supplementary material, which is available to authorized users.

P. Longa and C. Ràfols (Eds.): LATINCRYPT 2021, LNCS 12912, pp. 254–274, 2021.
https://doi.org/10.1007/978-3-030-88238-9_13

Wagner in [15], under the name *Integral cryptanalysis*. The main idea behind the integral attack is to find different properties of a set of ciphertexts corresponding to a set of plaintexts with a certain structure. These properties propagate through different operations of the cipher. Let us consider a set of plaintexts $\mathcal{P}$ from $(\mathbb{F}_2^m)^n$ and then any element of $\mathcal{P}$ can be seen as $(p_1, p_2, \cdots, p_n)$ where $p_i \in \mathbb{F}_2^m$, i.e., vector of m-bit words. Integral distinguisher exploits the propagation of some simple properties of the words from plaintext to ciphertext. The integral distinguisher considers the following properties: ALL (if the word position considers all possible values exactly once), BALANCED (if the word position is zero in the XOR sum of all elements), CONSTANT (if the word position is identical for all vectors). Based on these properties, an attacker can distinguish a cryptographic function from a random function. For example, the well-known 4-round integral distinguisher used in [12], to attack 6-round AES [8]. The integral distinguishers have since been also applied to a variety of ciphers [17,33,35].

The Division property was proposed as a generalization of the integral property by Todo at Eurocrypt 2015 [28] and was used in [29] to offer the first attack on the full MISTY1. The division property proposed by Todo was word-based division property, i.e., the propagation of the division property captures information only from the word level. In FSE 2016, Todo and Morii first introduced the bit-based division property [30]. In such bit-based division properties, the propagation captures information at the bit level which naturally captures more information than word-based division properties. The idea of the division property is the same as the integral property: consider an affine subspace of plaintexts and then check if the resulting set of ciphertexts has some balanced bits, i.e., their XOR sum is zero. To detect these balanced bits we consider the algebraic normal form (ANF) of a vectorial Boolean function. Suppose that $f : \mathbb{F}_2^n \to \mathbb{F}_2^n$ is a vectorial Boolean function that maps $x = (x_0, x_1, \cdots, x_{n-1})$ to $y = (f_0(x), f_1(x), \cdots, f_{n-1}(x))$. Let $X \subset \mathbb{F}_2^n$ be an input set and $Y = \{f(x) : x \in X\}$. The bit-based division property exploits the fact that, for some $i \in \{0, 1, \cdots, n-1\}$, $\bigoplus_{y \in Y} y_i = \bigoplus_{x \in X} f_i(x) = 0$ is predictable or not.

1.1   Related Work

The bit-based division property is an important tool for integral cryptanalysis. However, finding the bit-based division property is a tedious job. Direct programming approach is used in [29] to find bit-based division properties of SIMON-32 and SIMECK-32. Both ciphers have a block size of 32 bits. Unfortunately, this direct approach fails for larger block sizes used in modern ciphers.

In this case, automatic tools play a significant role. The main idea is to transform this bit-based property search problem into some mathematical problem and use an automatic tool to solve it. In this direction, Xiang et al. first proposed to use Mixed Integer Linear Programming (MILP) based tool in [34]. This approach has been used to attack many ciphers in the last few years [23,25,32]. A different approach suggested by Sun et al. [24] is to use SAT/SMT modeling [6]. Based on this method, Eskandari et al. studied many block ciphers in [11] and built a tool called SOLVATORE. In [14], the authors studied the bit-based division property for the ciphers with complex linear layers and modeled using SAT/SMT tool. Another approach is the use of Constraint Programming (CP) based tools. This approach was proposed in [26] to find the integral distinguisher of the PRESENT [4] block cipher. An extension of the integral cryptanalysis was proposed by Lambin et al. in [16], where they proposed to compose linear layers in the input and output to extend the distinguisher. With this approach, they found a 10-round distinguisher for the RECTANGLE [36] block cipher.

1.2   Our Contribution

Our work aims at using compact modeling of the Sbox to improve the automatic search of bit-based division properties. We use the SAT/SMT and the CP-based automatic approach to find bit-based division properties of all variants of the KNOT family [31] and Ascon [10]. We also test again some of the previous results on GIFT, Rectangle and PRESENT. While we check our approach for consistency, the comparison allows us to determine that for all tested models, our approach significantly reduces the running times of the tools. We express the propagation of bit-based division properties using Boolean logical formulas. We observe that modeling a formula in the Conjunctive Normal Form (CNF) instead of the table-based approach used in [14], gives a significant advantage in performance. We also provide a comparative analysis of these two methods. The above-mentioned tool SOLVATORE [11] was also modeled using the CNF, where the authors used the trivial approach to find the CNF of a function. Here we propose to use the Quine-McCluskey algorithm [19,21] to find the minimum size CNF. The Quine-McCluskey algorithm was previously used in the context of differential cryptanalysis in [1]. From our result, we can observe that for the KNOT and Ascon, the CP-based approach outperforms the SAT-based approach.

We also provide a concrete algorithm for finding lower data distinguishers. This algorithm is a formalization of two previous works in [11,24]. We used our algorithm on the KNOT and Ascon and found many distinguishers, which are more efficient. Table 1 compares the known results and our results.

Finally, we studied the direction provided in [16] to extend distinguishers by composing linear layers at the input and output. For the output layer, we used linear combinations instead of linear maps to reduce the search space, as suggested in [9]. Here we provide a formal way to find the optimal number of linear combinations that need to be considered, using Depth First Search (DFS) to find these. As an application of this theory, we found a new result that 18-round KNOT-256 and KNOT-384 have no integral distinguisher using conventional division property and we proved that more efficiently than before.

2   Preliminaries

2.1   Notations

The Hamming weight of $a \in \mathbb{F}_2^n$ is $wt(a) = \sum_{i=1}^{i=n} a_i$ and for any vector $\boldsymbol{a} = (a_0, a_1, \cdots, a_{m-1}) \in \mathbb{F}_2^{l_0} \times \mathbb{F}_2^{l_1} \times \cdots \times \mathbb{F}_2^{l_{m-1}}$, the vectorial Hamming weight of $\boldsymbol{a}$

Table 1. Summary of previous results and our best results

Primitive	#Rounds	Data	#Balanced bits	Source
KNOT-256	17	2^{255}	1	[31]
	17	2^{254}	7	Sect. 5
	18	Does not exist		Sect. 7
KNOT-384	17	2^{383}	1	[31]
	17	2^{380}	19	Sect. 5
	18	Does not exist		Sect. 7
KNOT-512	19	2^{511}	1	[31]
	19	2^{508}	139	Sect. 5
Ascon	5	2^{16}	320	[11]
	5	2^{12}	2	Sect. 6

is $W(\boldsymbol{a}) = (wt(a_0), wt(a_1), \cdots, wt(a_{m-1})) \in \mathbb{Z}^m$. For any $\boldsymbol{k} \in \mathbb{Z}^m$ and $\boldsymbol{k}' \in \mathbb{Z}^m$, we define $\boldsymbol{k} \succeq \boldsymbol{k}'$ if $k_i \geq k_i'$ for all i. For any integer $k \in \{0, 1, .., n\}$ we define the set $\mathbb{S}_k^n = \{a \in \mathbb{F}_2^n : k \leq wt(a)\}$ and for any vector $\boldsymbol{k} \in (\{0, 1, .., n\})^m$ we define the set $\mathbb{S}_{\boldsymbol{k}}^{m,n} = \{\boldsymbol{a} = (a_1, a_2, ..., a_m) \in (\mathbb{F}_2^n)^m : \boldsymbol{k} \preceq W(\boldsymbol{a})\}$. For any vector $u \in \mathbb{F}_2^n$ and $x \in \mathbb{F}_2^n$, we define the *bit product* $\pi_u : \mathbb{F}_2^n \to \mathbb{F}_2$ as $\pi_u(x) = \prod_{i=1}^{n} x_i^{u_i}$ and for any vector $\boldsymbol{u} \in (\mathbb{F}_2^n)^m$ and $\boldsymbol{x} \in (\mathbb{F}_2^n)^m$, we define the *vectorial bit product* $\pi_{\boldsymbol{u}} : (\mathbb{F}_2^n)^m \to \mathbb{F}_2$ as $\pi_{\boldsymbol{u}}(\boldsymbol{x}) = \prod_{i=1}^{m} \pi_{u_i}(x_i) = \prod_{i=1}^{m} \left(\prod_{j=1}^{n} x_{ij}^{u_{ij}} \right)$. The Algebraic Normal Form (ANF) of a function $f : \mathbb{F}_2^n \to \mathbb{F}_2$ can be defined as $f(x) = \bigoplus_{u \in \mathbb{F}_2^n} a_u^f \pi_u(x)$ and the degree of a function $f : \mathbb{F}_2^n \to \mathbb{F}_2$ is d if d is the degree of the largest monomial in the ANF of f, i.e., $d = \max_{u \in \mathbb{F}_2^n, a_u^f \neq 0} wt(u)$. We define $in_{i_1,i_2,...,i_p}$ is the vector in $\mathbb{F}_2^n$ with all coordinates 1 expect for the positions $i_1, i_2, ..., i_p$ and we define $out_{j_1,j_2,...,j_p}$ is the vector in $\mathbb{F}_2^n$ with all coordinates 0 expect for the positions $j_1, j_2, ..., j_p$. Similarly, we use $in_{(k,\ell)}$ to denote the binary matrix with all the elements are 1 except for (k, ℓ) position and $out_{(k,\ell)}$ to denote the binary matrix with all the elements are 0 except for (k, ℓ) position.

2.2 Definitions

Definition 1. *(Division Property [28]) A multi-set $X \subseteq \mathbb{F}_2^n$ is said to have the division property of order k, $\mathcal{D}_k^n$ for some $1 \leq k \leq n$, if the sum over all vectors $x \in X$ of the product $x^u = 0$, for all vectors u with hamming weight less than k, i.e.,*

$$\bigoplus_{x \in X} \pi_u(x) = 0, \forall u \in \mathbb{F}_2^n \text{ with } wt(u) < k.$$

Definition 2. *(Vectorial Division Property [28]) A multi-set $X \subseteq \mathbb{F}_2^{l_0} \times \mathbb{F}_2^{l_1} \times \cdots \times \mathbb{F}_2^{l_{m-1}}$ is said to have the division property $\mathcal{D}_{\mathbb{K}}^{l_0, l_1, \cdots l_{m-1}}$ for some set of m-dimensional vectors $\mathbb{K}$ whose i-th element takes a value between 0 to l_i, it fulfills the following conditions:*

$$\bigoplus_{x \in X} \pi_u(x) = \begin{cases} unknown, & \text{if there is } k \in \mathbb{K} \text{ s.t } W(u) \succeq k \\ 0, & otherwise \end{cases}$$

Moreover, if each l_i is restricted to 1, we will say bit-based division property and we will denote it by $\mathcal{D}_{\mathbb{K}}^{1,n}$.

Definition 3. (Balanced Position [28]) Let $Y \subseteq \mathbb{F}_2^n$ be a multi-set of vectors. A coordinate position $0 \le i < n$ is called balanced position if $\bigoplus_{y \in Y} y_i = 0$.

Definition 4. (Even Polynomial) Let f be a polynomial in the ring

$$\mathbb{F}_2[x_0, x_1, \ldots, x_{m-1}]/(x_0^2 + x_0, x_1^2 + x_1, \ldots, x_{n-1}^2 + x_{m-1})$$

with the algebraic normal form (ANF) $f(x_{m-1}, \cdots, x_0) = \bigoplus_{u \in \mathbb{F}_2^m} a_u^f \pi_u(x)$. Then f is called a even polynomial over a multiset X if the following holds $\forall u \in \mathbb{F}_2^m$:

$$a_u^f \bigoplus_{x \in X} \pi_u(x) = 0.$$

3   Propagation of Bit-Based Division Property

Let us consider a function $F : \mathbb{F}_2^n \to \mathbb{F}_2^n$. This function can be an Sbox, linear function or even a round function. We are interested in how the division property can propagate through this function. We consider the input set X as an affine subspace. Suppose X has division property $\mathcal{D}_{\{k_0\}}^{1,n}$ and after propagation through F, we get a division property $\mathcal{D}_{\{k_1\}}^{1,n}$. If $k_0 = (k_0^0, k_1^0, \cdots, k_{n-1}^0)$ and $k_1 = (k_0^1, k_1^1, \cdots, k_{n-1}^1)$, then we call $(k_0^0, k_1^0, \cdots, k_{n-1}^0, k_0^1, k_1^1, \cdots, k_{n-1}^1)$ a valid division trail through F. A formal definition of division trails was given in [34].

   Our main motivation is to model such a search problem that each solution of it be a valid division trail. Then we can solve that problem using various tools like constraint programming, SAT solver, etc. Suppose that we are given an r-round primitive $E_r : \mathbb{F}_2^n \to \mathbb{F}_2^n$. Let $(a_0, a_1, \cdots, a_{n-1})$ be the variables denoting the input division property vectors and $(b_0, b_1, \cdots, b_{n-1})$ be the variables denoting the output division property vectors. We set values to the input variables $(a_0, a_1, \cdots, a_{n-1})$ of the first round by a vector $k \in \{0, 1\}^n$ of our choice and find the balanced positions in the output vector from the last round. Once we have a set of balanced positions corresponding to an input division property k, we can distinguish E_r from a random function. For this, we take a set $X \subset \mathbb{F}_2^n$ of plaintexts and get an output set Y such that $Y = \{y = E_r(x) \mid x \in X\}$. The set X is an affine subspace, constructed corresponding to the input division property k. For each vector $x = (x_0, \cdots, x_{n-1}) \in X$, if the i-th coordinate of k is 1 then x_i can accepts all possible values from $\{0, 1\}$ and if the i-th coordinate of k is 0 then x_i is set to a fixed constant $c_i \in \{0, 1\}$. From the division property, we can guarantee that the balanced positions of the vectors of Y are balanced, which can distinguish E_r from a random function. As the size of the set X is $2^{wt(k)}$, the data complexity is $2^{wt(k)}$.

3.1   Modeling the Sbox

From the above discussion, we can observe that modeling a primitive is the main step in the attack. Xiang et al. [34] proposed an algorithm to accurately compute the propagation of bit-based division property through an Sbox. This algorithm takes the input division property vector $k = (k_0, k_1, \cdots, k_{n-1})$ as the input and outputs a set of vectors $\mathbb{K}_k$ such that the output multi-set has division property $\mathcal{D}_{\mathbb{K}_k}^{1,n}$. Here we have denoted the output set as $\mathbb{K}_k$ to attach it with the input property k. For any $(k, u) \in \mathbb{F}_2^n \times \mathbb{F}_2^n$ is a valid division trail if and only if $u \in \mathbb{K}_k$, where $\mathbb{K}_k$ is the output of the Algorithm on input k.

3.2   CNF from Division Trail

As discussed in the previous part we can form a division trail table T, such that

$$T = \{(a, b) \in \mathbb{F}_2^{2n} \mid b \in \mathbb{K}_a\}.$$

From the construction of T it is clear that $T^c = \mathbb{F}_2^{2n} \backslash T$ contains all the invalid division trails. We can consider a Boolean function F_S from $\mathbb{F}_2^{2n}$, corresponding to a given Sbox S with the following property:

$$F_S(a, b) = \begin{cases} 1, \text{ if } (a, b) \in T \\ 0, \text{ if } (a, b) \in T^c \end{cases}$$

Here we are interested in modeling this function to SAT/CP formula. One idea of this kind of modeling is the table-based approach, used in [14]. This table-based approach is the same as considering the disjunctive normal form (DNF) of F_S. However, we observe that the performance of this model is very low. Hence, we propose modeling using the conjunctive normal form (CNF) of the function F_s. The difference between the time requirements of these two methods suggests that we can significantly improve the performance by using the CNF instead of the DNF. Let us discuss how to compute the CNF of a given function F_S. We do so by first computing another function $G(x) = \overline{F_s(x)}$, i.e., $G(a, b) = 1$ if $(a, b) \in T^c$. The disjunctive normal form (DNF) of the function G can be trivially found, as used in [11]. Then we can again convert $G(x)$ to $\overline{G(x)}$ to get the CNF of $F_s(x)$ using De Morgan's laws. However, this approach results in a huge CNF representation. The number of terms in the CNF is the same as the size of T^c. To counter this effect, we propose to use the Quine-McCluskey algorithm [19, 21] to find a minimum size CNF.

We modeled the division property propagation problem using two different tools: as an SMT problem and as a Constraint programming problem. This is done to identify which of these two approaches are better for the CNF clauses. As we report in Sect. 5, CP based approach on the CNF, is more efficient.

There are many public solvers to solve SAT and SMT problems. Here we construct our model using the CVC [3] language and give it to an SMT solver. The SMT solver solves the satisfiability problem with the help of an SAT solver.

We used the STP $2.3.3^1$ [13] as the SMT solver and the Cryptominisat 5.7.1 [22] as the SAT solver. We modeled our CP problem in MiniZinc [20], which is a solver-independent open-source language that can be used to express CP models readable by multiple solvers. Then the model is given to the publicly available solver Chuffed[2] 0.10.4 [5].

4 Input Division Property and Output Division Property

Consider an SPN structure block cipher or a permutation. Each round function consists of parallel applications of a certain number of Sboxes, followed by a linear layer. We construct a model for each layer and repeat the procedure r times for an r-round primitive. Then we set values to the input variables $a = (a_0, a_1, \cdots, a_{n-1})$ and the output variables $b = (b_0, b_1, \cdots, b_{n-1})$, and solve the model. We now have to choose those values for a and b.

4.1 Input Division Property

Our initial division property is selected on the basis of the *embedded property*, introduced in [24], whose definition is recalled as follows.

Proposition 1 (Embedded Property [24]). *Let E_r be an r-round iterated encryption algorithm, R be the round function, which only composes of Substitution, Copy, XOR, Split and Concatenation operations. Suppose that the input and the output take values from $\mathbb{F}_2^n$ and k_0, k_1 are two initial division properties with $k_0 \succeq k_1$. If the output multi-set under k_0 does not have integral property, then the output multi-set under k_1 also has no integral property.*

Thus we consider n vectors with Hamming weight $n - 1$ as $in_i = (1, ..., 1, 0, 1, ..., 1)$ (0 is in the i-th position) for $0 \le i \le n - 1$. If we start from each of these in_i, i.e., set $a = in_i$ and cannot find any integral distinguisher then we can conclude that there is no integral distinguisher. We do not to check with the other initial properties according to the above Proposition 1.

4.2 Output Division Property

The choice of the output division property depends on when we need to stop the search, i.e., when we get a set without an integral property. This is described in the following proposition from [34].

Proposition 2 ([34]). *Let $\mathbb{X}$ be a multi-set with bit-based division property $\mathcal{D}_{\mathbb{K}}^n$, then $\mathbb{X}$ does not have integral property iff $\mathbb{K}$ contains all vectors of weight 1.*

Thus here, if the output multi-set (set of ciphertexts) has the division property $\mathbb{K}$ where $\mathbb{K}$ contains each out_j, then the output multi-set has no integral distinguishers. So we set the output variable with each out_j and solve the model.

---

[1] https://stp.github.io/.
[2] https://github.com/chuffed/chuffed.

4.3   Automatic Algorithm for Finding Division Properties

Now we recall an algorithm to find the maximum round r for which we can find an integral distinguisher from [24]. If for r-round, the system is consistent (satisfiable) for all in_i and out_j then there is no distinguisher, because from any input division property, the set of output division property contains all out_j. In that case, we set $r - 1$ as the highest possible round. On the other hand, if for some in_i and out_j, the model is not consistent with $a = in_i$ and $b = out_j$, then the j-th bit of the output multi-set is balanced. In that case, we can try finding a division trail for more rounds.

4.4   Reduction of Data Complexity

Till now, we have discussed how to find the maximal number of rounds with a division property. Suppose that for some in_i and out_j, the model is inconsistent with the input variable $a = in_i$ and output variable $b = out_j$, i.e., there is an integral distinguisher. This distinguisher uses a set of plaintext vectors $\mathbb{X} \subset \mathbb{F}_2^n$ such that the i-th bit is constant and the other bits take all possible ($\{0,1\}$) values. The data complexity of this distinguisher is 2^{n-1} plaintexts. We now discuss an idea from [24] to reduce the data complexity.

We first find an index set $\mathbb{S}$ such that for each $i \in \mathbb{S}$, if we set the initial division property as in_i, we have at least one j such that the j-th bit of the output multi-set is balanced. The set $\overline{\mathbb{S}} = \{0, 1, \cdots, n - 1\} \backslash \mathbb{S}$ is called the *necessary set* [24]. This name *necessary set* follows from the fact that we can get a balanced bit at the output only if we set $a_i = 1$ for all $i \in \overline{\mathbb{S}}$. The set $\mathbb{S}$ also called a *sufficient set* [24]. To choose an index i such that $a = in_i$, the set $\mathbb{S}$ is sufficient. Now if $\mid \mathbb{S} \mid > 1$, then we may set more than one $a_i = 0$ where $i \in \mathbb{S}$ and still have some balanced bits. Suppose we choose m indices $\{i_0, i_1, \cdots, i_{m-1}\}$ from $\mathbb{S}$ and set $a_i = 0$ for all $i \in \{i_0, i_1, \cdots, i_{m-1}\}$ and still have some balanced bit. In that case, we have an integral distinguisher with data complexity of 2^{n-m}.

Given the sufficient set $\mathbb{S}$, we can try with all possible subsets from $\mathbb{S}$, as suggested in [24], to see which offers the best data complexity. If we get a balanced bit for some subset, we stop this search; otherwise, we continue. This strategy brute forces all the subsets, i.e., its worst-case time complexity is $\binom{|\mathbb{S}|}{t}$ calls to the solver.

An improved idea proposed in [11], is to test only those combinations of indices from $\mathbb{S}$ which already have common balanced bits. Now we discuss the idea from [11] more formally and we provide an algorithm to use this search process. Let us consider a set OUT_i of all indices j such that the j-th bit is balanced when the input division property is in_i. We find the following set

$$IN_2 = \{\{i_0, i_1\} : (i_0 \neq i_1) \wedge (OUT_{i_0} \cap OUT_{i_1} \neq \phi), \forall i_0, i_1 \in \mathbb{S}\}.$$

We test if there are some balanced bits with initial division property in_{i_0, i_1} for each $\{i_0, i_1\} \in IN_2$. If we can find some balanced bit for some $\{i_0, i_1\}$ then we have a lower data distinguisher. Note that in this stage we are checking only with those out_j such that $j \in (OUT_{i_0} \cap OUT_{i_1})$, i.e., which are already balanced in the previous stage. This gives a significant advantage over searching for all out_j. The idea can be trivially generalized to IN_m where $IN_m = \{\{i_0, i_1, \cdots, i_{m-1}\} : (i_0 \neq i_1 \neq \cdots \neq i_{m-1}) \wedge ((\cap_{j=0}^{m-1} OUT_{i_j}) \neq \phi), \forall i_0, \cdots, i_{m-1} \in \mathbb{S}\}$. According to this, we can take $IN_1 = \mathbb{S}$.

This search starts from lowest value of m, i.e., $m = 2$ and increases by 1 if there is some balanced bits from an element of IN_m. To justify this we are proposing the following new Proposition 3.

Proposition 3. *Let m_0 and m_1 be two non-zero integers with $m_0 < m_1$. If we cannot get any integral distinguisher by setting the initial division property $a = in_{i_0, i_1, \cdots, i_{m_0-1}}$ for each $\{i_0, i_1, \cdots, i_{m_0-1}\} \in IN_{m_0}$ then there is no integral property from any index set of IN_{m_1}.*

Proof. If $m_1 > m_0$, then for any element $\{j_0, j_1, \cdots, j_{m_1-1}\} \in IN_{m_1}$ there is some element $\{i_0, i_1, \cdots, i_{m_0-1}\} \in IN_{m_0}$ such that $in_{i_0, i_1, \cdots, i_{m_0-1}} \succeq in_{j_0, j_1, \cdots, j_{m_1-1}}$. So the proof follows from the embedded property in Proposition 1.

It was also suggested in [11] to continue the process until we find some m such that IN_m is empty. But from the above Proposition 3 it also follows that we can stop our search when m is such that no element of IN_m leads to a balanced bit.

Algorithm 1 captures the above proposition. This algorithm outputs the size of the maximum possible combination from $\mathbb{S}$ for which we can get an integral distinguisher with data complexity 2^{n-t}. This algorithm also outputs a set $Z = \{i_0, i_1, \cdots, i_{t-1}\}$ of such a combination. Note that if the algorithm cannot find any larger combination, we can take any element from IN_1, so Z can be initialized with any one element from IN_1. In Algorithm 1 we initialized Z with an $i \in IN_1$ such that it gives a maximum number of balanced bits. Finally, once we have such a set Z we can get balanced bits corresponding to the initial division property $in_{i_0, i_1, \cdots, i_{n-1}}$. Here if we keep track of the list OUT from Algorithm 1, then we can use that to find balanced bits efficiently. In that case we search only on $\cap_{i \in \{i_0, i_1, \cdots, i_{t-1}\}} OUT[i]$ for balanced bits.

Remark 1. One important remark is that the time complexity of Algorithm 1 may not be feasible if the size of $\mathbb{S}$ is very large. The main work is needed here to compute the sets OUT_i for all $i \in \mathbb{S}$. For every element in $\mathbb{S}$ we need to call our model n times. If this is computationally infeasible, one can sample a smaller subset of $\mathbb{S}$ as we show in the next section.

5   Application to the KNOT Permutation

KNOT is a family of bit-slice lightweight authenticated encryption algorithms and hash functions [31], submitted to the NIST lightweight crypto competition [27]. The KNOT permutation is the main primitive used in the KNOT family and comprises three variants with different sizes: 256 bits, 384 bits and 512 bits (denoted by KNOT-b).

Algorithm 1. OptimalDistinguisher

Require: SAT/CP model for the primitive, Max round $r > 1$, Sufficient set $\mathbb{S}$
Ensure: t and Z such that t is the max possible size and Z is one combination of size t

1: $IN_1 = \mathbb{S}$
2: OUT is empty list of sets
3: **for** $i \in IN_1$ **do**
4:      $OUT_i = \phi$
5:      $a = (a_0, \cdots, a_{n-1}) = in_i$
6:      **for** $0 \le j < n$ **do**
7:          $b = (b_0, \cdots, b_{n-1}) = out_j$
8:          {solve the r-round model with a and b
9:          as first round and last round variable, respectively}
10:         **if** not satisfiable **then**
11:             $OUT_i = OUT_i \cup \{j\}$
12:         **end if**
13:     **end for**
14:     $OUT[i] = OUT_i$
15: **end for**
16: $Flag = True$
17: $t = 1$
18: $Z = \max_{i \in IN_1} |\ OUT[i]\ |$
19: **while** $Flag = True$ **do**
20:     $FLAG = False$
21:     $t = t + 1$
22:     compute IN_t
23:     **for** $\{i_0, i_1, \cdots, i_{t-1}\} \in IN_t$ **do**
24:         $a = in_{i_0, i_1, \cdots, i_{t-1}}$
25:         $B = \cap_{i \in \{i_0, i_1, \cdots, i_{t-1}\}} OUT[i]$
26:         **for** $(b_0, \cdots, b_{n-1}) \in B$ **do**
27:             $b = (b_0, \cdots, b_{n-1}) = out_j$
28:             {solve the r-round model with a and b
29:             as first round and last round variable, respectively}
30:             **if** not satisfiable **then**
31:                 $Flag = True$
32:                 $Z = \{i_0, i_1, \cdots, i_{t-1}\}$
33:                 break
34:             **end if**
35:         **end for**
36:         **if** $Flag = True$ **then**
37:             break
38:         **end if**
39:     **end for**
40: **end while**
41: $t = t - 1$
42: **return** t, Z

Table 2. KNOT's Sbox

x	0	1	2	3	4	5	6	7	8	9	A	B	C	D	E	F
$S(x)$	4	0	A	7	B	E	1	D	9	F	6	8	5	2	C	3

Table 3. Shift Row offsets for the KNOT permutation

b	c_1	c_2	c_3
256	1	8	25
384	1	8	55
512	1	16	25

5.1 Specification

The underlying permutations iteratively applies an SP-network round transformation. Each round is the composition of three operations: Add round constants, Sub Column, Shift Row. The round constants do not affect the division property. So we do not describe them here and refer the interested reader to [31]. Each b-bit state of the KNOT-b can be seen as a $4 \times \frac{b}{4}$ matrix, where $b = 256, 384$ or 512.

The operation of Sub Column is a parallel application of $\frac{b}{4}$ similar Sboxes to the 4 bits in the same column. The Sbox $S : \mathbb{F}_2^4 \to \mathbb{F}_2^4$ is given in Table 2. The Shift Row transformation left rotate each row by 0, c_1, c_2 and c_3 bits, respectively. The offsets c_1, c_2 and c_3 are different for different state size, given in Table 3.

5.2 Application of Our Model

We applied both SAT and CP models to KNOT. When the state size is b, we have in total $\frac{b}{4}$ many 4-bit Sboxes for each round. Thus we have a total $\frac{b}{4} \times r$ many constraints for r rounds. To implement r-round KNOT we have the variable matrices $a^0, a^1, a^2, ..., a^r$ of the form

$$a^i = \begin{bmatrix} a_{0,0}^i & a_{0,1}^i & a_{0,2}^i & \cdots & a_{0,\frac{b}{4}-1}^i \\ a_{1,0}^i & a_{1,1}^i & a_{1,2}^i & \cdots & a_{1,\frac{b}{4}-1}^i \\ a_{2,0}^i & a_{2,1}^i & a_{2,2}^i & \cdots & a_{2,\frac{b}{4}-1}^i \\ a_{3,0}^i & a_{3,1}^i & a_{3,2}^i & \cdots & a_{3,\frac{b}{4}-1}^i \end{bmatrix} \quad \forall i \in \{0, 1, ..., r\},$$

where each $a_{j,k}^i \in \{0, 1\}$. In our model, the variables are related with some constraints. Each column of a^i and $a^{(i+1)}$ are related with parallel application of $\frac{b}{4}$ Sboxes. Then a^i is rotated according to the shift row and we get b^i. Note that as this is only a permutation of variables we do not need to introduce new variables for b^i, instead we can just connect a^i and b^i according to shift row. The chain of propagation is as follows (omitted last shift row):

$$a^0 \xrightarrow{\text{Sbox}} a^1 \xrightarrow{\text{rotation}} b^1 \xrightarrow{\text{Sbox}} a^2 \xrightarrow{\text{rotation}} \cdots b^{r-1} \xrightarrow{\text{Sbox}} a^r.$$

Table 4. Distinguishers for the KNOT with input property $a = in_{(3,0)}$

KNOT-b	#Rounds	#Data	#Balanced-bits	SAT	SAT/CNF	CP	CP/CNF
KNOT-256	17	2^{255}	89	13 h	19 min	>15 h	12 min
KNOT-384	17	2^{383}	140	>15 h	45 min	>15 h	17 min
KNOT-512	19	2^{511}	269	>15 h	2.1 h	>15 h	70 min

5.3   Finding the Longest Division Properties

The authors of KNOT used the MILP-based search strategy to analyze KNOT's integral properties. They found $17, 17, 19$-round integral distinguishers for the sizes $b = 256$, 384 and 512, respectively. All of the distinguishers have data complexity of 2^{b-1} and in all cases, they found one balanced bit at position $(3, 0)$. To the best of our knowledge, this is the only available result on the KNOT in the context of the integral attacks. Also, the authors did not provide any time requirements for these findings.

We obtained several new results on the KNOT-256, KNOT-384 and KNOT-512. All of our experiments are conducted on the following 64-bit Linux platform: Intel Core i7-3520M CPU @ 2.90 GHz, 8.00 G RAM. We used the model proposed in Sect. 5.2 and solved it using SAT/SMT and CP based tools. All the source codes are available in public domain at https://github.com/ShibamCrS/AutomaticSearchforBBDP.

First, for all versions of KNOT, we considered the initial division property $in_{(k,\ell)}$ (all coordinates 1 except for the (k, ℓ)-th position) for each $0 \le k < 4$ and $0 \le \ell < \frac{b}{4}$. We are getting at least two balanced bits on the output states after 17-rounds KNOT-256 and KNOT-384 and 19-round KNOT-512. From this result, we can say that the *sufficient index set* $\mathbb{S}$ defined in Sect. 4.4 contains all of the b bits positions for $b = 256, 384, 512$. Secondly, if we set the input variables as

$$a^0 = in_{(3,0)} = \begin{cases} 0, & \text{if } (k, \ell) = (3, 0) \\ 1, & \text{otherwise} \end{cases}$$

then we can get many balanced bits after 17 rounds for the KNOT-256 and KNOT-384 and after 19 rounds for the KNOT-512, which spread over all the four rows. These results outperform the previous result in [31], where the authors found only one balanced bit in each version. The time requirements with the number of balanced positions are given in Table 4.

5.4   More Efficient Distinguishers

From the previous result, as the sufficient index set $\mathbb{S}$ is huge, here we cannot use the whole set on the data complexity reduction algorithm. Instead we used a subset $\mathbb{S}'$ of $\mathbb{S}$. If we consider only the first column, i.e., we set constant at positions $\mathbb{S}' = \{(0,0), (1,0), (2,0), (3,0)\}$.

Table 5. Distinguisher for 17-round KNOT-384 (data complexity 2^{380})

Constant positions	(0, 0), (1, 0), (2, 0), (3, 0)
Balanced positions at the third row	[24, 31, 38, 39, 40, 77, 78, 79, 80, 86, 87, 89]
Balanced positions at the fourth row	[40, 77, 79, 80, 86, 87, 89]

Table 6. Distinguisher for 19-round KNOT-512 (data complexity 2^{508})

Constant	(0, 0), (1, 0), (2, 0), (3, 0)
1st row	{0, 7, 8, 15, 16, 30, 31, 32, 40, 47, 55, 56, 64, 79, 80, 88, 112, 127}
2nd row	{0, 7, 8, 14, 15, 16, 23, 30, 31, 32, 39, 40, 47, 48, 55, 56, 63, 64, 79, 80, 87, 88, 95, 96, 103, 111, 112, 119, 127}
3rd row	{0, 5, 6, 7, 8, 14, 15, 16, 22, 23, 24, 29, 30, 31, 32, 38, 39, 40, 41, 47, 48, 55, 56, 57, 63, 64, 65, 70, 71, 79},
	{80, 81, 86, 87, 88, 89, 94, 95, 96, 102, 103, 104, 109, 110, 111, 112, 118, 119, 120, 126, 127}
4th row	{0, 5, 6, 7, 8, 14, 15, 16, 23, 29, 30, 31, 32, 39, 40, 41, 47, 48, 55, 56, 57, 63, 64, 65, 71, 79}
	{80, 81, 87, 88, 89, 95, 96, 103, 104, 109, 111, 112, 118, 119, 127}

KNOT-256: For the KNOT-256 we calculated the balanced bits for each constant positions in $\{(0,0),(1,0),(2,0),(3,0)\}$. Then we applied Algorithm 1 with $\mathbb{S}' = \{(0,0),(1,0),(2,0),(3,0)\}$ on 17 round KNOT-256. It gives the output $t = 2$ and $Z = \{(0,0),(1,0)\}$. Now we can get balanced positions with input Z. We get two balanced positions $(2,16)$ and $(2,56)$ after 17 rounds. By a similar approach we can get several distinguishers.

KNOT-384: For the KNOT-384 we took $\mathbb{S}' = \{(0,0),(1,0),(2,0),(3,0)\}$ and we apply Algorithm 1 for 17 rounds. It gives the outputs $t = 4$ and $Z = \{(0,0),(1,0),(2,0),(3,0)\}$. We get in total 19 many balanced bits from Z, spread over the last two rows given in Table 5.

KNOT-512. For the KNOT-512 also we found a lower complexity distinguisher on 19 rounds. Here also we took $\mathbb{S}' = \{(0,0),(1,0),(2,0),(3,0)\}$ and we apply Algorithm 1 which outputs $t = 4$ and $Z = \{(0,0),(1,0),(2,0),(3,0)\}$. We get in total 139 many balanced bits from Z, spread over all the four rows given in Table 6.

6 Other Results

To show the strength of our approach, we considered some well-known ciphers RECTANGLE [36], GIFT [2], PRESENT [4]. While we obtained results that do

Table 7. Division property results

Primitives	#Round	#Data	#Balanced bits	SAT	SAT(CNF)	CP	CP(CNF)
Ascon-320	5	2^{12}	2	>15 h	20 min	>15 h	10 min
RECTANGLE-64	9	2^{60}	16	70 s	35 s	50 s	40 s
RECTANGLE-64	10		No Distinguisher*	1.48 h	41 min	1.44 h	39 min
PRESENT-64	9	2^{60}	1	76 s	21 s	17 min	45 s
PRESENT-64	10		No Distinguisher*	1.5 h	24 min	1.7 h	38 min
GIFT-64	9	2^{61}	5	103 s	60 s	58 min	62 s
GIFT-64	10		No Distinguisher*	1.49 h	42 min	1.19 h	43 min

*Time required for exhaustive search with all possible in_i and out_j

not improve the previously known results, they demonstrate the clear advantage of using CNF models. The difference between the time requirements of two methods is given in the Table 7. We also implement our model to NIST lightweight candidate Ascon [10] and we obtain a distinguisher with data complexity 2^{12}. This result improves the previous result in [11], where data complexity was 2^{16}. The 12 active bit positions in the Ascon state matrix are $(0,0),(1,0),(2,0),(3,0),(4,0),\ (0,1),(1,1),(2,1),(3,1),(4,1),(0,2),(1,2)$.

7 Proving the Non-Existence of Longer Division Trails

In a very recent work in [16], Lambin et al. proposed a new way to extend the integral distinguisher. The main motivation of these types of extensions is that the division properties are not linearly invariant. If we consider a linear map L and an Sbox S then the division properties of $L \circ S$ and $S \circ L$ may be different from those of S and consequently, the division trail table may differ. Thus by choosing a proper L, we may get new distinguishers which were impossible when modeling S alone. Thus, for a given r-round primitive E_r, the authors of [16] proposed to consider $L_{out} \circ E_r \circ L_{in}$ instead of E_r where both L_{in} and L_{out} are linear mappings. This way, we may get some distinguisher on $L_{out} \circ E_r \circ L_{in}$ which is not possible on E_r. Lambin et al. also described some ideas to choose proper L_{in} and L_{out}. Note that the search space of these linear combinations is huge and this space needs to be reduced. On this direction, Lambin et al.'s first proposed the following Proposition 4.

Proposition 4. *Let S be an invertible m-bit Sbox and P be an m-bit permutation. Let $S_1 = S \circ P$ and $S_2 = P \circ S$ and $k \xrightarrow{S} k'$ be any valid division property propagation through S. Then both of the propagations*

$$P^{-1}(k) \xrightarrow{S_1} k' \text{ and } k \xrightarrow{S_2} P(k')$$

are also valid.

Proof of the above proposition is obvious. As we consider the bit-based division property, bit-permutation just permutes the division property vector. But this plays a crucial role in reducing the search space.

We focus on linear mapping which are block diagonals, each block corresponds to an m-bit Sbox in the Sbox layer (an $m \times m$ matrix). So we can write $L_{in} = (L_{in}^0, L_{in}^1, \cdots, L_{in}^{s-1})$ and $L_{out} = (L_{out}^0, L_{out}^1, \cdots, L_{out}^{s-1})$ where each L_{in}^j and L_{out}^j is an $m \times m$ matrix. To find the i-th block L_{in}^i Lambin et al. considered the following permutation equivalence classes

$$\mathcal{E}_{in}(L) = \{L' \in GL_m(\mathbb{F}_2)| \exists \text{ permutation } P \text{ s.t. } L' = L \circ P\}.$$

Similarly to find L_{out}^i we have

$$\mathcal{E}_{out}(L) = \{L' \in GL_m(\mathbb{F}_2)| \exists \text{ permutation } P \text{ s.t. } L' = P \circ L\}.$$

The number of these classes is $\frac{\prod_{i=0}^{m-1} 2^m - 2^i}{m!}$. This number is much lower than the total number of $m \times m$ invertible matrices, which is $\prod_{i=0}^{m-1} 2^m - 2^i$. Now if we can find each $\mathcal{E}_{in}(L)$ and $\mathcal{E}_{out}(L)$, we consider only **one** linear map from each of the classes. For example, if $m = 4$, there are in total 840 of such classes instead of 20160 matrices.

7.1   Further Reduction of the Search Space for L_{out}

We now discuss the method to find an optimal number of L_{out}. It was suggested in [9] that finding proper linear combinations of the output bits is enough to find an integral distinguisher instead of a linear map. Indeed, here our main motivation is that multiplying the output vectors with a matrix is the same as taking linear combinations. If we cannot get any balanced bit by linear combinations, we cannot get them by matrix multiplication. Thus, we check all possible nonzero linear combinations. This reduces the search space from $\frac{\prod_{i=0}^{m-1} 2^m - 2^i}{m!}$ to $2^m - 1$. If $m = 4$, it reduced from 840 to 15. However, checking for all those 15 linear combinations is also a huge task. We now discuss how to further reduce this number.

Let us consider an r-round primitive E_r. Here we want to take linear combinations of each Sbox output, not the whole state. For an $m \times m$ Sbox, there are $2^m - 1$ linear combinations. If the Sbox $S : \mathbb{F}_2^m \to \mathbb{F}_2^m$ maps $(x_{m-1}, \cdots, x_0)$ to $(y_{m-1}, \cdots, y_0)$ then any linear combination of $(y_{m-1}, \cdots, y_0)$ is also a Boolean function. Its ANF can be determined from the ANF of y_i's. If c is an integer with binary representation $(c_{m-1}, \cdots, c_0)$ then P_c is the linear combination corresponding to c, i.e.,

$$P_c = (c_{m-1}, \cdots, c_0) \cdot (y_{m-1}, \cdots, y_0) = \sum_{i=0}^{m-1} c_i y_i.$$

So there are $2^m - 1$ polynomials $P_1, P_2, \cdots, P_{2^m-1}$ corresponding to each Sbox. Each of these can be written as $P_c(x_{m-1}, \cdots, x_0) = \bigoplus_{u \in \mathbb{F}_2^m} a_u^{P_c} \pi_u(x)$.

7.2   Checking Polynomials

We now discuss the process to check a polynomial is even polynomial or not. To do so, we check each monomial present in the polynomial by our SAT/CP model. Suppose that we want to check a monomial $x_{j_0}^i x_{j_1}^i \cdots x_{j_k}^i$, where $(x_{m-1}^i, \cdots, x_0^i)$ is the input to the i-th Sbox of the last round. To check the monomial $x_{j_0}^i x_{j_1}^i \cdots x_{j_k}^i$ we set the output property as $out_{j_0,j_1,\cdots,j_k}$, where $out_{j_0,j_1,\cdots,j_k}$ is a vector with all zero except for positions $j_0, \cdots, j_k$. If we get the system unsatisfiable for some initial property, then we can say that the monomial is even. Consequently, if all the monomials in the ANF are even, then the polynomial is even polynomial and there is an integral distinguisher. One important thing is that we solve the model for $r-1$ rounds to decide whether a balanced bit exists after r rounds.

Let us consider an Sbox of size m. There are in total $2^m - 1$ linear combinations polynomial $P_1, \cdots, P_{2^m-1}$. Each P_i corresponds to the linear combination obtained from the binary representation of i. However, there is no need to check all $2^m - 1$ polynomials. We identify a subset of polynomials which are sufficient, i.e., if these polynomials are not even, then there is no division property. We define an order ($\sqsubseteq$) among the polynomials such that if $P_i \sqsubseteq P_j$ then we check if the polynomial P_i is even polynomial or not. Suppose P_i is not even, then there is no need to check for P_j. If P_i is even, we have a distinguisher and for more distinguishers, we can check P_j's such that $P_i \sqsubseteq P_j$. The definition of this order is as follows.

Definition 5. *Let us consider two polynomials P and Q from the ring*

$$\mathbb{F}_2[x_0, x_1, \ldots, x_{m-1}]/(x_0^2 + x_0, x_1^2 + x_1, \ldots, x_{n-1}^2 + x_{m-1}).$$

We say that Q is Dependent on P, denoted by $P \sqsubseteq Q$ if any monomial (term) in P divides at least one monomial (term) of Q.

Proposition 5. *If we have two linear combination polynomials P and Q with $P \sqsubseteq Q$ and we can find that P is not even, then Q is not even.*

Proof. If P is not even then according to Definition 4 of the even polynomial we can get some monomials in P which is not even, i.e., there is some $u \in \mathbb{F}_2^m$ such that $a_u^P = 1$ and $\bigoplus_{x \in \mathbb{F}_2^m} \pi_u(x)$ is unknown. As $P \sqsubseteq Q$, then that unknown term must divide some term of Q and that term of Q must be unknown according to the definition of division property. So Q can not be an even polynomial.

For example there are 15 polynomials for the KNOT Sbox. Let us consider P_4 and P_2, for which the terms of P_4 are $\{x_0, x_2x_1, x_1, x_2, x_3, 1\}$ and the terms of P_2 are $\{x_3x_0, x_3x_2x_1, x_1, x_3x_2, x_2\}$. We can observe that x_0, x_3 divides x_3x_0 and x_1, x_2, x_1x_2 divides $x_3x_2x_1$. Hence, $P_4 \sqsubseteq P_2$.

Minimal Number of Polynomials. Finally, we want to decide how many polynomials we need to check. According to the dependency relation defined above, we form a few clusters of polynomials so that all the polynomials present in a cluster depend on a single polynomial and then by checking that single polynomial, we can decide about all other polynomials in the cluster.

To form this cluster we consider a dependency graph $G = (V, E)$, where each vertex v_P in the vertex set V corresponds to a polynomial P and there is a directed edge from v_P to v_Q if and only if $P \sqsubseteq Q$. Then we choose a starting vertex v_P and try to construct a trail. It is clear that the order ($\sqsubseteq$) relation is transitive. So, for all the vertices v_Q that fall in the trail starting from v_P must satisfy $P \sqsubseteq Q$. Also, We have to find a trail of size as large as possible. The reason is that if the size of the trail is large, we can check a large number of polynomials at once. We use Depth First Search (DFS) from each vertex one by one for the task of finding a trail starting from that vertex.

Table 8. Trails from each vertex

Length	c
11	[4, 2, 3, 7, 11, 15, 6, 10, 14, 5, 13]
11	[8, 1, 3, 7, 11, 15, 5, 13, 9, 10, 14]
9	[12, 3, 7, 11, 15, 5, 13, 10, 14]
8	[1, 3, 7, 11, 15, 5, 13, 9]
8	[2, 3, 7, 11, 15, 6, 10, 14]
8	[6, 2, 3, 7, 11, 15, 10, 14]
8	[9, 1, 3, 7, 11, 15, 5, 13]
6	[5, 3, 7, 11, 15, 13]
6	[10, 3, 7, 11, 15, 14]
6	[13, 3, 7, 11, 15, 5]
6	[14, 3, 7, 11, 15, 10]
4	[3, 7, 11, 15]
4	[7, 3, 11, 15]
4	[11, 3, 7, 15]
4	[15, 3, 7, 11]

Table 9. Final trails of considerations

Starting	Trails
4	[4, 2, 3, 7, 11, 15, 6, 10, 14, 5, 13]
8	[8, 1, 9]
12	[12]

7.3   Application on the KNOT

The trails for the KNOT Sbox are given in Table 8 where the first element is the starting linear combination c. From Table 8 we can see that one of the maximum length trails can be formed from the polynomial P_4 (i.e., from the vertex v_{P_4}). First we remove all the vertices that are reachable from v_{P_4}, which are $\{v_{P_4}, v_{P_2}, v_{P_3}, v_{P_7}, v_{P_{11}}, v_{P_{15}}, v_{P_6}, v_{P_{10}}, v_{P_{14}}, v_{P_5}, v_{P_{13}}\}$ and then we move to the next cluster. As the next cluster starts with v_{P_8} and v_{P_8} does not belong to the previously removed cluster we can start a search from v_{P_8} and construct a cluster with remaining vertices. If v_{P_8} was already removed, just consider starting vertex of the next cluster on the list and so on. Finally, we have found the following trails given in Table 9. We note that this greedy approach may not be the most optimal sequence. However, determining the exact sequence seems to be an NP-complete problem. Furthermore, it seems that the greedy algorithm suffices.

According to this result first we need to check the following three polynomials:

$$y_2(x) = x_0 + x_2x_1 + x_1 + x_2 + x_3 + 1, \text{ linear combination for } 4 = (0, 1, 0, 0)$$
$$y_3(x) = x_1x_0 + x_1 + x_2 + x_3, \text{ linear combination for } 8 = (1, 0, 0, 0)$$
$$y_3(x) + y_2(x) = x_1x_0 + x_0 + x_2x_1 + 1, \text{ linear combination for } 12 = (1, 1, 0, 0)$$

If this set of polynomials are not even then we need not check further. Also, we can see that there are only 6 different monomials $\{x_0, x_1, x_2, x_3, x_0x_1, x_1x_2\}$ in all those three polynomials that we need to check. Among these 6, we start from x_0x_1 and x_1x_2 because none of the polynomials are even if these two are not even.

Let b^{r-1} be the input variables to the rth round Sbox S^{r-1} where $a^{r-1} \xrightarrow{\text{rotation}} b^{r-1}$. Let us take linear combination of the output of the first Sbox. Then to check x_0x_1 is even or not we set 1 to the positions $b_{0,0}^{r-1}$ and $b_{1,0}^{r-1}$ and to check x_1x_2 we set 1 to $b_{1,0}^{r-1}$ and $b_{2,0}^{r-1}$ as follows:

$$b^{r-1} = \begin{bmatrix} 1\,0\,0\cdots 0 \\ 1\,0\,0\cdots 0 \\ 0\,0\,0\cdots 0 \\ 0\,0\,0\cdots 0 \end{bmatrix} \text{ and } b^{r-1} = \begin{bmatrix} 0\,0\,0\cdots 0 \\ 1\,0\,0\cdots 0 \\ 1\,0\,0\cdots 0 \\ 0\,0\,0\cdots 0 \end{bmatrix}.$$

Finally, we solve the model in both cases with all possible input vectors $in_{(k,\ell)}$ of weight $b - 1$.

Result for the KNOT. For the KNOT-256 and KNOT-384, we searched for all initial vectors for all Sboxes after 17 rounds and we did not get any even monomial. This proves that we can not extend the integral distinguisher to 18 rounds by this method. In other words, the 18-round KNOT-256 and KNOT-384 have no integral distinguisher using a conventional division property. This follows from the fact that y_0, y_1, y_2, y_3 are also belong to the set of all linear combinations as we have $P_1 = y_0, P_2 = y_1, P_4 = y_2$ and $P_8 = y_3$. However, note that here for each column, we need to solve a 17-round SAT/CP model twice per Sbox, whereas in the usual method, we need to solve the 18-round model four times per Sbox. In other words, not only we proved a strong result about KNOT-256 and KNOT-384, we did so more efficiently. Our CP model takes 20 h for KNOT-256 and 50 h for KNOT-384 to complete this search, which is significantly more efficient compared to the usual method used in [31], which was terminated after several days.

Adding L_{in}. We also tried to add a linear layer L_{in} at the input. But we could not find any useful information for any versions of the KNOT and Ascon.

8   Conclusion

In this paper we provided several new distinguishers for the KNOT permutation and Ascon using the SAT and CP-based automatic tools. To model the division trail table of an Sbox we used the Quine-McCluskey method, which gives the minimal size CNF. We provided a compact algorithm to find the optimal distinguishers. Our model is much more efficient and accurate than the previous result on KNOT and Ascon. Finally, we provided a way to get the optimal number of linear combinations for extended integral attack and using this, we have shown that 18-round KNOT-256 and KNOT-384 have no integral distinguisher conventional division property.

Acknowledgements. The research described in this paper was supported in part by the Center for Cyber, Law, and Policy in conjunction with the Israel National Cyber Bureau in the Prime Minister's Office and by the Israeli Science Foundation through grants No. 880/18 and 3380/19. The authors were also supported by the Data Science Research Center (DSRC), University of Haifa.

References

1. Abdelkhalek, A., Sasaki, Y., Todo, Y., Tolba, M.F., Youssef, A.: MILP modeling for (large) S-boxes to optimize probability of differential characteristics. IACR Trans. Symmetric Cryptol. **2017**, 99–129 (2017)
2. Banik, S., Pandey, S.K., Peyrin, T., Sasaki, Yu., Sim, S.M., Todo, Y.: GIFT: a small present. In: Fischer, W., Homma, N. (eds.) CHES 2017. LNCS, vol. 10529, pp. 321–345. Springer, Cham (2017). https://doi.org/10.1007/978-3-319-66787-4_16
3. Barrett, C., Tinelli, C.: CVC3. In: Damm, W., Hermanns, H. (eds.) CAV 2007. LNCS, vol. 4590, pp. 298–302. Springer, Heidelberg (2007). https://doi.org/10.1007/978-3-540-73368-3_34
4. Bogdanov, A., et al.: PRESENT: an ultra-lightweight block cipher. In: Paillier, P., Verbauwhede, I. (eds.) CHES 2007. LNCS, vol. 4727, pp. 450–466. Springer, Heidelberg (2007). https://doi.org/10.1007/978-3-540-74735-2_31
5. Chu, G.: Improving combinatorial optimization: extended abstract. In: Proceedings of the Twenty-Third International Joint Conference on Artificial Intelligence, pp. 3116–3120. IJCAI 2013. AAAI Press (2013)
6. Cook, S.A.: The complexity of theorem-proving procedures. In: Proceedings of STOC 1971, pp. 151–158. ACM, New York, USA (1971)
7. Daemen, J., Knudsen, L., Rijmen, V.: The block cipher Square. In: Biham, E. (ed.) FSE 1997. LNCS, vol. 1267, pp. 149–165. Springer, Heidelberg (1997). https://doi.org/10.1007/BFb0052343

8. Daemen, J., Rijmen, V.: AES and the wide trail design strategy. In: Knudsen, L.R. (ed.) EUROCRYPT 2002. LNCS, vol. 2332, pp. 108–109. Springer, Heidelberg (2002). https://doi.org/10.1007/3-540-46035-7_7

9. Derbez, P., Fouque, P.A.: Increasing precision of division property. IACR Cryptol. ePrint Arch. **2021**, 22 (2020)

10. Dobraunig, C., Eichlseder, M., Mendel, F., Schläffer, M.: ASCON v1.2 - lightweight authenticated encryption and hashing. J. Cryptol. **34**(3), 1–42 (2020). https://doi.org/10.1007/s00145-021-09398-9

11. Eskandari, Z., Kidmose, A., Kölbl, S., Tiessen, T.: Finding integral distinguishers with ease. In: Cid, C., Jacobson Jr., M. (eds.) SAC 2018. LNCS, vol. 11349, pp. 115–138. Springer, Cham (2019). https://doi.org/10.1007/978-3-030-10970-7_6

12. Ferguson, N., et al.: Improved cryptanalysis of Rijndael. In: Goos, G., Hartmanis, J., van Leeuwen, J., Schneier, B. (eds.) FSE 2000. LNCS, vol. 1978, pp. 213–230. Springer, Heidelberg (2001). https://doi.org/10.1007/3-540-44706-7_15

13. Ganesh, V., Dill, D.L.: A decision procedure for bit-vectors and arrays. In: Damm, W., Hermanns, H. (eds.) CAV 2007. LNCS, vol. 4590, pp. 519–531. Springer, Heidelberg (2007). https://doi.org/10.1007/978-3-540-73368-3_52

14. Hu, K., Wang, Q., Wang, M.: Finding bit-based division property for ciphers with complex linear layers. IACR Trans. Symmetric Cryptol. **2020**(1), 396–424 (2020)

15. Knudsen, L., Wagner, D.: Integral cryptanalysis. In: Daemen, J., Rijmen, V. (eds.) FSE 2002. LNCS, vol. 2365, pp. 112–127. Springer, Heidelberg (2002). https://doi.org/10.1007/3-540-45661-9_9

16. Lambin, B., Derbez, P., Fouque, P.-A.: Linearly equivalent S-boxes and the division property. Des. Codes Cryptogr. **88**(10), 2207–2231 (2020). https://doi.org/10.1007/s10623-020-00773-4

17. Li, Y., Wu, W., Zhang, L.: Improved integral attacks on reduced-round CLEFIA block cipher. In: Jung, S., Yung, M. (eds.) WISA 2011. LNCS, vol. 7115, pp. 28–39. Springer, Heidelberg (2012). https://doi.org/10.1007/978-3-642-27890-7_3

18. Lucks, S.: The saturation attack — A bait for Twofish. In: Matsui, M. (ed.) FSE 2001. LNCS, vol. 2355, pp. 1–15. Springer, Heidelberg (2002). https://doi.org/10.1007/3-540-45473-X_1

19. McCluskey, E.J.: Minimization of boolean functions. Bell Syst. Tech. J. **35**(6), 1417–1444 (1956)

20. Nethercote, N., Stuckey, P.J., Becket, R., Brand, S., Duck, G.J., Tack, G.: MiniZinc: towards a standard CP modelling language. In: Bessière, C. (ed.) CP 2007. LNCS, vol. 4741, pp. 529–543. Springer, Heidelberg (2007). https://doi.org/10.1007/978-3-540-74970-7_38

21. Quine, W.V.: The problem of simplifying truth functions. Am. Math. Monthly **59**(8), 521–531 (1952). http://www.jstor.org/stable/2308219

22. Soos, M., Nohl, K., Castelluccia, C.: Extending SAT solvers to cryptographic problems. In: Kullmann, O. (ed.) SAT 2009. LNCS, vol. 5584, pp. 244–257. Springer, Heidelberg (2009). https://doi.org/10.1007/978-3-642-02777-2_24

23. Sun, L., Wang, W., Liu, R., Wang, M.: MILP-aided bit-based division property for ARX ciphers. Sci. China Inf. Sci. **61**(11), 1–3 (2018)

24. Sun, L., Wang, W., Wang, M.: Automatic search of bit-based division property for ARX ciphers and word-based division property. In: Takagi, T., Peyrin, T. (eds.) ASIACRYPT 2017. LNCS, vol. 10624, pp. 128–157. Springer, Cham (2017). https://doi.org/10.1007/978-3-319-70694-8_5

25. Sun, L., Wang, W., Wang, M.: MILP-aided bit-based division property for primitives with non-bit-permutation linear layers. IET Inf. Secur. **14**(1), 12–20 (2019)

26. Sun, S., et al.: Analysis of AES, skinny, and others with constraint programming. IACR Trans. Symmetric Cryptol. **2017**(1), 281–306 (2017)
27. National Institute of Standards and Technology: Report on Lightweight Cryptography: NiSTIR 8114. CreateSpace Independent Publishing Platform (2017)
28. Todo, Y.: Structural evaluation by generalized integral property. In: Oswald, E., Fischlin, M. (eds.) EUROCRYPT 2015. LNCS, vol. 9056, pp. 287–314. Springer, Heidelberg (2015). https://doi.org/10.1007/978-3-662-46800-5_12
29. Todo, Y.: Integral cryptanalysis on full MISTY1. J. Cryptol. **30**, 920–959 (2016)
30. Todo, Y., Morii, M.: Bit-Based division property and application to SIMON family. In: Peyrin, T. (ed.) FSE 2016. LNCS, vol. 9783, pp. 357–377. Springer, Heidelberg (2016). https://doi.org/10.1007/978-3-662-52993-5_18
31. Zhang, W., et al.: KNOT: algorithm specifications and supporting document. IACR Cryptol. ePrint Arch. (2020)
32. Wang, Q., Grassi, L., Rechberger, C.: Zero-Sum partitions of PHOTON permutations. In: Smart, N.P. (ed.) CT-RSA 2018. LNCS, vol. 10808, pp. 279–299. Springer, Cham (2018). https://doi.org/10.1007/978-3-319-76953-0_15
33. Wu, W., Zhang, L.: LBlock: a lightweight block cipher. In: Lopez, J., Tsudik, G. (eds.) ACNS 2011. LNCS, vol. 6715, pp. 327–344. Springer, Heidelberg (2011). https://doi.org/10.1007/978-3-642-21554-4_19
34. Xiang, Z., Zhang, W., Bao, Z., Lin, D.: Applying MILP method to searching integral distinguishers based on division property for 6 lightweight block ciphers. In: Cheon, J.H., Takagi, T. (eds.) ASIACRYPT 2016. LNCS, vol. 10031, pp. 648–678. Springer, Heidelberg (2016). https://doi.org/10.1007/978-3-662-53887-6_24
35. Z'aba, M.R., Raddum, H., Henricksen, M., Dawson, E.: Bit-Pattern based integral attack. In: Nyberg, K. (ed.) FSE 2008. LNCS, vol. 5086, pp. 363–381. Springer, Heidelberg (2008). https://doi.org/10.1007/978-3-540-71039-4_23
36. Zhang, W.T., Bao, Z.Z., Lin, D.D., Rijmen, V., Yang, B.H., Verbauwhede, I.: Sci. China Inf. Sci. **58**(12), 1–15 (2015). https://doi.org/10.1007/s11432-015-5459-7

TEDT2 – Highly Secure Leakage-Resilient TBC-Based Authenticated Encryption

Eik List[(✉)]

Bauhaus-Universität Weimar, Weimar, Germany
eik.list@uni-weimar.de

Abstract. Leakage-resilient authenticated encryption (AE) schemes received considerable attention during the previous decade. Two core security models of bounded and unbounded leakage have evolved, where the latter has been motivated in a very detailed and practice-oriented manner. In that setting, designers often build schemes based on (tweakable) block ciphers due to the small state size, such as the recent two-pass AE scheme TEDT from TCHES 1/2020. TEDT is interesting due to its high security guarantees of $O(n-\log(n^2))$-bit integrity under leakage and similar AE security in the black-box setting. Though, a detail limited it to provide only $n/2$-bit privacy under leakage.

In this work, we extend TEDT to TEDT2 in three aspects with the help of a tweakable block cipher with a $3n$-bit tweakey: we (1) adopt the idea from the design team of Romulus of replacing TEDT's previous internal hash function with Naito's MDPH, (2) move the nonce from the hash to the tag-generation function both for more efficiency, and (3) strengthen the security of the encryption to obtain beyond-birthday-bound security also under leakage.

Keywords: Symmetric-key cryptography · Authenticated encryption · Provable security · Leakage resilience

1 Introduction

1.1 Leakage-Resilient Authenticated Encryption

Authenticated encryption (AE) has been established as an invaluable cryptographic primitive [3,42] for various practical use cases that need the protection of both authenticity and the confidentiality of transmitted data. While the usual security notions treat the primitives as black boxes to the adversary, side channels [32,33] are a highly important threat to many systems. The protection of primitives against side-channel leakage – be it due to timing, memory accesses, power consumption, induced faults, or electromagnetic radiation – is usually left to the implementors and engineers. On a hardware level, the signal can be blurred by noise or special circuits, whereas on the implementation level, countermeasures include masking (i.e., secret sharing) [11,22] or shuffling [46]. Since side-channel protection is often inhibitive in terms of area, additional power consumption,

© Springer Nature Switzerland AG 2021
P. Longa and C. Ràfols (Eds.): LATINCRYPT 2021, LNCS 12912, pp. 275–295, 2021.
https://doi.org/10.1007/978-3-030-88238-9_14

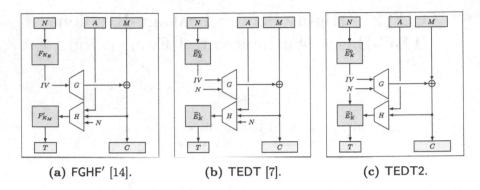

(a) FGHF' [14].   (b) TEDT [7].   (c) TEDT2.

Fig. 1. High-level comparison on existing two–pass designs and our proposal.

and efficiency, a line of research has been devoted to developing leakage-resilient schemes. The interested reader can find in-depth surveys in [6,31].

Schools of Thought. The literature on confidentiality with leakage could be categorized into three approaches: (1) "only computation leaks" (OCL) [36] with bounded leakage [21], (2) absence of oracles and hard-to-invert leakage [47], and (3) efficient simulatability of leakage [45]. The latter is still unsolved [34].

The former direction started with the framework by Barwell et al. [2] that contained notions capturing arbitrary non-adaptive leakage in the bounded-leakage setting. The approach has found widespread adoption, e.g. in [14,17,19]. Characteristic is that security is lacking while leakage occurs, but is guaranteed again once the leakage ends. Thus, schemes can provide nonce-misuse robustness in the sense of [43]. The second school of thought can be located by the group around Standaert. The school considers unbounded leakage with leveled implementations [40]. It has evolved stepwise with early focus on integrity [40], integrity with decryption leakage [9], and the composition with confidentiality [8], along to attempts to include misuse-resilience [7,25], to the recent summary at CRYPTO'20 [6]. In contrast to the bounded-leakage school, their notions cannot provide nonce-misuse resistance, but only resilience in the sense of [1].

Recent Schemes. The portfolio of leakage-resilient AE schemes has grown significantly recently, with focus on permutation-based designs like ISAP [15,16] and the generic Sponge and Duplex [14,17] in the OCL line of research. In contrast, the unbounded-leakage direction preferred leveled implementations with a few calls to a strongly protected primitive and the majority of computations to a more efficient, less protected primitive. Proposals using this approach often employed only a (tweakable) block cipher [7,25], but several permutation-based designs [5,10,26] with few calls to a protected block cipher followed.

Leveled block-cipher-based constructions such as TEDT are interesting for potentially higher efficiency compared to the permutation-based schemes; firstly, the latter employ a very small rate for the nonce absorption in the key-derivation phase [14,15]; secondly, tweakable block ciphers (TBCs) can be realized in a more lightweight manner compared to permutations, as shown by Naito et al.

[38]. Since a high-level view can help identify concepts, we will look briefly at FGHF′ and TEDT, which can be compared well, in the following (Table 1).

Table 1. Comparison between existing (T)BC-based leakage-resilient AE schemes and our proposal. Security in bits, #primitive calls for messages of at most m n-bit blocks and at most a-block associated data. • = see CCAmL2, – = not available, (x) = probably x-bit security, but no proof is known, $^{(*)}$ = keyed hashing, $^{(†)}$ = can be one call less depending on the hash-input length.

Scheme	Black-box bit Security			Leakage bit Security			#Primitive calls			
	CCA	CI	MR	CCAmL1	CCAmL2	CIML2	Enc	Hash	KDF	TGF
1 Pass										
TET [7]	(n)	(n)	–	$(n/2)$	–	(n)	$2m$	$2a$	1	1
AET-LR [23]	n	$n/2$	–	n	–	$(n/2)$	m	$a/2$ $^{(*)}$	1	1
2 Pass										
Romulus-LR-TEDT [29]	$n-\log(n^2)$	$n-\log(n^2)$	–	•	$n/2$	$n-\log(n^2)$	$2m$	$a+m+3^{(†)}$	1	1
TEDT [7]	$n-\log(n^2)$	$n-\log(n^2)$	–	•	$n/2$	$n-\log(n^2)$	$2m$	$2a+2m+4$	1	1
TEDT2 [This work]	$n-\log(n)$	$n-\log(n)$	–	•	$n-\log(n)$	$n-\log(n)$	$2m$	$a+m+2^{(†)}$	2	1
3 Pass										
FEMALE [25]	$n/2$	$n/2$	$n/2$	•	$n/2$	$n/2$	$4m$	$2a+2m+8$	2	1

Based on the analysis of Encrypt-then-MAC under leakage by [2], Degabriele et al. [14] suggested FGHF′, where the acronym reflects the structure. The result of a key-derivation function F takes the nonce and produces an IV for a pseudorandom stream generator G. H hashes the resulting ciphertext, nonce, and associated data and forwards the output to a keyed function F' to generate the tag. The high-level structure is similar in other designs, e.g., ISAP or TEDT. The latter, which stands for Tweakable Encrypt-Digest-and-Tag is built from a TBC and comes with strong security guarantees, a single small-size primitive, and a single key. It has only a few structural differences compared to FGHF′: TEDT employs a TBC, an invertible tag-generation function for integrity under decryption leakage, and uses the nonce as IV to G, as illustrated in Fig. 1.

1.2 Research Questions

TEDT is interesting for its efficiency and the leveled approach that spares the expensive protections for most primitive calls. However, the low-level view in the analysis by Guo et al. [25] may be hard to have a clear view of all details. We can identify three aspects of improvements, where we could use (1) a more efficient hash function, (2) the nonce in the finalization for more efficient authentication, and (3) a $2n$-bit tweakey in the encryption for higher security under leakage.

Firstly, TEDT employed Hirose's compression function with Merkle-Dåmgard strengthening [27] for hashing. Compared to TEDT, we can use Naito's proposal MDPH[$\tilde{\pi}$] from [37] that had also been suggested for Romulus-LR-TEDT [29] and AET-LR [23]. Like Romulus-LR-TEDT, we also suggest using a $3n$-bit TBC.

Thus, our proposal can process a $2n$-bit message block with each iteration of two primitive calls. Thus, the hash-function rate increases from $1/2$ to 1.

Secondly, both FGHF′ and TEDT process all inputs to the public hash function H nonce, associated data, and ciphertext. A similar approach is followed in the instantiation of FGHF′ and in ISAP, which use the nonce as an initialization vector. Using a TBC with $3n$-bit tweakey, we can spare to process the nonce during hashing and use it in the tag-generation function (TGF) instead.

Thirdly, TEDT uses two primitive calls per message block: one to derive a new key for the subsequent block and one to produce a keystream block that is added to the current message block. The resulting rate-$1/2$ encryption provided $O(n - \log(n))$-bit security in the single-user black-box setting, but only $n/2$-bit security under leakage due to collisions and a hybrid argument. We generalize the encryption to use a larger tweak efficiently. Using a TBC based on the TWEAKEY framework by Jean et al. [30], we obtain a longer tweakey for higher security, whose encryption need two primitive calls for the tweakey update per message block. To compensate for the additional call, we use the tweakey for processing two message blocks. We obtain a more secure rate-$1/2$ construction that provides $O(n - \log(n))$-bit security in both the black-box setting and under leakage, where we adopt from TEDT the assumption that the distinguishing advantage for the XORs of the plain/ciphertexts with the PRG keystream does not endanger the security.

Outline. The remainder of this work is structured as follows: After Sect. 2 gives general preliminaries, Sect. 3 provides a design rationale of our improvements before Sect. 4 describes our proposal. Section 5 explains our used security model before Sects. 6 and 7 summarize the results of the security analysis. Section 8 concludes this work. Due to space limitations, the analysis details are provided in a full version that will be published alongside this work.

2   Preliminaries

General Notations. We use uppercase characters for variables and functions, lowercase characters for indices, calligraphic characters $(\mathcal{X}, \mathcal{Y}, \ldots)$ for sets and spaces, and bold characters $(\mathbf{X}, \mathbf{Y}, \ldots)$ for vectors, matrices, and adversaries. For a non-negative integer x, we define $[x] =^{\text{def}} \{1, \ldots, x\}$ and $[0..x] =^{\text{def}} \{0, \ldots, x\}$. $\mathbb{F}_q^n$ denotes the n-dimensional extension of the field with characteristic q, where the elements of $\mathbb{F}_2^n$ can be represented as bit strings and ε is the empty string. For a list $\mathbf{L}$, we define $[]$ as the empty list and $\mathbf{L} \xleftarrow{\cup} x$ denotes appending an element x to $\mathbf{L}$. Given sets $\mathcal{X}$ and $\mathcal{Y}$, we define $\mathsf{Func}(\mathcal{X}, \mathcal{Y})$ for the set of all functions $F : \mathcal{X} \to \mathcal{Y}$, $\widetilde{\mathsf{Perm}}(\mathcal{T}, \mathcal{X})$ for the set of all tweakable permutations over $\mathcal{X}$, and $\mathsf{TBC}(\mathcal{K}, \mathcal{T}, \mathcal{X})$ for the sets of all tweakable block ciphers with key space $\mathcal{K}$ and tweak space $\mathcal{T}$ over $\mathcal{X}$. We define $X_1, X_2, \ldots \leftarrow \mathcal{X}$ for random uniform sampling $X_1, X_2, \ldots$, independently from each other and other samplings from $\mathcal{X}$. Furthermore, we define n-bit strings for arbitrary n as $X = (X_{n-1}, \ldots X_0)$ where X_i is the i-th least significant bit. We denote by $\mathrm{MSB}_c(X)$ and $\mathrm{LSB}_c(X)$ the c least significant bits of X.

Distinguishers. An adversary is a computationally unbounded algorithm that shall win a security game against a challenger. In this work, we focus on adversaries that are distinguishers. A distinguisher $\mathbf{A}$ is given access to one of two worlds and shall output a decision bit at the end of its interaction that shall denote which setting it interacted with. The challenger chooses one of the worlds by a fair coin toss at the start and provides $\mathbf{A}$ with access to either the real world $\mathcal{O}^1$ and an ideal world $\mathcal{O}^0$ with identical interfaces. We define

$$\underset{\mathbf{A}}{\Delta}(\underbrace{O_1^1, \dots, O_r^1}_{\mathcal{O}^1}; \underbrace{O_1^0, \dots, O_r^0}_{\mathcal{O}^0})(\mathbf{A}) \overset{\text{def}}{=} \left| \Pr\left[\mathbf{A}^{O_1^1, \dots, O_r^1} \Rightarrow 1\right] - \Pr\left[\mathbf{A}^{O_1^0, \dots, O_r^0} \Rightarrow 1\right] \right|,$$

where the probabilities are over the coins in the game, if any. Later, we will use labeled oracles, such as $\Delta_{\mathbf{A}}(\mathcal{E}_K, \mathcal{D}_K; \$, \bot)$, where we use $\bot$ as a function that always outputs the $\bot$ symbol as the indicator for a failed decryption: $\bot(X) = \bot$ for all X. We will use O_j to mean the j-th oracle in the sequence in each world, e.g., O_1 will refer to $\mathcal{E}_K$ or $\$$. We consider computationally unbounded distinguishers whose complexities are measured only by the number of queries to their oracles. Moreover, we assume that adversaries do not ask duplicate queries or queries to which they already know the answer. W.l.o.g., we focus on deterministic distinguishers since for any probabilistic distinguisher, there exists a deterministic one with at least the same success probability, cf. [18].

Notion Conventions. For a notion X, we write $\mathbf{Adv}_\Pi^X(\mathbf{A})$ for the advantage of $\mathbf{A}$ on some scheme Π. We define that $\mathbf{A}$ is a $(r_1, \dots, r_k)$-X-adversary for a notion X if $\mathbf{A}$ uses at most the resources $r_1, \dots, r_k$ (certain types of queries or blocks). We write $\mathbf{Adv}_\Pi^X(r_1, \dots, r_k) \overset{\text{def}}{=} \max_{\mathbf{A}} \left\{ \mathbf{Adv}_\Pi^X(\mathbf{A}) \right\}$ for the maximum advantage over all $(r_1, \dots, r_k)$-X-adversaries $\mathbf{A}$ on Π.

Query Restrictions. The security models we consider contain query restrictions that are necessary to prevent trivial wins of the adversary. We use $O_i \not\hookrightarrow O_j$ to say that $\mathbf{A}$ must not ask the result of an earlier query to O_i in a later query to O_j. We write $O_{i,N} \not\hookrightarrow O_{j,N}$ to indicate that $\mathbf{A}$ must not ask a query with a nonce N to $O_{j,N}$ if N was used in an earlier query to O_i. For sets of oracles $\mathcal{S}_i$, $\mathcal{S}_j$, we write $\mathcal{S}_i \not\hookrightarrow \mathcal{S}_j$ for $O_i \not\hookrightarrow O_j$ for each combination of $O_i, O_j \in \mathcal{S}_i \times \mathcal{S}_j$. For example, $O_1 \not\hookrightarrow \{O_1, O_2\}$ means that a result from O_1 must not be used as input to O_1 or O_2. Similarly, we write $\mathcal{S}_i \not\succ \mathcal{S}_j$ that a query to any oracle in $\mathcal{S}_j$ must not have occured earlier to any oracle in $\mathcal{S}_i$. Finally, we denote as $O_i \uparrow O_j$ that O_j accepts only those queries that have been used earlier as queries to O_i. This will be useful for models with several leaking oracles that allow $\mathbf{A}$ to collect additional leakage traces for earlier queries.

Nonce-Based Authenticated Encryption. Let $\mathcal{K}, \mathcal{N}, \mathcal{A}, \mathcal{M}, \mathcal{C}, \mathcal{T}$ be non-empty sets or spaces for keys, nonces, associated data, messages, ciphertexts, and tags, respectively. Following [39], a nonce-based AE (nAE) scheme consists of a pair of deterministic algorithms $\mathcal{E} : \mathcal{K} \times \mathcal{N} \times \mathcal{A} \times \mathcal{M} \to \mathcal{C} \times \mathcal{T}$ and $\mathcal{D} : \mathcal{K} \times \mathcal{N} \times \mathcal{A} \times \mathcal{C} \times \mathcal{T} \to \mathcal{M} \cup \{\bot\}$ for encryption and decryption, respectively. We assume correctness and tidiness: For all $K, N, A, M \in \mathcal{K} \times \mathcal{N} \times \mathcal{A} \times \mathcal{M}$, it holds

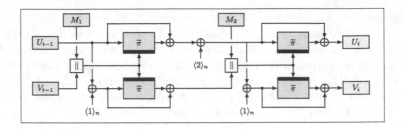

Fig. 2. Naito's hash function MDPH[$\tilde{\pi}$] [37], based on the double-block-length compression function [27] and the MDP mode [28].

Table 2. Number of primitive calls of $\tilde{\pi} \in \mathrm{TBC}(\mathbb{F}_2^n, \mathbb{F}_2^t, \mathbb{F}_2^n)$ in the hash functions. a and m denote the number of n-bit message blocks after padding each.

Scheme	Hash	MAC	$(a+m) \bmod 2$		
			t	0	1
TEDT [7]	Hirose [27]	HaT	n	$2a + 2m + 4$	
TEDT	Hirose [27]	HaT	$2n$	$a + m + 4$	$a + m + 5$
Romulus-LR-TEDT [29]	MDPH [28,37]	HaT	$2n$	$a + m + 2$	$a + m + 3$
TEDT2 [This work]	MDPH [28,37]	NHaT	$2n$	$a + m + 2$	$a + m + 1$

that $\mathcal{D}_K^{N,A}(\mathcal{E}_K^{N,A}(M)) = M$, and for all $(K,N,A,C,T) \in \mathcal{K} \times \mathcal{N} \times \mathcal{A} \times \mathcal{C} \times \mathcal{T}$ where $\exists M \in \mathcal{M}$ s.t. $\mathcal{E}_K^{N,A}(M) = (C,T)$, it holds that $\mathcal{E}_K^{N,A}(\mathcal{D}_K^{N,A}(C,T)) = (C,T)$.

3 Design Rationale

TEDT. From a high-level perspective, TEDT encrypts a message M as

$$IV \leftarrow \tilde{E}_K(N), \ C \leftarrow G[\tilde{E}](IV,N) \oplus M, \ (U,V) \leftarrow H[\tilde{E}](N,A,C), \ T \leftarrow \tilde{E}_K^V(U)$$

under a secret key K and a nonce N. G and H are based on the same TBC $\tilde{E} \in \mathrm{TBC}(\mathbb{F}_2^n, \mathbb{F}_2^n, \mathbb{F}_2^n)$, where G is a variant of the Bellare-Yee rekeying PRG [4]. In contrast to FGHF', TEDT uses an invertible tag-generation function F' inspired by [9]: instead of computing a leaking tag for a decryption query, the scheme inverts $F'^{-1}(T)$ and compares the output with the hash of nonce, associated data, and ciphertext. Since FGHF' and other permutation-based schemes output only a fraction of the state as tag, they are usually not efficiently invertible.

Reducing the Hash Function. TEDT2 employs three ways for more efficient hashing compared to TEDT. It adopts the use of a TBC with $3n$-bit tweakey from AET-LR [23] and Romulus-LR-TEDT [29], processing $2n$ bits of message material by each hash-function iteration with two calls, saving half of the primitive calls. Moreover, it adopts "Merkle-Dåmgard with permutation", MDPH [28]. In [37],

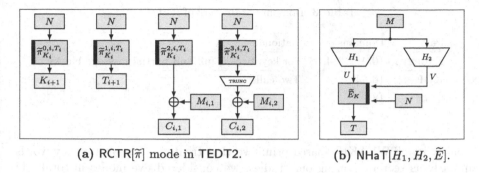

(a) RCTR[$\widetilde{\pi}$] mode in TEDT2.   (b) NHaT[$H_1, H_2, \widetilde{E}$].

Fig. 3. Encryption (left) and tag-generation function (right) of TEDT2.

Naito showed its indifferentiability for up to $O(2^n/n)$ queries when instantiated with the compression function from [27]. The construction is illustrated for two blocks in Fig. 2. Compared to [27] with Merkle-Dåmgard strengthening (MDS) [13,35], MDPH[$\widetilde{\pi}$] spares a compression-function call and allows smaller key-tweak inputs than Hirose's compression function with MDS [27]. Finally, TEDT2 need not hash the nonce. If the number of n-bit blocks of the padded hash-function input is even, TEDT2 saves an iteration (i.e., two calls) for messages of random length on average, which is detailed in Table 2.

Strengthening the Authentication and Hashing More Efficiently. Unkeyed hashing avoids the need for strong leakage protection. Though, the absence of a key allows an offline adversary to evaluate the hash function separately. For authentication, TEDT employed a variant of Cogliati et al.'s MAC Hash-as-Tweak (HaT) [12], which provides n-bit security independent of nonces, but with unkeyed hashing. Given an $n + t$-bit hash, it uses the n-bit part as state and the t-bit part as the tweak in a tweakable block cipher to generate the tag. Since we have a TBC with an $(n + t)$-bit tweak, we can employ the nonce in the finalization. We call the resulting MAC Nonce-and-Hash-as Tweak (NHaT).

The Encryption in TEDT. One iteration of the PRG G in TEDT computes $K_{i+1} = \widetilde{\pi}_{K_i}^{PK}(N \parallel \langle i \rangle_{\lfloor n/4 \rfloor - 1} \parallel 0)$ and $C_i = \widetilde{\pi}_{K_i}^{PK}(N \parallel \langle i \rangle_{\lfloor n/4 \rfloor - 1} \parallel 1)$, where PK is a user-dependent public constant. G provides beyond-birthday-bound security in the black-box setting [7], but the bound is tight under leakage using a hybrid argument of the form $\sigma \cdot \mathbf{Adv}_{F[\widetilde{\pi}]}^{\mathsf{LUP\text{-}2}}(p, \sigma)$, where $F[\widetilde{\pi}]$ represents one iteration of the PRG, σ the total number of blocks by the adversary and p the number of leakage measures per iteration. This is the bottleneck of TEDT due to the n-bit key size since $\mathbf{Adv}_{F[\widetilde{\pi}]}^{\mathsf{LUP\text{-}2}}(p, \sigma) \in O(\sigma/2^n)$. Over all σ blocks of the adversary, the term leads to a birthday bound of $O(\sigma^2/2^n)$.

Modes. Our aim for a mode was to obtain n-bit security under leakage. We assume an ephemeral-key scheme with (1) n-bit CPA security under nonce-respecting adversaries and leakage and (2) unpredictability of the iteration in $O(\sigma/2^{2n})$ to allow the use of a hybrid argument in the CCA analysis, and (3) a rate of at least $1/2$ comparable with G in TEDT. For security, we suggest a $2n$-bit

Table 3. Domain parameters of TEDT2.

Part	Domains	Rationale
ENCRYPT	$\{0,1,2,3,4,5\}$	For key, tweak, full and partial message blocks
KDF	$\{6,7\}$	Two calls
TGF	$\{8\}$	

tweakey in a TWEAKEY-based primitive that treats both n-bit tweakey words similarly as secrets. During our studies, we considered five modes in total: (1) Generalized TET [7] (GTET), (2) Generalized FEMALE [24] (GFBE), (3) Rekeying counter mode (RCTR), (4) Rekeying OCB (ROCB), and (5) Rekeying OTR (ROTR). In the full version of this work, we study them in more detail. For TEDT2, we opted for the RCTR, which is illustrated for $r = 2$ message blocks per iteration in Fig. 3a. Thus, an iteration needs two calls the primitive to derive the subsequent tweakey (K_{i+1}, T_{i+1}) from the previous $2n$-bit tweakey (K_i, T_i). To compensate the additional primitive call without lowering the rate, we use the tweakey for two primitive calls to derive $(C_{i,1}, C_{i,2})$. While this provides a side-channel adversary with six instead of three traces, it must recover a $2n$-bit tweakey compared to TEDT. While GTET and GFBE have a higher rate of $r/(r+1)$, RCTR has the advantage of being a PRG, which simplifies the decryption and is a direct extension of the PRG in TEDT.

The tweakey could be expanded further to $3n$ or $4n$ bits, etc. given a primitive with a larger tweak at the cost of increased state size. Such primitives have been announced by Peyrin [41] for more efficient hashing. Such a primitive will be slightly slower for encryption, but more efficient if the rate can be increased further. Though, this should be considered in detail under the concrete side-channel analysis, which cannot be addressed satisfactorily in the present work.

4   Definition of TEDT2

Primitive and Domains. We instantiate TEDT2 with a tweakable block cipher $\widetilde{E} \in \mathsf{TBC}(\mathbb{F}_2^n, \mathbb{F}_2^{2n}, \mathbb{F}_2^n)$. Concretely, we suggest Skinny-64-192, Skinny-128-384, or Deoxys-BC-128-384. We assume a TWEAKEY-based block cipher where key and tweak words are treated (almost) equivalently and in a generalizable manner. The tweak allows us to have a single primitive for all occasions using domains for the different purposes of key derivation, encryption, hashing, and tag generation. We assume that key derivation and tag generation use strongly protected implementations of $\widetilde{E}$, e.g. against simple (SPA) and differential-power analysis (DPA), and all other calls to $\widetilde{E}$ use a less protected implementation, e.g. against only SPA (cf. [6]).

Sets and Primitive. Define positive integers $k = \tau = n$, $d = 4$, and $\nu = n - d$. Let $\mathcal{K} = \mathbb{F}_2^k$, $\mathcal{N} = \mathbb{F}_2^\nu$, $\mathcal{A} = \mathbb{F}_2^{\leq n \cdot a_{max}}$, $\mathcal{M} = \mathcal{C} = \mathbb{F}_2^{\leq n \cdot m_{max}}$, and $\mathcal{T} = \mathbb{F}_2^\tau$ be spaces for keys, nonces, associated data, messages, ciphertexts, and authentication tags,

Algorithm 1. Definition of TEDT2.

11: **function** $\mathcal{E}[\widetilde{E}]_K^{N,A}(M)$
12:     $K_E \leftarrow \text{KDF}[\widetilde{E}]_K(N)$
13:     $C \leftarrow \text{ENCRYPT}[\widetilde{E}]_{K_E}(M)$
14:     $T \leftarrow \text{TGF}[\widetilde{E}]_K(N,A,C)$
15:     **return** (C,T)

16: **function** $\text{KDF}[\widetilde{E}]_K(N)$
17:     **return** $\widetilde{E}_K^{6,0,0}(N), \widetilde{E}_K^{7,0,0}(N)$

20: **function** $\text{TGF}[\widetilde{E}]_K(N,A,C)$
21:     $X \leftarrow \text{CONCAT}_n(A,C)$
22:     $(U,V) \leftarrow \text{HASH}[\widetilde{E}](X)$
23:     **return** $\widetilde{E}_K^{8,N,V}(U)$

25: **function** $\text{ENCRYPT}[\widetilde{E}]_K^N(M)$
26:     $(K_1,T_1) \leftarrow K$
27:     $(M_1,\ldots,M_m) \xleftarrow{2n} M$
28:     **for** $i \leftarrow 1..m-1$ **do**
29:         $K_{i+1} \leftarrow \widetilde{E}_{K_i}^{0,i,T_i}(N)$
30:         $T_{i+1} \leftarrow \widetilde{E}_{K_i}^{1,i,T_i}(N)$
31:         $S_i \leftarrow \widetilde{E}_{K_i}^{2,i,T_i}(N) \parallel \widetilde{E}_{K_i}^{3,i,T_i}(N)$
32:         $C_i \leftarrow S_i \oplus M_i$
33:     $(d_1,d_2) \leftarrow \text{GETDOMAINFORM}(|M_m|)$
34:     $S_m \leftarrow \widetilde{E}_{K_m}^{d_1,m,T_m}(N) \parallel \widetilde{E}_{K_m}^{d_2,m,T_m}(N)$
35:     $C_m \leftarrow \text{TRUNC}_{|M_m|}(S_m) \oplus M_m$
36:     **return** $(C_1 \parallel \cdots \parallel C_m)$

41: **function** $\text{CONCAT}_n(X,Y)$
42:     $X^* \leftarrow \text{PADZEROES}_n(X)$
43:     $Y^* \leftarrow \text{PADZEROES}_n(Y)$
44:     $L \leftarrow \langle|X|\rangle_{n/2} \parallel \langle|Y|\rangle_{n/2}$

46: **function** $\text{PADZEROES}_x(X)$
47:     $\ell \leftarrow |X| \bmod x$
48:     **if** $\ell \equiv 0$ **then return** X
49:     **return** $X \parallel 0^{x-\ell}$

51: **function** $\mathcal{D}[\widetilde{E}]_K(N,A,C,T)$
52:     $K_E \leftarrow \text{KDF}[\widetilde{E}]_K(N)$
53:     **if** $\text{VERIFY}[\widetilde{E}]_K(N,A,C,T)$ **then**
54:         **return** $\text{DECRYPT}[\widetilde{E}]_{K_E}^N(C)$
55:     **return** $\perp$

56: **function** $\text{VERIFY}[\widetilde{E}]_K(N,A,C,T)$
57:     $X \leftarrow \text{CONCAT}_n(A,C)$
58:     $(U,V) \leftarrow \text{HASH}[\widetilde{E}](X)$
59:     $U' \leftarrow \widetilde{D}_K^{8,N,V}(T)$
60:     **return** $U = U'$

61: **function** $\text{DECRYPT}[\widetilde{E}]_K^N(C)$
62:     **return** $\text{ENCRYPT}[\widetilde{E}]_K^N(C)$

66: **function** $\text{HASH}[\widetilde{E}](M)$
67:     $(M_{1,1}, M_{1,2}, \ldots, M_{m,1}, M_{m,2}) \xleftarrow{n} M$
68:     $(U_0,V_0) \leftarrow (0^n,0^n)$
69:     **for** $i \leftarrow 1..m$ **do**
70:         **if** $i = m$ **then** $U_{i-1} \leftarrow U_{i-1} \oplus \langle 2 \rangle$
71:         $K_i \leftarrow V_{i-1}$
72:         $T_i \leftarrow M_{i,1} \parallel M_{i,2}$
73:         $W_i \leftarrow U_{i-1} \oplus \langle 1 \rangle$
74:         $U_i \leftarrow \widetilde{E}_{K_i}^{T_i}(U_{i-1}) \oplus U_{i-1}$
75:         $V_i \leftarrow \widetilde{E}_{K_i}^{T_i}(W_i) \oplus W_i$
76:     **return** (U_m, V_m)

81: **function** $\text{TRUNC}_x(X)$
82:     **if** $|X| \leq x$ **then return** X
83:     **return** $\text{MSB}_x(X)$

86: **function** $\text{PAD}_x(X)$
87:     $\ell \leftarrow (|X| + 1) \bmod x$
88:     **if** $\ell \equiv 0$ **then return** $X \parallel 1$
89:     **return** $X \parallel 1 \parallel 0^{x-\ell}$

91: **function** $\text{GETDOMAINFORM}(\ell)$
92:     **if** $\ell = 2n$ **then return** $(2,3)$
93:     **else if** $n \leq \ell \wedge \ell < 2n$ **then return** $(2,5)$
94:     **else return** $(4,5)$

---

respectively. We define a domain space $\mathcal{D} = \mathbb{F}_2^d$ and a compound tweak space $\mathcal{T}_D = \mathcal{D} \times \mathcal{T}_1 \times \mathcal{T}_2 = \mathbb{F}_2^{2n}$, where $\mathcal{T}_1 = \mathbb{F}_2^{n-d}$ and $\mathcal{T}_2 = \mathbb{F}_2^n$. Thus, we define the nonce space as $\mathbb{F}_2^{n-d}$, to have d bits for the domain. We use the domains from Table 3 encoded as d-bit integers, e.g., $\langle 8 \rangle_d = 1000$. We will often use block indices, where we assume that they are encoded as $n - d$-bit integers, like domains. We define TEDT2 for at most $a_{\max} = 2^{n/2}$ n-bit blocks of associated data and at most $m_{\max} = 2^{n/2}$ blocks per message and at most $2^{n/2}$ messages.

Encryption and Decryption. The encryption $\mathcal{E}[\widetilde{E}]_K$ expects a nonce, associated data, and message $(N,A,M) \in \mathcal{N} \times \mathcal{A} \times \mathcal{M}$ and encrypts M under a key $K \in \mathcal{K}$ and the nonce to a tuple of ciphertext $C \in \mathcal{C}$ and tag $T \in \mathcal{T}$ such that $|M| = |C|$ and returns (C,T). The decryption algorithm $\mathcal{D}[\widetilde{E}]_K$ expects a nonce, associated data, ciphertext, and a tag $(N,A,C,T) \in \mathcal{N} \times \mathcal{A} \times \mathcal{C} \times \mathcal{T}$.

If the tuple is deemed invalid, the decryption outputs $\perp$. Otherwise, it decrypts C under the key $K \in \mathcal{K}$ and the nonce to the single possible message $M \in \mathcal{M}$ such that $\mathcal{E}[\widetilde{E}]_K^{N,A}(M) = (C,T)$ and outputs M. The algorithms are correct and tidy. Algorithm 1 defines the encryption and decryption procedures.

5 Security Model

Comparison to [7,24,25]**.** We follow the framework of unbounded leakage under oracle-free hard-to-invert leakage functions [7,25] since it captures leakage in all queries. The notions follow a convention of [PI,CI,CPA,CCA][m,M,-][L⟨i⟩] (for plaintext/ciphertext integrity, chosen-plain-/ciphertext attack), where m means nonce-misuse resilience, i.e., nonces may repeat except in challenge queries. L⟨i⟩ indicates leakage in i oracles; L2 means leakage in en- and decryption. Though, we differ in three minor aspects from their notions.

First, the notions from [25] used only a single challenge query, where CCAmL2 was extended to a multi-challenge variant in [24]. We will use multi-challenge but single-user notions (and denote this by a q) throughout this work since they are much more common and make our results comparable with those for TEDT, which was proven under multi-challenge notions muCIML2 and muCCAmL2 [7].

Second, we replace the left-or-right style for confidentiality with a real-or-random style, where the ideal world samples a message at random. We make this explicit by a -$ in the notions. While left-or-right and real-or-random notions are roughly equally strong, the latter seems more natural for avoiding dependencies on how an adversary chooses alternative messages. We stress that our real-or-random definitions only sample the message at random but process it with the same construction and key; they do not define an abstract ideal without the real construction since leakage of idealized objects is difficult to define (cf. [7,25,44]).

Third, we focus on information-theoretic distinguishers whose resources are bounded only by the numbers of queries and bits/blocks to the available oracles. Complexity-theoretic results can be derived in a straightforward manner.

We will write notions as distinguishing games. Note that we will usually add primitive oracles similar as in the ideal-cipher model in [7,25].

Leakage Functions. We inherit three usual assumptions that leakage functions Λ are (1) probabilistic, (2) oracle-free, and (3) not efficiently invertible from the notions of [7,25]. We use a non-empty random-coin set $\mathcal{R}$ and sample $R \twoheadleftarrow \mathcal{R}$ for every call to a leakage function (cf. [2]), which ensures that repeated calls may result in different leakage traces. We denote by $[L_i]_p = (L_1, \ldots, L_p)$ a p-element list of leakages L_i from the same leakage function Λ collected under independent random coins. Since leakage functions chosen by an adversary could compute some state in the future, they are usually prohibited from calling the primitives and are therefore called oracle-free (cf. [47]) to prevent future-computation attacks, where $\Lambda(K_i, \ldots)$ might otherwise leak outputs about K_j for a later occurring key $i < j$, which would render any confidentiality goal unachievable. This model reflects practice where leakages are a function of the primitive's

Algorithm 2. The qCIML2 experiment, adapted from [7] and [24,25].

11: **procedure** INITIALIZE	41: **function** $\widehat{\mathcal{D}}_K(N, A, C, T, \Lambda)$
12: $K \twoheadleftarrow \mathcal{K}; \mathcal{Q} \leftarrow \emptyset; b \twoheadleftarrow \{0,1\}$	42: $R \twoheadleftarrow \mathcal{R}$
	43: $M \leftarrow \mathcal{D}_K^{N,A}(C,T)$
21: **function** FINALIZE(b')	44: $L \leftarrow \Lambda_K^{N,A}(C,T;R)$
22: **return** $b = b'$	45: **return** (M, L)
31: **function** $\widehat{\mathcal{E}}_K(N, A, M, \Lambda)$	51: **function** $\widehat{\mathcal{D}}_K^{ch}(N, A, C, T, \Lambda)$
32: $R \twoheadleftarrow \mathcal{R}$	52: $R \twoheadleftarrow \mathcal{R}$
33: $(C,T) \leftarrow \mathcal{E}_K^{N,A}(M)$	53: $L \leftarrow \Lambda_K^{N,A}(C,T;R)$
34: $\mathcal{Q} \xleftarrow{\cup} \{(N,A,C,T)\}$	54: **if** $(N,A,C,T) \in \mathcal{Q} \vee b = 0$ **then return** $(\perp, L)$
35: $L \leftarrow \Lambda_K^{N,A}(M;R)$	55: $M \leftarrow \mathcal{D}_K^{N,A}(C,T)$
36: **return** (C,T,L)	56: **return** (M, L)

Algorithm 3. The qCCA\$mL2 experiment, adapted from [7] and [24,25].

11: **procedure** INITIALIZE	41: **function** FINALIZE(b')
12: $K \twoheadleftarrow \mathcal{K}; b \twoheadleftarrow \{0,1\}$	42: **return** $b = b'$
13: $\mathcal{Q}_N \leftarrow \emptyset; \mathcal{Q} \leftarrow \emptyset$	
14: $\mathcal{Q}_N^{ch} \leftarrow \emptyset; \mathcal{Q}^{ch} \leftarrow \emptyset$	51: **function** $\widehat{\mathcal{E}}_K^{ch}(N, A, M, \Lambda)$
	52: **if** $N \in \mathcal{Q}_N^{ch} \vee N \in \mathcal{Q}_N \vee M = \varepsilon$ **then**
21: **function** $\widehat{\mathcal{E}}_K(N, A, M, \Lambda)$	53: **return** $\perp$
22: **if** $N \in \mathcal{Q}_N^{ch}$ **then return** $\perp$	54: $M^* \leftarrow M$
23: $R \twoheadleftarrow \mathcal{R}$	55: $R \twoheadleftarrow \mathcal{R}$
24: $(C,T) \leftarrow \mathcal{E}_K^{N,A}(M)$	56: **if** $b = 0$ **then** $M^* \twoheadleftarrow \mathbb{F}_2^{|M|}$
25: $\mathcal{Q} \xleftarrow{\cup} \{(N,A,C,T)\}; \mathcal{Q}_N \xleftarrow{\cup} \{N\}$	57: $(C,T) \leftarrow \mathcal{E}_K^{N,A}(M^*)$
26: $L \leftarrow \Lambda_K^{N,A}(M;R)$	58: $\mathcal{Q}^{ch} \xleftarrow{\cup} \{(N,A,C,T)\}; \mathcal{Q}_N^{ch} \xleftarrow{\cup} \{N\}$
27: **return** (C,T,L)	59: $L \leftarrow \Lambda_K^{N,A}(C,T;R)$
	60: **return** (C,T,L)
31: **function** $\widehat{\mathcal{D}}_K(N, A, C, T, \Lambda)$	
32: **if** $(N,A,C,T) \in \mathcal{Q}^{ch}$ **then return** $\perp$	66: **function** $\widehat{\mathcal{D}}_K^{ch}(N, A, C, T, \Lambda)$
33: $R \twoheadleftarrow \mathcal{R}$	67: **if** $(N,A,C,T) \notin \mathcal{Q}^{ch}$ **then return** $\perp$
34: $M \leftarrow \mathcal{D}_K^{N,A}(C,T)$	68: $R \twoheadleftarrow \mathcal{R}$
35: $L \leftarrow \Lambda_K^{N,A}(C,T;R)$	69: $L \leftarrow \Lambda_K^{N,A}(C,T;R)$
36: **return** (M, L)	70: **return** L

in- and outputs. Moreover, we assume that leakage functions are not efficiently invertible in the sense of exponentially hard-to-invert functions [20].

We assume that leakage-function sets are used for the queries corresponding to their subscripts, i.e., $\mathcal{L}_E$ and $\mathcal{L}_D$ correspond $\mathcal{E}$ and $\mathcal{D}$ oracle(s), respectively. We mark leaking oracles by a hat, i.e. the leaking variant of $\mathcal{E}_K$ is $\widehat{\mathcal{E}}_K$, where leaking means that $\widehat{\mathcal{E}}_K$ takes a leakage function $\Lambda \in \mathcal{L}_E$ as an additional parameter that is called with the remaining parameters of $\mathcal{E}_K$ and random coins.

5.1 Notion for Authenticity

qCIML2 is a single-user variant of muCIML2 [7] and a distinguisher version of CIML2; every forgery allows distinguishing. qCIML2, as defined in Algorithm 2, splits the decryption queries into two oracles, one for collecting decryption leakage from earlier encryption queries, and one as a challenge oracle. Note that $\widehat{\perp}$ always outputs the decryption $\perp$, but also outputs decryption leakage.

Definition 1 (qCIML2). Let $\Pi = (\mathcal{E}_K, \mathcal{D}_K)$ be an nAE scheme, $K \twoheadleftarrow \mathcal{K}$, and $\mathcal{L}_E$ and $\mathcal{L}_D$ be sets of leakage functions. Let $\mathbf{A}$ be an adversary on Π. Then, the qCIML2 advantage of $\mathbf{A}$ on Π is defined as

$$\mathbf{Adv}^{\mathsf{qCIML2}}_{\mathcal{E}_K, \mathcal{D}_K, \mathcal{L}_E, \mathcal{L}_D}(\mathbf{A}) \overset{\text{def}}{=} \underset{\mathbf{A}}{\Delta}(\widehat{\mathcal{E}}_K, \widehat{\mathcal{D}}_K, \widehat{\mathcal{D}}^{ch}_K ; \widehat{\mathcal{E}}_K, \widehat{\mathcal{D}}_K, \widehat{\bot}) \quad \text{where} \quad O_1 \not\rightarrow O_3.$$

5.2   Notions for Confidentiality

We define qCCA\$mL2 in Algorithm 3 as a real-or-random variant of mCCAmL2 [24] or as a single-user variant of muCCAmL2 [7]. In the ideal world, the challenge encryption oracle $\widehat{\$}_{\mathcal{E}}$ encrypts a random string of $|M|$ bits with the real construction to produce a ciphertext and leakage. The challenge decryption oracle is defined similarly as $\widehat{\$}_{\mathcal{D}}$. Though, in both worlds, $\widehat{\$}_{\mathcal{D}}$ accepts only queries that were previous outputs from $\widehat{\$}_{\mathcal{E}}$ (denoted as $O_3 \uparrow O_4$) and outputs only the corresponding decryption leakages and not the decryption to avoid trivial wins.

qCPA\$mL2 is a real-or-random variant of the mCPAmL2 notion by [24], which differs from qCCA\$mL2 in the fact that it has no non-challenge decryption oracle. Thus, it is defined in Algorithm 3 without Lines 31–36.

Definition 2 (qCCA\$mL2 and qCPA\$mL2). Let $\Pi = (\mathcal{E}_K, \mathcal{D}_K)$ be an nAE scheme, $K \twoheadleftarrow \mathcal{K}$, and $\mathcal{L}_E$ and $\mathcal{L}_D$ be sets of leakage functions. Then, the qCCA\$mL2 advantage of an adversary $\mathbf{A}$ on Π is defined as

$$\mathbf{Adv}^{\mathsf{qCCA\$mL2}}_{\mathcal{E}_K, \mathcal{D}_K, \mathcal{L}_E, \mathcal{L}_D}(\mathbf{A}) \overset{\text{def}}{=} \underset{\mathbf{A}}{\Delta}(\widehat{\mathcal{E}}_K, \widehat{\mathcal{D}}_K, \widehat{\mathcal{E}}^{ch}_K, \widehat{\mathcal{D}}^{ch}_K ; \widehat{\mathcal{E}}_K, \widehat{\mathcal{D}}_K, \widehat{\$}_{\mathcal{E}}, \widehat{\$}_{\mathcal{D}}),$$

where $O_{3,N} \not\rightarrow O_{1,N}$, $\{O_{1,N}, O_{3,N}\} \not\rightarrow O_{3,N}$, $O_3 \not\rightarrow O_2$, $O_3 \uparrow O_4$. The qCPA\$mL2 advantage of an adversary $\mathbf{A}$ on Π is defined as

$$\mathbf{Adv}^{\mathsf{qCPA\$mL2}}_{\mathcal{E}_K, \mathcal{D}_K, \mathcal{L}_E, \mathcal{L}_D}(\mathbf{A}) \overset{\text{def}}{=} \underset{\mathbf{A}}{\Delta}(\widehat{\mathcal{E}}_K, \widehat{\mathcal{E}}^{ch}_K, \widehat{\mathcal{D}}^{ch}_K ; \widehat{\mathcal{E}}_K, \widehat{\$}_{\mathcal{E}}, \widehat{\$}_{\mathcal{D}}),$$

where $O_{2,N} \not\rightarrow O_{1,N}$, $\{O_{1,N}, O_{2,N}\} \not\rightarrow O_{2,N}$, $O_2 \uparrow O_3$.

We adapt two auxiliary notions, LUP-4 and XOR\$, from [6,7] that reflect practical attacks under leakage regarding its non-invertability and the indistinguishability of XORs, respectively. Algorithms 4 and 5 defines their experiments.

Unpredictability. For TEDT, the LUP-2 game [7] modeled the unpredictability under leakage of a single iteration of the used PRG. LUP-4 generalizes the notion to the setting in RCTR. It takes a larger tweakey $K_0, T_0 \in \mathbb{F}^n_2 \times \mathbb{F}^n_2$ from the adversary, samples $K_1 \twoheadleftarrow \mathbb{F}^n_2$ and $T_1 \twoheadleftarrow \mathbb{F}^n_2$ and uses them for p decryptions, as well as p calls of one iteration of the PRG in TEDT2 that generates two n-bit outputs and K_2, T_2. $\mathbf{A}$ can query the encryption p times to collect a vector of input- and output-leakages from all primitive calls except for the calls to $M_{0,1}$ and $M_{0,2}$, where it is not provided with input leakage. $\mathbf{A}$ outputs a set $\mathcal{K}'$ of q tuples (K_1, T_1) and wins iff the correct tweakey is contained.

Algorithm 4. LUP-4 experiment.

11: **procedure** INITIALIZE(K_0, T_0)	41: **function** $\widehat{\mathcal{E}}[\widetilde{E}](N, \Lambda^{\text{in}}, \Lambda^{\text{out}})$
12: $K_1 \twoheadleftarrow \mathbb{F}_2^n; T_1 \twoheadleftarrow \mathbb{F}_2^n$	42: **for** $i \leftarrow 1..p$ **do**
13: $M_{0,1} \leftarrow (\widetilde{E}_{K_0}^{0,0,T_0})^{-1}(K_1)$	43: $R_{0,1}^{\text{out}}, R_{0,2}^{\text{out}} \twoheadleftarrow \mathcal{R}$
14: $M_{0,2} \leftarrow (\widetilde{E}_{K_0}^{1,0,T_0})^{-1}(T_1)$	44: $K_1 \leftarrow \widetilde{E}_{K_0}^{0,0,T_0}(M_{0,1}); \ T_1 \leftarrow \widetilde{E}_{K_0}^{1,0,T_0}(M_{0,2})$
	45: $K_2 \leftarrow \widetilde{E}_{K_1}^{0,1,T_1}(N); \ T_2 \leftarrow \widetilde{E}_{K_1}^{1,1,T_1}(N)$
21: **function**	46: $Z_{1,1} \leftarrow \widetilde{E}_{K_0}^{2,1,T_0}(N); \ Z_{1,2} \leftarrow \widetilde{E}^{3,1,T_1}_{K_1}(N)$
LEAK$[\widetilde{E}](\Lambda^{\text{in}}, \Lambda^{\text{out}}, K, T, X, Y)$	47: $L_{0,1}^{\text{out}} \leftarrow \Lambda_0^{\text{out}}(K_0, (0, 0, T_0), K_1; R_{0,1}^{\text{out}})$
22: $R^{\text{in}}, R^{\text{out}} \twoheadleftarrow \mathcal{R}$	48: $L_{0,2}^{\text{out}} \leftarrow \Lambda_0^{\text{out}}(K_0, (1, 0, T_0), T_1; R_{0,2}^{\text{out}})$
23: $L^{\text{in}} \leftarrow \Lambda^{\text{in}}(K, T, X; R^{\text{in}})$	49: $L_0 \leftarrow L_{0,1}^{\text{out}}, L_{0,2}^{\text{out}}$
24: $L^{\text{out}} \leftarrow \Lambda^{\text{out}}(K, T, Y; R^{\text{out}})$	50: $L_{1,1}^{\text{in}}, L_{1,1}^{\text{out}} \leftarrow$ LEAK$[\widetilde{E}](\Lambda^{\text{in}}, \Lambda^{\text{out}}, K_1, (0, 1, T_1), N, K_2)$
25: **return** $(L^{\text{in}}, L^{\text{out}})$	51: $L_{1,2}^{\text{in}}, L_{1,2}^{\text{out}} \leftarrow$ LEAK$[\widetilde{E}](\Lambda^{\text{in}}, \Lambda^{\text{out}}, K_1, (1, 1, T_1), N, T_2)$
	52: $L_{1,3}^{\text{in}}, L_{1,3}^{\text{out}} \leftarrow$ LEAK$[\widetilde{E}](\Lambda^{\text{in}}, \Lambda^{\text{out}}, K_1, (2, 1, T_1), N, Z_{1,1})$
31: **function** FINALIZE$(\mathcal{K}')$	53: $L_{1,4}^{\text{in}}, L_{1,4}^{\text{out}} \leftarrow$ LEAK$[\widetilde{E}](\Lambda^{\text{in}}, \Lambda^{\text{out}}, K_1, (3, 1, T_1), N, Z_{1,2})$
32: win $\leftarrow |\mathcal{K}'| \le q \wedge$	54: $L_{1,1} \leftarrow L_{1,1}^{\text{in}}, L_{1,1}^{\text{out}}; \ L_{1,2} \leftarrow L_{1,2}^{\text{in}}, L_{1,2}^{\text{out}}$
33: $(K_1, T_1) \in \mathcal{K}'$	55: $L_{1,3} \leftarrow L_{1,3}^{\text{in}}, L_{1,3}^{\text{out}}; \ L_{1,4} \leftarrow L_{1,4}^{\text{in}}, L_{1,4}^{\text{out}}$
34: **if** win **then**	56: **return** $(K_2, T_2, Z_{1,1}, Z_{1,2},$
35: **return** 1	57: $[L_0]_p, [L_{1,1}]_p, [L_{1,2}]_p, [L_{1,3}]_p, [L_{1,4}]_p)$
36: **return** 0	

Algorithm 5. XOR$ experiment.

11: **function** INITIALIZE$(K, T, M, \Lambda^{\text{out}}, \Lambda^{\oplus})$	31: **function** $\widehat{\mathcal{E}}[\widetilde{E}]_K(\Lambda^{\text{out}}, \Lambda^{\oplus})$
12: $Y \twoheadleftarrow \mathbb{F}_2^n; b \twoheadleftarrow \{0, 1\}$	32: $R^{\text{out}}, R^{\oplus} \twoheadleftarrow \mathcal{R}$
13: $M^* \leftarrow M$	33: $Y \leftarrow \widetilde{E}_K^T(X); \ C \leftarrow Y \oplus M^*$
14: **if** $b = 0$ **then**	34: $L^{\text{out}} \leftarrow \Lambda^{\text{out}}(K, T, Y; R^{\text{out}})$
15: $M^* \twoheadleftarrow \mathbb{F}_2^n$	35: $L^{\oplus} \leftarrow \Lambda^{\oplus}(Y, C; R^{\oplus})$
16: $X \leftarrow (\widetilde{E}_K^T)^{-1}(Y)$	36: **for** $i \leftarrow 2..p$ **do**
	37: $R^{\text{out}}, R^{\oplus} \twoheadleftarrow \mathcal{R}$
21: **function** FINALIZE(b')	38: $Y \leftarrow \widetilde{E}_K^T(X); \ M^* \leftarrow C \oplus Y$
22: **return** $b = b'$	39: $L^{\text{out}} \leftarrow \Lambda^{\text{out}}(K, T, Y; R^{\text{out}})$
	40: $L^{\oplus} \leftarrow \Lambda^{\oplus}(Y, M^*; R^{\oplus})$
	41: **return** $(C, [L^{\text{out}}]_p, [L^{\oplus}]_p)$

Definition 3 (LUP-4). Let $\widetilde{\pi} \in \mathsf{TBC}(\mathbb{F}_2^n, \mathcal{T}_D, \mathbb{F}_2^n)$. Let $\mathcal{L}^{\text{in}}$ and $\mathcal{L}^{\text{out}}$ be sets of leakage functions. Let **A** be an adversary that provides $K_0, T_0 \in \mathbb{F}_2^n$ to and plays the LUP-4 experiment against $\widehat{\mathcal{E}}[\widetilde{\pi}]$, and outputs a set $\mathcal{K}' \subseteq (\mathbb{F}_2^n \times \mathbb{F}_2^n)^*$ with $|\mathcal{K}'| \le q$. The LUP-4 advantage of **A** is defined as

$$\mathbf{Adv}^{\mathsf{LUP\text{-}4}}_{\widehat{\mathcal{E}}[\widetilde{\pi}]_{K_0}^{*,*,T_0}, \mathcal{L}^{\text{in}}, \mathcal{L}^{\text{out}}}(\mathbf{A}) \overset{\text{def}}{=} \Pr\left[(K_1, T_1) \in \mathcal{K}'\right].$$

We define $\mathbf{Adv}^{\mathsf{LUP\text{-}4}}_{\widehat{\mathcal{E}}[\widetilde{\pi}], \mathcal{L}^{\text{in}}, \mathcal{L}^{\text{out}}}(p, q)$ as the maximum of all LUP-4 adversaries **A** on $\widehat{\mathcal{E}}[\widetilde{\pi}]$ that ask at most p queries and output a set of at most q guesses.

Indistinguishability of XOR. An implementation that shall provide confidentiality must protect all operations. An XOR that leaks a single bit can destroy privacy, but the probability may be non-negligible [6,7,26]. However, it should be addressed in the security analysis. Their works proposed a notion of Left-or-Right XOR security that can be evaluated in practice on an isolated component. The XOR$ game in Algorithm 5 is our real-or-random variant thereof for consistency, where the real world processes a message $M \in \mathbb{F}_2^n$ chosen by the adversary, and the ideal world samples and processes a message $M^* \twoheadleftarrow \mathbb{F}_2^n$.

Definition 4 (XOR$). Let $\widetilde{\pi} \in \mathsf{TBC}(\mathcal{K}, \mathcal{T}_D, \mathbb{F}_2^n)$ and $K_1 \twoheadleftarrow \mathcal{K}$. Let $\mathcal{L}^{\mathsf{out}}$, $\mathcal{L}_1^{\oplus}$, and $\mathcal{L}^{\oplus}$ be sets of leakage functions. Let **A** be a adversary that plays the XOR$ experiment given in Algorithm 5 against $\widehat{\mathcal{E}}[\widetilde{\pi}]$. Then, the XOR$ advantage of $\mathbf{A}^b \Rightarrow b'$, interacting with world b and outputting b' is defined as
$$\mathbf{Adv}^{\mathsf{XOR\$}}_{\widehat{\mathcal{E}}[\widetilde{\pi}]_K, \mathcal{L}^{\mathsf{out}}, \mathcal{L}^{\oplus}}(\mathbf{A}) \overset{\text{def}}{=} \left| \Pr\left[\mathbf{A}^1 \Rightarrow 1\right] - \Pr\left[\mathbf{A}^0 \Rightarrow 1\right] \right|.$$

We define $\mathbf{Adv}^{\mathsf{XOR\$}}_{\widehat{\mathcal{E}}[\widetilde{\pi}]_K, \mathcal{L}^{\mathsf{out}}, \mathcal{L}^{\oplus}}(p, q)$ for the maximum advantage over all XOR$ adversaries **A** on $\widehat{\mathcal{E}}[\widetilde{\pi}]_K$ that ask at most q queries under p measurements each.

6 Authentication Security Analysis of TEDT2

TEDT2 inherits the single-user CIML2 security from [7]. Since it is similar to the proof of TEDT, we provide a cleaned and slightly adapted description in the full version of this work. As for TEDT, we assume that all intermediate values may leak completely, except for the key K of the key-derivation and tag-generation functions. The leakage-function sets are defined as singletons $\mathcal{L}_E = \{\Lambda_E\}$ and $\mathcal{L}_D = \{\Lambda_D\}$, where on input (N, A, M), Λ_E and Λ_D return

- (K, S, X, Y) for each primitive call of the PRG G, where $S = (D, T, U) \in \mathcal{T}_D$,
- (X, S, Y) for each call to the key-derivation function,
- (N, U, V, T) for each call to the tag-generation function, and
- (A, B) for each XOR of $A \oplus B$.

We follow the steps by Berti et al. [7]:

(1) We replace the KDF and TGF by ideal secret tweakable keyed permutations, independent of each other and all other permutation calls.
(2) Then, we study the calls to the TGF and upper bound the probability of partial collisions and partial multi-collisions in V as bad events.
(3) Third, we upper bound the probability of forgeries for good transcripts.

The result is given in Theorem 1 and proven in the full version of this work.

Theorem 1 (qCIML2 Security). Let $\widetilde{\pi} \in \mathsf{TBC}(\mathcal{K}, \mathcal{T}_D, \mathbb{F}_2^n)$, $K \twoheadleftarrow \mathcal{K}$, and $n \geq 4$. Let **A** be a qCIML2-adversary on $\Pi[\widetilde{\pi}]_K = \mathsf{TEDT2}[\widetilde{\pi}]_K$ that makes at most q_c construction queries of at most σ message blocks and σ_a associated-data blocks in total and q_p primitive queries. Let q_e be the numbers of encryption construction queries, q_d the cumulative decryption construction queries to the oracles and μ be the number of encryption queries with repeating nonces in non-challenge encryption queries. Let $\sigma_p = 3\sigma + \sigma_a + 2q_c + q_p \leq 2^{n-3}$ be the number of ideal-primitive calls in all primitive and construction queries of **A**. Let the sets of leakage functions $\mathcal{L}_E$ and $\mathcal{L}_D$ be as defined in Sect. 6. Then

$$\mathbf{Adv}^{\mathsf{qCIML2}}_{\Pi[\widetilde{\pi}]_K, \widetilde{\pi}^{\pm}, \mathcal{L}_E, \mathcal{L}_D}(q_e, q_d, \sigma, q_p) \leq \mathbf{Adv}^{\mathsf{TPRP}}_{\widetilde{\pi}}(2q_c) + \mathbf{Adv}^{\mathsf{STPRP}}_{\widetilde{\pi}}(q_e, q_d)$$
$$+ \frac{2n(q_p + q_d) + 3(\sigma + \sigma_a) + 1}{2^n} + \frac{9\sigma_p^2 + 2\sigma_p + 8q_p(q_d + \mu)}{2^{2n}}.$$

7   Encryption Security Analysis of TEDT2

We adopt the definitions of $\widetilde{\pi}$ and K from Sect. 6. The leakage-function sets are singletons $\mathcal{L}_E = \{\Lambda_E\}$ and $\mathcal{L}_D = \{\Lambda_D\}$, where on input (N, A, M), Λ_E outputs

- $\Lambda^{\text{in}}(K, T, X)$ and $\Lambda^{\text{out}}(K, T, Y)$ for each call of $\widetilde{\pi}_K^T(X) = Y$ in ENCRYPT.
- $\Lambda^{\oplus}(A, B)$ for each XOR of two values $A \oplus B$ by internal actions
- All intermediate values during hashing, i.e., the hash function is unprotected.

On input (N, A, C, T), Λ_D returns the values corresponding to the above that occur during regular decryption in Algorithm 1. We let $\mathcal{L}^{\text{in}} = \{\Lambda^{\text{in}}\}$, $\mathcal{L}^{\text{out}} = \{\Lambda^{\text{out}}\}$, and $\mathcal{L}^{\oplus} = \{\Lambda^{\text{out}}\}$ be the leakage-function sets that contain the parts of Λ_E and Λ_D, respectively, that are used in the LUP-4 and XOR\$ notions.

Theorem 2. Let $\mathbf{A}$ be an qCCA\$mL2 adversary on $\Pi[\widetilde{\pi}]_K = \text{TEDT2}[\widetilde{\pi}]_K$ that asks at most q_e encryption queries and q_d decryption queries of at most σ blocks in total and q_p primitive queries. Let $F[\widetilde{\pi}]$ be an iteration of $\text{RCTR}[\widetilde{\pi}]$. Let $n \geq 4$, $\sigma \leq 2^{n-3}$, and let $\mathcal{L}_E$ and $\mathcal{L}_D$ be as defined at the top of Sect. 7. Then

$$\mathbf{Adv}^{\text{qCCA\$mL2}}_{\Pi[\widetilde{\pi}]_K, \widetilde{\pi}^{\pm}, \mathcal{L}_E, \mathcal{L}_D}(q_e, q_d, \sigma, q_p) \leq \frac{4q_p(\sigma + q_c) + 4(\sigma + q_c)^2}{2^{2n}}$$

$$+ \mathbf{Adv}^{\text{qCIML2}}_{\Pi[\widetilde{\pi}]_K, \widetilde{\pi}^{\pm}, \mathcal{L}_E, \mathcal{L}_D}(q_e, q_d, \sigma, q_p) + 2\sigma \cdot \mathbf{Adv}^{\text{LUP-4}}_{F[\widetilde{\pi}], \mathcal{L}^{\text{in}}, \mathcal{L}^{\text{out}}}(p, \sigma + q_c + q_p)$$

$$+ \sigma \cdot \mathbf{Adv}^{\text{XOR\$}}_{F[\widetilde{\pi}], \mathcal{L}^{\text{out}}, \mathcal{L}^{\oplus}}(p, 2\sigma + 2q_c + q_p).$$

The latter term reflects side-channel tweakey recovery and has a birthday-bound complexity of

$$O\left(\sigma \cdot \frac{\sigma + q_c + q_p}{c \cdot 2^{2n}}\right).$$

Following the argument by Berti et al. [7], the three leakage traces per tweakey should not render the value of c significant. While TEDT2 doubles the number of available traces for every tweakey to six, two n-bit values must be recovered. Thus, we assume that the resulting term of $c \cdot 2^{2n}$ that reflects six traces remains insignificant. The term $\sigma \cdot \mathbf{Adv}^{\text{XOR\$}}_{F[\widetilde{\pi}]}(p, 2q_c + 2\sigma + q_p)$ represents the distinguishing advantage in the case of "minimal message manipulation" and is inevitable for schemes that employ XOR during encryption.

Proof. The proof can follow the steps of the muCCAmL2 proof for TEDT in [7]. All queries of $\mathbf{A}$ will be stored in a transcript $\tau = \tau_c \cup \tau_p$. In this context, τ_c consists of the construction queries of $\mathbf{A}$ and their corresponding responses. τ_p represents the primitive queries of $\mathbf{A}$ to $\widetilde{\pi}^{\pm}$ and their associated responses. We have to show that

(1) Encryption queries provide confidentiality.
(2) Leakages from the decryption oracle do not affect confidentiality.

From Theorem 1, we can upper bound the advantage that TEDT2 is qCIML2-secure. Thus, unless **A** can forge, non-trivial decryption queries will yield only the $\perp$ symbol and leak only the invalid decryptions from $(\widetilde{\pi}_K^{8,N,H(A,C)})^{-1}(T)$. We can capture this as follows.

$$\underset{\mathbf{A}}{\Delta}(\widehat{\mathcal{E}}_K, \widehat{\mathcal{D}}_K, \widehat{\mathcal{E}}_K^{ch}, \widehat{\mathcal{D}}_K^{ch}, \widetilde{\pi}^{\pm}, \mathcal{L}_E, \mathcal{L}_D ; \widehat{\mathcal{E}}_K, \widehat{\mathcal{D}}_K, \widehat{\$}_{\mathcal{E}}, \widehat{\$}_{\mathcal{D}}, \widetilde{\pi}^{\pm}, \mathcal{L}_E, \mathcal{L}_D) \tag{1}$$

with the restrictions $O_{3,N} \not\sim O_{1,N}$, $\{O_{1,N}, O_{3,N}\} \not\sim O_{3,N}$, $O_3 \not\sim O_2$, and $O_3 \updownarrow O_4$. We can introduce an intermediate step of

$$\underset{\mathbf{A}}{\Delta}(\widehat{\mathcal{E}}_K, \widehat{\mathcal{D}}_K, \widehat{\mathcal{E}}_K^{ch}, \widehat{\mathcal{D}}_K^{ch}, \widetilde{\pi}^{\pm}, \mathcal{L}_E, \mathcal{L}_D ; \widehat{\mathcal{E}}_K, \widehat{\perp}, \widehat{\mathcal{E}}_K^{ch}, \widehat{\mathcal{D}}_K^{ch}, \widetilde{\pi}^{\pm}, \mathcal{L}_E, \mathcal{L}_D),$$

with the restrictions as for Eq. (1) plus $O_1 \not\sim O_2$. Its left-hand side is equivalent to that in Eq. (1) since every adversary that wanted to ask a query that was output from $O_1 \hookrightarrow O_2$ before could now use $O_3 \hookrightarrow O_4$ for this purpose. This setting can be reformulated as

$$\underset{\mathbf{A}}{\Delta}(\widehat{\mathcal{E}}_K, \widehat{\mathcal{D}}_K, \widehat{\mathcal{D}}_K, \widetilde{\pi}^{\pm}, \mathcal{L}_E, \mathcal{L}_D ; \widehat{\mathcal{E}}_K, \widehat{\mathcal{D}}_K, \widehat{\perp}, \widetilde{\pi}^{\pm}, \mathcal{L}_E, \mathcal{L}_D)$$
$$\leq \mathbf{Adv}_{\mathcal{E}[\widetilde{\pi}], \mathcal{D}[\widetilde{\pi}], \widetilde{\pi}^{\pm}, \mathcal{L}_E, \mathcal{L}_D}^{\mathsf{qCIML2}}(q_e, q_d, \sigma, q_p) \tag{2}$$

since the nonce restrictions to two encryption oracles are irrelevant. The remaining restrictions merge to $O_1 \not\sim O_3$ for Eq. (2), which yields the qCIML2 notion. The remaining step is to upper bound the distinguishing advantage of

$$\underset{\mathbf{A}}{\Delta}(\widehat{\mathcal{E}}_K, \widehat{\perp}, \widehat{\mathcal{E}}_K^{ch}, \widehat{\mathcal{D}}_K^{ch}, \widetilde{\pi}^{\pm}, \mathcal{L}_E, \mathcal{L}_D ; \widehat{\mathcal{E}}_K, \widehat{\perp}, \widehat{\$}_{\mathcal{E}}, \widehat{\$}_{\mathcal{D}}, \widetilde{\pi}^{\pm}, \mathcal{L}_E, \mathcal{L}_D)$$
$$= \underset{\mathbf{A}}{\Delta}(\widehat{\mathcal{E}}_K, \widehat{\mathcal{E}}_K^{ch}, \widehat{\mathcal{D}}_K^{ch}, \widetilde{\pi}^{\pm}, \mathcal{L}_E, \mathcal{L}_D ; \widehat{\mathcal{E}}_K, \widehat{\$}_{\mathcal{E}}, \widehat{\$}_{\mathcal{D}}, \widetilde{\pi}^{\pm}, \mathcal{L}_E, \mathcal{L}_D)$$
$$\leq \mathbf{Adv}_{\mathcal{E}[\widetilde{\pi}], \mathcal{D}[\widetilde{\pi}], \widetilde{\pi}^{\pm}, \mathcal{L}_E, \mathcal{L}_D}^{\mathsf{qCPA\$mL2}}(q_e, q_d, \sigma, q_p) \tag{3}$$

with the restrictions $O_{2,N} \not\sim O_{1,N}$, $\{O_{1,N}, O_{2,N}\} \not\sim O_{2,N}$, and $O_2 \updownarrow O_3$. The advantage in Eq. (3) for TEDT2 can be upper bounded by Lemma 1. its proof is deferred to the full version of this work. □

Lemma 1 (qCPA\$mL2 Security of TEDT2 with RCTR). Let $\widetilde{\pi} \leftarrow \mathrm{TBC}(\mathcal{K}, \mathcal{T}_D, \mathbb{F}_2^n)$. Let **A** be an qCPA\$mL2 adversary on $\Pi[\widetilde{\pi}]_K = \mathrm{TEDT2}[\widetilde{\pi}]_K$ that asks at most q_e encryption queries and q_d decryption queries of at most σ blocks in total and q_p primitive queries. Let $F[\widetilde{\pi}]$ be an iteration of $\mathrm{RCTR}[\widetilde{\pi}]$. Let $n \geq 2$, $\sigma \leq 2^{n-3}$, and let $\mathcal{L}_E$ and $\mathcal{L}_D$ be as defined at the top of Sect. 7. Then

$$\mathbf{Adv}_{\Pi[\widetilde{\pi}]_K, \widetilde{\pi}^{\pm}, \mathcal{L}_E, \mathcal{L}_D}^{\mathsf{qCPA\$mL2}}(q_e, q_d, \sigma, q_p) \leq \frac{4q_p(\sigma + q_c) + 4(\sigma + q_c)^2}{2^{2n}}$$
$$+ 2\sigma \mathbf{Adv}_{F[\widetilde{\pi}], \mathcal{L}^{\mathsf{in}}, \mathcal{L}^{\mathsf{out}}}^{\mathsf{LUP\text{-}4}}(p, \sigma + q_c + q_p) + \sigma \mathbf{Adv}_{F[\widetilde{\pi}], \mathcal{L}^{\mathsf{out}}, \mathcal{L}^{\oplus}}^{\mathsf{XOR\$}}(p, 2\sigma + 2q_c + q_p).$$

Comparison of Security Bounds. Figure 4 compares the single-user CCAmL2 and CIML2 bounds for TEDT with the corresponding qCCA\$mL2 and qCIML2

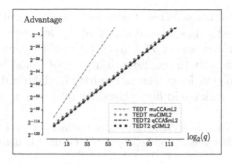

Fig. 4. Single-user CIML2 and CCAmL2 bounds of TEDT and qCIML2 and qCCA\$mL2 bounds for TEDT2, for $n = 128$ and where $q_c = q_p = \sigma = q$ are used.

bounds for TEDT2. The plot uses $n = 128$ and $q_c = q_p = \sigma$ as an example. It contains the bounds for the LUP-2 and LUP-4 terms, respectively, but must omit the terms for XOR\$ security since it strongly depends on the implementation and must be determined in practice. The lines that represent the qCCA\$mL2 and qCIML2 security bounds for TEDT2 almost overlap, which is natural since the qCCA\$mL2 bound contains the dominating bound for qCIML2 security. The difference in the terms of qCIML2 is largely due to the presentation. The main effect is the difference between the birthday-bound term for LUP-2 in the CCAmL2 bound of TEDT, while the $2n$-bit tweakey of TEDT2 leads to an improved bound.

8   Discussion and Future Work

Under the umbrella aim of maintaining qCIML2 and qCCA\$mL2 security, our core goals for TEDT2 were three-fold: to adopt a more efficient hash function, to render the authentication more efficient by moving the nonce to the tag-generation function, and to strengthen the encryption under leakage beyond the birthday bound. For this purpose, we adopted the more efficient hash function from Naito's result on MDPH and used a TBC with $3n$-bit tweakey to have a rate of about one while hashing. We could spare the effort for hashing the nonce and obtain higher security for the encryption mode and thus for the scheme under leakage, using a TWEAKEY-based TBC with $3n$-bit tweakey. We emphasize that the use of MDPH and a TBC with $3n$-bit tweakey has been also proposed for AET-LR and Romulus-LR-TEDT. We do not claim this adoption as a novel idea. We further stress that AET-LR used a more efficient sequential hashing of the associated data that used both state input and tweak, which is efficient and secure in the black-box setting but needs costly protection against DPAs [23] under leakage.

We identify several potential future improvements: the efficiency of the hash function can be further increased with longer tweaks, as suggested by Peyrin [41]. Concerning the PRG, the rate of $1/2$ may limit the applicability of our proposal in high-performance settings. While the same tweakey could be used for more blocks, this would need a fine-grained study of the leakage. Alternatively, other PRGs such as a generalization of TET from [7] might appear useful. Thanks to having modular proofs, only the confidentiality proof would have to be revised in this case. Finally, while our focus was on security in the usual single-user setting, an interesting future work could be to consider multiple users.

Acknowledgments. We thank the reviewers of Latincrypt 2021 for their highly fruitful comments. The author was supported by DFG Grant LU 608/9-1.

References

1. Ashur, T., Dunkelman, O., Luykx, A.: Boosting authenticated encryption robustness with minimal modifications. In: Katz, J., Shacham, H. (eds.) CRYPTO 2017. LNCS, vol. 10403, pp. 3–33. Springer, Cham (2017). https://doi.org/10.1007/978-3-319-63697-9_1
2. Barwell, G., Martin, D.P., Oswald, E., Stam, M.: Authenticated encryption in the face of protocol and side channel leakage. In: Takagi, T., Peyrin, T. (eds.) ASIACRYPT 2017. LNCS, vol. 10624, pp. 693–723. Springer, Cham (2017). https://doi.org/10.1007/978-3-319-70694-8_24
3. Bellare, M., Namprempre, C.: Authenticated encryption: relations among notions and analysis of the generic composition paradigm. In: Okamoto, T. (ed.) ASIACRYPT 2000. LNCS, vol. 1976, pp. 531–545. Springer, Heidelberg (2000). https://doi.org/10.1007/3-540-44448-3_41
4. Bellare, M., Yee, B.: Forward-security in private-key cryptography. In: Joye, M. (ed.) CT-RSA 2003. LNCS, vol. 2612, pp. 1–18. Springer, Heidelberg (2003). https://doi.org/10.1007/3-540-36563-X_1
5. Bellizia, D., et al.: Spook: sponge-based leakage-resistant authenticated encryption with a masked tweakable block cipher. IACR ToSC **2020**(S1), 295–349 (2020)
6. Bellizia, D., et al.: Mode-level vs. implementation-level physical security in symmetric cryptography. In: Micciancio, D., Ristenpart, T. (eds.) CRYPTO 2020. LNCS, vol. 12170, pp. 369–400. Springer, Cham (2020). https://doi.org/10.1007/978-3-030-56784-2_13
7. Berti, F., Guo, C., Pereira, O., Peters, T., Standaert, F.-X.: TEDT, a leakage-resist AEAD mode for high physical security applications. IACR Trans. Cryptogr. Hardw. Embed. Syst. **2020**(1), 256–320 (2020)
8. Berti, F., Koeune, F., Pereira, O., Peters, T., Standaert, F.-X.: Leakage-resilient and misuse-resistant authenticated encryption. IACR Cryptol. ePrint Arch. **2016**, 996 (2016)
9. Berti, F., Pereira, O., Peters, T., Standaert, F.-X.: On leakage-resilient authenticated encryption with decryption leakages. IACR ToSC **2017**(3), 271–293 (2017)
10. Cassiers, G., Guo, C., Pereira, O., Peters, T., Standaert, F.-X.: SpookChain: chaining a sponge-based AEAD with beyond-birthday security. In: Bhasin, S., Mendelson, A., Nandi, M. (eds.) SPACE 2019. LNCS, vol. 11947, pp. 67–85. Springer, Cham (2019). https://doi.org/10.1007/978-3-030-35869-3_7
11. Chari, S., Jutla, C.S., Rao, J.R., Rohatgi, P.: Towards sound approaches to counteract power-analysis attacks. In: Wiener, M. (ed.) CRYPTO 1999. LNCS, vol. 1666, pp. 398–412. Springer, Heidelberg (1999). https://doi.org/10.1007/3-540-48405-1_26

12. Cogliati, B., Lee, J., Seurin, Y.: New constructions of MACs from (tweakable) block ciphers. IACR Trans. Symmetric Cryptol. **2017**(2), 27–58 (2017)
13. Damgård, I.B.: Collision free hash functions and public key signature schemes. In: Chaum, D., Price, W.L. (eds.) EUROCRYPT 1987. LNCS, vol. 304, pp. 203–216. Springer, Heidelberg (1988). https://doi.org/10.1007/3-540-39118-5_19
14. Degabriele, J.P., Janson, C., Struck, P.: Sponges resist leakage: the case of authenticated encryption. In: Galbraith, S.D., Moriai, S. (eds.) ASIACRYPT 2019. LNCS, vol. 11922, pp. 209–240. Springer, Cham (2019). https://doi.org/10.1007/978-3-030-34621-8_8
15. Dobraunig, C., et al.: Isap v2.0. IACR ToSC **2020**(S1), 390–416 (2020)
16. Dobraunig, C., Eichlseder, M., Mangard, S., Mendel, F., Unterluggauer, T.: ISAP - Towards side-channel secure authenticated encryption. IACR ToSC **2017**(1), 80–105 (2017)
17. Dobraunig, C., Mennink, B.: Leakage resilience of the duplex construction. In: Galbraith, S.D., Moriai, S. (eds.) ASIACRYPT 2019. LNCS, vol. 11923, pp. 225–255. Springer, Cham (2019). https://doi.org/10.1007/978-3-030-34618-8_8
18. Dobraunig, C., Mennink, B.: Leakage resilience of the ISAP mode: a vulgarized summary. In: NIST LWC Workshop, vol. 2019, p. 23 (2019)
19. Dobraunig, C., Mennink, B.: Leakage resilient value comparison with application to message authentication. In: Canteaut, A., Standaert, F.-X. (eds.) EUROCRYPT 2021. LNCS, vol. 12697, pp. 377–407. Springer, Cham (2021). https://doi.org/10.1007/978-3-030-77886-6_13
20. Dodis, Y., Kalai, Y.T., Lovett, S.: On cryptography with auxiliary input. In: Mitzenmacher, M. (ed.) STOC, pp. 621–630. ACM (2009)
21. Dziembowski, S., Pietrzak, K.: Leakage-resilient cryptography. In: FOCS, pp. 293–302. IEEE Computer Society (2008)
22. Goubin, L., Patarin, J.: DES and differential power analysis the "duplication" method. In: Koç, Ç.K., Paar, C. (eds.) CHES 1999. LNCS, vol. 1717, pp. 158–172. Springer, Heidelberg (1999). https://doi.org/10.1007/3-540-48059-5_15
23. Guo, C., Khairallah, M., Peyrin, T.: AET-LR: rate-1 leakage-resilient AEAD based on the Romulus family. In: NIST LWC Workshop (2020)
24. Guo, C., Pereira, O., Peters, T., Standaert, F.-X.: Authenticated encryption with nonce misuse and physical leakages: definitions, separation results, and leveled constructions. IACR Cryptol. ePrint Arch. **2018**, 484 (2018). version 20190711:105233
25. Guo, C., Pereira, O., Peters, T., Standaert, F.-X.: Authenticated encryption with nonce misuse and physical leakage: definitions, separation results and first construction. In: Schwabe, P., Thériault, N. (eds.) LATINCRYPT 2019. LNCS, vol. 11774, pp. 150–172. Springer, Cham (2019). https://doi.org/10.1007/978-3-030-30530-7_8
26. Guo, C., Pereira, O., Peters, T., Standaert, F.-X.: Towards low-energy leakage-resistant authenticated encryption from the duplex sponge construction. IACR ToSC **2020**(1), 6–42 (2020)
27. Hirose, S.: Some plausible constructions of double-block-length hash functions. In: Robshaw, M. (ed.) FSE 2006. LNCS, vol. 4047, pp. 210–225. Springer, Heidelberg (2006). https://doi.org/10.1007/11799313_14
28. Hirose, S., Park, J.H., Yun, A.: A simple variant of the Merkle-Damgård scheme with a permutation. In: Kurosawa, K. (ed.) ASIACRYPT 2007. LNCS, vol. 4833, pp. 113–129. Springer, Heidelberg (2007). https://doi.org/10.1007/978-3-540-76900-2_7
29. Iwata, T., Khairallah, M., Minematsu, K., Peyrin, T.: New Results on Romulus. In: NIST LWC Workshop (2020)

30. Jean, J., Nikolić, I., Peyrin, T.: Tweaks and keys for block ciphers: the TWEAKEY framework. In: Sarkar, P., Iwata, T. (eds.) ASIACRYPT 2014. LNCS, vol. 8874, pp. 274–288. Springer, Heidelberg (2014). https://doi.org/10.1007/978-3-662-45608-8_15

31. Kalai, Y.T., Reyzin, L.: A survey of leakage-resilient cryptography. In: Goldreich, O. (ed.) Providing Sound Foundations for Cryptography: On the Work of Shafi Goldwasser and Silvio Micali, pp. 727–794. ACM (2019)

32. Kocher, P.C.: Timing attacks on implementations of Diffie-Hellman, RSA, DSS, and other systems. In: Koblitz, N. (ed.) CRYPTO 1996. LNCS, vol. 1109, pp. 104–113. Springer, Heidelberg (1996). https://doi.org/10.1007/3-540-68697-5_9

33. Kocher, P., Jaffe, J., Jun, B.: Differential power analysis. In: Wiener, M. (ed.) CRYPTO 1999. LNCS, vol. 1666, pp. 388–397. Springer, Heidelberg (1999). https://doi.org/10.1007/3-540-48405-1_25

34. Longo, J., Martin, D.P., Oswald, E., Page, D., Stam, M., Tunstall, M.J.: Simulatable leakage: analysis, pitfalls, and new constructions. In: Sarkar, P., Iwata, T. (eds.) ASIACRYPT 2014. LNCS, vol. 8873, pp. 223–242. Springer, Heidelberg (2014). https://doi.org/10.1007/978-3-662-45611-8_12

35. Merkle, R.C.: One way hash functions and DES. In: Brassard, G. (ed.) CRYPTO 1989. LNCS, vol. 435, pp. 428–446. Springer, New York (1990). https://doi.org/10.1007/0-387-34805-0_40

36. Micali, S., Reyzin, L.: Physically observable cryptography (extended abstract). In: Naor, M. (ed.) TCC 2004. LNCS, vol. 2951, pp. 278–296. Springer, Heidelberg (2004). https://doi.org/10.1007/978-3-540-24638-1_16

37. Naito, Y.: Optimally indifferentiable double-block-length hashing without post-processing and with support for longer key than single block. In: Schwabe, P., Thériault, N. (eds.) LATINCRYPT 2019. LNCS, vol. 11774, pp. 65–85. Springer, Cham (2019). https://doi.org/10.1007/978-3-030-30530-7_4

38. Naito, Y., Sasaki, Yu., Sugawara, T.: Lightweight authenticated encryption mode suitable for threshold implementation. In: Canteaut, A., Ishai, Y. (eds.) EUROCRYPT 2020. LNCS, vol. 12106, pp. 705–735. Springer, Cham (2020). https://doi.org/10.1007/978-3-030-45724-2_24

39. Namprempre, C., Rogaway, P., Shrimpton, T.: Reconsidering generic composition. In: Nguyen, P.Q., Oswald, E. (eds.) EUROCRYPT 2014. LNCS, vol. 8441, pp. 257–274. Springer, Heidelberg (2014). https://doi.org/10.1007/978-3-642-55220-5_15

40. Pereira, O., Standaert, F.-X., Vivek, S.: Leakage-resilient authentication and encryption from symmetric cryptographic primitives. In: Ray, I., Li, N., Kruegel, C. (eds.) ACM CCS, pp. 96–108. ACM (2015)

41. Peyrin, T.: Tweakable Block Cipher-Based Cryptography, 12 November 2020

42. Rogaway, P.: Authenticated-encryption with associated-data. In: Atluri, V. (ed.) ACM CCS, pp. 98–107. ACM (2002)

43. Rogaway, P., Shrimpton, T.: A provable-security treatment of the key-wrap problem. In: Vaudenay, S. (ed.) EUROCRYPT 2006. LNCS, vol. 4004, pp. 373–390. Springer, Heidelberg (2006). https://doi.org/10.1007/11761679_23

44. Standaert, F.-X.: Towards an open approach to side-channel resistant authenticated encryption. In: Chang, C-H., Rührmair, U., Holcomb, D.E., Schaumont, P. (eds.) ACM, p. 1. ACM (2019)

45. Standaert, F.-X., Pereira, O., Yu, Y.: Leakage-resilient symmetric cryptography under empirically verifiable assumptions. In: Canetti, R., Garay, J.A. (eds.) CRYPTO 2013. LNCS, vol. 8042, pp. 335–352. Springer, Heidelberg (2013). https://doi.org/10.1007/978-3-642-40041-4_19

46. Veyrat-Charvillon, N., Medwed, M., Kerckhof, S., Standaert, F.-X.: Shuffling against side-channel attacks: a comprehensive study with cautionary note. In: Wang, X., Sako, K. (eds.) ASIACRYPT 2012. LNCS, vol. 7658, pp. 740–757. Springer, Heidelberg (2012). https://doi.org/10.1007/978-3-642-34961-4_44
47. Yu, Y., Standaert, F.-X., Pereira, O., Yung, M.: Practical leakage-resilient pseudorandom generators. In: Al-Shaer, E., Keromytis, A.D., Shmatikov, V. (eds.) ACM CCS, pp. 141–151. ACM (2010)

Distributed Cryptographic Protocols

Weight-Based Nakamoto-Style Blockchains

Simon Holmgaard Kamp[1], Bernardo Magri[1], Christian Matt[2], Jesper Buus Nielsen[1], Søren Eller Thomsen[1(✉)], and Daniel Tschudi[2]

[1] Concordium Blockchain Research Center, Aarhus University, Aarhus, Denmark
{kamp,magri,jbn,sethomsen}@cs.au.dk
[2] Concordium, Zurich, Switzerland
{cm,dt}@concordium.com

Abstract. We propose a framework for building Nakamoto-style proof-of-work blockchains where blocks are treated differently in the "longest chain rule". The crucial parameter is a *weight function* assigning different weights to blocks according to their hash value. Our framework enables the analysis of different weight functions while proving all statements at the appropriate level of abstraction. This allows us to quickly derive protocol guarantees for different weight functions. We exemplify the usefulness of our framework by capturing the classical Bitcoin protocol as well as exponentially growing functions as special cases. We show the typical properties—chain growth, chain quality and common prefix—for both, and further show that the latter provide an additional guarantee, namely a weak form of *optimistic responsiveness*. More precisely, we prove for a certain class of exponentially growing weight functions that in periods without corruption, the confirmation time only depends on the unknown actual network delay instead of the known upper bound.

Keywords: Blockchain · Proof of work · Chain-selection rule · Block weight · Optimistic responsiveness

1 Introduction

In classical blockchains such as Nakamoto's Bitcoin [9], the parties run a distributed "lottery" to decide who is allowed to append the next block to the existing chain. When there is a winner of the lottery, a block is produced and disseminated to the other parties, that will perform a series of checks to guarantee that the block is valid and that the party that produced the block actually won the lottery. If all the checks are correct, the parties append the new block to their local view of the chain. Classical blockchains (also called Nakamoto-style, or NSB for short) usually assume the majority of the resources (e.g., computational power or stake) to be trusted, from which they can achieve totally ordered broadcast.

Bitcoin is a NSB based on proof-of-work (PoW) where a block is only considered valid and allowed to be appended to the chain if its hash value is below

P. Longa and C. Ràfols (Eds.): LATINCRYPT 2021, LNCS 12912, pp. 299–319, 2021.
https://doi.org/10.1007/978-3-030-88238-9_15

some threshold value T. The probability of this is proportional to T. The value T is computed in real time by the network such that a single valid block is created, on average, every 10 min. In a period where T is fixed[1] the "best-chain" rule for Bitcoin is determined by how many blocks are on the chain. Previous analyses of the Bitcoin protocol [4,5,10,11,14] show that under certain network assumptions, Bitcoin satisfies the properties of chain growth, chain quality and common prefix (introduced by [4]) for some choice of parameters.

The *block time* of a NSB is the average time between blocks. Existing analyses use at their core the fact that the block time is longer than the average network delay. This allows for honest block winners to typically having seen all previous honest blocks when they add a new block. This allows the longest chain to grow by one block when there is an honest winner. If blocks are produced faster than they propagate, then all "bets are off". Therefore the block time of existing NSB needs to be set conservatively to some worst case value. At a conceptual level, our study is motivated by the simple observation that on existing NSBs, whenever the block time is fixed to a constant, the protocols do not respond with higher throughput when the network is in fact much faster than the worst case assumed. At a technical level, our study departs from the observation that not all types of blocks are equal. In Bitcoin there are two types of blocks, those above the threshold T, which do not count at all, and those below T, which count as one block. However, blocks with hash below T/m for some integer m have average block time about m times as long as blocks with hash below T. Therefore, one could for instance consider counting blocks with hash below T/m with "weight" m or "weight" 2^m. That is, we can consider different *weight functions* assigning weights to blocks based on their hash values. This raises the following question:

Can we get better guarantees for NSBs if we assign different weights to the blocks?

In that vein, we provide a general framework to analyze PoW protocols under different weight functions. The main goal of the framework is to provide useful tools where one can easily explore and analyze the impact of different weight functions applied to a Bitcoin-like protocol. As a sanity check, we first instantiate the (standard) Bitcoin weight function in our framework (Sect. 4.2) and show similar bounds as previous work.

As evidence of the usefulness of our framework in exploring different weight functions, we show that a large class of weight functions achieves a weak form of "optimistic responsiveness" (c.f. [13]). In a nutshell, we show that in periods without corruption, the time it takes for blocks to be in a common prefix only depends on the actual network delay instead of a known upper bound.

---

[1] For simplicity, in this work we only consider the case of fixed participation. We leave the case of adaptive T as future work.

1.1   Overview of Our Results

Our contributions are twofold: (1) We provide a general framework for easy exploration and design of protocols with different weight functions and (2) we show that there are weight functions that are strictly better than the traditional longest chain rule of Bitcoin. We detail our contributions next:

Generic Framework. Our framework constitutes the backbone of a PoW blockchain where its valid block predicate and best-chain rule rely on a weight function that establishes a numerical value (i.e., weight) to each individual block in the chain. The best chain at any given time is the chain with more accumulated weight over all its blocks. We provide general lemmas for several bounds on the produced weight of a PoW protocol instantiated with any weight function. Furthermore, we derive for any weight function the concrete bounds that are needed for the main blockchain properties of growth, quality and common-prefix to be guaranteed, and calculate how these bounds translate into guarantees for the protocol. The main goal of our generic framework is that any weight function can be "plugged-in" to the framework and the parameters needed for the desired levels of guarantees can be obtained almost directly. This enables an easy exploration and design of protocols without needing to redo a series of complex and potentially error-prone proofs.

Weakly Optimistically Responsive Protocol. We introduce in Sect. 4 the class of T-capped weight functions, which are monotonically increasing weight functions that are constant if the input is larger than a threshold T. We show that a PoW blockchain that employs a particular weight function from such a class achieves chain growth, chain quality and common-prefix parameters similar to the ones achieved by Bitcoin in previous works [4,5]. We also note that instantiating a PoW protocol with a particular T-capped weight function can make it *weakly optimistically responsive*, i.e., under no corruption we show common-prefix guarantees for the protocol that are based on the *real* network delay, and not on the known upper bound.

Intuitively, a weight function needs to satisfy two properties: First, blocks produced at a good frequency with respect to the actual network delay should get enough weight to cancel out the weight of blocks that are produced too fast. Secondly, it should be difficult for the adversary to produce extremely heavy blocks as these can be used to cause huge rollbacks and violate common prefix. To satisfy both conditions, we let the weight functions grow exponentially until they reach a threshold, which is determined by the known upper bound $\hat{\Delta}_{\mathsf{Net}}$ on the network delay; above the threshold the weight remains constant. The cap ensures that the adversary cannot cause rollbacks longer than this upper bound with a single block. Growing exponentially below the threshold gives us responsiveness in the all-honest setting: Assume the actual network delay Δ_{Net} is much lower than the known upper bound $\hat{\Delta}_{\mathsf{Net}}$. Blocks produced at the right frequency with respect to Δ_{Net} are weighted much heavier than more frequent blocks. Thus, the honest parties essentially build a chain just with these blocks, and the lighter ones are negligible in comparison. It is not necessary to wait for even heavier blocks up to the threshold to get the desired properties. Note that this only provides responsiveness if there are no corrupted parties: A single dishonest party can with non-negligible probability produce a block with maximal possible weight, and thus cause a roll-back of honest blocks produced in $\hat{\Delta}_{\text{Net}}$ time.

While this may seem not particularly useful, the responsiveness can still greatly improve the throughput of the chain when the protocol is combined with a finality layer such as Casper the Friendly Finality Gadget [2], GRANDPA [16], or Afgjort [3], where blocks are declared as final (and cannot be rolled back) as soon as they are in the common-prefix of honest users. In that case, the time it takes for blocks to be in the common prefix in periods without corruption only depends on the actual network delay, and finalization ensures that all users know which blocks to trust. We leave it as interesting future work to analyze the feasibility of responsiveness in the face of active corruption.

Due to space constraints, all non-trivial proofs of lemmas and theorems are left out of this version. We refer to the full version of this paper [6] for these.

1.2 Related Work

The first formal analysis of NSB blockchains was given in the seminal paper [4] for a fixed threshold T, which was later extended to a variable threshold in [5], and to a different setting with more variable message delivery times, adaptive corruption, and spawning of new players in [11]. Ren [14] gives a simpler analysis of the standard Bitcoin protocol under the assumption that mining on Bitcoin can be modeled as a Poisson process.

Responsiveness was defined by Pass and Shi [12] as the property of a blockchain that achieves a liveness parameter expressed in terms of the actual network delay, independent of the conservative upper bound on the network delay used to instantiate the protocol. They show that a protocol tolerating up to a $\frac{1}{3}$ corruption can achieve responsiveness, and that this bound is tight. They later show in [13] that assuming only honest majority (and a delay for the corruption of parties) it is possible to obtain the weaker property of *optimistic responsiveness*, i.e., responsiveness under some additional "goodness" condition, while still providing security in the worst case. In particular, they show responsiveness in the case of more than $\frac{3}{4}$ honest computing power and an additional assumption of an honest *accelerator*. In [15] a lower bound is given for the latency in the *optimistic* setting of [13] alongside a protocol achieving this within a constant factor of the actual network delay.

Since [13] and [15] both require a committee and an accelerator, their results only hold assuming considerably delayed corruption, allowing the accelerator to make progress. Our generic weighted protocol, on the other hand, can tolerate immediate adaptive corruptions, as desired in the permissionless setting. However, our result is weaker with respect to the "goodness" condition since we only achieve responsiveness in the case of no corruption. Whether one can get responsiveness with non-zero fully adaptive corruption in the permissionless setting remains an open problem.

The concept of assigning different weights to blocks based on their hash value has already been considered in the context of proofs of proof of work [7,8]. The purpose there, and consequently the analysis, was completely different: Heavy blocks are used to link to older blocks in addition to the direct parents, to allow for faster verification of recent transactions without verifying the whole chain.

2   Our Generic Framework for Weight-Based Analysis

In this section we formally describe our generic framework and we introduce the concept of weight functions for PoW blockchains. In Sects. 2.2 and 2.4 we provide generic definitions and tools that will be used to show the properties of chain growth, chain quality and common prefix for PoW blockchains that leverages weight functions (in Sect. 3). Our analysis builds upon the ideas of previous work [4,14] and extends those to the more general setting of weighted blocks. We start by describing the blockchain model that we consider for our framework.

2.1   Blockchain Model

Network and Time. We assume that time is divided into *rounds* which correspond to the smallest unit of time of interest. We assume a network with bounded delay, which is parameterized by an upper bound Δ_{Net} on the network delivery time. It allows parties to multicast messages. That is, any message sent by an honest party in round r is guaranteed to arrive at all honest parties until round $r + \Delta_{\mathsf{Net}}$. As in, e.g., [11], we assume a gossip network, which ensures that all messages (sent by a dishonest sender and) received by an honest party in round r are received by all honest parties until round $r + \Delta_{\mathsf{Net}}$. Note that the latter can be achieved by resending all freshly received messages. The actual delay of messages (per message and party) can be set by the adversary (within Δ_{Net}). The delay Δ_{Net} is *not* known to the honest parties. However, we assume that honest parties know a rough upper bound $\hat{\Delta}_{\mathsf{Net}}$, potentially much larger than Δ_{Net}, on the network delay.

Random Oracle. Following [11], we assume every "party" can make at most one query to a random oracle in each round. The idea is that one round corresponds to the time it takes to evaluate the hash function on one CPU and is the smallest unit of time of interest. To model real-world parties with different amounts of computing power, one can assume that they control different amounts of these "one-query-per-round" parties. As in [1,4,11], we allow the corrupted parties to make their queries sequentially, while honest parties have to make the queries in parallel. We assume the range of the random oracle to be $\mathcal{H} := \{1, \ldots, 2^k\}$.

In the remainder of the paper, we let $q \in \mathbb{N}$ denote the number of parties in the protocol. As each party has one query this is also the maximal amount of queries that can be made to the oracle in each round.

304   S. H. Kamp et al.

Corruptions. We allow the adversary to adaptively corrupt up to a $\beta < \frac{1}{2}$ fraction of all parties before each round. Newly corrupted parties are then fully under the adversary's control from that round on. We denote by $\alpha := 1 - \beta$ the minimal fraction of participating parties that are honest at any time. Note that by our definition of the random oracle, there can be at most $q\beta$ random-oracle queries by corrupted parties in each round, and there are at least $q\alpha$ queries by honest parties in each round (since honest parties in our protocol query the random oracle in each round). We will thus for most of the paper only consider these upper and lower bounds on the numbers of dishonest and honest queries, and not explicitly map these to parties.

Mining. As in Bitcoin, miners in our protocol continuously take what they currently consider the best chain and try to extend it with a new block. The proof of work aspect corresponds to miners finding an input to a hash function with certain properties. In the Bitcoin protocol a valid block must satisfy (among others things) that its hash is smaller than some threshold T. The challenge of finding a nonce which makes the block hash small enough is what makes Bitcoin a proof-of-work blockchain. The threshold T is adjusted such that the block-production rate is approximately constant. The constant is chosen as a trade-off between performance and security. The block validity predicate of Bitcoin thus consists of checking the block hash along with some (for our purposes unimportant) syntactic well-formedness conditions on the block and its contents. In our protocol blocks are considered valid independent of their hash value. Instead, the hash of a block determines how much the block weighs when selecting the best-chain. To avoid having many low-weight blocks swarm the network we can use a *cutoff*. Since it does not impact the security of the protocol but merely a parameter that can be optimized for throughput, we will ignore it in this paper.

We define the round in which a block was mined to be the round in which the corresponding query to the random oracle was made.

Best Chain. In Bitcoin (with fixed difficulty), the length of the chain is what decides how "good" a chain is [4,9]. Thus, in Bitcoin, chains with more blocks are considered better. In our protocol we use a best-chain rule that is based on the accumulated weight of the blocks in a chain, i.e., the heavier a chain is, the better, as in bitcoin with variable difficulty [5].

No Insertions, Copies, and Predictions. To simplify our analysis and following [4], we assume throughout the paper that it never happens that a new block is added between two existing blocks (*insertion*), the same block occurs in two different positions (*copy*), or a block extends a block that is mined in a later round (*prediction*). As shown in [4], insertions and copies can only occur if there is a collision in the random oracle linking blocks together, which has negligible probability, and the probability of guessing a block is negligible as well.

2.2   Basic Definitions

In this section, we first present some basic definitions for the weight of a chain and the weight of a block. Then we present a categorization for certain good events which are important for the analysis, and finally we introduce the notation for upper and lower bounds on the weight produced.

Weight. We define the chain of a block B denoted $\mathsf{Chain}(B)$ to be the list of all blocks one gets by following the pointers in the chain from B up to the genesis block. We next define the concept of weight for blocks and chains.

Definition 1 (Weight functions, weight of blocks and chains). *We define a weight function to be a function of type $\mathcal{H} \to \mathbb{R}_{\geq 0}$. Let w be a weight function. We then define the weight of a block B to be $\mathsf{Weight}_\mathsf{w}(B) = \mathsf{w}(\mathsf{Hash}(B))$, and the weight of a chain C to be $\mathsf{Weight}_\mathsf{w}(C) = \sum_{B \in C} \mathsf{Weight}_\mathsf{w}(B)$.*

Next, we define the weight range, that is analogous to the depth of a block in Bitcoin.

Definition 2 (Weight range). *Given a weight function w, we define the* start weight *of a block B to be $\mathsf{StartWeight}_\mathsf{w}(B) := \mathsf{Weight}_\mathsf{w}(\mathsf{Chain}(B)) - \mathsf{Weight}_\mathsf{w}(B)$ and the* end weight *to be $\mathsf{EndWeight}_\mathsf{w}(B) := \mathsf{Weight}_\mathsf{w}(\mathsf{Chain}(B))$. We define the weight* range *of a block B to be $\mathsf{WeightRange}_\mathsf{w}(B) := (\mathsf{StartWeight}_\mathsf{w}(B), \mathsf{EndWeight}_\mathsf{w}(B)]$. Consequently, $|\mathsf{WeightRange}_\mathsf{w}(B)| = \mathsf{Weight}_\mathsf{w}(B)$.*

Good Events. Previous analyses [4,10,11,14] are based on the fact that in a certain amount of rounds a block is produced that has enough time to propagate to all honest parties before a new block is mined. Ren [14] takes a slightly different approach and defines this in terms of blocks rather than rounds. More concretely, he defines a "non-tailgater" to be an honest block mined at time t such that no other honest block is mined between time $t - \Delta_{\mathsf{Net}}$ and t. We believe that this is closer to the intuition for the proof, namely that once in a while an honest party mines a block that has enough time to propagate. In his analysis, mining is assumed to be a Poisson process and therefore no mining events occur simultaneously with positive probability. In our model, however, it can happen that several blocks are mined in the same round. If several blocks are mined in a round after Δ_{Net} empty rounds, we can count one of them as a "good" block.

To leverage this in the analysis, we introduce an order in the mined blocks that we call "proof-order". With the order fixed, one can choose, e.g., the first of these blocks as the "good" block.[2] More formally, we introduce an arbitrary but fixed total order on all blocks produced in the protocol. We order blocks

---

[2] The proof-order could be defined to take the block with maximal weight in each round instead of ordering them by the parties. This would give a slightly tighter analysis as there then would be slightly more "good" weight. For simplicity, have we chosen not to take this approach.

lexicographically first based on the production round (i.e., the round the block was created) and secondly on the party that made the query to the random oracle. Note that the production time of a block is well-defined, even for adversarial blocks as they also need to make a query to the random oracle in some round. We stress that this enumeration and induced order of blocks is completely unrelated to the total order of blocks that the protocol achieves, and only needed as an artifact of our proofs. To avoid confusion will we refer to the above as the *proof-order*.

We now use this order on blocks to precisely categorize certain "good" events (blocks mined with sufficient time between them). We further generalize previous notions to our setting with different weights, i.e., instead of requiring that no blocks are mined within a propagation period, we only require that no blocks above a certain threshold are mined within this period.

Definition 3 (h-(left-)isolation). *Let $h \in \mathcal{H}$, and let B be a block mined in round $r \in \mathbb{N}$. We say B is h-left-isolated if B is honest, $\mathsf{Hash}(B) > h$, and there is no block left of B in the proof-order with hash above h mined in rounds $[r - \Delta_{\mathsf{Net}}, r]$. If B is honest, $\mathsf{Hash}(B) > h$, and no other blocks with hash above h are mined in rounds $[r - \Delta_{\mathsf{Net}}, r + \Delta_{\mathsf{Net}}]$, we say B is h-isolated.*

Note that we define h-(left-)isolation with respect to the unknown upper bound Δ_{Net} on the network delay, not on the known bound $\hat{\Delta}_{\mathsf{Net}}$.

Remark 1. Similar notions have been defined in previous work [4,10,11,14]. We deviate from these definitions by defining (resp. left-) isolation to require that *no* blocks are mined on either side (resp. to the left) of a block, whereas earlier work had the requirement that no other *honest* block was mined within that period. We use the stricter definition because it simplifies some of the arguments (especially with respect to adaptive corruptions). Only considering honest blocks may potentially allow to prove tighter bounds, though. Note that we define the round in which a block was mined to be the round in which the corresponding query to the random oracle was made, so this is also well-defined for corrupted parties, who may send their block in a later round.

Left-isolated blocks are called "non-tailgaters" and isolated blocks are called "loners" by Ren [14]. Analogous notions to that of a round with a left-isolated block has in previous work been called an "effective-round" [10] and "isolated successful round" [4]. The event of a isolated block has in previous work been called "convergence opportunity" [11], "uniquely effective round" [10] and an "uniquely isolated successful round" [4]. We chose the terms "left-isolated" and "isolated" as we believe them to be more intuitive.

2.3 Bounds on Produced Weight

We now introduce some definitions for weight functions describing different bounds on weight that can be produced with a specific weight function. We start with the upper-bounds on how much weight a certain number of queries can produce. We will later use this fact to reason about how much weight any adversary can produce.

We say a weight function is $(\hat{W}_g, \hat{p}_g)$-upper-bounding for some parameter $g \leq q$ if the weight of all blocks mined in r rounds (for all $r \in \mathbb{N}$) with at most g queries (honest or dishonest) per round is at most $\hat{W}_g(r)$, except with probability $\hat{p}_g(r)$. Similarly, we introduce $(\hat{W}_g^{\leq h_0}, \hat{p}_g^{\leq h_0})$-below-threshold-upper-bounding to bound the weight produced by blocks with hash value at most h_0, and $(\hat{W}_g^{>h_0}, \hat{p}_g^{>h_0})$-above-threshold-upper-bounding to bound the weight produced by blocks with hash value more than h_0.

Definition 4. *Let* w *be a weight function, let* $g \in \mathbb{N}$, $h_0 \in \mathcal{H}$, *let* $\hat{W}_g, \hat{W}_g^{\leq h_0}$, $\hat{W}_g^{>h_0} : \mathbb{N} \to \mathbb{R}$, *and let* $\hat{p}_g, \hat{p}_g^{\leq h_0}, \hat{p}_g^{>h_0} : \mathbb{N} \to [0,1]$ *be monotonically decreasing. Further, let* $W_{g,r}$ *for* $r \in \mathbb{N}$ *be the random variable corresponding to the total weight of all blocks weighted with* w *mined in* r *consecutive rounds with at most* g *queries in each round, and similarly* $W_{g,r}^{\leq h_0}$ *($W_{g,r}^{>h_0}$) for* $r \in \mathbb{N}$ *be the random variable corresponding to the total weight of all blocks with hash value at most* h_0 *(more than* h_0*) weighted with* w *mined in* r *consecutive rounds with at most* g *queries in each round. We say* w *is* $(\hat{W}_g, \hat{p}_g)$*-upper-bounding if for all* $r \in \mathbb{N}$,*

$$\Pr[W_{g,r} \geq \hat{W}_g(r)] \leq \hat{p}_g(r),$$

w *is* $(\hat{W}_g^{\leq h_0}, \hat{p}_g^{\leq h_0})$-below-threshold-upper-bounding *if for all* $r \in \mathbb{N}$,

$$\Pr\left[W_{g,r}^{\leq h_0} \geq \hat{W}_g^{\leq h_0}(r)\right] \leq \hat{p}_g^{\leq h_0}(r),$$

and w *is* $(\hat{W}_g^{>h_0}, \hat{p}_g^{>h_0})$-above-threshold-upper-bounding *if for all* $r \in \mathbb{N}$,

$$\Pr\left[W_{g,r}^{>h_0} \geq \hat{W}_g^{>h_0}(r)\right] \leq \hat{p}_g^{>h_0}(r).$$

Next, we introduce the definition for lower-bounds on the amount of (left-) isolated weight, i.e., on how much weight is produced by honest parties with sufficient time in between. By our definition of (left-)isolated blocks, only honest blocks can be left-isolated. We therefore do not use a parameter g here, but always consider q queries in each round in total, with at least $q\alpha$ queries from honest parties. We introduce the notion of a $(\check{W}_{\mathsf{Iso}^h}, \check{p}_{\mathsf{Iso}^h})$-isolated-lower-bounding weight function. It means that the total weight of all h-isolated blocks mined in r consecutive rounds is at least $\check{W}_{\mathsf{Iso}^h}(r)$, except with probability $\check{p}_{\mathsf{Iso}^h}(r)$. Left-isolated-lower-bounding weight functions are defined analogously.

Definition 5. *Let* w *be a weight function, and let* $h_0 \in \mathcal{H}$, $\check{W}_{\mathsf{Iso}^{h_0}}$, $\check{W}_{\mathsf{LeftIso}^{h_0}} : \mathbb{N} \to \mathbb{R}$, *and let* $\check{p}_{\mathsf{Iso}^{h_0}}, \check{p}_{\mathsf{LeftIso}^{h_0}} : \mathbb{N} \to [0,1]$ *be monotonically decreasing. Further let* $W_{r,\mathsf{Iso}^{h_0}}$ *for* $r \in \mathbb{N}$ *be the random variable corresponding to the total weight of all h-isolated blocks weighted with* w *mined in* r *consecutive rounds, and let* $W_{r,\mathsf{LeftIso}^{h_0}}$ *for* $r \in \mathbb{N}$ *be the random variable corresponding to the* *total weight of all h-left-isolated blocks weighted with* w *mined in r consecutive rounds. We say* w *is* $\left(\check{W}_{\mathsf{Iso}^{h_0}}, \check{p}_{\mathsf{Iso}^{h_0}}\right)$-*isolated-lower-bounding if for all* $r \in \mathbb{N}$,

$$\Pr\left[W_{r,\mathsf{Iso}^{h_0}} \leq \check{W}_{\mathsf{Iso}^{h_0}}(r)\right] \leq \check{p}_{\mathsf{Iso}^{h_0}}(r),$$

and w *is* $\left(\check{W}_{\mathsf{LeftIso}^{h_0}}, \check{p}_{\mathsf{LeftIso}^{h_0}}\right)$-*left-isolated-lower-bounding if for all* $r \in \mathbb{N}$,

$$\Pr\left[W_{r,\mathsf{LeftIso}^{h_0}} \leq \check{W}_{\mathsf{LeftIso}^{h_0}}(r)\right] \leq \check{p}_{\mathsf{LeftIso}^{h_0}}(r).$$

2.4 Proving Bounds from Properties of the Weight Functions

In this section, we show how to derive some of the thresholds defined in Sect. 2.3.

Notation. In the remainder of the paper we define $p_{\leq h_0} := \frac{h_0}{2^k}$ to be the probability that a single random oracle query returns a value at most h_0, and $\mathsf{w}_{\max \leq h_0} := \max_{h \in \{1,\ldots,h_0\}} \mathsf{w}(h)$, $\mathsf{w}_{\max > h_0} := \max_{h \in \{h_0+1,\ldots,2^k\}} \mathsf{w}(h)$, and $\mathsf{w}_{\min > h_0} = \min_{h \in \{h_0+1,\ldots,2^k\}} \mathsf{w}(h)$ (for the weight function that is clear from the context).

First, we provide a simple upper-bound for the total weight above and below a threshold.

Lemma 1 (Weight above and below a threshold). *Let* w *be a weight function, let* $g \in \mathbb{N}$, *and* $h_0 \in \mathcal{H}$. *Then, for all* $\delta \in (0,1)$, w *is*

(i) $\left(\hat{W}_g^{\leq h_0}, \hat{p}_g^{\leq h_0}\right)$-*below-threshold-upper-bounding with*

$$\hat{W}_g^{\leq h_0} = \mathsf{w}_{\max \leq h_0} \cdot (1+\delta) \cdot g \cdot r \cdot p_{\leq h_0}, \qquad \hat{p}_g^{\leq h_0} = e^{-\frac{\delta^2 \cdot g \cdot r \cdot p_{\leq h_0}}{3}},$$

(ii) and $\left(\hat{W}_g^{> h_0}, \hat{p}_g^{> h_0}\right)$-*above-threshold-upper-bounding with*

$$\hat{W}_g^{> h_0}(r) = \mathsf{w}_{\max > h_0} \cdot (1+\delta) \cdot g \cdot r \cdot (1 - p_{\leq h_0}), \quad \hat{p}_g^{> h}(r) = e^{-\frac{\delta^2 \cdot g \cdot r \cdot (1 - p_{\leq h_0})}{3}}.$$

Proof. The probability to get a block below a threshold in just one query is $p_{\leq h_0}$ and above a threshold is $1 - p_{\leq h_0}$. The amount of blocks below/above a threshold can be upper bounded with Chernoff Each block below contributes with weight at most $\mathsf{w}_{\max \leq h_0}$, and blocks above with weight at most $\mathsf{w}_{\max > h_0}$. □

We next prove bounds on the number of (left-)isolated blocks and afterwards use this for a simple bound on the amount of (left-)isolated weight. The proof follows some ideas from Ren [14].

Lemma 2 (Amount of (left-)isolated blocks). *Let* r *be a number of consecutive rounds, let* $h_0 \in \mathcal{H}$, *let* $N_{r,\mathsf{LeftIso}^{h_0}}$ *denote the number of* h_0-*left-isolated* *blocks produced, and let $N_{r,\mathsf{Iso}^{h_0}}$ denote the number of h_0-isolated blocks produced during these r rounds. We then have for any $\delta \in (0,1)$,*

$$\Pr\left[N_{r,\mathsf{LeftIso}^{h_0}} \le (1-\delta)\cdot\alpha qr\cdot(1-p_{\le h_0})\cdot p_{\le h_0}^{q\Delta_{\mathsf{Net}}}\right] \le 2e^{-\frac{\delta^2\cdot\alpha qr\cdot\left(1-p_{\le h_0}\right)\cdot p_{\le h_0}^{q\Delta_{\mathsf{Net}}}}{16}},$$

(1)

$$\Pr\left[N_{r,\mathsf{Iso}^{h_0}} \le (1-\delta)\cdot\alpha qr\cdot(1-p_{\le h_0})\cdot p_{\le h_0}^{2\cdot q\Delta_{\mathsf{Net}}}\right] \le 3e^{-\frac{\delta^2\cdot\alpha qr\cdot\left(1-p_{\le h_0}\right)\cdot p_{\le h_0}^{2q\Delta_{\mathsf{Net}}}}{108}}.$$

(2)

Lemma 3. *Let* w *be a weight function and $h_0 \in \mathcal{H}$. Then, for all $\delta \in (0,1)$,*

(i) w *is* $\left(\breve{W}_{\mathsf{LeftIso}^{h_0}}, \breve{p}_{\mathsf{LeftIso}^{h_0}}\right)$*-left-isolated-lower-bounding with*

$$\breve{W}_{\mathsf{LeftIso}^h}(r) = \mathsf{w}_{\min>h_0}\cdot(1-\delta)\cdot\alpha qr\cdot(1-p_{\le h_0})\cdot(p_{\le h_0})^{q\Delta_{\mathsf{Net}}},$$

$$\breve{p}_{\mathsf{LeftIso}^h}(r) = 2e^{-\frac{\delta^2\cdot\alpha qr\cdot(1-p_{\le h_0})\cdot(p_{\le h_0})^{q\Delta_{\mathsf{Net}}}}{16}},$$

(ii) and w *is* $\left(\breve{W}_{\mathsf{Iso}^{h_0}}, \breve{p}_{\mathsf{Iso}^{h_0}}\right)$*-isolated-lower-bounding with*

$$\breve{W}_{\mathsf{Iso}^h}(r) = \mathsf{w}_{\min>h_0}\cdot(1-\delta)\cdot\alpha qr\cdot(1-p_{\le h_0})\cdot(p_{\le h_0})^{2q\Delta_{\mathsf{Net}}},$$

$$\breve{p}_{\mathsf{Iso}^h}(r) = 3\cdot e^{-\frac{\delta^2\cdot\alpha qr\cdot(1-p_{\le h_0})\cdot(p_{\le h_0})^{2q\Delta_{\mathsf{Net}}}}{108}}.$$

Proof. Each (left-)isolated block contributes at least $\mathsf{w}_{\min>h_0}$ weight. Hence, the bounds on the amount of (left-)isolated blocks from Lemma 2 directly imply the lower bounds on (left-)isolated weight. □

3   Proving Chain Properties

In this section we prove the standard properties of chain growth, chain quality, and common prefix for our generic framework by only assuming bounds on the produced weight, as introduced in Sect. 2. We consider a fixed weight function w for the entire section so we leave it out of the notations.

We warm-up with some fundamental lemmas that will be used as building blocks when proving the more complex theorems of the chain properties.

The following lemma is a generalization of Lemma 5 (i) in [14]. It intuitively says that if we only consider blocks above a certain hash, and enough time has passed since an honest block was mined, then a new honest block will have a different position in the chain than the previous block.

Lemma 4. *Let $h \in \mathcal{H}$ and let $B \ne B'$ be h-left-isolated blocks. Then, B and B' have disjoint weight ranges.*

Proof. We assume without loss of generality that B is mined first. The party P' who mines B' receives B within Δ_{Net} rounds, which is by definition of h-left-isolation before B' is mined. After receiving B, P' only extends chains with weight at least $\mathsf{EndWeight}(B)$. Hence, $\mathsf{EndWeight}(B) \leq \mathsf{StartWeight}(B')$, and thus, $\mathsf{WeightRange}(B) \cap \mathsf{WeightRange}(B') = \varnothing$. $\square$

The next lemma is a generalization of Lemma 5 (ii) in [14]. The lemma says that if we only consider honest blocks above a certain hash, then if such a block has had enough time to propagate before the next block is produced and no other block was mined in a period before, then this block will not share a position in the chain with any other block.

Lemma 5. *Let $h \in \mathcal{H}$ and let B be a h-isolated block. Further let $B' \neq B$ be an honest block with $\mathsf{Hash}(B') > h$. Then, B and B' have disjoint weight ranges.*

Proof. Let $B_0 \in \{B, B'\}$ be the block which is mined first. By definition of h-isolation, the other block is mined more than Δ_{Net} rounds later. As in the proof of Lemma 4, we can thus conclude that the party mining the second block knows B_0 beforehand and thus extends a chain with weight at least $\mathsf{EndWeight}(B_0)$. Hence, $\mathsf{WeightRange}(B) \cap \mathsf{WeightRange}(B') = \varnothing$. $\square$

3.1   Chain Growth

The chain growth property intuitively says that a chain will increase its weight by at least a fixed bound at every round. We give a formal definition of our weight-based chain growth property next.

Definition 6 (Chain Growth). *Let w be a weight function. The chain growth property with parameters $\rho \in \mathbb{N}$ and $\tau \in \mathbb{R}$, states that for any honest party P that has a chain C_1, it holds that after any ρ consecutive rounds P adopts a chain C_2 such that $\mathsf{Weight}(C_2) \geq \mathsf{Weight}(C_1) + (\rho \cdot \tau)$ for $\tau > 0$.*

Next, we show that the accumulated weight of the chain grows at least by the accumulated weight of the left-isolated blocks at each round, and therefore satisfies the property of Definition 6. We show a slightly more general version of chain growth as this is useful for proving chain quality later.

Theorem 1 (Chain Growth). *Let C_1 be the best chain of P_1 in round r_1 and let C_2 be the best chain of P_2 in round r_2, where $r_1 \leq r_2 - 2\Delta_{\mathsf{Net}} + 1$. For any $h_0 \in \mathcal{H}$ such that the weight function is $\left(\check{W}_{\mathsf{LeftIso}^{h_0}}, \check{p}_{\mathsf{LeftIso}^{h_0}}\right)$-left-isolated-lower-bounding, we have*

$$\Pr\left[\mathsf{Weight}(C_2) < \mathsf{Weight}(C_1) + \check{W}_{\mathsf{LeftIso}^{h_0}}(r_2 - r_1 - 2\Delta_{\mathsf{Net}} + 1)\right]$$
$$\leq \check{p}_{\mathsf{LeftIso}^{h_0}}(r_2 - r_1 - 2\Delta_{\mathsf{Net}} + 1).$$

When this theorem is instantiated with $P_1 = P_2$, we obtain chain growth for $\rho > 2\Delta_{\mathsf{Net}}$ and $\tau = \frac{\check{W}_{\mathsf{LeftIso}^{h_0}}(\rho - 2\Delta_{\mathsf{Net}})}{\rho}$ except with probability $\check{p}_{\mathsf{LeftIso}^{h_0}}(\rho - 2\Delta_{\mathsf{Net}})$.

3.2   Chain Quality

The chain quality property intuitively says that within any consecutive chunk of blocks of an honest party's chain, at least a ratio of the blocks was produced by honest parties. We give a formal definition next.

Definition 7 (Chain Quality). *The chain quality property with parameters $\Lambda \in \mathbb{R}$ and $\mu \in \mathbb{R}$, states that for any honest party P that has a chain C as their best chain, it holds that for any sequence of consecutive blocks with a weight range of size at least Λ in C, it holds that the ratio of honest weight is at least μ.*

We believe that it is more intuitive to reason about the chain quality property in terms of *elapsed time* instead of weight. Hence, we present our results for a "timed" version of the chain quality property,[3] which intuitively ensures that a fraction of honest weight is contained in a sequence of blocks that are mined within some time-period.

Theorem 2 (Chain quality). *Let P be an honest party with best chain $C = B_1 B_2 \ldots B_n$ and let $R = B_i \ldots B_j$ be any consecutive list of blocks in C with $1 \le i < j \le n$ where block B_i was mined in round r_i, B_j in round r_j, and $r_j - r_i \ge 2\Delta_{\mathsf{Net}}$. Further let $h_0 \in \mathcal{H}$ and $X \in \mathbb{R}$ such that the weight function is $\left(\check{W}_{\mathsf{LeftIso}^{h_0}}, \check{p}_{\mathsf{LeftIso}^{h_0}} \right)$-left-isolated-lower-bounding and $(\hat{W}_{q\beta}, \hat{p}_{q\beta})$-upperbounding such that for any $\rho \ge r_j - r_i$, we have $\check{W}_{\mathsf{LeftIso}^{h_0}}(\rho - 2\Delta_{\mathsf{Net}} + 1) \ge \hat{W}_{q\beta}(\rho) + X$. Finally let p_{bad} be the probability that the fraction of honest weight in R is less than $\frac{X}{\mathsf{Weight}(R)}$. Then,*

$$p_{\mathsf{bad}} \le \check{p}_{\mathsf{LeftIso}^{h_0}}(r_j - r_i - 2\Delta_{\mathsf{Net}} + 1) + \hat{p}_{q\beta}(r_j - r_i).$$

In Appendix A we state the weighted version of the chain quality as a corollary of Theorem 2 together with the fact that the amount of weight produced during a time period is bounded.

3.3   Common Prefix

The common prefix property is arguably the most important property of blockchains. It informally says that the chains of honest parties are always a common prefix of each other after removing some blocks on the chain. Next, we formally define the concept of "removing some blocks" of the chain in the form of pruning.

Definition 8 (Pruning). *Let C be a chain, $w \in \mathbb{R}$ be a weight, and let $r \in \mathbb{N}$ be a round. We define $C^{\mathsf{W}\lceil w}$ to be the longest prefix of C such that $\mathsf{Weight}(C^{\mathsf{W}\lceil w}) \le \mathsf{Weight}(C) - w$, i.e., blocks with total weight at least w are removed from the end of C. We further define $C^{\mathsf{R}>\lceil r}$ to be the chain containing all blocks from C that were mined until round r, i.e., all blocks mined after round r are removed from C.*

---

[3] We omit the formal definition here as it can be easily derived from Definition 7.

Similarly to chain quality, we believe it to be more intuitive to reason about the common-prefix property with respect to the absolute number of rounds (time). It states that for any pair of honest parties that adopted chains at different rounds, the oldest chain is a prefix of the most recent chain.

Definition 9 (Common Prefix). *For parameter $\rho \in \mathbb{N}$, let C_1 be the best chain of honest party P_1 in round r_1, and let C_2 be the best chain of honest party P_2 in round r_2 for $r_1 \leq r_2$. The common-prefix property says that $C_1^{\,\mathrm{R} > \lceil r_1 - \rho} \preceq C_2$.*

In Theorem 3 we prove that given certain restrictions on the weight function our protocol satisfies Definition 9. Similarly to [4] we prove this in two steps, by first showing a weaker version of the property that says that the best chain of any pair of honest players at the *same* round must be a prefix of each other. Afterwards, we extend the proof to capture the case where the honest parties might be at different rounds.

Theorem 3 (Common prefix). *Let $\rho \geq 2\Delta_{\mathsf{Net}} - 1$, let P_1, P_2 be (not necessarily different) honest parties, let $r_1 \leq r_2$ be rounds, and let C_1 be the best chain of P_1 in round r_1. Further let p_{bad} be the probability that P_2 has a best chain C_2 in round r_2 with $C_1^{\,\mathrm{R} > \lceil r_1 - \rho} \npreceq C_2$. We have*

(i) *For all $h_0 \in \mathcal{H}$ such that the weight function is $\left(\check{W}_{\mathsf{LeftIso}^{h_0}}, \check{p}_{\mathsf{LeftIso}^{h_0}} \right)$-left-isolated-lower-bounding and $\left(\hat{W}_q, \hat{p}_q \right)$-upper-bounding, and for all $\rho' \geq \rho$*

$$2 \cdot \check{W}_{\mathsf{LeftIso}^{h_0}} (\rho' - 2\Delta_{\mathsf{Net}} + 1) \geq \hat{W}_q(\rho'),$$

we have

$$p_{\mathsf{bad}} \leq 2\check{p}_{\mathsf{LeftIso}^{h_0}} (\rho - 2\Delta_{\mathsf{Net}} + 1) + 2\hat{p}_q(\rho).$$

(ii) *For all $h_0 \in \mathcal{H}$ such that the weight function is $\left(\hat{W}_q^{\leq h_0}, \hat{p}_q^{\leq h_0} \right)$-below-threshold-upper-bounding, $\left(\hat{W}_{q\beta}^{>h_0}, \hat{p}_{q\beta}^{>h_0} \right)$-upper-bounding, and $\left(\check{W}_{\mathsf{Iso}^{h_0}}, \check{p}_{\mathsf{Iso}^{h_0}} \right)$-isolated-lower-bounding, and for all $\rho' \geq \rho$*

$$\check{W}_{\mathsf{Iso}^{h_0}} (\rho' - 2\Delta_{\mathsf{Net}} + 1) \geq \hat{W}_q^{\leq h_0}(\rho') + \hat{W}_{q\beta}^{>h_0}(\rho'),$$

we have

$$p_{\mathsf{bad}} \leq 2\check{p}_{\mathsf{Iso}^{h_0}} (\rho - 2\Delta_{\mathsf{Net}} + 1) + 2\hat{p}_q^{\leq h_0}(\rho) + 2\hat{p}_{q\beta}^{>h_0}(\rho).$$

In Appendix A we prove the weighted version of the common-prefix property as a corollary of Theorem 3.

4   Applying the Framework to Capped Weight Functions

Our framework allows the exploration of infinitely many different weight functions. Intuitively, good weight functions should ensure that a majority of weight is produced by honest parties that have a nearly complete view of all other honest blocks, i.e., the winning events that produce most of the weight should on average occur so rarely that they have enough time to propagate before the next time such a rare event occurs. On the other hand the weight difference between such winning events should not be too large as this increases the variance and thus gives worse bounds on the probabilities.

These considerations led us to focus on a special class of functions which we call *capped weight functions* that we use our framework to analyze in this section. We first prove general conditions that ensures common prefix for this class of functions using only very loose bounds. Next, we derive a condition that such functions should satisfy to additionally provide a weak form of optimistic responsiveness. We then discuss how to pick such functions, and how additionally combining such a function with a finality layer provides very fast confirmation. Finally, we show how previous analyses of Bitcoin are subsumed by our framework, and present a weight function that is strictly better than the Bitcoin function with respect to the properties presented in this work.

4.1 Definitions and General Results

To derive concrete equations for the bounds the weight functions should satisfy, we instantiate Theorem 3 with the *loose* bounds from Sect. 2.4. The specific conditions we achieve for *any* weight function are captured by the lemma below.

Lemma 6. *Let* w *be a weight-function. Further let* $h_0 \in \mathcal{H}$. *We assume that* $w_{\min > h_0} > 0$. *Let* $\delta \in (0, 1)$ *and* $\rho > 2\Delta_{\mathsf{Net}} - 1$ *such that*

$$\alpha \cdot (1 - \delta) \cdot (1 - p_{\leq h_0}) \cdot (p_{\leq h_0})^{2q \Delta_{\mathsf{Net}}}$$
$$\geq \frac{\rho}{\rho - 2\Delta_{\mathsf{Net}} + 1} \left(\frac{w_{\max \leq h_0}}{w_{\min > h_0}} \cdot p_{\leq h_0} + \frac{w_{\max > h_0}}{w_{\min > h_0}} \cdot \beta \cdot (1 - p_{\leq h_0}) \right).$$

Let P_1, P_2 *be (not necessarily different) honest parties, let* $r_1 \leq r_2$ *be rounds, and let* C_1 *be the best chain of* P_1 *in round* r_1. *Finally let* p_{bad} *be the probability that* P_2 *has a best chain* C_2 *in round* r_2 *with* $C_1^{R > \lceil r_1 - \rho \rceil} \not\preceq C_2$. *We then have*

(i) for any β

$$p_{\mathsf{bad}} \leq 10 e^{- \frac{\delta^2 \cdot q\beta \cdot (\rho - 2\Delta_{\mathsf{Net}} + 1) \cdot (1 - p_{\leq h_0}) \cdot (p_{\leq h_0})^{2q \Delta_{\mathsf{Net}}}}{432}},$$

(ii) and for $\beta = 0$

$$p_{\mathsf{bad}} \leq 8 e^{- \frac{\delta^2 \cdot q \cdot (\rho - 2\Delta_{\mathsf{Net}} + 1) \cdot (1 - p_{\leq h_0}) \cdot (p_{\leq h_0})^{2q \Delta_{\mathsf{Net}}}}{432}}.$$

We now introduce the notion of a *capped-weight-function* to encapsulate the intuition for the properties a useful weight function should have.

Definition 10 (Capped weight functions). *Let* w *be a weight function, and* $T \in \mathcal{H}$. *We say that* w *is* T-*capped if for all* $h, h' \in \mathcal{H}$, *with* $h, h' > T$, *we have* $w(h) = w(h')$.

Using this definition we consider two special cases of the general common-prefix property: What should be satisfied to ensure common prefix under the worst case conditions and how fast do we achieve common prefix in the best case where the adversary only controls the network delay?

We next show one way to pick T such that the common-prefix property holds for the special case where w is T-capped weight function. To this end, we use Lemma 6 with $h_0 = T$. The specific conditions we achieve are captured by the lemma below.

Lemma 7. *Let P_1, P_2 be (not necessarily different) honest parties, let $r_1 \leq r_2$ be rounds, let $\epsilon_c := \alpha - \beta > 0$, let $\delta \in (0,1)$, and let C_1 be the best chain of P_1 in round r_1. Finally let p_{bad} be the probability that P_2 has a best chain C_2 in round r_2 with $C_1^{R > \lceil r_1 - \rho} \npreceq C_2$.. If $\rho > 2\hat{\Delta}_{\mathsf{Net}} - 1$ and w is a T-capped-weight-function that satisfies*

$$T \geq \left(\frac{\beta \cdot \rho}{\left(\beta + \frac{\epsilon_c}{2}\right)(1 - \delta)(\rho - 2\hat{\Delta}_{\mathsf{Net}} + 1)} \right)^{\frac{1}{2q\hat{\Delta}_{\mathsf{Net}}}} \cdot 2^k, \tag{3}$$

and

$$\frac{1}{2\hat{\Delta}_{\mathsf{Net}}} \cdot (1 - \delta) \cdot \frac{\epsilon_c}{2} \cdot (1 - p_{\leq T}) \cdot (p_{\leq T})^{2q\hat{\Delta}_{\mathsf{Net}} - 1} \geq \frac{\mathsf{w}_{\max \leq T}}{\mathsf{w}_{\min > T}}, \tag{4}$$

then

$$p_{\mathsf{bad}} \leq 10e^{-\frac{\delta^2 \cdot q\beta^2 \cdot \rho \cdot (1 - p_{\leq T})}{432\left(\beta + \frac{\epsilon_c}{2}\right)(1 - \delta)}}. \tag{5}$$

Furthermore, if $\rho > 2\Delta_{\mathsf{Net}} - 1$, $\alpha = 1$, $\beta = 0$, and for all $h_0 \leq T$

$$\frac{1}{2\hat{\Delta}_{\mathsf{Net}}} \cdot \frac{(1 - \delta)}{e \cdot 2q\hat{\Delta}_{\mathsf{Net}}} \geq \frac{\mathsf{w}_{\max \leq h_0}}{\mathsf{w}_{\min > h_0}}, \tag{6}$$

then

$$p_{\mathsf{bad}} \leq 8e^{-\frac{\delta^2 \cdot q \cdot (\rho - 2\Delta_{\mathsf{Net}} + 1)}{432 \cdot e \cdot (2q\Delta_{\mathsf{Net}} + 1)}}. \tag{7}$$

Choosing a Weight Function. In order to instantiate a T-capped weight function we suggest the following approach. Pick T such that it satisfies equation (3) for a sufficiently large ρ. Next pick the function such that it additionally ensures the condition from Eq. (4). For monotone functions this can simply be done by increasing the growth of the function such that $\frac{\mathsf{w}_{\max \leq T}}{\mathsf{w}_{\min > T}}$ is sufficiently small. When a T-capped weight function is instantiated like this, it provides common prefix except with the probability given by (5). To further satisfy equation (6) one can additionally increase the growth of the function until it is true for all $h_0 \leq T$.[4]

Waiting Time for Common Prefix. To ensure that parties are on a common prefix except with negligible probability, one has to wait until p_{bad} is negligible. If κ is the security parameter, this means that one has to wait ρ rounds such that $\rho \cdot q(1 - p_{\leq T}) = \Omega(\kappa)$. Note that $q(1 - p_{\leq T})$ is the expected number of blocks with hash above the threshold T produced in each round. This means one needs to wait for $\Omega(\kappa)$ blocks above the threshold. This matches the bounds derived for the plain Bitcoin backbone, e.g., in [4].

In the case without corruption, one has to wait ρ rounds such that $\rho \cdot \frac{1}{\Delta_{Net}} = \Omega(\kappa)$. Note that this only depends on Δ_{Net}, not on $\hat{\Delta}_{Net}$. Hence, the protocol is responsive in this case!

Chain Growth and Chain Quality. Note that this approach automatically ensures some chain growth and chain quality as the preconditions for Theorem 1 and Theorem 2 are weaker than the precondition for Theorem 3. One can also obtain tighter bounds by optimizing for this, but we leave that for future work.

Finality Layers. A practical issue of the responsiveness that is provided by Lemma 7 is that it is hard to know whether there are actively corrupted nodes or not. This means that even in the good case without corruption, where all parties quickly agree on blocks, parties typically do not know for sure that there is no corruption, and thus cannot confirm transactions quickly. As a solution to this issue, we propose to use a finality layer, such as Casper the Friendly Finality Gadget [2], GRANDPA [16], or Afgjort [3]. These act as an additional layer on top of a NSB, where a committee votes on blocks to become final, and finalized blocks are never rolled back by adjusting the chain-selection rule to prefer chains with more finalized blocks. In such finality layers, a block can be declared final as soon as enough committee members vote for that block. In the optimistic case, this happens as fast as the actual network conditions allow in our responsive blockchain, as all honest parties will in fact have the same common-prefix and thus vote for the same. And given the decision from the finalization committee, one can immediately trust these finalized blocks, yielding a high overall efficiency.

---

[4] In our analysis, we need to set $\frac{w_{max} \leq h_0}{w_{min} > h_0}$ sufficiently small to satisfy both conditions (4) and (6). Note that no condition places a lower bound on this fraction. This means the weight function can be chosen to grow arbitrarily fast.

The trade-off that is hidden in our analysis is that faster growing functions lead to less responsiveness if there is some corruption. That is because it becomes easier to produce very heavy blocks that can roll back a huge number of lighter blocks. The growth of the function should thus not be set higher than necessary. We leave exploring this trade-off for future work.

4.2   Examples of Capped Weight Functions

In this section, we provide two concrete instantiations of weight functions using our framework. For means of comparison, we first instantiate the standard Bitcoin weight function and afterwards a capped-exponential weight function, which we compare to the Bitcoin protocol.

Bitcoin Weight. The Bitcoin protocol originally considers the best chain to be the one that is the longest. Each block added to a chain can therefore be considered as incrementing the weight of the chain with 1. If a block is invalid it does not change the weight of a chain and it can thus be thought of as having weight 0. With this interpretation, the Bitcoin weight function with threshold T can be defined as[5]

$$w_T^{BC}(h) := \begin{cases} 0, & \text{if } h \leq T, \\ 1, & \text{else.} \end{cases}$$

This is clearly an instance of a T-capped-weight-function. Thus, the approach from Sect. 4.1 can be applied for picking T, i.e., simply set T such that (3) is an equality.

For $w = w_T^{BC}$, we have $w_{\min>T} = 1$ and $w_{\max \leq T} = 0$. Hence, Eq. (4) is trivially satisfied and (5) thus provides the probability bound for the common-prefix violations. As explained in Sect. 4.1, this matches known bounds.

There only exists a single h_0 such that condition (6) is satisfied, namely $h_0 = T$. This matches well with the intuition: Bitcoin is clearly not reactive as T needs to be set based on the *worst case network delay* to ensure security.

Capped Exponential Weight. We now provide an example weight function that can be instantiated such that we obtain an optimistically responsive protocol. For some parameter $c \in \mathbb{R}$ and a threshold $T \in \mathcal{H}$, we define

$$w_{c,T}^{EXP}(h) := \begin{cases} e^{hc}, & \text{if } h \leq T, \\ e^{(T+1)c}, & \text{else.} \end{cases}$$

Let $h \in \mathcal{H}$, $h \leq T$. We then have for $w = w_{c,T}^{EXP}$,

$$\frac{w_{\max \leq h}}{w_{\min>h}} = \frac{w_{c,T}^{EXP}(h)}{w_{c,T}^{EXP}(h+1)} = \frac{e^{hc}}{e^{(h+1)c}} = e^{-c}.$$

Again we pick T such that (3) is an equality. We now pick c such that both Eq. (4) and Eq. (6) are satisfied for all h_0. In other words, we pick c such that both

$$e^{-c} = \frac{w_{\max \leq T}}{w_{\min>T}} \leq \frac{1}{2\hat{\Delta}_{\text{Net}}} \cdot (1-\delta) \cdot \frac{\epsilon_c}{2} \cdot (1 - p_{\leq T}) \cdot (p_{\leq T})^{2q\hat{\Delta}_{\text{Net}}-1},$$

---

[5] To adapt to our framework we negate the condition on the valid block predicate. Note that this is without loss of generality.

and

$$e^{-c} = \frac{\mathsf{w}_{\max \le h_0}}{\mathsf{w}_{\min > h_0}} \le \frac{1}{2\hat{\Delta}_{\mathsf{Net}}} \cdot \frac{(1-\delta)}{e \cdot 2q\hat{\Delta}_{\mathsf{Net}}},$$

are satisfied. Such a c exists as both right hand sides are constant and e^{-c} drops exponentially in c. Instantiating w in this way provides a protocol that under worst case conditions performs as the Bitcoin protocol but in good conditions is perfectly responsive to the actual network delay.

5   Conclusions and Directions for Future Work

We have provided a framework for analyzing blockchain protocols with different weight functions. Using this framework, we have shown how to obtain a protocol that is responsive during periods without corruption. After this first step introducing the relevant concepts, several interesting questions remain open: Are there other weight functions with even better guarantees? Is it possible to achieve graceful degradation with respect to responsiveness under some corruption? How can our analysis be extended to variable thresholds to handle changing participation? We believe that our framework provides the right tools for investigating these and further questions.

A   Weight-Based Chain Quality and Common Prefix

In this section we state the weighted variant of the chain quality and common prefix theorems. We start with chain quality and we use Theorem 2 together with the fact that the amount of weight produced during a time period is bounded; moreover, we use the collective mining rate to do this mapping, which is by no means a tight bound.

Corollary 1 (Weighted chain quality). *Let P be an honest party, let R be any consecutive list of blocks from the best chain of this party, and let $\rho \in \mathbb{N}$, $\rho \ge 2\Delta_{\mathsf{Net}}$ be the largest value such that $\hat{W}_q(\rho) \le \mathsf{Weight}(R)$. Further, let $h_0 \in \mathcal{H}$ and $X \in \mathbb{R}$ such that the weight function is $\left(\check{W}_{\mathsf{LeftIso}^{h_0}}, \check{p}_{\mathsf{LeftIso}^{h_0}} \right)$-left-isolated-lower-bounding and $(\hat{W}_{q\beta}, \hat{p}_{q\beta})$-upper-bounding such that for any $\rho' \ge \rho$, we have $\check{W}_{\mathsf{LeftIso}^{h_0}}(\rho' - 2\Delta_{\mathsf{Net}} + 1) \ge \hat{W}_{q\beta}(\rho') + X$. Let p_{bad} be the probability that the fraction of honest weight in R is less than $\frac{X}{\mathsf{Weight}(R)}$. Then,*

$$p_{\mathsf{bad}} \le \check{p}_{\mathsf{LeftIso}^{h_0}} (\rho - 2\Delta_{\mathsf{Net}} + 1) + \hat{p}_{q\beta}(\rho) + \hat{p}_q(\rho).$$

Proof. By our assumption on the weight function, it took at least ρ rounds to produce R, except with probability $\hat{p}_q(\rho)$. We can thus apply Theorem 2 to conclude the proof of the corollary.   □

We next show the weighted common-prefix property.

Corollary 2 (Weighted common prefix). *Let $\omega \in \mathbb{R}$, and let $\rho \in \mathbb{N}$ be the largest value such that $\hat{W}_q(\rho) \leq \omega$ and $\rho \geq 2\Delta_{\mathsf{Net}} - 1$. Further let $h_0 \in \mathcal{H}$ such that the weight function is $\left(\check{W}_{\mathsf{LeftIso}^{h_0}}, \check{p}_{\mathsf{LeftIso}^{h_0}}\right)$-left-isolated-lower-bounding and $(\hat{W}_q, \hat{p}_q)$-upper-bounding, and for all $\rho' \geq \rho$, we have $2 \cdot \check{W}_{\mathsf{LeftIso}^{h_0}}(\rho' - 2\Delta_{\mathsf{Net}} + 1) \geq \hat{W}_q(\rho')$. Let P_1, P_2 be (not necessarily different) honest parties, let $r_1 \leq r_2$ be rounds, and let C_1 be the best chain of P_1 in round r_1. Then, the probability that P_2 has a best chain C_2 in round r_2 with $C_1^{\mathsf{W}\lceil \omega} \npreceq C_2$ is at most*

$$2\check{p}_{\mathsf{LeftIso}^{h_0}}(\rho - 2\Delta_{\mathsf{Net}} + 1) + 2\hat{p}_q(\rho).$$

Proof. By our assumption on the weight function, there is at most $\hat{W}_q(\rho) < \omega$ weight produced in ρ rounds, except with probability $\hat{p}_q(\rho)$. In this case, all blocks on $C_1^{\mathsf{W}\lceil \omega}$ are mined before round $r_1 - \rho$, i.e., $C_1^{\mathsf{W}\lceil \omega} \preceq C_1^{\mathsf{R}>\lceil r_1 - \rho}$. Therefore, we have $C_1^{\mathsf{R}>\lceil r_1 - \rho} \npreceq C_2$. We can thus apply Theorem 3 to conclude the proof of the theorem. $\qquad \square$

References

1. Badertscher, C., Maurer, U., Tschudi, D., Zikas, V.: Bitcoin as a transaction ledger: a composable treatment. In: Katz, J., Shacham, H. (eds.) CRYPTO 2017. LNCS, vol. 10401, pp. 324–356. Springer, Cham (2017). https://doi.org/10.1007/978-3-319-63688-7_11
2. Buterin, V., Griffith, V.: Casper the friendly finality gadget. CoRR, abs/1710.09437 (2017)
3. Dinsdale-Young, T., Magri, B., Matt, C., Nielsen, J.B., Tschudi, D.: Afgjort: a partially synchronous finality layer for blockchains. In: Galdi, C., Kolesnikov, V. (eds.) SCN 2020. LNCS, vol. 12238, pp. 24–44. Springer, Cham (2020). https://doi.org/10.1007/978-3-030-57990-6_2
4. Garay, J., Kiayias, A., Leonardos, N.: The bitcoin backbone protocol: analysis and applications. In: Oswald, E., Fischlin, M. (eds.) EUROCRYPT 2015. LNCS, vol. 9057, pp. 281–310. Springer, Heidelberg (2015). https://doi.org/10.1007/978-3-662-46803-6_10
5. Garay, J., Kiayias, A., Leonardos, N.: The bitcoin backbone protocol with chains of variable difficulty. In: Katz, J., Shacham, H. (eds.) CRYPTO 2017. LNCS, vol. 10401, pp. 291–323. Springer, Cham (2017). https://doi.org/10.1007/978-3-319-63688-7_10
6. Kamp, S.H., Magri, B., Matt, C., Nielsen, J.B., Thomsen, S.E., Tschudi, D.: Weight-based Nakamoto-style blockchains. Cryptology ePrint Archive, Report 2020/328 (2020). https://eprint.iacr.org/2020/328
7. Kiayias, A., Lamprou, N., Stouka, A.-P.: Proofs of proofs of work with sublinear complexity. In: Clark, J., Meiklejohn, S., Ryan, P.Y.A., Wallach, D., Brenner, M., Rohloff, K. (eds.) FC 2016. LNCS, vol. 9604, pp. 61–78. Springer, Heidelberg (2016). https://doi.org/10.1007/978-3-662-53357-4_5
8. Kiayias, A., Miller, A., Zindros, D.: Non-interactive proofs of proof-of-work. Cryptology ePrint Archive, Report 2017/963 (2017). https://eprint.iacr.org/2017/963
9. Nakamoto, S.: Bitcoin: a peer-to-peer electronic cash system (2009). http://www.bitcoin.org/bitcoin.pdf

10. Niu, J., Feng, C., Dau, H., Huang, Y.C., Zhu, J.: Analysis of Nakamoto consensus, revisited. Cryptology ePrint Archive, Report 2019/1225 (2019). https://eprint.iacr.org/2019/1225
11. Pass, R., Seeman, L., Shelat, A.: Analysis of the blockchain protocol in asynchronous networks. In: Coron, J.-S., Nielsen, J.B. (eds.) EUROCRYPT 2017. LNCS, vol. 10211, pp. 643–673. Springer, Cham (2017). https://doi.org/10.1007/978-3-319-56614-6_22
12. Pass, R., Shi, E.: Hybrid consensus: efficient consensus in the permissionless model. In: 31st International Symposium on Distributed Computing, DISC 2017, Vienna, Austria, 16–20 October 2017, pp. 39:1–39:16 (2017)
13. Pass, R., Shi, E.: Thunderella: blockchains with optimistic instant confirmation. In: Nielsen, J.B., Rijmen, V. (eds.) EUROCRYPT 2018. LNCS, vol. 10821, pp. 3–33. Springer, Cham (2018). https://doi.org/10.1007/978-3-319-78375-8_1
14. Ren, L.: Analysis of Nakamoto consensus. Cryptology ePrint Archive, Report 2019/943 (2019). https://eprint.iacr.org/2019/943
15. Shrestha, N., Abraham, I., Ren, L., Nayak, K.: On the optimality of optimistic responsiveness. In: Ligatti, J., Ou, X., Katz, J., Vigna, G. (eds.) ACM CCS 2020, pp. 839–857. ACM Press, November 2020
16. Stewart, A., Kokoris-Kogia, E.: Grandpa: a byzantine finality gadget (2020)

LOVE a Pairing

Diego F. Aranha[1,4]([✉]), Elena Pagnin[2,4], and Francisco Rodríguez-Henríquez[3,4]

[1] Aarhus University, Aarhus, Denmark
dfaranha@cs.au.dk
[2] Lund University, Lund, Sweden
elena.pagnin@eit.lth.se
[3] Cryptography Research Centre, Technology Innovation Institute, Abu Dhabi, UAE
[4] Computer Science Department, Cinvestav, Mexico
francisco@cs.cinvestav.mx

Abstract. The problem of securely outsourcing the computation of a bilinear pairing has been widely investigated in the literature. Designing an efficient protocol with the desired functionality has, however, been an open challenge for a long time. Recently, Di Crescenzo et al. (CARDIS'20) proposed the first suite of protocols for *securely and efficiently* delegating pairings with online inputs under the presence of a *malicious server*. We progress along this path with the aim of LOVE (Lowering the cost of Outsourcing and Verifying Efficiently) a pairing. Our contributions are threefold. First, we propose a protocol (LOVE) that improves the efficiency of Di Crescenzo et al.'s proposal for securely delegating pairings with online, public inputs. Second, we provide the first implementation of efficient protocols in this setting. Finally, we evaluate the performance of our LOVE protocol in different application scenarios by benchmarking an implementation using BN, BLS12 and BLS24 pairing-friendly curves. Interestingly, compared to Di Crescenzo et al.'s protocol, LOVE is up to 29.7% faster for the client, up to 24.9% for the server and requires 23–24% less communication cost depending on the choice of parameters. Furthermore, we note that our LOVE protocol is especially suited for subgroup-secure groups: checking the correctness of the delegated pairing requires up to 56.2% less computations than evaluating the pairing locally (no delegation). This makes LOVE the most efficient protocol to date for securely outsourcing the computation of a pairing with online public inputs, even when the server is malicious.

1 Introduction

Cryptographic bilinear pairings (a.k.a. pairings, in short) have proven to be an extremely versatile building block to realize novel and advanced cryptographic tools including identity-based encryption [12], short signatures [14], aggregate signatures [13], and zero knowledge-Succinct Non-interactive ARgument of Knowledge (zk-SNARK) [27]. Very recently, pairings found applications in isogeny-based cryptography, to compress public keys in key exchange [45] and to construct verifiable delay functions [21].

© Springer Nature Switzerland AG 2021
P. Longa and C. Ràfols (Eds.): LATINCRYPT 2021, LNCS 12912, pp. 320–340, 2021.
https://doi.org/10.1007/978-3-030-88238-9_16

Pairing-based protocols critically rely on an efficient implementation of the pairing, which has computational cost far more expensive than any other of the protocol's building blocks. Several clever algorithmic breakthroughs [8,41], capitalized on efficient software and hardware implementations (see [1], [36, Chapter 11] for a comprehensive overview), producing an impressive reduction of the latency associated to a pairing. Nonetheless, as of 2015, the timing cost for the execution of a single pairing on the BN curve at the 128-bit security level, was five to six times higher than the one of a scalar multiplication (over $\mathbb{G}_1$) [46, Table II]. The considerably higher cost of evaluating a pairing motivated a line of research on how to outsource this computation in a secure and efficient way.

Secure and Efficient Pairing Delegation. For many years, researchers and developers have addressed the problem of how a resource-constrained device (Client), can safely delegate the computation of a pairing to a much more powerful computational entity (Server). This setting is particularly relevant in the Internet of the Things (IoT): if secure and efficient pairing delegation is possible, IoT devices (acting as clients) can manage advanced pairing-based protocols without having to pay the cost of locally evaluating pairings. Intuitively, a protocol for secure and efficient pairing delegation should provide mechanisms allowing the client to verify the correctness of the output returned by the server. With respect to efficiency, we want the client's computational costs associated to such delegation be strictly less expensive than the action of computing the pairing solely on the client's device. However, the verification normally involves the computation of costly exponentiations (over $\mathbb{G}_T$), membership tests (in $\mathbb{G}_T$), and at times, additional lighter operations such as scalar multiplications (on $\mathbb{G}_1$ and $\mathbb{G}_2$). Progressive efficiency improvements on pairing evaluation rapidly closed the gap between the cost of verifying the delegated pairing and actually computing the pairing locally. As a result, many of the pairing delegation protocols with the verifiability property proposed to date [16,17,25,31], fail to meet the efficiency requirement stated above. This situation has called to question the whole idea of delegating a pairing in the first place.

In 2020, Di Crescenzo, Khodjaeva, Kahrobaei and Shpilrain put forth a promising solution to realize efficient pairing delegation in the offline/online setting [20]. In a nutshell, this means that the protocol splits into two subsequent phases: an offline phase (run by the client only), followed by an online phase when the inputs to the pairing are disclosed and the client interacts with the server. The key idea is that the offline phase is independent of the pairing inputs, can be run at any point in time, and collects the bulk of the computation required from the client. In contrast, the online phase should be as lightweight as possible for the client, so that verifying the outsourced pairing computation is less expensive than evaluating the pairing locally on the client device. In this paper, we carefully investigate about the efficiency claims of [20] in the context of the new parameter recommendations for pairings at the 128- and 192-bit security level. We additionally introduce minor changes to the original protocol to further optimize its efficiency and test our implementation on a simulated client-server interaction.

Our Contributions. This paper provides the first implementation of a secure and efficient protocol for pairing delegation in the offline/online setting. We focus only on the case of public inputs, because our experimental results indicate that delegating a pairing with private inputs remains inefficient and more expensive than performing the local computation. Concretely, we take the most efficient protocols proposed in [20] and make slight but clever modifications with the aim of LOVE (Lowering the cost of Outsourcing and Verifying Efficiently) a pairing. As a result, we obtain the most efficient protocols to date for securely outsourcing the computation of a pairing with online public inputs, even in cases where we cannot trust the server. We formally prove the security for our 'adjusted' protocol LOVE. Finally, we experimentally evaluate LOVE with several choices of curves at different security levels. As a byproduct (and a result of independent interest), we provide updated costs for scalar multiplication and exponentiation in pairing groups using optimized implementations. Interestingly, in lieu of the new optimizations, the performance improvement of delegating a pairing is lower than the reported in previous work, when state of the art implementations are used and the cost of membership checks in $\mathbb{G}_T$ is considered. Furthermore, our results reinforce the observation stated in [6] that even at the cost of a small performance penalty for its individual building blocks, choosing subgroup-secure parameters provides an overall better performance when the whole protocol is analyzed.

Applications. Delegating the computation of a pairing on public inputs may seem a task with little use, yet, we will argue next that it has interesting implications in the realm of efficient verification.

First of all, such a scheme can be deployed to realize server-aided signature verification for schemes that involve pairings in the verification process. This setting has been studied, e.g., in [37], and becomes of particular interest for verifications that involve several pairing computations, e.g. [4]. We note that, if one assumes a trusted set up (for instance, a set up that outputs $\gamma = e(P_1, P_2)$), verifiers could leverage the pairing γ provided by the set up in their offline phase, and thus run the signature verification without needing to ever compute a pairing locally. This simple observation is of particular interest for IoT devices, where one may wish to minimize the code loaded on a constrained device without compromising too much its limited computing resources.

Another venue of application for delegating the computation of a pairing on public inputs is the recent isogeny-based Verifiable Delay Function (VDF) construction presented in [21]. VDFs [11], have important applications for Blockchain proof of space and stake, design of trustworthy randomness beacons and benchmarking of high-end servers, among others. In a VDF setting, given an input challenge x and public parameters pp, the Prover must compute a function $Eval(pp, x) \mapsto (y, \pi)$, where y is the output of the function $Eval$ and π is its proof. A second entity, known as the Verifier, must compute a decision function $Verify(pp, x, y, \pi) \mapsto \{True, False\}$, which determines whether the Prover satisfactorily completed its task or not. By design running $Eval$ shall take time comparable with a prescribed delay T; more formally, it should be computationally intractable, regardless of the amount of parallelization employed by the Prover, to calculate $Eval$ in time less than T. Moreover, once y along with its proof π are produced, the output y should be easily verifiable by anyone in a much shorter Polylog(T) time. Recently, De Feo, Masson, Petit and Sanso proposed in [21] an isogeny-based VDF construction that uses a pairing for its verification algorithm. In this protocol, the verifier sets up the scheme, and checks the correctness of the evaluation's output by computing two pairings (and by performing other, less expensive checks). Notably, the pairings' inputs are public values, so it seems natural to apply our technique: include the pairing delegation setup in the VDF set up, and enjoy a more efficient verification procedure. This change clearly increases the computational demands on the Prover (running $Eval$) and thus its delay, which is a desirable feature in the VDF setting, and at the same time it speeds up the verification. At the moment, the improvement we described above only works for one of the pairings (the right hand side one, on line 2. of Verify in Fig. 1 and 2 of [21]) and assuming that the verifier knows the point Q at set up time.

1.1 Related Work

The seminal work on secure pairing delegation protocols is due to Girault and Lefranc [25] who formalized this notion as *Server-Aided Verification*. The aim of [25] was to improve the efficiency of signature verification by relying on a server to carry out the expensive pairing computation. This approach sparked a long line of research, which includes more expressive models for server-aided verification [18,37,43], security notions for pairing delegation (in the framework of verifiable computation) [17], and several constructions aiming at concrete efficiency and/or better security [16,20,30,31,42,44]. Paradoxically, the state of the art in this matter seems to suggest that delegating a pairing computation in a secure and verifiable way inherently requires more computations than evaluating the pairing locally. To overcome this problem, Di Crescenzo et al. [20] adopted a new strategy. Instead of relying on the standard server-aided verification syntax (two-message protocol), they considered an offline phase (traditionally called key generation, which runs independently of the computational input), and an online phase where the pairing arguments are disclosed and the verifier (acting as a client) interacts with the server. The offline/online approach seems a winning concept: it allows the verifier to run the bulk of computations during the offline phase, which may happen at any point in time before the actual pairing computation is needed. Once the pairing arguments are disclosed, the verifier enjoys more efficient procedures that rely on the output of the expensive offline phase. While this setting is promising, [20] provides no concrete implementation of the suggested protocols and the efficiency estimates are extrapolated from a hypothetical text-book implementation using the well-known, but by now outdated, performance figures from [15].

Interestingly, the problem of pairing delegation appears to be easier in the *batch* setting, where the client wants to compute several pairings $e(A_i, B_i)$ for $A_i \in \mathbb{G}_1$ and $B_i \in \mathbb{G}_2$. The first solution came out in 2007, when Tsang, Chow and Smith [40] proposed the first batch pairing delegation protocols and related security notions. They classified the possible pairing arguments in 16 types (all combinations of public/secret, variable/constant inputs) and proposed protocols tailored to 4 of these settings. Unfortunately, their main protocol was limited to pairings sharing the same secret first argument and involved costly exponentiation in the target group. Later, Mefenza and Vergnaud [34] proposed new efficient batch pairing delegation protocols in the same settings by adopting the endomorphism idea from Guillevic and Vergnaud [30] and reducing the size of exponents. Performance improvements ranged from 40% to 74% at the 128-bit security level in comparison with previous work.

2 Preliminaries

Notation. We denote by λ (resp. σ) the computational (resp. statistical) security parameter of a scheme. We use *choosing at random* or *randomly choosing* to refer to sampling from the given set according to the uniform distribution, and denote this by $x \overset{\$}{\leftarrow} X$. We denote by $\mathsf{poly}(\lambda)$ a generic polynomial function in the variable λ, and by negl a negligible function, that is $\mathsf{negl}(\lambda) < 1/\mathsf{poly}(\lambda)$, for any poly and large enough values of λ. We denote by $\mathsf{cost}(\cdot)$ a function that, given as input an algorithm returns its computational cost (in some desired computational model). Unless otherwise specified, all groups we work with have order q, which is a 2λ-bit prime; and P_i denotes a generator of the group cyclic group $\mathbb{G}_i$. We denote by $\mathsf{Bool}(\cdot)$ the boolean function that returns 1 if the statement given in input is true/satisfied, and 0 otherwise.

The parameters $p, q, \phi_k(p)$ and k, denote the base field prime, the pairing group order and the k-th cyclotomic polynomial evaluated at p and the embedding degree, respectively. These parameters are formally defined next.

2.1 Pairings

Let E be an elliptic curve defined over the finite field $\mathbb{F}_p$, where p is a large prime. Denote by $E(\mathbb{F}_p)$ the set of points $(x, y) \in \mathbb{F}_p$ that satisfy the elliptic curve equation along with the point at infinity denoted by $\mathcal{O}$. It is known that $E(\mathbb{F}_p)$ forms an additive Abelian group with respect to the elliptic point addition operation. Let $\#E$ denote the cardinality of $E(\mathbb{F}_p)$, and let q be a large prime that divides $\#E$ with $\gcd(q, p) = 1$. Then, the *embedding degree* of a curve is defined as the smallest integer k, such that q divides $p^k - 1$. Let $\mathbb{F}_{p^k}$ be an *extension field* of $\mathbb{F}_p$ of degree k, and let $\mathbb{F}_{p^k}^*$ be the field composed by the non-zero elements of $\mathbb{F}_{p^k}$. We say that $\mathbb{G}_1, \mathbb{G}_2$ and $\mathbb{G}_T$ are an order-q subgroup of $E(\mathbb{F}_p)$, an order-q subgroup of $E(\mathbb{F}_{p^k})$, and the order-q subgroup of $\mathbb{F}_{p^k}^*$, respectively. Groups $\mathbb{G}_1, \mathbb{G}_2$ are typically written additively, while group $\mathbb{G}_T$ is always written multiplicatively.

The standard procedure for computing a pairing is based on an iterative algorithm, proposed by Victor Miller in 1986 [35]. Let $R \in E(\mathbb{F}_{p^k})$ and let s be a non-negative integer. A *Miller function* $f_{s,R}$ of length s is a function in

$\mathbb{F}_{p^k}(E)$ with divisor $(f_{s,R}) = s(R) - (sR) - (s-1)(\infty)$, where ∞ denotes the point at infinity. Miller's algorithm calculates a value f that is only unique up to a multiplicative power of q. The *reduced* Tate pairing computes a *final exponentiation* step, where the value f is raised to the power $(p^k - 1)/q$. This exponentiation is known as the final exponentiation, and maps the result into the desired subgroup of q-th roots of unity. For even embedding degree k and k-th cyclotomic polynomial $\psi_k(\cdot)$, the final exponentiation is split in the *easy* and *hard* parts as $(p^k - 1)/q = [(p^{k/2} - 1) \cdot (p^{k/2} + 1)/\phi_k(p)] \cdot [\phi_k(p)/q]$. This way one gets a bilinear pairing, whose main properties are summarized below.

A pairing is an efficiently-computable map $e : \mathbb{G}_1 \times \mathbb{G}_2 \to \mathbb{G}_T$ defined over groups of prime order q, that enjoys the following properties:

Bilinearity. $e(aP_1, bP_2) = e(P_1, P_2)^{ab}$, $\forall a, b \xleftarrow{\$} \mathbb{Z}_q, P_1 \in \mathbb{G}_1$ and $P_2 \in \mathbb{G}_2$
Non-degeneracy. If P_1 and P_2 are generators of $\mathbb{G}_1$ and $\mathbb{G}_2$ respectively, then $g_T = e(P_1, P_2)$ is a generator for $\mathbb{G}_T$.

The pairing e is of Type 1 (symmetric) if $\mathbb{G}_1 = \mathbb{G}_2$. This implies that the curve is equipped with a *distortion map* to produce a linearly independent second argument for non-degeneracy. The pairing e is of Type 3 (asymmetric) if $\mathbb{G}_1 \neq \mathbb{G}_2$ and there are no homomorphisms between the two groups. In the latter case a *twist* is typically used to compress group elements in $\mathbb{G}_2$.

The state of the art in pairing-based cryptography employs the optimal Ate pairing [41] operating on a *family* of curves of small embedding degree, called *pairing-friendly* [22]. Pairing-friendly curves are specified by means of associated parameterized polynomial formulae for the prime modulus p and the prime order subgroup q. For the sake of efficiency, these formulae are instantiated using *seeds* with low Hamming weight (cf. Table 1). Known pairing-friendly families offer different trade-offs between the field sizes (for security in $\mathbb{G}_T$), and curve orders (for security in $\mathbb{G}_1$ and $\mathbb{G}_2$). With the aim of achieving a better performance, we normally choose larger embedding degrees when targeting higher security levels. This design decision allows us to work with moderate sizes of the base field and the curve order.

Selecting a suitable pairing-friendly curve and its associated finite fields and pairing parameters requires trying many *seeds* with low Hamming weight, until a curve with the right performance properties and security requirements is found, inside the chosen family. Design aspects to be considered include the existence of endomorphisms to accelerate scalar multiplication and exponentiation in the pairing groups, the degree of the twist, an optimized *towering* to represent $\mathbb{F}_{p^k}$, efficient ways to test for membership or to hash bit strings to group elements, among others. Security requirements include the hardness of solving the discrete logarithm problem in all groups, and the necessity of verifying that group elements have the right order and were not maliciously selected. The latter is alleviated by choosing curves providing *subgroup security* [6], which mandates that $E(\mathbb{F}_p)$ and $E(\mathbb{F}_{p^k})$ do not contain subgroups significantly smaller than the subgroups $\mathbb{G}_1$ and $\mathbb{G}_2$, both of prime order q. The related $\mathbb{G}_T$-strength security notion applies this idea to $\mathbb{G}_T$ only [38]. Checking the order of group elements is called *subgroup membership testing*.

After the TNFS algorithm was proposed to solve the discrete logarithm in parameterized composite-degree extension fields [32], prime-order Barreto-Naehrig curves [9] lost the top performance spot at 128-bit security. Currently, the families that offer better performance are Barreto-Lynn-Scott curves (BLS) [7] with embedding degree 12 at the 128-bit security level, and 24 at the 192-bit security level [5]. The corresponding curve with embedding degree 48 has been considered for the 256-bit security level [33].

3   Delegating Pairings with Online Public Inputs

In this section, we recall part of Di Crescenzo et al.'s work [20] both for completeness and for providing more intuitive notations, descriptions, as well as a more rigorous formalism. Concretely, we begin by presenting a formal framework for offline/online pairing delegation, and a suitable security model. Our goal here is to spell out the details of the intuitions provided in [20], by having rigorous definitions, which simplify the well-established VC model of [24] to the case of pairing delegation. We then describe the original protocol for online public inputs provided in [20], with an improved notation, and along with correctness, security and efficiency considerations.

3.1   Modeling Offline/Online Pairing Delegation Protocols

We describe a formal model for offline/online pairing delegation. In a nutshell, this model makes use of correctness and (output) security as introduced for verifiable computation (VC) by Gennaro, Gentry and Parno [24]. These notions are, however, adapted (and simplified) to the special setting of our work. We prefer to re-name the standard VC algorithms (KeyGen, ProbGen, Compute, and Verify) to something with a more explicit meaning for our setting, namely (offSetup, onSetup, Compute, and onVerify).

Definition 1 (Offline/Online Pairing Delegation). *An offline/online protocol for pairing delegation consists of the five algorithms* (GlobalSetup, offSetup, onSetup, Compute, onVerify) *with the following syntax:*

GlobalSetup(λ) $\rightarrow$ bilin.group *this is a randomized algorithm that takes as input a value λ (the computational security parameter) and returns the description of a bilinear group* bilin.group $= (q, \mathbb{G}_1, P_1, \mathbb{G}_2, P_2, \mathbb{G}_T, e)$, *where q is a 2λ-bit prime, and e is a pairing. We assume* bilin.group *is implicitly available to all subsequent algorithms. (This is a one-time set up).*

offSetup(σ) $\rightarrow$ off.pp *this is a randomized algorithm that takes as input a value σ (the statistical security parameter). It returns some values* off.pp. *(This algorithm is run in by the* client *during the offline phase).*

onSetup(off.pp, (A, B)) $\rightarrow$ (pub, sec) *this is a randomized algorithm that takes as input* off.pp, *and a pairing argument $(A, B) \in \mathbb{G}_1 \times \mathbb{G}_2$. It returns a public value* pub, *and a secret value* sec. *(This algorithm is run by the* client, *and is the first algorithm of the online phase. At this point* off.pp *and* sec *are only known to the* client, *while* pub *will be sent to the* server).

Compute(pub) → out *this is a deterministic algorithm that takes as input the public value* pub; *and returns a public output* out. *(This algorithm is run by the* server, *and is the second algorithm of the online phase).*

Verify(sec, out) → value *this is a deterministic algorithm that takes as input the secret value* sec *(generated by the online setup) and the server's output* out. *It returns a value* value $\in \{\mathbb{G}_T \cup \perp\}$. *(This algorithm is run by the* client, *and is the last algorithm of the online phase. It is designed to verify the correctness of the computation carried out by the* server*).*

Figure 1 displays a graphical summary of the syntax introduced in Definition 1.

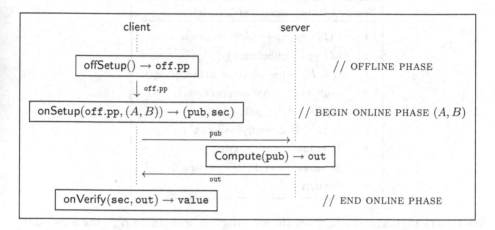

Fig. 1. Diagram visualizing the model for offline/online pairing delegation. Notably, the pairing arguments (A, B) are revealed only at the start of the online phase. The one-time GlobalSetup is omitted from the picture.

A protocol for offline/online delegation of a pairing computation is correct if for all possible input arguments $(A, B) \in \mathbb{G}_1 \times \mathbb{G}_2$, (and for any possible randomness used by offSetup and onSetup) the protocol execution returns value $= e(A, B)$, assuming all algorithms are run honestly. This is formalized by the following definition (which is closely similar to the correctness for VC in [24], but tailored to our case of interest).

Definition 2 (Correctness). *A protocol for offline/online pairing delegation is correct if for any value of λ and σ, and for all of possible input arguments $(A, B) \in \mathbb{G}_1 \times \mathbb{G}_2$ it holds that:*

$$Prob \left[\text{value} = e(A, B) \middle| \begin{array}{l} \text{bilin.group} \leftarrow \text{GlobalSetup}(\lambda) \\ \text{off.pp} \leftarrow \text{offSetup}(\sigma) \\ (\text{pub, sec}) \leftarrow \text{onSetup}(\text{off.pp}, (A, B)) \\ \text{out} \leftarrow \text{Compute(pub)} \\ \text{value} \leftarrow \text{onVerify(sec, out)} \end{array} \right] = 1.$$

A protocol for offline/online delegation of a pairing computation is secure if no adversary (in the shoes of a malicious server) is able to produce a value out* that is not rejected by the verifier and that results in a incorrect output value* $\neq e(A, B)$. This is formalized in the following security definition and the experiment $\mathbf{Exp}_{\mathcal{A}}^{\mathsf{sec}}$. Notably, $\mathbf{Exp}_{\mathcal{A}}^{\mathsf{sec}}$ is a simplification of the security experiment for VC in [24]: we reduce the number of adversarial queries to a single one, since in the setting of [20], every new input (A, B) requires a new run of offSetup. Our adversary is a pair of algorithms $\mathcal{A} = (\mathcal{A}_1, \mathcal{A}_2)$ that share an internal state st.

Security Experiment $\mathbf{Exp}_{\mathcal{A}}^{\mathsf{sec}}(n, \sigma)$

1 :   bilin.group $\leftarrow$ GlobalSetup(n)

2 :   off.pp $\leftarrow$ offSetup(σ)

3 : $((A, B), st) \leftarrow \mathcal{A}_1(n, \sigma, \text{bilin.group})$

4 :   (pub, sec) $\leftarrow$ onSetup(off.pp, (A, B))

5 :   out* $\leftarrow \mathcal{A}_2(st, \text{pub}, (A, B))$

6 :   value* $\leftarrow$ onVerify(sec, out*)

7 :   **if** value* $= \bot$ **return** 0

8 :   **if** value* $= e(A, B)$ **return** 0

9 :   **return** 1

We remark that, in order to reach the winning condition in $\mathbf{Exp}_{\mathcal{A}}^{\mathsf{sec}}$, the adversary needs to produce an output out* that is not rejected by the verification (i.e., value* $\neq \bot$) and that yields an incorrect value value* $\neq e(A, B)$. Such an output would indeed fool the client into accepting an incorrect value as the result of the outsourced pairing computation. A protocol is secure if any adversary has only negligible probability of winning the security experiment $\mathbf{Exp}_{\mathcal{A}}^{\mathsf{sec}}$.

Definition 3 (Security). *A protocol for offline/online pairing delegation is said to be secure if for any probabilistic, polynomial time algorithm $\mathcal{A} = (\mathcal{A}_1, \mathcal{A}_2)$ it holds that:*

$$Prob\left[\mathbf{Exp}_{\mathcal{A}}^{\mathsf{sec}}(\lambda, \sigma) = 1\right] \leq 2^{-\sigma} + \mathsf{negl}(\lambda).$$

Regarding efficiency, we cannot use the amortized efficiency framework of VC, where the computational cost of running KeyGen –our offSetup– can be amortized over several executions of the core delegation protocol. In our case, for security reasons, the output of offSetup can be used only for a single pairing delegation. As we discussed already in the introduction, it is hopeless to expect a pairing delegation protocol be efficient in the strictest sense; the best we can hope to achieve is efficiency in the online verification. This is formalized in the following definition.

Definition 4 (Efficient Online Verification). *A protocol for offline/online pairing delegation is said to have efficient online verification if* (cost(onSetup) +

$\mathsf{cost(onVerify))} < \mathsf{cost}(e(\cdot,\cdot))$, *i.e., the cost of running the online phase on the client-side is less than the cost of computing the pairing on the client's device.*

3.2 Di Crescenzo et al.'s Protocol

In [20], Di Crescenzo et al. propose five different protocols for securely delegating the computation of $e(A, B)$, given the points $A \in \mathbb{G}_1, B \in \mathbb{G}_2$. The most efficient protocol (described in Section 3 of [20], and here in Figure 2) works in the setting where (A, B) are public. In the protocol description, the value q (which determines the size of the field from which r is sampled), depends on the security parameter λ (that sets up the bilinear group). The value σ, instead, represents the parameter for statistical security that delivers the information theoretic security guarantee of the protocol. Finally, we recall that the handle $\mathtt{bilin.group} = (q, \mathbb{G}_1, P_1, \mathbb{G}_2, P_2, \mathbb{G}_T, e)$ generated by $\mathsf{GlobalSetup}(\lambda)$, is available to all algorithms.

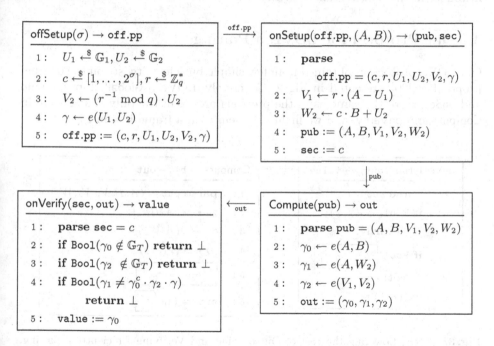

Fig. 2. Di Crescenzo et al.'s protocol for secure pairing delegation with online public inputs (see Section 3 in [20]). This description uses a different, more intuitive notation. The GlobalSetup is not included explicitly as it is trivial.

Correctness. The correctness is trivial by inspection. By line 2 in Compute and line 5 in onVerify it follows that $\mathtt{value} = \gamma_0 = e(A, B)$, since for correctness all parties are required not to deviate from the algorithms descriptions, and all communication happens via a perfect, noise-free channel.

330   D. F. Aranha et al.

Security. The security essentially relies on the fact that an adversary (playing the role of a malicious **server**) cannot guess the challenge value c, except with probability $2^{-\sigma}$ (which is small by construction). We refer the reader to [20] for a detailed security proof.

Efficiency. Regarding efficient online verification, we would need to estimate the client's computational cost in the online phase, i.e., $\mathsf{cost}(\mathsf{onSetup})+\mathsf{cost}(\mathsf{onVerify})$ and compare it to the cost of computing the pairing $\mathsf{cost}(e(\cdot,\cdot))$. This is already done by [20] in an abstract way through a theoretical complexity analysis based on cost estimates extracted from Bos et al.'s work [15]. Interestingly, this efficiency analysis disregards the cost of membership testing in $\mathbb{G}_T$ which can be quite significant for some parameters [6]. In contrast, we aim to provide concrete efficiency analysis of complete algorithm executions (see Sect. 5). To this end, we implement the protocol in Fig. 2, collect actual computational complexity and timings, and compare its performance against our LOVE variant (that we introduce in the next section, Fig. 3).

4 Our Protocol for LOVE a Pairing

Our LOVE protocol is obtained from few simple but clever twists on the original proposal of [20] presented in Fig. 2. Concretely, LOVE's GlobalSetup, offSetup and onSetup are the same as in the previous proposal; the only changes are in Compute and onVerify, and we highlight them with a frame box in Fig. 3.

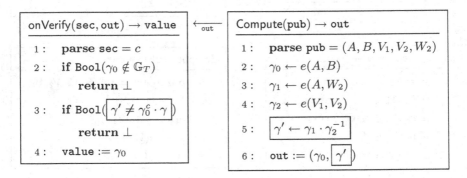

Fig. 3. LOVE: Lowering the cost of Outsourcing and Verifying Efficiently a pairing. The algorithms GlobalSetup, offSetup and onSetup are exactly as in Fig. 2. For clarity, we frame the points in which LOVE differs from the previous proposal.

Correctness. The correctness of our LOVE protocol (depicted in Fig. 3) is evident by inspection: $\mathtt{value} := \gamma_0$ (line 4 in onVerify) and $\gamma_0 \leftarrow e(A,B)$ (line 2 in Compute).

Security. The security proof for LOVE follows from the same arguments as the one for original protocol given in [20]. For completeness, we present below the full proof for our LOVE variant using the formalism of the offline/online framework introduced in Sect. 3.1.

In the security experiment $\mathbf{Exp}_{\mathcal{A}}^{\mathsf{sec}}(\lambda, \sigma)$, $\mathcal{A}$ chooses the pairing argument $(A, B) \in \mathbb{G}_1 \times \mathbb{G}_2$, and receives the string $\mathsf{pub} = (A, B, V_1, V_2, W_1)$. The adversary wins the game if she can forge an output $\mathsf{out}^* = (\gamma_0^*, \gamma'^*)$ on which onVerify returns $\mathsf{value} \notin \{\perp, e(A, B)\}$, i.e., the verification does not reject the forgery and returns a value different from the correct one.

Since we work with cyclic groups, each element has a unique representation as a multiple of a generator. For convenience let us describe the elements in pub in terms of their respective discrete logarithms (convention: lower case Latin letters denote the dlog of the corresponding capital case group element): $A = a \cdot P_1$, $B = b \cdot P_2$, $U_1 = u_1 \cdot P_1$, $V_1 = v_1 \cdot P_1$, $U_2 = u_2 \cdot P_2$, $V_2 = v_2 \cdot P_2$, $W_2 = w_2 \cdot P_2$. By construction we have:

$$\begin{cases} v_1 = ra - ru_1 \\ v_2 = r^{-1}u_2 \\ w_2 = cb + u_2 \end{cases} \tag{1}$$

where u_1, u_2 are uniform random variables (u.r.v.) on $\mathbb{Z}_q$, r is a u.r.v. on $\mathbb{Z}_q^*$, and c is a u.r.v. on $[1, \ldots, 2^\sigma]$. We make no assumptions on the distributions of a and b since these may be chosen by the adversary.

Our first step is to prove that pub leaks no information about c. We do so by showing that the distribution of (v_1, v_2, w_2), seen as the Cartesian product of the random variables obtained as the combination of (a, b, c, r, u_1, u_2) defined in System (1), is independent of the distribution of (a, b, c). Formally,

$$Prob[\{(v_1, v_2, w_2)\} | \{(a, b, c)\}] = Prob[\{(v_1, v_2, w_2)\}] + \mathsf{negl}(\lambda).$$

Proposition 1. $Prob[\{(v_1, v_2, w_2)\}]$ *is negligibly close to* q^{-3} *(u.r.v. on* $\mathbb{Z}_q^3$*).*

This is immediate since adding a u.r.v. defined on $\mathbb{Z}_q$ to any r.v. on any subset of $\mathbb{Z}_q$ yields a u.r.v. on $\mathbb{Z}_q$ (this is the argument for v_1 and w_2); and any r.v. on any subset of $\mathbb{Z}_q$ multiplied by a u.r.v. on $\mathbb{Z}_q$ yields a u.r.v. with overwhelming probability, i.e., except when either variable takes the value 0 (this is the argument for v_2). The latter event has probability q^{-1} which is negligible in the security parameter λ ($r \neq 0$ since it is invertible).

Our next goal is to show that the same statement holds even when conditioning the probability to a given event $\{(a, b, c)\} \in \mathbb{Z}_q \times \mathbb{Z}_q \times [1, \ldots, 2^\sigma]$.

Proposition 2. $Prob[\{(v_1, v_2, w_2)\} | \{(a, b, c)\}]$ *is negligibly close to* q^{-3}.

This is immediate for the same reasoning as Proposition 1. In detail, $w_2 = cb + u_2$ is uniformly distributed over $\mathbb{Z}_q$ since so is u_2, even conditioned to (b, c). Whenever $u_2 \neq 0$, $v_2 = r^{-1}u_2$ is uniformly distributed since so is r, and this holds independently of b, c and w_2. Finally, $v_1 = ra - ru_1$ is uniformly distributed since so is u_1 (and $r \neq 0$ since it is invertible by construction), and this holds independently of a, b, c and v_2, w_2.

Once established that pub leaks no information about c to $\mathcal{A}$ (except with a negligible probability in λ), we can move on to consider $\mathcal{A}$'s forgery attempts.

Proposition 3. *Given $\gamma = e(U_1, U_2) \in \mathbb{G}_T$, for any eligible forgery, i.e., for any $(\gamma_0^*, \gamma'^*) \in \mathbb{G}_T^2$ with $\gamma_0^* \neq e(A, B)$, there exists a unique value c, for which it holds that $\gamma'^* = \gamma_0^{*c} \cdot \gamma$.*

Because $\mathbb{G}_T$ is a multiplicative group, we can re-write the probabilistic verification check as $\gamma_0^{*c} = \gamma'^* \cdot \gamma^{-1}$. Since $\mathbb{G}_T$ is cyclic and of prime order, any element of $\mathbb{G}_T$ is a generator (except for its unit). Thus, $c = DLog_{\gamma_0^*}(\gamma_0^{*c}) = DLog_{\gamma_0^*}(\gamma'^* \cdot \gamma^{-1})$ is unique, modulus q (the group order).

Proposition 4. *For any $\mathsf{out}^* = (\gamma_0^*, \gamma'^*) \in \mathbb{G}_T^2$ such that $\gamma_0^* \neq e(A, B)$, $\mathbf{Exp}_{\mathcal{A}}^{\mathsf{sec}}(\lambda, \sigma)$ outputs 1 with probability at most $2^{-\sigma} + \mathsf{negl}(\lambda)$.*

By Propositions 1 and 2, the string pub does not leak any information about c. This implies that, for a malicious server, all values in $[1, \ldots, 2^\sigma]$ are still equally likely for c, even when conditioning over the $\mathcal{A}$'s view pub. By Proposition 3, the probability that any two values $(\gamma_0^*, \gamma'^*) \in \mathbb{G}_T$ satisfy the probabilistic test is one divided by the number of possible values c can take. Since to $\mathcal{A}$ all values of c are still equally likely, we get: $Prob[\mathbf{Exp}_{\mathcal{A}}^{\mathsf{sec}}(\lambda, \sigma) = 1] \leq 2^{-\sigma} + \mathsf{negl}(\lambda)$, which corresponds to $\mathcal{A}$ randomly guessing the value γ'^* that passes the verification equation (there are only 2^σ such values, given that $\gamma_0^*, \gamma \in \mathbb{G}_T$ and $c \in [1, \ldots 2^\sigma]$), or $\mathcal{A}$'s view leaking some information about c.   □

Efficiency. The next section collects the actual computational complexity, timings and performance comparison against the original proposal of [20]. Here we provide only high-level arguments by counting the main operations of both protocols. Compared to the original protocol in Fig. 2, the onVerify algorithm of LOVE saves one membership test for a $\mathbb{G}_T$ group element, and one multiplication in $\mathbb{G}_T$. Regarding communication, LOVE beats the original protocol by transmitting one less $\mathbb{G}_T$-element. Moreover, from the server side, LOVE's optimization also allows to compute γ' as a product of pairings and share the final exponentiation, which brings potential additional efficiency gains.

5   Implementation Results

We implemented LOVE and Di Crescenzo et al.'s protocol [20] using four different sets of parameters with the help of the RELIC cryptographic library [2]. The first choice is the legacy BN-254 curve previously used to set speed records [3] at the 128-bit security level, whose security guarantees have been degraded to a security level lying somewhere between 100 and 110 bits. The second choice is the curve BN-382, adjusted for new security levels. The third choice is BLS12-381 with embedding degree $k = 12$ and 255-bit prime-order subgroup popularized by the ZCash cryptocurrency [10]. The fourth choice is BLS12-383, a $\mathbb{G}_T$-strong curve generated by Scott [38,39] for applications where subgroup membership checking is performance-critical.[1] The last choice is the BLS24-509 curve originally proposed by Costello [19] and recently suggested by Guillevic as promising at the 192-bit security [28]. RELIC provides dedicated Assembly acceleration for Intel 64-bit platforms for all these curves using a shared codebase, which means that finite field arithmetic is implemented using essentially the same techniques, which permits fair comparisons across different curves and protocols.[2] Given that our choices of λ range from 100 to 192, in order to improve protocol performance we selected a much lower statistical security level of $\sigma = 50$ bits in comparison to 128 used in [20].

Table 1. Parametrization and concrete parameters for the BN, BLS12 and BLS24 pairing-friendly curves used in our implementation. For the specified seed choice z_0, the curve BN-254 provides around 100 bits of security; and the curves BN-382, BLS12-381 and BLS12-383 provide a conjectured 128-bit security level. The curve BLS24-509 yields a conjectured security level of 192-bits.

	BN curves: $k = 12$	BLS12 curves: $k = 12$	BLS12 curves: $k = 12$
$p(z)$	$36z^4 + 36z^3 + 24z^2 + 6z + 1$	$(z-1)^2(z^4 - z^2 + 1)/3 + z$	$(z-1)^2(z^8 - z^4 + 1)/3 + z$
$q(z)$	$36z^4 + 36z^3 + 18z^2 + 6z + 1$	$z^4 - z^2 + 1$	$z^8 - z^4 + 1$
$t(z)$	$6z^2 + 1$	$z + 1$	$z + 1$
$h(z)$	1	$(z-1)^2/3$	$(z-1)^2/3$

E	b	z_0	$\lceil \log_2 p \rceil$	$\lceil \log_2 q \rceil$	$\lceil \log_2 h \rceil$
BN-254	2	$-(2^{62} + 2^{55} + 1)$	254	254	1
BN-382	2	$-(2^{94} + 2^{78} + 2^{67} + 2^{64} + 2^{48} + 1)$	382	382	1
BLS12-381	4	$-(2^{63} + 2^{62} + 2^{60} + 2^{57} + 2^{48} + 2^{16})$	381	255	126
BLS12-383	4	$2^{64} + 2^{51} + 2^{24} + 2^{12} + 2^9$	383	256	126
BLS24-509	1	$-2^{51} - 2^{28} + 2^{11} - 1$	509	408	100

Table 1 summarizes the main parameters corresponding to the BN [9], BLS12 and BLS24 [7] families of elliptic curves. Note that all of these curves are parameterized by an integer z, and they are defined by an equation of the form $Y^2 = X^3 + b$, and have a twist of degree $d = 6$. Table 1 also reports the salient parameters of the BN, BLS12 and BLS24 curve instantiations using a concrete choice of seed z_0, suitable for implementing pairing-based protocols at the 128- and 192-bit security level (this last security level is only achieved by the curve BLS24-509). The requirements for these security levels are in good agreement with the recommendations recently given in [28,29].

---

[1] Following the definition given in [38], a curve is said to be $\mathbb{G}_T$-strong, if $\phi_k(p)/q$ does not have small factors.

[2] The resulting code is available in the library repository for reproducibility.

Membership Testing in $\mathbb{G}_T$. The traditional way of performing a subgroup membership test for a group element g, i.e., to explicitly verify whether or not $g \in \mathbb{G}_T$, is to exponentiate g by the group order q to check whether g^q is equal to the identity. An alternative way is first checking if g belongs to the cyclotomic subgroup of order $\phi_k(p)$. Thanks to the Frobenius endomorphism, this is an inexpensive operation (see below). If this test is passed, the second check consists of raising g to a power given by the cofactor $\phi_k(p)/q$, such that the final result lies in the right subgroup. For $\mathbb{G}_T$, the first strategy is usually more efficient because the cofactor $\phi_k(p)/q$ is typically considerably large, having, for the curve families considered in this paper, a bitlength at least three times larger than that of q.

For the specific case of prime-order BN curves, we know that $q = p + 1 - t$, so testing for membership can be done by checking that $g^q = g^{p+1-t} \overset{?}{=} 1_T$, or $g^p \overset{?}{=} g^{6z^2}$, which costs an efficient Frobenius map and an exponentiation by the short exponent $6z^2$ [38]. The exponentiation can be performed after checking that g is in the cyclotomic subgroup of order $p^4 - p^2 + 1$ through the equation $g \cdot g^{p^4} \overset{?}{=} g^{p^2}$, which only requires a few applications of powers of the Frobenius and one multiplication. In the cyclotomic subgroup, faster [26] and compressed squarings [3] are available and are favored due to the low Hamming weight of the exponent.

The case for BLS12 curves is split into the two options, but we start by checking for cyclotomic subgroup membership in both. The BLS12-383 curve is $\mathbb{G}_T$-strong, so further checks can be omitted. For BLS12-381, the situation is more complicated, as the cofactor is known to be composite but hard to factor. A conservative way involves exploiting $g^q = g^{(p+1-t)/h} \overset{?}{=} 1_T$ to check $g^p \overset{?}{=} g^z$ and $g^h \neq 1_T$, as implemented in the MIRACL library[3]. A faster way consists of following the recommendation in [6] to perform the exponentiation by the group order with the 4-GLS method using the Frobenius as an efficient endomorphism in $\mathbb{G}_T$ [23]. The 4-dimensional decomposition is fixed and sparse for the group order, such that the exponentiation requires only an exponentiation by sparse z, two multiplications and two applications of the Frobenius.

For the BLS24-509 curve, we first check for membership in the cyclotomic subgroup of order $p^8 - p^4 + 1$ and then proceed with the same conservative and fast strategies as in the BLS12 curve, namely, exploiting the group order equation or optimizing the 8-GLS exponentiation. The latter approach only involves an exponentiation by z followed by four multiplications and four Frobenius.

5.1   Timings for Operations in Pairing Groups

We implemented the conservative and fast membership testing in $\mathbb{G}_T$ as described in the previous section, and benchmarked the other pairings group operations on a high-end Intel Core i7-6700K Skylake processor running at 4.0 GHz, with HyperThreading (HT) and TurboBoost (TB) turned off to reduce measurement noise. RELIC was built for each curve using the available configuration presets with GCC 11.0.1 on a Fedora 34 operating system.

---

[3] https://github.com/miracl/MIRACL/.

The target platform is obviously not representative of an embedded system, but to keep comparisons fair we do not make usage of any memory-heavy operation that would benefit either the pairing computation or the additional protocol operations in one platform or another. In particular, the protocols we implemented do not require fixed-base scalar multiplications or exponentiations that could benefit from large precomputed tables in any of the groups.

Timings can be found in Table 2, for scalar multiplication in the unknown point case for $\mathbb{G}_1$ and $\mathbb{G}_2$ using endomorphisms and a left-to-right w-NAF algorithm with $w = 4$. Exponentiation of a variable base in $\mathbb{G}_T$ does not rely on precomputation and uses cyclotomic squarings and GLS endomorphisms with a simple NAF algorithm, since inversion in a cyclotomic subgroup is just conjugation. We also include timings for operations with short scalar/exponents using a simple NAF approach to show savings for shorter 50-bit challenges. We hope these results can update the figures from [15] with current parameters, and note that the rate at which the cost of performing operations increases from $\mathbb{G}_1$ to $\mathbb{G}_2$, and to $\mathbb{G}_T$ is lower than [15], indicating that we employ a more efficient implementation of extension field arithmetic.

Table 2. Timings of pairing group operations implemented in RELIC reported in 10^3 cycles in a Skylake processor, averaged over 10^4 executions (HT and TB disabled). The operations are scalar multiplication or exponentiation by a random integer $r \xleftarrow{\$} \mathbb{Z}_q^*$ or a short 50-bit scalar c, and membership testing in $\mathbb{G}_T$ (both conservative and fast variants). The pairing computation is split between Miller loop and Final exponentiation.

Operation\Curve	BN-254	BN-382	BLS12-381	BLS12-383	BLS24-509
$[r]P$ in $\mathbb{G}_1$	214	587	402	404	969
$[c]P$ in $\mathbb{G}_1$, short c	72	133	134	134	210
$[r]Q$ in $\mathbb{G}_2$	381	1268	836	879	5231
$[c]Q$ in $\mathbb{G}_2$, short c	139	305	322	322	1631
g^r in $\mathbb{G}_T$	601	1952	1317	1318	8323
g^c in $\mathbb{G}_T$, short c	282	633	634	634	2487
Cons. Test in $\mathbb{G}_T$	262	895	683	–	2483
Fast test in $\mathbb{G}_T$	–	–	382	–	1660
$e(P, Q)$	1086	3664	3255	3187	16730
Miller Loop	641	2183	1469	1446	5924
Final Exp	445	1481	1786	1741	10806

5.2 Timings for Delegated Pairing Computation

We implemented the original protocol due to Di Crescenzo et al. and our LOVE variant in the same benchmarking machine, and collected the timings in Table 3. We implemented both the public and the private input versions for completeness, and adopted the fast membership check for a best-case scenario. The protocol operations include preco (corresponding to the client's offSetup), the server-side portion of the computation server (Compute) and client-side online algorithms client (onSetup and onVerify). We first note that the offline setup of both protocols is the same, so no significant performance difference is observed in that step. Compared to [20], LOVE has significant improvements for the client in all curves, except for BLS12-383 because the main savings come from skipping one subgroup membership checking. In the public inputs case, the LOVE's improvements range from 18.0% to 29.7%; while in the private inputs case, they decrease to around 10.3% and 14.9%. From the server's point of view, the savings are between 20.2% and 24.9% for public inputs; and 15.1% to 18.7% for private inputs. These extra savings come from interleaving products of pairings inside Compute for the LOVE protocol. We do not take the communication latency in consideration for our performance estimates, but a simple analysis of how many bytes are transmitted points out that LOVE saves 23–24% communication cost depending on the choice of parameters by reducing by one the number of $\mathbb{G}_T$ elements transmitted.

Now considering the cost of computing a pairing, we observe performance improvements of LOVE in comparison with local computation ranging from

Table 3. Timings from running the pairing delegation protocols implemented in RELIC reported in 10^3 cycles in a Skylake processor, averaged over 10^4 executions (HT and TB disabled). For all protocols the statistical security parameter is set to $\sigma = 50$. The label preco refers to the offline precomputation (offSetup), client to the client-side online computation (onSetup and onVerify), and server to server-side online computation (Compute). We mark in bold the combination of parameter and setting that provides a performance improvement over computing the pairing locally. In these cases, we display between parenthesis the corresponding efficiency gain computed as $(1 - \mathsf{cost}(\mathsf{client})/\mathsf{cost}(e(P, Q)))$. Higher percentage values imply larger efficiency gains.

Protocol\Curve	BN-254	BN-382	BLS12-381	BLS12-383	BLS24-509
cost($e(P, Q)$)	1086	3664	3255	3187	16730
[20] (preco)	2055	6520	5207	5225	27659
[20] (client)	1183	**3459** (5.6%)	**2167** (33.4%)	**1472** (53.8%)	**8928** (46.6%)
[20] (server)	3284	11070	9889	9710	50363
LOVE (preco)	2050	6516	5199	5217	27657
LOVE (client)	**916** (15.7%)	**2433** (33.6%)	**1768** (45.7%)	**1397** (56.1%)	**7322** (56.2%)
LOVE (server)	2595	8829	7600	7442	37800
Priv-[20] (preco)	4892	15607	12100	12219	65852
Priv-[20] (client)	2452	7071	4406	3358	18459
Priv-[20] (server)	4404	14800	13237	12991	67179
Priv-LOVE (preco)	4892	15619	1209	12219	65845
Priv-LOVE (client)	2130	6017	3953	3304	16298
Priv-LOVE (server)	3704	12560	10887	10701	54591

15.7% to 56.2%. The speedup is higher for the curves BLS12-383 and BLS24-509 because of the $\mathbb{G}_T$-strong property. LOVE provides speedups even in the BN-254 and BN-382 curves, where [20] underperforms. Neither protocol is efficient in the private inputs case. The significantly lower performance of Di Crescenzo et al.'s protocol, even in the favourable setting when $\sigma = 50$ reduces the impact of $\mathbb{G}_T$ exponentiations, directly contradicts the estimates given in [20]. We attribute this effect to the lack of membership checks in the performance estimates and an inaccurate extrapolation from [15] to new security levels.

6 Conclusions

In this paper, we introduced LOVE: the most efficient protocol to date for secure offline/online delegation of a pairing computation. While developing and analyzing LOVE we identified interesting questions that stem out of our research.

For instance, is there a secure way to leverage the first pairing delegation to efficiency advantage of delegating one-more pairing? In other words, can 'batch delegation' of n pairings be secure and more efficient than just repeating LOVE n times? An orthogonal direction would be to investigate if one can securely delegate other building blocks of the verification, such as hash-to-point or membership tests.

Also, protocol-tailored solutions might be interesting. For instance, in the context of Groth's zk-SNARK [27], the verifier needs to compute l scalar multiplications in $\mathbb{G}_1$, 3 executions of the Miller's loop and 1 computation of the final exponentiation (here l is a parameter of the zk-SNARK protocol). In this setting, can we design a secure and efficient delegation protocol for the computation of the three Miller loops and the final exponentiation? These are all components needed for the computation of a pairing, but we are not aware of works that outsource these components, instead of the whole pairing.

Finally, we identified the need for efficient and reliable $\mathbb{G}_T$-membership testing. Since the BLS12-381 curve is being considered for standardization[4], we suggest starting a computational effort to find out the integer factorization of the $\mathbb{G}_T$ cofactor of this curve or bounds on its prime factors to better understand its subgroup security.

Acknowledgments. This work was partly funded by:the strategic research area ELLIIT. The first author is also affiliated to the DIGIT Centre for Digitalisation, Big Data and Data Analytics; and the Concordium Blockchain Research Center at Aarhus University.

References

1. Aranha, D.F., Barreto, P.S.L.M., Longa, P., Ricardini, J.E.: The realm of the pairings. In: Lange, T., Lauter, K., Lisoněk, P. (eds.) SAC 2013. LNCS, vol. 8282, pp. 3–25. Springer, Heidelberg (2014). https://doi.org/10.1007/978-3-662-43414-7_1

---

[4] https://datatracker.ietf.org/doc/html/draft-irtf-cfrg-bls-signature-04.

2. Aranha, D.F., Gouvêa, C.P.L., Markmann, T., Wahby, R.S., Liao, K.: RELIC is an Efficient LIbrary for Cryptography. https://github.com/relic-toolkit/relic
3. Aranha, D.F., Karabina, K., Longa, P., Gebotys, C.H., López, J.: Faster explicit formulas for computing pairings over ordinary curves. In: Paterson, K.G. (ed.) EUROCRYPT 2011. LNCS, vol. 6632, pp. 48–68. Springer, Heidelberg (2011). https://doi.org/10.1007/978-3-642-20465-4_5
4. Aranha, D.F., Pagnin, E.: The simplest multi-key linearly homomorphic signature scheme. In: Schwabe, P., Thériault, N. (eds.) LATINCRYPT 2019. LNCS, vol. 11774, pp. 280–300. Springer, Cham (2019). https://doi.org/10.1007/978-3-030-30530-7_14
5. Barbulescu, R., Duquesne, S.: Updating key size estimations for pairings. J. Cryptol. **32**(4), 1298–1336 (2019)
6. Barreto, P.S.L.M., Costello, C., Misoczki, R., Naehrig, M., Pereira, G.C.C.F., Zanon, G.: Subgroup security in pairing-based cryptography. In: Lauter, K., Rodríguez-Henríquez, F. (eds.) LATINCRYPT 2015. LNCS, vol. 9230, pp. 245–265. Springer, Cham (2015). https://doi.org/10.1007/978-3-319-22174-8_14
7. Barreto, P.S.L.M., Lynn, B., Scott, M.: Constructing elliptic curves with prescribed embedding degrees. In: Cimato, S., Persiano, G., Galdi, C. (eds.) SCN 2002. LNCS, vol. 2576, pp. 257–267. Springer, Heidelberg (2003). https://doi.org/10.1007/3-540-36413-7_19
8. Barreto, P.S.L.M., Lynn, B., Scott, M.: Efficient implementation of pairing-based cryptosystems. J. Cryptol. **17**(4), 321–334 (2004)
9. Barreto, P.S.L.M., Naehrig, M.: Pairing-friendly elliptic curves of prime order. In: Preneel, B., Tavares, S. (eds.) SAC 2005. LNCS, vol. 3897, pp. 319–331. Springer, Heidelberg (2006). https://doi.org/10.1007/11693383_22
10. Ben-Sasson, E., et al.: Decentralized anonymous payments from bitcoin. In: IEEE Symposium on Security and Privacy, pp. 459–474. IEEE Computer Society (2014)
11. Boneh, D., Bonneau, J., Bünz, B., Fisch, B.: Verifiable delay functions. In: Shacham, H., Boldyreva, A. (eds.) CRYPTO 2018. LNCS, vol. 10991, pp. 757–788. Springer, Cham (2018). https://doi.org/10.1007/978-3-319-96884-1_25
12. Boneh, D., Franklin, M.: Identity-based encryption from the Weil pairing. In: Kilian, J. (ed.) CRYPTO 2001. LNCS, vol. 2139, pp. 213–229. Springer, Heidelberg (2001). https://doi.org/10.1007/3-540-44647-8_13
13. Boneh, D., Gentry, C., Lynn, B., Shacham, H.: Aggregate and verifiably encrypted signatures from bilinear maps. In: Biham, E. (ed.) EUROCRYPT 2003. LNCS, vol. 2656, pp. 416–432. Springer, Heidelberg (2003). https://doi.org/10.1007/3-540-39200-9_26
14. Boneh, D., Lynn, B., Shacham, H.: Short signatures from the Weil pairing. J. Cryptol. **17**(4), 297–319 (2004). https://doi.org/10.1007/s00145-004-0314-9
15. Bos, J.W., Costello, C., Naehrig, M.: Exponentiating in pairing groups. In: Lange, T., Lauter, K., Lisoněk, P. (eds.) SAC 2013. LNCS, vol. 8282, pp. 438–455. Springer, Heidelberg (2014). https://doi.org/10.1007/978-3-662-43414-7_22
16. Canard, S., Devigne, J., Sanders, O.: Delegating a pairing can be both secure and efficient. In: Boureanu, I., Owesarski, P., Vaudenay, S. (eds.) ACNS 2014. LNCS, vol. 8479, pp. 549–565. Springer, Cham (2014). https://doi.org/10.1007/978-3-319-07536-5_32
17. Chevallier-Mames, B., Coron, J.-S., McCullagh, N., Naccache, D., Scott, M.: Secure delegation of elliptic-curve pairing. In: Gollmann, D., Lanet, J.-L., Iguchi-Cartigny, J. (eds.) CARDIS 2010. LNCS, vol. 6035, pp. 24–35. Springer, Heidelberg (2010). https://doi.org/10.1007/978-3-642-12510-2_3

18. Chow, S.S., Au, M.H., Susilo, W.: Server-aided signatures verification secure against collusion attack. Inf. Secur. Tech. Rep. **17**(3), 46–57 (2013)
19. Costello, C., Lauter, K., Naehrig, M.: Attractive subfamilies of BLS curves for implementing high-security pairings. In: Bernstein, D.J., Chatterjee, S. (eds.) INDOCRYPT 2011. LNCS, vol. 7107, pp. 320–342. Springer, Heidelberg (2011). https://doi.org/10.1007/978-3-642-25578-6_23
20. Di Crescenzo, G., Khodjaeva, M., Kahrobaei, D., Shpilrain, V.: Secure and efficient delegation of pairings with online inputs. In: Liardet, P.-Y., Mentens, N. (eds.) CARDIS 2020. LNCS, vol. 12609, pp. 84–99. Springer, Cham (2021). https://doi.org/10.1007/978-3-030-68487-7_6
21. De Feo, L., Masson, S., Petit, C., Sanso, A.: Verifiable delay functions from supersingular isogenies and pairings. In: Galbraith, S.D., Moriai, S. (eds.) ASIACRYPT 2019. LNCS, vol. 11921, pp. 248–277. Springer, Cham (2019). https://doi.org/10.1007/978-3-030-34578-5_10
22. Freeman, D., Scott, M., Teske, E.: A taxonomy of pairing-friendly elliptic curves. J. Cryptol. **23**(2), 224–280 (2010)
23. Galbraith, S.D., Scott, M.: Exponentiation in pairing-friendly groups using homomorphisms. In: Galbraith, S.D., Paterson, K.G. (eds.) Pairing 2008. LNCS, vol. 5209, pp. 211–224. Springer, Heidelberg (2008). https://doi.org/10.1007/978-3-540-85538-5_15
24. Gennaro, R., Gentry, C., Parno, B.: Non-interactive verifiable computing: outsourcing computation to untrusted workers. In: Rabin, T. (ed.) CRYPTO 2010. LNCS, vol. 6223, pp. 465–482. Springer, Heidelberg (2010). https://doi.org/10.1007/978-3-642-14623-7_25
25. Girault, M., Lefranc, D.: Server-aided verification: theory and practice. In: Roy, B. (ed.) ASIACRYPT 2005. LNCS, vol. 3788, pp. 605–623. Springer, Heidelberg (2005). https://doi.org/10.1007/11593447_33
26. Granger, R., Scott, M.: Faster squaring in the cyclotomic subgroup of sixth degree extensions. In: Nguyen, P.Q., Pointcheval, D. (eds.) PKC 2010. LNCS, vol. 6056, pp. 209–223. Springer, Heidelberg (2010). https://doi.org/10.1007/978-3-642-13013-7_13
27. Groth, J.: On the size of pairing-based non-interactive arguments. In: Fischlin, M., Coron, J.-S. (eds.) EUROCRYPT 2016. LNCS, vol. 9666, pp. 305–326. Springer, Heidelberg (2016). https://doi.org/10.1007/978-3-662-49896-5_11
28. Guillevic, A.: A short-list of pairing-friendly curves resistant to special TNFS at the 128-bit security level. In: Kiayias, A., Kohlweiss, M., Wallden, P., Zikas, V. (eds.) PKC 2020. LNCS, vol. 12111, pp. 535–564. Springer, Cham (2020). https://doi.org/10.1007/978-3-030-45388-6_19
29. Guillevic, A., Masson, S., Thomé, E.: Cocks-pinch curves of embedding degrees five to eight and optimal ate pairing computation. Des. Codes Cryptogr. **88**(6), 1047–1081 (2020)
30. Guillevic, A., Vergnaud, D.: Algorithms for outsourcing pairing computation. In: Joye, M., Moradi, A. (eds.) CARDIS 2014. LNCS, vol. 8968, pp. 193–211. Springer, Cham (2015). https://doi.org/10.1007/978-3-319-16763-3_12
31. Kang, B.G., Lee, M.S., Park, J.H.: Efficient delegation of pairing computation. IACR Cryptol. ePrint Arch. **2005**, 259 (2005)
32. Kim, T., Barbulescu, R.: Extended tower number field sieve: a new complexity for the medium prime case. In: Robshaw, M., Katz, J. (eds.) CRYPTO 2016. LNCS, vol. 9814, pp. 543–571. Springer, Heidelberg (2016). https://doi.org/10.1007/978-3-662-53018-4_20

33. Mbang, N.M., Aranha, D.F., Fouotsa, E.: Computing the optimal ate pairing over elliptic curves with embedding degrees 54 and 48 at the 256-bit security level. Int. J. Appl. Cryptogr. 4(1), 45–59 (2020)
34. Mefenza, T., Vergnaud, D.: Verifiable outsourcing of pairing computations. Technical report
35. Miller, V.S.: The Weil pairing, and its efficient calculation. J. Cryptol. 17(4), 235–261 (2004). https://doi.org/10.1007/s00145-004-0315-8
36. Mrabet, N.E., Joye, M. (eds.): Guide to Pairing-Based Cryptography. Chapman and Hall/CRC, London (2017)
37. Pagnin, E., Mitrokotsa, A., Tanaka, K.: Anonymous single-round server-aided verification. In: Lange, T., Dunkelman, O. (eds.) LATINCRYPT 2017. LNCS, vol. 11368, pp. 23–43. Springer, Cham (2019). https://doi.org/10.1007/978-3-030-25283-0_2
38. Scott, M.: Unbalancing pairing-based key exchange protocols. Cryptology ePrint Archive, Report 2013/688 (2013). http://eprint.iacr.org/
39. Scott, M.: Pairing implementation revisited. Cryptology ePrint Archive, Report 2019/077 (2019). https://eprint.iacr.org/2019/077
40. Tsang, P.P., Chow, S.S.M., Smith, S.W.: Batch pairing delegation. In: Miyaji, A., Kikuchi, H., Rannenberg, K. (eds.) IWSEC 2007. LNCS, vol. 4752, pp. 74–90. Springer, Heidelberg (2007). https://doi.org/10.1007/978-3-540-75651-4_6
41. Vercauteren, F.: Optimal pairings. IEEE Trans. Inf. Theory 56(1), 455–461 (2010)
42. Wang, Z.: A new construction of the server-aided verification signature scheme. Math. Comput. Model. 55(1–2), 97–101 (2012)
43. Wu, W., Mu, Y., Susilo, W., Huang, X.: Server-aided verification signatures: definitions and new constructions. In: Baek, J., Bao, F., Chen, K., Lai, X. (eds.) ProvSec 2008. LNCS, vol. 5324, pp. 141–155. Springer, Heidelberg (2008). https://doi.org/10.1007/978-3-540-88733-1_10
44. Wu, W., Mu, Y., Susilo, W., Huang, X.: Provably secure server-aided verification signatures. Comput. Math. Appl. 61(7), 1705–1723 (2011)
45. Zanon, G.H., Simplicio, M.A., Pereira, G.C., Doliskani, J., Barreto, P.S.: Faster key compression for isogeny-based cryptosystems. IEEE Trans. Comput. 68(5), 688–701 (2019)
46. Zavattoni, E., Perez, L.J.D., Mitsunari, S., Sánchez-Ramírez, A.H., Teruya, T., Rodríguez-Henríquez, F.: Software implementation of an attribute-based encryption scheme. IEEE Trans. Comput. 64(5), 1429–1441 (2015)

Implementing Secure Reporting of Sexual Misconduct - Revisiting WhoToo

Alejandro Hevia[✉] and Ilana Mergudich-Thal[✉]

Department of Computer Science, University of Chile, Santiago, Chile
{ahevia,imergudi}@dcc.uchile.cl

Abstract. Reporting sexual assault or harassment is notoriously difficult, and even though more victims are coming forward every year, a significant percentage of victims do not formally report it (Morgan and Oudekerk - U.S. Department of Justice). Studies have shown that most sexual assault episodes occur by repeat perpetrators and that people are more likely to report if they know that other victims of the same aggressor exist (Callisto Homepage). Recently, the WhoToo protocol (Kuykendall, Krawczyk and Rabin - POPETS 2019) presented a system in which the identities of the accuser and the accused are protected until a certain pre-specified number (quorum) of victims reports the same perpetrator. We revisit this protocol from an implementation perspective, shedding light on necessary clarifications and optimizations.

We first identify several key operations whose implementation was left unclear. One of such operations, if implemented in a straightforward fashion by using other WhoToo subroutines would compromise anonymity. Fixes for another were simple but required a new (but straightforward) security proof. Such fixes, although rather minor, are important for a system whose design emphasizes practicality and fast operations.

Our second contribution concerns efficiency. Using a Distributed Input PRF and a variant of Robust Anonymous IBE Encryption, we improve detection of duplicated and matching accusations. Given N accusations, our solution requires $O(1)$ instead of $O(N)$ distributed operations (the most expensive primitive in WhoToo) to detect duplicates and matching accusations once the quorum is reached. Our results give raise to WhoToo$^+$, a practical and more efficient variant of WhoToo that preserves the original security guarantees.

Keywords: Privacy-preserving reporting of sexual misconduct · Anonymity · Secure multiparty computation · Efficient implementations

1 Introduction

Sexual harassment is a common problem across all countries and contexts. In educational settings it is specially prevalent. A recent study by Pontificia

I. Mergudich-Thal—Supported by ANID - Subdirección de Capital Humano/Magíster Nacional/2020.

© Springer Nature Switzerland AG 2021
P. Longa and C. Ràfols (Eds.): LATINCRYPT 2021, LNCS 12912, pp. 341–362, 2021.
https://doi.org/10.1007/978-3-030-88238-9_17

Universidad Católica de Chile has shown that, in one of the biggest universities in the country, 39,9% of students declare that they have been victims of sexual harassment, yet 65% of them did not formally report it [21]. Similar numbers have been reported for female students at other universities [8,18], showing that a significant number of victims never come forward. On the other hand, research has shown that people are more likely to report sexual assault if they know other victims of the same perpetrator exist [7]. Furthermore, an overwhelming majority of sexual misconduct episodes are caused by offenders who have committed sexual assault before [7]. Project Callisto [24] was the first to address this problem considering all these factors. They proposed a protocol in which the identity of the accuser and the accused remain hidden until two victims accuse the same perpetrator. Since then, two other protocols based on the same premise have been proposed: WhoToo [20] and SAE [4]. Both define a quorum q so that accusations are revealed only when q accusations against a certain person are submitted. The first provides strong security guarantees, however, it can become increasingly inefficient as the number of unopened accusations in the system grows. SAE is significantly more efficient than WhoToo and even though its security guarantees are stronger than Callisto, it reveals information about matching accusations (accusing the same perpetrator) before the quorum is reached.

We started our project aiming to implement WhoToo as securely and efficiently as possible. Rather surprisingly, even if the protocol provides significant security improvements over previous protocols, we uncovered and corrected two gaps in the specification of key aspects (these gaps were not trivial, as they could possibly compromise the protocol security), and identify some other aspects whose design can be significantly improved in terms of efficiency.

1.1 Contributions

We revisit the WhoToo protocol, both correcting two key operations whose implementations were left unclear and significantly improving the protocol's efficiency. First, we identify an inconsistency in a key element used to evaluate whether a quorum of accusations has been reached. The protocol uses a random encrypted polynomial, yet the operations in which the polynomial is used are defined for polynomials in the clear (not encrypted). A straightforward modification with a randomization step fixes the issue, yet it requires a new security proof which we provide. Then, we identify another operation whose specification leaves an implementation gap. WhoToo describes how to securely compare two ElGamal encodings. The protocol, however, requires the simultaneous comparison of two *pairs* of ElGamal encodings. In this case, the solution is not as simple, as a straightforward clarification would compromise either the anonymity of the accuser or the accused. Instead of concocting a local fix for the issue, we take a step back and re-examine the particular phase where it arises. Our solution then solves this issue while carrying a positive side effect: efficiency.

Our second contribution is indeed improving WhoToo's efficiency. When receiving a new accusation, the protocol from Kuykendall et al. must compare it with every element of a list of unopened accusations, in order to achieve two goals: (1) preventing duplicated accusations (those involving the same pair accuser-accused), and (2) identifying all existent accusations for a given accused, when the quorum has been reached. WhoToo's strategy to deal with these tasks becomes increasingly inefficient as the number of unopened accusations grows: it takes $O(N)$ *interactive distributed operations* to review a total number of N unopened accusations in the system, for each of the abovementioned goals. Inspired by SAE [4], we propose an alternative to the duplicate revision (goal (1)) requiring only a constant number of (interactive distributed) operations, by employing a distributed input pseudorandom function (DIPRF) in a new way. Additionally, by relying on a different technique – a variant of strongly robust identity-based encryption (IBE) – we reduce the number of interactive distributed operations required to identify existent accusations (goal (2)) from $O(N)$ to a constant number too.[1] This last technique may have applications to other server-based privacy-preserving protocols and is of independent interest.

We provide security proofs for our modified protocol WhoToo$^+$, together with the first open-source implementation of WhoToo$^+$(and WhoToo). Due to space constrains, the security definitions are mostly informal and more complete proofs can be found on the full version [17].

1.2 Related Work

Project Callisto: The first protocol specifically designed for privacy-preserving sexual assault accusations [24]. Its design criteria was explicitly motivated by the fact that "those who experience unwanted sexual contact may be more willing to report it if they know that others have spoken up as well" [24] attempting to privately preserve the names of accusers and accused so they can be compared with those of new reports. Using cryptographic tools, Callisto hides all identities until a second accusation is made against the same perpetrator.

Kuykendall, Krawczyk, and Rabin [20] describe three attacks against Callisto, showing that there is no binding between the accuser's identity and the accusation, and that the identities of the accusers and the accused are not entirely protected.

WhoToo: Following Callisto's principles, Kuykendall, Krawczyk and Rabin [20] propose WhoToo, a distributed protocol that provides a stronger binding between the accuser's identity and their accusation, as well as stronger security definitions to protect the identities of the accusers and accused. Furthermore, WhoToo works for any fixed quorum q, in contrast to Callisto where the quorum was fixed to 2. Below, we present a brief summary of WhoToo. A more complete picture is described in the next sections as WhoToo is indeed the base of our proposed protocol.

---

[1] Our protocol still takes $O(N)$ local operations for goals (1) and (2) but they are *local* operations as opposed to *distributed* operations.

The protocol relies on threshold cryptography, so $t+1$ out of n servers need to agree in order to reveal any information, for some fixed $1 \le t \le n$. Accusations are stored in privacy-preserving multisets, represented as (encrypted) polynomials whose roots are the accused people's identifiers. Therefore, in order to add an accusation, the servers multiply the existing set (polynomial) by $(x-s)$, where s represents the perpetrator's identifier. Checking if the quorum has been reached is simply done by checking if the $(q-1)^{th}$-derivative of the polynomial evaluated at s is zero. Multiset confidentiality and robustness follows from the servers computing over encrypted polynomials using verifiable secret sharing.

WhoToo seeks to protect all identities and avoid leaking information while at most t servers are corrupt. The protocol relies on a clever combination of ElGamal encryption, verifiable secret sharing, and group signatures based on signatures of knowledge. The authors claim that this protocol would be feasible in practice, yet they do not provide an implementation.

SAE: Secure Allegation Escrows (SAE) [4] is a distributed protocol for anonymous allegations that is based in the same quorum principles as Callisto and WhoToo. It provides accusation confidentiality, accuser anonymity, accountability, and scalability as long as there is an honest majority. Adding a new accusation requires $O(1)$ distributed operations. Arun et al. introduce a *Distributed Input Verifiable Pseudo-Random Function* (DVRF), which is computed over a distributed input and key. They describe a bucketing algorithm for accusation matching, where each server locally can locally check if the quorum has been reached by verifying if enough repeated DVRF values exist. Even though this achieves a matching algorithm that needs no distributed operations, it comes at a price: servers get to know if there are repeated values before the quorum is reached. This information leak could be used for potential attacks by a malicious user and an honest but curious server. A corrupted user colluded with an honest but curious escrow server, for example, could make a false accusation against a specific identifier and recover the number of accusations (with equal or lower quorum) made against that identifier.

ORGANIZATION: The rest of the paper is organized as follows. First, in Sect. 2, we present some preliminaries needed to understand both the original WhoToo protocol and our extension. Then, in Sect. 3, we review some tools and definitions used in our solution WhoToo$^+$. We then identify and correct two operations that where left unclear in the WhoToo protocol, adding a new security proof for the modified protocol. Afterwards, we present the optimizations that WhoToo$^+$ provides, introducing the new schemes and describing the necessary modifications. Then, we outline the security proofs for the modified protocol. Finally, we briefly analyze the efficiency of WhoToo$^+$ and compare it to the original protocol.

2 Preliminaries

In this section we present the main components of the WhoToo Protocol.

SECURITY REQUIREMENTS AND THREAT MODEL: The WhoToo protocol provides secrecy, anonymity, accountability and metadata hiding. Secrecy means all information about a submitted accusation is protected until the quorum is reached. Anonymity ensures that the identities of the accuser and the accused are protected until the quorum is reached. Accountability guarantees that the identity of the accuser is bound to a real world identity. Finally, metadata hiding establishes that other than the total number of accusations in the system, no partial information about the accusations and its matches is leaked.

WhoToo and WhoToo$^+$ use the standard static threat model for threshold cryptography, where an adversary can control up to t servers and any number of users. Moreover, all communication for user key generation occurs over an *authenticated* and *confidential* channel, while accusation submission occurs over an *anonymous* and *confidential* channel.

2.1   WhoToo: An Introduction

This section provides an informal description of the WhoToo Protocol [20]. At a high level, each accuser can submit an accusation against a certain person and the identities of the accuser and the accused remain hidden until the quorum is reached, namely, until a pre-specified number of accusers file accusations against the same person.

PARTICIPATING PARTIES: The protocol strongly relies on threshold cryptography, where in order to compute or reveal any information that could reveal private values, $t + 1$ of the n servers need to agree or cooperate. This group of servers is called the Distributed Authority ($\mathcal{DA}$). The cooperation guarantees that as long as no more than t servers are corrupted, all operations are performed correctly and no server learns private values.

Accusers can be any user U of the system which are identified with a public key R computed by the $\mathcal{DA}$ during registration. The identity of the accused is represented by an arbitrary string D: a name, e-mail or any unique identifier. For simplicity, we assume this value is unique but in practice the accuser can file different accusations for every identity under which the accused is known [20].

REGISTRATION: WhoToo assumes there exists an external registration authority which verifies the identities of the potential accusers. All registered users are valid accusers. We envision the system used in a community where all members may submit accusations.

For every user U in this list, the $\mathcal{DA}$ computes a public key R and registers that the key R corresponds to user U. It also computes a private key α which is only obtained by U.

SUBMITTING ACCUSATIONS: In order to submit an accusation against D from a user with identifier R, the user needs to provide encodings c_D and c_R of these values. These values are intrinsically linked to D and R respectively, yet reveal no useful information about D and R unless $t + 1$ $\mathcal{DA}$ servers cooperate. Moreover, the $\mathcal{DA}$ needs to be able to make computations on the encoded values in order to know if there are a certain number of accusations against the same D without revealing anything about D.

To achieve this, two main tools are used. First, using verifiable secret sharing [23], the user distributes shares of D to every server so if $t + 1$ or more of them cooperate they can recover the secret, yet t or less servers learn nothing about it. A linear secret sharing scheme allows efficient computation of some operations from the shared values without revealing D. Additionally, R and D are encoded using a threshold public key encryption scheme. Any user can encrypt using the public key while cooperation is needed in order to recover the plaintext as the secret key is distributed among the $\mathcal{DA}$ servers. Both of these schemes preserve anonymity of the accuser and the accused as long as at most t servers are corrupted.

Finally, the user also signs these encodings with their private key α, guaranteeing accountability. It also provides zero-knowledge proofs for the encoded values so that the $\mathcal{DA}$ can verify that there are no malformed accusations while preserving anonymity.

DISCARDING MALFORMED AND DUPLICATED ACCUSATIONS: Once the $\mathcal{DA}$ receives an accusation from a user, it verifies the signature and zero-knowledge proofs, and discards any malformed accusations. Then, it must verify that it is not a duplicated accusation, namely, that there is not already an accusation from the same R to the same D in the system. This is non-trivial as the check must not reveal anything about R or D other than if both are equal to a previous accusation. In order to do this, WhoToo introduces a distributed equality testing that verifies if two ciphertexts encode the same plaintext. They use this to compare the new accusation to every other c_R and c_D in the system.

FINDING MATCHING ACCUSATIONS: Accusations are stored in privacy-preserving multisets, represented as polynomials where the roots are the accused people's identifiers. In order to add an accusation, the servers multiply the existing set by $(x - D)$ and checking if the quorum has been reached is done by verifying if the $(q - 1)^{th}$-derivative of the polynomial evaluated at D is zero.

The polynomial coefficients are encrypted using threshold public key encryption that is multiplicatively homomorphic. This allows to efficiently implement the required set operations (adding a new element and checking if the quorum has been reached) described above. The $\mathcal{DA}$ servers use their shares of D to multiply the existing encoded polynomial by $(x - D)$ when adding a new accusation.

Once the quorum is reached, the $\mathcal{DA}$ needs to identify the individual matching accusations. WhoToo uses the same equality testing used to discard duplicated accusations to compare c_D of the last submitted accusation to every other accusation in the system.

Once the matching accusations and its respective accusers are identified, this information is given to the corresponding authority.

2.2 WhoToo$^+$ Overview

In WhoToo$^+$, we provide additional steps during registration and accusation submission, which together with significant changes during verification, duplicate revision and finding matching accusations, allow us to correct some inconsistencies found in WhoToo and improve efficiency. Consequently, WhoToo$^+$ achieves scalability, making it practical for real world implementation, even under a significant backlog of unopened accusations. An overview of these changes is next.

REGISTRATION: The $\mathcal{DA}$ servers calculate k tokens for each valid user R using a distributed message authentication scheme (MAC), and privately send the shares to each user who reconstructs the tokens. No one else learns the value of these tokens.

SUBMITTING ACCUSATIONS: The user also provides a sharing of the secret R. The user must submit one of the tokens from the registration which the $\mathcal{DA}$ uses to validate the correctness of the sharing.

DISCARDING MALFORMED AND DUPLICATED ACCUSATIONS: In order to check for duplicated accusations, instead of using the distributed equality testing proposed in WhoToo, we produce a combined distributed input $x = f(R, D)$ with an injective f. The $\mathcal{DA}$ computes a distributed input PRF on input x which then each server locally compares with previous submissions to detect duplicates.

FINDING MATCHING ACCUSATIONS: During this phase, we also propose an alternative to the equality testing used in the original protocol. Using a threshold variant of Robust Anonymous IBE, the $\mathcal{DA}$s can *distributively compute* a valid encoding for a specific identity D starting from only the shares of D. When an accusation is received, the $\mathcal{DA}$ servers use their shares of D to compute an encoding ρ_D, without learning anything about D. Once the quorum is reached and D is revealed, the servers compute and publish sk_D. Each server can attempt to decrypt $\rho_{D'}$ using sk_D for every other accusation (other than the one which triggered the quorum being reached); if successful, then it is a matching accusation. Since the IBE scheme is strongly robust (meaning ciphertexts do not reveal the intended recipient even when valid secret keys of different recipients are known), the privacy of not matching accusations is preserved.

3 Building Blocks

This section describes the components and notation used in the WhoToo$^+$ construction. We follow the original WhoToo presentation.

NOTATION, ASSUMPTIONS, AND MODEL: In what follows, we write $[n]$ to denote $\{1, \ldots, n\}$ for $n \in \mathbb{Z}$. If S is a set, $x \in_R S$ denotes picking x uniformly at random from the elements in S. If V is an algorithm, running V and assigning its output to variable a is denoted by $a \leftarrow V$. When describing distributed protocols which share values among the players or servers, we use the notation $\{x_i\}$ or simply $\{x\}$ to denote that x is a shared value among servers and x_i to denote the share of x corresponding to the i-th server. The protocols presented in this paper rely on a variety of standard Diffie-Hellman assumptions which consider probabilistic polynomial-time (PPT) adversaries. Due to space constraints, we refer the reader to [4,20]. Also, all hash functions used here are treated as random oracles for the security proofs.

BILINEAR GROUPS: Let $(\mathbb{G}_1, \mathbb{G}_2, \mathbb{G}_T, e, g_1, g_2)$ be a Type-3 bilinear group with prime order p, where g_1 and g_2 are generators of $\mathbb{G}_1$ and $\mathbb{G}_2$ respectively. We suggest using the curves BLS12-381 or BN254.

ELGAMAL ENCRYPTION: WhoToo and WhoToo$^+$ use three variants of ElGamal encryption [11]. The first one is the (standard) multiplicatively homomorphic ElGamal, which allows encryption of group elements, using the following primitives:

ElGamal.Setup: Choose $x \in_R \mathbb{Z}_p$ and $h \in_R \mathbb{G}_1$, and set $g \leftarrow h^{1/x}$. Output $sk \leftarrow x$ and $pk \leftarrow (g, h)$.

ElGamal.Enc(pk, m): Choose $a \in_R \mathbb{Z}_p$ and output $(c_1, c_2) \leftarrow (g^a, h^a m)$.

ElGamal.Dec$(sk, (c_1, c_2))$: Output c_2/c_1^x.

The second one is an extension of ElGamal to encrypt strings [1] which uses a symmetric key authenticated encryption scheme (AuthEnc, AuthDec) with keyspace $\mathcal{K}$ and a hash function $H_\mathcal{K}$ with codomain $\mathcal{K}$:

ElGamal.EncString(pk, m): Choose $a \in_R \mathbb{Z}_p$ and output $(c_1, c_2) \leftarrow (g^a,$ AuthEnc$(H_\mathcal{K}(h^a), m))$.

ElGamal.DecString$(sk, (c_1, c_2))$: Output AuthDec$(H_\mathcal{K}(c_1^x), c_2)$.

Finally, in our setting, the secret key $sk = \{x\}$ for the ElGamal scheme must be secret shared among the servers, so we use a variant that adds distributed decryption to the previous ElGamal extension:

ElGamal.DistDec$(c_1, c_2, \{x\})$: Compute $d \leftarrow$ SecShare.Exp$(c_1, \{x\})$ and output c_2/d. Here SecShare.Exp is the distributed exponentiation protocol described later in this section.

ElGamal.DistDecString$(c_1, c_2, \{x\})$: Compute $d \leftarrow$ SecShare.Exp$(c_1, \{x\})$ and output AuthDec$(H(d), c_2)$.

The first and third ElGamal variants are CPA-secure under the Decisional Diffie-Hellman assumption. The extension to strings is CCA-secure under the strong computational Diffie-Hellman assumption if $H_\mathcal{K}$ is a random oracle [1].

ZERO-KNOWLEDGE PROOFS: We require proofs of plaintext knowledge to detect when users submit malformed accusations [20]. These proofs are standard, based on the Schnorr's protocol [25], applying the Fiat-Shamir heuristic [12] to make it non-interactive.

ElGamal.Prove(c, a, ρ): Given c, an ElGamal encryption of m with randomness a, output π, a non interactive proof of knowledge of m. Here ρ is the value used to derive the random oracle challenge.

ElGamal.Verify(pk, π, c, ρ): Check if π is a valid zero-knowledge proof for the plaintext encoded in c.

3.1   Distributed Operations

THRESHOLD OPERATIONS: Both WhoToo and WhoToo$^+$ strongly rely on threshold cryptography, and in particular, on the following threshold operations. They require a group $\mathbb{G}$ with generators g and h. In WhoToo$^+$, $\mathbb{G} = \mathbb{G}_1$ and $g = g_1$ unless stated otherwise.

VERIFIABLE SECRET SHARING (VSS): All threshold operations are based on VSS which requires Shamir Secret Sharing [26]. In Shamir's protocol, in order to share a value $x \in \mathbb{Z}_p$, a random polynomial P of degree $t \leq n$ is chosen such that $P(0) = x$, and then shares $x_i = P(i)$ are sent to the i-th server. In this way, t or less servers learn nothing about x, but any greater number of servers can recover the secret. Recovery is done by simply publishing the x_i's and using Lagrange interpolation. Pedersen VSS [23] introduced share verification by asking the party that wants to share x to compute both the sharing of x and the sharing of a random value $r \in \mathbb{Z}_p$. At the same time, it must compute verification values $v_i \leftarrow g^{a_i} h^{b_i}$, for $i = 0, ..., t$, where a_i and b_i are the coefficients of the polynomials used for secret sharing x and r respectively. Observe that $x = a_0$ and $r = b_0$. When each server $\mathcal{DA}_i$ receives its shares, it verifies them by checking if $g^{x_i} h^{r_i} = \prod_{j=0}^{t} v_j^{i^j}$ were x_i and r_i are the shares of $\mathcal{DA}_i$ for x and r respectively. We use the convention that if the operation outputs shares, they are output locally to the servers themselves (each server obtaining their own single share), as opposed to the case it outputs values, which are publicly revealed. This functionality is captured in the following three operations:

SecShare.Encode(x): output^2 $\{\omega\} = (\{x\}, \{r\})$, v, e_0 and r, where r is the random value used for Pedersen VSS, v are the Pedersen verification values and $e_0 \leftarrow g^r$.

SecShare.Verify(w_i, v): Compute Pedersen verification, as described above. Output false if verification fails and true otherwise [9].

SecShare.Reconstruct($\{x\}$): Reconstruct the secret x from its shares.

Many other operations can be build on top of Pedersen VSS such as reconstructing g^x without reconstructing x, or operating on the shares to compute shares for a given function of x. We use several of them: Add, Multiply, Invert, among others, which given shared inputs, output the shares of the corresponding operation. For example, SecShare.Add($\{x\}, \{y\}$) outputs $\{z\}$ where $z = x + y$. We enumerate some of them here and provide a full list in [17].

SecShare.Gen(): Generates a shared secret $\{x\}$ in a distributed manner so $x \in_R \mathbb{Z}_p$ is unknown to t servers or less [14].

SecShare.Exp(b,$\{x\}$): Reconstruct b^x from the shares $\{x\}$ directly by releasing b^{x_i} and performing interpolation on the exponent, namely computing $b^x = \prod (b^{x_i})^{\lambda_i}$, for Lagrange coefficients λ_i [20].

SecShare.ExpLocal($b, \{x\}$, U): Output the pair (b^{x_i}, π_i) privately to user U, where π_i and a zero-knowledge proof of equality of discrete logarithm for b^{x_i} and g^{x_i}. This operation is called PublicExponentiate in [4].

---

^{2} For this work, we slightly modify the semantics for the function SecShare.Encode(x) so all shares $\{w\}$ are received by the party who invokes the function.

SecShare.CheckConsistent($\{\omega\}, e_0$): Extract $(\{s\}, \{r\}) \leftarrow \{\omega\}$ and output true if $e_0 = $ SecShare.Exp$(g, \{r\})$ and false otherwise [20].

For conciseness' sake, we sometimes use a simpler notation, where secret share addition, multiplication, share inversion, and exponentiation are written in infix notation. For example, given shares $\{x\}$ and $\{y\}$, their addition is denoted by $\{x\} + \{y\}$, their multiplication by $\{x\} \cdot \{y\}$, inverting $\{x\}$ by $\{x\}^{-1}$, and exponentiation of $b \in G$ by $b^{\{x\}}$. By $\{x\} \xleftarrow{\$} G$ we will also denote running SecShare.Gen(), and share reconstruction by $x \leftarrow \{x\}$.

The following operations can be easily implemented from the previous operations, but we name them to make the presentation easier:

SecShare.Gen(g): Given a generator g of G, generates a shared secret $\{x\}$ in a distributed manner for $x \in_R \mathbb{Z}_p$, and outputs a public value $g^x \in G$ [14].

SecShare.GenInv(g): Given a generator g of G, generate a random shared secret $\{x\}$ in a distributed manner and output a public value $g^{1/x}$ [13]. This is equivalent to computing $g^{\{y\}}$ where $\{x\} \xleftarrow{\$} G$, $\{y\} \leftarrow \{x\}^{-1}$.

SecShare.ExpRR($(e_0, e_1), \{x\}$): Given (e_0, e_1) an ElGamal encryption of g^m, output an encryption of g^{mx} [20].

SecShare.MultExp($b_1, b_2, \{x\}, \{y\}$): Reconstructs $b_1^x \cdot b_2^y$ without exposing b_1^x nor b_2^y. The procedure is new, needed for WhoToo$^+$. It is described in [17]. We use the simpler notation $\{z\} \leftarrow b_1^{\{x\}} \cdot b_2^{\{y\}}$.

All of these operations are secure multiparty computations and therefore the view of the honest servers can be computationally simulated using only public outputs (the verification values), a fact we use in the security proofs. Indeed, with the exception of SecShare.ExpLocal, the operations that take a shared value $\{x\}$ and produce (the shares of) a new shared value $\{y\}$ (e.g. $\{y^{-1}\} = $ SecShare.Invert($\{x\}$)) mentioned above, also publicly output new verification values. To keep things simple, we do not include these values in the notation. Each operation also provides *correctness*, meaning that the reconstruction does actually recover the secret shared value.

3.2　Distributed Group Signatures

A group signature scheme allows any member of set of participants to sign a message on behalf of a group without disclosing their identity unless a special participant, the group manager, wishes to trace and expose the signer. In [20], Kuykendall et al. present a distributed variant of the Boneh, Boyen, and Shacham group signature [6] where the manager is distributed among the servers. This scheme is used to validate an accuser's identity and reveal it once their accusation has reached the quorum. BBS signatures provide a signature of knowledge of a private key α together with an ElGamal encryption of R. To prevent disclosure of the identity of the signer, the private key to decrypt the second value is distributed among the servers.

The distributed operations we need for both WhoToo and WhoToo$^+$ are the following:

DistBBS.Setup(g_1, g_2): The servers compute secret keys $\{x\}$ and $\{\gamma\}$, $h \leftarrow g^x$, $w \leftarrow g_2^\gamma$, and publish public keys $pkeg \leftarrow (g_1, h, w)$.

DistBBS.UserKeyIssue$_U(\{\gamma\})$: The servers compute the private key $\{\alpha\}$ for user U and send them their shares so that U can reconstruct α. They also compute the public key $R \leftarrow g_1^{1/(\alpha+\gamma)}$.

BBS.Sign(pk, sk_U, m): Compute $c_R \leftarrow$ ElGamal.Enc($pkeg, R$) and σ, the signature of knowledge of sk_U. Output (c_r, σ).

BBS.Verify(pk, m, c, σ): Verify that σ is a valid signature of knowledge.

DistBBS.Trace($c_R, \{x\}$): Output ElGamal.DistDec($c_R, \{x\}$).

Under the security notions of [5] this scheme is correct, fully anonymous and fully traceable under the k-strong Diffie Hellman assumption in $\mathbb{G}_1$, as long as the secret sharing operations are secure. The implementation of these functions is detailed in [20].

3.3 Privacy-Preserving Multisets

One of the innovative aspects of WhoToo was the efficient use of new privacy-preserving data structures. One of them is the multisets proposed by Kissner and Song [19], constructed from encoded polynomials. In this solution, a set is represented by a polynomial $F(x)$ and elements in the multiset are represented as the roots of $F(x)$. Adding a new element s is done by multiplying $F(x)$ with $(x - s)$, and checking if the quorum has been reached after adding a value s is done by calculating $F^{(q-1)}(x)$, the $(q-1)^{th}$-derivative of $F(x)$ and verifying if $F^{(q-1)}(s) = 0$. We follow the description and notation from [20], and let $e_F = (e_{F_0}, e_{F_1}, ..., e_{F_d})$ represent the *encoded* coefficients of polynomial $F(x) = F_0 + F_1 x + ... + F_d x^d$, where e_{F_i} is an ElGamal encryption of g^{F_i}. Thus, given an ElGamal encryption scheme, any polynomial F can be represented by an encoded polynomial e_F. Polynomials can be operated with the following distributed operations:

PrivatePoly.Subtract(e_F, e_G): Output e_H where $H = F - G$.

Private.Poly.Differentiate(e_F, ℓ): Output e_G where G is the ℓth-derivative of F.

PrivatePoly.Multiply(e_F, R): Given an encoded polynomial F and a polynomial R in the clear, output e_G where $G = F \cdot R$.

PrivatePoly.MultiplyLinear($e_F, \{s\}$): Output e_G where $G = F \cdot (x - s)$.

PrivatePoly.ZeroTest($e_F, \{s\}$): Output true if $F(s) = 0$, false otherwise.

For a detailed description of these operations, see [20]. Using these operations over polynomials, Kuykendall et al. define the following privacy-preserving multiset operations:

Set.Init(): Output e_{g^0}. This creates the set.

Set.Add($e_F, \{s\}$): Output PrivatePoly.MultiplyLinear(e_F, s). Adding a value s to F is simply multiplying F by $(x - s)$.

Set.Quorum($e_F, \{s\}$): Output true if $(x - s)^q$ divides F and false otherwise. Value q is the pre-specified quorum for the protocol.

In terms of security notions, we say the data structure is correct if all operations over the multiset (additions, and evaluating if any element has multiplicity q) properly correlates to the above operations over the polynomials. Also, the structure achieves (computational) hiding if any PPT adversary with limited interaction with the data structure (who gets to choose some elements to add, sees some of the other additions but does not get to see all added elements) does not obtain any information other than the size of the set and what it can infer from the multiplicity tests (see [19] for formal definitions). The WhoToo protocol [20] required that these operations achieve perfect completeness and computational hiding of the elements of the set. The only information revealed should be the size of the set, e.g., the degree of the polynomial.

A FIRST GAP: As we mentioned in the introduction, our analysis detected some minor inconsistencies in the specification of Set.Quorum, steaming from its use of PrivatePoly.Multiply, PrivatePoly.MultiplyLinear and PrivatePoly.ZeroTest. We thus provide a detailed description of all these operation in the following section.

4   Two Issues in WhoToo

In this section, we discuss two key aspects of the WhoToo protocol that (we believe) require some clarifications before a secure and working version of the protocol can be properly implemented. Although they are arguably small, finding a secure working solution seems to require, in one case, revisiting the security proof of a key component of the protocol and, in the other case, coming up with a secure yet not obvious subprotocol to compare *four* encrypted values in a pairwise fashion.

4.1   Securely Evaluating Quorum in WhoToo

There is an inconsistency between functions PrivatePoly.Multiply and Set.Quorum as stated in the published version of [20]. The first function takes two arguments: an encoded polynomial e_F and a polynomial R in the clear. Yet, in [20, Fig. 5], Set.Quorum invokes PrivatePoly.Multiply with *two encoded polynomials*. (The syntax is consistent with this interpretation as SecShare.Gen returns an encoding of the shared value when implementing with Pedersen VSS, as suggested in the paper.)

Of course, at first glance, the most reasonable explanation is a typo. Indeed, it seems we may simply take R (the second and random polynomial) in the clear. This solution, however, requires revisiting Lemma 6.5 [20, page 423] because this version of the Set.Quorum protocol does not hide all information on the set. We notice that since R is "in the clear", taking the derivative of the encoding of $(F \cdot R)'$ and then evaluating it on s (say obtaining a value s^*) reveals information, as s^* only depends on (the actual, non-encoded) F and the publicly known polynomial R. A concrete attack is described in the full version [17].

To prevent this attack, we decided to put forward a simple but robust modification of PrivatePoly.ZeroTest so value s^* is randomized if not null before being publicly exposed. This randomization is done using protocol MsgRand before decryption [20], details in [17]. In this way, we can have the random polynomial R in the clear without leaking any information. We prove the following two lemmas in the full version [17].

Lemma 4.1. *The modified PrivatePoly.ZeroTest does not reveal any information other than if the shared value s is a root of the encrypted polynomial e_F.*

Lemma 4.2. *The modified Set.Quorum hides all elements of the set, revealing only its size and whether or not the multiplicity of a shared value s is above of a fixed threshold.*

4.2   Identifying Duplicate Accusations

In WhoToo, in order to validate accusations, servers need to remove duplicate accusations. They are those that identify the same pair of accused D and accuser R. To eliminate them, servers must check whether a given pair $(s = H(D), R)$ has already appeared in some previous valid accusations, on the list Accusations of unopened accusations. The protocol uses $s = H(D) \in \mathbb{Z}_p$ as the identifier for the accused so that it can be secret shared. To guarantee privacy, values s and R are both encoded (encrypted) using a multiplicatively homomorphic ElGamal. Let $e_{s'}$ and $c_{R'}$ be encodings associated to an existing (valid) accusation in the set Accusations, say the i-th accusation on the list. The WhoToo protocol provides Equal, a distributed equality testing operation that, given two encodings, divides, randomized, and decrypts the result, so the only exposed value is 1 if the plaintexts are equal, and a uniformly random value if not. We could certainly use Equal($e_s, e_{s'}$) to compare whether two encodings e_s and $e_{s'}$ have equal plaintexts s and s'. Protocol Equal indeed works perfectly and does not reveal additional information when two encodings are compared. However, it does not suffice in order to identify duplicate accusations, as we need to do more: we must compare e_s and c_R from *two different accusations, simultaneously*. The original description for this step (WhoToo.VerifyAcc, line 4) calls for Equal on inputs $(e_s, c_R), (e_{s'}, c_{R'})$. The meaning of such call is confusing, at least, as the input comprises *four* ciphertexts, not two. No description nor explanation is given about how this equality test must be computed with four ciphertexts. At this point, the most natural solution is to compare them sequentially, say first $(e_s, e_{s'})$ and then $(c_R, c_{R'})$. This approach, unfortunately, compromises the anonymity of the accuser. Consider the case that $s = s'$ but $R \neq R'$. If we apply the above strategy, everyone learns that there are two accusations against s, and since later we learn that $R \neq R'$, the accusations are not duplicated, thus valid. If the comparison is made starting with $(c_R, c_{R'})$, it is easy to see that the anonymity of the accuser may be compromised this time. Even though no individual value for the "unequal" plaintext is computed, learning that there are other accusations in the system with the same identities would clearly compromise anonymity.

It is not trivial to adapt Equal for multiple inputs. The fact that it is unclear and left open for the protocol implementer to decide, could potentially compromise the security of the entire protocol.

In the following section we provide an alternative to this process which preserves anonymity and, in fact, is more efficient.

5 Improving WhoToo

WhoToo uses the distributed equality testing mentioned in the previous section in two different components of the protocol: to identify repeated accusations (same pair accuser, accused, the case above) and to identify accusations for the same *accused*, in order to identify the accusations that triggered the quorum. In each of these components, the test is used to compare a specific accusation to all other unopened accusations. Therefore, the $\mathcal{DA}$ must compute as many distributed operations as there are unopened accusations. If there is a big backlog of accusations that have not reached the quorum, this becomes very inefficient. We propose alternatives to each of these components where the $\mathcal{DA}$ only needs to compute a constant number of distributed operations to obtain the same information.

5.1 Duplicate Revision

As mentioned in the previous section, this component aims to check whether a new accusation has already been submitted, by detecting if the same accuser R has already submitted an accusation against the same $s = H(D)$. Instead of following the (rather problematic) WhoToo approach, we propose an alternative inspired upon the SAE protocol. We use a *distributed input pseudorandom function* (DIPRF) introduced in SAE [4]. This DIPRF is a distributed variant of the distributed verifiable PRF from [10].

Distributed Input Pseudorandom Functions (DIPRF): A DIPRF is a pseudo-random function where the key and input are secret shared among the computing parties. It outputs a sharing of the calculated pseudo-random value, which can be sent directly to a user U or simply reconstructed by the servers. The DIPRF introduced in SAE [4] can be securely and efficiently computed among the servers. Their function is also verifiable, but we ignore that feature. Indeed, we use the following result from [10]:

Proposition 1. *Given a bilinear group $\mathbb{G}$ with generator g where a q-Decisional Bilinear Diffie Hellman Inversion assumption holds, with $sk \in_R \mathbb{Z}_q$ and $pk = g^{sk}$, $F_{sk}(x) = e(g, g)^{(1/(x+sk))}$ is a PRF.*

A slight modification gives us a DIPRF over Type-III pairings, namely $F_{sk}(x) = e(g_1, g_2)^{1/(x+sk)}$. We further extend it, based on a similar construction in [4], to obtain a distributed-input PRF variant whose sk is secret shared. It is shown in Fig. 1. The security is discussed in [17].

OUR SOLUTION: The intuition for our solution is the following. We create an input that non-malleably combines the values R and s, and let the servers jointly

---

DIPRF.Setup():

1. $g \in_R \mathbb{G}$
2. $(\{sk_d\}, pk_d = g^{sk_d}) \leftarrow$ SecShare.Gen(g)
3. Publish pk_d

DIPRF.Calculate($\{sk_d\}, \{x\}$, recipients):

1. $\{t\} \leftarrow \{sk_d\} + \{x\}$
2. $\{exp\} \leftarrow \{t\}^{-1}$
3. if recipients = all_DAs:
   (a) output $e(g, g)^{\{exp\}}$
4. else if recipients = U:
   (a) $\{res\} \leftarrow$ SecShare.ExpLocal
       $(e(g, g), \{exp\}, U)$
       Shares of $\{res\}$ are sent to user U
5. else if recipients = none:
   (a) $\{res\} \leftarrow e(g, g)^{\{exp\}}$

DIMAC.Setup():

1. $(pk_m, \{sk_m\}) \leftarrow$ DIPRF.Setup()
2. $V = \emptyset$

DIMAC.Tag($\{sk_m\}, \tau, U$):

1. $\{j\} \xleftarrow{\$} \mathbb{Z}_p$
2. $\{p_j\} \leftarrow$ DIPRF.Calculate($\{sk_m\}, \{j\}$, none)
3. $\{x\} \leftarrow \tau + \{p_j\}$
4. $\{d_j\} \leftarrow$ DIPRF.Calculate($\{sk_m\}, \{x\}, U$)
5. Send shares of j and d_j to user U.

DIMAC.Verify($\{sk\}, \{\tau\}, d_j, j$):

1. if $(d_j, j) \in V$: output False
2. $\{p_j\} \leftarrow$ DIPRF.Calculate($\{sk_m\}, j$, none)
3. $\{x\} \leftarrow \{\tau\} + \{p_j\}$
4. $d'_j \leftarrow$ DIPRF.Calculate($\{sk_m\}, \{x\}$, all_DAs)
5. $V \leftarrow V \cup \{(d'_j, j)\}$
6. output $d_j = d'_j$

Fig. 1. Distributed input PRF and MAC. Operations involving shares use arguments with braces (e.g. $\{x\}$) as described in Sect. 3.1.

compute the DIPRF on that input. Then for every new accusation the servers only need to compute this value once and compare it with the previously stored ones. If a majority of servers agree that the new DIPRF value has not been calculated before, then the accusation is not duplicated.

Since we can not use R directly, we define $\tau = H'(R)$. When the accusation is prepared, the user must provide a secret sharing of τ. The combined input for the DIPRF will be $\{x\} = \{s\} + \{\tau\}$. Under the random oracle model, the value $s + \tau$ uniquely identify a valid pair of accused and accuser, except with negligible probability [17].

Avoiding Mismatched Accusations: If we only use the DIPRF in this way, a corrupted user could send shares of τ that do not match R, namely $\tau \neq H'(R)$. In order to ensure that there is no mismatch between R and τ, we build a Distributed Input MAC using the DIPRF in a somewhat standard way. The resulting DIMAC scheme is described in Fig. 1.

Using the DIMAC scheme, we modify the protocol so that the $\mathcal{DA}$ computes τ during initialization and then calculates k values $T = \text{DIMAC}(\{sk\}, \tau)$, sending the shares of each T directly to the user, so that no servers learn any of the values of the DIMACs. Each value T is a pair (d_j, j), where j is a random value added to the DIPRF input. Our protocol uses k random j's to prevent reusing τ's and to prevent a malicious user from sending another user's τ and a random $(d_{j'}, j')$, which even though would fail verification, would reveal and invalidate (spend) a real user's DIMAC.

When making a new accusation, a user U sends their shares of τ with any unused d_j and the corresponding j to the $\mathcal{DA}$. To ensure the shares of τ correspond to the value given during initialization, the $\mathcal{DA}$ verifies (recomputes) the DIMAC. As a consequence of this approach, our protocol only allows each user to submit at most k different accusations. We believe this is a reasonable tradeoff.

5.2 Matching Accusations

Once Set.Quorum returns true, all accusations against the same perpetrator must be opened. In order to find the matching accusations, WhoToo performs a linear scan, distributively comparing each e_s in the Accusations set to the last accusation. If $N = |\text{Accusations}|$, this means that every time the quorum is reached, N interactive distributed operations must be computed.

A naive approach to reduce this number is to generate public and private keys (pk_s, sk_s) for every possible s and encrypt every sk_s with the servers' public key. When making an accusation against s, the user could include an encryption of some value (say 1) with pk_s. Let $\rho_s = Enc_{pk_s}(1)$. Then, once the quorum is reached for a certain s, the servers could cooperate to obtain sk_s and each server could locally try to decrypt every ρ_s in the Accusations set. If the decrypted value is 1, then it is a matching accusation. This approach would require only one distributed operation, nevertheless, it has two significant issues: (1) generating and encrypting keys for every possible s is extremely inefficient and (2) we need to ensure that no information about accusations that do not match is revealed, which would require a robust encryption scheme that can guarantee $Dec_{sk_s}(Enc_{pk_{s'}}(1)) \neq 1$ for every $s \neq s'$.

We propose a distributed variant of a Strongly-Robust Identity-Based encryption scheme, which allows to have a similar approach solving both issues.

Strongly Robust Distributed IBE: An Identity-Based Encryption is a public key encryption scheme in which any user can use public parameters and a specific identifier ID to compute a public key for that ID [16]. The corresponding secret key is computed by a centralized trusted authority using a master secret key, public parameters and the given ID. Notice that secret keys to decrypt messages encrypted with public keys can be created after the message is encrypted.

Going back to our problem, we first notice that using IBE encryption solves the first issue above, as secret keys can be computed when needed instead of precomputing them for all possible identities. To solve the second issue, we need a new property for our (IBE) encryption scheme: *Strong Robustness* [3]. Strongly robust IBE guarantees that $Dec_{sk_{ID}}(Enc_{sk_{ID'}}(m)) = \perp$ for all m and for all $ID = ID'$. Indeed, this ensures that no information is revealed when trying to decrypt a message encrypted for a specific identity with a (valid) secret key that does not match that identity. This security notion is formalized as SROB [3].

FROM IBE TO DISTRIBUTED IBE: In our setting, however, we do not have a centralized trusted authority, so we create a variant with a distributed authority. To achieve our goal, the servers operate as a distributed key center, providing secret keys to decrypt IBE encrypted messages to any identity. Indeed, they first compute a shared master private key and publish public parameters that anyone can use to encrypt for any identifier ID. Furthermore, the servers (not the users) compute all IBE encryptions. Interestingly, our solution does not need to encrypt any message (the empty message suffices), it simply must provide an *identity-based* proof that the ciphertext was generated for the correct ID.

To describe our solution, we present the scheme we use as starting point, and how we modify it to make it distributed.

IBE SYNTAX: More formally, an identity-based encryption scheme is a 4-tuple (Setup,KeyGen,Enc, Dec) where Setup, on input λ (the security parameter), creates public parameters *params* and a master private key *msk*, KeyGen, on input *params* and a given ID, creates the corresponding secret key sk_{ID}, Enc, on input message M, encrypts it under a given ID using *params*, and Dec, on input ciphertext C and a secret key sk_{ID} returns the corresponding plaintext M.

We start from an identity-based encryption scheme proposed by Gentry [16] which was later modified to work with Type-3 bilinear groups and to achieve strongly robust ANON-IND-ID-CCA security by Okano et al. [22]. To obtain a strongly robust scheme (SROB), Okano et al. apply the transform proposed by Abdalla, Bellare and Neven [3]. Since our threat model is weaker (the servers will generate the IBE ciphertext, so no chosen-ciphertext is needed), we can simply use the original IBE scheme with the modifications for Type-3 pairings, which is ANON-IND-ID-CPA secure as long as the truncated decision q-ABDHE assumption holds for $(\mathbb{G}, \mathbb{G}_T, e)$ [16]. In the modified version, we require the truncated decision q-$ABDHE$ assumption to hold for $(\mathbb{G}_1, \mathbb{G}_2, \mathbb{G}_T, e)$. Furthermore, since we do not encrypt any message, we do not need IND-CPA security, therefore, we aim to construct a strongly robust ANON-ID-CPA secure scheme.

THE BASIC SCHEME: Consider a bilinear group $(\mathbb{G}_1, \mathbb{G}_2, \mathbb{G}_T, e, g_1, g_2)$ with no efficient known isomorphism between $\mathbb{G}_1$ and $\mathbb{G}_2$ of prime order p where g_1 and g_2 are generators of $\mathbb{G}_1$ and $\mathbb{G}_2$ respectively. Let $H : \{0,1\}^* \rightarrow \mathbb{Z}_p$ be a universal one-way hash function. The following scheme IBE is a straightforward simplification of the scheme by Okano et al. [22].

IBE.Setup(): The authority chooses random $g', h' \in \mathbb{G}_T$ and $h \in \mathbb{G}_2$. Then, it chooses a random value msk from $\mathbb{Z}_p$ as master private key, and a public key $g_1' \leftarrow g_1^{msk}$. The private output is msk and the public output is $params = (g', h', g_1, g_1', g_2, h)$ and msk.

IBE.KeyGen($params, \{msk\}, ID$): The authority computes a random $r_{ID} \in \mathbb{Z}_p$ and $h_{ID} \leftarrow (h \cdot g_2^{-r_{ID}})^{1/(msk-ID)}$. The output is the private key $sk_{ID} = (r_{ID}, h_{ID} = (h \cdot g_2^{-r_{ID}})^{1/(msk-ID)})$.

IBE.Enc($params, \{ID\}$): The authority chooses random values $dec, s \in \mathbb{Z}_p$ and computes $com \leftarrow g'^{ID}h'^{dec}$, $C_1 \leftarrow g_1'^s g_1^{-sID}$, $C_2 \leftarrow e(g_1, g_2)^s$, and $C_3 \leftarrow h'^{dec}e(g_1, h)^{-s}$. It outputs ciphertext $C \leftarrow (com, C_1, C_2, C_3)$.

IBE.Dec($params, sk_{ID}, C, ID$): Given sk_{ID}, it computes $h'^{dec} \leftarrow e(C_1, h_{ID}) \cdot C_2^{r_{ID}} \cdot C_3$ and outputs true if $com = g'^{ID}h'^{dec}$ otherwise it outputs false.

DistIBE.Setup():

1. $g', h' \xleftarrow{R} \mathbb{G}_T$
2. $(\{\alpha_i\}_{t,n}, g_1' = g_1^\alpha) \leftarrow$ SecShare.Gen(g_1)
3. $h \xleftarrow{R} \mathbb{G}_2$
4. $params \leftarrow (g', h', g_1, g_1', g_2, h, H)$
5. $\{msk\} \leftarrow \{\alpha\}$
6. **output** $params, \{msk\}$

DistIBE.KeyGen$(params, \{msk\}, ID)$:

1. $\{\gamma\} \leftarrow \{msk\} - ID$
2. $\{\gamma_{Inv}\} \leftarrow \{\gamma\}^{-1}$
3. $r_{ID} \xleftarrow{\$} \mathbb{Z}_p$
4. $h_{ID} \leftarrow (h g_2^{-r_{ID}})^{\{\gamma_{Inv}\}}$
5. $sk_{ID} \leftarrow (ID, r_{ID}, h_{ID})$
6. **output** sk_{ID}

DistIBE.Enc$(params, \{ID\})$:

1. $\{dec\} \xleftarrow{\$} \mathbb{Z}_p$
2. $com \leftarrow g'^{\{ID\}} \cdot h'^{\{dec\}}$
3. $\{s\} \xleftarrow{\$} \mathbb{Z}_p$
4. $\{t\} \xleftarrow{\$} \mathbb{Z}_p$
5. $\{tInv\} \leftarrow \{t\}^{-1}$
6. $\{x\} \leftarrow \{t\} \cdot \{ID\}$
7. $a \leftarrow g_1'^{\{t\}} \cdot (g_1^{-1})^{\{x\}}$
8. $\{y\} \leftarrow \{s\} \cdot \{tInv\}$
9. $C_1 \leftarrow a^{\{y\}}$
10. $C_2 \leftarrow e(g_1, g_2)^{\{s\}}$
11. $C_3 \leftarrow h'^{\{dec\}} \cdot (e(g_1, h)^{-1})^{\{s\}}$
12. $C \leftarrow (com, C_1, C_2, C_3)$
13. **output** C

DistIBE.Dec$(params, sk_{ID}, C, ID)$:

1. $h'^{dec} \leftarrow e(C_1, h_{ID}) C_2^{r_{ID}} C_3$
2. **output** $com = g'^{ID} h'^{dec}$

Fig. 2. Strongly Robust Distributed IBE. Operations involving shares use arguments with braces (e.g. $\{x\}$) as described in Sect. 3.1.

Lemma 5.1 ([22]). *Scheme IBE is ANON-ID-CPA secure and strongly robust (SROB) under the q-ABDHE assumption for $(\mathbb{G}_1, \mathbb{G}_2, \mathbb{G}_T, e)$.*

THE DECENTRALIZED SCHEME: The scheme above can be adapted for a distributed trusted central authority. The scheme, called DistIBE, is in Fig. 2. We remark that, despite the name, DistIBE.Dec is not distributed since sk_{ID} is known by everyone, so this operation is simply performed locally by each server.

In terms of security notions, we adapt both ANON-ID-CPA and SROB to the distributed setting in the obvious way. See [17] for details and proof of the following lemma.

Lemma 5.2. *DistIBE is ANON-ID-CPA secure and strongly robust (SROB) under the q-ABDHE assumption for $(\mathbb{G}_1, \mathbb{G}_2, \mathbb{G}_T, e)$ in the distributed setting.*

Our Solution: When an accusation is received, the servers encrypt a message with ID $= s$, which they obtain as a shared secret from the user in Who-Too.Accuse, and add it to Accusations. We will call this value ρ_s. Similarly to the naive approach, once the quorum is reached and s is revealed, the servers jointly compute the private key for $ID = s$ and then locally try to decrypt every ρ_s in Accusations with that key. If the value can be decrypted with that key, then it is an accusation against s.

Because it is a strongly robust scheme, the main result is a test of whether the message can be decrypted by that key, a test that anyone who knows the secret key for identity ID can perform. We can think of this scheme as an instance of searchable encryption [2], where the keywords that can be searched for are the identities.

```
WhoToo+.Initialize():

 1. ValidAccuser← GetUsers()
 2. (pk, {msk}) ← DistBBS.Setup()
 3. (pk_d, {sk_d}) ← DIPRF.Setup()
 4. (pk_m, {sk_m}) ← DIMAC.Setup()
 5. (params, {msk_IBE}) ← DistIBE.Setup()
 6. IdentityMap ← ∅
 7. for each U ∈ ValidAccusers:
    (a) R ← DistBBS.UserKeyIssue_U({msk})
    (b) τ ← H'(R)
    (c) IdentityMap[R]← U
    (d) for i ∈ [k]:
        i. d_j,j ← DIMAC.Tag({sk_m}, τ, U)
 8. S ← Set.Init()
 9. Accusations← ∅
10. UniqueAccs ← ∅

WhoToo+.Accuse():

 1. U :
    (a) (acc_i)_{i∈[n]} ← WhoToo.PrepareAcc(D)
    (b) Send acc_i to server DA_i of the DA
        over anonymous confidential channel
 2. DA_i : if not WhoToo.VerifyAcc(acc_i): halt
 3. ρ_s ← DistIBE.Enc(params, {s})
 4. S ← Set.Add(S, {s})
 5. Accusations ← Accusations ∪{(c_R, ρ_s, c_D)}
 6. if Set.Quorum(S, {s})
    (a) Run WhoToo.OpenAccusations
        (ρ_s, {s}, c_D)

WhoToo+.OpenAccusations(ρ_s, {s}, c_D):

 1. Accusers ← ∅
 2. s ← {s}
 3. D ← Null
 4. sk_{ID} ← DistIBE.KeyGen
        (params, {msk_IBE}, s)
 5. for each (c_{R'}, ρ_{s'}, c_{D'}) ∈ Accusations
 6.    if DistIBE.Dec(params, sk_{ID}, ρ_{s'})
 7.        R' ← ElGamal.DistDec(skeg, c_{R'})
 8.        U ← IdentityMap[R']
 9.        Accusers ← Accusers∪{U}
10.        D' ← ElGamal.DistDec(skeg, c_{D'})
11.        if H(D') = s: D ← D'
12. if D =Null: halt
13. Run Investigate(D, Accusers)
```

```
WhoToo+.PrepareAcc(D):

 1. s ← H(D)
 2. {ω}, v, e_0, r_s ← SecShare.Encode(s)
 3. e_s ← (e_0, v_0)
 4. r_D ←$ Z_p
 5. c_D ← ElGamal.EncString(pkeg, D, r_D)
 6. {ω_τ}, v_τ, e_{0τ}, r_τ ← SecShare.Encode(τ)
 7. for each i ∈ [n]
    (a) m_i ← c_D||ω_i||v||e_0;
    (b) (c_R, σ) ← BBS.Sign(m_i, sk_U)
    (c) π_0 ← ElGamal.Prove(e_s, r_s, c_R||σ)
    (d) π_1 ← ElGamal.Prove(c_D, r_D, c_R||σ)
    (e) acc_i ← (c_R, c_D, ω_i, ω_{τ_i}, v, v_τ, e_0,
                 e_{0τ}, σ, π_0, π_1, d_j, j)
 8. output (acc_i)_{i∈[n]}

WhoToo+.VerifyAcc(c_R, c_D, ω_i, ω_{τ_i}, v, v_τ,
                   e_0, e_{0τ}, σ, π_0, π_1, d_j, j):

 1. e_s ← (e_0, v_0)
 2. m_i ← c_D||ω_i||v||e_0
 3. (s_i, r_i) ← ω_i
 4. τ_i, r_{τ_i} ← ω_{τ_i}
 5. if any of the following fail: output False
    (a) DIMAC.Verify({sk_m}, {ω_τ}, d_j, j)
    (b) ElGamal.Verify(pkeg, π_0, e_s, c_R||σ)
    (c) ElGamal.VerifyString(pkeg, π_1,
                             c_D, c_R||σ)
    (d) BBS.Verify(pk, m_i, c_R, σ)
    (e) SecShare.Verify(ω_i, v)
    (f) SecShare.Verify(ω_{τ_i}, v_τ)
    (g) SecShare.CheckConsistent({r_s}, v, e_0)
    (h) SecShare.CheckConsistent({r_τ}, v_τ, e_{0τ})
 6. {x} ← {s} + {τ}
 7. p ← DIPRF.Calculate({sk_d}, {x}, all_DAs)
 8. if p in UniqueAccs: output False
 9. UniqueAccs ← UniqueAccs∪{p}
10. output true
```

Fig. 3. The WhoToo+ Protocol. Operations involving shares use arguments with braces (e.g. $\{x\}$) as described in Sect. 3.1.

5.3 The Full WhoToo+ Description:

Figure 3 presents a full description of WhoToo+, including the modifications needed to use DIPRF for duplicate revision and DistIBE for finding matched accusations. Changes are shown in gray. See [17] for a more detailed description.

6 Security Analysis

In this section, we discuss the security argument for the WhoToo+ protocol. To obtain composability under threshold adversaries, we heavily rely on the fact that the secret sharing operations SecShare (used to implement several of the distributed operations used here) are simulatable (given the appropriate ideal

```
                                    Accuse:
                                      1. ValidAccusers ← GetUsers()
  Initialize:                         2. Receive D from user U
                                      3. if U ∉ ValidAccusers: halt
  1. ValidAccusers ← GetUsers()       4. else if (D, U) ∈ UniqueAccs: halt
  2. Accusers ← ∅                     5. else:
  3. UniqueAccs ← ∅                      (a) Accusers[D] ← Accusers[D]∪{U}
                                         (b) UniqueAccs ← UniqueAccs ∪{(D, U)}
                                         (c) if |Accusers[D]| ≥ q:
                                               i. Run Investigate(D, Accusers[D])
```

Fig. 4. $\mathcal{F}_{\text{WhoToo}+}$: ideal functionality for WhoToo$^+$ [20].

functionality) from only public outputs under a static adversary that corrupts up to $t < n/2$ servers, under the discrete logarithm assumption [15].

Theorem 1. *Let $\mathcal{A}$ be a real world adversary attacking* WhoToo$^+$ *protocol and corrupting up to t servers and any number of users. Under the assumption stated above, the execution of* WhoToo$^+$ *protocol under $\mathcal{A}$ can be simulated by an ideal adversary given the ideal functionality $\mathcal{F}_{\text{WhoToo}+}$ (Fig. 4).*

Due to space constraints, we only sketch the proof. Let A be a PPT adversary that statically corrupts up to t out of the $n \geq 2t + 1$ servers and an arbitrary number of users. Our argument proceed in steps, considering a sequence of games $G_1, \ldots, G_{13}$, where G_1 is the WhoToo$^+$ protocol in real world under the real world adversary $A_1 = A$, and G_{13} is the ideal world with functionality $F_{\text{WhoToo}+}$ and ideal adversary A_{13}. In each game G_i for $i = 2, \ldots, 13$, we show how adversary A_{i-1} can be replaced by a new adversary A_i in such a way that the view for all players and adversary A_{i-1} in game G_1 is computationally indistinguishable from the view for all players and adversary A_i. To move between games, we first use that under the discrete logarithm assumption, each secret sharing operation SecShare from Sect. 3.1 can be simulated against a PPT adversary that statically corrupts a minority of the servers and any number of users given the outputs of the corresponding functionality [15]. Indeed, for DIPRF, the DIMAC, and the DistBBS scheme, we use that these primitives depend on the distributed key generation protocol by Gennaro et al. [14] (which is simulatable), they can be simulated as so the keys are known to the simulator. We also use that the security of all the distributed schemes is reduced to the security of the basic (non distributed) version.

7 Efficiency Analysis

In this section we compare the efficiency between WhoToo and WhoToo$^+$. Let N be the total number of accusations in the system and m the total number of valid users. Notice that all generations of random values can be pre-computed. Table 1 presents the main results, showing the total number of online and offline distributed operations required for duplicate revision (DR), matching accusations (MA) and verifying if the quorum has been reached (Quorum).

Table 1. Efficiency comparison given a total number N of accusations, m valid users, a maximum number k of accusations per user and quorum q.

	RD offline	RD online	MA offline	MA online	Quorum offline	Quorum online	Total offline	Total online
WhoToo	0	$6N$	0	$3N$	$N+q+5$	$N+2$	$N+2$	$10N+2$
WhoToo$^+$	$5(mk+1)$	6	12	14	$N+q+5$	$N+2$	$5mk+N$ $+q+22$	$N+22$

Our modifications lower the number of online distributed operations from $10N+2$ to $N+22$, making WhoToo$^+$ more efficient if there is a backlog of at least 3 accusations. WhoToo$^+$'s efficiency still depends on the number of accusations in the system because the process of determining if the quorum has been reached depends on the size of the multiset that records the accusations. Even though the number of offline distributed operations increases, they can be pre-computed and do not affect scalability.

When running the prototype on an Intel Core i9 CPU and 32 GB of RAM, initialization for 1000 users and $k = 3$ took approximately 45 min. We believe this is a reasonable amount of time for a practical solution. Submitting a new accusation with a backlog of 100 unopened accusations takes 19 s if it does not reach the quorum, and 27 s if it does, while WhoToo takes 42 and 70 s respectively.

References

1. Abdalla, M., Bellare, M., Rogaway, P.: The oracle Diffie-Hellman assumptions and an analysis of DHIES. In: Naccache, D. (ed.) CT-RSA 2001. LNCS, vol. 2020, pp. 143–158. Springer, Heidelberg (2001). https://doi.org/10.1007/3-540-45353-9_12
2. Abdalla, M., et al.: Searchable encryption revisited: consistency properties, relation to anonymous IBE, and extensions. In: Shoup, V. (ed.) CRYPTO 2005. LNCS, vol. 3621, pp. 205–222. Springer, Heidelberg (2005). https://doi.org/10.1007/11535218_13
3. Abdalla, M., Bellare, M., Neven, G.: Robust encryption. J. Cryptol. **31**(2), 307–350 (2017). https://doi.org/10.1007/s00145-017-9258-8
4. Arun, V., Kate, A., Garg, D., Druschel, P., Bhattacharjee, B.: Finding safety in numbers with secure allegation escrows. In: NDSS 2020. The Internet Society (2020)
5. Bellare, M., Micciancio, D., Warinschi, B.: Foundations of group signatures: formal definitions, simplified requirements, and a construction based on general assumptions. In: Biham, E. (ed.) EUROCRYPT 2003. LNCS, vol. 2656, pp. 614–629. Springer, Heidelberg (2003). https://doi.org/10.1007/3-540-39200-9_38
6. Boneh, D., Boyen, X., Shacham, H.: Short group signatures. In: Franklin, M. (ed.) CRYPTO 2004. LNCS, vol. 3152, pp. 41–55. Springer, Heidelberg (2004). https://doi.org/10.1007/978-3-540-28628-8_3
7. Callisto Homepage. https://www.mycallisto.org/. Accessed 10 Mar 2021
8. Cantor, D., et al.: Report on the AAU Campus Climate Survey on Sexual Assault and Misconduct. Westat for the Association of American Universities (AAU) (2020)

9. Chor, B., Goldwasser, S., Micali, S., Awerbuch, B.: Verifiable secret sharing and achieving simultaneity in the presence of faults (extended abstract). In: FOCS, pp. 383–395. IEEE Computer Society (1985)
10. Dodis, Y., Yampolskiy, A.: A verifiable random function with short proofs and keys. In: Vaudenay, S. (ed.) PKC 2005. LNCS, vol. 3386, pp. 416–431. Springer, Heidelberg (2005). https://doi.org/10.1007/978-3-540-30580-4_28
11. Elgamal, T.: A public key cryptosystem and a signature scheme based on discrete logarithms. IEEE Trans. Inf. Theory 31(4), 469–472 (1985)
12. Fiat, A., Shamir, A.: How To prove yourself: practical solutions to identification and signature problems. In: Odlyzko, A.M. (ed.) CRYPTO 1986. LNCS, vol. 263, pp. 186–194. Springer, Heidelberg (1987). https://doi.org/10.1007/3-540-47721-7_12
13. Gennaro, R., Jarecki, S., Krawczyk, H., Rabin, T.: Robust threshold DSS signatures. In: Maurer, U. (ed.) EUROCRYPT 1996. LNCS, vol. 1070, pp. 354–371. Springer, Heidelberg (1996). https://doi.org/10.1007/3-540-68339-9_31
14. Gennaro, R., Jarecki, S., Krawczyk, H., Rabin, T.: Secure distributed key generation for discrete-log based cryptosystems. J. Cryptol. 20(1), 51–83 (2006). https://doi.org/10.1007/s00145-006-0347-3
15. Gennaro, R., Rabin, M.O., Rabin, T.: Simplified VSS and fast-track multiparty computations with applications to threshold cryptography. In: PODC 1998, pp. 101–111. ACM (1998)
16. Gentry, C.: Practical identity-based encryption without random oracles. In: Vaudenay, S. (ed.) EUROCRYPT 2006. LNCS, vol. 4004, pp. 445–464. Springer, Heidelberg (2006). https://doi.org/10.1007/11761679_27
17. Hevia, A., Mergudich-Thal, I.: Implementing Secure Reporting of Sexual Misconduct - Revisiting WhoToo (Full Version) (2021)
18. Ibáñez, M.J.: Universidad de Chile presenta primeros resultados de estudio de acoso sexual. https://www.uchile.cl/noticias/124410/u-de-chile-presenta-primeros-resultados-de-estudio-de-acoso-sexual. Accessed 18 May 2020
19. Kissner, L., Song, D.: Privacy-preserving set operations. In: Shoup, V. (ed.) CRYPTO 2005. LNCS, vol. 3621, pp. 241–257. Springer, Heidelberg (2005). https://doi.org/10.1007/11535218_15
20. Kuykendall, B., Krawczyk, H., Rabin, T.: Cryptography for #MeToo. POPETS 2019(3), 409–429 (2019)
21. Lizama-Lefno, A., Hurtado-Quiñones, A.: Acoso Sexual en el Contexto Universitario: Estudio Diagnóstico Proyectivo de la Situación de Género en la Universidad de Santiago de Chile 2019. Pensamiento Educativo. Revista de Investigación Educacional Latinoamericana, pp. 1–14 (2019)
22. Okano, H., Emura, K., Ishibashi, T., Ohigashi, T., Suzuki, T.: Implementation of a strongly robust identity-based encryption scheme over type-3 pairings. IJNC 10(2), 174–188 (2020)
23. Pedersen, T.P.: Non-interactive and information-theoretic secure verifiable secret sharing. In: Feigenbaum, J. (ed.) CRYPTO 1991. LNCS, vol. 576, pp. 129–140. Springer, Heidelberg (1992). https://doi.org/10.1007/3-540-46766-1_9
24. Rajan, A., Qin, L., Archer, D.W., Boneh, D., Lepoint, T., Varia, M.: Callisto: a cryptographic approach to detecting serial perpetrators of sexual misconduct. In: COMPASS 2018, pp. 1–4 (2018)
25. Schnorr, C.P.: Efficient signature generation by smart cards. J. Cryptol. 4(3), 161–174 (1991)
26. Shamir, A.: How to share a secret. Commun. ACM 22(11), 612–613 (1979)

Stronger Notions and a More Efficient Construction of Threshold Ring Signatures

Alexander Munch-Hansen[✉], Claudio Orlandi, and Sophia Yakoubov

Aarhus University, Aarhus, Denmark
{almun,orlandi,sophia.yakoubov}@cs.au.dk

Abstract. We consider *threshold ring signatures* (introduced by Bresson *et al.* [BSS02]), where any t signers can sign a message while anonymizing themselves within a larger (size-n) group. The signature proves that t members of the group signed, without revealing anything else about their identities.

Our contributions in this paper are two-fold. First, we strengthen existing definitions of threshold ring signatures in a natural way; we demand that a signer cannot be de-anonymized even by their fellow signers. This is crucial, since in applications where a signer's anonymity is important, we do not want that anonymity to be compromised by a single insider. Our definitions demand non-interactive signing, which is important for anonymity, since truly anonymous interaction is difficult or impossible in many scenarios.

Second, we give the first rigorous construction of a threshold ring signature with size independent of n, the number of users in the larger group. Instead, our signatures have size linear in t, the number of signers. This is also a very important contribution; signers should not have to choose between achieving their desired degree of anonymity (possibly very large n) and their need for communication efficiency.

Keywords: Threshold ring signatures · Anonymity · Unique ring signatures · Compact signatures

1 Introduction

It is often desirable for parties to anonymously sign on behalf of a group. A *group signature scheme* [Cv91] enables this; the signature proves that a member of the group signed, but does not reveal which one. However, the downside of group signatures is that the group must be set up and maintained by a trusted *group manager*.[1] *Threshold* (group) signatures similarly allow any t of the parties in

---

[1] *List signatures* [CSST06] are a related primitive. Like group signatures, list signatures require a group manager to set up the keys and parameters. However, in a list signature scheme, signers may only sign a certain amount of times before their anonymity is revoked.

© Springer Nature Switzerland AG 2021
P. Longa and C. Ràfols (Eds.): LATINCRYPT 2021, LNCS 12912, pp. 363–381, 2021.
https://doi.org/10.1007/978-3-030-88238-9_18

a group to sign on behalf of the group together. The signature proves that t members of the group signed without revealing which ones. But, as in group signatures, trusted setup is required for each group.

A *ring signature scheme* (introduced by Rivest *et al.* [RST01]) enables signing on behalf of a group without the need for interactive or trusted setup. Instead, everyone independently generates a key pair, and publishes their public key. The signer chooses the group (or ring) to anonymize herself amongst at signing time, and does so using that ring's public keys. In this paper, we focus on *threshold ring signature schemes* (introduced by Bresson *et al.* [BSS02]), which are a natural extension of ring signature schemes. In a threshold ring signature scheme, any t signers can sign a message together while anonymizing themselves within a larger (size-n) group. Like a ring signature scheme, a threshold ring signature scheme allows the signers to pick the larger group they want to anonymize themselves amongst in an ad-hoc way at signing time.

We make two major contributions in this paper: a strengthening of threshold ring signature definitions, and a new construction with more compact signatures. Our new definition demands that a signer cannot be de-anonymized even by their fellow signers. In applications where a signer's anonymity is important, this protects their anonymity from insiders.

Our construction has signatures of size linear in t, the number of signers. All prior rigorous constructions have signatures with size dependent on n, the size of the larger group. Compact signatures are important; signers should not have to choose between achieving their desired degree of anonymity (possibly very large n) and their need for communication efficiency.

1.1 Application: Whistleblowing

We can imagine a set of people within a large corporation wanting to blow the whistle on some corrupt activity within that organization; however, they are afraid to come forward publicly because of the repercussions they might face. On the other hand, blowing the whistle anonymously may not be effective, since it is important that the public believe that the message came from within the organization, from a sufficient number of organization members (and that it thus has credibility). Threshold ring signatures are the perfect solution. The whistle-blowers form a size-t sub-group, and anonymize themselves within the entire size-n organization. Anyone can then verify that t members of the organization all blew the whistle on the corrupt activity.

Small signature sizes are important here, since often the size n of an organization is unreasonably large. In this application, it also becomes especially important that each individual whistleblower retain anonymity, even against their fellow whistleblowers. Otherwise, in order to de-anonymize *all* of the whistle-blowers, all the organization administration would have to do is get *one* of the whistleblowers' cooperation.

1.2   Our Contributions

As we mentioned earlier, we make two contributions: we give a stronger definition of threshold ring signatures, and a construction that meets those definitions while achieving signatures with size $O(t)$.

Stronger Definitions. Our most significant definitional contribution is a strengthening of the anonymity property. We require that an adversary not be able to tell the difference between signatures produced by two different subsets of signers of the same size t (within the same group of size n), as long as the two subsets contain the same corrupt parties. All previous definitions of anonymity [YLA+11, PBB12, OTYO18, HS20] do not allow the sets of signers to contain any corrupt parties at all; this is a dealbreaker in many applications, where one insider should not be able to bring down the entire group.

We use a strong syntax that fits well with our stronger notion of anonymity. We require that signers be able to produce *partial* signatures locally, without interacting with their fellow signers; the partial signatures should preserve the signers' anonymity, and should be combinable into a threshold signature by any third party. Having such a noninteractive structure is crucial for preserving anonymity against fellow signers; if signing were interactive, signers might learn their peers' identities via e.g. their IP addresses.

Construction with Succinct Signatures. We build the first threshold ring signature scheme with signatures of size $O(t)$; all previous constructions have signatures with size dependent on n. For groups of signers of size t significantly smaller than the larger group of size n they wish to anonymize themselves amongst, this is crucial.

Naively, to produce a threshold ring signature, each of the t signers could produce a ring signature, and their threshold ring signature would simply be a concatenation of these. The issue here is that a verifier would need to be convinced that these ring signatures were produced by distinct signers. An immediate solution to this would be a zero-knowledge proof that each signature was generated using a different secret key; however, this proof would be large, inefficient, and producing it would require interaction between the signers.

Instead, we base our threshold ring signature scheme on a primitive called a unique ring signature scheme (URS), introduced by Franklin and Zhang [FZ12][2]. A unique ring signature scheme is a ring signature scheme which allows the linking of two signatures produced by the same signer on the same message with respect to the same ring. We can construct a threshold ring signature simply by concatenating t unique ring signatures. A verifier can check that no two unique

---

[2] A similar approach to building a threshold ring signature scheme was mentioned by Yuen *et al.* [YLA+13] where they would instead use a traceable ring signature scheme [FS06]; however, it was not formalized or proven. As far as we can tell, the definition of security they use for a traceable ring signature scheme does not seem to allow such a proof.

ring signatures were produced by the same signer, and so is convinced that t of the n users signed the message.

Any unique ring signature scheme (secure under our definitions, which are slightly modified from those of Franklin and Zhang) can be used to construct a threshold ring signature scheme in such a way. We present a new, intuitive unique ring signature scheme with signatures of size $O(1)$ which draws inspiration from the construction of Dodis *et al.* [DKNS04]. Unlike the work of Yuen *et al.*, we leverage a random oracle, allowing us to get smaller unique signatures. We additionally use an RSA accumulator [Bd94][3] and the generalized DDH assumption. These assumptions are more standard than the Link-Decisional RSA assumption used in some traceable ring signature constructions [TW05, ACST06]. Existing constructions [FZ13] require an OR-proof showing that the signer is within the ring that the message is being signed with respect to. This leads to a signature size that scales with the size of the ring. We are the first to propose a URS with signatures of size independent of the ring size.

At a high level, our unique ring signature scheme works as follows: each signer in the ring hashes the message (together with the set of n public keys belonging to the super-set of users), and raises it to the power of their secret signing key. By the generalized DDH assumption, this does not reveal the signer's identity. Each signer then proves using non-interactive zero knowledge (NIZK) that they used a signing key corresponding to one of the public keys belonging to the ring.[4] It may seem that such a proof must be linear in the number n of public keys, but we get around that by using an *accumulator* [Bd94] (a compact representation of an arbitrarily large set that supports efficient proofs of membership) to represent the set of public keys, like in the construction of Dodis *et al.* [DKNS04].

As required by our definitions, our construction is completely non-interactive; each of the t signers produces a unique ring signature independently, and those signatures are then simply concatenated to produce the threshold ring signature. This concatenation can be done by any third party. An important consequence of this is that the scheme is *flexible*, meaning that a signer can contribute a partial signature at any point, resulting in a threshold signature with a threshold t that is larger by 1.

---

[3] We could instead use a bilinear map accumulator [CKS09]; however, the use of such an accumulator would require an a-priori upper bound on the ring size.

[4] Our use of NIZK proofs requires the presence of a common reference string (CRS). At first glance, since a CRS is a form of setup, this might seem to make our construction a group signature scheme instead of a ring signature scheme. However, there is a qualitative difference between a CRS (which is a global and reusable trusted setup) and a per-user trusted setup (in group signatures, parties' secret keys need to be distributed by a trusted party). In particular, once the CRS is generated in a trusted way (perhaps using an MPC ceremony), the parties in our system can generate their own keys independently.

1.3 Fully Compact Threshold Ring Signatures

While our threshold ring signature scheme is the first scheme to give signatures of size independent of the ring size n, the signature size does still depend linearly on the threshold t. A natural question to ask is,

Is it possible to build a threshold ring signature scheme
with signatures of constant size?

The answer is that it *is* possible; any threshold ring signature scheme can be altered to have constant-size signatures with the use of succinct non-interactive arguments of knowledge (SNARKs). This can be done simply by allowing any third party—or perhaps one of the signers—to take the produced signature (whose size might depend on n or t) and replace it with a SNARK of a verifying signature for the given ring. Since SNARK sizes do not depend on the statement being proven or the witness for that statement, this yields a constant-size signature.

While this transformation is optimal from an asymptotic point of view, the non-black box use of public-key cryptography inside a SNARK would make this construction prohibive in practice.[5]

1.4 Related Work

Work	Signature Size	Adversarial Keys?	Assumptions
Our work	**$O(t)$**	**Yes**	**Generalized DDH, RSA, RO**
Bresson *et al.* [BSS02]	$O(n \log n)$	No	RSA, RO
Petzoldt *et al.* [PBB12]	$O(n)$	No	Quadratic MQ-problem, RO
Liu *et al.* [YLA+13]	$O(t\sqrt{n})$	No	Q-Strong DH, Subgroup Decision in $\mathcal{G}_q$, DDH-Inversion
Zhou *et al.* [ZZY+17]	$O(n)$	No	Syndrome Decoding Problem, Indistinguishability of Goppa Codes, RO
Chen *et al.* [CHGL18]	$O(n)$	No	Ideal Lattice, Shortest Independent Vector Problem, RO
Okamoto *et al.* [OTYO18]	$O(tn)$	No	Discrete Log, RO, Trusted Dealer
Haque *et al.* [HS20]	$O(n)$	Yes	(Any) Trapdoor Commitments, QROM
Haque *et al.* [HKSS20]	$O(t)$	No	SPB hashing, NIWI

Fig. 1. Threshold ring signature constructions

In Fig. 1 we list some known threshold ring signature constructions, their signature sizes, whether they support adversarial key generation, and the assumptions they leverage. All prior constructions of threshold ring signatures have signatures whose size depends on the number n of users in the ring $\mathcal{R}$. This is not ideal, as the threshold t may be much smaller than n.

---

[5] Even the most basic public-key type operation, a scalar multiplication in an elliptic curve, requires billions of gates [JLE17] when represented by a circuit. This needs to be multiplied by a function of n for any existing threshold ring signature, or t for our construction. While this is the state of the art, we cannot of course rule out that more efficient constructions might emerge in the future, and this could be an interesting venue for further research.

Concurrent Work. Haque *et al.* [HKSS20], posted shortly after this paper, also construct threshold ring signatures of size $O(t)$. The advantage of their work is that their construction does not require a common reference string (CRS), which our construction uses for non-interactive zero knowledge (NIZK) proofs. They get around the need for a CRS by using NIWI (non-interactive witness-indistinguishable) proofs instead of NIZK proofs. However, the advantage of our work is that we support adversarially generated public keys. In the scheme of Haque *et al.*, an adversary who is able to generate and register keys himself is immediately able to break anonymity and unforgeability.[6]

Relying on honestly generated keys is significantly riskier than relying on an honestly generated CRS. CRS generation occurs once, and therefore efficiency is not too much of a concern: we can ensure security e.g. via secure multiparty computation (which can be slow), by involving a large number of parties all of whom are extremely unlikely to collude. However, taking such measures in the generation of every party's key pair, which can happen frequently, would be unreasonable.

1.5   Outline

In Sect. 2, we define ring and threshold ring signatures. In Sect. 3, we describe our threshold ring signature construction. Please refer to the full version [MOY20] for a description of the tools and assumptions necessary for our constructions, such as cryptographic accumulators.

2   (Threshold) Ring Signature Definitions

In this section, we recall the definitions of ring signatures and threshold ring signatures (focusing on the latter).

2.1   Ring Signature Definitions

Ring signatures were originally defined by Rivest *et al.* [RST01] as a natural extension of group signature schemes. Group signatures require some trusted authority to act as a group manager, predefining groups of signers and distributing keys to members of those groups. These keys can then be used to anonymously sign messages on behalf of the entire group. However, requiring a trusted authority that distributes—and knows—signers' keys can be a big drawback. Ring signatures instead allow signers to generate their own key pairs, and to form groups in an ad-hoc way.

---

[6] This is by design; in the proof of anonymity, the authors need to create simulated NIWI proofs that are independent of the identities of the signers. They do this by additionally allowing a witness to demonstrate a relationship between two keys in the ring, where this relationship never holds between keys that are honestly generated. If an adversary was able to register maliciously generated keys, she could register two keys that *do* have this relationship, and use this to forge signatures with arbitrarily high threholds, as long as those two corrupt keys are in the ring in question.

Ring Signature Syntax. A ring signature scheme is defined as a tuple of four algorithms (setup, keygen, sign, verify):

setup(1^λ) → pp:
An algorithm that takes a security parameter λ and outputs a set of public parameters pp. These public parameters pp include the security parameter itself, and any global parameters which can be used within the other algorithms.

keygen(pp) → (pk, sk):
An algorithm that takes the public parameters pp and outputs a key pair (pk, sk).

sign(pp, msg, $\{pk_j\}_{j \in \mathcal{R}}$, sk_i) → σ:
An algorithm that takes the public parameters, a message $msg \in \{0,1\}^*$ to be signed, the set of public keys of the users within the ring $\{pk_j\}_{j \in \mathcal{R}}$, and the secret key sk_i of the signer $i \in \mathcal{R}$ (which must correspond to a public key within the set of public keys $\{pk_j\}_{j \in \mathcal{R}}$). Outputs a signature σ on the message msg.

verify(pp, msg, $\{pk_i\}_{i \in \mathcal{R}}$, σ) → accept/reject:
An algorithm that takes the public parameters, the message, the set of public keys of the users within the ring, and a signature σ. Outputs accept or reject, reflecting the validity of the signature σ on the message msg.

An important property of ring signatures is *setup freeness*, which requires that signers' keys be generated independently. (We note that most ring signature schemes do have a setup algorithm that is run by a trusted authority. However, this authority does not produce the secret keys for the signers; its only job is to produce the public parameters such as moduli and generators used throughout the scheme. The signers can then generate their keys independently using those public parameters.)

Ring Signature Security Definitions. Informally, a ring signature scheme must satisfy the following properties [Liu19, BSS02, DKNS04]:

- *Correctness* requires that a correctly generated signature must verify.
- *Unforgeability* requires that an adversary should not be able to forge a signature on behalf of another user.
- *Anonymity* requires that a signature should completely hide the identity of the signer, even if the adversary has access to a signing oracle.
- *Unlinkability* requires that no adversary should be able to determine whether two signatures were produced by the same signer, even if the adversary has access to a signing oracle.

Remark 1. Note that anonymity implies unlinkability, and vice versa; however, when access to signing oracles is removed, this is no longer the case.

We omit the formal definitions of ring signatures from this paper, focusing instead on *threshold* ring signatures.

2.2   Threshold Ring Signature Definitions

Threshold ring signatures are similar to ring signatures, but instead of allowing any one signer to anonymize themselves among a set of signers, a threshold ring signature scheme allows any t signers to anonymize themselves among a larger set (or ring) of signers $\mathcal{R}$. A verifier can then check that at least t signers in the ring $\mathcal{R}$ signed the message. Note that a ring signature scheme can be viewed as a threshold ring signature scheme with $t = 1$.

Threshold Ring Signature Syntax. A threshold ring signature scheme is usually defined as a tuple of four algorithms (setup, keygen, sign, verify), where sign is interactive and requires the secret keys of t of the signers. We instead choose to define a threshold ring signature scheme as a tuple of five algorithms, by adding combisign. We let sign be locally executed by each signer i (requiring only that signer's secret key sk_i), and produce *partial* signatures σ_i; combisign can then be run by any third party to combine those partial signatures into a threshold signature.

We describe the syntax of combisign below. Notice that it does not require the secret keys of any of the signers.

combisign(pp, $\{\sigma_i\}_{i \in S}, t) \rightarrow \sigma$:
   An algorithm that takes partial signatures $\{\sigma_i\}_{i \in S}$ from t signers, and outputs a combined signature σ.

The syntax of setup, keygen, sign and verify remain unchanged from those of a ring signature scheme, except that sign outputs partial signatures, and verify takes the threshold t as input.

This syntax specification is very strong. In particular, it demands the following desirable properties:

Setup Freeness
   Every signer can generate their own key pair. This is a feature of all ring signature schemes.
Dynamic Choice of Ring Size n
   Different sets of signers can choose rings of different sizes.
Dynamic Choice of Threshold t
   Arbitrarily many signers' partial signatures can be combined into a single threshold signature; the signers don't need to know t when they produce their partial signature. Verification takes a threshold t, and checks that at least that many signers have signed. The upside of this is what is called *flexibility* [OTYO18], meaning that signers can contribute their partial signatures after others have signed. Our syntax demands a weak notion of flexibility where signers can contribute their signatures before combination via combisign; if combisign is as simple as e.g. concatenation of the partial signatures, the stronger notion of flexibility—where signers can contribute even after combination—follows.
   The downside of this flexibility is that the number of signers cannot be hidden by a signature σ.

Non-interactive Signing

As per our syntax, parties generate partial signatures locally; those partial signatures can be combined into a threshold signature by any third party. Non-interactive signing is essential in ensuring the signers' privacy (even against their peers), since anonymous interactive signing would require anonymous communication, which is often difficult to achieve in practice.

Threshold Ring Signature Security Definitions. We base our security definitions on Bresson *et al.* [BSS02] and Haque *et al.* [HS20]. (In particular, we require security against an adversary who can generate and register public keys, as required by Haque *et al.*) We strengthen the definition of anonymity to require that signers remain anonymous even to their fellow signers.

Additionally, both of our security games are defined using *partial* signatures, where a complete signature will be formed by combining the partial signatures of all the signers. This allows for a simple statement of the games while still demanding security against fellow members of the signing rings $\mathcal{R}$. An adversary wins the unforgeability game if he is able to forge a partial signature, and he wins the anonymity game if he is able to distinguish between two partial signatures.

Definition 1 (TRS). *A threshold ring signature scheme is* secure *if it satisfies correctness (Definition 2), unforgeability (Definition 3), and anonymity (Definition 4).*

Definition 2 (Correctness for TRS). *Correctness requires that verification return* accept *on any honestly generated signature.*

More formally, let **TRS** $=$ (setup, keygen, sign, combisign, verify) *be a TRS scheme. We say that* **TRS** *is correct if for all security parameters* $\lambda \in \mathbb{N}$, *for all messages* $msg \in \{0,1\}^*$, *all rings* $\mathcal{R}$, *and all signer sets* $\mathcal{S} \subseteq \mathcal{R}$:

$$\Pr\left[\begin{array}{l} \text{pp} \leftarrow \textbf{TRS}.\text{setup}(1^\lambda), \\ \{(pk_i, sk_i) \leftarrow \textbf{TRS}.\text{keygen}(\text{pp})\}_{i \in \mathcal{R}}, \\ \{\sigma_i \leftarrow \textbf{TRS}.\text{sign}(\text{pp}, msg, \{pk_j\}_{j \in \mathcal{R}}, sk_i)\}_{i \in \mathcal{S}}, \\ \sigma \leftarrow \textbf{TRS}.\text{combisign}(\text{pp}, \{\sigma_i\}_{i \in \mathcal{S}}, t = |\mathcal{S}|) : \\ \textbf{TRS}.\text{verify}(\text{pp}, msg, \{pk_j\}_{j \in \mathcal{R}}, \sigma, t = |\mathcal{S}|) = \text{accept} \end{array}\right] = 1$$

Definition 3 (Unforgeability for TRS). *Unforgeability requires that no efficient adversary* $\mathcal{A}$ *is able to forge a valid signature* σ *for some ring* $\mathcal{R}$ *and message* msg^* *for which* $\mathcal{A}$ *has issued fewer than t corruption queries (on signers in* $\mathcal{R}$) *or signing queries (for ring* $\mathcal{R}$ *and message* msg^*), *where t is the threshold.*

More formally, let **TRS** $=$ (setup, keygen, sign, combisign, verify) *be a TRS scheme. Consider the game* $\text{Game}_{\textbf{TRS},\mathcal{A}}^{Unforge}(1^\lambda)$ *in Fig. 2 between a probabilistic polynomial-time adversary* $\mathcal{A}$ *and a challenger* $\mathcal{CH}$.

We say that **TRS** *is unforgeable if for any efficient adversary* $\mathcal{A}$,

$$\Pr[\mathcal{A} \text{ wins } \text{Game}_{\textbf{TRS},\mathcal{A}}^{unforge}(1^\lambda)] \leq \text{negl}(\lambda)$$

for some negligible function $\text{negl}(\lambda)$.

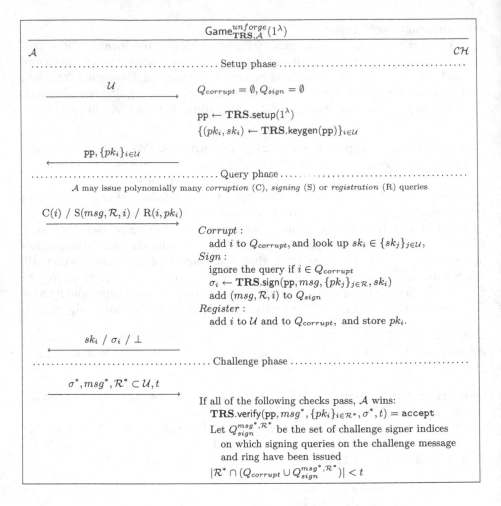

Fig. 2. The unforgeability game for TRS

Remark 2. Note that in the unforgeability game, the challenger responds to signing queries with partial signatures. This is to capture that the adversary might know some of the secret keys (due to corruption queries), and is therefore only interested in seeing the partial signatures by the honest parties. The same holds true for the anonymity game.

Definition 4 (Anonymity for TRS). *Anonymity requires that no efficient adversary $\mathcal{A}$ be able to distinguish between partial signatures produced by two different signers in the same ring.*

More formally, let **TRS** $=$ (setup, keygen, sign, combisign, verify) *be a TRS scheme. Consider the game* $\text{Game}_{\text{TRS},\mathcal{A}}^{anon}(1^\lambda)$ *in Fig. 3 between a probabilistic polynomial-time adversary $\mathcal{A}$ and a challenger $\mathcal{CH}$.*

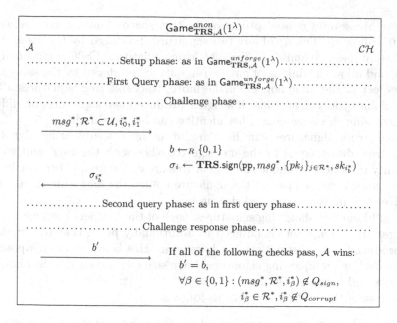

Fig. 3. The anonymity game for TRS

We say that **TRS** *is* anonymous *if for any efficient adversary $\mathcal{A}$,*

$$\Pr[\mathcal{A}\ wins\ \mathsf{Game}_{\mathsf{TRS},\mathcal{A}}^{anon}(1^\lambda)] \leq \frac{1}{2} + \mathsf{negl}(\lambda)$$

for some negligible function $\mathsf{negl}(\lambda)$.

3 Our Threshold Ring Signature Construction

A natural approach to building threshold ring signatures is having each of the t signers produce a ring signature, and then appending to the list of t signatures a zero knowledge proof that all of the signatures were produced using distinct signing keys. However, this approach has two downsides.

1. Producing the zero knowledge proof requires interaction among the signers.
2. The zero knowledge proof may be complex. (One way to do this is to commit to the secret keys used, order the commitments by secret key, prove that each key was used to produce the corresponding signature, and use t range proofs to prove that each committed key is strictly larger than the previous one - since we need to prove that the signatures were produced by t *distinct* signers).

In order to circumvent these two issues, we leverage *unique ring signatures (URS)* [FZ12, FZ13], which allow the linking of two signatures produced by the same signer on the same message with respect to the same ring.

There are several related primitives in this space. *Linkable ring signatures* [LWW04] allow the linking of any two signatures produced by the same signer, regardless of message and ring. *Traceable* ring signatures [FS06] additionally use nonces, and allow the linking of any two signatures produced by the same signer with respect to the same nonce. Furthermore, traceable ring signatures allow a notion of anonymity revocation; if a signer produced two signatures on different messages using the same nonce, her identity can be recovered.

Unique ring signatures can be thought of as traceable ring signatures, with nonces always equal to the message together with the ring, and without anonymity revocation. Unique ring signatures are called unique because in most constructions, there is a part of the signature (called the *tag*) which is deterministic given the message, ring and signing key.

To build our threshold ring signatures, each of the t signers produce a *unique* ring signature; then, there is no need to additionally prove that the signatures were produced using distinct signing keys, since this is immediately apparent.[7] If the underlying unique ring signatures have size $O(1)$, then the threshold ring signatures will have size $O(t)$.

The rest of this section proceeds as follows:

1. In Sect. 3.1, we state the definition of a *unique ring signature scheme* (URS) [FZ12].
2. In Sect. 3.2, we construct a URS scheme with signatures of size $O(1)$.
3. In Sect. 3.3, we use our URS scheme to construct a TRS scheme with signatures of size $O(t)$.

3.1   Unique Ring Signature Definitions

We leverage the notion of *unique ring signature (URS)* schemes, as defined by Franklin and Zhang [FZ12]. We modify the definitions of Franklin and Zhang to allow the adversary to register its own public keys.

Unique Ring Signature Syntax. We define a unique ring signature scheme as a tuple of five algorithms (setup, keygen, sign, verify, link). The setup, keygen, sign and verify algorithms all have the same input and output behavior as the corresponding ring signature algorithms. The link algorithm (described below) allows any verifier to determine whether two signatures were produced by the same signer (on the same message).

link(pp, msg, $\{pk_j\}_{j \in \mathcal{R}}$, σ_0, σ_1) → {linked, unlinked}:
   An algorithm that takes a message msg, public keys belonging to members of

---

[7]   A similar idea was mentioned by Yuen *et al.* [YLA+13]; however, it was not formalized or proven. In particular, a stronger linkability property is needed from the underlying traceable ring signature scheme in order for the TRS construction to be secure. Additionally, since Yuen *et al.* focus on avoiding the random oracle assumption and we do not, we obtain a TRS construction with size $O(t)$ signatures, while they obtain a TRS construction with size $O(t\sqrt{n})$ signatures.).

a ring $\mathcal{R}$, and two signatures σ_0, σ_1. Outputs linked or unlinked, depending on whether the two signatures were produced by the same signer.

Franklin and Zhang avoid the need for a link algorithm by requiring that a part (called the *tag*) of every signature be uniquely determined by the message, ring and signing key; however, we introduce the link algorithm, which is a more general formalization of this requirement.

Unique Ring Signature Security Definitions. Informally, a unique ring signature scheme must satisfy the following properties:

- *Correctness* requires that a correctly generated signature must verify (this is inherited from ring signatures)
- *Uniqueness* requires that no $t - 1$ corrupt signers can produce t signatures that verify for the same message and ring and appear unlinked (we present this property as Definition 6).
- *Anonymity* requires that no adversary can determine whether two signatures that verify for different messages or under different rings were produced by the same signer (we present this property as Definition 7).

Definition 5 (URS). *A unique ring signature scheme is* secure *if it satisfies correctness, uniqueness (Definition 6) and anonymity (Definition 7).*

Definition 6 (Uniqueness for URS). *Let* **URS** $=$ (setup, keygen, sign, verify, link) *be a URS scheme. Consider the game* $\mathsf{Game}_{\mathbf{URS},\mathcal{A}}^{unique}(1^\lambda)$ *in Fig. 4 between a probabilistic polynomial-time adversary $\mathcal{A}$ and a challenger $\mathcal{CH}$.*

We say that **URS** *is* unique *if for any efficient adversary $\mathcal{A}$,*

$$\Pr[\mathcal{A} \text{ wins } \mathsf{Game}_{\mathbf{URS},\mathcal{A}}^{unique}(1^\lambda)] \leq \mathsf{negl}(\lambda)$$

for some negligible function $\mathsf{negl}(\lambda)$.

Definition 7 (Anonymity for URS). *Given two signatures for different messages it should be infeasible for an adversary to determine whether they were created by the same signer or not. More formally, let* **URS** $=$ (setup, keygen, sign, verify, link) *be a URS scheme. Consider the game* $\mathsf{Game}_{\mathbf{URS},\mathcal{A}}^{anon}(1^\lambda)$ *in Fig. 5 between a probabilistic polynomial-time adversary $\mathcal{A}$ and a challenger $\mathcal{CH}$.*

We say that **URS** *is* anonymous *if for any efficient adversary $\mathcal{A}$,*

$$\Pr[\mathcal{A} \text{ wins } \mathsf{Game}_{\mathbf{URS},\mathcal{A}}^{anon}(1^\lambda)] \leq \frac{1}{2} + \mathsf{negl}(\lambda)$$

for some negligible function $\mathsf{negl}(\lambda)$.

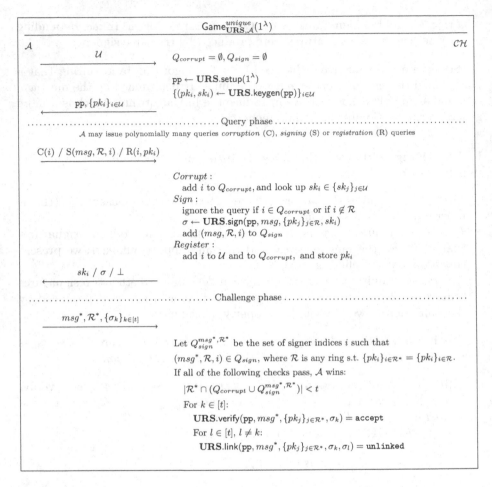

Fig. 4. The uniqueness game for URS. Note that t verifying pairwise-unlinked signatures only count as a win for the adversary if the adversary has not corrupted (or queried the signing oracle on the appropriate message and ring for) t or more of the relevant parties.

3.2   A Unique Ring Signature Scheme

We describe a unique ring signature scheme in Construction 1 in terms of an underlying accumulator scheme **ACC**, a non-interactive zero-knowledge argument of knowledge scheme **NIZKAoK**, a group $\mathbb{G}$ (of order p, with generator g) in which the generalized DDH problem is hard, and a random oracle H which maps arbitrary strings to elements in $\mathbb{G}$. We refer to the full version [MOY20] for a description of these building blocks.

The non-interactive zero-knowledge argument of knowledge scheme **NIZKAoK** will be used for the relation $\mathcal{R}_{\mathsf{sig}}$, which is described below.

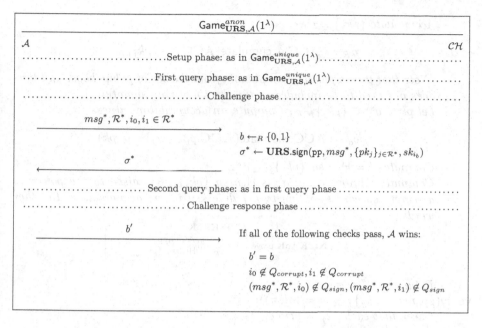

$$\mathsf{Game}^{anon}_{\mathbf{URS},\mathcal{A}}(1^\lambda)$$

$\mathcal{A}$ .... $\mathcal{CH}$

..............................Setup phase: as in $\mathsf{Game}^{unique}_{\mathbf{URS},\mathcal{A}}(1^\lambda)$..............................

..........................First query phase: as in $\mathsf{Game}^{unique}_{\mathbf{URS},\mathcal{A}}(1^\lambda)$..........................

....Challenge phase...

$msg^*, \mathcal{R}^*, i_0, i_1 \in \mathcal{R}^*$

$\xrightarrow{\hspace{4cm}}$

$\qquad\qquad b \leftarrow_R \{0,1\}$

$\qquad\qquad \sigma^* \leftarrow \mathbf{URS}.\mathsf{sign}(\mathsf{pp}, msg^*, \{pk_j\}_{j\in\mathcal{R}^*}, sk_{i_b})$

$\xleftarrow{\hspace{3cm}\sigma^*\hspace{3cm}}$

..........................Second query phase: as in first query phase..........................

....Challenge response phase...

$\xrightarrow{\hspace{2cm}b'\hspace{2cm}}$

If all of the following checks pass, $\mathcal{A}$ wins:

$b' = b$

$i_0 \notin Q_{corrupt}, i_1 \notin Q_{corrupt}$

$(msg^*, \mathcal{R}^*, i_0) \notin Q_{sign}, (msg^*, \mathcal{R}^*, i_1) \notin Q_{sign}$

Fig. 5. The anonymity game for URS. Note that, if the adversary queried the signing oracle on either of the challenge signer identities with the challenge message and ring, he could legitimately link the output of the signing oracle to one of the signatures, helping him determine whose secret key was used to produce it. So, if such a signing query was asked, we do not count the adversary's win.

$$\mathcal{R}_{\mathsf{sig}} \begin{pmatrix} \phi = (\mathbb{G}, g, \mathbf{ACC}.\mathsf{pp}, \\ a_{\mathcal{R}}, \sigma', h), \\ w = (pk, sk, w_a) \end{pmatrix} = \begin{pmatrix} (pk = g^{sk}) \\ \wedge \mathbf{ACC}.\mathsf{verify}(\mathbf{ACC}.\mathsf{pp}, a_{\mathcal{R}}, pk, w_a) \\ \wedge (\sigma' = h^{sk}) \end{pmatrix}$$

Construction 1

$\mathsf{setup}(1^\lambda)$:
- *Sample a DDH group $(\mathbb{G}, g, p)$ with security parameter 1^λ.*
- *Run $\mathbf{ACC}.\mathsf{pp} \leftarrow \mathbf{ACC}.\mathsf{setup}(1^\lambda)$.*
- *Run $(\mathbf{NIZKAoK}.\mathsf{crs}, \mathbf{NIZKAoK}.\mathsf{td}) \leftarrow \mathbf{NIZKAoK}.\mathsf{setup}(1^\lambda, \mathcal{R}_{\mathsf{sig}})$.*
- *Set $\mathsf{pp} = ((\mathbb{G}, g, p), \mathbf{ACC}.\mathsf{pp}, \mathbf{NIZKAoK}.\mathsf{crs})$.*

$\mathsf{keygen}(\mathsf{pp})$:
- *Pick $sk \leftarrow \mathbb{Z}_p$ at random.*
- *Set $pk = g^{sk}$.*
- *If pk is not prime (when interpreted as an integer), redo the first two steps until it is. (We require the public keys to be prime so that they are within the domain of the RSA accumulator.)*

$\mathsf{sign}(\mathsf{pp}, msg, \{pk_j\}_{j\in\mathcal{R}}, sk)$:
- *Check that each pk_j is prime.*

- *Accumulate $\{pk_j\}_{j\in\mathcal{R}}$ as*

$$a_\mathcal{R} \leftarrow \textbf{ACC}.\text{accumulate}(\textbf{ACC}.\text{pp}, \{pk_j\}_{j\in\mathcal{R}}).$$

(Note that this is publicly computable from the set of public keys, and thus does not need to be included in the threshold ring signature.)
- *Let $pk = g^{sk} \in \{pk_j\}_{j\in\mathcal{R}}$. Compute an accumulator witness*

$$w_a \leftarrow \textbf{ACC}.\text{witcreate}(\textbf{ACC}.\text{pp}, \{pk_j\}_{j\in\mathcal{R}}, pk) .$$

- *Compute $\sigma' = \mathsf{H}(msg, \{pk_j\}_{j\in\mathcal{R}})^{sk}$.*
- *Compute π proving that σ' is $\mathsf{H}(msg, \{pk_j\}_{j\in\mathcal{R}})$ raised to the power of a secret key corresponding to a public key in the accumulator. In other words,*

$$\pi \leftarrow \textbf{NIZKAoK}.\text{prove} \begin{pmatrix} \textbf{NIZKAoK}.\text{crs}, \\ \phi = (\mathbb{G}, g, \textbf{ACC}.\text{pp}, \\ \quad a_\mathcal{R}, \sigma', \mathsf{H}(msg, \{pk_j\}_{j\in\mathcal{R}})), \\ w = (pk, sk, w_a) \end{pmatrix}$$

- *Return $\sigma = (\sigma', \pi)$.*

verify($\text{pp}, msg, \{pk_j\}_{j\in\mathcal{R}}, \sigma = (\sigma', \pi)$):
- *Check that each pk_j is prime.*
- *Accumulate $\{pk_j\}_{j\in\mathcal{R}}$ as*

$$a_\mathcal{R} \leftarrow \textbf{ACC}.\text{accumulate}(\textbf{ACC}.\text{pp}, \{pk_j\}_{j\in\mathcal{R}})$$

- *Verify the proof π; return*

$$\begin{aligned} NIZKAoK.\text{verify}(&\textbf{NIZKAoK}.\text{crs}, \phi = \\ &(\mathbb{G}, g, \textbf{ACC}.\text{pp}, a_\mathcal{R}, \sigma', \mathsf{H}(msg, \{pk_j\}_{j\in\mathcal{R}})), \pi). \end{aligned} \quad (1)$$

link($\text{pp}, msg, \{pk_j\}_{j\in\mathcal{R}}, \sigma_0 = (\sigma'_0, \pi_0), \sigma_1 = (\sigma'_1, \pi_1)$):
    return linked *if $\sigma'_0 = \sigma'_1$, and* unlinked *otherwise.*

Theorem 1. *If* **NIZKAoK** *is a secure non-interactive zero knowledge argument of knowledge, if* **ACC** *is a secure accumulator, if* H *is a random oracle, and if the generalized DDH problem is hard in* $\mathbb{G}$, *then Construction 1 is a secure unique ring signature scheme (Definition 5).*

The proof of Theorem 1 can be found in the full version [MOY20].

3.3   A Threshold Ring Signature Scheme

We build threshold ring signatures out of unique ring signatures in a generic way. If the underlying unique ring signatures have size $O(1)$, then the resulting threshold ring signatures have size $O(t)$, where t is the threshold. We require the additional assumption that no message msg is ever signed twice by the same ring $\mathcal{R}$. This is because we use the underlying unique ring signature scheme to sign the message together with the ring; if the same message is signed twice by the same ring, then the partial signatures will be linkable across the two threshold signature instances, and in this case we cannot guarantee anonymity.

We describe our TRS construction formally below, in terms of the underlying URS. (We assume the public keys are always ordered in a canonical way (e.g. lexicographically), so that in the underlying URS, the same message and set of keys always hashes to the same value.)

Construction 2

setup(1^λ): *Return* **URS**.pp $\leftarrow$ **URS**.setup(1^λ).

keygen(pp): *Return* $(sk, pk) \leftarrow$ **URS**.keygen(**URS**.pp).

sign(pp, $msg, sk_i, \{pk_j\}_{j\in\mathcal{R}}$): *Return* $\sigma_i \leftarrow$ **URS**.sign(**URS**.pp, $msg, \{pk_j\}_{j\in\mathcal{R}}, sk_i$).

combisign(pp, $\{\sigma_i\}_{i\in\mathcal{S}}, t = |\mathcal{S}|$): *Return* $\sigma = \{\sigma_i\}_{i\in\mathcal{S}}$. *(So simple!)*[8]

verify(pp, $msg, \{pk_j\}_{j\in\mathcal{R}}, \sigma = \{\sigma_i\}_{i\in\mathcal{S}}, t$):
  - *If* $|\sigma| < t$, *return* reject.
  - *For* $\sigma_i \in \sigma$, *if* **URS**.verify(**URS**.pp, $msg, \{pk_j\}_{j\in\mathcal{R}}, \sigma_i$) = reject, *return* reject.
  - *For all pairs of different signatures* σ_i, σ_j *in* σ, *if* **URS**.link(**URS**.pp, msg, $\{pk_j\}_{j\in\mathcal{R}}, \sigma_i, \sigma_j$) = linked, *return* reject.[9]
  - *Return* accept.

Remark 3. Note that, since combisign simply takes a concatenation of the partial signatures, our construction satisfies flexibility [OTYO18]. Flexibility requires that a signer $i \in \mathcal{R}$ can take an existing threshold signature σ on message msg using the ring $\mathcal{R}$ that verifies with threshold t, and create a signature σ^* on the same msg and $\mathcal{R}$, that verifies with threshold $t + 1$. This is trivially achieved in our construction; signer i simply produces his own partial signature σ_i, and appends it to the existing signature.

Remark 4. Note that there is an immediate transformation from this construction to a *linkable threshold ring signature scheme*. Our threshold ring signature scheme uses a unique ring signature scheme as a primitive, providing a way of using the signatures to verify the distinctness of the t signers while disallowing linking across signatures. If one instead uses a regular linkable ring signature scheme (where signatures from the same signer are linkable across messages and rings), our TRS construction (Construction 2) would also be linkable across multiple signatures. See Munch-Hansen [MH20] for details.

Theorem 2. *If URS is a secure unique ring signature scheme (Definition 5), then Construction 2 is a secure threshold ring signature scheme (Definition 1).*

The proof of Theorem 2 can be found in the full version [MOY20].

---

[8] The signing set $\mathcal{S}$ is only mentioned here for the sake of clarity. The set of signers is never leaked to the party who performs the combining of the signatures, as each signature is anonymous and does not leak the individual signers.

[9] Recall that the link algorithm simply checks equality of two sub-strings in σ_i, σ_j. Thus the running time of verify can be made $O(t\log(t))$ by sorting these strings and checking for repeated entries.

Acknowledgements. The authors would like to thank the anonymous reviewers for their useful feedback. This research was supported by: the Concordium Blockhain Research Center, Aarhus University, Denmark; the Carlsberg Foundation under the Semper Ardens Research Project CF18-112 (BCM); the European Research Council (ERC) under the European Unions's Horizon 2020 research and innovation programme under grant agreement No 669255 (MPCPRO); the European Research Council (ERC) under the European Unions's Horizon 2020 research and innovation programme under grant agreement No 803096 (SPEC) and the Defense Advanced Research Projects Agency (DARPA) under Contract No. HR001120C0085. Any opinions, findings and conclusions or recommendations expressed in this material are those of the author(s) and do not necessarily reflect the views of the Defense Advanced Research Projects Agency (DARPA).

References

[ACST06] Au, M.H., Chow, S.S.M., Susilo, W., Tsang, P.P.: Short linkable ring signatures revisited. In: Atzeni, A.S., Lioy, A. (eds.) EuroPKI 2006. LNCS, vol. 4043, pp. 101–115. Springer, Heidelberg (2006). https://doi.org/10.1007/11774716_9

[Bd94] Benaloh, J., de Mare, M.: One-way accumulators: a decentralized alternative to digital signatures. In: Helleseth, T. (ed.) EUROCRYPT 1993. LNCS, vol. 765, pp. 274–285. Springer, Heidelberg (1994). https://doi.org/10.1007/3-540-48285-7_24

[BSS02] Bresson, E., Stern, J., Szydlo, M.: Threshold ring signatures and applications to ad-hoc groups. In: Yung, M. (ed.) CRYPTO 2002. LNCS, vol. 2442, pp. 465–480. Springer, Heidelberg (2002). https://doi.org/10.1007/3-540-45708-9_30

[CHGL18] Chen, J., Hu, Y., Gao, W., Liang, H.: Lattice-based threshold ring signature with message block sharing. KSII Trans. Internet Inf. Syst. **13**, 1003–1019 (2018)

[CKS09] Camenisch, J., Kohlweiss, M., Soriente, C.: An accumulator based on bilinear maps and efficient revocation for anonymous credentials. In: Jarecki, S., Tsudik, G. (eds.) PKC 2009. LNCS, vol. 5443, pp. 481–500. Springer, Heidelberg (2009). https://doi.org/10.1007/978-3-642-00468-1_27

[CSST06] Canard, S., Schoenmakers, B., Stam, M., Traoré, J.: List signature schemes. Discrete Appl. Math. **154**(2), 189–201 (2006). Coding and Cryptography

[Cv91] Chaum, D., van Heyst, E.: Group signatures. In: Davies, D.W. (ed.) EUROCRYPT 1991. LNCS, vol. 547, pp. 257–265. Springer, Heidelberg (1991). https://doi.org/10.1007/3-540-46416-6_22

[DKNS04] Dodis, Y., Kiayias, A., Nicolosi, A., Shoup, V.: Anonymous identification in *Ad hoc* groups. In: Cachin, C., Camenisch, J.L. (eds.) EUROCRYPT 2004. LNCS, vol. 3027, pp. 609–626. Springer, Heidelberg (2004). https://doi.org/10.1007/978-3-540-24676-3_36

[FS06] Fujisaki, E., Suzuki, K.: Traceable ring signature. Cryptology ePrint Archive, Report 2006/389 (2006). https://eprint.iacr.org/2006/389

[FZ12] Franklin, M., Zhang, H.: A framework for unique ring signatures. Cryptology ePrint Archive, Report 2012/577 (2012). https://eprint.iacr.org/2012/577

[FZ13] Franklin, M., Zhang, H.: Unique ring signatures: a practical construction. In: Sadeghi, A.-R. (ed.) FC 2013. LNCS, vol. 7859, pp. 162–170. Springer, Heidelberg (2013). https://doi.org/10.1007/978-3-642-39884-1_13

[HKSS20] Haque, A., Krenn, S., Slamanig, D., Striecks, C.: Logarithmic-size (linkable) threshold ring signatures in the plain model. Cryptology ePrint Archive, Report 2020/683 (2020). https://eprint.iacr.org/2020/683

[HS20] Haque, A., Scafuro, A.: Threshold ring signatures: new definitions and post-quantum security. In: Kiayias, A., Kohlweiss, M., Wallden, P., Zikas, V. (eds.) PKC 2020. LNCS, vol. 12111, pp. 423–452. Springer, Cham (2020). https://doi.org/10.1007/978-3-030-45388-6_15

[JLE17] Jayaraman, B., Li, H., Evans, D.: Decentralized certificate authorities. CoRR, abs/1706.03370 (2017)

[Liu19] Liu, J.K.: Ring signature. In: Li, K.-C., Chen, X., Susilo, W. (eds.) Advances in Cyber Security: Principles, Techniques, and Applications, pp. 93–114. Springer, Singapore (2019). https://doi.org/10.1007/978-981-13-1483-4_5

[LWW04] Liu, J.K., Wei, V.K., Wong, D.S.: Linkable spontaneous anonymous group signature for ad hoc groups. In: Wang, H., Pieprzyk, J., Varadharajan, V. (eds.) ACISP 2004. LNCS, vol. 3108, pp. 325–335. Springer, Heidelberg (2004). https://doi.org/10.1007/978-3-540-27800-9_28

[MH20] Munch-Hansen, A.: Stronger notions and a more efficient construction of threshold ring signatures, 06 2020

[MOY20] Munch-Hansen, A., Orlandi, C., Yakoubov, S.: Stronger notions and a more efficient construction of threshold ring signatures. Cryptology ePrint Archive, Report 2020/678 (2020). https://eprint.iacr.org/2020/678

[OTYO18] Okamoto, T., Tso, R., Yamaguchi, M., Okamoto, E.: A k-out-of-n ring signature with flexible participation for signers. IACR Cryptol. ePrint Arch. **2018**, 728 (2018)

[PBB12] Petzoldt, A., Bulygin, S., Buchmann, J.: A multivariate based threshold ring signature scheme. Cryptology ePrint Archive, Report 2012/194 (2012). https://eprint.iacr.org/2012/194

[RST01] Rivest, R.L., Shamir, A., Tauman, Y.: How to leak a secret. In: Boyd, C. (ed.) ASIACRYPT 2001. LNCS, vol. 2248, pp. 552–565. Springer, Heidelberg (2001). https://doi.org/10.1007/3-540-45682-1_32

[TW05] Tsang, P.P., Wei, V.K.: Short linkable ring signatures for e-voting, e-cash and attestation. In: Deng, R.H., Bao, F., Pang, H.H., Zhou, J. (eds.) ISPEC 2005. LNCS, vol. 3439, pp. 48–60. Springer, Heidelberg (2005). https://doi.org/10.1007/978-3-540-31979-5_5

[YLA+11] Yuen, T.H., Liu, J.K., Au, M.H., Susilo, W., Zhou, J.: Threshold ring signature without random oracles, 01 2011

[YLA+13] Yuen, T.H., Liu, J.K., Au, M.H., Susilo, W., Zhou, J.: Efficient linkable and/or threshold ring signature without random oracles. Comput. J. **56**(4), 407–421 (2013)

[ZZY+17] Zhou, G., Zeng, P., Yuan, X., Chen, S., Choo, K.-K.: An efficient code-based threshold ring signature scheme with a leader-participant model. Secur. Commun. Netw. (2017)

Improved Threshold Signatures, Proactive Secret Sharing, and Input Certification from LSS Isomorphisms

Diego F. Aranha[1]([✉]), Anders Dalskov[2], Daniel Escudero[1],
and Claudio Orlandi[1]

[1] Aarhus University, Aarhus, Denmark
dfaranha@cs.au.dk
[2] Partisia, Aarhus, Denmark

Abstract. In this paper we present a series of applications steming from a formal treatment of linear secret-sharing isomorphisms, which are linear transformations between different secret-sharing schemes defined over vector spaces over a field $\mathbb{F}$ and allow for efficient multiparty conversion from one secret-sharing scheme to the other. This concept generalizes the folklore idea that moving from a secret-sharing scheme over $\mathbb{F}_p$ to a secret sharing "in the exponent" can be done non-interactively by multiplying the share unto a generator of e.g., an elliptic curve group. We generalize this idea and show that it can also be used to compute arbitrary bilinear maps and in particular pairings over elliptic curves.

We include the following practical applications originating from our framework: First we show how to securely realize the Pointcheval-Sanders signature scheme (CT-RSA 2016) in MPC. Second we present a construction for dynamic proactive secret-sharing which outperforms the current state of the art from CCS 2019. Third we present a construction for MPC input certification using digital signatures that we show experimentally to outperform the previous best solution in this area.

1 Introduction

A (t, n)-secure secret-sharing scheme allows a secret to be distributed into n shares in such a way that any set of at most t shares are independent of the secret, but any set of at least $t + 1$ shares together can completely reconstruct the secret. In *linear* secret-sharing schemes (LSSS), shares of two secrets can be added together to obtain shares of the sum of the secrets. A popular example of a $(n - 1, n)$-secure LSSS is additive secret sharing, whereby a secret $s \in \mathbb{F}_p$ (here $\mathbb{F}_p$ denotes integers modulo a prime p) is secret-shared by sampling uniformly random $s_1, \ldots, s_n \in \mathbb{F}_p$ subject to $s_1 + \cdots + s_n \equiv s \bmod p$. Another well-known example of a (t, n)-secure LSSS is Shamir secret sharing [Sha79] that distributes a secret $s \in \mathbb{F}_p$ by sampling a random polynomial $f(x)$ over $\mathbb{F}_p$ of degree at most t such that $f(0) = s$, and where the i-th share is defined as $s_i = f(i)$.

© Springer Nature Switzerland AG 2021
P. Longa and C. Ràfols (Eds.): LATINCRYPT 2021, LNCS 12912, pp. 382–404, 2021.
https://doi.org/10.1007/978-3-030-88238-9_19

Linear secret-sharing schemes are information-theoretic in nature: they do not rely on any computational assumption and therefore tend to be very efficient. Furthermore, they are widely used in multiple applications like distributed storage [GGJR00] or secure multiparty computation [CDM00]. Linear secret-sharing schemes can be augmented with techniques from public-key cryptography, such as elliptic-curve cryptography. As an example, consider (a variant of) Feldman's scheme for verifiable secret sharing[1] [Fel87]: To distribute a secret $s \in \mathbb{F}_p$, the dealer samples a polynomial of degree at most t such that $f(0) = s$, say $f(x) = s + r_1 x + \cdots + r_t x^t$, and sets the i-th share to be $s_i = f(i)$. On top of this, the dealer publishes $s \cdot G, r_1 \cdot G, \ldots, r_t \cdot G$, where G is a generator of an elliptic-curve group $\mathbb{G}$ of order p for which the discrete-log problem is hard. Each party can now detect if its share s_i is correct by computing $s_i \cdot G$ and checking that it equals $s \cdot G + i^1(r_1 G) + i^2(r_2 G) + \cdots + i^t(r_t G)$.

While the general idea of using secret sharing "in the exponent" has been used multiple times in the literature, we find that this has been done in a rather ad-hoc way. Thus, a more formal and general treatment of these techniques is currently missing.

1.1 Our Contributions

In this work we expand the range of applications which benefits from performing "MPC in the exponent" by considering the case of secure signatures, proactive secret sharing and input certification, providing novel protocols in each of these settings that improve over the state of the art. We also provide experimental results for some of our protocols. Furthermore, we generalize the idea of "secret sharing in the exponent" by using a formal mathematical definition of linear secret sharing, extending it to general vector spaces—of which elliptic curves are particular cases—and using linear transformations between these vector spaces to convert from one secret-shared representation to a different one. Less expressive frameworks were presented in prior work like [DKO+20, ST19, CCXY18], to cite some examples. Among other things our extensions show how generic multiplication triples over $\mathbb{F}_p$ can be used to securely compute general bilinear maps, of which bilinear *pairings* are a particular case.

The contributions made in this work are summarized below. This listing also serves as an overview of the rest of the paper.

– We show how generic multiplication triples can be used to compute securely any bilinear map, after presenting an adequate mathematical foundation for LSS isomorphisms. As we have mentioned, this is achieved by formalizing the concept of **linear secret-sharing isomorphisms** (LSS isomorphisms) which can be seen as a generalization of the idea of "putting the share in the exponent". Due to space constraints in this proceeding version, this and other contributions can be found in the full version of this paper [ADEO20].

---

[1] A verifiable secret-sharing scheme is one in which parties can verify that the dealer shared the secret correctly.

- We demonstrate how LSS isomorphisms allow computation of scalar products and furthermore show that it is possible to use our techniques to compute bilinear pairings over secret-shared data using any secure computation protocol. This can be found in the full version too.
- To illustrate the usefulness of our LSS isomorphisms, we provide 3 applications. The first of these is a demonstration of how digital signatures can be computed and verified on secret-shared data. This is done in Sect. 3.
- Our second application demonstrates a protocol for dynamic proactive secret-sharing (PSS). This uses the digital signatures and the result is a dynamic PSS protocol with better communication complexity than the current state of the art. This is done in Sect. 4.
- Our final application is input certification. We present a method for verifying that a certain party provided input to a secure computation that was previously certified by a trusted party. We benchmark our protocol experimentally and show that it significantly outperforms the previous best solution for input certification for any number of inputs. The protocol is presented in Sect. 5, and our experiments are presented in Sect. 6.

1.2 Related Work

As already mentioned, the idea of "putting the shares in the exponent" is folklore and dates back at least to verifiable secret sharing [Fel87]. It has since then been used in a variety of other contexts such as e.g. threshold decryption [CDI05,Sho00], attribute-based encryption [GPSW06], polynomial commitments [KZG10], etc. More recent works [DKO+20,ST19] have made use of this idea to develop generic protocols for MPC over elliptic curves, mostly motivated by threshold ECDSA signatures (a task which has received much attention lately due to its impact on developing secure key-management solutions for cryptocurrencies). Compared to previous work, our approach is to describe the folklore idea in the most general framework, applying it to *any* linear secret-sharing scheme and also any vector space isomorphism, since we believe that by providing a more general framework we can enable a wider class of applications, as demonstrated by the example applications in this paper. Other works have formalized a similar notion, like the K-linear secret-sharing schemes from [CCXY18]. However, transformations across these schemes have not been considered in full generality before.

In a recent work [FN20] the authors present protocols to securely compute over elliptic curves (and also over lattices). The authors consider key generation of elliptic-curve ElGamal, as well as decryption, based on generic MPC protocols. In addition, a protocol for solving the discrete log of a secret-shared value is presented. We present an alternative to such a decoding scheme in the full version.

In [CKR+20] the authors construct protocols for multiplying matrices and other bilinear operations such as convolutions based on the observation that the widely used Beaver multiplication technique [Bea92] extends to these operations as well. This turns out to be a particular instantiation of our framework from Sect. 2 when the vector spaces are instantiated with matrix spaces and the bilinear map is instantiated with matrix product.

Multiple works have addressed the problem of proactive secret-sharing. It was originally proposed in [HJKY95, OY91], and several works have built on top of these techniques [HJJ+97, SLL08, BELO15, BELO14, MZW+19], including ours. Among these, the closest to our work is the state-of-the-art [MZW+19], which also makes use of pairing-friendly elliptic curves to ensure correctness of the transmitted message. However, a crucial difference is that in their work, a commitment scheme based on elliptic curves, coupled with the technique of "putting the share in the exponent" is used to ensure each player *individually* behaves correctly. Instead, in our work, we use elliptic curve computation on the secret rather than on the shares, which reduces the communication complexity, as shown in Sect. 4.

Finally, not many works have been devoted to the important task of input certification in MPC. For general functions, the only works we are aware of are [BB16, KMW16, ZBB17, BJ18]. Among these, only [BJ18] tackles the problem from a more general perspective, having multiple parties and different protocols. In [BJ18], the concept of signature schemes with privacy is introduced, which are signatures that allow for an interactive protocol for verification, in such a way that the privacy of the message is preserved. The authors of [BJ18] present constructions of this type of signatures, and use them to solve the input certification problem. However, the techniques from [BJ18] differ from ours at a fundamental level: Their protocols first computes a commitment of the MPC inputs, and then engage in an interactive protocol for verification to check the validity of these inputs. Furthermore, these techniques are presented separately for two MPC protocols: one from [DN07] and one from [DKL+13]. Instead, our results apply to *any* MPC protocol based on linear secret-sharing schemes, and moreover, is much simpler and efficient as no commitments, proofs of knowledge, or special verification protocol are needed.

2 LSS Isomorphisms and Bilinear Maps

Let $\mathbb{F}$ be a prime field of order p. We use $a \in_R A$ to represent that a is sampled uniformly at random from the finite set A.

2.1 Linear Secret Sharing

In this section we define the notion of linear secret sharing that we will use throughout this paper. Most of the presentation here can be seen as a simplified version of [CDN15, Section 6.3], but it can also be regarded as a generalization since we consider arbitrary vector spaces. Similar notions have been considered in the literature before. For example, the same concept presented in a slightly different way has been consider in [CCXY18] under the term of general K-linear secret-sharing schemes.

Definition 1. *Let* $\mathbb{F}$ *be a field. A linear secret sharing scheme (LSSS) $\mathcal{S}$ over $\mathbb{F}$ for n players is defined by a matrix $M \in \mathbb{F}^{m \times (t+1)}$, where $m \geq n$, and a function* label : $\{1, \ldots, m\} \to \{1, \ldots, n\}$. *We say M is the matrix for $\mathcal{S}$. We can apply* label *to the rows of M in a natural way, and we say that player $P_{\text{label}(i)}$ owns the i-th row of M. For a subset A of the players, we let M_A be the matrix consisting of the rows owned by players in A.*

To secret-share a value $s \in \mathbb{F}$, the dealer samples uniformly at random a vector $\boldsymbol{r}_s \in \mathbb{F}^{t+1}$ such that its first entry is s, and sends to player P_i each row of $M \cdot \boldsymbol{r}_s$ owned by this player.[2] We write $[\![s, \boldsymbol{r}_s]\!]$ for the vector of shares $M \cdot \boldsymbol{r}_s$, or simply $[\![s]\!]$ if the randomness vector $\boldsymbol{r}_s$ is not needed. Observe that the parties can obtain shares of $s_1 + s_2$ from shares of s_1 and shares of s_2 by locally adding their respective shares. We denote this by $[\![s_1 + s_2]\!] = [\![s_1]\!] + [\![s_2]\!]$.

The main properties of a secret sharing scheme are privacy and reconstruction, which are defined with respect to an access structure. In this work, and for the sake of simplicity, we consider only threshold access structures. That said, our results generalize without issue to more general access structures as well.

Definition 2. *An LSSS $\mathcal{S} = (M, \text{label})$ is $(t, t+1)$-secure if the following holds:*

- *(Privacy) For all $s \in \mathbb{F}$ and for every subset A of players with $|A| \leq t$, the distribution of $M\boldsymbol{r}_s$ is independent of s*
- *(Reconstruction) For every subset A of players with $|A| \geq t+1$ there is a reconstruction vector $\boldsymbol{e}_A \in \mathbb{F}^{m_A}$ such that $\boldsymbol{e}_A^\mathsf{T}(M_A \boldsymbol{r}_s) = s$ for all $s \in \mathbb{F}$.*

2.2 LSS over Vector Spaces

Let V be a finite-dimensional $\mathbb{F}$-vector space, and let $\mathcal{S} = (M, \text{label})$ be an LSSS over $\mathbb{F}$. Since V is isomorphic to $\mathbb{F}^k$ for some k, we can use the LSSS $\mathcal{S}$ to secret-share elements in V by simply sharing each one of its k components. This is formalized as follows.

Definition 3. *A linear secret-sharing scheme over a finite-dimensional $\mathbb{F}$-vector space V is simply an LSSS $\mathcal{S} = (M, \text{label})$ over $\mathbb{F}$. To share a secret $v \in V$, the dealer samples uniformly at random a vector $\boldsymbol{r}_v \in V^{t+1}$ such that its first entry is v, and sends to player P_i each row of $M \cdot \boldsymbol{r}_v \in V^m$ owned by this player. $(t, t+1)$-security is preserved. To reconstruct, a set of parties A with $|A| > t$ uses the reconstruction vector $\boldsymbol{e}_A$ as $\boldsymbol{e}_A^\mathsf{T}(M_A \boldsymbol{r}_v) = v$.*

As before, given $v \in V$ we use the notation $[\![v, \boldsymbol{r}_v]\!]_V$, or simply $[\![v]\!]_V$, to denote the vector in V^m of shares of v. Similar notions have appeared in the literature under the name *multi-linear* [BBPT14] or *folded-linear* [BBFP21] secret sharing.

---

[2] Note that the use of the vector $\boldsymbol{r}_v$ here where all but one entries are random is similar to e.g., the choice of a random polynomial with a fixed 0-coefficient in Shamir's secret sharing.

2.3 LSS Isomorphisms

Let U and V be two finite-dimensional $\mathbb{F}$-vector spaces, and let $\phi : V \to U$ be a vector-space isomorphism (we extend the definition of ϕ to operate on vectors over V pointwise when convenient). According to the definition in Sect. 2.2, any given LSSS $\mathcal{S} = (M, \text{label})$ over $\mathbb{F}$ can be seen as an LSSS over V or over U. However, the fact that there is a vector-space isomorphism from V to U implies that, for any $v \in V$, the parties can locally get $[\![\phi(v)]\!]_U$ from $[\![v]\!]_V$. We formalize this below.

Definition 4. *Let U and V be two finite-dimensional $\mathbb{F}$-vector spaces, and let $\phi : V \to U$ be a vector-space isomorphism. Let $\mathcal{S} = (M, \text{label})$ be an LSSS over V. We say that the pair $(\mathcal{S}, \phi)$ is a linear secret-sharing isomorphism.*

The following simple proposition illustrates the value of considering LSS isomorphisms.

Proposition 1. *Let U and V be two finite-dimensional $\mathbb{F}$-vector spaces, and let $(\mathcal{S}, \phi)$ be a LSS isomorphism from U to V. Given $v \in V$ and $[\![v, r_v]\!]_V$, applying ϕ to each share leads to $[\![\phi(v), \phi(r_v)]\!]_U$.*

Proof. Observe that $\phi([\![v, r_v]\!]_V) = \phi(Mr_v) = M\phi(r_v) = [\![\phi(v), \phi(r_v)]\!]_U$. $\qquad\square$

Remark 1 (About generalizing to LSS homomorphisms). In the definition above we could have considered, more generally, LSS *homomorphisms*, where the mapping $\phi : V \to U$ is a homomorphism that is not necessarily a bijection. If ϕ is not surjective we can simply restrict the codomain to the vector space $\phi(V) \subseteq U$. However, when ϕ is not injective, then $(t, t + 1)$-security may not hold on the resulting LSSS over $\phi(V)$, which makes the notion meaningless. This can be seen, for example, if ϕ is the zero mapping, in which case the resulting scheme over $\phi(V) = \{0\}$ only allows sharing the value 0 with zero-shares.

2.4 LSSS with Bilinear Maps

In Sect. 2.3 we saw how the parties could locally convert from sharings in one vector space to another vector space, provided there is a linear transformation between the two. The goal of this section is to extend this to the case of bilinear maps. More precisely, let U, V, W be $\mathbb{F}$-vector spaces of dimension d, and let $\mathcal{S} = (M, \text{label})$ be an LSSS over $\mathbb{F}$. From Sect. 2.2, $\mathcal{S}$ is also an LSSS over U, V and W. Let $\psi : U \times V \to W$ be a bilinear map, that is, the functions $\psi(\cdot, v)$ for $v \in V$ and $\psi(u, \cdot)$ for $u \in U$ are linear.

We show how the parties can obtain $[\![\psi(u, v)]\!]_W$ from $[\![u]\!]_U$ and $[\![v]\!]_V$, for $u \in U$ and $v \in V$. Unlike the case of a linear transformation, this operation requires communication among the parties. Intuitively, this is achieved by using a generalization of "multiplication triples" [Bea92] to the context of bilinear maps. At a high level, the parties preprocess "bilinear triples" $([\![\alpha]\!]_U, [\![\beta]\!]_V, [\![\psi(\alpha, \beta)]\!]_W)$

where $\alpha \in U$ and $\beta \in V$ are uniformly random, open $\delta = u - \alpha$ and $\epsilon = v - \beta$, and compute $[\![\psi(u, v)]\!]_W$ as

$$\psi(\delta, \epsilon) + \psi(\delta, [\![\beta]\!]_V) + \psi([\![\alpha]\!]_U, \epsilon) + [\![\psi(\alpha, \beta)]\!]_W = [\![\psi\,(\delta + \alpha, \epsilon + \beta)]\!]_W$$
$$= [\![\psi\,(u, v)]\!]_W.$$

In the full version we formalize this intuition and define a protocol Π_{bilinear} parameterized by the map ψ, which takes as input $[\![u]\!]_U$, $[\![v]\!]_V$ and outputs $[\![w]\!]_W$ with $w = \psi(u, v)$.

3   Threshold Signature Schemes

In this section we show how our techniques can be used to securely sign and verify messages that are secret shared, using keys that are similarly secret-shared. More precisely, we present here three protocols: First, a key generation protocol Π_{Keygen} for generating $(\text{pk}, [\![\text{sk}]\!])$ securely where pk is a public key and $[\![\text{sk}]\!]$ a secret-shared private key. Second, a signing protocol Π_{Sign} protocol that on input a secret shared message $[\![m]\!]$ and $[\![sk]\!]$ output from Π_{Keygen} outputs $[\![\sigma]\!]$ where σ is a signature on m under sk. Finally, we present a verification protocol Π_{Verify} which on input $[\![m]\!]$, $[\![\sigma]\!]$ and pk outputs $[\![b]\!]$ where b is a value indicating whether or not σ is a valid signature on m under the private key corresponding to the public key pk.

We choose to use the signature scheme [PS16] by Pointcheval and Sanders (henceforth PS) as our starting point. The primary reason for choosing the PS scheme is that signatures are short and independent of the message length, and that messages do not need to be hashed prior to signing.[3]

Primitives for MPC. For this section, and for the rest of the paper, we will rely on the existence of several functionalities to securely compute on secret-shared data. We list them here in brief. Also, for a functionality/protocol $\mathcal{F}_{\text{abc}}/\Pi_{\text{abc}}$, we denote by $\mathcal{C}_{\text{abc}}$ its total communication cost, in bits.

- $\mathcal{F}_{\text{MulTriple}}$ outputs a triple $([\![a]\!], [\![b]\!], [\![c]\!])$ where $c = ab$.
- $\mathcal{F}_{\text{DotProd}}$ takes as input $([\![x_i]\!])_{i=1}^{L}$ and $([\![y_i]\!])_{i=1}^{L}$, and produces $[\![z]\!]$, where $z = \sum_{\ell=1}^{L} \phi(x_\ell y_\ell)$.
- $\mathcal{F}_{\text{Mul}}$ takes two inputs $[\![x]\!]$ and $[\![y]\!]$, and outputs $[\![w]\!]$ where $w = xy$. $\mathcal{F}_{\text{Mul}}$ is a particular case of $\mathcal{F}_{\text{DotProd}}$ for $L = 1$ (with ϕ the identity function).
- $\mathcal{F}_{\text{Rand}}(K)$ outputs $[\![x]\!]$ where $x \in K$, where K is a $\mathbb{F}$-vector space. Notice that it is enough to have a functionality which samples a secret-shared field element: to get a secret point, parties can locally apply an appropriate LSS isomorphism to obtain a secret-shared group element.
- $\mathcal{F}_{\text{Coin}}(K)$ outputs a uniformly random $s \in K$ to all parties.

---

[3] A downside of e.g., ECDSA signatures is that messages have to be hashed first, which creates a significant problem when messages are secret-shared, as hashing secret-shared data is quite expensive.

The functionalities above are defined irrespectively of whether the adversary is passive (that is, they respect the protocol specification) or active (the adversary may deviate arbitrarily).[4] The following functionality only makes sense for settings with active security.

- $\mathcal{F}_{\mathsf{DotProd}*}$ takes as input $(\llbracket x_i \rrbracket)_{i=1}^{L}$ and $(\llbracket y_i \rrbracket)_{i=1}^{L}$, and produces $\llbracket z + \delta \rrbracket$, where $z = \sum_{\ell=1}^{L} \phi(x_\ell y_\ell)$ and $\delta \in \mathbb{F}$ is an error provided by the adversary.

The reason to consider this dot product functionality, which produces incorrect results, is that (1) for some secret-sharing schemes this functionality can be instantiated with a communication complexity that is independent of the length L, and (2) that it suffices for some of the applications we consider later on. How these functionalities are instantiated depends naturally on the choice of secret-sharing scheme. We discuss instantiations for popular secret sharing schemes, including the ones we will focus on what follows (additive and Shamir secret sharing), in the full version.

3.1 The PS Signature Scheme

The PS signature scheme [PS16] signs a vector of messages $\mathbf{m} \in \mathbb{F}^r$ as follows (we present the multi-message variant here):

- Setup(1^λ): Output $pp \leftarrow (p, \mathbb{G}_1, \mathbb{G}_2, \mathbb{G}_T, e)$ where $\mathbb{G}_1 \neq \mathbb{G}_2$ and where no efficient homomorphism exists between $\mathbb{G}_1$ and $\mathbb{G}_2$ (i.e., a type-3 pairing).
- Keygen(pp): Select random $H \leftarrow \mathbb{G}_2$ and $(x, y_1, \ldots, y_r) \leftarrow \mathbb{F}^{r+1}$. Compute $(X, Y_1, \ldots, Y_r) = (xH, y_1 H, \ldots, y_r H)$ set $\mathsf{sk} = (x, y_1, \ldots, y_r)$ and $\mathsf{pk} = (H, X, Y_1, \ldots, Y_r)$.
- Sign($\mathsf{sk}, \mathbf{m}$): Select random $G \leftarrow \mathbb{G}_1 \setminus \{0\}$ and output the signature $\sigma = (G, (x + \sum_{i=1}^{r} m_i y_i) \cdot G)$.
- Verify($\mathsf{pk}, \mathbf{m}, \sigma$): Parse σ as (σ_1, σ_2). If $\sigma_1 \neq 0$ and $e(\sigma_1, X + \sum m_i Y_i) = e(\sigma_2, H)$ output 1. Otherwise output 0.

The remainder of this section will focus on how to instantiate the threshold PS signature scheme securely.

3.2 Threshold PS Signatures

The Π_{Keygen} protocol presented below shows how to generate keys suitable for signing messages of r blocks. The protocol proceeds as follows: parties invoke $\mathcal{F}_{\mathsf{Coin}}$ and $\mathcal{F}_{\mathsf{Rand}}$ a suitable number of times to generate the private key and then use an appropriate LSS isomorphism to compute the public key.

---

[4] One caveat is that the shares on their own may not define the secret if the adversary is allowed to change the corrupt parties' shares, which is the case for an active adversary. This is an issue for example with additive secret sharing and an dishonest majority (which can be fixed by adding homomorphic MACs), but not for Shamir secret sharing with an honest majority. We discuss this in detail in the full version.

Protocol Π_{Keygen}

Inputs: $pp = (p, \mathbb{G}_1, \mathbb{G}_2, \mathbb{G}_T, e)$, r
Outputs: $(\mathsf{pk}, [\![\mathsf{sk}]\!])$

1. Parties invoke $\mathcal{F}_{\mathsf{Coin}}(\mathbb{G}_2)$ to obtain H, and invoke $\mathcal{F}_{\mathsf{Rand}}(\mathbb{F})$ a total of $r+1$ times to obtain $([\![x]\!], [\![y_1]\!], \ldots, [\![y_r]\!])$.
2. Let $\phi_2 : \mathbb{F} \to \mathbb{G}_2$ be LSS-isomorphism given by $\phi_2 : x \mapsto xH$. Using ϕ_2, compute $[\![X]\!]_{\mathsf{G}_2} = \phi_2([\![x]\!])$ and $[\![Y_i]\!]_{\mathsf{G}_2} = \phi_2([\![y_i]\!])$ for $i = 1, \ldots, r$.
3. Parties open $X \leftarrow [\![X]\!]_{\mathsf{G}_2}$ and $Y_i \leftarrow [\![y_i]\!]_{\mathsf{G}_2}$ for $i = 1, \ldots, r$. Output the pair $(\mathsf{pk}, [\![\mathsf{sk}]\!])$ where $\mathsf{pk} = (H, X, Y_1, \ldots, Y_r)$ and $[\![\mathsf{sk}]\!] = ([\![x]\!], [\![y_1]\!], \ldots, [\![y_r]\!])$.

The communication complexity of Π_{Keygen} is $\mathcal{C}_{\mathsf{Keygen}} = \mathcal{C}_{\mathsf{Coin}}(1) + \mathcal{C}_{\mathsf{Rand}}(r + 1) + \mathcal{C}_{\mathsf{Open}}(r+1)$ field elements.

Next up is computing Sign on secret-shared inputs (assumed to be generated by a $\mathcal{F}_{\mathsf{Input}}$ functionality) given the tools we have described so far. The Π_{Sign} protocol below outputs a signature $(\sigma_1, [\![\sigma_2]\!]_{\mathsf{G}_1})$. The reasons for keeping σ_1 public are (1) that it simplifies things when we use this later, and (2) makes signing more efficient. If, however, σ_1 cannot be revealed then Π_{Pairing} is needed for step 3.

Protocol Π_{Sign}

Inputs: $[\![\mathsf{sk}]\!] = ([\![x]\!], [\![y_1]\!], \ldots, [\![y_r]\!])$, $[\![\mathbf{m}]\!] = ([\![m_1]\!], \ldots, [\![m_r]\!])$
Outputs: $[\![\sigma]\!]$

1. Parties obtain $\sigma_1 \in_R \mathbb{G}_1$ by invoking $\mathcal{F}_{\mathsf{Coin}}(\mathbb{G}_1)$. If $\sigma_1 = 0$, repeat this step.
2. Parties invoke $[\![z]\!] \leftarrow \mathcal{F}_{\mathsf{DotProd}}(([\![y_i]\!])_{i=1}^r, ([\![m_i]\!])_{i=1}^r)$ and then compute $[\![w]\!] = [\![x]\!] + [\![z]\!]$.
3. Parties use the LSS isomorphism $x \mapsto x \cdot \sigma_1$ to compute locally $[\![\sigma_2]\!]_{\mathsf{G}_1} \leftarrow \Pi_{\mathsf{ScalarMul}}([\![w]\!], \sigma_1)$.
4. Output $(\sigma_1, [\![\sigma_2]\!]_{\mathsf{G}_1})$.

Protocol Π_{Sign} produces a correct signature with communication complexity $\mathcal{C}_{\mathsf{Coin}}(1) + \mathcal{C}_{\mathsf{DotProd}}(r)$.

Finally, we show a verification protocol Π_{Verify} in which a secret-shared $\mathbb{G}_T$ element $[\![b]\!]_{\mathsf{G}_T}$ where $b = 1_{\mathbb{G}_T}$ if the signature was valid, or a uniform random group element otherwise. While this is not a bit, it nevertheless carries the same information. Below the signature we verify is $(\sigma_1, [\![\sigma_2]\!]_{\mathsf{G}_1})$, however if this is not the case (in particular, if σ_1 is secret-shared) then Π_{Pairing} is needed in step 4.

Protocol Π_{Verify}

Inputs: $\mathsf{pk} = (H, X, Y_1, \ldots, Y_r)$, $[\![\mathbf{m}]\!] = ([\![m_i]\!])_{i=1}^r$, $\sigma = (\sigma_1, [\![\sigma_2]\!]_{\mathbb{G}_1})$
Outputs: $[\![b]\!]_{\mathbb{G}_T} = [\![1_{\mathbb{G}_T}]\!]$ if $\mathsf{Verify}(\mathsf{pk}, \mathbf{m}, \sigma) = 1$ and a random value otherwise.

1 If $\sigma_1 = 0$ then output $[\![\mu]\!]_{\mathbb{G}_T} \leftarrow \mathcal{F}_{\text{Rand}}(\mathbb{G}_T)$.
2 Compute $[\![\alpha]\!]_{\mathbb{G}_T} = e([\![\sigma_2]\!], H)$ using the LSS isomorphism $x \mapsto xH$.
3 Locally compute $[\![\beta]\!]_{\mathbb{G}_T} = e(\sigma_1, X + \sum_{i=1}^r [\![m_i]\!]Y_i)$ using LSS isomorphisms.
4 Output $[\![b]\!]_{\mathbb{G}_T} \leftarrow \Pi_{\text{ScalarMul}}([\![\rho]\!], [\![\alpha]\!]_{\mathbb{G}_T}/[\![\beta]\!]_{\mathbb{G}_T})$ where $[\![\rho]\!]$ was obtained by invoking $\mathcal{F}_{\text{Rand}}$.

The communication complexity of the Π_{Verify} protocol is $\mathcal{C}_{\text{Rand}}(1) + \mathcal{C}_{\text{ScalarMul}}(1)$. We now argue security.

Lemma 1. *Protocol Π_{Verify} outputs a secret-sharing of $1_{\mathbb{G}_T}$ if $\sigma = (\sigma_1, [\![\sigma_2]\!]_{\mathbb{G}_1})$ is a valid signature on $[\![\mathbf{m}]\!]$ with public key pk, otherwise the protocol outputs a secret-sharing of a uniformly random element.*

Proof. Note that $[\![\alpha]\!]_{\mathbb{G}_T}/[\![\beta]\!]_{\mathbb{G}_T} = [\![e(\sigma_1, X + \sum_i m_i Y_i)/e(\sigma_2, H)]\!]_{\mathbb{G}_T}$ which is $1_{\mathbb{G}_T}$ if and only if $e(\sigma_1, X + \sum_i m_i Y_i) = e(\sigma_2, H)$; that is, if the signature is valid. Thus we have that the distribution of $[\![b]\!]_{\mathbb{G}_T} = [\![(a/\beta)^\rho]\!]_{\mathbb{G}_T}$ is either uniformly random (if $\alpha \neq \beta$), or $1_{\mathbb{G}_T}$ (if $\alpha = \beta$). To see that $[\![b]\!]_{\mathbb{G}_T}$ is uniformly random when $\alpha \neq \beta$ it suffices to note that α/β is a generator of $\mathbb{G}_T$ and that ρ was picked at random. □

It is likewise possible to see that any successful attack on ($\Pi_{\text{Keygen}}, \Pi_{\text{Sign}}, \Pi_{\text{Verify}}$) can easily be turned into an attack on the original PS signature scheme, in particular on the EUF-CMA [GMR88] property of the PS signature scheme.

We consider an ideal threshold signature functionality roughly equivalent to the $\mathcal{F}_{\text{tsig}}$ functionality presented in [CGG+20], the main difference being that we do not consider key refreshment. It is possible to show that $\Pi_{\text{PS}} = (\Pi_{\text{Keygen}}, \Pi_{\text{Sign}}, \Pi_{\text{Verify}})$ securely realizes this functionality

The $\mathcal{F}_{\text{tsig}}$ functionality records a message as signed once it has received a sign request from $t+1$ parties. During verification, $\mathcal{F}_{\text{tsig}}$ receives a tuple (m, σ, pk) and does one of three things: If (m, σ, b) was previously recorded, then b is returned (that is, the signature was previously verified and b was the result); If m was never signed, then $b = 0$ is returned, and if (m, σ) was not previously verified but m was signed, then $b = \mathsf{Verify}(\mathsf{pk}, m, \sigma)$ is returned.

Importantly, distinguishing between Π_{PS} and $\mathcal{F}_{\text{tsig}}$ happens only if the adversary manages to input a pair (m, σ, pk) such that m was never signed, but $1 = \mathsf{Verify}(\mathsf{pk}, m, \sigma)$. However, this corresponds *precisely* to breaking the EUF-CMA property of the PS signature scheme.

Due to our black-box use of the MPC functionality, the security of the resulting threshold-signature scheme will inherit the same security properties (e.g., number of parties, honest vs. dishonest majority, passive vs. active security, stand-alone vs. UC security, etc.) as the MPC protocol used to implement the functionality.

Extensions to Other Schemes. Our techniques, here presented for the PS signature scheme, could easily generalize to any other "sufficiently algebraic" signature scheme (a formal definition of "algebraic signatures" has recently appeared in [DHH+21]). In fact, most signatures used for anonymous credentials are similarly algebraic e.g., CL [CL04], BBS+ [CL04, ASM06], Boneh-Boyen [BB04], as well as algebraic MACs [CMZ14, CPZ20] (note that one can see PS signatures as an instance of an algebraic MAC from [CMZ14] instantiated in a group with a pairing to enable public verification).

4   Applications to Proactive Secret Sharing

Secret sharing allows a dealer to distribute a secret such that an adversary with only access to some subset of the shares cannot learn anything about the secret. However as time passes it becomes harder to argue that no leakage beyond this subset takes place, and thus that the secret remains hidden from the adversary. Proactive Secret-sharing (PSS) deals with this problem by periodically "refreshing" (or *proactivizing*) shares such that shares between two proactivization stages become "incompatible".

Typically, the case of interest in the PSS setting is honest majority, since in this case the value of the underlying secret is determined by the shares from the honest parties only. In this section we focus on Shamir secret-sharing, and we denote such sharings by $[\![\cdot]\!]$. We assume that $2t + 1 = n$. Multiple PSS schemes have been proposed for this case, but for the special situation of *dynamic PSS* (a PSS scheme is dynamic if the number of parties and threshold can change between each proactivization), CHURP is presented in [MZW+19]. In a nutshell, CHURP first performs an optimistic proactivization and, if cheating is detected, falls back to a slower method that is able to detect cheaters.

In what follows we show how to use the protocols for signatures developed in Sect. 3 to obtain a conceptually simple and efficient dynamic PSS with abort. We first develop a highly efficient protocol for proactivizing a secret that guarantees privacy, but allows the adversary to tamper with the transmitted secret. Then, we use our signatures to transmit a signature on the secret, that can be checked by the receiving committee. In this way, due to the unforgeability properties of the signature scheme, an adversary cannot make the receiving committee accept an incorrectly transmitted message. This construction leads to a 9-fold improvement in terms of communication with respect to the optimistic protocol from [MZW+19].

We say that the parties have *consistent sharings* of a secret x if each P_i knows a value s_i such that there exists a polynomial $f(x)$ of degree at most t with $f(i) = s_i$ and $f(0) = s$.

4.1   Proactive Secret Sharing

We present here the definitions of proactive secret sharing, or PSS for short. We remark that our goal is not to provide formal definitions of these properties but rather a high level description of what a PSS scheme is, so that we can present in a clear manner our optimizations to the work of [MZW+19].

In a PSS scheme a set of n parties have consistent Shamir shares of a secret $[\![s]\!] = (s_1, \ldots, s_n)$ with threshold t. At a given stage, a proactivization mechanism is executed, from which the parties obtain $[\![s']\!] = (s'_1, \ldots, s'_m)$. A PSS scheme satisfies:

- *(Correctness).* It must hold that $s = s'$
- *(Privacy).* An adversary corrupting a set of at most t parties before the proactivization, and also a (potentially different) set of at most t' parties after the proactivization, cannot learn anything about the secret s.

The PSS schemes we consider in this work are *dynamic* in that the set of parties holding the secret before the proactivization step may be different than the set of parties holding the secret afterwards. Note that the number of parties, as well as the threshold, can change as part of the proactivization.

4.2 Partial PSS

In what follows we denote by $C = \{P_i\}_{i=1}^n$ and $C' = \{P'_i\}_{i=1}^m$ the old and new committees, respectively. Furthermore, we denote $\mathcal{U} = \{P_i\}_{i=1}^{t+1}$ and $\mathcal{U}' = \{P'_i\}_{i=1}^{t'+1}$. As mentioned before, we consider Shamir secret-sharing, with threshold $t < n/2$ (resp. $t' < m/2$). This ensures that the corrupt parties cannot modify their shares without resulting in an error, thanks to error-detection (further details on this can be found in the full version). Our protocol $\Pi_{\mathsf{PartialPSS}}$ is inspired by the protocol from [BELO15], except that, since we do not require the transmitted message to be correct, we can remove most of the bottlenecks like the use of hyper-invertible matrices or consistency checks to ensure parties send shares consistently.

Protocol $\Pi_{\mathsf{PartialPSS}}([\![s]\!]^C)$

Inputs A shared value $[\![s]\!]^C = (s_1, \ldots, s_n)$ among a committee C.
Output: Either a consistently shared value $[\![s']\!]^{C'}$ or abort. If all parties behave honestly then $s' = s$.

1. Each $P_i \in C$ samples $s_{i1}, \ldots, s_{i,t+1} \in_R \mathbb{F}$ such that $s_i = \sum_{j=1}^{t+1} s_{ij}$ and sends s_{ij} to P_j for $j = 1, \ldots, t+1$.
2. Each $P_i \in \mathcal{U}$ samples $r_{ki} \in_R \mathbb{F}$ for $k = 1, \ldots, t'$, and sets $r_{0,i} = 0$.
3. Each $P_i \in \mathcal{U}$ sets $a_{ij} = s_{ji} + \sum_{k=0}^{t'} r_{ki} \cdot j^k$ and sends a_{ij} to P'_j, for each $j = 1, \ldots, m$.
4. Each $P'_j \in C'$ sets $s'_j := \sum_{i=1}^{t'+1} a_{ij}$.
5. The parties in C' output the shares $(s'_1, \ldots, s'_m)$.

Theorem 1. *Protocol $\Pi_{\mathsf{PartialPSS}}$ satisfies the following properties.*

1. *Assume that initially the parties in C had consistent shares of a secret s. Then the protocol results in the parties in C' having consistent shares of $s+\delta$, where δ is an additive error known by the adversary.*
2. *An adversary simultaneously controlling t parties in C and t' parties in C' does not learn anything about the secret input s.*

The proof appears in the full version.

Extending to Group Elements. $\Pi_{\mathsf{PartialPSS}}$ can be extended to proactivize shares $[\![\alpha]\!]_{\mathbb{G}}^{C}$, where $\mathbb{G}$ is an elliptic curve group by running the same protocol "in the exponent". More formally, the LSS isomorphism $x \mapsto x \cdot G$, where G is a generator of $\mathbb{G}$, is used. This will be used later on in our protocol. Finally, observe that $\Pi_{\mathsf{PartialPSS}}$ communicates a total of $n(n+1)$ field elements.

4.3   Simple and Efficient PSS with Abort

The protocol $\Pi_{\mathsf{PartialPSS}}$ presented in the previous section guarantees privacy and consistency of the new sharings, but it does not satisfy the main property of a PSS, which is guaranteeing that the secret remains the same. More precisely, a malicious party may disrupt the output as $[\![s + \gamma]\!]^{C'} \leftarrow \Pi_{\mathsf{PartialPSS}}([\![s]\!]^{C})$, where γ is some value known by the adversary. This is of course not ideal, but it can be fixed by making use of the signature protocols proposed in Sect. 3. In a nutshell, the committee C uses $\Pi_{\mathsf{PartialPSS}}$ to send to C' not only the secret s, but also a signature on this secret using a secret-key shared by C. Then, upon receiving shares of the message-signature pair, the parties in C' proceed to verifying this pair securely using C's public key, and if this check passes then it can be guaranteed that the message was correct, since the adversary cannot produce a valid message-signature pair for a new message.

The protocol is presented more formally in Protocol Π_{PSS} below. The setup regarding secret/public key pairs is also presented in the protocol.

Protocol $\Pi_{\mathsf{PSS}}([\![s]\!]^{C})$

Inputs: A shared value $[\![s]\!]^{C} = (s_1, \ldots, s_n)$ among a committee C.
Output: Consistent shares $[\![s]\!]^{C'}$ or abort.
Setup: Parties in C have a shared secret-key $[\![\mathsf{sk_C}]\!]^{C}$, and its corresponding public key $\mathsf{pk_C}$ is known by the parties in C'. This can be easily generated by using protocol Π_{Keygen} from Section 3.

1. Parties in C call $(\sigma_1, [\![\sigma_2]\!]^{C}) \leftarrow \Pi_{\mathsf{Sign}}([\![\mathsf{sk_C}]\!]^{C}, [\![s]\!]^{C})$.
2. Parties in $C \cup C'$ call $[\![s']\!]^{C'} \leftarrow \Pi_{\mathsf{PartialPSS}}([\![s]\!]^{C})$ and $[\![\sigma'_2]\!]^{C'} \leftarrow \Pi_{\mathsf{PartialPSS}}([\![\sigma_2]\!]^{C})$.
3. $P_1, \ldots, P_{t+1}$ all send σ_1 to the parties in C'. If some party in $P_j \in C'$ receives two different σ_1 from two different parties, then the parties abort.
4. Parties in C' call $[\![v]\!]^{C'} \leftarrow \Pi_{\mathsf{Verify}}([\![s']\!]^{C'}, (\sigma_1, [\![\sigma'_2]\!]^{C'}), \mathsf{pk_C})$ and open v using error detection. If $v = 0_{\mathbb{G}_T}$ then the parties in C' output $[\![s']\!]^{C'}$. Else, they abort.

Intuitively, the protocol guarantees that the parties do not abort if and only if the message is transmitted correctly. This follows from the unforgeability of the signature scheme: If an adversary can cause the parties to accept with a wrong message/signature pair, then this would constitute a forged signature. The fact that privacy is maintained regardless of whether the parties abort or not is more subtle, but essentially follows from the fact that decision to abort can be shown to be *independent* of the secret (thus ruling out a selective failure attack). Put differently, a decision depends only on the error introduced by the adversary which is independent of the secret.

We summarize these properties in Theorem 2 below. In our proof we do not reduce to the unforgeability of the signature scheme, but instead to a hard problem over elliptic curves directly. This is easier and cleaner in our particular setting, given that the signatures are produced and checked within the same protocol. The computational problem we reduce the security of Protocol Π_{PSS} to is the following, which can be seen as a natural variant of Computational Diffie-Hellman (CDH) problem over $\mathbb{G}_1$.

Definition 5 (co-CDH Assumption). *Let* $\mathbb{G} \in \mathbb{G}_1$ *and* $G' \in \mathbb{G}_2$ *be generators. Given* (G, G', aG, bG') *for* $a, b, \in_R \mathbb{F}$, *an adversary cannot efficiently find* $(ab)G$.

With this assumption at hand, which is assumed to hold for certain choices of pairing settings (see [FG12]), we can prove the following about the security of Π_{PSS}.

Theorem 2. *Protocol* Π_{PSS} *instantiates the PSS-with-abort functionality described in Sect. 4.1, that is, if the parties do not abort in the protocol* Π_{PSS}, *then the parties in* C' *have shares* $[\![s]\!]^{C'}$, *where* $[\![s]\!]^C$ *was the input provided to the protocol. Furthermore, privacy of s is satisfied regardless of whether the parties abort or not.*

The proof appears in the full version.

Although we did not address this in our security arguments, the setup needed for the protocol Π_{PSS}, namely that the parties in C have a shared secret-key for which the parties in C' know the corresponding public key, can be reused for multiple successful proactivizations. Intuitively, this holds because, if the adversary cheats in the proactivization, Theorem 2 shows that this is detected with overwhelming probability, and if the adversary does not cheat then no extra information about the secret-key from the committee C is leaked to the adversary.

Communication Complexity. The communication complexity of the Π_{PSS} protocol when proactivizing L values is $\mathcal{C}_{\mathsf{PartialPSS}}(L+1) + \mathcal{C}_{\mathsf{Sign}}(L) + \mathcal{C}_{\mathsf{Verify}}(L)$. We ignore the opening of $[\![v]\!]$ at the end as this is independent of L. Recall that $\mathcal{C}_{\mathsf{Sign}}(L) = \mathcal{C}_{\mathsf{Coin}}(1) + \mathcal{C}_{\mathsf{DotProd}}(L)$, and $\mathcal{C}_{\mathsf{Verify}}(L) = \mathcal{C}_{\mathsf{Rand}}(1) + \mathcal{C}_{\mathsf{ScalarMul}}(1)$ For the case of Shamir secret sharing, $\mathcal{C}_{\mathsf{Rand}}(1) = 2n \log |\mathbb{F}|$, using the protocol from [DN07] and amortizing over multiple calls to $\mathcal{F}_{\mathsf{Rand}}$. Also, $\mathcal{C}_{\mathsf{DotProd}}(L) =$

$5.5n \log |\mathbb{F}|$, and $\mathcal{C}_{\mathsf{ScalarMul}}(1) = 5.5n \log |\mathbb{F}|$ too, using a specialized bilinear protocol $\Pi_{\mathsf{DotProd}}^{\mathsf{shm}}$ for Shamir SS that we describe in the full verison. We ignore the cost $\mathcal{C}_{\mathsf{Coin}}(1)$ since it can be instantiated non-interactively using a PRG.

Given the above, the total communication complexity of the Π_{PSS} protocol is

$$\log(|\mathbb{F}|) \cdot ((L+1) \cdot n \cdot (n+1) + 13n) \text{ bits.}$$

Comparison with CHURP. The dynamic PSS protocol proposed in [MZW+19], is to our knowledge state-of-the-art in terms of communication complexity. At a high level, CHURP is made of two main protocols, Opt-CHURP, which is able to detect malicious behavior during the proactivization but is not able to point out which party or parties cheated, and Exp-CHURP, which performs proactivization while enabling cheater detection at the expense of requiring more communication. Since in this work we have described a PSS protocol *with abort*, we compare our protocol against Opt-CHURP.

The total communication complexity of Opt-CHURP is $9Ln^2 \log |\mathbb{F}|$ bits in point-to-point channels, plus $256n$ bits over a blockchain,[5] so our novel method presents a 9-fold improvement over the state of the art. Furthermore, although not mentioned in our protocol, a lot of the communication that appears in the $13n$ term in our Π_{PSS} protocol can be regarded as preprocessing, that is, it is independent of the message being transmitted and can be computed in advance, before the proactivization phase.

We note that our novel protocol Π_{PSS} is conceptually much more simple than Opt-CHURP. Unlike in Opt-CHURP, our protocol does not require the expensive use of commitments and proofs at the individual level (i.e. *per party*) in order to ensure correctness of the transmitted value. Instead, we compute a *global* signature of the secret and check its validity after the proactivization.

Finally, we present an optimization if multiple shared elements are to be proactivized in the full version.

5   Applications to Input Certification

MPC does not put any restriction on what kind of inputs are allowed, yet such a property has its place in many applications. For example, one might want to ensure that the two parties in the classic *millionaires problem* [Yao82] do not lie about their fortunes.

Signatures seem like the obvious candidate primitive for certifying inputs in MPC: A trusted party $\mathcal{T}$ will sign all inputs x_i of party P_i that need certification. Then, after P_i have shared its input $[\![x_i']\!]$, which it may change if it is misbehaving, parties will verify that $[\![x_i']\!]$ is a value that was previously signed by $\mathcal{T}$. While this approach clearly works (if P_i could get away with sharing x_i', then P_i produced a forgery) it is nevertheless hindered by the fact that signature verification is expensive to compute on secret-shared values, arising from the fact that the usual

---

[5] For a more detailed derivation of this complexity, see the full version.

first step in verifying a signature is hashing the message, which is prohibitively expensive in MPC. In this section we show that by using our secure PS signatures from Sect. 3, this approach is no longer infeasible, and in fact, it is quite efficient.

5.1 Certifying Inputs with PS Signatures

We consider a setting in which n parties $P_1, \ldots, P_n$ wish to compute a function $f(\mathbf{x}_1, \ldots, \mathbf{x}_n)$, where $\mathbf{x}_i \in \mathbb{F}^L$ corresponds to the input of party P_i. We assume that all parties hold the public key pk of some trusted authority $\mathcal{T}$, who provided each P_i with a PS signature (σ_1^i, σ_2^i) on its input $\mathbf{x}_i$. We also assume a functionality $\mathcal{F}_{\text{Input}}$ that, on input $\mathbf{x}_i$ from P_i, distributes to the parties consistent shares $[\![x_{i1}]\!], \ldots, [\![x_{iL}]\!]$. We also assume the existence of a broadcast channel.

Our protocol, $\Pi_{\text{CertInput}}$, allows a party P_i to distribute shares of its input, only if this input has been previously certified. (If multiple parties are providing inputs, just repeat the protocol for all P_i's).

Protocol $\Pi_{\text{CertInput}}$

Input: Index $i \in \{1, \ldots, n\}$ and $((x_j)_{j=1}^L, \sigma_1, \sigma_2)$ from P_i.
Output: $[\![x_j]\!]$ if $\text{Verify}(\text{pk}, [\![x_j]\!], (\sigma_1, \sigma_2)) = 1$ for all $j = 1, \ldots, L$, or abort.

1. P_i calls $\mathcal{F}_{\text{Input}}$ to distribute $(([\![x_j]\!])_{j=1}^L, [\![\sigma_2]\!]_{\mathbb{G}_1})$. Also, P_i broadcasts σ_1 to all parties.
2. Parties call $[\![b]\!]_{\mathbb{G}_T} \leftarrow \Pi_{\text{Verify}}(\text{pk}, ([\![x_j]\!])_{j=1}^L, \sigma_1, [\![\sigma_2]\!]_{\mathbb{G}_1})$.
3. Parties open $[\![b]\!]_{\mathbb{G}_T}$, who output $([\![x_j]\!])_{j=1}^L$ if $b = 1_{\mathbb{G}_T}$ and abort otherwise.

Complexity Analysis. The communication complexity of the protocol $\Pi_{\text{CertInput}}$ is $\mathcal{C}_{\text{Input}}(L) + \mathcal{C}_{\text{Verify}}(L) + \mathcal{C}_{\text{Open}}(1)$ bits.

Security. The $\Pi_{\text{CertInput}}$ protocol provides security in the sense defined in [BJ18]. In a nutshell, $\Pi_{\text{CertInput}}$ guarantees that, *if* $\Pi_{\text{CertInput}}$ succeeds, then the inputs provided by the parties were certified by some authority. Indeed, this follows immediately from the security of the protocols presented in Sect. 3: If a corrupt P_i sends an incorrect share to an *honest* party, then that directly corresponds to creating a forgery in the PS signature scheme.[6]

We present an optimization if multiple parties are intended to provide input in the full version.

Comparison with [BJ18]. Certifying inputs for MPC with the help of signatures has been studied previously in [BJ18]. However, the approach followed in that work is conceptually much more complex than the one we presented here. At a

---

[6] Notice that in the case the protocol does not succeed, nothing can be said about what caused it to abort. If this property is desired, then the protocol underlying $\Pi_{\text{CertInput}}$ have to support *identifiable abort*.

high level, instead of verifying the signature in MPC, the parties jointly produce commitments of the secret-shared inputs, and then each input owner uses these commitments, together with the signatures, to prove via an interactive protocol (that roughly resembles a zero-knowledge proof of knowledge) "possession" of the signatures. Furthermore, the protocols presented in [BJ18] depend on the underlying secret-sharing scheme used, and two ad-hoc constructions, one for Shamir secret-sharing (using the MPC protocol from [DN07]) and another one for additive secret sharing (using the MPC protocol from [DKL+13]), are presented. Instead, our approach is completely general and applies to any linear secret-sharing scheme, as defined in Sect. 2.

There are no claims about round complexity in [BJ18], but we counted eight rounds of communication and two zero-knowledge proofs that can be made non-interactive. Our protocol requires only 3 rounds: one to distribute the signature and shares of the inputs, another to perform arithmetic in $\mathbb{G}_T$ in MPC for verifying the signature, and the final opening of the verification result.

We present in Sect. 6.1 a more experimental and quantitative comparison between our work and [BJ18]. We observe that, in general, our approach is at least 2 times more efficient in terms of computational and communication costs.

6   Implementation and Benchmarking

We implemented our protocols with the RELIC toolkit [AGM+] using the 128-bit-secure pairing-friendly BLS12-381 curve. This curve has embedding degree $k = 12$ and a 255-bit prime-order subgroup, and became popular after it was adopted by the ZCash cryptocurrency [BCG+14]. It is now in the process of standardization due to its attractive performance characteristics, including an efficient towering of extensions, efficient GLV endomorphisms for scalar multiplications, cyclotomic squarings for fast exponentiation in $\mathbb{G}_T$, among others. In terms of security, the choice is motivated by recent attacks against the DLP in $\mathbb{G}_T$ [KB16] and is supported by the analysis in [MSS16]. Our implementation makes use of all optimizations implemented in RELIC, including Intel 64-bit Assembly acceleration, and extend the supported algorithms to allow computation of arbitrarily-sized linear combinations of $\mathbb{G}_2$ points through Pippenger's algorithm. We take special care to batch operations which can be performed simultaneously, for example merging scalar multiplications together or combining the two pairing computations within MPC signature verification as a product of pairings. We deliberately enabled the variable-time but faster algorithms in the library relying on the timing-attack resistance built in MPC, since computations are performed essentially over ephemeral data. The resulting code was included in the library.

We benchmarked our implementation on an Intel Core i7-7820X Skylake CPU clocked at 3.6 GHz with HyperThreading and TurboBoost turned off to reduce noise in the benchmarks. Each procedure was executed 10^4 times and the averages are reported in Table 1. It can be seen from the table that the MPC versions of scalar multiplications and exponentiations introduce a computational

Table 1. Efficiency comparison between local computation and two-party computation of the main operations in pairing groups and PS signature computation/verification. We display execution times in 10^3 clock cycles (cc) for each of the main operations in the protocols and report the average for each of the two parties.

Operation	Local (cc)	Two-party (cc)
Scalar multiplication in $\mathbb{G}_1$	386	612
Scalar multiplication in $\mathbb{G}_2$	1,009	1,796
Exponentiation in $\mathbb{G}_T$	1,619	2,772
Pairing computation	3,107	4,063
PS key generation (1 msg)	2,670	4,723
PS signature computation (1 msg)	626	654
PS signature verification (1 msg)	5,153	8,065
PS key generation (10 msgs)	11,970	23,464
PS signature computation (10 msgs)	656	668
PS signature verification (10 msgs)	10,144	12,953

Table 2. Efficiency comparison between our certified input protocol from Sect. 5 and the one presented in [BJ18]. Performance numbers are measured in millions of clock cycles (cc), and communication cost is represented in thousands of bytes (KB). Figures are presented per party with highest runtime/communication cost.

	Number of messages						
	1	10	10^2	10^3	10^4	10^5	10^6
Ours	8.07	12.95	62.71	357.45	2,334.74	22,281.05	220,572.62
Comm.	0.93	1.22	4.10	32.90	320.90	3,209.00	32,090.00
[BJ18]	11.45	18.69	103.95	970.20	9,723.00	111,090.00	-
Comm.	1.02	2.81	20.70	200.00	1,950.00	19,500.00	195,000.00

overhead ranging from 1.59 to 1.78, while pairing computation becomes only 30% slower. For the PS protocol, key generation and signature verification in MPC are penalized in comparison to local computation by less than a 2-factor, while the cost of signature computation stays essentially the same. There is no performance penalty for signature computation involving many messages because of the batching possibility in the PS signature scheme.

6.1   Certified Inputs

Here we compare our protocol for input certification from Sect. 5 with the experimental results reported in [BJ18]. We choose [BJ18] as our point of comparison as it is the only other work which performs input certification using a general n-party protocol. In their paper, the experiments are conducted with three parties. To perform a fair comparison, we converted the timings from the second half of Table 2 in [BJ18] to clock cycles using the reported CPU frequency of 2.1 GHz for an Intel Sandy Bridge Xeon E5-2620 machine. We used as reference the largest running time or transmission cost of the running parties (input provider and another party) reported in [BJ18], since the computation would be bounded by the maximum running time and the communication latency by the maximum bandwidth requirement. Each procedure in our implementation was executed 10^4 times for up to 10^2 messages, after which we decreased the number of executions linearly with the increase in number of messages. Our results are shown in Table 2, and show that our implementations are already faster for small numbers of messages, but improve on related work by a factor of 2–5 when the number of messages is at least 100. Similar savings can be observed in communication. While the two benchmarking machines are different (Intel Sandy Bridge and Skylake), our implementations do not make use of any performance feature specific to Skylake, such as more advanced vector instruction sets. Hence we claim that the performance of our implementations would not be different enough in Sandy Bridge to explain the difference, and just converting performance figures to clock cycles makes the results generally comparable. The efficiency improvements are also large enough that they would be preserved if our implementation were scaled up to three parties as in [BJ18].

Acknowledgments. The authors would like to thank Greg Zaverucha and the anonymous reviewers for useful feedback on earlier versions of this paper.

This work has received funding from the European Research Council (ERC) under the European Union's Horizon 2020 research and innovation programme under grant agreements No 669255 (MPCPRO) and No 803096 (SPEC), the Concordium Blockhain Research Center at Aarhus University (COBRA), the Carlsberg Foundation under the Semper Ardens Research Project CF18-112 (BCM), and the Danish Independent Research Council under Grant-ID DFF-6108-00169 (FoCC). The first and last authors are affiliated to the DIGIT Centre for Digitalisation, Big Data and Data Analytics at Aarhus University.

References

[ADEO20] Aranha, D., Dalskov, A., Escudero, D., Orlandi, D.: Improved threshold signatures, proactive secret sharing and input certification from LSS isomorphisms. Cryptology ePrint Archieves Report 2020/691 (2020). https://eprint.iacr.org/2020/691

[AGM+] Aranha, D.F., Gouvêa, C.P.L., Markmann, T., Wahby, R.S., Liao, K.: RELIC is an Efficient LIbrary for Cryptography. https://github.com/relic-toolkit/relic

[ASM06] Au, M.H., Susilo, W., Mu, Y.: Constant-size dynamic k-TAA. In: De Prisco, R., Yung, M. (eds.) SCN 2006. LNCS, vol. 4116, pp. 111–125. Springer, Heidelberg (2006). https://doi.org/10.1007/11832072_8

[BB04] Boneh, D., Boyen, X.: Short Signatures Without Random Oracles. In: Cachin, C., Camenisch, J.L. (eds.) EUROCRYPT 2004. LNCS, vol. 3027, pp. 56–73. Springer, Heidelberg (2004). https://doi.org/10.1007/978-3-540-24676-3_4

[BB16]   Blanton, M., Bayatbabolghani, F.: Efficient server-aided secure two-party function evaluation with applications to genomic computation. PoPETs **2016**(4), 144–164 (2016)

[BBFP21] Bamiloshin, M., Ben-Efraim, A., Farràs, O., Padró, C.: Common information, matroid representation, and secret sharing for matroid ports. Des. Codes Cryptogr. **89**(1), 143–166 (2020). https://doi.org/10.1007/s10623-020-00811-1

[BBPT14] Beimel, A., Ben-Efraim, A., Padró, C., Tyomkin, I.: Multi-linear secret-sharing schemes. In: Lindell, Y. (ed.) TCC 2014. LNCS, vol. 8349, pp. 394–418. Springer, Heidelberg (2014). https://doi.org/10.1007/978-3-642-54242-8_17

[BCG+14] Ben-Sasson, E., et al.: Decentralized anonymous payments from bitcoin. In: 2014 IEEE Symposium on Security and Privacy, pp. 459–474. IEEE Computer Society Press, May 2014

[Bea92]   Beaver, D.: Efficient multiparty protocols using circuit randomization. In: Feigenbaum, J. (ed.) CRYPTO 1991. LNCS, vol. 576, pp. 420–432. Springer, Heidelberg (1992). https://doi.org/10.1007/3-540-46766-1_34

[BELO14] Baron, J., El Defrawy, K., Lampkins, J., Ostrovsky, R.: How to withstand mobile virus attacks, revisited. In: Halldórsson, M.M., Dolev, S. (eds.) 33rd ACM PODC, pp. 293–302. ACM, July 2014

[BELO15] Baron, J., Defrawy, K.E., Lampkins, J., Ostrovsky, R.: Communication-optimal proactive secret sharing for dynamic groups. In: Malkin, T., Kolesnikov, V., Lewko, A.B., Polychronakis, M. (eds.) ACNS 2015. LNCS, vol. 9092, pp. 23–41. Springer, Cham (2015). https://doi.org/10.1007/978-3-319-28166-7_2

[BJ18]   Blanton, M., Jeong, M.: Improved Signature schemes for secure multi-party computation with certified inputs. In: Lopez, J., Zhou, J., Soriano, M. (eds.) ESORICS 2018. LNCS, vol. 11099, pp. 438–460. Springer, Cham (2018). https://doi.org/10.1007/978-3-319-98989-1_22

[CCXY18] Cascudo, I., Cramer, R., Xing, C., Yuan, C.: Amortized complexity of information-theoretically secure MPC revisited. In: Shacham, H., Boldyreva, A. (eds.) CRYPTO 2018. LNCS, vol. 10993, pp. 395–426. Springer, Cham (2018). https://doi.org/10.1007/978-3-319-96878-0_14

[CDI05]   Cramer, R., Damgård, I., Ishai, Y.: Share conversion, pseudorandom secret-sharing and applications to secure computation. In: Kilian, J. (ed.) TCC 2005. LNCS, vol. 3378, pp. 342–362. Springer, Heidelberg (2005). https://doi.org/10.1007/978-3-540-30576-7_19

[CDM00]   Cramer, R., Damgård, I., Maurer, U.: General secure multi-party computation from any linear secret-sharing scheme. In: Preneel, B. (ed.) EURO-CRYPT 2000. LNCS, vol. 1807, pp. 316–334. Springer, Heidelberg (2000). https://doi.org/10.1007/3-540-45539-6_22

[CDN15]   Cramer, R., Bjerre Damgård, I., Nielsen, J.B.: Secure Multiparty Computation, Cambridge University Press, Cambridge (2015)

[CGG+20] Canetti, R., Gennaro, R., Goldfeder, S., Makriyannis, N.: Udi Peled. Uc non-interactive, proactive, threshold ecdsa with identifiable aborts. In: Proceedings of the 2020 ACM SIGSAC Conference on Computer and Communications Security (CCS 2020), pp. 1769–1787, New York, NY, USA, Association for Computing Machinery (2020)

[CKR+20] Chen, H., Kim, M., Razenshteyn, I., Rotaru, D., Song, Y., Wagh, S.: Maliciously secure matrix multiplication with applications to private deep learning. In: Moriai, S., Wang, H. (eds.) ASIACRYPT 2020. LNCS, vol. 12493, pp. 31–59. Springer, Cham (2020). https://doi.org/10.1007/978-3-030-64840-4_2

[CL04] Camenisch, J., Lysyanskaya, A.: Signature schemes and anonymous credentials from bilinear maps. In: Franklin, M. (ed.) CRYPTO 2004. LNCS, vol. 3152, pp. 56–72. Springer, Heidelberg (2004). https://doi.org/10.1007/978-3-540-28628-8_4

[CMZ14] Chase, M., Meiklejohn, S., Zaverucha. G.: Algebraic MACs and keyed-verification anonymous credentials. In: Ahn, G.-J., Yung, M., Li, N. (eds.) ACM CCS 2014, pp. 1205–1216. ACM Press, November 2014

[CPZ20] Chase, M., Perrin, T., Zaverucha, G.: The signal private group system and anonymous credentials supporting efficient verifiable encryption. In: Ligatti, J., Ou, X., Katz, J., Vigna, G. (eds.) ACM CCS 2020, pp. 1445–1459. ACM Press, November 2020

[DHH+21] Döttling, N., Hartmann, D., Hofheinz, D., Kiltz, E., Schäge, S., Ursu, B.: On the impossibility of short algebraic signatures. Cryptology ePrint Archive, Report 2021/738 (2021). https://eprint.iacr.org/2021/738

[DKL+13] Damgård, I., Keller, M., Larraia, E., Pastro, V., Scholl, P., Smart, N.P.: Practical covertly secure MPC for dishonest majority - or: breaking the SPDZ limits. In: Crampton, J., Jajodia, S., Mayes, K. (eds.) ESORICS 2013. LNCS, vol. 8134, pp. 1–18. Springer, Heidelberg (2013)

[DKO+20] Dalskov, A., Orlandi, C., Keller, M., Shrishak, K., Shulman, H.: Securing DNSSEC Keys via Threshold ECDSA from Generic MPC. In: Chen, L., Li, N., Liang, K., Schneider, S. (eds.) ESORICS 2020. LNCS, vol. 12309, pp. 654–673. Springer, Cham (2020). https://doi.org/10.1007/978-3-030-59013-0_32

[DN07] Damgård, I., Nielsen, J.B.: Scalable and unconditionally secure multiparty computation. In: Menezes, A. (ed.) CRYPTO 2007. LNCS, vol. 4622, pp. 572–590. Springer, Heidelberg (2007). https://doi.org/10.1007/978-3-540-74143-5_32

[Fel87] Feldman, P.: A practical scheme for non-interactive verifiable secret sharing. In: 28th FOCS, pp. 427–437. IEEE Computer Society Press, Washington, October 1987

[FG12] Fiore, D., Gennaro. R.: Publicly verifiable delegation of large polynomials and matrix computations, with applications. In: Yu, T., Danezis, G., Gligor, V.D. (eds.) ACM CCS 2012, pp. 501–512. ACM Press, October 2012

[FN20] Falk, B.H., Noble, D.: Secure computation over lattices and elliptic curves. Cryptology ePrint Archive, Report 2020/926 (2020). https://eprint.iacr.org/2020/926

[GGJR00] Garay, J.A., Gennaro, R., Jutla, C., Rabin, T.: Secure distributed storage and retrieval. Theor. Comput. Sci. 243(1–2), 363–389 (2000)

[GMR88] Goldwasser, S., Micali, S., Rivest, R.L.: A digital signature scheme secure against adaptive chosen-message attacks. SIAM J. Comput. 17(2), 281–308 (1988)

[GPSW06] Goyal, V., Pandey, O., Sahai, A., Waters, B.: Attribute-based encryption for fine-grained access control of encrypted data. In: Juels, A., Wright, R.N., De Capitani di Vimercati, S. (eds.) ACM CCS 2006, pp. 89–98. ACM Press, October/November (2006). Cryptology ePrint Archive Report 2006/309

[HJJ+97] Herzberg, A., Jakobsson, M., Jarecki, S., Krawczyk, H., Yung, M.: Proactive public key and signature systems. In: Graveman, R., Janson, P.A., Neuman, C., Gong, L. (eds.) ACM CCS 97, pp. 100–110. ACM Press, April 1997

[HJKY95] Herzberg, A., Jarecki, S., Krawczyk, H., Yung, M.: Proactive secret sharing Or: how to cope with perpetual leakage. In: Coppersmith, D. (ed.) CRYPTO 1995. LNCS, vol. 963, pp. 339–352. Springer, Heidelberg (1995). https://doi.org/10.1007/3-540-44750-4_27

[KB16] Kim, T., Barbulescu, R.: Extended tower number field sieve: a new complexity for the medium prime case. In: Robshaw, M., Katz, J. (eds.) CRYPTO 2016. LNCS, vol. 9814, pp. 543–571. Springer, Heidelberg (2016). https://doi.org/10.1007/978-3-662-53018-4_20

[KMW16] Katz, J., Malozemoff, A.J., Wang, X.: Efficiently enforcing input validity in secure two-party computation. Cryptology ePrint Archive, Report 2016/184 (2016). https://eprint.iacr.org/2016/184

[KZG10] Kate, A., Zaverucha, G.M., Goldberg, I.: Constant-size commitments to polynomials and their applications. In: Abe, M. (ed.) ASIACRYPT 2010. LNCS, vol. 6477, pp. 177–194. Springer, Heidelberg (2010). https://doi.org/10.1007/978-3-642-17373-8_11

[MSS16] Menezes, A., Sarkar, P., Singh, S.: Challenges with assessing the impact of NFS advances on the security of pairing-based cryptography. In: Mycrypt, vol.10311 LNCS, pp. 83–108. Springer (2016)

[MZW+19] Deepak Maram, S.K., et al.: CHURP: dynamic-committee proactive secret sharing. In: Cavallaro, L., Kinder, J., Wang, K., Katz, J. (eds.) ACM CCS 2019, pp. 2369–2386. ACM Press, November 2019

[OY91] Ostrovsky, R., Yung, M.: How to withstand mobile virus attacks (extended abstract). In: Logrippo, L. (ed) 10th ACM PODC, pp. 51–59. ACM, August 1991

[PS16] Pointcheval, D., Sanders, O.: Short randomizable signatures. In: Sako, K. (ed.) CT-RSA 2016. LNCS, vol. 9610, pp. 111–126. Springer, Cham (2016). https://doi.org/10.1007/978-3-319-29485-8_7

[Sha79] Shamir, A.: How to share a secret. Commun. Assoc. Comput. Mach. 22(11), 612–613 (1979)

[Sho00] Shoup, V.: Practical threshold signatures. In: Preneel, B. (ed.) EUROCRYPT 2000. LNCS, vol. 1807, pp. 207–220. Springer, Heidelberg (2000). https://doi.org/10.1007/3-540-45539-6_15

[SLL08] Schultz, D.A., Liskov, B., Liskov, M.: Mobile proactive secret sharing. In: Bazzi, R.A., Patt-Shamir, B. (eds.) 27th ACM PODC, p. 458. ACM, August 2008

[ST19] Smart, N.P., Talibi Alaoui, Y.: Distributing any elliptic curve based protocol. In: Albrecht, M. (ed.) IMACC 2019. LNCS, vol. 11929, pp. 342–366. Springer, Cham (2019). https://doi.org/10.1007/978-3-030-35199-1_17

[Yao82]   Chi-Chih Yao, A.: Protocols for secure computations (extended abstract). In: 23rd FOCS, pp. 160–164. IEEE Computer Society Press, November 1982

[ZBB17]   Zhang, Y., Blanton, M., Bayatbabolghani, F.: Enforcing input correctness via certification in garbled circuit evaluation. In: Foley, S.N., Gollmann, D., Snekkenes, E. (eds.) ESORICS 2017. LNCS, vol. 10493, pp. 552–569. Springer, Cham (2017). https://doi.org/10.1007/978-3-319-66399-9_30

Multiparty Computation

Full-Threshold Actively-Secure Multiparty Arithmetic Circuit Garbling

Eleftheria Makri[1,2(✉)] and Tim Wood[1,3]

[1] imec-COSIC, KU Leuven, Leuven, Belgium
emakri@esat.kuleuven.be
[2] ABRR, Saxion University of Applied Sciences, Enschede, The Netherlands
[3] University of Bristol, Bristol, UK

Abstract. In this work, we show how to garble arithmetic circuits with full active security in the general multiparty setting, secure in the full-threshold setting (that is, when only one party is assumed honest). Our solution allows interfacing Boolean garbled circuits with arithmetic garbled circuits. Previous works in the arithmetic circuit domain focused on the two-party setting, or on semi-honest security and assuming an honest majority – notably, the work of Ben-Efraim (Asiacrypt 2018) in the semi-honest, honest majority security model, which we adapt and extend. As an additional contribution, we improve on Ben-Efraim's selector gate. A selector gate is a gate that given two arithmetic inputs and one binary input, outputs one of the arithmetic inputs, based on the value of the selection bit input. Our new construction for the selector gate reduces the communication cost to almost half of that of Ben-Efraim's gate. This result applies both to the semi-honest and to the active security model.

Keywords: Arithmetic garbling · Active security · Efficient selector gate

1 Introduction

Garbled circuits have been an indispensable cryptographic tool in the field of secure computation since the seminal work of Yao [26]. From a theoretical point of view, garbled circuits are important as they provide the means by which we can construct *constant-round* secure computation protocols, originally only in the two-party setting, but later generalised to the multiparty setting, following the paradigm of Beaver et al. [5]. In the two-party setting, garbled circuits are typically *Boolean* circuits executed between two asymmetric parties – a garbler and an evaluator. However, many secure computation problems require arithmetic operations to emulate integer arithmetic, which are inefficient to realise with a Boolean circuit (e.g., requiring 1000 AND gates for an addition mod p and 100000 AND gates for a multiplication mod p, for $p \approx 2^{128}$). Towards the goal of efficient constant-round computation of arithmetic circuits, one theoretical approach was given by Applebaum et al. [2] and more recently a practical solution was proposed by Ball et al. [4], in the two-party setting.

© Springer Nature Switzerland AG 2021
P. Longa and C. Ràfols (Eds.): LATINCRYPT 2021, LNCS 12912, pp. 407–430, 2021.
https://doi.org/10.1007/978-3-030-88238-9_20

In this work we focus on *multiparty* arithmetic garbling. The work of Ben-Efraim [6] was the first to explore multiparty garbling of arithmetic circuits, and gave protocols secure in the presence of a passive adversary in the honest-majority setting. The goal of multiparty arithmetic garbling protocols is the functionality $\mathcal{F}_{AC}$ for computing an arithmetic circuit, given in Fig. 1. This functionality is the goal of all Multiparty Computations (MPC), but offers only security *with abort* instead of full *robustness*, in which honest parties can always obtain the correct output after the initial inputs are provided, or *fairness*, in which honest parties always receive the output if the corrupt parties receive it.

Functionality $\mathcal{F}_{AC}$

Let S denote the ideal-world adversary and $A \subsetneq [n]$ the indexing set of corrupt parties.

Evaluate On input $(\mathsf{Evaluate}, C, \mathbf{x}^i)$ from each party P_i, or S if $i \in A$, if C is an arithmetic circuit over $\mathbb{F}_p$ and $\mathbf{x}^i \in \mathbb{F}_p^{t_i}$ for all i such that $\sum_{i=1}^n t_i$ is the arity of C, send $y := C(\mathbf{x}^1, \ldots, \mathbf{x}^n)$ to S and await a message Abort or OK from S. If the message is OK, then send y to all honest parties and halt; otherwise, send the message Abort to all honest parties and halt.

Fig. 1. Functionality $\mathcal{F}_{AC}$ for evaluating an arithmetic circuit, secure *with abort*.

In our approach, we allow a (limited) combination of arithmetic and Boolean circuits, as this appears to be desirable for many real-world applications. From the simplest motivating example that one can consider, such as the one of conditional summation that Ben-Efraim [6] suggests, to the most complicated computations, such as evaluation of Machine Learning (ML) algorithms, a combination of arithmetic with Boolean gates is required to yield an efficient solution. Machine Learning as a Service is becoming increasingly popular, and when privacy concerns arise, secure computation solutions should be deployed. The most commonly used ML algorithms (e.g., Support Vector Machines (SVMs) and Neural Networks) contain one or more components that require linear operations – for which arithmetic operations are more appropriate – and one or more components that require non-linear operations, such as argmax or sign computation – where Boolean computation is best. Thus it seems sensible to attempt to support both types of gates to achieve efficient solutions to realistic applications.

Related Work. Our work combines the work of Ben-Efraim [6], and Ball et al. [4], and extends them in such a way as to achieve full-threshold active security by using recent actively-secure secret-sharing-based MPC to construct the circuit, a technique initiated by Lindell et al. [19]. In the work of Ball et al., which is based on some of the techniques discussed also in the work of Malkin et al. [21], the authors propose a two-party arithmetic garbling scheme, secure in the presence of a semi-honest adversary, where the arithmetic takes place in a ring isomorphic to a cyclic group of primorial modulus. They show how to use a Chinese Remainder Theorem (CRT) representation of the inputs (and intermediate values) of the circuit to achieve great performance gains over the straightforward conversion of ring elements to binary. In this approach, garbling of linear gates (e.g., addition and scalar multiplication) requires no communication and can be viewed as an arithmetic analogue of the FreeXOR technique due to Kolesnikov and Schneider [18] for Boolean circuits; multiplication, exponentiation by (public) constant, and high fan-in gates are also significantly improved beyond the naïve implementations. However, operations such as comparison of two numbers remain challenging, and prohibitively costly in the CRT representation. To overcome this issue, Ball et al. suggested a method to convert CRT numbers to a positional number system other than the binary system, namely the primorial mixed radix (PMR) system. Although highly improved over the straightforward (convert to binary) approach, the solution is still costly.

The work of Ben-Efraim [6] is secure in the presence of a passive adversary and assumes an honest majority, and involves a circuit construction comprising a mixture of arithmetic and Boolean gates. Ben-Efraim's construction also allows linear operations to be performed for free, while for multiplication gates a "designated" solution is proposed, inspired by the half-gates approach of Zahur et al. [27], extended to the multiparty setting. This is because projection gates (that is, gates that convert values in one ring to the equivalent values in another ring) are difficult to achieve in the multiparty setting, unlike the two-party setting, where as shown by Ball et al. [4], general projection gates are feasible.

Unfortunately, row-reduction techniques [22,24] in the Boolean setting, and also applied in [4], cannot be directly applied in the multiparty setting as protocols for more than two parties are (usually) symmetrical – that is, every party acts both as garbler and evaluator. However, by elegantly re-applying a variation of the half-gates approach [27], Ben-Efraim proposes a construction for a "designated" selector gate solution (i.e., a gate which selects one out of two arithmetic inputs u and v, based on a third, binary input b) that reduces computation cost. Specifically, after describing the construction of a straightforward selector (projecting the bit to characteristic p, and then performing a multiplication using the standard multiplexing equation $u + (v - u)b$), Ben-Efraim demonstrates the designated selector gate, which has the same communication cost as the straightforward one ($2p + 2$ ciphertexts), but it improves the computation cost by 33% (i.e., 2 decryptions for the designated construction, instead of 3).

Concurrently and independently of our work, Ball et al. [3] propose a series of optimisations over the previous state-of-the-art in the two-party setting [4], which is tailored to the garbling of neural networks. One of their main technical contributions is the new mixed-modulus half-gate, which allows efficiently multiplying circuit wires from different domains. This can be thought of as a generalisation of the alternative selector gate that we present in this work, as we can only multiply bit wires by arithmetic wires, while their construction is not limited to bits. While our method can only treat mixed-modulus half-gate multiplications if one of the two domains is the $\mathbb{F}_2$, the approach of Ball et al. [3] is generalisable to multiplication of wires from any (different) domain. This is achieved by exploiting the asymmetry between the parties in the two-party case, where we can choose certain labels to only be used in one of the parties' half-gates. This does not extend to the multiparty garbling setting, which is our focus, because all parties play the role of the garbler. Still, we maintain that garbled multiplication of an integer by a bit is indeed the most commonly occurring mixed-modulus multiplication (e.g., selector gates). Note that the communication cost of our approach is almost the same as the cost of the approach of Ball et al. [3] (in the case of multiplying by a bit). The second contribution of that work is an improved mixed-radix addition, which is important for increasing the efficiency of the non-linear parts of a garbled neural network. Mixed-radix operations (other than the ones where the one operand is base 2) do not appear to extend readily to the multiparty case.

Our Contribution. We continue the study of Ben-Efraim [6] of multiparty garbling of circuits that contain both arithmetic and Boolean gates. Ben-Efraim [6] showed how to construct a designated selector gate in this setting, based on an extension of the half-gate technique. The communication cost of Ben-Efraim's [6] selector gate is the same as in the straightforward construction, while that work manages to reduce the computation cost by approximately 33% (i.e., 2 decryptions instead of 3 at evaluation time). We propose an *alternative designated selector gate*, which while it requires again 3 decryptions at evaluation time, it *reduces the communication cost to almost half* of that of Ben-Efraim's solution. We achieve this by making use of preprocessed data called daBits, proposed by Rotaru and Wood [25] and improved on in [1].

The other contribution of this work is to show how to perform multiparty garbling of both arithmetic circuits with *active security in the full-threshold multiparty setting*. We achieve this by using an authentication subprotocol akin to those in MASCOT [16] and in $\text{SPD}\mathbb{Z}_{2^k}$ [11] to apply the Boolean circuit garbling approach by Hazay et al. [14] to arithmetic garbling. One can view our contribution as extending the work of Hazay et al. [14] to the arithmetic case and combining it with recent arithmetic garbling techniques.

Paper Organisation. In Sect. 2 we introduce the assumed (full-threshold active) security model; the universal composability (UC) framework of Canetti [10]; secret sharing; (multiparty) garbling; and the half-gates optimisation. In Sect. 3, we explain how we achieve active security against $n-1$ out of the total n parties. Due to space considerations, we defer the proofs of Lemma 1, and Theorem 1 to the full version of the paper [20]. In Sect. 4, we give the construction of our alternative selector gate, and in Sect. 5, we provide an efficiency evaluation and comparison to previous work. Section 6 concludes our work.

2   Preliminaries

Security Model. The protocols in this work are proved secure in the universal composability (UC) framework of Canetti [10]. We consider an active, static adversary that can corrupt up to $n - 1$ out of the n total parties. An active adversary may deviate arbitrarily from the protocol description, and a static adversary can choose which parties it will corrupt at the beginning of the protocol execution but not thereafter. Consequently, the functionalities are assumed to know at the beginning of their execution the set of corrupt parties: in the more general setting, the ideal-world adversary sends special "corruption" messages so that the functionality knows how to interact with different parties. Security is parameterised by the statistical security parameter, σ, and the computational security parameter, κ. We do not provide an implementation but typically one sets $\kappa \in \{64, 96, 128\}$ and $\sigma \in \{40, 80\}$ with $\sigma < \kappa$. We will make use of the standard functionalities $\mathcal{F}_{\mathsf{Rand}}$ given in Fig. 2 and $\mathcal{F}_{\mathsf{Commit}}$ given in Fig. 3.

Functionality $\mathcal{F}_{\mathsf{Rand}}$

On input (Rand, X) from all parties, sample $x \xleftarrow{\$} X$ uniformly and send x to all honest parties and $\mathcal{S}$.

Fig. 2. Functionality $\mathcal{F}_{\mathsf{Rand}}$ for agreeing on random strings sampled uniformly from a specified domain.

Functionality $\mathcal{F}_{\mathsf{Commit}}$

The ideal-world adversary is denoted by $\mathcal{S}$ and the indexing set of corrupt parties by A.

Initialise On input $(\mathsf{Initialise}, \mathsf{sid})$ from all honest parties, initialise a database DB.

Commit On input $(\mathsf{Commit}, x, i, \mathsf{sid})$ from party P_i, sample $\mathsf{id}_{x,i}$, store $(\mathsf{id}_{x,i}, x)$ in DB, and send $\mathsf{id}_{x,i}$ to all honest parties and $\mathcal{S}$.

Open On input $(\mathsf{Open}, \mathsf{id}_{x,i}, \mathsf{sid})$ from all parties and $\mathcal{S}$, retrieve $(\mathsf{id}_{x,i}, x)$ in DB;
- If $i \in A$ then await a message OK or Abort from $\mathcal{S}$. If the message is OK then send x to all honest parties; otherwise, send the message Abort to all honest parties and halt.
- If $i \in [n] \setminus A$, then send x to all honest parties and $\mathcal{S}$ and continue.

Fig. 3. Standard commitment functionality.

Secret-Sharing. We use the notation $\langle x \rangle$ to denote that the secret x is additively shared amongst the n parties: that is, the dealer samples $\{x^i\}_{i=1}^{n-1}$ uniformly at random from $\mathbb{F}$, sets $x_n := x - \sum_{i=1}^{n-1} x^i$, and for each $i \in [n]$ sends x^i (i.e., the ith additive share of x) to party P_i.

We denote an *authenticated* shared value x by $[\![x]\!]$, which means that x is shared as above, and additionally there is some procedure for verifying that the sharing of x is not modified by the adversary. In the full-threshold setting, this is typically achieved by secret-sharing an information-theoretic Message Authentication Code (MAC) on every secret, as is done in BDOZ [8], TinyOT [23] and SPDZ [12]. The details of how secrets are authenticated in $\mathbb{F}_p$ and verified for correctness are not important for this work. If an error is introduced on any variable written as $[\![x]\!]$, this will be detected by the honest parties.

Garbling. We assume the reader is familiar with circuit garbling, but provide an overview here. A garbled circuit is a randomised version of a circuit that allows multiple parties to evaluate a function on the union of their private inputs without revealing anything more about their private inputs than what can be inferred from their own inputs and the output alone. In the two-party setting, this procedure is asymmetric; the high-level idea is as follows: one party, called the garbler, generates a "garbled" version of a circuit, hardwiring its own inputs in the circuit; then the other party, called the evaluator, evaluates the garbled circuit on its inputs (given some encoding information by the garbler that is provided in such a way that the garbler does not learn the evaluator's inputs) to obtain a "garbled" encoding of the output. At the end, the two parties communicate to reveal the final output to both.

Now we make things more concrete. Each fan-in-2 gate $g : \mathbb{F}^2 \to \mathbb{F}$ in the circuit with input wires u and v and output wire w is expressed as a table with one row for each $(\alpha, \beta) \in \mathbb{F}^2$ so that a row in the table has the form $(\alpha, \beta, g(\alpha, \beta))$. The garbler then samples a key for each possible value of α, β and $\gamma := g(\alpha, \beta)$. These keys typically live in some finite extension of the base field $\mathbb{F}^\ell$ where ℓ is $O(\kappa)$, so that the keys live in $O(2^\kappa)$, but general garbling does not prescribe how these keys should look except that certain garbling optimisations constrain the encryption scheme to have certain properties. The values in the input/output table are replaced with their corresponding encryption keys. Finally, the keys corresponding to the output wire w of the table are encrypted first under the key corresponding to the input on wire u input, and then under the key corresponding to the input on wire v input. In practice, the encryption function is a pseudorandom one-time-pad using a pseudorandom function (PRF) taking two keys, and using the gate index as a nonce so that the entry for input (α, β) in the table representation of gate g is converted to a ciphertext:

$$\widetilde{g}_{\alpha,\beta} := F_{\mathsf{k}_{u,\alpha},\mathsf{k}_{v,\beta}}(g) + \mathsf{k}_{w,g(\alpha,\beta)},$$

where g is a gate index and acts as a nonce for the encryption, and $\mathsf{k}_{w,g(\alpha,\beta)}$ is the key. All of these $|\mathbb{F}|^2$ ciphertexts (i.e., the final column of the table) are handed to the evaluator. To begin evaluating, the evaluator is handed keys corresponding to its inputs and decrypts gates by computing $\widetilde{g}_{\alpha,\beta} - F_{k_{u,\alpha}, k_{v,\beta}}(g)$. This results in a key that can be used to decrypt the next gate in the circuit (after the evaluator has also obtained the output key of another gate from elsewhere in the circuit). The evaluation involves proceeding iteratively through the circuit in this way, decrypting using pairs of keys, until a final output key is obtained.

To hide the inputs of the evaluator from the garbler when obtaining the initial gate input keys, the keys are sent using oblivious transfer (OT). Oblivious transfer is a channel in which a sender sends many messages, and the receiver selects one, with the guarantees that the sender cannot know which option the receiver selected and the receiver learns nothing about the messages it did not pick. In circuit garbling, for each wire on which the evaluator has input, the garbler sends the $|\mathbb{F}|$ different possible keys and the evaluator chooses the one corresponding to its input.

The circuit has the values of the garbler hardwired in. This is achieved, for example, by only encrypting under the "v" keys if the garbler provides the input on wire u for a given gate. However, this way the *order* of the ciphertexts may reveal to the evaluator the input of the garbler. To hide the garbler's input from the evaluator, the ciphertexts are randomly permuted using so-called *permutation* or *masking* values chosen by the garbler. In the arithmetic case, this is a rotation of the table rows. In order to evaluate the gates correctly, when evaluating a gate, in addition to learning the output key, the evaluator must learn a so-called *external* or *signal* value, which is the real value v masked with the masking value λ, that is, $e := v + \lambda$, so that it knows which ciphertexts to decrypt for each gate despite the rows being permuted. The ciphertexts are then

$$\widetilde{g}_{\alpha,\beta} := F_{k_{u,\alpha}, k_{v,\beta}}(g) + \left(k_{w, g(\alpha - \lambda_u, \beta - \lambda_v) + \lambda_w} \big\| (g(\alpha - \lambda_u, \beta - \lambda_v) + \lambda_w) \right),$$

where $g(\alpha - \lambda_u, \beta - \lambda_v) + \lambda_w$ is the masked output wire (i.e., external) value. (The reader should think of the key as being in $\mathbb{F}^\ell$ for some ℓ of size $O(\kappa)$, and the external value as being in $\mathbb{F}$, and $F : \mathbb{F}^\ell \times \mathbb{F}^\ell \times \{0,1\}^{\log_2(|g|)} \to \mathbb{F}^{\ell+1}$.) The reader is referred to the original work of Beaver et al. [5] for a complete discussion of the permutation method (known as *point-and-permute*).

A technique known as FreeXOR, generalised for arithmetic circuits by Ben-Efraim et al. [7], can be employed to allow linear gates to be evaluated for free: the garbler chooses a global difference R and then for every non-linear gate, the wire key for the value 0 is a random element $k_{w,0}$ of $\mathbb{F}$ and the wire key for each value $\gamma \in \mathbb{F}_p \setminus \{0\}$ is set to $k_{w,\gamma} := k_{w,0} + \gamma \cdot R$. Then for linear (i.e., addition) gates, the output 0 wire key is defined as $k_{w,0} := k_{u,0} + k_{v,0}$ and the corresponding mask as $\lambda_w := \lambda_u + \lambda_v$. Other gates are computed as:

$$\widetilde{g}_{\alpha,\beta} := F_{k_{u,\alpha}, k_{v,\beta}}(g)$$
$$+ \left(k_{w,0} + (g(\alpha - \lambda_u, \beta - \lambda_v) + \lambda_w R) \big\| (g(\alpha - \lambda_u, \beta - \lambda_v) + \lambda_w) \right).$$

Note that instead of encrypting a concatenation of the masking bit with the key, the garbler can use a form of authenticated encryption, and then the evaluator decrypts ciphertexts until it finds a valid decrypted message and considers this the output key. This technique will be used in the garbling described later.

Half Gates. During the evaluation of the circuit, the signal values learnt by the evaluator "contain" the real values (in the sense that they are linearly dependent on them); likewise, the keys contain information regarding the real values. The idea behind half-gates is to exploit this information to reduce the amount of garbling required: during evaluation, the evaluator can compute the product of a signal value e_u with a key k_{v,e_v} to obtain "almost" a key for the product $v_u \cdot v_v$, and then can correct the errors that arise from the masking values using garbled gates (i.e., ciphertexts) in the more usual way[1]. In a sense, the difficult part of the multiplication gate, namely the cross-term $v_u \cdot v_v$ in the output key $k_{w,e_w} = k_{w,0} + (\lambda_w + v_u v_v)R$, is computed by computing $e_u \cdot k_{v,e_v}$. The reason this is useful is that the errors that must be corrected in the product are each functions in the value of only *one* of the two real wire values v_u or v_v (and a combination of the (fixed) masking values). This means that the ciphertexts containing the corrections can be generated independently for each pair of inputs in $\mathbb{F}_p^2$ into the gate, which means only $p+p$ ciphertexts are needed, rather than $p \cdot p$ as required by garbling in the conventional manner.

To design a half gate, one observes what can be obtained from products of signal value with keys of input wires, namely from $e_u \cdot k_{v,e_v}$, or from $e_v \cdot k_{u,e_u}$. For example,

$$e_u k_{v,e_v} = (v_u + \lambda_u)(k_{v,0} + (v_v + \lambda_v)R)$$
$$= v_u k_{v,0} + \lambda_u k_{v,0} + v_u v_v R + \lambda_u v_v R + v_u \lambda_v R + \lambda_u \lambda_v R$$
$$= v_u v_v R + \underbrace{v_u k_{v,0} + v_u \lambda_v R +}_{\text{Dependent on } v_u} \underbrace{\lambda_u v_v R}_{\text{Dependent on } v_v} + \underbrace{\lambda_u k_{v,0} + \lambda_u \lambda_v R}_{\text{Dependent on neither}}$$

Now since the goal is to obtain $k_{w,e_w} = k_{w,0} + (\lambda_w + v_u v_v)R$, for every $\gamma \in \mathbb{F}_p$ the garbler generates two ciphertexts: one encrypting

$$k_{w,g,0} + \lambda_w R - ((\gamma - \lambda_u)(k_{v,0} + \lambda_v R) + (\lambda_u k_{v,0} + \lambda_u \lambda_v R)),$$

and the other encrypting

$$k_{w,e,0} - (\gamma - \lambda_v)(\lambda_u R).$$

The output wire key is set to $k_{w,0} := k_{w,g,0} + k_{w,e,0}$. The evaluator will decrypt the ciphertexts corresponding to $\gamma = e_u$ for the first half gate and $\gamma = e_v$ for the second; since $e_u - \lambda_u = v_u$ and $e_v - \lambda_v = v_v$, they will obtain the correct key by summing the two resulting plaintexts and the value $e_u k_{v,e_v}$. Note that in the original two-party protocols, one gate input was assumed to come from the garbler and the other from the evaluator, so the evaluator would also be involved in the garbling of the half gates. This results in reduced communication since each party knows one of the wire masks. In the multiparty setting described later, no party knows the wire masks, so the main saving comes from reducing the quadratic cost p^2 to the linear cost $2 \cdot p$.

---

[1] This is analogous to the key-switching operation required for relinearisation of ciphertexts in somewhat-homomorphic encryption (SHE) schemes, where one first does a "naïve" multiplication, and then corrects the errors.

Some recent papers evaluate over a ring of primorial modulus rather than over a prime field in order to reduce the size of multiplication gates from $(\sum_{i=1}^{t} p_i)^2$ to $\sum_{i=1}^{t} p_i^2$ total ciphertexts. However, using the half-gate technique, the cost is the same regardless of the modulus, at $2 \cdot \sum_{i=1}^{t} p_i$ ciphertexts. The CRT approach is also useful for performing non-linear operations such as computing powers. These operations are quite expensive even in the passive security setting. While it may be useful to have an actively-secure protocol for arithmetic circuits over a composite modulus ring, there are difficult challenges to overcome arising from the presence of zero divisors; thus we leave this to future work.

We evaluate the garbled circuits in $\mathbb{F}_p$, for which the straightforward garbling approach requires that p be small enough to allow parties to send $O(p)$ ciphertexts per multiplication gate, but large enough so that the PRF keys used for encryption are computationally secure. To do this, we evaluate circuits in $\mathbb{F}_p$, but take keys in an extension field, specifically $\mathbb{F}_{p^{\ell_\kappa}}$, where $\ell_\kappa := 1 + \lceil \kappa / \log p \rceil$.

Multiparty Garbling. In multiparty garbling, originally developed by Beaver et al. [5], all parties act as garbler and evaluator. Lindell et al. [19] showed how to use actively-secure secret-sharing-based MPC to compute a multiparty garbled circuit with active security. Using MPC, each party generates keys for a circuit, and the masking values are chosen randomly and are unknown to the parties. This way for each gate, each party holds n ciphertexts, indexed by j:

$$\tilde{g}_{\alpha,\beta}^j := \sum_{i=1}^{n} F_{k_{u,\alpha}^i, k_{v,\beta}^i}(g,j) + \left(k_{w,0}^j + (g(\alpha - \lambda_u, \beta - \lambda_v) + \lambda_w)R^j \right).$$

Since each party P_i generates one set of keys (those indexed by i), the external values on the wires can be learnt by each party examining the output plaintext m^i from its own circuit and setting $e_w := (m^i - k_{w,0}^i) \cdot R^{i^{-1}}$ and $k_{w,e_w}^i := m^i$.

In many ways, the protocol we present in this work is a straightforward generalisation of garbling protocols over $\mathbb{F}_2$. Notice that for a Boolean circuit, the half-gate approach is no more efficient than the naïve approach, unless we are in the two-party setting in which one party is the garbler and one the evaluator, rather than all being both as in the multiparty setting.

PRF Assumption. To encrypt a gate, a single-keyed PRF is evaluated on a nonce and used to one-time-pad encrypt a key. To make use of the (generalised) FreeXOR technique, the following assumption is required.

Let $F : \mathbb{F}_{p^{\ell_\kappa}} \times \mathbb{N} \to \mathbb{F}_{p^{\ell_\kappa}}$ be a keyed pseudorandom function (PRF). Define the oracle $\mathcal{O}_{F,R}$ in the following way:

$$\mathcal{O}_{F,R} : \mathbb{F}_{p^{\ell_\kappa}} \times \mathbb{F}_p \times \mathbb{N} \times \mathbb{F}_p \to \mathbb{F}_{p^{\ell_\kappa}}$$

$$\mathcal{O}_{F,R}(k, \gamma, x, \delta) \mapsto F_{k+\gamma \cdot R}(x) + \delta \cdot R$$

Now define $\mathcal{F}_{\mathsf{RO}}$ to be an oracle that, on input a query $m = (k, \gamma, x, \delta) \in \mathbb{F}_{p^{\ell_\kappa}} \times \mathbb{F}_p \times \mathbb{N} \times \mathbb{F}_p$, if m has not been queried before, samples $r \xleftarrow{\$} \mathbb{F}_{p^{\ell_\kappa}}$ and outputs r, and otherwise outputs whatever was sampled previously.

The following definition was given by Hazay et al. [14] for Boolean functions, and a similar definition for arithmetic circuits was given by Ball et al. [4].

Definition 1 (Circular Correlation Robustness). *For the oracles above, define* legal queries *as those with inputs in the correct domain, and additionally:*

1. *The oracle may not be queried when $\gamma = 0$.*
2. *The oracle may not be queried twice for the same δ unless at least one other variable changes.*

Then we say that F is circular correlation robust *if for all probabilistic polynomial-time distinguishers $\mathcal{D}$, it holds that*

$$\left| \Pr_{R \xleftarrow{\$} \mathbb{F}_{p^{\ell_\kappa}}} [\mathcal{D}^{\mathcal{O}_{F,R}}(1^\kappa)] - \Pr[\mathcal{D}^{\mathcal{F}_{RO}}(1^\kappa)] \right| = O(2^{-\kappa})$$

In the garbling protocols, the PRF is queried on values (g, j), where $g \in \mathbb{N}$ is the gate index and $j \in [n]$ is the party index, parsed as a natural number $\lceil \log n / \log 10 \rceil \cdot g + j$.

The choice for this definition comes from the fact that parties should not be able to distinguish between keys generated using global differences and uniform keys in the field. Note that while the keys generated for each wire are only in some coset $\mathsf{k}_{w,0} + \{\gamma R : \gamma \in \mathbb{F}_p\}$ of $\mathbb{F}_{p^{\ell_\kappa}}$, the distinguisher is only allowed to query once per key per nonce for a fixed δ. This corresponds to the fact that in the garbling, the evaluator(s) can only decrypt a single ciphertext.

3   Full-Threshold Active Security

We define an n-party arithmetic garbling protocol by extending the state-of-the-art techniques used by Hazay et al. [14] for Boolean garbling to arithmetic garbling, using actively-secure MPC over $\mathbb{F}_p$ as a black box, and using the half-gate techniques described for arithmetic circuits by Ben-Efraim [6]. In this section we describe the actively-secure garbling of the "standard" multiplication gate, since using the classical garbling techniques one can replace the multiplication function with any gate $g : \mathbb{F}_p^2 \to \mathbb{F}_p$; our techniques for active security also apply to other gates, and indeed in the protocol later we garble multiplication half gates. Many of the techniques due to Hazay et al. [14] apply almost immediately to the arithmetic case and so the exposition here closely follows theirs. We will first explain the components of the garbling protocol at a high level, then discuss how to realise these different parts, and finally we will give the complete protocol.

3.1   Overview

In the arithmetic analogue of the multiparty garbling protocol of Beaver et al. [5], with the half-gates optimisations [6,27], we aim to produce a set of $p^2 \cdot n$

ciphertexts, indexed by $j \in [n]$ and $(\alpha, \beta) \in \mathbb{F}_p^2$, for each multiplication gate, of the form:

$$\widetilde{g}_{\alpha,\beta}^j := \left(\sum_{i=1}^n F_{\mathsf{k}_{u,\alpha}^i, \mathsf{k}_{v,\beta}^i}(g, j) \right) + \mathsf{k}_{w,0}^j + R^j \cdot ((\alpha - \lambda_u) \cdot (\beta - \lambda_v) + \lambda_w),$$

where the wire masks λ_u, λ_v and λ_w are not known to any party and the keys indexed by i are generated by P_i. For now, the reader can think of $\mathsf{k}_{u,\alpha}$, $\mathsf{k}_{v,\beta}$, $\mathsf{k}_{w,0}$ and R^j as lying in a finite extension of $\mathbb{F}_p$ – the same space as the codomain of the PRF. The approach of Hazay et al. for Boolean circuits to produce these ciphertexts with active security is to generate a secret-shared version of $\widetilde{g}_{\alpha,\beta}^j$ for every $j \in [n]$ and open them, in the following way:

1. Use a generic "Bit-MPC" functionality, $\mathcal{F}_{\mathsf{BitMPC}}$, for parties to obtain authenticated secret-shared random bits $[\![\lambda_u]\!]$, $[\![\lambda_v]\!]$ and $[\![\lambda_w]\!]$ and to compute $[\![\lambda_u \cdot \lambda_v]\!]$.
2. Use correlated oblivious transfer (COT) to compute the products by the global differences: for each $j \in [n]$ to compute secret-shared versions of:

$$R^j \cdot \lambda_u, \quad R^j \cdot \lambda_v, \quad R^j \cdot (\lambda_w + \lambda_u \cdot \lambda_v).$$

3. *Locally* combine the secret-shared values with local PRF evaluations to obtain a sharing of each gate $\widetilde{g}_{\alpha,\beta}^j$.
4. Open all the sharings.

A key observation, first made by Lindell et al. [19], is that the sharings need not be authenticated, as the parties will abort during circuit evaluation with overwhelming probability if the adversary introduces errors. This means that the PRF evaluations need neither be authenticated, nor proved correct using a zero-knowledge proof. Authentication is required on the wire masks to ensure the multiplication is performed correctly. Thus, only *one* secure Bit-MPC multiplication is required per AND gate, along with an amortised COT operation.

Our approach here is to give the simple generalisation for the field $\mathbb{F}_p$, noting that the keys must live in the space $\mathbb{F}_{p^{\ell_\kappa}}$, where $\ell_\kappa := 1 + \lceil \kappa / \log p \rceil$. We first describe the replacement of $\mathcal{F}_{\mathsf{BitMPC}}$ with MPC over a field, denoted by $\mathcal{F}_{\mathsf{MPC}}$, and second show how to replace COT with correlated oblivious product evaluation (COPE) (also known as vector oblivious linear function evaluation (vOLE)).

3.2   Secret-Sharing-Based Wire Mask Arithmetic

For arithmetic circuits, the bit masks are replaced with masks in $\mathbb{F}_p$ and the functionality $\mathcal{F}_{\mathsf{BitMPC}}$ is replaced with $\mathcal{F}_{\mathsf{MPC}}$, shown in Fig. 4. Instead of *any* generic $\mathcal{F}_{\mathsf{MPC}}$ functionality, we model here a secret-sharing-based functionality, which can be instantiated with any actively secure protocol for secret-sharing-based arithmetic MPC. We denote by $[\![x]\!]$ an authenticated secret shared value x that is stored internally by $\mathcal{F}_{\mathsf{MPC}}$. Then, x^i denotes party P_i's additive share of x. In the garbling protocol, just as in the work of Hazay et al. [14], to obtain a wire mask λ_u, each party samples $\lambda_u^i \xleftarrow{\$} \mathbb{F}_p$ and calls $\mathcal{F}_{\mathsf{MPC}}$ to create an authenticated sharing of this value; then they call **Add** to obtain $[\![\lambda_u]\!] = \sum_{i=1}^n [\![\lambda_u^i]\!]$. They do similarly for λ_v and λ_w so that the parties obtain $[\![\lambda_u]\!]$, $[\![\lambda_v]\!]$ and $[\![\lambda_w]\!]$, and then call **Multiply** to multiply $[\![\lambda_u]\!]$ and $[\![\lambda_v]\!]$, and obtain $[\![\lambda_{uv}]\!] = [\![\lambda_u \cdot \lambda_v]\!]$.

Functionality $\mathcal{F}_{\mathsf{MPC}}$

The functionality assumes n parties $P_1, \ldots, P_n$, and the ideal-world adversary $\mathcal{S}$, who controls a subset of parties $I \subset [n]$. If a command is received where sid differs from what was sent during **Initialise**, ignore the command and await the next. At any point, the ideal-world adversary $\mathcal{S}$ can send the message Abort and the functionality sends the message Abort to all honest parties and halts.

Initialise On input (Initialise, $\mathbb{F}$, sid), store the field $\mathbb{F}$ and initialise a new database, DB := $\varnothing$.

Input On input (Input, i, id$_1$, ..., id$_\ell$, x_1, ... x_ℓ, sid) from P_i and (Input, i, id$_1$, ... id$_\ell$, $\bot$, sid) from all other parties, where $x_i \in \mathbb{F}$ and id$_i$ are distinct new identifiers, append the ℓ entries (id$_i$, x_i) to DB.

Add On input (Add, id$_x$, id$_y$, id$_z$, sid) from all parties, where id$_x$ and id$_y$ are identifiers in the database and id$_z$ is a new identifier, retrieve (id$_x$, x) and (id$_y$, y) from memory and append the entry (id$_z$, $x + y$) to DB.

Multiply On input (Multiply, id$_x$, id$_y$, id$_z$, sid) from all parties, where id$_x$ and id$_y$ are identifiers in the database and id$_z$ is a new identifier, retrieve (id$_x$, x) and (id$_y$, y) from memory and compute $z := x \cdot y$. Receive shares $z^i \in \mathbb{F}$ from $\mathcal{S}$, for $i \in I$, randomly sample honest parties' shares $z^j \in \mathbb{F}$ for $j \notin I$ s.t. $\sum_{i=1}^n z^i = z$, send z^i to P_i, $i \in [n]$, and append (id$_z$, z) to DB.

Output On input (Output, id$_x$, sid) from all parties, retrieve the entry (id$_x$, x) from DB, send x to $\mathcal{S}$, and await a message OK or Abort; if the message is OK then send x to all honest parties, and otherwise send the message Abort to all honest parties and halt.

Fig. 4. Functionality $\mathcal{F}_{\mathsf{MPC}}$ for performing general MPC, secure *with abort*.

3.3   Wire Mask/Global Difference Products

In the garbling protocol, for every wire w the parties require (unauthenticated) sharings of $R^j \cdot \lambda_w$ for every $j \in [n]$. Since λ_w is additively shared, the parties actually compute sharings of $R^j \cdot \lambda_w^i$ for every $j \in [n]$ and $i \neq j$. Since the global difference is fixed for all gates in the circuit, in the Boolean case such sharings can be generated using COT, in which a sender chooses a fixed correlation, namely R^j, and the receiver inputs their sharing of the mask λ_w^i; then the sender obtains some $q^{j,i}$ and the receiver some $t^{i,j}$ such that $q^{j,i} + t^{i,j} = \lambda_w^i \cdot R^j$. Hazay et al.'s [14] protocol for computing the wire mask/global difference products is called $\Pi_{\mathsf{Bit \times String}}$, since $R^j \in \mathbb{F}_{2^k}$ and the masks are bits.

We can apply essentially the same techniques here, and correctness of the protocol follows in exactly the same way. The difference is that we are now interested in masks in $\mathbb{F}_p$ and global differences in $\mathbb{F}_{p^{\ell_\kappa}}$. Thus, we must use the correlated oblivious product evaluation (COPE) presented in Fig. 5, which is an extension of the protocol $\Pi_{\mathsf{Bit} \times \mathsf{String}}$ [14], operating in any finite field, instead of only in $\mathbb{F}_2$. Note that $\mathcal{F}_{\mathsf{COPE}}$ accepts inputs from the sender in $\mathbb{F}_{p^{\ell_\kappa}}$, but in our protocol the inputs are assumed to be in $\mathbb{F}_p$, as they are circuit wire masks. Thus a corrupt sender could send an element of $\mathbb{F}_{p^{\ell_\kappa}} \setminus \mathbb{F}_p$ in the instance of $\mathcal{F}_{\mathsf{COPE}}$. However, the follow-up checks that take place during the execution of the subprotocol $\Pi_{\mathsf{Mask} \times \mathsf{Diff}}$ (Fig. 6) ensure that secrets lie in $\mathbb{F}_p$. A functionality such as $\mathcal{F}_{\mathsf{OLE}}^{t,1}$ by Ghosh et al. [13] that accepts input from the sender in a small field, from the receiver in an extension field and outputs a sharing in the larger field could be used, but for a technical reason it is not amenable to OT extension [15] as is $\mathcal{F}_{\mathsf{COPE}}$ and is therefore less efficient when performing a large number of multiplications. Realising a product functionality more efficiently would improve the overall efficiency of the garbling protocol and we leave this for future work.

Functionality $\mathcal{F}_{\mathsf{COPE}}$ (from [16])

Let $\mathbf{g} : \mathbb{F}^{\lceil \log |\mathbb{F}| \rceil} \to \mathbb{F}$ be any map such that for every $x \in \mathbb{F}$, if $\mathbf{x} \in \{0,1\}^{\lceil \log |\mathbb{F}| \rceil}$ represents its bit-decomposition, then $\mathbf{g}(\mathbf{x}) = x$. Let $\mathbf{g}^{-1}(x)$ denote the bit-decomposition of x, which is well-defined by uniqueness of decomposition.

Initialise On receiving the message $(\mathsf{Initialise}, \mathbb{F}, P_j, P_i, \mathsf{sid}_{j,i})$ from parties P_i and P_j, await $\Delta \in \mathbb{F}$ from P_j, store Δ, and set $\boldsymbol{\Delta} := \mathbf{g}^{-1}(\Delta)$.

Extend On receiving the message $(\mathsf{Extend}, \mathsf{sid}_{j,i})$ from both parties,

1. – If P_i and P_j are honest then await $x \in \mathbb{F}$ from P_i, sample $q \xleftarrow{\$} \mathbb{F}$ and set
$$t = x \cdot \Delta - q$$
    – If P_i is corrupt and P_j is honest then await $t \in \mathbb{F}$ and $\mathbf{x} \in \mathbb{F}^{\lceil \log |\mathbb{F}| \rceil}$ from $\mathcal{S}$ and set
$$q = \mathbf{g}(\mathbf{x} * \boldsymbol{\Delta}) - t$$
    where $*$ denotes the coordinatewise product.
    – If P_i is honest and P_j is corrupt then await $x \in \mathbb{F}$ from P_i and $q \in \mathbb{F}$ from $\mathcal{S}$ and compute
$$t := x \cdot \Delta - q.$$

2. Send t to P_i and q to P_j.

Fig. 5. Functionality for correlated oblivious product evaluation.

The subprotocol for mutliplying global differences with wire masks is given in Fig. 6.

Subprotocol $\Pi_{\mathsf{Mask} \times \mathsf{Diff}}$

Initialise For every ordered pair of parties (P_j, P_i), call an instance of $\mathcal{F}_{\mathsf{COPE}}$, denoted by $\mathcal{F}_{\mathsf{COPE}}^{(j,i)}$ with P_i as the sender and P_j as the receiver, with input $(\mathsf{Initialise}, \mathbb{F}_{p^{\ell_\kappa}}, P_j, P_i, \mathsf{sid}_{j,i})$, and input R^j from P_j.

Multiply To compute unauthenticated sharings $(\langle x_k \cdot R^i \rangle)_{k=1}^m$ from authenticated sharings $(\llbracket x_k \rrbracket)_{k=1}^m$ for which the parties additionally hold $(\langle x_k \rangle)_{k=1}^m$, the parties do the following:

1. **Mask** The parties generate $\ell_\sigma := \lceil \sigma / \log p \rceil$ masks: for each $l \in [\ell_\sigma]$,

   (a) For each $i \in [n]$, party P_i samples $x_{m+l}^i \xleftarrow{\$} \mathbb{F}_p$ and calls $\mathcal{F}_{\mathsf{MPC}}$ with input $(\mathsf{Input}, i, x_{m+l}^i, \mathsf{id}_{x_{m+l}^i})$ while each party P_j, $j \neq i$, provides corresponding input $(\mathsf{Input}, i, \perp, \mathsf{id}_{x_{m+l}^i})$.

   (b) The parties obtain $\llbracket x_{m+l} \rrbracket = \sum_{i=1}^n \llbracket x_{m+l}^i \rrbracket$ by creating a new identifier $\mathsf{id}_{x_{m+l}}$ and calling the **Add** procedure of $\mathcal{F}_{\mathsf{MPC}}$ multiple times.

2. **Generate** For each $j \in [n]$,

   (a) For every $i \neq j$,

      i. P_i and P_j call $\mathcal{F}_{\mathsf{COPE}}^{(i,j)}$ with input $(\mathsf{Extend}, \mathsf{sid}_{i,j})$:

         A. P_i provides $x_1^i, \ldots, x_{m+l}^i$ as input.

         B. P_i receives $(t_k^{i,j})_{k=1}^{m+l}$ and P_j receives $(q_k^{j,i})_{k=1}^{m+l}$.

      ii. It holds that $q_k^{j,i} + t_k^{i,j} = x_k^i R^j$. Party P_i sets $z_k^{i,j} := t_k^{i,j}$.

   (b) Party P_j sets $z_k^{j,j} := x_k^j R^j + \sum_{i \neq j} q_k^{j,i}$.

3. **Check**

   (a) Call $\mathcal{F}_{\mathsf{Rand}}$ with input $(\mathsf{Rand}, \mathbb{F}_p^{\ell_\sigma \times m})$ to obtain a matrix $H = (\chi_{l,k})_{l \in [\ell_\sigma], k \in [m]}$.

   (b) Let $\mathbf{x} := (x_k)_{k=1}^m$ and $\hat{\mathbf{x}} := (x_{m+l})_{l=1}^{\ell_\sigma}$. The parties compute $\llbracket \mathbf{c} \rrbracket := H \cdot \llbracket \mathbf{x} \rrbracket + \llbracket \hat{\mathbf{x}} \rrbracket$ and call $\mathcal{F}_{\mathsf{MPC}}$ with input $(\mathsf{Output}, \mathsf{id}_\mathbf{c}, \mathsf{sid})$ to obtain $\mathbf{c}$. If it aborts, then the parties abort.

   (c) Each party P_i computes $\mathbf{c}^{i,j} := H \cdot (z_k^{i,j})_{k=1}^m + (z_{m+l}^{i,j})_{l=1}^{\ell_\sigma}$ and $\mathbf{c}^{i,i} := -\mathbf{c} \cdot R^i + H \cdot (z_k^{i,i})_{k=1}^m + (z_{m+l}^{i,i})_{l=1}^{\ell_\sigma}$.

   (d) Each party P_i calls $\mathcal{F}_{\mathsf{Commit}}$ with input $(\mathsf{Commit}, \mathbf{c}^{i,j}, i, \mathsf{sid})$ for all $j \in [n]$.

   (e) When $\mathsf{id}_{\mathbf{c}^{i,j}}$ has been received from $\mathcal{F}_{\mathsf{Commit}}$ for all $i, j \in [n]^2$, call $\mathcal{F}_{\mathsf{Commit}}$ with input $(\mathsf{Open}, \mathsf{id}_{\mathbf{c}^{i,j}}, \mathsf{sid})$.

   (f) Check that $\sum_{i=1}^n \mathbf{c}^{i,j} = \mathbf{0}$ for all $j \in [n]$. If so, then each party P_i (locally) outputs $(z_k^{i,j})_{k \in [m], j \in [n]}$; otherwise, they abort.

Fig. 6. Subprotocol $\Pi_{\mathsf{Mask} \times \mathsf{Diff}}$ for multiplying global differences with wire masks.

For active security, it is necessary to check that each P_j provides the same global difference R^j with every other P_i, and that every P_i provides the same sharing λ_w^i with every other P_j. Observe that

$$\left(x^j \cdot R^j + \sum_{i \neq j} q^{j,i} \right) + \left(\sum_{i \neq j} t^{i,j} \right) = R^j \cdot \left(x^j + \sum_{j \neq i} (q^{j,i} + t^{i,j}) \right) = R^j \cdot \left(\sum_{i=1}^n x^i \right)$$

where the first summand is computed by party P_j and for each $i \neq j$, $t^{i,j}$ is held by P_i. The fact that this relationship must hold (by design) can be used to check correctness of a *batch* of secrets $\{[\![x_k]\!]\}_{k=1}^m$ as follows: parties can take an additional mask $[\![x_{m+1}]\!]$, reveal a random linear combination $c := x_{m+1} + \sum_{k=1}^m \chi_k x_k, \chi_k \in \mathbb{F}_p \forall k$, and check for all $j \in [n]$ that $\langle z^j \rangle$ defined by

$$z^{i,j} := t^{i,j}_{m+1} + \sum_{k=1}^m \chi_k \cdot t^{i,j}_k \qquad (i \neq j)$$

and

$$z^{j,j} := -c \cdot R^j + \left(x^j_{m+1} \cdot R^j + \sum_{i \neq j} q^{j,i}_{m+1} \right) + \sum_{k=1}^m \chi_k \cdot \left(x^j_k \cdot R^j + \sum_{i \neq j} q^{j,i}_k \right)$$

is an additive sharing of 0. It is shown in the proof of Lemma 1 (provided in the full version of the paper [20]) that the probability that parties are inconsistent but all of the n sharings $\{\langle z^i \rangle\}_{i=1}^n$ are zero is bounded above by p^{-1}; thus the check is performed independently $\ell_\sigma := \lceil \sigma / \log p \rceil$ times in parallel to ensure at least σ bits of statistical security.

Concrete Instantiation. One of the reasons that the protocol of Hazay et al. [14] is so efficient is that the functionality $\mathcal{F}_{\mathsf{BitMPC}}$ can be realised using the n-party variant [9] of the TinyOT [23] protocol, in which bits are authenticated exactly via sharings of $b^i \cdot R^j$, where R^j is taken to be the secret key of P_j. Thus sharings of the wire mask/global difference products are immediately available to the parties by the correctness of the $\mathcal{F}_{\mathsf{BitMPC}}$ functionality, without the need for a separate $\Pi_{\mathsf{Bit \times String}}$ protocol. However, currently the most efficient protocols in the setting of a large prime field use a different form of authentication and so this optimisation cannot be directly applied here. Instead, we can use, for example, the most recent version of the SPDZ protocol [12] known as Overdrive [17]. Note that in MASCOT [16], pairwise MACs are generated and then combined to create global MACs, so it may be that this approach, which then obviates the need to perform the protocol $\Pi_{\mathsf{Mask \times Diff}}$ separately, is better in practice.

Lemma 1, states that an adversary succeeds in cheating without detection in $\Pi_{\mathsf{Mask \times Diff}}$ with negligible probability in the statistical security parameter, σ.

Lemma 1. *For the outputs* $(z^{i,j}_k)_{i,j \in [n]}$ *of the subprotocol* $\Pi_{\mathsf{Mask \times Diff}}$ *it holds that* $\sum_{i=1}^n z^{i,j}_k = x^i_k \cdot R^j$ *for all j except with probability at most* $2^{-\sigma}$.

Notice that in order to establish a unique signal value after decrypting ciphertexts, it is necessary to multiply by R^{-1}, which means that R must be invertible. However, since R is sampled from a field, the random choice is invertible except if it is 0, which happens with probability $p^{-\ell_\kappa} < 2^{-\kappa} < 2^{-\sigma}$.

3.4   The Complete Garbling and Evaluation Protocols

Following the analysis of the necessary components for garbling we now present the complete garbling and evaluation protocols. The subprotocol for garbling is given in Fig. 7, and the one for evaluation in Fig. 8.

Subprotocol Π_{Garble}

For simplicity, the session identifiers for functionalities are taken as implicit.

Initialise

1. Agree on a new session identifer, a computational and statistical security parameter, κ and σ, and a circuit C to evaluate, with circuit input wires W_{IN}, circuit output wires W_{OUT}, and a set of gates G comprised of a set of multiplication gates G_{MUL}, a set of addition gates G_{ADD}, and a set of selection gates G_{SEL}. Let $\mathtt{PID}() : W_{\mathrm{IN}} \rightarrow [n]$ denote the map determining which party provides input on which wire.
2. Set $\ell_\kappa := \lceil \kappa / \log p \rceil$.
3. For each $i \in [n]$, P_i samples $R^i \overset{\$}{\leftarrow} \mathbb{F}_{p^{\ell_\kappa}}$ and then the parties execute the procedure **Initialise** from $\Pi_{\mathsf{Mask} \times \mathsf{Diff}}$.
4. Call an instance of $\mathcal{F}_{\mathsf{MPC}}$ with input $(\mathsf{Initialise}, \mathbb{F}_p, \mathsf{sid})$.

Wire Masks and Keys

Circuit Input Wires For circuit input wire $w \in W_{\mathrm{IN}}$, let $i := \mathtt{PID}(w)$ and then do the following:

1. Party P_i samples $\lambda_w \overset{\$}{\leftarrow} \mathbb{F}_p$ and calls $\mathcal{F}_{\mathsf{MPC}}$ with this value as input.
2. Each party P_j, $j \in [n]$, samples a key $\mathsf{k}^j_{w,0} \overset{\$}{\leftarrow} \mathbb{F}_{p^{\ell_\kappa}}$ and for each $\alpha \in \mathbb{F}_p$ sets $\mathsf{k}^j_{w,\alpha} := \mathsf{k}^j_{w,0} + \alpha \cdot R^j$.

Addition Output Wires For each wire w that is an output of an addition gate with input wires u and v, do the following:

1. Compute $[\![\lambda_w]\!] = [\![\lambda_u + \lambda_v]\!]$ by calling $\mathcal{F}_{\mathsf{MPC}}$.
2. For each $i \in [n]$, party P_i computes $\mathsf{k}^i_{w,0} := \mathsf{k}^i_{u,0} + \mathsf{k}^i_{v,0}$ and for each $\alpha \in \mathbb{F}_p$ sets $\mathsf{k}^i_{w,\alpha} := \mathsf{k}^i_{w,0} + \alpha \cdot R^i$.

Multiplication Output Wires For a wire w that is an output of a multiplication gate with input wires u and v,

1. For each $\mathsf{x} \in \{\mathsf{g}, \mathsf{e}\}$,
   (a) For each $i \in [n]$, party P_i samples $\lambda^i_{w,\mathsf{x}} \overset{\$}{\leftarrow} \mathbb{F}_p$ and calls $\mathcal{F}_{\mathsf{MPC}}$ with this value as input.
   (b) Compute $[\![\lambda_{w,\mathsf{x}}]\!] := [\![\sum_{i=1}^n \lambda^i_{w,\mathsf{x}}]\!]$ by calling $\mathcal{F}_{\mathsf{MPC}}$.
   (c) For each $i \in [n]$, party P_i samples a key $\mathsf{k}^i_{w,\mathsf{x},0} \overset{\$}{\leftarrow} \mathbb{F}_{p^{\ell_\kappa}}$ and for each $\gamma \in \mathbb{F}_p$ sets $\mathsf{k}^i_{w,\mathsf{x},\gamma} := \mathsf{k}^i_{w,\mathsf{x},0} + \gamma \cdot R^i$.
2. For each $i \in [n]$, party P_i sets $\mathsf{k}^i_{w,0} := \mathsf{k}^i_{w,\mathsf{g},0} + \mathsf{k}^i_{w,\mathsf{e},0}$ and for all $\gamma \in \mathbb{F}_p$ sets $\mathsf{k}^i_{w,\gamma} := \mathsf{k}^i_{w,0} + \gamma \cdot R^i$.

Wire Mask/Global Difference Products

Multiplication Gates For each $g \in G_{\mathrm{MUL}}$, let u and v be the input wires and w the output wire; then do the following:

1. Compute $[\![\lambda_{uv}]\!] := [\![\lambda_u \cdot \lambda_v]\!]$ by calling $\mathcal{F}_{\mathsf{MPC}}$.
2. Execute the procedure **Multiply** from $\Pi_{\mathsf{Mask} \times \mathsf{Diff}}$ on the set $\{\lambda_u, \lambda_v, \lambda_{uv}, \lambda_{w,\mathsf{g}}, \lambda_{w,\mathsf{e}}\}_{g \in G_{\mathrm{MUL}}}$ to obtain, for all $i \in [n]$, (unauthenticated) sharings

$$\left\{ \langle R^i \cdot \lambda_u \rangle, \langle R^i \cdot \lambda_v \rangle, \langle R^i \cdot \lambda_{uv} \rangle, \langle R^i \cdot \lambda_{w,\mathsf{g}} \rangle, \langle R^i \cdot \lambda_{w,\mathsf{e}} \rangle \right\}_{g \in G_{\mathrm{MUL}}}.$$

3. For each $i \in [n]$, for each $\gamma \in \mathbb{F}_p$, set

$$\langle \rho_{i,g,\mathsf{g},\gamma} \rangle := -\gamma \cdot \langle R^i \cdot \lambda_v \rangle + \langle R^i \cdot \lambda_{uv} \rangle + \langle R^i \cdot \lambda_{w,\mathsf{g}} \rangle$$

$$\langle \rho_{i,g,\mathsf{e},\gamma} \rangle := -\gamma \cdot \langle R^i \cdot \lambda_u \rangle + \langle R^i \cdot \lambda_{w,\mathsf{e}} \rangle$$

Garbling

Multiplication Gates For each $g \in G_{\mathrm{MUL}}$, for each $i \in [n]$, for each $\gamma \in \mathbb{F}_p$,

1. The parties compute the garbler half gate:
   - P_i sets $\tilde{g}^{i,i}_{\mathsf{g},\gamma} := F_{\mathsf{k}^i_{u,\gamma}}(g,i) + \mathsf{k}^i_{w,\mathsf{g},0} + \rho^i_{i,g,\mathsf{g},\gamma}$
   - For every $j \neq i$, P_j sets $\tilde{g}^{i,j}_{\mathsf{g},\gamma} := F_{\mathsf{k}^j_{u,\gamma}}(g,i) + \rho^j_{i,g,\mathsf{g},\gamma}$
2. The parties compute the evaluator half gate:
   - Party P_i sets $\tilde{g}^{i,i}_{\mathsf{e},\gamma} := F_{\mathsf{k}^i_{v,\gamma}}(g,i) + \mathsf{k}^i_{w,\mathsf{e},0} - \gamma \cdot \mathsf{k}^i_{u,0} + \rho^i_{i,g,\mathsf{e},\gamma}$
   - Every party P_j, $j \neq i$, sets $\tilde{g}^{i,j}_{\mathsf{e},\gamma} := F_{\mathsf{k}^j_{v,\gamma}}(g,i) + \rho^j_{i,g,\mathsf{e},\gamma}$

Fig. 7. Subprotocol Π_{Garble} for garbling a circuit.

Subprotocol Π_{Eval}

Input Wires For each wire $w \in W$ which is an input wire, the parties do the following:

    1. Let $i = \mathrm{PID}(w)$: then party P_i computes and broadcasts $e_w := v_w + \lambda_w$, where $v_w \in \mathbb{F}_p$, is P_i's input.

    2. For each $i \in [n]$, party P_i broadcasts k^i_{w,e_w}.

Opening For each $g \in G_{\mathrm{MUL}}$, for each $\mathsf{x} \in \{\mathsf{g}, \mathsf{e}\}$, for each $i \in [n]$,

    1. For each $j \in [n]$, for each $\gamma \in \mathbb{F}_p$, P_i broadcasts $\widetilde{g}^{j,i}_{\mathsf{x},\gamma}$.

    2. All parties compute $\widetilde{g}^i_{\mathsf{x},\gamma} := \sum_{j=1}^n \widetilde{g}^{i,j}_{\mathsf{x},\gamma}$.

Circuit Evaluation Traversing the circuit in topological order, for every gate G with input wires u and v and output wire w, the parties do the following:

  – If g is an addition gate, each party does the following:

    1. Set the external wire value to be $e_w := e_u + e_v$.

    2. Compute the output keys as: for each $i \in [n]$, $\mathsf{k}^i_{w,e_w} := \mathsf{k}^i_{u,e_u} + \mathsf{k}^i_{v,e_v}$.

  – If g is a multiplication gate, each party does the following:

    1. For each $i \in [n]$, compute

$$\mathsf{k}^i_{w,e_w} := \underbrace{\widetilde{g}^i_{\mathsf{g},e_u} - \sum_{j=1}^n F_{\mathsf{k}^j_{u,\mathsf{g},e_u}}(g,i)}_{\text{Garbler half gate}} + \underbrace{\widetilde{g}^i_{\mathsf{e},e_v} - \sum_{j=1}^n F_{\mathsf{k}^j_{v,\mathsf{e},e_v}}(g,i)}_{\text{Evaluator half gate}} + e_v \cdot \mathsf{k}^i_{u,e_u}.$$

    2. Each party P_i determines the signal value e_w by computing $e_w := (\mathsf{k}^i_{w,e_w} - \mathsf{k}^i_{w,0}) \cdot (R^i)^{-1}$.

Output To obtain the output of wire $w \in W_{\mathrm{OUT}}$, call $\mathcal{F}_{\mathsf{MPC}}$ to execute the procedure **Output** to reveal the value $e_w - [\![\lambda_w]\!]$.

Fig. 8. Subprotocol Π_{Eval} for evaluating the garbled circuit.

Theorem 1. *The execution of the subprotocol Π_{Garble} followed by the execution of the subprotocol Π_{Eval}, making use of the subprotocol $\Pi_{\mathsf{Mask} \times \mathsf{Diff}}$, UC-securely realises the functionality $\mathcal{F}_{\mathsf{AC}}$ in the presence of a static, active adversary that corrupts up to $n-1$ parties, in the $\mathcal{F}_{\mathsf{Commit}}, \mathcal{F}_{\mathsf{COPE}}, \mathcal{F}_{\mathsf{MPC}}, \mathcal{F}_{\mathsf{Rand}}$-hybrid model, assuming the PRF F satisfies correlation-robustness.*

The proof of Theorem 1 can be found in the full version of the paper [20].

All of the protocols in this section can be realised using protocols (with minor modifications) given in MASCOT [16]; however, the two parts of the computation outlined above are most optimally performed using a mixed approach: using the Overdrive protocol [17] to realise $\mathcal{F}_{\mathsf{MPC}}$, and using MASCOT-like protocols to perform the Wire Mask/Global Difference products. The reason is that Overdrive is more efficient over large prime fields, as opposed to large extension fields such as $\mathbb{F}_{2^k}$ for which MASCOT is better.

4 Selector Gate

It was argued by Ben-Efraim [6] that a selector gate taking a Boolean selection bit and choosing between field elements is a desirable feature of garbling protocols as the selection bit is likely to come from the evaluation of some Boolean subcircuit. Such a construction was given in [6]; in this section we give an alternative construction, which we call the alternative selector gate, which, specifically, takes one input in $\mathbb{F}_2$, held as a signal bit with a corresponding key in $\mathbb{F}_{2^\kappa}$ and viewed as output from a Boolean circuit, and two inputs in $\mathbb{F}_p$, and outputs one of the field elements according to the selection bit. Note that if the selection bit is also a field element then the standard $2 \cdot p$ ciphertexts for general field/field multiplication is required, as is the case in Ben-Efraim's work [6].

Multifield Shared Bits. Rotaru and Wood [25] showed how to generate secret-sharings of uniformly-random bits shared in two fields with authentication in each; these were called daBits, for doubly-authenticated bits. This can be viewed as an actively-secure version of the multi-field bits discussed by Ben-Efraim, which can be used in arithmetic garbling of selector gates. The protocol for generating such bits uses authentication in a black-box way, and so any actively-secure MPC protocol can be used to generate them. In this work, we use daBits shared in $\mathbb{F}_p$ and $\mathbb{F}_{2^\kappa}$ for our selector gates.

4.1 New Selector Gate

Recall that the standard cost of multiplication in $\mathbb{F}_p$ is $p \cdot p$ ciphertexts; the garbler/evaluator half-gate approach reduces this to $p + p$ ciphertexts. The main observation driving our alternative selector gate is that the actual selection operation is a multiplication of a bit by an element in $\mathbb{F}_p$, and thus the goal is to reduce the naïve $2 \cdot p$ ciphertexts to (almost) $2 + p$.

A selection gate based on selection bit b between the values on wires u and v is computed via the standard multiplexer $u + (v - u) \cdot b$. Since linear operations are garbled without communication or preprocessing, we focus on the product of the wire $w := v - u \in \mathbb{F}_p$ with the bit $b \in \mathbb{F}_2$; the output wire is denoted by z.

The point is that while the previous approach by Ben-Efraim involved converting the bit to $\mathbb{F}_p$ using a so-called *projection gate* and evaluating a standard multiplication gate in $\mathbb{F}_p$, we can use daBits to perform this projection directly. We will now explain how to garble the new selector gate; this explanation is followed by a formal protocol description.

Let b' be the Boolean wire, and let b be the $\mathbb{F}_p$ wire to which we wish to convert. We let the wire mask output of the Boolean wire be a daBit $\lambda_{b'} \in \{0,1\}$ and convert it to an $\mathbb{F}_p$ wire using $2n$ ciphertexts in $\mathbb{F}_{p^{\ell_\kappa}}$ as follows: for every $\beta \in \{0,1\}$, for every $j \in [n]$,

$$g_\beta^j := \sum_{i=1}^{n} F_{\mathsf{k}_{b',\beta}^i}(g,j) + \mathsf{k}_{b,0}^j + ((\beta + \lambda_{b'} - 2 \cdot \beta \cdot \lambda_{b'}) + \lambda_b) \cdot R^j,$$

where $k_{b',\beta}^i \in \mathbb{F}_{2^\kappa}$ for all $i \in [n]$ and λ_b is a uniform mask in $\mathbb{F}_p$. Since the PRF used in previous sections takes keys of length at least κ bits, we may assume the same PRF is used here, with additional padding if necessary. Here, we use the fact that in any field, if a and b are in $\{0,1\}$ then their XOR is computed as

$$a \oplus b = a + b - 2 \cdot a \cdot b,$$

which means that we can remove the mask in $\mathbb{F}_p$ since the mask $\lambda_{b'}$ used in the garbling of the Boolean circuit was a daBit. The two ciphertexts (for each $i \in [n]$) are indexed by the two possible Boolean external values, which is denoted by $e_{b'}$; the external value on the output, denoted by e_b, is not needed in the next steps, but can be computed by the evaluators in the usual way (i.e., by P_i comparing the output key indexed by i to its own p keys). In doing so, the evaluators learn either $0 + \lambda_b$ or $1 + \lambda_b$, but do not learn which they hold. In fact, this external value e_b is never used by the evaluators.

The multiplication gate is then computed in two halves:

$$g_{g,\alpha}^j := \sum_{i=1}^{n} F_{k_{w,\alpha}^i}(g,j) + k_{g,z,0}^j - \alpha(k_{b,0}^j + \lambda_b R^j)$$

$$g_{e,\beta}^j := \sum_{i=1}^{n} F_{k_{b,\beta}^i}(g,j) + k_{e,z,0}^j - (\beta + \lambda_{b'} - 2\beta\lambda_{b'})\lambda_w R^j + \lambda_z R^j$$

Now when evaluating, the parties will obtain e_w and $e_{b'}$, will compute $a := \mathsf{Dec}(g_{g,e_w})$ and $b := \mathsf{Dec}(g_{e,e_{b'}})$ and will compute

$$
\begin{aligned}
k_{z,e_z} &= a + b + e_w k_{b,e_b} \\
&= \left(k_{g,z,0}^j - e_w(\cancel{k_{b,0}^j} + \lambda_b R^j)\right) + \left(k_{e,z,0}^j - (e_{b'} + \lambda_{b'} - 2e_{b'}\lambda_{b'})\lambda_w R^j + \lambda_z R^j\right) \\
&\quad + e_w(\cancel{k_{b,0}^j} + e_b R^j) \\
&= \left(k_{g,z,0}^j - e_w \lambda_b R^j\right) + \left(k_{e,z,0}^j - v_b \lambda_w R^j + \lambda_z R^j\right) + e_w e_b R^j \\
&= \left(k_{g,z,0}^j - (v_w + \lambda_w)\lambda_b R^j\right) + \left(k_{e,z,0}^j - v_b \lambda_w R^j + \lambda_z R^j\right) \\
&\quad + (v_w + \lambda_w)(v_b + \lambda_b)R^j \\
&= \left(k_{g,z,0}^j - \cancel{(v_w + \lambda_w)\lambda_b R^j}\right) + \left(k_{e,z,0}^j - v_b \lambda_w R^j + \lambda_z R^j\right) \\
&\quad + ((v_w + \lambda_w)v_b + \cancel{(v_w + \lambda_w)\lambda_b})R^j \\
&= k_{g,z,0}^j + \left(k_{e,z,0}^j + \lambda_z R^j - \cancel{v_b \lambda_w R^j}\right) + ((v_w + \cancel{\lambda_w})v_b)R^j \\
&= k_{z,0}^j + (v_w v_b + \lambda_z)R^j.
\end{aligned}
$$

In total, this requires $p + 4$ ciphertexts per party: 2 for the conversion, 2 for the first half gate and p for the second.

We do not provide a complete proof of the security of the alternative selector gate as it follows straightforwardly from the security of the selector gate of Ben-Efraim [6]. The high-level intuition is that the keys $k_{g,z,0}^j$ and $k_{e,z,0}^j$ are sampled

---

Subprotocol Π_{Select}

This subprotocol takes a gate with Boolean input wire b' and arithmetic inputs u and v and output wire $z = u + (v - u) \cdot b'$.

Wire Masks and Keys
  Wire Mask/Global Difference Products
    Selection Gates If g is a selection gate with input wires u and v, selection bit wire b, and output wire z,

1. If b' is the Boolean input wire, let $\lambda_{b'}$ be the $\mathbb{F}_p$ daBit mask stored as $[\![\lambda'_b]\!]$ in $\mathcal{F}_{\mathsf{MPC}}$.
2. Generate an $\mathbb{F}_p$ wire mask $[\![\lambda_b]\!]$:
    (a) For each $i \in [n]$, party P_i samples $\lambda_b^i \xleftarrow{\$} \mathbb{F}_p$ and calls $\mathcal{F}_{\mathsf{MPC}}$ with this value as input.
    (b) Compute $[\![\lambda_b]\!] := [\![\sum_{i=1}^n \lambda_b^i]\!]$ by calling $\mathcal{F}_{\mathsf{MPC}}$.
3. Each party P_i samples a key $\mathsf{k}_{b,0}^i \xleftarrow{\$} \mathbb{F}_{p^{\ell_\kappa}}$.
4. Generate an $\mathbb{F}_p$ output wire mask $[\![\lambda_z]\!]$ in the same way as for $[\![\lambda_b]\!]$, above.
5. Let $[\![\lambda_u]\!]$ and $[\![\lambda_v]\!]$ be the masks stored in $\mathcal{F}_{\mathsf{MPC}}$ for wires u and v, respectively, generated when garbling an addition or multiplication gate or input wire. Set $[\![\lambda_w]\!] := [\![\lambda_v]\!] - [\![\lambda_u]\!]$ by calling $\mathcal{F}_{\mathsf{MPC}}$.
6. Let $\mathsf{k}_{u,0}^i$ and $\mathsf{k}_{v,0}^i$ be the keys previously generated by party P_i for wires u and v. For each $i \in [n]$, party P_i sets $\mathsf{k}_{w,0}^i := \mathsf{k}_{v,0}^i - \mathsf{k}_{u,0}^i$.
7. For each $i \in [n]$, party P_i samples a wire key $\mathsf{k}_{w,\mathsf{g},0}^i \xleftarrow{\$} \mathbb{F}_{p^{\ell_\kappa}}$ and sets $\mathsf{k}_{w,\mathsf{e},0}^i := \mathsf{k}_{w,0}^i - \mathsf{k}_{w,\mathsf{g},0}^i$.
8. Compute $[\![\lambda_{b'w}]\!] := [\![\lambda_{b'} \cdot \lambda_w]\!]$ by calling $\mathcal{F}_{\mathsf{MPC}}$.
9. Execute $\Pi_{\mathsf{Mask} \times \mathsf{Diff}}$ to obtain

$$\left\{ \langle R^i \cdot \lambda_{b'} \rangle, \langle R^i \cdot \lambda_b \rangle, \langle R^i \cdot \lambda_w \rangle, \langle R^i \cdot \lambda_{b'w} \rangle, \langle R^i \cdot \lambda_z \rangle \right\}.$$

10. For each $i \in [n]$, for each $\alpha \in \mathbb{F}_p$ and $\beta \in \{0,1\}$, set

$$\langle \rho_{i,g,b,\beta} \rangle := (1 - 2 \cdot \beta) \cdot \langle R^j \cdot \lambda_{b'} \rangle + \langle R^j \cdot \lambda_b \rangle$$
$$\langle \rho_{i,g,\mathsf{g},\alpha} \rangle := -\alpha \cdot \langle R^j \cdot \lambda_b \rangle$$
$$\langle \rho_{i,g,\mathsf{e},\beta} \rangle := -\beta \cdot \langle R^j \cdot \lambda_w \rangle - (1 - 2 \cdot \beta) \cdot \langle R^j \cdot \lambda_{b'w} \rangle + \langle R^j \cdot \lambda_z \rangle.$$

Garbling
  Selection Gates If g is a selection gate with input wires u and v and selection bit wire b,

1. The parties generate ciphertexts for converting the Boolean input wire b' to an $\mathbb{F}_p$ wire b: for every $i \in [n]$,
    – P_i sets $\tilde{g}_{b,\beta}^{i,i} := F_{\mathsf{k}_{b,\beta}^i}(g,i) + \mathsf{k}_{b,0}^i + \beta \cdot R^i + \rho_{i,g,b,\beta}^i$
    – For every $j \neq i$, P_j sets $\tilde{g}_{b,\beta}^{i,j} := F_{\mathsf{k}_{b,\beta}^j}(g,i) + \rho_{i,g,b,\beta}^j$
2. The parties compute the gates for the product of wire $w := (v - u)$ with wire b:
    (a) The parties compute the garbler half gate:
        – P_i sets $\tilde{g}_{\mathsf{g},\alpha}^{i,i} := F_{\mathsf{k}_{\mathsf{g},z,\alpha}^i}(g,i) + \mathsf{k}_{\mathsf{g},z,0}^i - \alpha \cdot \mathsf{k}_{b,0}^i + \rho_{i,g,\mathsf{g},\alpha}^i$
        – For every $j \neq i$, P_j sets $\tilde{g}_{\mathsf{g},\alpha}^{i,j} := F_{\mathsf{k}_{\mathsf{g},z,\alpha}^j}(g,i) + \rho_{i,g,\mathsf{g},\alpha}^j$
    (b) The parties compute the evaluator half gate:
        – P_i sets $\tilde{g}_{\mathsf{e},\beta}^{i,i} := F_{\mathsf{k}_{\mathsf{e},b,\beta}^i}(g,i) + \mathsf{k}_{\mathsf{e},z,0}^i + \rho_{i,g,\mathsf{e},\beta}^i$
        – For every $j \neq i$, P_j sets $\tilde{g}_{\mathsf{e},\beta}^{i,j} := F_{\mathsf{k}_{\mathsf{e},b,\beta}^j}(g,i) + \rho_{i,g,\mathsf{e},\beta}^j$

Fig. 9. Subprotocol Π_{Select} for garbling a selector gate.

uniformly at random, and independently of one another, and so their sum $k_{z,0}$ is also uniformly random, as is required of 0 keys; furthermore, the wire mask λ_z is uniform and not known to any individual party, so the external value of the output wire perfectly hides the real value $v_w \cdot v_b$. The complete protocol for garbling these new selector gates is given in Fig. 9. The evaluation protocol is the same as the evaluation of a multiplication gate and is therefore omitted.

5 Evaluation in Comparison to Previous Work

We evaluate our work in comparison to all previous works in the field of arithmetic garbling; both in the two-party, and in the multiparty paradigm. As shown in Table 1, we are the only work providing full-threshold active security, and proving our garbling techniques UC-secure under the named assumptions. Previous work provided either two-party, passively secure constructions [3,4], or multiparty, passively secure constructions in the honest majority setting [6].

Recall that, in the multiparty setting, projection gates (significantly increasing the efficiency of previous work [3,4]) are non-trivial to construct, and are not universal (i.e., tailored techniques per gate are required). Given that in the multiparty setting all parties play the role of the garbler, we cannot exploit the asymmetry between garbler and evaluator that two-party solutions enjoy. In addition, as already pointed out by Ben-Efraim [6], each garbled table row in the multiparty setting requires n ciphertexts, versus a single ciphertext in the two-party setting, and each row decryption requires n^2 PRF calls in the multiparty setting, versus a single PRF call in the two-party setting. These values are reflected in our cost description provided in Table 1.

For the works that did not suggest an improved version of a specific garbled gate (e.g., multiplication gates in both our work, and the work of Ball et al. [3]), we assume the same cost as the cost of the best previous technique of which they make use. Our work almost halves the communication cost of the selector gate, compared to the previous work in the multiparty setting [6], at the cost of losing the $\sim$33% improvement of computation cost that Ben-Efraim's approach enjoys (in addition to the generation of daBits). This is an overall improvement, given that the main bottleneck is the communication cost, and that the computation cost is dominated by hash function calls, which are efficient. Garbling is a technique suitable for secure computation over unreliable networks, where continuous connectivity cannot be guaranteed. Although most of the communication happens during the preprocessing phase, the communication cost remains the main bottleneck of garbling. Performing one additional PRF call during the online phase, given that it comes at such a significant efficiency increase of the offline phase, is less of a concern, since PRFs are a symmetric primitive, with significant hardware optimisations on modern processors. Our selector gate remains competitive even with the related work in the two party setting [3], where we consider a selector gate to be the so-called cross-modulus multiplication for $q = 2$. We require $p + 4$ ciphertexts per party, while Ball et al. [3] require $p + 1$. This minor difference comes mainly from the fact that we cannot deploy the row reduction techniques in the multiparty setting. Note that the cost of our protocols that comes from applying actively secure MPC techniques, instead of the passively secure approach in previous works, is not digested in Table 1.

Table 1. Comparison of our garbling techniques with the garbling of [4], [6], and [3], in terms of security model supported, number of parties supported, number of ciphertexts required per multiplication and selection gate, and number of decryptions required per multiplication and selection gate.

Protocol	Model	Parties	Multiplication		Selection	
			#Ciphertexts	#Decryptions	#Ciphertexts	#Decryptions
[4]	Passive	2	$6p - 5$	6	$2p - 1$	2
[6]	Passive	n	$2p \cdot n$	$2n^2$	$(2p + 2) \cdot n$	$2n^2$
[3]	Passive	2	$6p - 5$	6	$p + 1$	2
Ours	Active	n	$2p \cdot n$	$2n^2$	$(p + 4) \cdot n$	$3n^2$

6 Conclusion

Our work continues the study of multiparty arithmetic garbling initiated by Ben-Efraim [6]. Specifically, we extend the previous work from the semi-honest, honest majority setting, to the full-threshold actively-secure setting. Given the practical importance of circuits, which combine Boolean and arithmetic gates, we follow this paradigm, also considered in the work of Ben-Efraim [6]. We consider a selector gate as suggested by Ben-Efraim [6] (essentially a multiplexer); we extend it to the full-threshold actively-secure equivalent, and show how to garble such a gate, while almost halving the communication cost it incurs.

Representations of Boolean circuits have clear advantages over arithmetic circuits when it comes to non-linear operations. On the other hand, appropriate representations of arithmetic circuits are orders of magnitude more efficient than Boolean circuits for linear operations on arithmetic values. Garbling techniques that enable the construction of circuits, which integrate both Boolean and arithmetic gates, are essential to treat numerous real-world application scenarios, and allow computation of arbitrary circuits in constant rounds. This is the reason why the design of such garbling schemes is on the rise. It remains an interesting open problem to devise techniques that allow a seamless and efficient conversion between the two representations with active security in the multiparty setting.

Acknowledgements. The authors would like to thank Dragos Rotaru and the anonymous reviewers for their valuable feedback on this manuscript.

References

1. Aly, A., Orsini, E., Rotaru, D., Smart, N.P., Wood, T.: Zaphod: efficiently combining LSSS and garbled circuits in scale. In: Proceedings of the 7th ACM Workshop on Encrypted Computing & Applied Homomorphic Cryptography, pp. 33–44 (2019)

2. Applebaum, B., Ishai, Y., Kushilevitz, E.: How to garble arithmetic circuits. In: Ostrovsky, R. (ed.) 52nd Annual Symposium on Foundations of Computer Science, Palm Springs, CA, USA, 22–25 October 2011, pp. 120–129. IEEE Computer Society Press (2011)
3. Ball, M., Carmer, B., Malkin, T., Rosulek, M., Schimanski, N.: Garbled neural networks are practical. Cryptology ePrint Archive, Report 2019/338 (2019). https://eprint.iacr.org/2019/338
4. Ball, M., Malkin, T., Rosulek, M.: Garbling gadgets for boolean and arithmetic circuits. In: Weippl, E.R., Katzenbeisser, S., Kruegel, C., Myers, A.C., Halevi, S. (eds.) ACM CCS 2016: 23rd Conference on Computer and Communications Security, Vienna, Austria, 24–28 October 2016, pp. 565–577. ACM Press (2016)
5. Beaver, D., Micali, S., Rogaway, P.: The round complexity of secure protocols (extended abstract). In: 22nd Annual ACM Symposium on Theory of Computing, Baltimore, MD, USA, 14–16 May 1990, pp. 503–513. ACM Press (1990)
6. Ben-Efraim, A.: On multiparty garbling of arithmetic circuits. In: Peyrin, T., Galbraith, S. (eds.) ASIACRYPT 2018, Part III. LNCS, vol. 11274, pp. 3–33. Springer, Cham (2018). https://doi.org/10.1007/978-3-030-03332-3_1
7. Ben-Efraim, A., Lindell, Y., Omri, E.: Optimizing semi-honest secure multiparty computation for the internet. In: Weippl, E.R., Katzenbeisser, S., Kruegel, C., Myers, A.C., Halevi, S. (eds.) ACM CCS 2016: 23rd Conference on Computer and Communications Security, Vienna, Austria, 24–28 October 2016, pp. 578–590. ACM Press (2016)
8. Bendlin, R., Damgård, I., Orlandi, C., Zakarias, S.: Semi-homomorphic encryption and multiparty computation. In: Paterson, K.G. (ed.) EUROCRYPT 2011. LNCS, vol. 6632, pp. 169–188. Springer, Heidelberg (2011). https://doi.org/10.1007/978-3-642-20465-4_11
9. Burra, S.S., et al.: High performance multi-party computation for binary circuits based on oblivious transfer. Cryptology ePrint Archive, Report 2015/472 (2015). http://eprint.iacr.org/2015/472
10. Canetti, R.: Universally composable security: a new paradigm for cryptographic protocols. Cryptology ePrint Archive, Report 2000/067 (2000). http://eprint.iacr.org/2000/067
11. Cramer, R., Damgård, I., Escudero, D., Scholl, P., Xing, C.: SPDZ$_{2^k}$: efficient MPC mod 2^k for dishonest majority. In: Shacham, H., Boldyreva, A. (eds.) CRYPTO 2018, Part II. LNCS, vol. 10992, pp. 769–798. Springer, Cham (2018). https://doi.org/10.1007/978-3-319-96881-0_26
12. Damgård, I., Pastro, V., Smart, N., Zakarias, S.: Multiparty computation from somewhat homomorphic encryption. In: Safavi-Naini, R., Canetti, R. (eds.) CRYPTO 2012. LNCS, vol. 7417, pp. 643–662. Springer, Heidelberg (2012). https://doi.org/10.1007/978-3-642-32009-5_38
13. Ghosh, S., Nielsen, J.B., Nilges, T.: Maliciously secure oblivious linear function evaluation with constant overhead. In: Takagi, T., Peyrin, T. (eds.) ASIACRYPT 2017, Part I. LNCS, vol. 10624, pp. 629–659. Springer, Cham (2017). https://doi.org/10.1007/978-3-319-70694-8_22
14. Hazay, C., Scholl, P., Soria-Vazquez, E.: Low cost constant round MPC combining BMR and oblivious transfer. In: Takagi, T., Peyrin, T. (eds.) ASIACRYPT 2017, Part I. LNCS, vol. 10624, pp. 598–628. Springer, Cham (2017). https://doi.org/10.1007/978-3-319-70694-8_21
15. Ishai, Y., Kilian, J., Nissim, K., Petrank, E.: Extending oblivious transfers efficiently. In: Boneh, D. (ed.) CRYPTO 2003. LNCS, vol. 2729, pp. 145–161. Springer, Heidelberg (2003). https://doi.org/10.1007/978-3-540-45146-4_9

16. Keller, M., Orsini, E., Scholl, P.: MASCOT: Faster malicious arithmetic secure computation with oblivious transfer. In: Weippl, E.R., Katzenbeisser, S., Kruegel, C., Myers, A.C., Halevi, S. (eds.) ACM CCS 2016: 23rd Conference on Computer and Communications Security, Vienna, Austria, 24–28 October 2016, pp. 830–842. ACM Press (2016)

17. Keller, M., Pastro, V., Rotaru, D.: Overdrive: making SPDZ great again. In: Nielsen, J.B., Rijmen, V. (eds.) EUROCRYPT 2018, Part III. LNCS, vol. 10822, pp. 158–189. Springer, Cham (2018). https://doi.org/10.1007/978-3-319-78372-7_6

18. Kolesnikov, V., Schneider, T.: Improved garbled circuit: free XOR gates and applications. In: Aceto, L., Damgård, I., Goldberg, L.A., Halldórsson, M.M., Ingólfsdóttir, A., Walukiewicz, I. (eds.) ICALP 2008, Part II. LNCS, vol. 5126, pp. 486–498. Springer, Heidelberg (2008). https://doi.org/10.1007/978-3-540-70583-3_40

19. Lindell, Y., Pinkas, B., Smart, N.P., Yanai, A.: Efficient constant round multiparty computation combining BMR and SPDZ. In: Gennaro, R., Robshaw, M. (eds.) CRYPTO 2015, Part II. LNCS, vol. 9216, pp. 319–338. Springer, Heidelberg (2015). https://doi.org/10.1007/978-3-662-48000-7_16

20. Makri, E., Wood, T.: Full-Threshold Actively-Secure Multiparty Arithmetic Circuit Garbling. Cryptology ePrint Archive, Report 2019/1098 (2019). https://eprint.iacr.org/2019/1098

21. Malkin, T., Pastro, V., Shelat, A.: An algebraic approach to garbling (2016, Unpublished manuscript)

22. Naor, M., Pinkas, B., Sumner, R.: Privacy preserving auctions and mechanism design. In: 1st ACM Conference on Electronic Commerce, EC 1999, pp. 129–139. Citeseer (1999)

23. Nielsen, J.B., Nordholt, P.S., Orlandi, C., Burra, S.S.: A new approach to practical active-secure two-party computation. In: Safavi-Naini, R., Canetti, R. (eds.) CRYPTO 2012. LNCS, vol. 7417, pp. 681–700. Springer, Heidelberg (2012). https://doi.org/10.1007/978-3-642-32009-5_40

24. Pinkas, B., Schneider, T., Smart, N.P., Williams, S.C.: Secure two-party computation is practical. In: Matsui, M. (ed.) ASIACRYPT 2009. LNCS, vol. 5912, pp. 250–267. Springer, Heidelberg (2009). https://doi.org/10.1007/978-3-642-10366-7_15

25. Rotaru, D., Wood, T.: Marbled circuits: mixing arithmetic and boolean circuits with active security. Cryptology ePrint Archive, Report 2019/207 (2019). https://eprint.iacr.org/2019/207

26. Yao, A.C.-C.: Protocols for secure computations (extended abstract). In: 23rd Annual Symposium on Foundations of Computer Science, Chicago, Illinois, 3–5 November 1982, pp. 160–164. IEEE Computer Society Press (1982)

27. Zahur, S., Rosulek, M., Evans, D.: Two halves make a whole. In: Oswald, E., Fischlin, M. (eds.) EUROCRYPT 2015, Part II. LNCS, vol. 9057, pp. 220–250. Springer, Heidelberg (2015). https://doi.org/10.1007/978-3-662-46803-6_8

The Cost of IEEE Arithmetic in Secure Computation

David W. Archer[1], Shahla Atapoor[2], and Nigel P. Smart[2,3(✉)]

[1] Galois Inc., Portland, USA
dwa@galois.com
[2] imec-COSIC, KU Leuven, Leuven, Belgium
{shahla.atapoor,nigel.smart}@kuleuven.be
[3] University of Bristol, Bristol, UK

Abstract. Programmers are used to the rounding and error properties of IEEE double precision arithmetic, however in secure computing paradigms, such as provided by Multi-Party Computation (MPC), usually a different form of approximation is provided for real number arithmetic. We compare the two standard variants using for LSSS-based MPC, with an implementation of IEEE compliant double precision using binary circuit-based MPC. We compare the relative performance, and conclude that the addition cost of IEEE compliance maybe too great for some applications. Thus in the secure domain standards bodies may wish to examine a different form of real number approximations.

1 Introduction

Multi-Party Computation (MPC) is a technique which enables a set of parties to compute a function on their own joint private input, whilst at the same time revealing nothing about their private inputs to each other; other than what can be deduced from the output of the function. Most MPC protocols fall into one of two broad categories: garbled circuits or linear-secret-sharing-scheme-based (LSSS-based) MPC. The garbled-circuit approach began with the work of Yao [29], who gave a two party protocol in which one party 'garbles' (or encrypts) a binary circuit (along with their input) and then another party 'evaluates' the garbled circuit using their own input. By contrast, the LSSS-based approach [7, 12] involves the parties dividing each secret value into several *shares*, over a finite field $\mathbb{F}_p$, and perform computations on the shares, and then reconstruct the secret at the end by combining the shares to determine the output.

Since their invention in the mid 1980s such technologies have come a long way. The garbled circuit (GC) based approach of Yao was generalized to the honest-majority multi-party setting by Beaver et al. [6]. Where now the collection of parties "garble" the binary circuit, and then later the same collection of parties jointly evaluating the garbled circuit. Recent work [17,28] (which we denote by HSS and WRK respectively) have given very efficient multi-party protocols for binary circuits using this methodology for the dishonest majority setting.

© Springer Nature Switzerland AG 2021
P. Longa and C. Ràfols (Eds.): LATINCRYPT 2021, LNCS 12912, pp. 431–452, 2021.
https://doi.org/10.1007/978-3-030-88238-9_21

The other line of LSSS based work has also had considerable recent practical advances, e.g. [8,15], for the case of large prime p and full threshold access structures, or [13] for the case of honest majority style access structures for a large prime. For 'small prime' LSSS based MPC Araki et al. [5] propose a method for the threshold case of $(n, t) = (3, 1)$ using replicated sharing. This method is relatively easy to generalize to any Q2 access structure represented by replicated sharing.

In all settings, the state-of-the-art is now protocols which provide so-called active (a.k.a. malicious security), namely they allow honest parties to detect when adversarial parties arbitrarily deviate from the protocol. In addition, recent work has also focused on combining the two approaches so as to get the advantages of working with function representations given by binary circuits, as well as function representations tailored to the LSSS-based approaches (working with large basic data types, i.e. integers modulo p). The work [3], implemented in the Scale-Mamba system [2], combines the HSS protocol [17] in the GC world with either the SPDZ protocol [15] (for full threshold adversaries) or the Smart-Wood protocol [27] (for non-full threshold adversaries) in the LSSS world. This conversation is itself based on so-called daBits, introduced in [25].

In real applications one does not want to work either directly with binary circuit based representations of functions, nor does one want to work with integers modulo p. After all many practical real world applications involve processing real numbers. But real numbers are not native datatypes in MPC systems, just as they are not native in normal computing, thus approximations have to be made. In standard (in-the-clear) computing we approximate real numbers by floating point operations; with the IEEE-754 representation being the standard.

For efficiency reasons much prior work on real number arithmetic in secure computation has mainly focused on fixed point operations. This follows from the work of Catrina and Saxena [11], who showed how to perform efficient fixed point operations within an LSSS-based MPC system. Over the years various authors have examined efficient LSSS-based MPC arithmetic on such fixed point numbers, e.g. [4,20,21]. However, as is well known in standard in-the-clear computation, fixed point arithmetic is not particularly suitable for many real world applications.

Using a floating point representation is possible with an MPC system. By utilizing binary circuits one can implement the IEEE-754 representation as a circuit and then execute them, so as to produce true IEEE-754 compliant secure floating point operations. However, unlike normal circuit design, the binary circuits for GC-operations are composed purely of AND, XOR and NOT gates; with the major cost associated to AND gates. Thus we need to produce circuits which are optimized for this cost metric and not the usual electronic circuit style cost metrics. We present a solution to this circuit creation problem in this work, and present gate counts and run-times of our IEEE-754 compliant circuits.

Utilizing an LSSS-based MPC system one can often obtain a more efficient form of floating point arithmetic, using the methodology of [1]. This tries to emulate the real number arithmetic, not in a computer whose native operations are modulo a power-of-two (as in IEEE-754 format), but in a computing machine whose native arithmetic is modulo a large prime number p. The methodology of [1] gives a number of tunable values, such as the usual mantissa and exponent sizes, but also a 'statistical security' parameter which controls how close 'leaked' values are from uniformly random values[1]. The paper [18] also implements floating point arithmetic but in a passively secure honest-majority three party setting, utilizing secret sharing modulo 2^v. The work *approximates* IEEE arithmetic using a technique similar to [1], but tuned for the case of sharing modulo 2^v. This work was extended and improved in [20].

In this work, we compare the binary circuit based approach for IEEE-754 arithmetic (which follows the IEEE-754 standard with respect to round errors), with the approach of [1] which follows a different approach to rounding errors. As remarked above a modern trend is to utilize the two types of MPC systems together. Thus we also present methodologies to convert from the IEEE-754 representation to the representation used in [1]. Our work is most closely related to that of [24], which combines, as we do, a binary circuit approach for IEEE 754 arithmetic with a linear secret sharing approach for other MPC operations. They also use the CBMC-GC approach to obtain the binary circuits. However, their MPC implementation is restricted to passive security and the honest-majority three party setting (as opposed to our actively secure approach for general access structures). The evaluation of the circuits in [24] is performed by classical garbling, as opposed to our approach (in the honest majority setting) of utilizing an LSSS-based protocol. Thus in the three party case, we achieve roughly a five fold performance improvement for basic operations such as addition and multiplication, whilst at the same time we achieve active security.

We aim to answer the question; what is the performance penalty one incurs from requiring adherence to the IEEE-754 standard? We present run-times for all the above variants, and compare these against run-times for the fixed point representation mentioned above. We only examine the basic floating point operations of addition, multiplication and division. For higher level functions (such as $\sin, \cos, \mathsf{sqrt}, \log$ etc.) there are often specific protocols in the secure computation domain for these functions which differ from the 'standard' methodologies, see [1,4]. We conclude that the performance penalty for utilizing IEEE-754 compliant arithmetic as opposed to a tailored form of arithmetic for MPC computations may be too great.

2   Preliminaries

In this section, we introduce three forms of approximating real numbers, as well as our MPC-black box. The key set in all our methodologies is $\mathbb{Z}_{\langle k \rangle}$, which we define as the set of integers $\{x \in \mathbb{Z} : -2^{k-1} \leq x \leq 2^{k-1} - 1\}$, which we embed into $\mathbb{F}_p$ via the map $x \mapsto x \pmod{p}$, assuming $k < \log_2 p$. We let $[n]$ denote the set $\{1, \ldots, n\}$. We assume a statistical security parameter sec, which one can

---

[1] The closer they are to uniformly random, then the less information is leaked.

think of as being equal to 40. This measures the statistical distance between various distributions in the underlying protocols.

2.1 MPC-Black Box

Here we describe our two MPC systems (one GC-based and one LSSS-based) and how they fit together using the 'Zaphod' methodology given in [3]. The systems are in the active security with abort paradigm, i.e. if a malicious party deviates from the protocol then the protocol will abort with overwhelming probability.

LSSS-Based MPC: We let $[\![\cdot]\!]_p$ denote an (authenticated) linear secret sharing scheme (LSSS) over the finite field $\mathbb{F}_p$ (for a large prime p) which realizes either a full threshold access structure or a Q2-access structure (a Q2-access structure [22], for readers not familiar with this terminology, can be thought of as a generalization of a threshold system in which the threshold t satisfies $t < n/2$). There are various MPC protocols that enable actively secure MPC with abort to be carried out using such an LSSS, e.g. [13,15,27].

The simplest LSSS is the one which supports full threshold access structures. In this situation, a secret $x \in \mathbb{F}_p$ is held secure by n parties, by each party holding a value $x_i \in \mathbb{F}_p$ so that $x = \sum x_i \pmod{p}$. This produces an unauthenticated sharing which we denote by $\langle x \rangle_p$. To ensure correctness in the presence of active adversaries such a secret sharing needs to be authenticated with a distributed MAC value, i.e. each party also holds $\gamma_i \in \mathbb{F}_p$ such that $\alpha \cdot x = \sum \gamma_i$ for some fixed global secret MAC key α; see [14,15] for details and how one can define MPC in this context in the pre-processing model. Such authentication is called a SPDZ-style MAC, and the combined sharing of x we denote by $[\![x]\!]_p$.

For threshold Q2-access structures, which can tolerate up to t corrupt parties out of n, where $t < n/2$, one can define the secret sharing scheme using Shamir's secret sharing [26]. In this method, a secret $x \in \mathbb{F}_p$ is shared as the zero'th coefficient of a polynomial $f(X)$ of degree t with player i being given the share $f(i)$. Share reconstruction can be performed using Lagrange interpolation. Active security of the underlying MPC protocol is achieved using the error detection properties of the Reed-Solomon code associated to the Shamir sharing, see [27]. Thus we automatically obtain a sharing $[\![x]\!]_p$ which authenticates itself to be correct.

We can also consider LSSS-based MPC over a small prime p, for example $p = 2$. Utilizing Shamir sharing is impossible here, without using relatively expensive field extensions, thus it is common in this situation to represent the Q2-access structure via replicated sharing. This is only possible when the number of maximally unqualified sets[2] (i.e. $n!/(t! \cdot (n-t)!)$) is 'small'. For such Q2-access structures over $\mathbb{F}_2$ we use a generalization of the method of [5]. This protocol uses Maurer's passively secure multiplication protocol [22] to generate passively secure multiplication triples over $\mathbb{F}_2$. These are then turned into actively secure

---

[2] A maximally unqualified set is a set of parties which cannot recover the secret, but for which adding an arbitrary additional player will make the set qualified.

triples using the method of [5] [Protocol 3.1]. Finally, the triples are consumed in a standard secret sharing based online phase, using the methodology of [27] to ensure active security, whilst using the techniques of [19] to reduce the total amount of communication performed. Again, the use of Q2 access structures ensures that the sharing authenticates itself. We let $[\![x]\!]_2$ denote such an authenticated sharing of a bit $x \in \mathbb{F}_2$ using this replicated sharing.

GC-Based n-party MPC: For full threshold access structures we cannot use the trick of utilizing replicated sharing, thus to execute binary circuits in the full threshold case we turn to general n-party Garbled Circuit based MPC; i.e. constant round protocols based on the HSS protocol [17]. Being an n-party GC protocol the data is still secret shared between the parties, but with a different sharing to that used above. We first pick a large finite field of characteristic two, in our case we select $\mathcal{K} = \mathbb{F}_{2^{128}}$. The size is determined so that an event with probability $1/|\mathcal{K}|$ can be considered negligible. For each element $x \in \mathbb{F}_2$ (resp. $\mathcal{K}$), we denote $\langle x \rangle_2$ (resp. $\langle x \rangle_{\mathcal{K}}$) the *unauthenticated* additive sharing of x over $\mathbb{F}_2$ (resp. $\mathcal{K}$), where $x = \sum_{i \in [n]} x_i$, with party P_i holding $x_i \in \mathbb{F}_2$ (resp. $\mathcal{K}$).

To obtain active security with abort we need to authenticate these sharings. However, for technical reasons, this is done using a BDOZ-style MAC introduced by Bendlin et al. [8], as opposed to a SPDZ-style MAC, introduced in [15]. In particular every party P_i authenticates their share b_i towards party P_j, for each $j \neq i$, by holding a MAC $M_i^j \in \mathcal{K}$, such that $M_i^j = K_j^i + b_i \cdot \Delta_j \in \mathcal{K}$, where P_j holds the local key $K_j^i \in \mathcal{K}$ and the fixed global MAC key $\Delta_j \in \mathcal{K}$. This defines an n-party authenticated representation of a bit, denoted by $[\![b]\!]_2$, where $b = \sum_{i=1}^n b_i$ and each P_i holds the bit-share b_i, $n-1$ MACs M_i^j, $n-1$ local keys K_i^j and Δ_i, i.e. $[\![b]\!]_2 = \{b_i, \Delta_i, \{M_i^j, K_i^j\}_{j \neq i}\}_{i \in [n]}$.

We denote by $[\![b]\!]_2$ a bit that is linearly secret shared according to $\langle \cdot \rangle_2$ and *authenticated* according to the pairwise MACs. The extension to vectors of shared bits is immediate. We let $[\![\mathbf{b}]\!]_2$ denote a secret sharing of a vector $\mathbf{b}$, the sharing of the i-bit will be denoted by $[\![\mathbf{b}^{(i)}]\!]_2$, whilst the i-bit of the clear vector $\mathbf{b}$ will be denoted by $\mathbf{b}^{(i)}$. Using such sharings one can create an n-party MPC protocol to evaluate binary circuits, see [17] for details.

Combining the Binary and Large Prime Variants: To combine the binary and large prime worlds we use the Zaphod methodology [3], which we briefly recap on. Our interest is in the function dependent online phase, so we focus on the online functionalities only. When using the mapping from binary to arithmetic circuits the data being transferred has bit length bounded by 64. In other words every data item x is an element of $\mathbb{Z}_{\langle 2^{64} \rangle}$. We will be interested in the 'large prime' regime of Zaphod, so we will require that $64 + \mathsf{sec} < \log_2 p$, for a statistical security parameter sec. This guarantees that selecting $\log_2 p$ bits b_i at random and then forming, for $x \in \mathbb{Z}_{\langle 2^{64} \rangle}$,

$$x + \sum_{i=0}^{\lceil \log_2 p \rceil} b_i \cdot 2^i \pmod{p}$$

will statistically hide the value of x.

Functionality $\mathcal{F}_{\mathsf{MPC}}$ - Zaphod Evaluation

The functionality runs with parties $P_1, \ldots, P_n$ and an ideal adversary Adv. Let A be the set of corrupt parties. Given a set I of valid identifiers, all values are stored in the form $(varid, domain, x)$, where $varid \in I$, $domain \in \{\mathbb{F}_2^{64}, \mathbb{F}_p\}$ and $x \in domain$. We assume p is restricted as in the main text.

Initialize: On input $(Init)$ from all parties, the functionality activates. If $(Init)$ was received before, do nothing.

Input: On input $(Input, P_i, varid, domain, x)$ from P_i and $(input, P_i, varid, domain)$ from all other parties, with $varid$ a fresh identifier, store $(varid, domain, x)$.

Evaluate: Upon receiving $(\{varid_j\}_{j \in m}, varid, domain, C_{\bar{f}})$, from all parties, where $\bar{f} : \{domain\}^m \to domain$ and $varid$ is a fresh identifier, if $\{varid_j\}_{j \in [m]}$ were previously stored, proceed as follows:
   1. Retrieve $(varid_j, domain, x_j)$, for each $j \in [m]$
   2. Store $(varid, domain, x_{m+1} \leftarrow \bar{f}(x_1, \ldots, x_m))$

Output: On input $(Output, varid, domain, type)$, from all parties with $type \in \{0, \ldots, n\}$ (if $varid$ is present in memory):
   1. If $type = 0$ (**Public Output**): Retrieve $(varid, y)$ and send it to Adv. If the adversary sends $\mathsf{Deliver}$, send y to all parties.
   2. Otherwise (**Private Output**): Send $(varid)$ to Adv. Upon receiving $\mathsf{Deliver}$ from Adv, send y to P_i.

Abort: The adversary can at any time send abort, upon which send abort to all honest parties and halt.

Fig. 1. Functionality $\mathcal{F}_{\mathsf{MPC}}$ - Zaphod Evaluation

In Fig. 1 and Fig. 2 we provide the functionalities for our MPC black box. Each value in $\mathcal{F}_{\mathsf{MPC}}$ is uniquely identified by an identifier $varid \in I$, where I is a set of valid identifiers, and a domain set $domain \in \{\mathbb{F}_p, \mathbb{F}_2^{64}\}$. One can see $\mathcal{F}_{\mathsf{MPC}}$-*Zaphod Evaluation* as a combination of two MPC black boxes, specified by the set assigned to $domain$, along with two conversion routines, namely ConvertToField and ConvertToBinary, given in $\mathcal{F}_{\mathsf{MPC}}$-*Zaphod Conversion*. If $domain = \mathbb{F}_p$, the MPC black box provides arithmetic operations over the finite field $\mathbb{F}_p$, whereas if $domain = \mathbb{F}_2^{64}$, it enables one to execute arbitrary binary circuits over binary vectors of length 64, i.e. function with arguments and results in the set $\mathbb{F}_2^{64}$.

$\mathcal{F}_{\mathsf{MPC}}$-*Zaphod Conversion* permits parties to switch between the two MPC black boxes. Note that we have defined ConvertToBinary and ConvertToField to ensure that they are mutual inverses of each other (if the $\mathbb{F}_p$-input element is fewer than 64 bits in length when in the centered interval $(-p/2, \ldots, p/2]$). The algorithms to implement the conversion functions given below are given in [3]. To ease notation we will write these two operations, for $x \in \mathbb{Z}_{\langle 2^{64} \rangle}$, as $[\![x]\!]_p \leftarrow \mathsf{convert}([\![\mathbf{x}]\!]_2)$ and $[\![\mathbf{x}]\!]_2 \leftarrow \mathsf{convert}([\![x]\!]_p)$. A trivial modification of the protocol 'Convert To Field' allows us to perform an unsigned conversion (i.e. when we think of the bits $[\![\mathbf{x}]\!]_2$ representing an integer $x \in [0, \ldots, 2^{64})$, which we will denote by $[\![x]\!]_p \leftarrow \mathsf{convert}^u([\![\mathbf{x}]\!]_2)$.

Functionality $\mathcal{F}_{\mathsf{MPC}}$ - Zaphod Conversion

Convert To Field: On input $(Convert, varid_1, \mathbb{F}_2^{64}, varid_2, \mathbb{F}_p)$:
1. Retrieve $(varid_1, \mathbb{F}_2^{64}, \mathbf{x})$ and convert $\mathbf{x}$ to an element $y \in \mathbb{F}_p$ by setting $y \leftarrow -x_{63} \cdot 2^{63} + \sum_{i=0}^{62} x_i \cdot 2^i$.
2. Store $(varid_2, \mathbb{F}_p, y)$.

Convert To Binary: On input $(Convert, varid_1, \mathbb{F}_p, varid_2, \mathbb{F}_2^{64})$:
1. Retrieve $(varid_1, \mathbb{F}_p, x)$ as an integer in the range $(-p/2, \ldots, p/2)$.
2. Express $y = x \pmod{2^{64}}$ as $y = \sum_{i=0}^{64} y_i \cdot 2^i$ for $y_i \in \{0,1\}$
3. Consider the values y_i as elements in $\mathbb{F}_2$ and pack them into a vector $\mathbf{y} \in \mathbb{F}_2^{64}$.

Fig. 2. Functionality $\mathcal{F}_{\mathsf{MPC}}$ - Zaphod Conversion

To describe our protocols we will let $[\![\mathbf{x}]\!]_2$, for a boldface $\mathbf{x}$, denote a vector of 64 secret shared bits in the binary arithmetic based side of the computation. We let $[\![x]\!]_2$ for a non-boldface value x denote a single shared bit $x \in \{0,1\}$ in the binary side of the computation. An execution of **Output**, for $type = 0$, we will denote by $x \leftarrow \mathsf{Open}([\![x]\!]_p)$ (resp. $\mathbf{x} \leftarrow \mathsf{Open}([\![x]\!]_2)$.

We let $[\![\mathbf{x}]\!]_2 + [\![\mathbf{y}]\!]_2$ (resp. $[\![x]\!]_2 \cdot [\![y]\!]_2$) denote the execution of the Garbled Circuit to evaluate the addition (resp. multiplication) of two 64-bit integers. Likewise, we let $[\![\mathbf{x}]\!]_2 \oplus [\![\mathbf{y}]\!]_2$ denote the bit-wise XOR of the two secret 64-bit bitstrings $\mathbf{x}$ and $\mathbf{y}$, and $[\![x]\!]_2 \cdot [\![\mathbf{y}]\!]_2$ denote the secure bitwise AND of the single shared bit x with the secret bits of the vector $\mathbf{y}$. Clearly operations such as left/right-shift (i.e. $[\![x]\!]_2 \ll 3$) can be done for free, as they are just moving data around in memory. We let $[\![\mathbf{x}]\!]_2^{(i)}$ denote the i-th bit of $\mathbf{x}$, with bit zero representing the least significant bit.

A value $[\![x]\!]_p$ will always represent a shared value $x \in \mathbb{F}_p$. We let $[\![x]\!]_p + [\![y]\!]_p$ (resp. $[\![x]\!]_p \cdot [\![y]\!]_p$) denote addition (resp. multiplication) modulo $\mathbb{F}_p$. If we know $x \in \mathbb{Z}_{\langle 2^{64} \rangle}$ then we can also perform shift operations such as $[\![x]\!]_p \ll 3$, however these are more expensive and require specific protocols which are outlined in [10] (amongst other works).

2.2 IEEE-754

The accepted standard for floating-point arithmetic operations is the IEEE-754 standard, first published in 1985. We use version IEEE-754-2008, published in August 2008. We note that the relevant international standard, ISO/IEC/IEEE 60559:2011 is identical to IEEE-754-2008. IEEE-754 defines representations of finite numbers, infinities, and non-numeric values (so-called "NaNs"); a set of defined arithmetic operations on representable numbers; rounding modes to be used in generating correct outputs of those operations; and a variety of error conditions that may arise during those operations. In this paper we concentrate on the double precision binary format of the IEEE-754 standard.

The IEEE representation has 64 bits in total with the least significant bit (lsb) b_0 (which we assume placed to the right) and the most significant bit (msb) b_{63} (which we assume placed to the left). The three parts of the representation are the sign bit, in position b_{63}, the exponent, in positions $b_{62} \cdots b_{52}$, and the mantissa in positions $b_{51} \cdots b_0$.

If the sign bit is equal to one, then the number is negative. The eleven bits of exponent represent a number $e \in [0, \ldots, 2047]$, which becomes the 'real' exponent after subtracting the number 1023. The mantissa gives an integer $m \in [0, \ldots, 2^{52} - 1]$, although this is not the 'mathematically correct' mantissa as the initial trailing one bit in the msb position has already been deleted. There are two special cases for e, corresponding to the cases of the eleven bits being all zeros or all ones. If $e = 0$ and $m = 0$ then this represents the value zero (which can be positive or negative depending on b_{63}). If $e = 2047$ and $m = 0$ then we have either $+\infty$ or $-\infty$ depending on the sign bit b_{63}. When $e = 2047$ and $m \neq 0$ then we have the special number NaN, meaning 'Not a Number'. Thus assuming $e \neq 2047$ the real number represented by this representation is given by

$$(-1)^{b_{63}} \cdot \left(1 + \sum_{i=1}^{52}(b_{52-i} \cdot 2^{-i})\right) \cdot 2^{e-1023}.$$

2.3   Secure-Floats via $\mathbb{F}_p$-Arithmetic

The standard floating point representation in LSSS-based MPC over a finite field $\mathbb{F}_p$ of odd characteristic is due to [1], which itself builds on the work of [10]. Unlike [1] we always carry around a value err, which the reader should think of as a value which corresponds to the NaN in IEEE-754 arithmetic.

Floating point numbers are defined by two global, public integer parameters (ℓ, k) which define the size of the mantissa and the exponent respectively. Each floating point number is represented as a five-tuple (v, p, z, s, err), where

- $v \in [2^{\ell-1}, 2^{\ell})$ is an $\ell+1$-bit significant with its most significant bit always set to one (note here the msb is not dropped as in the IEEE format).
- $p \in \mathbb{Z}_{\langle k \rangle}$ is the signed exponent.
- z is a bit to define whether the number is zero or not.
- s is a sign bit (equal to zero if non-negative).
- err is the error flag (equal to zero if no rounding or arithmetic error has occurred, it holds a non-zero value otherwise).

Thus assuming err $= 0$ this tuple represents the value $u = (1 - 2 \cdot s) \cdot (1 - z) \cdot v \cdot 2^p$. We adopt the conventions that when $u = 0$ we also have $z = 1, v = 0$ and $p = 0$, and when err $\neq 0$ then the values of v, p, z and s are meaningless.

Such errors can be triggered by 'higher level' functions such as trying to compute $\sqrt{-1}$ or $\log(-1)$, they can be triggered by division by zero operations or an underflow/overflow operation. An underflow or overflow occurs when the value p from a computation falls out of the range $\mathbb{Z}_{\langle k \rangle}$. When an error occurs in an operation the err flag is incremented by one. Thus the operation $z \leftarrow x/0 + y$ results in $z.\mathsf{err} = 1$, whereas $z \leftarrow x/0 + y/0$ results in $z.\mathsf{err} = 2$ (assuming in both cases $x.\mathsf{err} = y.\mathsf{err} = 0$.

Following the documentation of Scale-Mamba [2] we refer to such a floating point value as an sfloat (secure-float) when the values $(v, p, z, s, \mathsf{err})$ are all secret shared. In which case, we write $(\llbracket v \rrbracket_p, \llbracket p \rrbracket_p, \llbracket z \rrbracket_p, \llbracket s \rrbracket_p, \llbracket \mathsf{err} \rrbracket_p)$. Unlike in [1] the value err is kept permanently masked. When an sfloat value $(\llbracket v \rrbracket_p, \llbracket p \rrbracket_p, \llbracket z \rrbracket_p, \llbracket s \rrbracket_p, \llbracket \mathsf{err} \rrbracket_p)$ is unmarked, first the value $\llbracket b \rrbracket_p \leftarrow (\llbracket \mathsf{err} \rrbracket_p = 0)$ is computed. Then the five values $(\llbracket b \rrbracket_p \cdot \llbracket v \rrbracket_p, \llbracket b \rrbracket_p \cdot \llbracket p \rrbracket_p, \llbracket b \rrbracket_p \cdot \llbracket z \rrbracket_p, \llbracket b \rrbracket_p \cdot \llbracket s \rrbracket_p, 1 - \llbracket b \rrbracket_p)$ are opened. In this way no information leaks, including how many errors were accumulated, when a value with $\mathsf{err} \neq 0$ is transferred from the secure to the insecure domain.

Arithmetic is implemented using the algorithms in [1], with correctness and security maintained as long as $2 \cdot \ell + \mathsf{sec} < \log_2 p$, for the statistical security parameter sec. In particular, $2^{-\mathsf{sec}}$ represents the statistical distance between values leaked by the algorithms in $\mathbb{F}_p$, and uniformly random values chosen from $\mathbb{F}_p$.

2.4 Fixed Point Representation

For comparison, we also compare how the above two methods compare against the standard LSSS-based approach to approximating floating point values; namely a fixed point representation first given in [11], which also utilizes the work in [10]. We define $\mathbb{Q}_{\langle k, f \rangle}$ as the set of rational numbers $\{x \in \mathbb{Q} : x = \overline{x} \cdot 2^{-f}, \overline{x} \in \mathbb{Z}_{\langle k \rangle}\}$. We represent $x \in \mathbb{Q}$ as the integer $x \cdot 2^f = \overline{x} \in \mathbb{Z}_{\langle k \rangle}$, which is then represented in $\mathbb{F}_p$ via the mapping used above. Thus $x \in \mathbb{Q}$ is in the range $[-2^e, 2^e - 2^{-f}]$ where $e = k - f$. As we are working with fixed point numbers we assume that the parameters f and k are public. For the algorithms to work (in particular fixed point multiplication and division) we require that $f < k$ and $2 \cdot k + \mathsf{sec} < \log_2 p$, again for the statistical security parameter sec. Again the documentation of Scale-Mamba [2] we refer to such a fixed point value as an sfix when the value $\overline{x}$ is secret shared as $\llbracket \overline{x} \rrbracket_p$.

3 Generating Circuits for IEEE Arithmetic

In this section, we implement circuits for floating-point arithmetic operations which are suitable for MPC based on binary circuit computation. While some of this machinery (with respect to NaN computations etc.) may at first glance appear superfluous, leading to more complex circuits than necessary; however, floating point implementations that lack this machinery may fail to meet the expectations of real-world users. Thus for our work to be as relevant to real-world settings as possible, we choose to implement fully IEEE-754-compliant circuit designs.

Unfortunately, because IEEE-754 is the recognized standard, and because floating-point performance is a key competitive metric for hardware implementations such as those found in modern microprocessors, IEEE-754 compatible arithmetic circuit designs are generally proprietary and optimized for the hardware. In our application we require combinatorial circuits which are optimized for low AND-depth. To achieve our goal of IEEE-754 compliance without readily available compliant circuit designs, we choose to generate our own standard-compliant circuit designs. To do so, we choose one of the few thoroughly tested open-source IEEE-754 compliant software libraries, the Berkeley SoftFloat library, release 2c [16], from which we automatically derive circuit designs using a C-to-circuit compiler designed for MPC applications (CBMC-GC) [9].

```
float64 float64_add(float64 a,float64 b)
{ flag aSign, bSign;
   aSign = extractFloat64Sign(a);
   bSign = extractFloat64Sign(b);
   if ( aSign == bSign )
   { return addFloat64Sigs(a,b,aSign); }
   else
   {  return subFloat64Sigs(a,b,aSign); } }
```

Fig. 3. The original SoftFloat C-code for IEEE-754 double addition

For each circuit of interest in this work, we started with the relevant main function in the SoftFloat library, and modified the circuit to make it acceptable as input to the CBMC-GC compiler. The necessary edits in each case were minor: changing the name of the relevant function to mpc_main so that CBMC-GC would compile that function; renaming the input and output arguments to match the expectations of the compiler and modifying the code to contain only a single output assignment statement and return point, with a specific output naming convention, at the end of the function. Figure 3 shows as an example the original SoftFloat code for IEEE-754 compliant 64-bit floating-point addition, whilst Fig. 4 shows the same function after modification for compilation by CBMC-GC.

CBMC-GC is a compilation pipeline designed to convert software functions written in the C programming language into circuit specifications suitable for use in secure multi-party computation – most particularly, garbled circuit computation. The compiler CBMC proceeds by first unrolling loops in the source algorithm. Next, the compiler converts the algorithm into static single-assignment form. Finally, the compiler uses multiple passes of optimization techniques with the aim of reducing gate count in the resulting circuit or reducing depth of that circuit. Optimization begins with conversion of the circuit into and-inverter graph (AIG) form – Boolean networks comprised of 2-input AND gates and inverter gates. During AIG construction, CBMC-GC employs structural hashing [23] to prevent addition of redundant AND gates, resulting in an AIG with

```
void mpc_main(float64 INPUT_X_a,
              float64 INPUT_Y_b)
{ flag aSign, bSign;
  float64 temp_output, OUTPUT_A_x;
  aSign = extractFloat64Sign(INPUT_X_a);
  bSign = extractFloat64Sign(INPUT_Y_b);
  if ( aSign == bSign )
   { temp = addFloat64Sigs(INPUT_X_a,
                INPUT_Y_b,aSign);
     goto done;  }
  else { temp =
     subFloat64Sigs(INPUT_X_a,
            INPUT_Y_b,aSign);
     goto done; }
  done:
    OUTPUT_A_X = temp; }
```

Fig. 4. SoftFloat C-code after modification for CBMC-GC

partial canonicity. The compiler uses constant propagation techniques to further reduce unnecessary gates (those that result in constant outputs due to one or more inputs being constant). The compiler also applies heuristic re-write rules to reduce subcircuit complexity, and employs SAT sweeping [30] to identify additional circuit nodes that realize equivalent logical functions, and then remove such redundancies.

When optimizing for minimum depth, CBMC-GC precedes these optimization passes with a step of "aggregating" gates – parallelizing otherwise sequential structures of gates in order to achieve lower circuit depth. For the addition circuit, we specify no compiler flags. For the multiplication circuit, we specify the "–low-depth" flag, so that the compiler optimizes for the lowest possible gate depth. For the division circuit, which is programmed using an iterative approximation loop, we specify compiler flags that limit the loop unrolling to a factor of 24. We choose this unrolling depth to closely match the number of stages typically used in modern microprocessor floating-point division pipelines, thus the output is (experimentally) indistinguishable from the output of the circuits used in a modern microprocessor. Finally, we use the circuit-utils tool in the CBMC-GC tool suite to convert the optimized circuit into the "Bristol Fashion" used by the Scale-Mamba suite. We have the Bristol format converter remove OR gates as well, resulting in circuits that contain only AND, XOR, and INV gates.

Eventually, we obtain the following circuit sizes for our three basic operations of IEEE-754 compliant floating-point addition, multiplication, and division:

	No. ANDs	No. XORs	No. INVs	AND depth
add	5385	8190	2062	235
mul	19626	21947	3326	129
div	82269	84151	17587	3619

In the above table, we also present the AND-depth of the circuit; since when operating in the Q2-domain using an LSSS-based MPC engineer modulo 2 the dominant cost is not the number of AND gates but the depth of the AND gates in the circuit.

4 Converting Between Representations

Converting between the two representations is mathematically trivial from a functional perspective. However, our conversion needs to be executed in the secure domain, and thus we need to ensure that no sensitive data leaks during the conversion and in addition, we must use constructions which can be executed reasonably efficient in the secure domain.

We first present two trivial extensions to the conversion algorithms in [3] which were given earlier. The conversion algorithms work by utilizing a correlated randomness source, called daBits. A call $([\![b]\!]_2, [\![b]\!]_p) \leftarrow$ daBits produces a doubly-shared bit $b \in \{0,1\}$, which is shared with respect to the two different methodologies. Having such a correlated randomness source allows us to perform conversions. See [3,25] for how such correlated randomness is produced.

The first conversion algorithm, which we denote by $[\![x]\!]_p \leftarrow$ convert$([\![x]\!]_2)$, converts a single bit x from the binary-world to the LSSS-world. This is executed as follows:

1. $([\![r]\!]_2, [\![r]\!]_p) \leftarrow$ daBits.
2. $[\![v]\!]_2 \leftarrow [\![x]\!]_2 \oplus [\![r]\!]_2$.
3. $v \leftarrow$ Open$([\![v]\!]_2)$.
4. $[\![x]\!]_p \leftarrow v + [\![r]\!]_p - 2 \cdot v \cdot [\![r]\!]_p$.

The converse algorithm takes a value $[\![x]\!]_p$ in the LSSS-world, which we know to represent a value $x \in \{0,1\} \subset \mathbb{F}_p$ and converts it to a shared bit in the binary-world; an operation which we denote by $[\![x]\!]_2 \leftarrow$ convert$([\![x]\!]_p)$. The procedure for this is a little more complex, and requires that sec $+ 1 \leq \min\{64, \log_2 p\}$, which will hold in practice in any case. This operation proceeds as follows:

1. For $i = 0, \ldots,$ sec execute $([\![r_i]\!]_2, [\![r_i]\!]_p) \leftarrow$ daBits.
2. $[\![r]\!]_p \leftarrow \sum_{i=0}^{\text{sec}} [\![r_i]\!]_p \cdot 2^i$.
3. $[\![v]\!]_p \leftarrow [\![x]\!]_p + [\![r]\!]_p$.

4. $v \leftarrow \mathsf{Open}(\llbracket v \rrbracket_p)$.
5. $\llbracket x \rrbracket_2 \leftarrow v - \llbracket r \rrbracket_2$.

This works as the value $v = x + r$ is guaranteed to hold a 64-bit unsigned integer, and it is also statistically hiding of the single bit x. The final subtraction is performed using a binary circuit for 64-bit subtraction.

We can now present our two algorithms for conversion between a secure IEEE floating point double, held as a bit vector $\llbracket x \rrbracket_2$ in the binary circuit world, and an sfloat value $(\llbracket v \rrbracket_p, \llbracket p \rrbracket_p, \llbracket z \rrbracket_p, \llbracket s \rrbracket_p, \llbracket \mathsf{err} \rrbracket_p)$ in the LSSS world; and vice-versa. These algorithms are given in Fig. 5 and Fig. 6, with the main complexity coming from needing to deal with the variable values ℓ and k representing the sizes of the mantissa and exponent in the sfloat datatype. We mark the lines which cost nothing in the secure domain with a comment of "free".

IEEE to sfloat

Input: $\llbracket x \rrbracket_2$.
Output: $(\llbracket v \rrbracket_p, \llbracket p \rrbracket_p, \llbracket z \rrbracket_p, \llbracket s \rrbracket_p, \llbracket \mathsf{err} \rrbracket_p)$, (with parameters ℓ and k).

1. $\llbracket s \rrbracket_p \leftarrow \mathsf{convert}(\llbracket x^{(63)} \rrbracket_2)$.
2. $\llbracket z \rrbracket_2 \leftarrow (\llbracket x \rrbracket_2 = 0)$
3. $\llbracket v \rrbracket_2 \leftarrow \llbracket x \rrbracket_2 \ll 11$.   //free
4. $\llbracket v^{(63)} \rrbracket_2 \leftarrow 1 - \llbracket z \rrbracket_2$.   //free
5. If $\ell \geq 64$ then
   (a) $\llbracket v \rrbracket_p \leftarrow \mathsf{convert}^u(\llbracket v \rrbracket_2)$.
   (b) $\llbracket v \rrbracket_p \leftarrow \llbracket v \rrbracket_p \ll (\ell - 64)$.
6. If $\ell < 63$ then
   (a) $\llbracket v \rrbracket_2 \leftarrow \llbracket v \rrbracket_2 \gg (64 - \ell)$.   //free
   (b) $\llbracket v \rrbracket_p \leftarrow \mathsf{convert}(\llbracket v \rrbracket_2)$.
7. $\llbracket x' \rrbracket_2 \leftarrow \llbracket x \rrbracket_2$.   //free
8. $\llbracket x'^{(63)} \rrbracket_2 \leftarrow 0$.   //free
9. $\llbracket p \rrbracket_2 \leftarrow \llbracket x' \rrbracket_2 \gg 52$.   //free
10. $\llbracket p' \rrbracket_2 \leftarrow (-(\ell - 1) - 1023) + \llbracket p \rrbracket_2$
11. $\llbracket p \rrbracket_p \leftarrow \mathsf{convert}(\llbracket p' \rrbracket_2)$.
12. $\llbracket z \rrbracket_p \leftarrow \mathsf{convert}(\llbracket z \rrbracket_2)$.
13. $\llbracket e \rrbracket_2 \leftarrow (\llbracket p \rrbracket_2 = 2047)$.
14. If $k < 11$ then
   (a) $\mathsf{mask} \leftarrow 2^{64} - 1 - (2^k - 1)$.   //free
   (b) $\llbracket t \rrbracket_2 \leftarrow \llbracket p' \rrbracket_2 \ \& \ \mathsf{mask}$.
   (c) $\llbracket e' \rrbracket_2 \leftarrow \llbracket t^{(63)} \rrbracket_2$.   //free
   (d) $\llbracket e'' \rrbracket_2 \leftarrow (\llbracket t \rrbracket_2 = 0)$.
   (e) $\llbracket e \rrbracket_2 \leftarrow \llbracket e \rrbracket_2 \oplus (1 - \llbracket e' \rrbracket_2) \cdot (1 - \llbracket e'' \rrbracket_2)$.
15. $\llbracket \mathsf{err} \rrbracket_p \leftarrow \mathsf{convert}(\llbracket e \rrbracket_2)$.
16. Return $(\llbracket v \rrbracket_p, \llbracket p \rrbracket_p, \llbracket z \rrbracket_p, \llbracket s \rrbracket_p, \llbracket \mathsf{err} \rrbracket_p)$.

Fig. 5. IEEE to sfloat

IEEE to sfloat: Algorithm Fig. 5, shows how we can securely convert a number from IEEE in the binary-world to sfloat in the LSSS-world. Step 1 extracts the single bit corresponding to the sign bit. This uses our optimized methodology for doing such conversions given earlier. In step 2 we test whether the shared vector $\mathbf{x}$ is equal to zero. This is done by forming $[\![z]\!]_2 \leftarrow \prod_{i=0}^{63}(1 - [\![\mathbf{x}^{(i)}]\!]_2)$.

In steps 3–6b we are extracting the mantissa v. A naive way to do this would be to take 64 bits of the IEEE representation, shift by 12 to the left and then shift back by 12 to right. Then, to obtain the 52 bit mantissa, we dd one bit in the most significant bit position which is bit position 52 and finally convert the value to the $[\![v]\!]_p$ used in sfloat, at which point we could adjust this to cope with the required value of ℓ. However, this would be very inefficient. We try to maintain as much of the bit-shifting operations in the $[\![\cdot]\!]_2$ domain, as their bit-shifts come for free. Thus we first shift left by eleven places and then add the one bit into the top position (which only needs to happen if the value $\mathbf{x}$ is non-zero, thus we use $[\![z]\!]_2$ for this). We then have two cases to consider, if $\ell \geq 64$ then we actually need to shift the value up even more, but we are already using 64-bits. Thus we convert, using the unsigned conversion routine (Step 5a) to a modulo p value, and then perform the shift up in this domain (which is relatively expensive but unavoidable given the basic instructions available to us). When $\ell < 63$ we perform the shift down in the binary domain (Step 6a) and then do the conversion (using an unsigned conversion as we know the top bit is zero).

Steps 7–9 extract the bits of the IEEE exponent p, whereas step 10 converts it to the correct exponent for the sfloat representation. Now obtaining $[\![z]\!]_p$ and $[\![p]\!]_p$ is relatively straight forward. Note, to obtain $[\![z]\!]_p$ we use the optimized bit conversion protocol given earlier in this section.

Steps 13 onwards deal with computing the error flag $[\![\text{err}]\!]_p$. This is first computed using bit operations in the modulo two domain, and then converted to $[\![\text{err}]\!]_p$ using the above optimized conversion (in the penultimate step). We need to set the flag err if either $[\![p]\!]_2$ represents the value 2047, or there is an error introduced due to a low value of k in the sfloat representation. The first test, in step 13, is accomplished by setting $[\![e]\!]_2 \leftarrow \prod_{i=0}^{11}[\![\mathbf{p}^{(i)}]\!]_2$. The second test, in steps 14a–14e, test whether the value of $[\![\mathbf{p}']\!]_2$ lies outside the range $[-2^{k-1}, \ldots, 2^{k-1} - 1]$ or not.

sfloat *to IEEE.* Algorithm Fig. 6, shows how we can convert a number from sfloat to IEEE. In steps 1–6, we are computing the mantissa of IEEE from $[\![v]\!]_p$. To do so, first we need to get rid of the most significant bit of $[\![v]\!]_p$ (step 1) as the sfloat representation stores the msb, whereas IEEE does not. Since bit-shifting in the $[\![\cdot]\!]_p$ domain is expensive, whereas bit-shifting in the $[\![\cdot]\!]_2$ domain costs nothing we do a complete shift (step 3) when $\ell > 64$ down to 53-bits, but when $\ell < 64$ we delay the shifting until we have converted $[\![v]\!]_p$ to $[\![\mathbf{v}]\!]_2$ (step 5).

---

sfloat to IEEE

Input: $(\llbracket v \rrbracket_p, \llbracket p \rrbracket_p, \llbracket z \rrbracket_p, \llbracket s \rrbracket_p, \llbracket \mathrm{err} \rrbracket_p)$, (with parameters ℓ and k).
Output: $\llbracket \mathbf{x} \rrbracket_2$.

1. $\llbracket v' \rrbracket_p \leftarrow \llbracket v \rrbracket_p - 2^{\ell-1} \cdot (1 - \llbracket z \rrbracket_p)$.
2. $\ell' \leftarrow \ell$.
3. If $\ell > 64$ then
     (a) $\ell' \leftarrow 53$
     (b) $\llbracket v' \rrbracket_p \leftarrow \llbracket v' \rrbracket_p \gg (\ell - 53)$.
4. $\llbracket \mathbf{v} \rrbracket_2 \leftarrow \mathrm{convert}(\llbracket v' \rrbracket_p)$.
5. If $\ell' < 53$ then $\llbracket \mathbf{v} \rrbracket_2 \leftarrow \llbracket \mathbf{v} \rrbracket_2 \ll (53 - \ell')$.   //free
6. Else $\llbracket \mathbf{v} \rrbracket_2 \leftarrow \llbracket \mathbf{v} \rrbracket_2 \gg (\ell' - 53)$.   //free
7. $\llbracket \mathrm{ok} \rrbracket_p \leftarrow (\llbracket \mathrm{err} \rrbracket_p == 0)$.
8. $\llbracket \mathrm{ok} \rrbracket_2 \leftarrow \mathrm{convert}(\llbracket \mathrm{ok} \rrbracket_p)$.
9. $\llbracket \mathbf{p} \rrbracket_2 \leftarrow \mathrm{convert}((1 - \llbracket z \rrbracket_p) \cdot (\llbracket p \rrbracket_p + \ell + 1023 - 1))$.
10. If $k > 11$ then
      (a) $\llbracket \mathbf{t} \rrbracket_2 \leftarrow \llbracket \mathbf{p} \rrbracket_2 \,\&\, \mathrm{0xFFFFFFFFFFFFF800}$
      (b) $\llbracket \mathrm{ok} \rrbracket_2 \leftarrow \llbracket \mathrm{ok} \rrbracket_2 \,\&\, (\llbracket \mathbf{t} \rrbracket_2 == 0)$.
11. $\llbracket \mathbf{s} \rrbracket_2 \leftarrow \mathrm{convert}(\llbracket s \rrbracket_p)$.
12. $\llbracket \mathbf{x} \rrbracket_2 \leftarrow (\llbracket \mathbf{p} \rrbracket_2 \ll 52) \oplus \llbracket \mathbf{v} \rrbracket_2$.   //free
13. $\llbracket \mathbf{x}^{(63)} \rrbracket_2 \leftarrow \llbracket \mathbf{s} \rrbracket_2$.
14. $\llbracket \mathbf{z} \rrbracket_2 \leftarrow \mathrm{convert}(\llbracket z \rrbracket_p)$.
15. $\mathrm{NaN} \leftarrow \mathrm{0x7FF0000000000001}$
16. $\llbracket \mathbf{x} \rrbracket_2 \leftarrow (1 - \llbracket \mathbf{z} \rrbracket_2) \,\&\, \llbracket \mathbf{x} \rrbracket_2$.
17. $\llbracket \mathbf{x} \rrbracket_2 \leftarrow (\llbracket \mathrm{ok} \rrbracket_2 \,\&\, \llbracket \mathbf{x} \rrbracket_2) \oplus ((1 - \llbracket \mathrm{ok} \rrbracket_2) \,\&\, \mathrm{NaN})$.
18. Return $\llbracket \mathbf{x} \rrbracket_2$.

Fig. 6. sfloat to IEEE

In step 7–8, we are dealing with the error flag which says if we should end up with NaN or not. To make it easier to follow we define ok flag which will be one when the error flag is zero. In step 9, we are converting the exponent of the sfloat into the IEEE exponent. When $k > 11$ this value could overflow the allowed IEEE representation, so this is detected in step 10 and the ok flag is updated accordingly.

The sign bit is dealt with in step 11 using the optimized bit conversion protocol which was explained earlier. In steps 12–13, we need to pack all the preceding values together to obtain the IEEE representation. This leaves us with dealing with the two special values of zero and NaN. These are dealt with in steps 14–17, where we use a fixed NaN value of $\mathrm{0x7FF0000000000001}$.

5 Experimental Results

In this section, we give results on our implementation of different operations namely, addition, multiplication, division, as well as our conversion algorithms of IEEE to sfloat and sfloat to IEEE which are presented in Sect. 4. These are given in the Full Threshold case for $n = 2, \ldots, 8$ parties and in the threshold case for (n, t) values with $t < n/2$ and $n = 3, \ldots, 8$. In the latter case, we do not present run times for $(n, t) = (8, 3)$ as in this situation the number of maximally unqualified sets starts to become too big for our replicated secret sharing based technique for evaluating binary circuits. For the large prime sharing in the threshold case we utilize Shamir sharing.

The experiments were done in Scale-Mamba version 1.11 [2]. The sfloat data type was instantiated using mantissas with bit length $l = 53$ and (signed) exponents with bit length $k = 11$. To satisfy the required equation $2 \cdot \ell + \kappa < \log_2 p$, for sfloat, we used a prime with 148 bit length and statistical security parameter $\kappa = 40$. In all experiments we measured the online run time averaged over 500 runs.

For the basic operations on IEEE values using binary circuit based MPC (Fig. 7) the runtime of the Full-Threshold variants grows with the number of parties. The average online time per operation in this case ranges for addition from $0.025\,\mathrm{s}$ (for $n = 2$) to $0.216\,\mathrm{s}$ (for $n = 8$), for multiplication from $0.092\,\mathrm{s}$ (for $n = 2$) to $0.672\,\mathrm{s}$ (for $n = 8$), for division from $0.634\,\mathrm{s}$ (for $n = 2$) to $3.27\,\mathrm{s}$ (for $n = 8$). For the threshold variants we see a range of run-times depending on the precise values of (n, t), growing as functions of n and t. The range of values is in the threshold case for addition from $0.013\,\mathrm{s}$ to $0.035\,\mathrm{s}$, for multiplication from $0.022\,\mathrm{s}$ to $0.041\,\mathrm{s}$, for division from $0.191\,\mathrm{s}$ to $0.643\,\mathrm{s}$. So depending on the number of parties and the precise operation the performance of the threshold variants are between 2 and 6 times faster than their full threshold counterparts. This behavior is to be expected as the IEEE operations are performed via binary circuits. In the full threshold case these are done via the HSS protocol, which is low round complexity but requires a lot of data to be sent and a lot of computation to be performed. When in the threshold case this is performed using a replicated LSSS, which requires higher round complexity but the total amount of data sent and computation performed is less.

We next turn to the sfix operations. Recall sfix addition is a local operation, and involves no communication thus it is very fast in all situations irrespective of the underlying access structure or the number of parties, taking roughly $0.2\,\mu\mathrm{s}$ on average per addition. For multiplication, the run times scales with the number of parties, and the threshold, ranging from $0.001\,\mathrm{s}$ to $0.0004\,\mathrm{s}$ for $n = 8$ in the Full Threshold case. For division, again, the runtime scales with the number of parties; ranging from $0.0026\,\mathrm{s}$ for $n = 2$ to 0.0082 for $n = 8$ in the Full Threshold

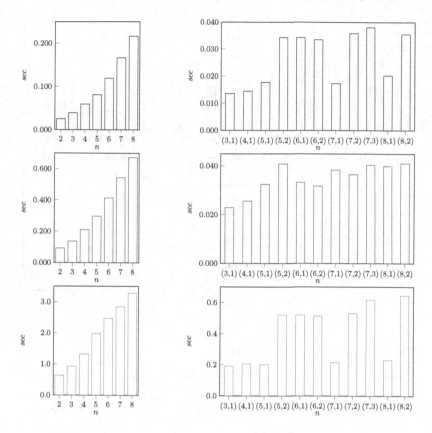

Fig. 7. Execution time in sec to execute the binary circuit based IEEE-754 operations addition (blue), multiplication (red), division (green) for Full Threshold access structure with n players (left column) and Shamir access structures (n, t) (right column) (Color figure online)

case. For the case of threshold Shamir sharing the times are roughly twice as fast as in the Full Threshold case. See Fig. 8 for details. Thus using sfix instead of IEEE arithmetic equates to savings (in execution times) of orders of magnitude.

The main issue with sfix operations is the inherent precision loss in fixed-point operations, thus we next turn to examine the performance (in Fig. 9) of the sfloat operations. Recall these are approximations to real numbers much like standard IEEE arithmetic, but not exactly the same, as they are more flexible and tunable to the MPC environment. Much like the sfix operations, the sfloat operations do not require the execution of binary circuits. The run time of the

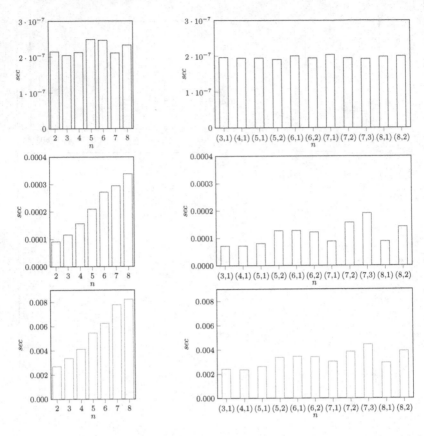

Fig. 8. Execution time in sec to execute the LSSS-based sfix operations addition (blue), multiplication (red), division (green) for Full Threshold access structure with n players (left column) and Shamir access structures (n, t) (right column) (Color figure online)

Shamir based threshold access structures is about half that of the Full Threshold access structures we tested. In the Full Threshold case, we obtain execution times ranging from 0.005 s–0.018 s for addition, 0.002 s–0.008 s for multiplication and 0.004 s–0.010 s for division.

In summary for the basic operations we have a trade off between accuracy sfix-sfloat-IEEE and speed IEEE-sfloat-sfix. For multiplication the performance improvement between sfloat and sfix is a factor of two, whereas the performance improvement between sfloat and IEEE multiplication is a factor of around one hundred.

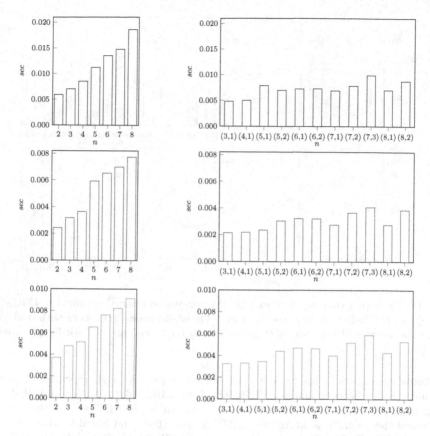

Fig. 9. Execution time in sec to execute the LSSS-based sfloat operations addition (blue), multiplication (red), division (green) for Full Threshold access structure with n players (left column) and Shamir access structures (n, t) (right column) (Color figure online)

Finally, we turn to the conversion routines between sfloat and IEEE representations given in Sect. 4. We see that since these operations require a combination of LSSS-based operations over the large field, as well as binary circuit based operations over $\mathbb{F}_2$, there is less of a pronounced difference between the run times for Full Threshold and those for thresholds with $t < n/2$. The conversion from IEEE to sfloat is roughly 2–4 times faster than the conversion from sfloat to IEEE. The timings are given in Fig. 10.

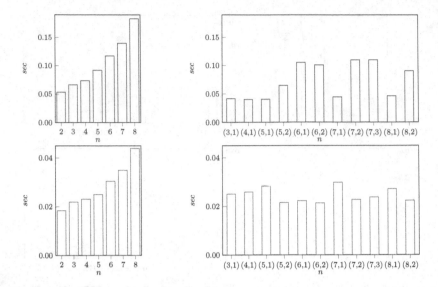

Fig. 10. Execution time in sec to execute the conversion operations sfloat to IEEE-764 (blue) and IEEE-764 to sfloat (red) for Full Threshold access structure with n players (left column) and Shamir access structures (n, t) (right column) (Color figure online)

Acknowledgments. This work was supported in part by CyberSecurity Research Flanders with reference number VR20192203, by ERC Advanced Grant ERC-2015-AdG-IMPaCT, by the FWO under an Odysseus project GOH9718N, by the Defense Advanced Research Projects Agency (DARPA) and Space and Naval Warfare Systems Center, Pacific (SSC Pacific) under contract No. FA8750-19-C-0502, and by the Office of the Director of National Intelligence (ODNI), Intelligence Advanced Research Projects Activity (IARPA) via Contract No. 2019-1902070006. The views and conclusions contained herein are those of the authors and should not be interpreted as necessarily representing the official policies, either express or implied, of the ERC, DARPA, the FWO, ODNI, IARPA, or the U.S. Government. The U.S. Government is authorized to reproduce and distribute reprints for governmental purposes notwithstanding any copyright annotation therein.

References

1. Aliasgari, M., Blanton, M., Zhang, Y., Steele, A.: Secure computation on floating point numbers. In: ISOC Network and Distributed System Security Symposium - NDSS 2013, San Diego, CA, USA, 24–27 February 2013. The Internet Society (2013)
2. Aly, A., et al.: SCALE and MAMBA v1.11: documentation (2021). https://homes.esat.kuleuven.be/~nsmart/SCALE/Documentation.pdf

3. Aly, A., Orsini, E., Rotaru, D., Smart, N.P., Wood, T.: Zaphod: efficiently combining LSSS and garbled circuits in SCALE. In: Brenner, M., Lepoint, T., Rohloff, K. (eds.) Proceedings of the 7th ACM Workshop on Encrypted Computing & Applied Homomorphic Cryptography, WAHC@CCS 2019, London, UK, 11–15 November 2019, pp. 33–44. ACM (2019)
4. Aly, A., Smart, N.P.: Benchmarking privacy preserving scientific operations. In: Deng, R.H., Gauthier-Umaña, V., Ochoa, M., Yung, M. (eds.) ACNS 2019. LNCS, vol. 11464, pp. 509–529. Springer, Cham (2019). https://doi.org/10.1007/978-3-030-21568-2_25
5. Araki, T., et al.: Optimized honest-majority MPC for malicious adversaries - breaking the 1 billion-gate per second barrier. In: 2017 IEEE Symposium on Security and Privacy, San Jose, CA, USA, 22–26 May 2017, pp. 843–862. IEEE Computer Society Press (2017)
6. Beaver, D., Micali, S., Rogaway, P.: The round complexity of secure protocols (extended abstract). In: 22nd Annual ACM Symposium on Theory of Computing, Baltimore, MD, USA, 14–16 May 1990, pp. 503–513. ACM Press (1990)
7. Ben-Or, M., Goldwasser, S., Wigderson, A.: Completeness theorems for non-cryptographic fault-tolerant distributed computation (extended abstract). In: 20th Annual ACM Symposium on Theory of Computing, Chicago, IL, USA, 2–4 May 1988, pp. 1–10. ACM Press (1988)
8. Bendlin, R., Damgård, I., Orlandi, C., Zakarias, S.: Semi-homomorphic encryption and multiparty computation. In: Paterson, K.G. (ed.) EUROCRYPT 2011. LNCS, vol. 6632, pp. 169–188. Springer, Heidelberg (2011). https://doi.org/10.1007/978-3-642-20465-4_11
9. Buescher, N., Holzer, A., Weber, A., Katzenbeisser, S.: Compiling low depth circuits for practical secure computation. In: Askoxylakis, I., Ioannidis, S., Katsikas, S., Meadows, C. (eds.) ESORICS 2016. LNCS, vol. 9879, pp. 80–98. Springer, Cham (2016). https://doi.org/10.1007/978-3-319-45741-3_5
10. Catrina, O., de Hoogh, S.: Improved primitives for secure multiparty integer computation. In: Garay, J.A., De Prisco, R. (eds.) SCN 2010. LNCS, vol. 6280, pp. 182–199. Springer, Heidelberg (2010). https://doi.org/10.1007/978-3-642-15317-4_13
11. Catrina, O., Saxena, A.: Secure computation with fixed-point numbers. In: Sion, R. (ed.) FC 2010. LNCS, vol. 6052, pp. 35–50. Springer, Heidelberg (2010). https://doi.org/10.1007/978-3-642-14577-3_6
12. Chaum, D., Crépeau, C., Damgård, I.: Multiparty unconditionally secure protocols (extended abstract). In: 20th Annual ACM Symposium on Theory of Computing, Chicago, IL, USA, 2–4 May 1988, pp. 11–19. ACM Press (1988)
13. Chida, K., et al.: Fast large-scale honest-majority MPC for malicious adversaries. Cryptology ePrint Archive, report 2018/570 (2018). https://eprint.iacr.org/2018/570
14. Damgård, I., Keller, M., Larraia, E., Pastro, V., Scholl, P., Smart, N.P.: Practical covertly secure MPC for dishonest majority – or: breaking the SPDZ limits. In: Crampton, J., Jajodia, S., Mayes, K. (eds.) ESORICS 2013. LNCS, vol. 8134, pp. 1–18. Springer, Heidelberg (2013). https://doi.org/10.1007/978-3-642-40203-6_1
15. Damgård, I., Pastro, V., Smart, N., Zakarias, S.: Multiparty computation from somewhat homomorphic encryption. In: Safavi-Naini, R., Canetti, R. (eds.) CRYPTO 2012. LNCS, vol. 7417, pp. 643–662. Springer, Heidelberg (2012). https://doi.org/10.1007/978-3-642-32009-5_38
16. Hauser, J.: Berkeley SoftFloat (2018). http://www.jhauser.us/arithmetic/SoftFloat.html

17. Hazay, C., Scholl, P., Soria-Vazquez, E.: Low cost constant round MPC combining BMR and oblivious transfer. In: Takagi, T., Peyrin, T. (eds.) ASIACRYPT 2017. LNCS, vol. 10624, pp. 598–628. Springer, Cham (2017). https://doi.org/10.1007/978-3-319-70694-8_21

18. Kamm, L., Willemson, J.: Secure floating point arithmetic and private satellite collision analysis. Int. J. Inf. Secur. **14**(6), 531–548 (2014). https://doi.org/10.1007/s10207-014-0271-8

19. Keller, M., Rotaru, D., Smart, N.P., Wood, T.: Reducing communication channels in MPC. In: Catalano, D., De Prisco, R. (eds.) SCN 2018. LNCS, vol. 11035, pp. 181–199. Springer, Cham (2018). https://doi.org/10.1007/978-3-319-98113-0_10

20. Kerik, L., Laud, P., Randmets, J.: Optimizing MPC for robust and scalable integer and floating-point arithmetic. In: Clark, J., Meiklejohn, S., Ryan, P.Y.A., Wallach, D., Brenner, M., Rohloff, K. (eds.) FC 2016. LNCS, vol. 9604, pp. 271–287. Springer, Heidelberg (2016). https://doi.org/10.1007/978-3-662-53357-4_18

21. Liedel, M.: Secure distributed computation of the square root and applications. In: Ryan, M.D., Smyth, B., Wang, G. (eds.) ISPEC 2012. LNCS, vol. 7232, pp. 277–288. Springer, Heidelberg (2012). https://doi.org/10.1007/978-3-642-29101-2_19

22. Maurer, U.M.: Secure multi-party computation made simple. Discrete Appl. Math. **154**(2), 370–381 (2006)

23. Mishchenko, A., Chatterjee, S., Jiang, R., Brayton, R.: FRAIGs: a unifying representation for logic synthesis and verification (2005)

24. Pullonen, P., Siim, S.: Combining secret sharing and garbled circuits for efficient private IEEE 754 floating-point computations. In: Brenner, M., Christin, N., Johnson, B., Rohloff, K. (eds.) FC 2015. LNCS, vol. 8976, pp. 172–183. Springer, Heidelberg (2015). https://doi.org/10.1007/978-3-662-48051-9_13

25. Rotaru, D., Wood, T.: MArBled circuits: mixing arithmetic and Boolean circuits with active security. In: Hao, F., Ruj, S., Sen Gupta, S. (eds.) INDOCRYPT 2019. LNCS, vol. 11898, pp. 227–249. Springer, Cham (2019). https://doi.org/10.1007/978-3-030-35423-7_12

26. Shamir, A.: How to share a secret. Commun. Assoc. Comput. Mach. **22**(11), 612–613 (1979)

27. Smart, N.P., Wood, T.: Error detection in monotone span programs with application to communication-efficient multi-party computation. In: Matsui, M. (ed.) CT-RSA 2019. LNCS, vol. 11405, pp. 210–229. Springer, Cham (2019). https://doi.org/10.1007/978-3-030-12612-4_11

28. Wang, X., Ranellucci, S., Katz, J.: Global-scale secure multiparty computation. In: Thuraisingham, B.M., Evans, D., Malkin, T., Xu, D. (eds.) ACM CCS 2017: 24th Conference on Computer and Communications Security, Dallas, TX, USA, 31 October–2 November 2017, pp. 39–56. ACM Press (2017)

29. Yao, A.C.C.: How to generate and exchange secrets (extended abstract). In: 27th Annual Symposium on Foundations of Computer Science, Toronto, Ontario, Canada, 27–29 October 1986, pp. 162–167. IEEE Computer Society Press (1986)

30. Zhu, Q., Kitchen, N., Kuehlmann, A., Sangiovanni-Vincentelli, A.L.: SAT sweeping with local observability don't-cares. In: Sentovich, E. (ed.) Proceedings of the 43rd Design Automation Conference, DAC 2006, San Francisco, CA, USA, 24–28 July 2006, pp. 229–234. ACM (2006)

Honest Majority MPC with Abort with Minimal Online Communication

Anders Dalskov[1]([✉]) and Daniel Escudero[2]

[1] Partisia, Aarhus, Denmark
[2] Aarhus University, Aarhus, Denmark
escudero@cs.au.dk

Abstract. In this work we focus on improving the communication complexity of the *online phase* of honest majority MPC protocols. To this end, we present a general and simple method to compile arbitrary secret-sharing-based passively secure protocols defined over an arbitrary ring that are secure up to additive attacks in a malicious setting, to actively secure protocols with abort. The resulting protocol has a total communication complexity in the online phase of $1.5(n-1)$ shares, which amounts to 1.5 shares per party asymptotically. An important aspect of our techniques is that they can be seen as generalization of ideas that have been used in other works in a rather *ad-hoc* manner for different secret-sharing protocols. Thus, our work serves as a way of unifying key ideas in recent honest majority protocols, to understand better the core techniques and similarities among these works. Furthermore, for $n = 3$, when instantiated with replicated secret-sharing-based protocols (Araki et al. CCS 2016), the communication complexity in the online phase amounts to only 1 ring element per party, matching the communication complexity of the BLAZE protocol (Patra & Suresh, NDSS 2020), while having a much simpler design.

1 Introduction

Multiparty Computation, or MPC for short, is a cryptographic technique that allows multiple parties to compute a given function f on private inputs without revealing anything beyond the output of the computation, even if an adversary collectively corrupts a subset of the parties. Different types of MPC protocols exist depending on the desired security level and desired guarantees about the output of the computation. For example, regarding the level of security, a typical dividing line lies in the fraction of parties is allowed to corrupt: In the dishonest majority setting the adversary is allowed to corrupt all but one of

This work has been supported by the European Research Council (ERC) under the European Union's Horizon 2020 research and innovation programme under grant agreements No 669255 (MPCPRO), and the Danish Independent Research Council under Grant-ID DFF-6108-00169 (FoCC). The first author did this work while a student at Aarhus University.

P. Longa and C. Ràfols (Eds.): LATINCRYPT 2021, LNCS 12912, pp. 453–472, 2021.
https://doi.org/10.1007/978-3-030-88238-9_22

the parties, whereas in the honest majority setting the adversary can only corrupt less than half of the parties. The adversary in the former scenario is much stronger and therefore much harder to achieve, and protocols in this setting, like [6,19,22,29,30], are computationally expensive and must rely in computational hardness assumptions. In contrast, honest majority protocols are possible without relying on computational assumptions [8,11,23], which makes them more resilient to attacks, as well as more efficient due to their simplicity and absence of a computational security parameter.

Another dividing line is drawn with respect to the type of corruption the adversary is allowed to make. Typically, two types of corruptions are considered: passive and active corruptions, with the former type consisting of corrupt parties respecting the protocol specifications (but trying to learn as much as they can from sent/received messages); in contrast, actively corrupt parties can deviate arbitrarily. Finally, regarding the output of the computation there are three typical notions considered: guaranteed output delivery, where the honest parties must be able to get output regardless of the adversarial behavior, fairness, where the honest parties must get output *if* the adversary gets output, and security with abort, where either the honest parties get the correct output or they abort.

Many protocols have been designed and optimized for different scenarios and use-cases. However, in spite of being an active and fruitful research field for more than three decades, state-of-the-art MPC protocols still add a considerable overhead with respect to plain "insecure" computation, which puts some applications out of reach for the time being. Most of the complexities appear from the interactive nature of MPC, which require parties to constantly communicate typically large amounts of data distributed across multiple rounds, which is highly dependent on the network conditions. Hence, an important task in MPC today is minimizing the communication complexity of the protocols for all kind of adversarial settings. One successful approach at achieving this consists of splitting the computation into an offline and online phase [7], with the former consisting of all the interaction that is independent of the parties' inputs and the latter, which tends to be orders of magnitude more efficient, made of the execution that requires knowledge of the parties' inputs. Given this separation, it is natural to optimize mostly the online phase since it dictates the total latency from the time the inputs are provided to the time the output is obtained.

Among all the possible adversarial settings, it is fair to say that honest majority MPC with abort is one of the scenarios that has received a lot of attention due to its practical, concrete efficiency [2,18,24,32,35], and it has been used already for applications like secure training and prediction of machine learning models [3,16,21,34,37]. Moreover, several recent works have focused on improving the concrete communication complexity of protocols in these settings. For example, BLAZE [36] achieves secure computation for three parties and one active corruption over rings with a communication complexity in the online phase of only 1 ring element per party. For an arbitrary number of parties, very recently, Goyal and Song [27] showed how to improve the overall communication complexity of Shamir-based honest majority protocols by presenting a novel method to check the correctness of multiplication gates with a communication complexity that is essentially independent of (specifically, logarithmic in) the circuit size, achieving an amortized communication complexity of 6 field elements per multiplication gate, distributed as 4 elements in the offline phase and 2 elements in the online phase.

1.1 Our Contribution

In this work we focus on improving the communication complexity of the *online phase* of honest majority MPC protocols that achieve security with abort. To this end, we present a general method to obtain from *any* secret-sharing-based passively secure protocol defined over an arbitrary ring that is secure up to additive attacks in a malicious setting, an actively secure protocol with abort over the same ring. The resulting protocol has a total communication complexity in the online phase of $1.5(n - 1)$ shares, where n is the number of parties, which amounts to 1.5 shares per party asymptotically. For three parties, when instantiated with protocols based on replicated secret-sharing [4], the communication complexity in the online phase amounts to only $1.5 \cdot 2 = 3$ shares in total, or 1 share per party, which matches the communication complexity of state-of-the-art protocols like BLAZE [36], while having a much simpler and generalizable design.

In addition to this, our construction has the appealing feature that, in the online phase, a secure dot product of arbitrary length can be computed with a communication complexity that is independent of the length of the input vectors.[1] This is in contrast to other protocols, specially these in the dishonest-majority setting, that require L secure multiplications to produce a dot product of length L. This feature enables highly efficient secure linear algebra, which can be applied for example to linear machine learning models such as linear regression or neural networks.

Our main protocol, presented in Sect. 3, is considerably simple and general, and provides great efficiency. Furthermore, it achieves the strongest privacy notion in the online phase, namely, perfect security. On top of matching the online complexity of state-of-the-art protocols, our protocol allows us to interpret the core techniques behind some of the most efficient protocols for specific settings like 3 and 4-party computation, namely [16,17,36], in a unified framework which highlights the main tools used in these works to achieve such low communication complexity. These protocols are constructed in an ad-hoc manner, introducing specific building blocks that seem to be inherently entangled to the particular setting (3-4 parties). However, our techniques enable the identification of a common and generalizable pattern behind these constructions. This is generally very useful as, on top of achieving good efficiency for more general

---

[1] More precisely, at the time of securely computing the dot product only the cost of a single multiplication must be paid. However, this does not rule out the potential cost that had to be paid to obtain shares of the inputs to this dot product in a first place.

settings instead of only scenarios with 3 and 4 parties, it enhances the understanding of these protocol by establishing clear relations among their design. We discuss this in the full version of this work.

The communication pattern of our protocol allows almost half of the parties to be shut down during most of the online phase, which saves in costs and reduces communication channels. However, in some concrete settings it would be ideal if these parties could be shut down during *all* of the online phase, as this could potentially help saving in operational costs. As an additional contribution, we present in Sect. 4 a variant of our first protocol that allows to shut down essentially half of the parties during the whole online phase.

Finally, we note that the description of our protocols from Sects. 3 and 4 considers computation over a field $\mathbb{F}$. We discuss in the full version of this work how to extend our protocols from Sects. 3 and 4 to the ring setting. One of the necessary steps to achieve this involves extending the results from [27], which are set over fields, to the ring setting, which may be of independent interest.

1.2   Overview of Our Techniques

First Protocol. Our compiler is conceptually simple and efficient, and requires little modifications to the underlying MPC protocol that is used as a basis. We achieve our results by leveraging a function-dependent preprocessing that reduces the communication complexity of a multiplication gate in the online phase to that of opening one single shared element, coupled with the simple but crucial observation that, in the honest-majority setting, only $t + 1$ parties are required to open a shared value non-robustly.

To provide a high level description of the techniques mentioned above, let us illustrate our compiler for the case of Shamir secret-sharing over a field $\mathbb{F}$. Let $[x]_d$ denote a degree-d sharing of $x \in \mathbb{F}$. We assume the existence of a method to multiply two shared values $[z]_t \leftarrow [x]_t \cdot [y]_t$, where $z = x \cdot y + \delta$ and δ is an additive error known by the adversary in the case of an active attack. For our compiled protocol, we define an alternative type of sharings: We write $\langle x \rangle$ if the parties have shares of a random mask $[\lambda_x]_t$, together with the public value $e_x = x - \lambda_x$. This method for secret-sharing is inspired by the work of Ben-Efraim et al. [10] that shows how to reduce the communication of the SPDZ protocol by half by making use of a circuit-dependent preprocessing. Furthermore, the core idea of having a masked version of a secret together with shares of the mask has been used already in previous works, such as [28] and the works we consider in the full version. We write $\langle x \rangle = ([\lambda_x]_t, e_x)$.

Processing addition gates in the scheme $\langle \cdot \rangle$ can be done locally, while processing multiplication gates require some interaction: To obtain $\langle x \cdot y \rangle$ from $\langle x \rangle$ and $\langle y \rangle$ we assume that the parties have shares $[\lambda_x \cdot \lambda_y]_t$ from a preprocessing phase, which we produce in our work via the protocol from [27]. Let $[\lambda_z]_t$ be the random mask that will be used for this multiplication. The parties can obtain $e_z = x \cdot y - \lambda_z$ by opening $e_x e_y + e_x [\lambda_y]_t + e_y [\lambda_x]_t + [\lambda_x \lambda_y] - [\lambda_z]_t$, thus preserving the invariant. Notice that the shares $([\lambda_x]_t, [\lambda_y]_t, [\lambda_x \lambda_y]_t)$ correspond to

circuit-dependent multiplication triples, which can be preprocessed very efficiently using the novel batch-checking technique of Goyal and Song [27].

Using the techniques sketched above, each multiplication gate in the online
phase reduces to opening one single shared value. However, the most efficient
method for achieving this, which uses the "king idea" from [23], requires $n - 1$
parties to send their share to one single party (the "king"), who then reconstructs
the secret and sends the result to the other parties. Overall, this implies an overall
communication complexity of $2 \cdot (n - 1)$ field elements. To further reduce this
count, we notice that it is not necessary for all the parties to send their share to
the king. Indeed, a subset of t parties, plus the king, suffices, as these together
hold $t + 1$ shares—enough to reconstruct the secret. Assuming $n = 2t + 1$, this
reduces the number of field elements transmitted to $t + (n - 1) = \frac{3}{2}(n - 1)$.

The optimization above comes with a downside in terms of security: By using
$t + 1$ shares to reconstruct the secret rather than all the n shares, it is possible
for a malicious party to fool an honest king into reconstructing an incorrect
value.[2] To overcome this issue we observe that, even if the intermediate shares
were opened non-robustly using only $t + 1$ shares, the parties still have full
degree-t shares of these values. To verify that the openings were done correctly,
we let the parties take a random linear combination of these shared values,
open this single result *robustly* (i.e. using all the shares), and then compare the
opened value against the corresponding combination of the values that were non-
robustly opened during the execution of the protocol. This idea can be seen as
an adaptation of the "partial opening" procedure of the SPDZ protocol to the
honest majority setting.

Second Protocol. Due to the fact that we open shared values using only $t + 1$
parties, we can set the communication pattern of the protocol sketched above
in such a way that only some *fixed* subset of $t + 1$ parties communicates during
the online phase, until the output phase. In the final check, the parties in this
subset would broadcast the intermediate opened values to the other t parties,
and the check would then be executed.

The fact that all the parties need to be available for the final check is a downside if one wants to shut down these parties "for good", once the online phase
has started. To allow the $t + 1$ parties that are active during the online phase
to perform the final correctness check without the help of the other parties, we
resort to a rather standard technique in the dishonest majority setting involving
the use of MACs: A value x is shared as $[x]$ together with $[r \cdot x]$ for a random
and global $[r]$. Then, to check that $[x]$ is opened correctly, the $t + 1$ parties that
were active during the online phase (among which a dishonest majority may
be corrupt) use the MAC $[r \cdot x]$ and the key $[r]$. Furthermore, this check can
be easily batched so that its communication complexity is independent of the
number of openings being verified.

---

[2] As presented here, a corrupt king can already disrupt the reconstruction of the secret
even if all n shares are used. This is handled in [23] by considering multiple kings
and using error correction techniques.

Extension to Rings. Most of the techniques used in our work carries over seamlessly to the ring setting. For example, the online phase of our first protocol from Sect. 3 does not exploit any specific property of fields, and so works the same over $\mathbb{Z}_{2^k}$. The main issue appears in the offline phase, given that the protocol from [27] that we use to produce the necessary preprocessing material only works over fields. To extend the protocol from [27] to the ring setting, we observe that the core technique used in this protocol is basic polynomial interpolation, which can be made to work over $\mathbb{Z}_{2^k}$ by taking a Galois ring extension of large enough degree, as done in [1]. This idea was already used in [12] for the three-party setting, whereas our results are applicable to an arbitrary number of parties and any linear secret-sharing scheme.

Finally, the online phase of our second protocol from Sect. 4 does not work directly over $\mathbb{Z}_{2^k}$ as it relies on the AMD code $(x, r \cdot x, r)$, which does not provide any integrity of $\mathbb{Z}_{2^k}$ due to the lack of invertible elements. Fortunately, the work of [19] shows how to extend this integrity mechanism to the ring $\mathbb{Z}_{2^k}$ by operating over a larger ring $\mathbb{Z}_{2^{k+\kappa}}$, where κ is the statistical security parameter. We show in the full version of our work that this technique also applies to our protocol.

1.3   Related Work

Honest majority MPC with a small communication footprint has been studied in a number of works in the last decade or so. One attractive feature of such protocols, is that they work well for a large number of parties where it is reasonable to assume that not everyone colludes (in particular, where only a minority colludes). This setting was investigated in [5], which demonstrated a concretely efficient protocol for large number of parties, based on a protocol adapted from [9].

While [9] has a linear communication complexity, recent research (which we have already mentioned) have brought this down to logarithmic [27]. Moreover, for the specific setting of 3 and 4 parties, specialized protocols have been shown to be concretely efficient [20, 31, 33, 36].

Compiling honest majority protocols from passive to active security have also been studied previously. [18] shows how to efficient convert a passively secure honest majority protocol with the same properties we require (security against an active adversary up to additive attacks), into an active secure protocol with a concretely very small overhead. The authors of [2] show, employing a similar approach as [18], how to get a similar compiler for ring based protocols. Finally, the work of [13] also aims at reducing communication in honest majority secure computation, and they also achieve 1.5 field elements per party while also achieving guaranteed output delivery, but their work is set in the computational setting, whereas our results are information-theoretic.

2   Preliminaries

2.1   Notation

We let n be the number of parties among which t are corrupt. In the honest majority setting it holds that $t < n/2$, but for simplicity in the presentation, we will assume that $n = 2t + 1$.[3] Let $\mathcal{R}$ be a ring of the form $\mathbb{Z}_{p^k}$ or $\mathrm{GF}(p^k)$ for some prime p and some non-negative integer k. We write $s \in_R A$ when s is uniformly sampled from a finite set A. We let κ denote the statistical security parameter.

2.2   Security Definition

In this work we assume a synchronous network of secure point-to-point channels, together with a broadcast channel. We consider simulation-based security, which can be either the universally composability framework [15] or the stand-alone setting [26] as our techniques apply to both. We focus on providing security with abort, in which the adversary can make the honest parties abort at any point in the protocol; in particular, the adversary itself may get output before the honest parties and immediately abort the computation. We assume the existence of a broadcast channel with abort (that is, the parties either get the value that was broadcast, or they abort), and we assume that when an honest party aborts, *all* honest parties abort, which can be easily achieved using the broadcast channel. Since the broadcast channel allows for abort, it can be efficiently instantiated via echo-broadcast by letting the sender distribute the value to be broadcast via the point-to-point channels, and then letting the receiving parties exchange hashes of his value and abort if an inconsistency is detected.

When measuring communication complexity, $M + \mathsf{BC}(N)$ means that M ring elements are communicated over point-to-point channels, and N ring elements are communicated over the broadcast channel. With the broadcast method sketched above, we would have that $\mathsf{BC}(N) = (n-1) \cdot N$, which amounts to the messages sent by the broadcaster (we ignore the cost of the hash exchange as it is independent of N).

2.3   Linear Secret-Sharing

We consider a linear secret-sharing scheme (LSSS) $[\cdot]$ over $\mathcal{R}$. Such a scheme for our purposes consists of a randomized injective function $\mathsf{share} : \mathcal{R} \to (\mathcal{R}^m)^n$ such that the following holds for all $x \in \mathcal{R}$. Below, we let $\mathsf{share}(x) = \{x_i\}_{i=1}^n$.

- *Privacy.* For any subset $J \subseteq \{1, \ldots, n\}$ such that $|J| \leq t$, the mutual information between $\{x_i\}_{i \in J}$ and x is 0.

---

[3] Some technical complications arise if $2t + 1 < n$, like the fact that the set of honest parties is strictly larger than $t + 1$, so different subsets of honest parties may reconstruct shared secrets to different values. This is not really a problem with the protocols, but it introduces some notational overhead that we would like to avoid.

- *Reconstruction.* There is a function rec : $(\mathcal{R}^m)^{t+1} \to \mathcal{R}$ such that, for any subset $J \subseteq \{1, \ldots, n\}$ such that $|J| = t + 1$, it holds that $\mathsf{rec}\,(\{x_i\}_{i \in J}) = x$ (the function rec is implicitly taking the set J as a parameter).
- *Linearity.* Given $\{y_i\}_{i=1}^{n} = \mathsf{share}(y)$, it holds that $\{x_i + y_i\}_i$ lies in the image of $\mathsf{share}(x + y)$.[4]

To ease the notation a bit, we may write $[x]^J := \{x_i\}_{i \in J}$, and $[x] := [x]^{\{1, \ldots, n\}}$.

The definition of rec is extended to more than $t + 1$ shares as follows: Let $K \subseteq \{1, \ldots, n\}$ such that $|K| \geq t+1$. We write $\mathsf{rec}\,(\{x_i\}_{i \in K}) = x$ if, for all $J \subseteq K$ with $|J| = t+1$, it holds that $\mathsf{rec}\,(\{x_i\}_{i \in J}) = x$. Else, we write $\mathsf{rec}\,(\{x_i\}_{i \in K}) = \bot$. In the former case we say that the shares $\{x_i\}_{i \in K}$ are *consistent*, and in the latter case we say they are *inconsistent*.

An important factor of honest-majority secret-sharing (and one which does not hold for a dishonest-majority) is that, when the sharings are consistent, it is ensured that the correct value will be reconstructed. More precisely, if the adversary modifies the t entries in $[x]$ corresponding to the corrupt parties, but if $\mathsf{rec}\,([x]) = x' \neq \bot$, then it is guaranteed that $x' = x$. Indeed, if H denotes the set of honest parties, which satisfies $|H| = n - t = t + 1$, then $\mathsf{rec}\,([x]) = x' \neq \bot$ implies that $\mathsf{rec}\,\left([x]^H\right) = x'$. But since the shares $[x]^H$ are not modified, this implies that $x' = x$.

2.4   Reconstruction Protocols

In the previous section we defined secret-sharing as a set of functions, but in practice it is used as a set of protocols for distributing and reconstructing data among n parties. In this section we discuss different ways in which the parties can reconstruct a shared value $[x] = \{x_i\}_i$, where party P_i has the share x_i. We consider two variants: Robust opening, where the value that is opened is guaranteed to be correct, and a much more efficient non-robust—or "loose"— opening, where the value that is opened may be incorrect. As we will see in subsequent sections, a key optimization in this work lies in using loose openings for the majority of our protocols in a way which does not harm correctness or privacy. Our subprotocols for reconstruction are presented in Fig. 1.

Improving Communication Complexity. The public reconstruction protocols Π_{Rec} and Π_{LooseRec}, as described in Fig. 1, have a communication complexity that is quadratic in the number of parties as they require (almost) all parties sending shares to all other parties. This can be improved to linear communication in n as follows: For $\Pi_{\mathsf{LooseRec}}([x])$, the $t + 1$ parties $P_1, \ldots, P_{t+1}$ send their shares to P_1, who reconstructs x using these shares, and broadcasts this value to all parties. The total communication is then t ring elements over point-to-point channels, plus 1 ring element over the broadcast channel.

---

[4] This extends naturally to multiplication by constants. Furthermore, addition by a constant z can be obtained by the parties generating public shares $[z]$ (e.g., by letting $z_1 = z$ and $z_i = 0$ for $1 < i < n$), and then using the linearity between shared values.

Reconstruction Protocols

ROBUST RECONSTRUCTION

$\Pi_{\mathsf{PrivRec}}([x], i)$. *Robustly reconstructs* x *towards party* P_i. Each party P_j sends its share x_j to P_i, who invokes rec on the received shares and outputs what rec outputs.

$\Pi_{\mathsf{Rec}}([x])$. *Robustly reconstructs* x *towards all parties.*
  1. Parties call $\Pi_{\mathsf{PrivRec}}([x], i)$ for all $i \in \{1, \ldots, n\}$.
  2. If P_i outputs $\perp$ from its reconstruction above, then P_i aborts.

- -

LOOSE RECONSTRUCTION

$\Pi_{\mathsf{LoosePrivRec}}([x], i)$. *Non-robustly reconstructs* x *towards party* P_i. Each party P_j for $j = 1, \ldots, t+1$ sends its share x_j to P_i, who invokes rec on the received shares and outputs whatever rec outputs.

$\Pi_{\mathsf{LooseRec}}([x])$. *Non-robustly reconstructs* x *towards all parties.* Each party P_j for $j = 1, \ldots, t+1$ broadcasts its share x_j. Each party invokes rec on the received shares and outputs whatever rec outputs.

Fig. 1. Different reconstruction protocols we use in our work

Unfortunately, this does not work for Π_{Rec} since the king can lie about the reconstructed value. To handle this, one can use the techniques from [23] to obtain linear *amortized* complexity in n (for multiple simultaneous openings). In a nutshell, this works by batching a sequence of secrets to be opened into a vector, and encoding this vector using a linear error-correcting code. Then, each secret in the codeword is opened by using the king idea from above with a different king for each symbol, and then error correction/detection is applied to the resulting opened codeword.

2.5 Sampling Shares of Random Values

We assume two functionalities for sampling shared randomness:

- $\mathcal{F}_{\mathsf{Rand}}$: Produces a shared value $[r]$ where $r \in_R \mathcal{R}$.
- $\mathcal{F}_{\mathsf{Coin}}$: Produces a value $r \in_R \mathcal{R}$ known to all parties.

$\mathcal{F}_{\mathsf{Rand}}$ can be instantiated, for example, using the techniques outlined in [23], which are based on Vandermonde matrices, although more efficient instantiations of $\mathcal{F}_{\mathsf{Rand}}$ exist for particular secret-sharing schemes like replicated secret sharing cf. [2, 18]. $\mathcal{F}_{\mathsf{Coin}}$ can be instantiated by calling $\mathcal{F}_{\mathsf{Rand}}$ to sample $[r]$, followed by $r \leftarrow \mathsf{rec}([r])$, or by cointossing using a commitment functionality $\mathcal{F}_{\mathsf{Commit}}$.

2.6 Correct Multiplication

We assume a functionality $\mathcal{F}_{\mathsf{CorrectMult}}$ that takes as input two shared values $[x], [y]$, and returns $[x \cdot y]$. This functionality will be only used in the preprocessing. An instantiation of this functionality is discussed in the full version.

3   Optimizing the Online Phase

In this section we present our first protocol whose online phase is optimized so that the parties only send, in total, $\frac{3}{2}(n-1) \cdot k \cdot \log(p)$ bits per multiplication gate. On top of being conceptually very simple, our optimization allows for a communication pattern in which only $t+1$ parties are present for most of the online phase, except that the remaining t parties must return for the output phase. In Sect. 4 we present a protocol for which this is not required, that is, only $t+1$ parties are required to run all of the online phase, including the output phase.

We begin by presenting in Sect. 3.1 the secret-sharing construction we will use in our protocols. Then, in Sect. 3.2, we present an intuitive overview of our protocol, and finally, in Sect. 3.3, we describe our protocol in detail, analyze its complexity and discuss its security.

3.1   Masked Secret-Sharing

Let $[\cdot]$ be a secret-sharing scheme over $\mathcal{R}$, as defined in Sect. 2.3. We define the following LSSS over $\mathcal{R}$ that builds on top of $[\cdot]$:

- $\mathsf{share}_{\langle \cdot \rangle}(x)$: Sample a random mask $\lambda_x \in \mathcal{R}$, call $\mathsf{share}_{[\cdot]}(\lambda_x)$ and append to each share the value $\mu_x = x - \lambda_x$. We denote this by $\langle x \rangle = ([\lambda_x], \mu_x = x - \lambda_x)$.
- $\mathsf{rec}_{\langle \cdot \rangle}([\lambda_x], \mu_x)$: Call $\lambda_x \leftarrow \mathsf{rec}_{[\cdot]}([\lambda_x])$ and if $\lambda_x \neq \bot$ then output $\lambda_x + \mu_x$, else output $\bot$.

It is easy to see that this new scheme is additively homomorphic. Indeed, given $\langle x \rangle = ([\lambda_x], \mu_x)$ and $\langle y \rangle = ([\lambda_y], \mu_y)$ parties can compute shares of the sum as $\langle z \rangle = ([\lambda_x + \lambda_y], \mu_x + \mu_y)$.

3.2   General Overview

We begin by providing a high-level view of our protocol. To this end, it is instructive to begin with a very simple and naive protocol that makes use of the original LSSS $[\cdot]$, together with correct multiplication triples. We consider this below, as well as optimizations.

Naive Protocol. As we mentioned in Sect. 2.3, a crucial property of honest majority LSSS is that either the correct value is reconstructed or an abort signal is generated. This property can be leveraged to obtain simple and efficient actively MPC protocol, presented in Fig. 2.

It is easy to see that this protocol satisfies security with abort. First, correctness holds given that addition gates are local and the formula used for the multiplication gates satisfies

$$d \cdot b + e \cdot a + c + d \cdot e = x \cdot y,$$

A Naive Protocol

Input phase. To share its input x_i, P_i proceeds as follows:

1. In a preprocessing phase the parties generate consistent shares $[r_i]$ where $r_i \in \mathcal{R}$ is uniformly random and only known to P_i. Such consistent shares can be generated efficiently as sketched in Section 2.5.
2. To share x_i, P_i broadcasts the value $x_i - r_i$, and the parties compute the shares $[x_i] = (x_i - r_i) + [r_i]$. If a proper broadcast channel is used, the resulting shares are guaranteed to be consistent.

Addition gates. Addition gates are handled locally by using the linearity property of the LSSS.

Multiplication gates. To multiply $[x]$ and $[y]$, the parties proceed as follows:

1. In a preprocessing phase, sample random shares $([a], [b], [c])$, where $c = a \cdot b$. Such triples can be generated as presented in the full version of this work.
2. In the online phase, the parties reconstruct $d \leftarrow \Pi_{\mathsf{Rec}}([x] - [a])$, $e \leftarrow \Pi_{\mathsf{Rec}}([y] - [b])$ (aborting if this is either reconstruction outputs $\perp$), and locally compute $[x \cdot y] = d[b] + e[a] + [c] + d \cdot e$.

Output gates. If party P_i is intended to learn the value of $[x]$, the parties call $\Pi_{\mathsf{PrivRec}}([x], i)$.

Fig. 2. A simple protocol for secure computation with abort.

as can be verified. In regards to privacy, begin by observing that every shared value throughout the computation is consistent. This is because consistent sharings are assumed to be produced in the preprocessing, and a proper broadcast channel is used in the input phase, which ensures this also extends to the input sharings and also for subsequent wires in the circuit as these are computed using only linear operations.

Finally, notice that due to the robustness properties of the LSSS and the consistency of the sharings, the adversary cannot cheat in any opening without causing an abort, so the only values opened are the $d = x - a$ and $e = y - b$ from the multiplication gates, which leak nothing about the inputs x and y given that a and b are uniformly random elements in $\mathcal{R}$ unknown to the adversary.

Remark 1. In the template above we pushed all the complexities of dealing with the additive errors to the preprocessing, where the multiplication triples are produced. This is good for the problem we have at hand, which is optimizing the communication complexity in the online phase. However, a different approach would be to deal with the additive errors in a "post-processing" phase, that is, one may allow additive errors during the multiplications in the online phase (for which one could either use potentially incorrect triples, or use the assumed multiplication produce directly in the online phase, avoiding extra preprocessing), and then perform some check that guarantees that these errors are zero.

This is what is done by many of the existing honest-majority protocols that have been proposed in recent years. For example, this approach is taken in [25], where cut-and-choose and triple sacrificing techniques are used to ensure all multiplications are handled correctly. This approach is also considered in [27], where, instead of using their novel triple verification techniques in the preprocessing phase, as we do here, the authors use the check after the online phase has been executed to check all multiplications are correct. [24] also follows a similar "post-processing" approach.

Optimizing the Naive Protocol. The basic template presented above can be (and has been) optimized in many different ways. However, in our work we aim at optimizing the online phase as much as possible, which implies that our preprocessing phase may be more inefficient than some of the existing works. The two optimizations we incorporate to the basic template sketched above are the following:

1. We use the secret sharing scheme $\langle \cdot \rangle$ instead of $[\cdot]$, and we handle multiplication gates as described in Fig. 2 instead of using triples directly in the online phase (correct triples must still be preprocessed). This lowers the complexity of a multiplication gate from two openings to only one opening.[5]
2. Instead of performing each opening robustly, the parties perform the openings using Π_{LooseRec}, which is cheaper but may cause reconstructed values to be incorrect. After all loose openings are done, but before the final output gates, the correctness of these openings is checked by taking a random linear combination of the opened values, and opening robustly the same linear combination over the corresponding shares.[6]

The first optimization only has an effect on the amount of communication in the online phase. However, the second optimization, on top of reducing the overall amount of bits sent, contributes in a much more impactful way: By using loose openings instead of robust openings, and by cleverly rearranging the communication pattern, the online phase can be run by just the parties $P_1, \ldots, P_{t+1}$, while the remaining parties $P_{t+2}, \ldots, P_n$ only have to come back for the final check. Removing communication channels among the parties is likely to have a much more noticeable impact in the efficiency than merely lowering the communication complexity. Furthermore, as these servers do not participate for the majority of the computation, this also frees up computing resources and is more energy efficient.

We remark that, even though we described the masked secret-sharing construction and the naive starting protocol over the arbitrary ring $\mathcal{R}$, in our actual protocol below the computation ring $\mathcal{R}$ is assumed to be a field (which we will denote as $\mathbb{F}$). We discuss in the full version how to extend our protocol so that it also works over a ring of the form $\mathbb{Z}_{2^k}$.

---

[5] This optimization was already introduced in [10] in the context of the SPDZ protocol.

[6] This is similar to what is done in the SPDZ protocol [22], where values are "partially opened" for each multiplication gate (that is, without using the MACs), and only at the end of the computation these openings are checked by taking a random linear combination.

Protocol $\Pi_{\mathsf{MPCLowOnline}}$

OFFLINE PHASE

- For every wire in the circuit x the parties call $[\lambda_x] \leftarrow \mathcal{F}_{\mathsf{Rand}}$.
- For every input gate x corresponding to a party P_i, the parties call $\Pi_{\mathsf{PrivRec}}([\lambda_x], i)$.
- For every multiplication gate with inputs x, y and output z, the parties call $[\lambda_x \lambda_y] \leftarrow \mathcal{F}_{\mathsf{CorrectMult}}([\lambda_x], [\lambda_y])$.

ONLINE PHASE

Input Gates. For every input gate x owned by party P_i, the parties do the following:
1. P_i uses the broadcast channel to send $\mu_x = x - \lambda_x$ to all parties.
2. Upon receiving this value, the parties set $\langle x \rangle = ([\lambda_x], \mu_x)$

Addition Gates. For every addition gate with inputs $\langle x \rangle = ([\lambda_x], \mu_x)$ and $\langle y \rangle = ([\lambda_y], \mu_y)$, the parties locally set $\langle x + y \rangle = ([\lambda_x] + [\lambda_y], \mu_x + \mu_y)$.

Multiplication Gates. For every multiplication gate with inputs $\langle x \rangle = ([\lambda_x], \mu_x)$ and $\langle y \rangle = ([\lambda_y], \mu_y)$, the parties proceed as follows:
1. Call $\mu_z \leftarrow \Pi_{\mathsf{LooseRec}}(\mu_x \mu_y + \mu_x [\lambda_y] + \mu_y [\lambda_x] + [\lambda_x \lambda_y] - [\lambda_z])$
2. Set $\langle x \cdot y \rangle = ([\lambda_z], \mu_z)$.

Checking Phase. Before any output gate is reconstructed, the parties proceed as follows. Let $[\eta_1], \ldots, [\eta_M]$ be the shares that were loosely opened to $\eta_1', \ldots, \eta_M'$ during the computation phase (these correspond to $[\mu_z]$ for every wire z that is the output of a multiplication gate).
1. For $i = 1, \ldots, M$ call $\alpha_i \leftarrow \mathcal{F}_{\mathsf{Coin}}$.
2. Let $[\eta] = \sum_{i=1}^M \alpha_i \cdot [\eta_i]$ and $\eta' = \sum_{i=1}^M \alpha_i \cdot \eta_i'$. The parties call $z \leftarrow \Pi_{\mathsf{Rec}}(\eta' - [\eta])$. If $z \neq 0$ then the parties abort.

Output Gates. If the parties did not abort above, then for every output gate $\langle x \rangle = ([\lambda_x], \mu_x)$ that is supposed to be learned by P_i, the parties call $\Pi_{\mathsf{PrivRec}}([\lambda_x], i)$, and if it succeeds then P_i outputs $\mu_x + \lambda_x$.

Fig. 3. Our first protocol with low online communication. The algebraic structure used for the computation is assumed to be a field $\mathbb{F}$ with $|\mathbb{F}| \geq 2^\kappa$.

3.3 Main Protocol

With the above intuitive explanation of our protocol, we proceed to a more formal description of our protocol shown in Fig. 3.

Remark 2. Observe that in the online phase the additions and multiplications can be handled only by $P_1, \ldots, P_{t+1}$, by performing the openings only among these parties. Hence, most of the online phase involves communication only among $P_1, \ldots, P_{t+1}$, which in practical terms means that parties $P_{t+2}, \ldots, P_n$ can go offline until the checking phase is reached. At this point, the offline parties must rejoin the computation, receive the partially opened values from the other parties and participate in the checking and output procedures. Having the ability to shut down parties has many relevant effects in practice. For instance, it can help in saving operational costs, as well as allowing parties to allocate resources more effectively by, say, placing most of the computation on the more powerful servers. Additionally, shutting down communication channels is particularly good in wide area networks, where strong use of communication is heavily penalized.

It can be checked that

$$\mu_x \mu_y + \mu_x \lambda_y + \mu_y \lambda_x + \lambda_x \lambda_y - \lambda_z = x \cdot y - \lambda_z,$$

which shows that the multiplication gates lead to correct $\langle \cdot \rangle$-sharings of the product of the inputs, and in particular shows that the protocol produces the right output if all openings are done correctly. Furthermore, to see that the protocol preserves privacy, observe that, before the checking phase, all intermediate values remain private since the only openings done throughout the protocol are the the values $\mu_x = x - \lambda_x$, and since the masks λ_x are uniformly random and secret-shared among the parties, μ_x looks uniformly random as well.

It only remains to be checked that openings are correct with high probability. As in the protocol, let $[\eta_1], \ldots, [\eta_M]$ be the shares that were loosely opened to $\eta'_1, \ldots, \eta'_M$ during the computation phase. Write $\eta'_i = \eta_i + \delta_i$, that is, we express the loosely opened value as the correct one plus an additive error from the adversary. In the checking phase, parties open

$$\eta' - \eta = \sum_{i=1}^{M} \alpha_i(\eta'_i - \eta_i) = \sum_{i=1}^{M} \alpha_i(\eta_i + \delta_i - \eta_i) = \sum_{i=1}^{M} \alpha_i \delta_i,$$

and check whether it is 0. Because each α_i is sampled *after* the adversary introduces the error δ_i (specifically, α_i is sampled after the computation concludes), the above sum is 0 with high probability if and only if $\delta_i = 0$ for all $i = 1, \ldots, M$.

A formal proof of security is provided in the full version.

Communication Complexity. The offline phase of our protocol consists of sampling the masks $[\lambda_x]$ and preprocessing the triples $([\lambda_x], [\lambda_y], [\lambda_z])$. This process overall has linear communication complexity with respect to the number of parties n. For the online phase, which is of our particular interest, the total communication per multiplication gate, ignoring the check phase and the calls to $\mathcal{F}_{\mathsf{Coin}}$, amounts to one call to Π_{LooseRec} which equals $t + \mathsf{BC}(1)$ ring elements. Using the broadcast protocol with abort sketched in Sect. 2.2, this amounts to $t + (n - 1) = \frac{3}{2}(n - 1)$.

4   Removing the Extra Parties from the Output Phase

As we discussed before, our protocol from Sect. 3 has the appealing feature that most of the online phase can be run by only $t + 1$ parties. More precisely, the only part in which the extra t parties are required is in the preprocessing and in the output phase. This not only helps in saving in communication, but it allows these extra t parties to be turned off during the online phase. However, it would be ideal if the online phase could be run in its entirety, including the output phase, by $t + 1$ parties only. This would allow these extra t parties to be switched off "for good" once the offline phase is finished, which can represent noticeable savings in many practical scenarios, as for example, when parties run on rented servers.

In this section we show how to run the entire online phase with only $t+1$ active parties. The price for this optimization, is that slightly more communication have to be done in the offline phase. Another downside is that the ring $\mathcal{R}$ has to be a field $\mathbb{F}$, although we show in the full version how to overcome this limitation.

We begin by providing a general overview of our protocol in Sect. 4.1, and then we describe our protocol in detail in Sect. 4.2, together with its complexity analysis and security proof.

4.1 General Overview

The intuition behind our protocol is that, if $2t+1$ participates in the offline phase, then it suffices—by being clever as to what kind of material is produced during preprocessing—to only have $t+1$ parties participate in the online phase.

More precisely, consider the case of a field $\mathbb{F}$, and let us revisit our protocol from Sect. 3. Recall that the online phase can be run by $t+1$ parties only since, after the preprocessing is done, only openings are required during the online phase. However, since the threshold of the secret-sharing scheme is t, $t+1$ parties only do not provide enough redundancy, which allows an active adversary to additively tamper these opened values. We solved this issue in our previous protocol from Sect. 3 as follows. Let $[\eta_1], \ldots, [\eta_M]$ the shares that were opened to $\eta'_1, \ldots, \eta'_M$.

1. The parties sample random public values $\alpha_1, \ldots, \alpha_M \in \mathbb{F}$. Let $[\eta] = \sum_{i=1}^{M} \alpha_i [\eta_i]$ and $\eta' = \sum_{i=1}^{M} \alpha_i \eta'_i$.
2. It suffices to check that $[\eta]$ opens to η', which is done by opening $\eta' - [\eta]$ using all of the $2t+1$ parties, which guarantees that this value is correct.

In the protocol we present in this section we replicate the same steps, except that we do not want to involve the extra t parties to open $[\eta]$ robustly. As mentioned above, $t+1$ parties alone cannot open $[\eta]$ robustly, and so we resort to a technique from the dishonest majority MPC literature: Instead of sharing a value $v \in \mathbb{F}$ as $[v]$, it is shared as $([v], [r \cdot v])$, where $r \in \mathbb{F}$ is a global (i.e. it is the same for all shared values) random key that is also shared as $[r]$. This "new" sharing scheme is easily verified to be linear and therefore its invariant can be kept throughout the whole computation.

The fact that $[r]$ is hidden, and that the sharing $([v], [r \cdot v])$ is linear, can be used to ensure correctness, provided errors inserted by the adversary during the check are independent of the honest parties shares. In order to enforce this, we take a "commit-and-open" approach. In more detail, to open a value $[v]$, each P_i first commits to their share $v^{(i)}$ of v using an ideal commitment functionality $\mathcal{F}_{\mathsf{Commit}}()$, after which they call Π_{LooseRec} where the received share is checked against the committed value. While this still permits the adversary to reveal the *wrong* value, the error that is induced is nevertheless going to be independent of the honest parties shares. Note that this commit-and-open is only needed in the checking and output phase of the protocol; during computation, invoking Π_{LooseRec} suffices.

Using this technique, once the M values $[\eta_1], \ldots, [\eta_M]$ have been opened to $\eta_1 + \delta_1, \ldots, \eta_M + \delta_m$ by the $t + 1$ parties running the online phase, these parties can also check the correctness of these openings without involving the other t parties by using the extra sharings $[r \cdot \eta_1], \ldots, [r \cdot \eta_M], [r]$ as follows:

1. Like in our protocol from Sect. 3, begin by sampling random public values $\alpha_1, \ldots, \alpha_M$. Let $[r \cdot \eta] = \sum_{i=1}^{M} \alpha_i [r \cdot \eta_i]$ and $\eta' = \sum_{i=1}^{M} \alpha_i(\eta_i + \delta_i)$. Also, let $[\beta] = [r \cdot \eta] - \eta' \cdot [r]$.
2. The parties loosely open $\beta + \epsilon \leftarrow [\beta]$ and abort if this is not equal to 0.

It is easy to see that the check passes if and only if $r \cdot \left(\sum_{i=1}^{M} \alpha_i \delta_i\right) = \epsilon$, which happens with probability at most $1/|\mathbb{F}|$ if there is at least one δ_i that is non-zero.[7] This idea is already widely used in other dishonest-majority protocols like [6,19,22,29,30], but, to the best of our knowledge, our work is the first to make use of this technique in the honest-majority setting with the goal of reducing the amount of parties needed for robust opening.[8]

Observe that the communication complexity of the online phase of this new approach is essentially the same as the one from the protocol in Sect. 3 because $\mathcal{F}_{\mathsf{Commit}}$ can be instantiated efficiently in UC with global setup [14], and given that the online phase is comprised mostly of loose openings. However, the offline phase of this new approach is more expensive since, on top of generating the necessary multiplication triples, it also generates the necessary MACs, which essentially doubles the required amount of preprocessed material.

4.2   Full Protocol Description

We present our optimized protocol in full detail in Fig. 4.

As we mentioned already, this protocol can be seen as an adaptation of [10] to the honest majority setting, where a dishonest majority is used for the online phase. Its security follows directly from the security of [10], which essentially boils down to the following two observations. First, privacy is preserved throughout the protocol execution because of the same reason as in $\Pi_{\mathsf{MPCLowOnline}}$ (only masked values μ_x are ever opened). Secondly, in the checking phase the sharing $[\beta]$ is opened to $\beta + \epsilon$. It is easy to see that $\beta + \epsilon$ is equal to 0 if and only if $r \cdot \sum_{i=1}^{M} \alpha_i \delta_i = \epsilon$ and that this happens with low probability if there is some $\delta_i \neq 0$. Indeed, in this case we have $\sum_{i=1}^{M} \alpha_i \delta_i \neq 0$ with overwhelming probability, which in turn implies that $r = \epsilon \cdot \left(\sum_{i=1}^{M} \alpha_i \delta_i\right)^{-1}$. However, this cannot be the case except with negligible probability as it implies the adversary could compute r before it was opened; an impossible task considering r is a uniform random value. A similar argument holds for the check done in the output phase.

---

[7] For simplicity we assume that $|\mathbb{F}|$ is big enough so that $1/|\mathbb{F}|$ is negligible. The general case is easily handled by iterating the current construction with multiple r's.

[8] [18] also uses this idea, but in a different way and with a different goal. In [18], the MACs are used not to ensure correct openings, since a complete honest majority is used for reconstruction, but to disallow additive attacks after multiplications.

Protocol $\Pi_{\mathsf{MPCLowChannels}}$

OFFLINE PHASE

- The parties call $[r] \leftarrow \mathcal{F}_{\mathsf{Rand}}$.
- For every wire in the circuit x the parties call $[\lambda_x] \leftarrow \mathcal{F}_{\mathsf{Rand}}$.
- For every input gate x corresponding to a party P_i, the parties call $\Pi_{\mathsf{PrivRec}}([\lambda_x], i)$.
- For every multiplication gate with inputs x, y and output z, the parties call $[\lambda_x \lambda_y] \leftarrow \mathcal{F}_{\mathsf{CorrectMult}}([\lambda_x], [\lambda_y])$.
- For every wire in the circuit x the parties call $[r\lambda_x] \leftarrow \mathcal{F}_{\mathsf{CorrectMult}}([r], [\lambda_x])$. For every multiplication gate with inputs x and y, the parties call $[r\lambda_x\lambda_y] \leftarrow \mathcal{F}_{\mathsf{CorrectMult}}([r], [\lambda_x\lambda_y])$

- -

ONLINE PHASE

Input Gates. For every input gate x owned by party P_i, the parties do the following:
1. P_i uses the broadcast channel to send $\mu_x = x - \lambda_x$ to all parties.
2. Upon receiving this value, the parties set $\langle x \rangle = ([\lambda_x], \mu_x)$
Only the parties $P_1, \ldots, P_{t+1}$ participate in what follows.
Addition Gates. For every addition gate with inputs $\langle x \rangle = ([\lambda_x], \mu_x)$ and $\langle y \rangle = ([\lambda_y], \mu_y)$, the parties locally set $\langle x + y \rangle = ([\lambda_x] + [\lambda_y], \mu_x + \mu_y)$.
Multiplication Gates. For every multiplication gate with inputs $\langle x \rangle = ([\lambda_x], \mu_x)$ and $\langle y \rangle = ([\lambda_y], \mu_y)$, the parties proceed as follows:
1. Call $\mu_z \leftarrow \Pi_{\mathsf{LooseRec}}(\mu_x\mu_y + \mu_x[\lambda_y] + \mu_y[\lambda_x] + [\lambda_x\lambda_y] - [\lambda_z])$
2. Set $\langle x \cdot y \rangle = ([\lambda_z], \mu_z)$.
Checking Phase. Before any output gate is reconstructed, the parties proceed as follows. Let $[\eta_1], \ldots, [\eta_M]$ be the shares that were loosely opened to $\eta'_1, \ldots, \eta'_M$ during the computation phase (these correspond to $[\mu_z]$ for every wire z that is the output of a multiplication gate). Notice that the parties also have shares $[r \cdot \eta_i]$ for every $i = 1, \ldots, M$.
1. For $i = 1, \ldots, M$ call $\alpha_i \leftarrow \mathcal{F}_{\mathsf{Coin}}$.
2. Let $[r \cdot \eta] = \sum_{i=1}^{M} \alpha_i [r \cdot \eta_i]$, $\eta' = \sum_{i=1}^{M} \alpha_i \eta'_i$ and $[\beta] = [r \cdot \eta] - \eta' \cdot [r]$.
3. Each P_i commits to their share $\beta^{(i)}$ of β using $\mathcal{F}_{\mathsf{Commit}}$.
4. Finally, parties open and check the commitments, compute $\beta = \mathsf{rec}([\beta])$ and abort if a party refuses to open their commitment, or if $\beta \neq 0$.
Output Gates. If no honest party aborted above, the parties $P_1, \ldots, P_{t+1}$ proceed as follows to open the final output gate x.
1. Parties commit-and-open $[\lambda_x]$ for all output wires x, aborting if this fails.
2. Let $[\rho] = [r\lambda_x] - \lambda'_x[r]$. The parties commit-and-open their share of $[\rho]$ to the other parties, and abort if $\rho \neq 0$ or if the commit-and-open fails.
3. If the procedure above does not abort, the parties output $\mu_x + \lambda'_x$.

Fig. 4. Our second protocol with minimal online complexity. In this protocol, the online phase can be run by only $t + 1$ parties, unlike the protocol from Fig. 3. This protocol requires the underlying algebraic structure to be a large enough field $\mathbb{F}$.

Finally, observe that since parties $P_{t+2}, \ldots, P_n$ disconnected, they would not be receiving output. If they were supposed to receive output, they could return to the final output phase. The difference with respect to our protocol from Sect. 3 is that, in this case, these returning parties do not need to participate in the protocol, they only need to receive the shares from the other parties.

A formal proof of security is presented in the full version.

Communication Complexity. Our protocol communicates a linear number of field elements (in n) in the offline phase, as in protocol $\Pi_{\mathsf{MPCLowOnline}}$. For the online phase, ignoring the final checking phase, the protocol requires $t + \mathsf{BC}(1)$ field elements communicated per multiplication gate. Since the broadcast involves only the parties $P_1, \ldots, P_{t+1}$, we have that $\mathsf{BC}(1) = t$, so the communication per multiplication gate is of $t + t = n - 1$ field elements.

References

1. Abspoel, M., Cramer, R., Damgård, I., Escudero, D., Yuan, C.: Efficient information-theoretic secure multiparty computation over $\mathbb{Z}/p^k\mathbb{Z}$ via Galois rings. In: Hofheinz, D., Rosen, A. (eds.) TCC 2019, Part I. LNCS, vol. 11891, pp. 471–501. Springer, Cham (2019). https://doi.org/10.1007/978-3-030-36030-6_19
2. Abspoel, M., Dalskov, A., Escudero, D., Nof, A.: An efficient passive-to-active compiler for honest-majority MPC over rings (2021, to appear at ACNS 2021)
3. Abspoel, M., Escudero, D., Volgushev, N.: Secure training of decision trees with continuous attributes (2021, to appear at PoPETs 2021)
4. Araki, T., Furukawa, J., Lindell, Y., Nof, A., Ohara, K.: High-throughput semi-honest secure three-party computation with an honest majority. In: Weippl, E.R., Katzenbeisser, S., Kruegel, C., Myers, A.C., Halevi, S. (eds.) ACM CCS 2016: 23rd Conference on Computer and Communications Security, pp. 805–817. ACM Press, October 2016
5. Barak, A., Hirt, M., Koskas, L., Lindell, Y.: An end-to-end system for large scale P2P MPC-as-a-service and low-bandwidth MPC for weak participants. In: Lie, D., Mannan, M., Backes, M., Wang, X. (eds.) ACM CCS 2018: 25th Conference on Computer and Communications Security, pp. 695–712. ACM Press, October 2018
6. Baum, C., Cozzo, D., Smart, N.P.: Using TopGear in overdrive: a more efficient ZKPoK for SPDZ. In: Paterson, K.G., Stebila, D. (eds.) SAC 2019. LNCS, vol. 11959, pp. 274–302. Springer, Cham (2020). https://doi.org/10.1007/978-3-030-38471-5_12
7. Beaver, D.: Efficient multiparty protocols using circuit randomization. In: Feigenbaum, J. (ed.) CRYPTO 1991. LNCS, vol. 576, pp. 420–432. Springer, Heidelberg (1992). https://doi.org/10.1007/3-540-46766-1_34
8. Beerliová-Trubíniová, Z., Hirt, M.: Efficient multi-party computation with dispute control. In: Halevi, S., Rabin, T. (eds.) TCC 2006. LNCS, vol. 3876, pp. 305–328. Springer, Heidelberg (2006). https://doi.org/10.1007/11681878_16
9. Beerliová-Trubíniová, Z., Hirt, M.: Perfectly-secure MPC with linear communication complexity. In: Canetti, R. (ed.) TCC 2008. LNCS, vol. 4948, pp. 213–230. Springer, Heidelberg (2008). https://doi.org/10.1007/978-3-540-78524-8_13
10. Ben-Efraim, A., Nielsen, M., Omri, E.: Turbospeedz: double your online SPDZ! Improving SPDZ using function dependent preprocessing. In: Deng, R.H., Gauthier-Umaña, V., Ochoa, M., Yung, M. (eds.) ACNS 2019. LNCS, vol. 11464, pp. 530–549. Springer, Cham (2019). https://doi.org/10.1007/978-3-030-21568-2_26
11. Ben-Sasson, E., Fehr, S., Ostrovsky, R.: Near-linear unconditionally-secure multiparty computation with a dishonest minority. In: Safavi-Naini, R., Canetti, R. (eds.) CRYPTO 2012. LNCS, vol. 7417, pp. 663–680. Springer, Heidelberg (2012). https://doi.org/10.1007/978-3-642-32009-5_39
12. Boyle, E., Gilboa, N., Ishai, Y., Nof, A.: Practical fully secure three-party computation via sublinear distributed zero-knowledge proofs. In: Cavallaro, L., Kinder, J., Wang, X., Katz, J. (eds.) ACM CCS 2019: 26th Conference on Computer and Communications Security, pp. 869–886. ACM Press, November 2019

13. Boyle, E., Gilboa, N., Ishai, Y., Nof, A.: Efficient fully secure computation via distributed zero-knowledge proofs. In: Moriai, S., Wang, H. (eds.) ASIACRYPT 2020, Part III. LNCS, vol. 12493, pp. 244–276. Springer, Cham (2020). https://doi.org/10.1007/978-3-030-64840-4_9

14. Camenisch, J., Drijvers, M., Gagliardoni, T., Lehmann, A., Neven, G.: The wonderful world of global random oracles. In: Nielsen, J.B., Rijmen, V. (eds.) EURO-CRYPT 2018, Part I. LNCS, vol. 10820, pp. 280–312. Springer, Cham (2018). https://doi.org/10.1007/978-3-319-78381-9_11

15. Canetti, R.: Universally composable security: a new paradigm for cryptographic protocols. In 42nd Annual Symposium on Foundations of Computer Science, pp. 136–145. IEEE Computer Society Press, October 2001

16. Chaudhari, H., Choudhury, A., Patra, A., Suresh, A.: ASTRA: high throughput 3pc over rings with application to secure prediction. In: Proceedings of the 2019 ACM SIGSAC Conference on Cloud Computing Security Workshop, pp. 81–92 (2019)

17. Chaudhari, H., Rachuri, R., Suresh, A.: Trident: efficient 4PC framework for privacy preserving machine learning. In: 27th Annual Network and Distributed System Security Symposium, NDSS 2020, San Diego, California, USA, 23–26 February 2020. The Internet Society (2020)

18. Chida, K., et al.: Fast large-scale honest-majority MPC for malicious adversaries. In: Shacham, H., Boldyreva, A. (eds.) CRYPTO 2018, Part III. LNCS, vol. 10993, pp. 34–64. Springer, Cham (2018). https://doi.org/10.1007/978-3-319-96878-0_2

19. Cramer, R., Damgård, I., Escudero, D., Scholl, P., Xing, C.: SPDZ$_{2^k}$: efficient MPC mod 2^k for dishonest majority. In: Shacham, H., Boldyreva, A. (eds.) CRYPTO 2018, Part II. LNCS, vol. 10992, pp. 769–798. Springer, Cham (2018). https://doi.org/10.1007/978-3-319-96881-0_26

20. Dalskov, A., Escudero, D., Keller, M.: Fantastic four: honest-majority four-party secure computation with malicious security. Cryptology ePrint Archive, Report 2020/1330 (2020). https://eprint.iacr.org/2020/1330

21. Dalskov, A.P.K., Escudero, D., Keller, M.: Secure evaluation of quantized neural networks. Proc. Priv. Enh. Technol. 2020(4), 355–375 (2020)

22. Damgård, I., Keller, M., Larraia, E., Pastro, V., Scholl, P., Smart, N.P.: Practical covertly secure MPC for dishonest majority – or: breaking the SPDZ limits. In: Crampton, J., Jajodia, S., Mayes, K. (eds.) ESORICS 2013. LNCS, vol. 8134, pp. 1–18. Springer, Heidelberg (2013). https://doi.org/10.1007/978-3-642-40203-6_1

23. Damgård, I., Nielsen, J.B.: Scalable and unconditionally secure multiparty computation. In: Menezes, A. (ed.) CRYPTO 2007. LNCS, vol. 4622, pp. 572–590. Springer, Heidelberg (2007). https://doi.org/10.1007/978-3-540-74143-5_32

24. Eerikson, H., Keller, M., Orlandi, C., Pullonen, P., Puura, J., Simkin, M.: Use your brain! Arithmetic 3PC for any modulus with active security. In: Kalai, Y.T., Smith, A.D., Wichs, D. (eds.) ITC 2020: 1st Conference on Information-Theoretic Cryptography, pp. 5:1–5:24. Schloss Dagstuhl, June 2020

25. Furukawa, J., Lindell, Y., Nof, A., Weinstein, O.: High-throughput secure three-party computation for malicious adversaries and an honest majority. In: Coron, J.-S., Nielsen, J.B. (eds.) EUROCRYPT 2017, Part II. LNCS, vol. 10211, pp. 225–255. Springer, Cham (2017). https://doi.org/10.1007/978-3-319-56614-6_8

26. Goldreich, O.: Foundations of Cryptography: Basic Tools, vol. 1. Cambridge University Press, Cambridge (2001)

27. Goyal, V., Song, Y.: Malicious security comes free in honest-majority MPC. Cryptology ePrint Archive, Report 2020/134 (2020). https://eprint.iacr.org/2020/134

28. Katz, J., Kolesnikov, V., Wang, X.: Improved non-interactive zero knowledge with applications to post-quantum signatures. In: Lie, D., Mannan, M., Backes, M., Wang, X. (eds.) ACM CCS 2018: 25th Conference on Computer and Communications Security, pp. 525–537. ACM Press, October 2018

29. Keller, M., Orsini, E., Scholl, P.: MASCOT: Faster malicious arithmetic secure computation with oblivious transfer. In: Weippl, E.R., Katzenbeisser, S., Kruegel, C., Myers, A.C., Halevi, S. (eds.) ACM CCS 2016: 23rd Conference on Computer and Communications Security, pp. 830–842. ACM Press, October 2016

30. Keller, M., Pastro, V., Rotaru, D.: Overdrive: making SPDZ great again. In: Nielsen, J.B., Rijmen, V. (eds.) EUROCRYPT 2018, Part III. LNCS, vol. 10822, pp. 158–189. Springer, Cham (2018). https://doi.org/10.1007/978-3-319-78372-7_6

31. Koti, N., Pancholi, M., Patra, A., Suresh, A.: SWIFT: super-fast and robust privacy-preserving machine learning. Cryptology ePrint Archive, Report 2020/592 (2020). https://eprint.iacr.org/2020/592

32. Lindell, Y., Nof, A.: A framework for constructing fast MPC over arithmetic circuits with malicious adversaries and an honest-majority. In: Thuraisingham, B.M., Evans, D., Malkin, T., Xu, D. (eds.) ACM CCS 2017: 24th Conference on Computer and Communications Security, pp. 259–276. ACM Press, October 2017

33. Mazloom, S., Le, P.H., Ranellucci, S., Gordon, S.D.: Secure parallel computation on national scale volumes of data. In: Capkun, S., Roesner, F. (eds.) USENIX Security 2020: 29th USENIX Security Symposium, pp. 2487–2504. USENIX Association, August 2020

34. Mohassel, P., Rindal, P.: ABY^3: A mixed protocol framework for machine learning. In: Lie, D., Mannan, M., Backes, M., Wang, X. (eds.) ACM CCS 2018: 25th Conference on Computer and Communications Security, pp. 35–52. ACM Press, October 2018

35. Nordholt, P.S., Veeningen, M.: Minimising communication in honest-majority MPC by batchwise multiplication verification. In: Preneel, B., Vercauteren, F. (eds.) ACNS 2018. LNCS, vol. 10892, pp. 321–339. Springer, Cham (2018). https://doi.org/10.1007/978-3-319-93387-0_17

36. Patra, A., Suresh, A.: BLAZE: blazing fast privacy-preserving machine learning. In: ISOC Network and Distributed System Security Symposium - NDSS 2020. The Internet Society, February 2020

37. Wagh, S., Gupta, D., Chandran, N.: SecureNN: 3-party secure computation for neural network training. Proc. Priv. Enh. Technol. **2019**(3), 26–49 (2019)

Author Index

Printed in the United States
by Baker & Taylor Publisher Services

Printed in the United States
by Baker & Taylor Publisher Services